EVERYMAN, I will go with thee,

and be thy guide,

In thy most need to go by thy side

JOHN FORSTER

Born in 1812 and educated at University College, London. Barrister, 1843, but devoted a large part of his life to journalism and literature. Died in 1876.

JOHN FORSTER

The Life of
Charles Dickens

IN TWO VOLUMES · VOLUME ONE

NEW EDITION

WITH NOTES AND AN INDEX BY A. J. HOPPÉ

AND ADDITIONAL AUTHOR'S FOOTNOTES

DENT: LONDON
EVERYMAN'S LIBRARY
DUTTON: NEW YORK

© Notes and editing, J. M. Dent & Sons Ltd, 1966, 1969

All rights reserved. No part of this publication may be
reproduced, stored in a retrieval system, or transmitted,
in any form or by any means, electronic, mechanical,
photocopying, recording or otherwise, without the prior
permission of J. M. Dent & Sons Ltd

Made in Great Britain
at the
Aldine Press · Letchworth · Herts
for
J. M. DENT & SONS LTD
Aldine House · Bedford Street · London
First included in Everyman's Library 1927
New, augmented edition 1966
Further revised, 1969

NO. 781

ΣDN: 460 00701 j

To the daughters of Charles Dickens

MY GOD-DAUGHTER MARY

and

HER SISTER KATE

this book is dedicated by their friend
and their father's friend and executor

JOHN FORSTER

CONTENTS
VOLUME ONE

BOOK FIRST

CHILDHOOD AND YOUTH

1812–36. ÆT. 1–24

BOOK SECOND

FIRST FIVE YEARS OF FAME

1836–41. ÆT. 24–9

BOOK THIRD

AMERICA

1841–2. ÆT. 29–30

BOOK FOURTH

LONDON AND GENOA

1843–5. Æt. 31–3

BOOK FIFTH

LONDON, LAUSANNE AND PARIS

1845–7. Æt. 33–5

VOLUME TWO

BOOK SIXTH

AT THE SUMMIT

1847–52. ÆT. 35–40

BOOK SEVENTH

CONTINENT REVISITED

1852–6. ÆT. 40–44

BOOK EIGHTH

PUBLIC READER

1856–67. ÆT. 44–55

CONTENTS
BOOK NINTH
AUTHOR
1836–70. ÆT. 24–58

BOOK TENTH
AMERICA REVISITED
1867–8. ÆT. 55–6

BOOK ELEVENTH
SUMMING UP
1868–70. ÆT. 56–8

BOOK TWELFTH
THE CLOSE
1870. ÆT. 58

APPENDIX

ILLUSTRATIONS

VOLUME 1

VOLUME 2

PREFACE

WHEN Forster's *Life of Dickens* was published in Everyman's Library in 1927, it contained the full and latest text of the work but only some of the author's prolific footnotes, and an incomplete names-only index. This edition reprints the text of that Everyman edition, but it has three new features: (1) additional author's footnotes numbering 166; (2) an index more worthy of the work; (3) some post-Forster notes by the present editor.

Forster's footnotes are of course an integral part of his work, most of them containing further extracts from Dickens's letters. As it is economically impossible to reset the whole work, the additional footnotes, taken from the three-volume 1872–4 edition, are placed at the end of each volume, each note being given an asterisked number followed by the relevant page number in brackets; and the number of each note is given in the margin of the page of the text to which it belongs. It will readily be seen that many of these additional footnotes are important, and that all of them enhance the quality of contemporaneity which characterizes Forster's biography, whether they are about Dickens's books, his relations with his family and friends, and with authors and publishers, his travels at home and abroad, or his public life and public readings here and in America.

The new index aims at a sufficiency of detailed biographical references and a closer identification where thought helpful, by description or full names, of most of the many people who figure in the work, including members of three generations of the Dickens family. A perusal of the index may give the reader a conspectus of the chief events, people and places in Dickens's life and writing career.

The editor's notes are also placed at the end of each volume with numbers marked † (followed by the page numbers), which are also given in the margin of the relevant pages. These notes are intended to provide a modern edition of Forster's *Dickens* for the general reader, summarizing as they do a good deal of the material which, in the course of many years since the work was originally published, has been revealed about matters and people in Dickens's life only briefly mentioned by Forster, or mentioned without names, or not mentioned at all. Familiar examples are the case of Maria Beadnell, the original of lovely young Dora of *David Copperfield*, who later became faded Flora of *Little Dorrit*, and the club-land quarrel between Thackeray and Edmund Yates in which Dickens was so deeply and unhappily involved. But the matters which inevitably loom largest in the notes are Dickens's separation from his wife and his friendship with Ellen Ternan; on these still controversial matters so much has now appeared in print—basic documents, contemporary letters and memoirs, as well as second-hand stories and speculative reconstructions—that a statement of the main features of the present position seems to be a necessary appendage to Forster's *Life*. Much of the data in the notes, including Dickens letters and memoranda up till recently unpublished, derives of course from later biographical works, particularly those published in the last decade or so; grateful acknowledgment of these sources is made in the notes. Attention is also drawn to the list on pages xvii and xviii of selected books on Dickens by other authors, among which Professor Edgar Johnson's comprehensive biography is outstanding.

The late Dame Una Pope-Hennessy wrote in her biography in 1945: 'The first and greatest book on Charles Dickens was written seventy years ago. John Forster, its author, apologized for making the letters he had received from his friend, "letters of unexampled candour and truthfulness", the basis of his narrative, but it turned out to be an excellent method of presentation. . . . Despite its planned limitations, the book remains and must remain the indispensable monument to friendship and genius that it was constructed to be.' Dame Una's was the first biography of Dickens to be written after the publication of the three-volume edition of the *Letters* in 1938, of which much use has been made in later biographies and which are quoted as necessary in my notes. It was not until early 1965 that there was published the first volume of the Pilgrim Edition of Dickens's *Letters*, editing of which began in 1949 and which is expected to be completed in twelve volumes. Therein further light may in due course be cast on some aspects of

Dickens's life; in the meantime it should here be recorded that in the preface in vol. i six pages out of twenty-two deal with Forster and his *Life of Dickens,* particularly with the letters to himself, 'nearly a thousand', from which Forster quoted. Great scholarship is going into this definitive edition of the *Letters*; several discrepancies, 'small distortions' or ambiguities by Forster in dating, transcribing or ascribing some of the letters in the *Life* are pointed out in the preface and in annotations, but on the whole Forster comes out of this searching scrutiny very well. Some details of this critical examination in the Pilgrim *Letters* have been added to my note † 28 (ii., 464). 'Forster had believed', write the editors of the *Letters*, 'his biography should try to present Dickens as the man he actually was. The story of Dickens's books was therefore Forster's first care. His aim was also to give the *Life* something of "the value of autobiography". Forster believed that over the years Dickens had revealed himself more fully to him than to anyone else . . .' which was, as a footnote adds, 'almost certainly true'. It seems, then, safe to reassert that this utterly contemporary biography, by his closest friend and confidant, will always occupy a fundamental place in the vast library of books about Dickens.

A. J. H.

March 1965.

NOTE TO NEW EDITION

WITH this edition Forster's *Dickens* is restored to its place as Nos. 781–2 in Everyman's Library. I have made a few adjustments in the above Preface, which was printed in the edition published in 1966 in a format different from that of the Library proper.

Another fifteen 'additional author's footnotes' have now been inserted, increasing the number of these extra footnotes from 166 to 181, which reduces to thirty-five the fifty still omitted in 1966 according to the estimate, which I accept, of *The Times Literary Supplement* reviewer. Among these further fifteen are certainly the longest, and in my opinion the only ones of significant biographical interest, left out of the 1966 edition. It would have been nice to print every single word of all the footnotes, and to place them at the foot of each relevant page, but the economics of publishing today (at Everyman's price) mean that the 1927 printing plates (which I repeat give Forster's final text complete) must be used and the hitherto omitted footnotes gathered together at the end of each volume. I am glad to say that, meeting one *TLS* point of criticism, a place has now been found in the text for the two pages of artist's trial sketches of Mr Dombey (vol. ii, pp. 110–11) omitted from the 1927 and 1966 editions. The list of other books about Dickens (vol. i, p. xviii) has been brought up to date and a few omissions repaired.

It is a remarkable fact that, in spite of the ever-growing importance of Forster's *Dickens* to all Dickensians, and indeed to everybody interested in English literary history, the only edition of it in print for the past thirty years has been the one in Everyman's Library, which has now been 'up-dated' and is here reissued, after a little further editorial attention, in time for the centenary of Dickens's death in 1970.

A. J. H.

August 1969.

JOHN FORSTER: BIBLIOGRAPHICAL NOTE

BIOGRAPHIES, ETC. Biographical sketch by Prof. Henry Morley, in the *Handbook of the Dyce and Forster Collections in the South Kensington Museum*, 1880; by the Rev. Whitwell Elwin in *Catalogue of the Forster Collection*, 1888; *A Catalogue of the Paintings, MSS., Autograph Letters, Pamphlets, etc., bequeathed by John Forster*, 1893; *John Forster, by one of his friends* [Percy H. Fitzgerald], 1903; *John Forster and his Friendships*, by Richard Renton, 1912.

WORKS. Contributed many articles to the *Examiner*, of which he was appointed chief literary and dramatic critic, 1833; edited the *Foreign Quarterly Review*, 1842–3; edited the *Daily News*, 1846 (succeeding Dickens); edited the *Examiner*, 1847–56.

Published *Lives of the Statesmen of the Commonwealth*, 1840; *A Treatise on the Popular Progress in English History*, 1840; *The Life and Adventures of Oliver Goldsmith*, 1848 (2nd edition improved and entitled *Life and Times of Oliver Goldsmith*, 1854, edited by G. T. Bettany, 1890, abridged and annotated by Roger Ingpen, 1903); *Historical and Biographical Essays* (2 vols. of essays from the *Foreign Quarterly Review* and *Edinburgh Quarterly*), 1858; *Arrest of the Five Members by Charles the First*, 1860; *The Debates on the Grand Remonstrance, November and December, 1641*, 1860; *Sir John Eliot: a Biography*, in 2 vols., with a portrait, 1864 (2nd edition, 1872); *Walter Savage Landor*, in 2 vols., 1869; vol. i of *Works and Life of W. S. Landor*, 1876.

The Life of Jonathan Swift; only vol. i published, the second volume unfinished at his death in 1876. *Dramatic essays of John Forster*, reprinted from the *Examiner*, with notes by W. Archer and R. W. Lowe, 1896.

The Life of Charles Dickens, with portraits, in 3 vols., 1872–4; Library edition, in 2 vols., 1876; another edition, with 40 illustrations, 1879; abridged and revised by George Gissing, with portraits and facsimiles, 1903; Fireside edition, with 32 illustrations, 1907; annotated by B. W. Matz, with 500 portraits, facsimiles and other illustrations, in 2 vols., 1911; new edition, edited and annotated by J. W. T. Ley, 1928. Translated into French by Th. Bentzon (pseudonym of Thérèse Blanc), about 1879; into Italian by C. Casoretti, 1879.

CHARLES DICKENS: BIBLIOGRAPHICAL NOTE

WORKS. An alphabetical list of Dickens's works, and miscellaneous pieces referred to in the *Life*, is given in the index at the end of the Charles Dickens entry.

BOOKS ABOUT DICKENS BY OTHER AUTHORS. The following is a selection of the innumerable biographical and critical works written about Charles Dickens: *Anecdote Biographies of Thackeray and Dickens*, by R. H. Stoddard,

1874; *Dickens*, in English Men of Letters Series, by Dr A. W. Ward, 1882; *The Childhood and Youth of Charles Dickens*, by Robert Langton, 1883; *Dickens as I Knew Him*, by George Dolby, 1885; *Life of Charles Dickens*, by Sir F. T. Marzials, 1887; *My Father as I Recall Him*, by Mary Dickens, 1897; *Charles Dickens, a Critical Study*, by George Gissing, 1898; *Charles Dickens, his Life, Writings and Personality*, by F. G. Kitton, 1901; *Charles Dickens, the Story of His Life and Writings*, by B. W. Matz, 1902; *The Life of Charles Dickens, as Revealed by his Writings*, by P. H. Fitzgerald, 2 vols., 1905; *Charles Dickens*, by G. K. Chesterton, 1906; *Charles Dickens and His Friends*, by W. Teignmouth Shore, 1909; *The Dickens Companion*, by Sir J. A. Hammerton, 1910; *Criticisms and Appreciations of the Works of Charles Dickens*, by G. K. Chesterton, 1911; *Dickens in America*, ed. by W. G. Wilkins, 1911; *Memories of Charles Dickens*, by P. H. Fitzgerald, 1913; *Charles Dickens*, by Wilhelm Dibelius (Leipzig and Berlin), 1916; *The Dickens Circle: The Novelist's Friendships*, by J. W. T. Ley, 1919; *The Dickens Encyclopaedia*, by Arthur L. Hayward, 1924 (reprinted 1969); *Dickens*, by Walter Dexter, 1927; *Dickens's Own Story*, by Sir W. Robertson Nicoll, 1927; *Dickens, a Portrait in Pencil*, by R. Straus, 1928; *Memories of My Father*, by Sir H. F. Dickens, 1928; *The Man Charles Dickens*, by E. Wagenknecht, 1929; *Dickens*, by Sir Osbert Sitwell, 1932; *The Sentimental Journey, A Life of Charles Dickens*, by Hugh Kingsmill, 1934; *The Life of Charles Dickens*, by Thomas Wright, 1935; *Dickens and Daughter*, by Gladys Storey, 1939; *The Dickens World*, by Humphry House, 1941; *Charles Dickens*, by Una Pope-Hennessy, 1945; *Dickens, Dali, and Others*, by George Orwell, 1946; *Dickens*, by Hesketh Pearson, 1949; *Charles Dickens*, by Jack Lindsay, 1950; *Dickens and Ellen Ternan*, by Ada Nisbet, 1952; *Charles Dickens, His Tragedy and Triumph*, by Edgar Johnson, 2 vols., 1952; *Dickens, Romancier*, by Sylvère Monod, 1953; *Dickens at Work*, by John Butt and Kathleen Tillotson, 1957; *Charles Dickens, a Critical Introduction*, by K. J. Fielding, 1958 (enlarged 1965); *Dickens Incognito*, by Felix Aylmer, 1959; *The Speeches of Charles Dickens*, ed. K. J. Fielding, 1960; *The Love-Lives of Charles Dickens*, by C. G. L. DuCann, 1961; *Charles Dickens, a Pictorial Biography*, by J. B. Priestley, 1961; *The Imagination of Charles Dickens*, by A. O. J. Cockshut, 1961; *The Dickens Critics*, ed. by George H. Ford and Lauriat Lane, Jr., 1961; *Dickens and Crime*, by Philip Collins, 1962; *Dickens and Education*, by Philip Collins, 1963; *Dickens in his Time*, by Ivor Brown, 1963; *The Charles Dickens Companion*, by Michael and Mollie Hardwick, 1965; *The Making of Charles Dickens*, by Christopher Hibbert, 1967. See also *The Dickensian*, vol. i, 1905 to vol. lxiv, 1968, continuing thrice yearly to a volume.

LETTERS. *The Letters of Charles Dickens*, ed. by Georgina Hogarth and Mamie Dickens, 1880–2, 1893, the same, *With Letters to Wilkie Collins*, selected by Georgina Hogarth, 1908; *Mr and Mrs Charles Dickens, His Letters to Her*, ed. by Walter Dexter, 1935; *The Letters of Charles Dickens*, ed. by Walter Dexter, 3 vols., 1938. The Pilgrim Edition of *The Letters of Charles Dickens*, editing of which was begun in 1949 by the late Humphry House, started publication, ed. by Madeline House and Graham Storey, in February 1965 with vol. i and is announced to be completed in due course in 12 volumes containing about 12,000 letters.

BOOK FIRST

CHILDHOOD AND YOUTH

1812–36. ÆT. 1–24

THE LIFE OF
CHARLES DICKENS

I

CHARLES DICKENS, the most popular novelist of the century, and one of the greatest humorists that England has produced, was born at Landport, in Portsea, on Friday, the seventh of † I February, 1812.

His father, John Dickens, a clerk in the navy pay-office, was at this time stationed in the Portsmouth Dockyard. He had made acquaintance with the lady, Elizabeth Barrow, who became afterwards his wife, through her elder brother, Thomas Barrow, also engaged on the establishment at Somerset House; and she bore him in all a family of eight children, of whom two died in infancy. The eldest, Fanny (born 1810), was followed by Charles (entered in the baptismal register of Portsea as Charles John Huffham, though on the very rare occasions when he subscribed that name he wrote Huffam); by another son, named Alfred, who died in childhood; by Letitia (born 1816); by another daughter, Harriet, who died also in childhood; by Frederick (born 1820); by Alfred Lamert (born 1822); and by Augustus (born 1827).

Walter Scott tells us, in his fragment of autobiography, speaking of the strange remedies applied to his lameness, that he remembered lying on the floor in the parlour of his grandfather's farmhouse, swathed up in a sheepskin warm from the body of the sheep, being then not three years old. David Copperfield's memory goes beyond this. He represents himself seeing so far back into the blank of his infancy as to discern therein his mother and her servant, dwarfed to his sight by stooping down or kneeling on the floor, and himself going unsteadily from the one to the other. He admits this may be

fancy, though he believes the power of observation in numbers
of very young children to be quite wonderful for its closeness
and accuracy, and thinks that the recollection of most of us
can go farther back into such times than many of us suppose.
But what he adds is certainly not fancy. "If it should appear
from anything I may set down in this narrative that I was a
child of close observation, or that as a man I have a strong
memory of my childhood, I undoubtedly lay claim to both of
these characteristics." Applicable as it might be to David
Copperfield, this was unaffectedly true of Charles Dickens.

He has often told me that he remembered the small front
garden to the house at Portsea, from which he was taken away
when he was two years old, and where, watched by a nurse
through a low kitchen window almost level with the gravel
walk, he trotted about with something to eat, and his little
elder sister with him. He was carried from the garden one day
to see the soldiers exercise; and I perfectly recollect that, on
our being at Portsmouth together while he was writing *Nickleby*,
he recognised the exact shape of the military parade seen by
him as a very infant, on the same spot, a quarter of a century
before.

When his father was again brought up by his duties to London
from Portsmouth, they went into lodgings in Norfolk Street,
Middlesex Hospital; and it lived also in the child's memory that
they had come away from Portsea in the snow. Their home,
shortly after, was again changed, the elder Dickens being
placed upon duty in Chatham Dockyard; and the house where
he lived in Chatham, which had a plain-looking whitewashed
plaster front and a small garden before and behind, was in
St. Mary's Place, otherwise called the Brook, and next door to
a Baptist meeting-house called Providence Chapel, of which a
Mr. Giles he presently mentioned was minister. Charles at this
* I time was between four and five years old; and here he stayed
till he was nine. Here the most durable of his early impressions
were received; and the associations that were around him when
he died were those which at the outset of his life had affected
him most strongly.

The house called Gadshill Place stands on the strip of highest
ground in the main road between Rochester and Gravesend.
Very often had we travelled past it together, many years before
it became his home; and never without some allusion to what
he told me when first I saw it in his company, that amid the
recollections connected with his childhood it held always a

prominent place, for, upon first seeing it as he came from Chatham with his father, and looking up at it with much admiration, he had been promised that he might himself live in it or in some such house when he came to be a man, if he would only work hard enough. Which for a long time was his ambition. The story is a pleasant one, and receives authentication at the opening of one of his essays on travelling abroad, when as he passes along the road to Canterbury there crosses it a vision of his former self.

"So smooth was the old high road, and so fresh were the horses, and so fast went I, that it was midway between Gravesend and Rochester, and the widening river was bearing the ships, white-sailed or black-smoked, out to sea, when I noticed by the wayside a very queer small boy.

"'Holloa!' said I, to the very queer small boy, 'where do you live?'

"'At Chatham,' says he.

"'What do you do there?' says I.

"'I go to school,' says he.

"I took him up in a moment, and we went on. Presently the very queer small boy says, 'This is Gadshill we are coming to, where Falstaff went out to rob those travellers, and ran away.'

"'You know something about Falstaff, eh?' said I.

"'All about him,' said the very queer small boy. 'I am old (I am nine), and I read all sorts of books. But *do* let us stop at the top of the hill, and look at the house there, if you please!'

"'You admire that house?' said I.

"'Bless you, sir,' said the very queer small boy, 'when I was not more than half as old as nine, it used to be a treat for me to be brought to look at it. And now I am nine, I come by myself to look at it. And ever since I can recollect, my father, seeing me so fond of it, has often said to me, *If you were to be very persevering, and were to work hard, you might some day come to live in it.* Though that's impossible!' said the very queer small boy, drawing a low breath, and now staring at the house out of window with all his might.

"I was rather amazed to be told this by the very queer small boy; for that house happens to be *my* house, and I have reason to believe that what he said was true."

The queer small boy was indeed himself. He was a very little and a very sickly boy. He was subject to attacks of violent spasms which disabled him for any active exertion. He was never a good little cricket-player; he was never a first-rate hand at marbles, or peg-top, or prisoner's base; but he had great pleasure in watching the other boys, officers' sons for the most part, at these games, reading while they played; and he had always the belief that this early sickness had brought to himself one inestimable advantage, in the circumstances of his weak health having strongly inclined him to reading. It will not appear, as my narrative moves on, that he owed much to his parents, or was other than in his first letter to Washington Irving he described himself to have been, a "very small and not-over-particularly-taken-care-of boy"; but he has frequently been heard to say that his first desire for knowledge, and his earliest passion for reading, were awakened by his mother, from whom he learnt the rudiments, not only of English, but also, a little later, of Latin. She taught him regularly every day for a long time, and taught him, he was convinced, thoroughly well. I once put to him a question in connection with this to which he replied in almost exactly the words he placed five years later in the mouth of David Copperfield: "I faintly remember her teaching me the alphabet; and when I look upon the fat black letters in the primer, the puzzling novelty of their shapes, the easy good nature of O and S always seem to present themselves before me as they used to do."

Then followed the preparatory day-school, a school for girls and boys to which he went with his sister Fanny, and which was in a place called Rome (pronounced Room) Lane. Revisiting Chatham in his manhood, and looking for the place, he found it had been pulled down to make a new street "ages" before: but, out of the distance of the ages, arose nevertheless a not dim impression that it had been over a dyer's shop; that he went up steps to it; that he had frequently grazed his knees in doing so; and that in trying to scrape the mud off a very unsteady little shoe, he generally got his leg over the scraper. Other similar memories of childhood have dropped from him occasionally in his lesser writings; whose readers may remember how vividly portions of his boyhood are reproduced in his fancy of the Christmas-tree, and will hardly have forgotten what he says, in his thoughtful little paper on Nurse's stories, of the doubtful places and people to which children may be introduced before they are six years old, and forced, night after night, to go back to against their wills, by servants to whom they are entrusted. That childhood exaggerates what it sees, too, has he not tenderly told? How he thought the Rochester High Street must be at least as wide as Regent Street, which he afterwards discovered to be little better than a lane; how the public clock in it, supposed to be the finest clock in the world, turned out to be as moon-faced and weak a clock as a man's eyes ever saw; and how, in its town hall, which had appeared to him once so glorious a structure that he had set it up in his mind as the model on which the genie of the lamp built the palace for Aladdin, he had painfully to recognise a mere mean little heap of bricks, like a chapel gone demented. Yet not so painfully, either, when second thoughts wisely came. "Ah! who was I that I should quarrel with the town for being changed to me, when I myself had come back, so changed, to it? All my early readings and early imaginations dated from this place, and I took them away so full of innocent construction and guileless belief, and I brought them back so worn and torn, so much the wiser, and so much the worse!"

And here I may at once expressly mention, what already has been hinted, that even as Fielding described himself and his belongings in Captain Booth and Amelia, and protested always that he had writ in his books nothing more than he had seen in life, so it may be said of Dickens in more especial relation to David Copperfield. Many guesses have been made since his death, connecting David's autobiography with his own; accounting, by means of such actual experiences, for the so frequent recurrence in his writings of the prison-life, its humour and pathos, described in them with such wonderful reality; and discovering, in what David tells Steerforth at school of the stories he had read in his childhood, what it was that had given the bent to his own genius. There is not only truth in all this, but it will very shortly be seen that the identity went deeper than any had supposed, and covered experiences not less startling in the reality than they appear to be in the fiction.

Of the "readings" and "imaginations" which he describes as brought away from Chatham, this authority can tell us. It is one of the many passages in *Copperfield* which are literally true, and its proper place is here. "My father had left a small collection of books in a little room upstairs to which I had access (for it adjoined my own), and which nobody else in our house ever troubled. From that blessed little room, *Roderick Random, Peregrine Pickle, Humphrey Clinker, Tom Jones, The Vicar of Wakefield, Don Quixote, Gil Blas* and *Robinson Crusoe* came out, a glorious host, to keep me company. They kept alive my fancy, and my hope of something beyond that place and time—they, and the *Arabian Nights,* and the *Tales of the Genii*

—and did me no harm; for, whatever harm was in some of them, was not there for me; *I* knew nothing of it. It is astonishing to me now, how I found time, in the midst of my porings and blunderings over heavier themes, to read those books as I did. It is curious to me how I could ever have consoled myself under my small troubles (which were great troubles to me), by impersonating my favourite characters in them. . . . I have been Tom Jones (a child's Tom Jones, a harmless creature) for a week together. I have sustained my own idea of Roderick Random for a month at a stretch, I verily believe. I had a greedy relish for a few volumes of voyages and travels—I forget what, now—that were on those shelves; and for days and days I can remember to have gone about my region of our house, armed with the centre-piece out of an old set of boot-trees: the perfect realisation of Captain Somebody, of the Royal British Navy, in danger of being beset by savages, and resolved to sell his life at a great price. . . . When I think of it, the picture always rises in my mind, of a summer evening, the boys at play in the churchyard, and I sitting on my bed reading as if for life. Every barn in the neighbourhood, every stone in the church, and every foot of the churchyard, had some association of its own, in my mind, connected with these books, and stood for some locality made famous in them. I have seen Tom Pipes go climbing up the church steeple; I have watched Strap, with the knapsack on his back, stopping to rest himself upon the wicket-gate; and I *know* that Commodore Trunnion held that club with Mr. Pickle in the parlour of our little village alehouse." Every word of this personal recollection had been written down as fact, some years before it found its way into *David Copperfield*; the only change in the fiction being his omission of the name of a cheap series of novelists then in course of publication, by means of which his father had become happily the owner of so large a lump of literary treasure in his small collection of books.

The usual result followed. The child took to writing himself; and became famous in his childish circle for having written a tragedy called *Misnar, the Sultan of India*, founded (and very literally founded, no doubt) on one of the *Tales of the Genii*. Nor was this his only distinction. He told a story offhand so well, and sang small comic songs so especially well, that he used to be elevated on chairs and tables, both at home and abroad, for more effective display of these talents; and when he first told me of this, at one of the Twelfth-night parties on his eldest son's birthday, he said he never recalled it that his own shrill little voice of childhood did not again tingle in his ears, and he blushed to think what a horrible little nuisance he must have been to many unoffending grown-up people who were called upon to admire him.

His chief ally and encourager in such displays was a youth of some ability, much older than himself, named James Lamert, stepson to his mother's sister, and therefore a sort of cousin, who was his great patron and friend in his childish days. Mary, the eldest daughter of Charles Barrow, himself a lieutenant in the navy, had for her first husband a commander in the navy called Allen, on whose death by drowning at Rio Janeiro she had joined her sister, the navy pay-clerk's wife, at Chatham; in which place she subsequently took for her second husband Doctor Lamert, an army surgeon, whose son James, even after he had been sent to Sandhurst for his education, continued still to visit Chatham from time to time. He had a turn for private theatricals; and as his father's quarters were in the ordnance hospital there, a great rambling place otherwise at that time almost uninhabited, he had plenty of room in which to get up his entertainments. The staff-doctor himself played his part, and his portrait will be found in *Pickwick*.

By Lamert, I have often heard him say, he was first taken to the theatre at the very tenderest age. He could hardly, however, have been younger than Charles Lamb, whose first experience was of having seen *Artaxerxes* when six years old; and certainly not younger than Walter Scott, who was only four when he saw *As You Like It* on the Bath stage, and remembered having screamed out, *"Ain't they brothers?"* when scandalised by Orlando and Oliver beginning to fight. But he was at any rate old enough to recollect how his young heart leapt with terror as the wicked King Richard, struggling for life against the virtuous Richmond, backed up and bumped against the box in which he was; and subsequent visits to the same sanctuary, as he tells us, revealed to him many wondrous secrets, "of which not the least terrific were, that the witches in *Macbeth* bore an awful resemblance to the thanes and other proper inhabitants of Scotland; and that the good King Duncan couldn't rest in his grave, but was constantly coming out of it, and calling himself somebody else."

During the last two years of Charles's residence at Chatham, he was sent to a school kept in Clover Lane by the young Baptist minister already named, Mr. William Giles. I have the picture of him here very strongly in my mind as a sensitive, thoughtful, feeble-bodied little boy, with an amount of experience as well as fancy unusual in such a child, and with a dangerous kind of wandering intelligence that a teacher might turn to good or evil, happiness or misery, as he directed it. Nor does the influence of Mr. Giles, such as it was, seem to have been other than favourable. Charles had himself a not ungrateful sense in after years that this first of his masters, in his little-cared-for childhood, had pronounced him to be a boy of capacity; and when, about half-way through the publication of *Pickwick*, his old teacher sent a silver snuff-box with admiring inscription to "the inimitable Boz," it reminded him of praise far more precious obtained by him at his first year's examination in the Clover Lane academy, when his recitation of a piece out of the *Humorist's Miscellany* about Doctor Bolus had received, unless his youthful vanity bewildered him, a double encore. A habit, the only bad one taught him by Mr. Giles, of taking for a time, in very moderate quantities, the snuff called Irish Blackguard, was the result of this gift from his old master; but he abandoned it after some few years, and it was never resumed.

It was in the boys' playing-ground near Clover Lane in which the school stood that, according to one of his youthful memories, he had been, in the hay-making time, delivered from the dungeons of Seringapatam, an immense pile ("of haycock"), by his countrymen the victorious British ("boy next door and his two cousins"), and had been recognised with ecstacy by his affianced one ("Miss Green"), who had come all the way from England ("second house in the terrace"), to ransom and marry him. It was in this playing-field, too, as he has himself recorded, he first heard in confidence from one whose father was greatly connected, "being under Government," of the existence of a terrible banditti called *the radicals*, whose principles were that the prince regent wore stays; that nobody had a right to any salary; and that the army and navy ought to be put down; horrors at which he trembled in his bed, after supplicating that the radicals might be speedily taken and hanged. Nor was it the least of the disappointments in his visit of after life to the scenes of his boyhood to have found this play-field swallowed up by a railway station. It was gone, with its two beautiful trees of hawthorn; and where the hedge, the turf and all the buttercups and daisies had been, there was nothing but the stoniest of jolting roads.

He was not much over nine years old when his father was recalled from Chatham to Somerset House, and he had to leave this good master, and the old place endeared to him by recollections that clung to him afterwards all his life long. It was here he had made the acquaintance not only of the famous books that David Copperfield specially names, of *Roderick Random, Peregrine Pickle, Humphrey Clinker, Tom Jones, The Vicar of Wakefield, Don Quixote, Gil Blas, Robinson Crusoe, The Arabian Nights,* and the *Tales of the Genii,* but also of the *Tatler, The Spectator, The Idler,* the *Citizen of the World,* and Mrs. Inchbald's *Collection of Farces.* These latter had been, as well, in the little library to which access was open to him; and of all of them his earliest remembrance was the having read them over and over at Chatham, not for the first, the second, or the third time. They were a host of friends when he had no single friend; and, in leaving the place, he has been often heard to say he seemed to be leaving them too, and everything that had given his ailing little life its picturesqueness or sunshine. It was the birthplace of his fancy; and he hardly knew what store he had set by its busy varieties of change and scene, until he saw the falling cloud that was to hide its pictures from him for ever. The gay, bright regiments always going and coming, the continual paradings and firings, the successions of sham-sieges and sham-defences, the plays got up by his cousin in the hospital, the navy pay-yacht in which he had sailed to Sheerness with his father, and the ships floating out in the Medway, with their far visions of sea— he was to lose them all. He was never to watch the boys at their games any more, or see them sham over again the sham-sieges and defences. He was to be taken away to London inside the stage-coach *Commodore;* and Kentish woods and fields, Cobham park and hall, Rochester cathedral and castle, and all the wonderful romance together, including a red-cheeked baby he had been wildly in love with, were to vanish like a dream. "On the night before we came away," he told me, "my good master came flitting in among the packing-cases to give me Goldsmith's *Bee* as a keepsake. Which I kept for his sake, and its own, a long time afterwards." A longer time afterwards he recollected the stage-coach journey, and in one of his published papers said that never had he forgotten, through all the intervening years, the smell of the damp straw in which he was packed and forwarded, like game, carriage paid. "There was no other inside passenger, and I consumed my sandwiches in solitude and dreariness, and it rained hard all the way, and I thought life sloppier than I expected to find it."

The earliest impressions received and retained by him in

London were of his father's money involvements; and how first he heard mentioned "the deed," representing in fact that crisis of his father's affairs which is ascribed in fiction to Mr. Micawber's. He knew it in later days to have been a composition with creditors; though at this earlier date he was conscious of having confounded it with parchments of a much more demoniacal description. One result from the awful document soon showed itself in enforced retrenchment. The family had to take up its abode in a house in Bayham Street, Camden Town.

Bayham Street was about the poorest part of the London suburbs then, and the house was a mean small tenement, with a wretched little back-garden abutting on a squalid court. Here was no place for new acquaintances to him: not a boy was near with whom he might hope to become in any way familiar. A washerwoman lived next door, and a Bow Street officer lived over the way. Many, many times has he spoken to me of this, and how he seemed at once to fall into a solitary condition apart from all other boys of his own age, and to sink into a neglected state at home which had always been quite unaccountable to him. "As I thought," he said on one occasion very bitterly, "in the little back garret in Bayham Street, of all I had lost in losing Chatham, what would I have given, if I had had anything to give, to have been sent back to any other school, to have been taught something anywhere!" He was at another school already, not knowing it. The self-education forced upon him was teaching, all unconsciously as yet, what, for the future that awaited him, it most behoved him to know.

That he took, from the very beginning of this Bayham Street life, his first impression of that struggling poverty which is nowhere more vividly shown than in the commoner streets of the ordinary London suburb, and which enriched his earliest writings with a freshness of original humour and quite unstudied pathos that gave them much of their sudden popularity, there cannot be a doubt. "I certainly understood it," he has often said to me, "quite as well then as I do now." But he was not conscious yet that he did so understand it, or of the influence it was exerting on his life even then. It seems almost too much to assert of a child, say at nine or ten years old, that his observation of everything was as close and good, or that he had as much intuitive understanding of the character and weaknesses of the grown-up people around him, as when the same keen and wonderful faculty had made him famous among men. But my experience of him led me to put implicit faith in the assertion

he unvaryingly himself made, that he had never seen any cause
to correct or change what in his boyhood was his own secret
impression of anybody, whom he had, as a grown man, the
opportunity of testing in later years.

How it came that, being what he was, he should now have
fallen into the misery and neglect of the time about to be
described, was a subject on which thoughts were frequently
interchanged between us; and on one occasion he gave me a
sketch of the character of his father which, as I can here repeat
it in the exact words employed by him, will be the best preface
I can make to what I feel that I have no alternative but to tell.
"I know my father to be as kindhearted and generous a man as
ever lived in the world. Everything that I can remember of his
conduct to his wife, or children, or friends, in sickness or affliction, is beyond all praise. By me, as a sick child, he has watched
night and day, unweariedly and patiently, many nights and days.
He never undertook any business, charge or trust that he did
not zealously, conscientiously, punctually, honourably discharge.
His industry has always been untiring. He was proud of me, in
his way, and had a great admiration of the comic singing. But,
in the ease of his temper, and the straitness of his means, he
appeared to have utterly lost at this time the idea of educating
me at all, and to have utterly put from him the notion that
I had any claim upon him, in that regard, whatever. So I
degenerated into cleaning his boots of a morning, and my own;
and making myself useful in the work of the little house; and
looking after my younger brothers and sisters (we were now six
in all); and going on such poor errands as arose out of our
poor way of living."

The cousin by marriage of whom I have spoken, James Lamert,
who had lately completed his education at Sandhurst, and was
waiting in hopes of a commission, lived now with the family in
Bayham Street, and had not lost his taste for the stage, or his
ingenuities in connection with it. Taking pity on the solitary
lad, he made and painted a little theatre for him. It was the
only fanciful reality of his present life; but it could not supply
what he missed most sorely, the companionship of boys of his
own age, with whom he might share in the advantages of school,
and contend for its prizes. His sister Fanny was at about this
time elected as a pupil to the royal academy of music; and he
has told me what a stab to his heart it was, thinking of his own
disregarded condition, to see her go away to begin her education,
amid the tearful good wishes of everybody in the house.

Nevertheless, as time went on, his own education still unconsciously went on as well, under the sternest and most potent of teachers; and, neglected and miserable as he was, he managed gradually to transfer to London all the dreaminess and all the romance with which he had invested Chatham. There were then at the top of Bayham Street some almshouses, and were still when he revisited it with me nearly twenty-seven years ago; and to go to this spot, he told me, and look from it over the dust-heaps and dock-leaves and fields (no longer there when we saw it together) at the cupola of St. Paul's looming through the smoke, was a treat that served him for hours of vague reflection afterwards. To be taken out for a walk into the real town, especially if it were anywhere about Covent Garden or the Strand, perfectly entranced him with pleasure. But, most of all, he had a profound attraction of repulsion to St. Giles's. If he could only induce whomsoever took him out to take him through Seven Dials, he was supremely happy. "Good Heaven!" he would exclaim, "what wild visions of prodigies of wickedness, want, and beggary, arose in my mind out of that place!" He was all this time, the reader will remember, still subject to continual attacks of illness, and, by reason of them, a very small boy even for his age.

That part of his boyhood is now very near of which, when the days of fame and prosperity came to him, he felt the weight upon his memory as a painful burthen until he could lighten it by sharing it with a friend; and an accident I will presently mention led him first to reveal it. There is, however, an interval of some months still to be described, of which, from conversations or letters that passed between us, after or because of this confidence, and that already have yielded fruit to these pages, I can supply some vague and desultory notices. The use thus made of them, it is due to myself to remark, was contemplated then; for though, long before his death, I had ceased to believe it likely that I should survive to write about him, he had never withdrawn the wish at this early time strongly expressed, or the confidences, not only then, but to the very eve of his death reposed in me, that were to enable me to fulfil it. The fulfilment indeed he had himself rendered more easy by partially uplifting the veil in *David Copperfield*.

The visits made from Bayham Street were chiefly to two connections of the family, his mother's elder brother and his godfather. The latter, who was a rigger, and mast, oar and block maker, lived at Limehouse in a substantial handsome

sort of way, and was kind to his godchild. It was always a great
treat to him to go to Mr. Huffham's; and the London night-
sights as he returned were a perpetual joy and marvel. Here,
too, the comic-singing accomplishment was brought into play
so greatly to the admiration of one of the godfather's guests,
an honest boat-builder, that he pronounced the little lad to be
a "progidy." The visits to the uncle, who was at this time
fellow-clerk with his father in Somerset House, were nearer
home. Mr. Thomas Barrow, the eldest of his mother's family,
had broken his leg in a fall; and, while laid up with this illness,
his lodging was in Gerard Street, Soho, in the upper part of the
house of a worthy gentleman then recently deceased, a bookseller named Manson, father to the partner in the celebrated
firm of Christie and Manson, whose widow at the time carried
on the business. Attracted by the look of the lad as he went
upstairs, these good people lent him books to amuse him;
among them Miss Porter's *Scottish Chiefs*, Holbein's *Dance of
Death*, and George Colman's *Broad Grins*. The latter seized his
fancy very much; and he was so impressed by its description
of Covent Garden, in the piece called the "Elder Brother," that
he stole down to the market by himself to compare it with the
book. He remembered, as he said in telling me this, snuffing up
the flavour of the faded cabbage-leaves as if it were the very
breath of comic fiction. Nor was he far wrong, as comic fiction
then, and for some time after, was. It was reserved for himself
to give sweeter and fresher breath to it. Many years were to
pass first, but he was beginning already to make the trial.

His uncle was shaved by a very odd old barber out of Dean
Street, Soho, who was never tired of reviewing the events of
the last war, and especially of detecting Napoleon's mistakes,
and rearranging his whole life for him on a plan of his own.
The boy wrote a description of this old barber, but never had
courage to show it. At about the same time, taking for his model
the description of the canon's housekeeper in *Gil Blas*, he
sketched a deaf old woman who waited on them in Bayham
Street, and who made delicate hashes with walnut ketchup. As
little did he dare to show this, either; though he thought it,
himself, extremely clever.

In Bayham Street, meanwhile, affairs were going on badly;
the poor boy's visits to his uncle, while the latter was still kept
a prisoner by his accident, were interrupted by another attack
of fever; and on his recovery the mysterious "deed" had again
come uppermost. His father's resources were so low, and all

his expedients so thoroughly exhausted, that trial was to be made whether his mother might not come to the rescue. The time was arrived for her to exert herself, she said; and she "must do something." The godfather down at Limehouse was reported to have an Indian connection. People in the East Indies always sent their children home to be educated. She would set up a school. They would all grow rich by it. And then, thought the sick boy, "perhaps even I might go to school myself."

A house was soon found at number four, Gower Street North; a large brass plate on the door announced MRS. DICKENS'S ESTABLISHMENT; and the result I can give in the exact words of the then small actor in the comedy, whose hopes it had raised so high. "I left, at a great many other doors, a great many circulars calling attention to the merits of the establishment. Yet nobody ever came to school, nor do I recollect that anybody ever proposed to come, or that the least preparation was made to receive anybody. But I know that we got on very badly with the butcher and baker; that very often we had not too much for dinner; and that at last my father was arrested." The interval between the sponging-house and the prison was passed by the sorrowful lad in running errands and carrying messages for the prisoner, delivered with swollen eyes and through shining tears; and the last words said to him by his father before he was finally carried to the Marshalsea, were to the effect that the sun was set upon him for ever. "I really believed at the time," said Dickens to me, "that they had broken my heart." He took afterwards ample revenge for this false alarm by making all the world laugh at them in *David Copperfield*.

The readers of Mr. Micawber's history who remember David's first visit to the Marshalsea prison, and how upon seeing the turnkey he recalled the turnkey in the blanket in *Roderick Random*, will read with curious interest what follows, written as a personal experience of fact two or three years before the fiction had even entered into his thoughts.

"My father was waiting for me in the lodge, and we went up to his room (on the top story but one), and cried very much. And he told me, I remember, to take warning by the Marshalsea, and to observe that if a man had twenty pounds a year, and spent nineteen pounds nineteen shillings and sixpence, he would be happy; but that a shilling spent the other way would make him wretched. I see the fire we sat before now; with two bricks inside the rusted grate, one on each side, to prevent its burning too many coals. Some other debtor shared the room with him, who came in by and by; and as the dinner was a joint-stock repast, I was sent up to 'Captain Porter' in the room overhead, with Mr. Dickens's compliments, and I was his son, and could he, Captain P., lend me a knife and fork?

"Captain Porter lent the knife and fork, with his compliments in return. There was a very dirty lady in his little room; and two wan girls, his daughters, with shock heads of hair. I thought I should not have liked to borrow Captain Porter's comb. The Captain himself was in the last extremity of shabbiness; and if I could draw at all, I would draw an accurate portrait of the old, old brown great-coat he wore, with no other coat below it. His whiskers were large. I saw his bed rolled up in a corner; and what plates and dishes and pots he had, on a shelf; and I knew (God knows how) that the two girls with the shock heads were Captain Porter's natural children, and that the dirty lady was not married to Captain P. My timid, wondering station on his threshold was not occupied more than a couple of minutes, I dare say; but I came down again to the room below with all this as surely in my knowledge, as the knife and fork were in my hand."

How there was something agreeable and gipsy-like in the dinner after all, and how he took back the Captain's knife and fork early in the afternoon, and how he went home to comfort his mother with an account of his visit, David Copperfield has also accurately told. Then, at home, came many miserable daily struggles that seemed to last an immense time, yet did not perhaps cover many weeks. Almost everything by degrees was sold or pawned, little Charles being the principal agent in those sorrowful transactions. Such of the books as had been brought from Chatham, *Peregrine Pickle, Roderick Random, Tom Jones, Humphrey Clinker*, and all the rest, went first. They were carried off from the little chiffonier, which his father called the library, to a bookseller in the Hampstead Road, the same that David Copperfield describes as in the City Road; and the account of the sales, as they actually occurred and were told to me long before David was born, was reproduced word for word in his imaginary narrative. "The keeper of this bookstall, who lived in a little house behind it, used to get tipsy every night, and to be violently scolded by his wife every morning. More than once, when I went there early, I had audience of him in a turn-up bedstead, with a cut in his forehead or a black eye, bearing witness to his excesses over night (I am afraid he was quarrelsome in his drink); and he, with a shaking hand, endeavouring to find the needful shillings in one or other of the pockets of his clothes, which lay upon the floor, while his wife, with a baby in her arms and her shoes down at heel, never left off rating him. Sometimes he had lost his money, and then he would ask me to call again; but his wife had always got some (had taken his, I dare say, while he was drunk), and secretly completed the bargain on the stairs, as we went down together."

The same pawnbroker's shop, too, which was so well known to David, became not less familiar to Charles; and a good deal of notice was here taken of him by the pawnbroker, or by his principal clerk who officiated behind the counter, and who, while making out the duplicate, liked of all things to hear the lad conjugate a Latin verb, and translate or decline his *musa* and *dominus*. Everything to this accompaniment went gradually; until at last, even of the furniture of Gower Street number four, there was nothing left except a few chairs, a kitchen table and some beds. Then they encamped, as it were, in the two parlours of the emptied house, and lived there night and day.

All which is but the prelude to what remains to be described.

II

HARD EXPERIENCES IN BOYHOOD

1822-4

THE incidents to be told now would probably never have been known to me, or indeed any of the occurrences of his childhood and youth, but for the accident of a question which I put to him one day in the March or April of 1847.

I asked if he remembered ever having seen in his boyhood our friend the elder Mr. Dilke, his father's acquaintance and contemporary, who had been a clerk in the same office in Somerset House to which Mr. John Dickens belonged. Yes, he said, he recollected seeing him at a house in Gerrard Street, where his uncle Barrow lodged during an illness, and Mr. Dilke had visited him. Never at any other time. Upon which I told him that someone else had been intended in the mention made to me, for that the reference implied not merely his being met accidentally, but his having had some juvenile employment in a warehouse near the Strand; at which place Mr. Dilke, being with the elder Dickens one day, had noticed him, and received, in return for the gift of a half-crown, a very low bow. He was silent for several minutes; I felt that I had unintentionally touched a painful place in his memory; and to Mr. Dilke I never spoke of the subject again. It was not, however, then, but some weeks later, that Dickens made further allusion to my thus having struck unconsciously upon a time of which he never could lose the remembrance while he remembered anything, and the recollection of which, at intervals, haunted him and made him miserable, even to that hour.

Very shortly afterwards, I learnt in all their detail the incidents that had been so painful to him, and what then was said to me or written respecting them revealed the story of his boyhood. The idea of *David Copperfield*, which was to take all the world into his confidence, had not at this time occurred to him; but what it had so startled me to know, his readers were afterwards told with only such change or addition as for the time might sufficiently disguise himself under cover of his hero. For, the poor little lad, with good ability and a most sensitive nature, turned at the age of ten into a "labouring hind" in the service of "Murdstone and Grinby," and conscious already of what made it seem very strange to him that he could so easily have been thrown away at such an age, was indeed himself. His was the secret agony of soul at finding himself "companion to Mick Walker and Mealy Potatoes," and his the tears that mingled with the water in which he and they rinsed and washed out bottles. It had all been written, as fact, before he thought of any other use for it; and it was not until several months later, when the fancy of *David Copperfield*, itself suggested by what he had so written of his early troubles, began to take shape in his mind, that he abandoned his first intention of writing his own life. Those warehouse experiences fell then so aptly into the subject he had chosen, that he could not resist the temptation of immediately using them; and the manuscript recording them, which was but the first portion of what he had designed to write, was embodied in the substance of the eleventh and earlier chapters of his novel. What already had been sent to me, however, and proof-sheets of the novel interlined at the time, enable me now to separate the fact from the fiction; and to supply to the story of the author's childhood those passages, omitted from the book, which, apart from their illustration of the growth of his character, present to us a picture of tragical suffering, and of tender as well as humorous fancy, unsurpassed in even the wonders of his published writings.

The person indirectly responsible for the scenes to be described was the young relative James Lamert, the cousin by his aunt's marriage of whom I have made frequent mention, who got up the plays at Chatham, and after passing at Sandhurst had been living with the family in Bayham Street in the hope of obtaining a commission in the army. This did not come until long afterwards, when, in consideration of his father's services, he received it, and relinquished it then in favour of a younger brother; but he had meanwhile, before the family removed from Camden Town, ceased to live with them. The husband of a sister of his (of the same name as himself, being indeed his cousin, George Lamert), a man of some property, had recently embarked in an odd sort of commercial speculation; and had taken him into his office, and his house, to assist in it. I give now the fragment of the autobiography of Dickens.

"This speculation was a rivalry of 'Warren's Blacking,

30, Strand,'—at that time very famous. One Jonathan Warren (the famous one was Robert), living at 30, Hungerford Stairs, or Market, Strand (for I forget which it was called then), claimed to have been the original inventor or proprietor of the blacking recipe, and to have been deposed and ill-used by his renowned relation. At last he put himself in the way of selling his recipe, and his name, and his 30, Hungerford Stairs, Strand (30, Strand, very large, and the intermediate direction very small), for an annuity; and he set forth by his agents that a little capital would make a great business of it. The man of some property was found in George Lamert, the cousin and brother-in-law of James. He bought this right and title, and went into the blacking business and the blacking premises.

"—In an evil hour for me, as I often bitterly thought. Its chief manager, James Lamert, the relative who had lived with us in Bayham Street, seeing how I was employed from day to day, and knowing what our domestic circumstances then were, proposed that I should go into the blacking warehouse, to be as useful as I could, at a salary, I think, of six shillings a week. I am not clear whether it was six or seven. I am inclined to believe, from my uncertainty on this head, that it was six at first, and seven afterwards. At any rate, the offer was accepted very willingly by my father and mother, and on a Monday morning I went down to the blacking warehouse to begin my business life.

"It is wonderful to me how I could have been so easily cast away at such an age. It is wonderful to me that, even after my descent into the poor little drudge I had been since we came to London, no one had compassion enough on me—a child of singular abilities: quick, eager, delicate, and soon hurt, bodily or mentally—to suggest that something might have been spared, as certainly it might have been, to place me at any common school. Our friends, I take it, were tired out. No one made any sign. My father and mother were quite satisfied. They could hardly have been more so, if I had been twenty years of age, distinguished at a grammar-school, and going to Cambridge.

"The blacking warehouse was the last house on the left-hand side of the way, at old Hungerford Stairs. It was a crazy, tumble-down old house, abutting of course on the river, and literally overrun with rats. Its wainscotted rooms and its rotten floors and staircase, and the old grey rats swarming down in the cellars, and the sound of their squeaking and scuffling coming up the stairs at all times, and the dirt and decay of the place, rise up visibly before me, as if I were there again. The counting-house was on the first floor, looking over the coal-barges and the river. There was a recess in it, in which I was to sit and work. My work was to cover the pots of paste-blacking: first with a piece of oil-paper, and then with a piece of blue paper; to tie them round with a string; and then to clip the paper close and neat all round, until it looked as smart as a pot of ointment from an apothecary's shop. When a certain number of grosses of pots had attained this pitch of perfection, I was to paste on each a printed label; and then go on again with more pots. Two or three other boys were kept at similar duty downstairs on similar wages. One of them came up, in a ragged apron and a paper cap, on the first Monday morning, to show me the trick of using the string and tying the knot. His name was Bob Fagin; and I took the liberty of using his name, long afterwards, in *Oliver Twist*.

"Our relative had kindly arranged to teach me something in the dinner-hour; from twelve to one, I think it was; every day. But an arrangement so incompatible with counting-house business soon died away, from no fault of his or mine; and for the same reason, my small work-table, and my grosses of pots, my papers, string, scissors, paste-pot and labels, by little and little, vanished out of the recess in the counting-house, and kept company with the other small work-tables, grosses of pots, papers, string, scissors and paste-pots downstairs. It was not long before Bob Fagin and I, and another boy whose name was Paul Green, but who was currently believed to have been christened Poll (a belief which I transferred, long afterwards, again, to Mr. Sweedlepipe, in *Martin Chuzzlewit*), worked generally, side by side. Bob Fagin was an orphan, and lived with his brother-in-law, a waterman. Poll Green's father had the additional distinction of being a fireman, and was employed at Drury Lane theatre; where another relation of Poll's, I think his little sister, did imps in the pantomimes.

"No words can express the secret agony of my soul as I sunk into this companionship; compared these everyday associates with those of my happier childhood; and felt my early hopes of growing up to be a learned and distinguished man crushed in my breast. The deep remembrance of the sense I had of being utterly neglected and hopeless; of the shame I felt in my position; of the misery it was to my young heart to believe that, day by day, what I had learned, and thought, and delighted in, and raised my fancy and my emulation up by, was passing away from me, never to be brought back any more; cannot be written.

My whole nature was so penetrated with the grief and humiliation of such considerations, that even now, famous and caressed and happy, I often forget in my dreams that I have a dear wife and children; even that I am a man; and wander desolately back to that time of my life.

"My mother and my brothers and sisters (excepting Fanny in the royal academy of music) were still encamped, with a young servant-girl from Chatham Workhouse, in the two parlours in the emptied house in Gower Street North. It was a long way to go and return within the dinner-hour, and, usually, I either carried my dinner with me, or went and bought it at some neighbouring shop. In the latter case, it was commonly a saveloy and a penny loaf; sometimes, a fourpenny plate of beef from a cook's shop; sometimes, a plate of bread and cheese, and a glass of beer, from a miserable old public-house over the way; the Swan, if I remember right, or the Swan and something else that I have forgotten. Once, I remember tucking my own bread (which I had brought from home in the morning) under my arm, wrapped up in a piece of paper like a book, and going into the best dining-room in Johnson's alamode beef-house in Clare Court, Drury Lane, and magnificently ordering a small plate of alamode beef to eat with it. What the waiter thought of such a strange little apparition, coming in all alone, I don't know; but I can see him now, staring at me as I ate my dinner, and bringing up the other waiter to look. I gave him a halfpenny, and I wish, now, that he hadn't taken it."

I lose here for a little while the fragment of direct narrative, but I perfectly recollect that he used to describe Saturday night as his great treat. It was a grand thing to walk home with six shillings in his pocket, and to look in at the shop windows, and think what it would buy. Hunt's roasted corn, as a British and patriotic substitute for coffee, was in great vogue just then; and the little fellow used to buy it, and roast it on the Sunday. There was a cheap periodical of selected pieces called the *Portfolio* which he had also a great fancy for taking home with him. The new proposed "deed," meanwhile, had failed to propitiate his father's creditors; all hope of arrangement passed away; and the end was that his mother and her encampment in Gower Street North broke up and went to live in the Marshalsea. I am able at this point to resume his own account.

"The key of the house was sent back to the landlord, who was very glad to get it; and I (small Cain that I was, except that I had never done harm to anyone) was handed over as a lodger to a reduced old lady, long known to our family, in Little College Street, Camden Town, who took children in to board, and had once done so at Brighton; and who, with a few alterations and embellishments, unconsciously began to sit for Mrs. Pipchin in *Dombey*, when she took in me.

"She had a little brother and sister under her care then; somebody's natural children, who were very irregularly paid for; and a widow's little son. The two boys and I slept in the same room. My own exclusive breakfast, of a penny cottage loaf and a pennyworth of milk, I provided for myself. I kept another small loaf, and a quarter of a pound of cheese, on a particular shelf of a particular cupboard: to make my supper on when I came back at night. They made a hole in the six or seven shillings, I know well; and I was out at the blacking warehouse all day, and had to support myself upon that money all the week. I suppose my lodging was paid for, by my father. I certainly did not pay it myself; and I certainly had no other assistance whatever (the making of my clothes, I think, excepted), from Monday morning until Saturday night. No advice, no counsel, no encouragement, no consolation, no support, from anyone that I can call to mind, so help me God.

"Sundays Fanny and I passed in the prison. I was at the academy in Tenterden Street, Hanover Square, at nine o'clock in the morning, to fetch her; and we walked back there together at night.

"I was so young and childish, and so little qualified—how could I be otherwise?—to undertake the whole charge of my own existence that, in going to Hungerford Stairs of a morning, I could not resist the stale pastry put out at half-price on trays at the confectioners' doors in Tottenham Court Road; and I often spent in that the money I should have kept for my dinner. Then I went without my dinner, or bought a roll, or a slice of pudding. There were two pudding shops between which I was divided, according to my finances. One was in a court close to St. Martin's Church (at the back of the church), which is now removed altogether. The pudding at that shop was made with currants, and was rather a special pudding, but was dear: two penn'orth not being larger than a penn'orth of more ordinary pudding. A good shop for the latter was in the Strand, somewhere near where the Lowther Arcade is now. It was a stout, hale pudding, heavy and flabby; with great raisins in it, stuck in whole, at great distances apart. It came up hot, at about noon every day: and many and many a day did I dine off it.

"We had half an hour, I think, for tea. When I had money enough, I used to go to a coffee-shop, and have half a pint of coffee, and a slice of bread and butter. When I had no money, I took a turn in Covent Garden Market, and stared at the pine-apples. The coffee-shops to which I most resorted were, one in Maiden Lane; one in a court (non-existent now) close to Hunger-ford Market; and one in St. Martin's Lane, of which I only recollect that it stood near the church, and that in the door there was an oval glass plate, with COFFEE-ROOM painted on it, addressed towards the street. If I ever find myself in a very different kind of coffee-room now, but where there is such an inscription on glass, and read it backward on the wrong side MOOR-EEFFOC (as I often used to do then, in a dismal reverie), a shock goes through my blood.

"I know I do not exaggerate, unconsciously and unintention-ally, the scantiness of my resources and the difficulties of my life. I know that if a shilling or so were given me by anyone, I spent it in a dinner or a tea. I know that I worked, from morn-ing to night, with common men and boys, a shabby child. I know that I tried, but ineffectually, not to anticipate my money, and to make it last the week through by putting it away in a drawer I had in the counting-house, wrapped into six little parcels, each parcel containing the same amount, and labelled with a different day. I know that I have lounged about the streets, insufficiently and unsatisfactorily fed. I know that, but for the mercy of God, I might easily have been, for any care that was taken of me, a little robber or a little vagabond.

"But I held some station at the blacking warehouse too. Besides that my relative at the counting house did what a man so occupied, and dealing with a thing so anomalous, could, to treat me as one upon a different footing from the rest, I never said, to man or boy, how it was that I came to be there, or gave the least indication of being sorry that I was there. That I suffered in secret, and that I suffered exquisitely, no one ever knew but I. How much I suffered, it is, as I have said already, utterly beyond my power to tell. No man's imagination can overstep the reality. But I kept my own counsel, and I did my work. I knew from the first that, if I could not do my work as well as any of the rest, I could not hold myself above a slight and contempt. I soon became at least as expeditious and as skilful with my hands as either of the other boys. Though perfectly familiar with them, my conduct and manners were different enough from theirs to place a space between us. They, and the men, always spoke of me as 'the young gentleman.' A certain man (a soldier once) named Thomas, who was the foreman, and another named Harry, who was the carman and wore a red jacket, used to call me 'Charles' sometimes, in speaking to me; but I think it was mostly when we were very confidential, and when I had made some efforts to entertain them over our work with the results of some of the old readings, which were fast perishing out of my mind. Poll Green uprose once, and rebelled against the 'young-gentleman' usage; but Bob Fagin settled him speedily.

"My rescue from this kind of existence I considered quite hopeless, and abandoned as such, altogether; though I am solemnly convinced that I never, for one hour, was reconciled to it, or was otherwise than miserably unhappy. I felt keenly, however, the being so cut off from my parents, my brothers, and sisters; and, when my day's work was done, going home to such a miserable blank; and *that*, I thought, might be corrected. One Sunday night I remonstrated with my father on this head, so pathetically and with so many tears, that his kind nature gave way. He began to think that it was not quite right. I do believe he had never thought so before, or thought about it. It was the first remonstrance I had ever made about my lot, and perhaps it opened up a little more than I intended. A back-attic was found for me at the house of an insolvent court agent, who lived in Lant Street in the Borough, where Bob Sawyer lodged many years afterwards. A bed and bedding were sent over for me, and made up on the floor. The little window had a pleasant prospect of a timber-yard; and when I took possession of my new abode, I thought it was a Paradise."

There is here another blank, which it is, however, not difficult to supply from letters and recollections of my own. What was to him of course the great pleasure of his paradise of a lodging was its bringing him again, though after a fashion sorry enough, within the circle of home. From this time he used to breakfast "at home," in other words in the Marshalsea; going to it as early as the gates were open, and for the most part much earlier. They had no want of bodily comforts there. His father's income, still going on, was amply sufficient for that; and in every respect indeed but elbow-room, I have heard him say the family lived more comfortably in prison than they had done for a long time out of it. They were waited on still by the maid-of-all-work from Bayham Street, the orphan girl of the Chatham Workhouse, from whose sharp little worldly and also kindly ways he took his first impression of the marchioness in the *Old Curiosity Shop*. She too had a lodging in the neighbourhood that she might be early on the scene of her duties; and when Charles met her, as he would do occasionally, in his lounging-place by London Bridge, he would occupy the time before the gates opened by telling her quite astonishing fictions about the wharves and the tower. "But I hope I believed them myself," he would say. Besides breakfast, he had supper also in the prison; and got to his lodging generally at nine o'clock. The gates closed always at ten.

I must not omit what he told me of the landlord of this little lodging. He was a fat, good-natured, kind old gentleman. He was lame, and had a quiet old wife; and he had a very innocent grown-up son, who was lame, too. They were all very kind to the boy. He was taken with one of his old attacks of spasm one night, and the whole three of them were about his bed until morning. They were all dead when he told me this, but in another form they live still very pleasantly as the Garland family in the *Old Curiosity Shop*.

He had a similar illness one day in the warehouse, which I can describe in his own words. "Bob Fagin was very good to me on the occasion of a bad attack of my old disorder. I suffered such excruciating pain that time, that they made a temporary bed of straw in my old recess in the counting-house, and I rolled about on the floor, and Bob filled empty blacking-bottles with hot water, and applied relays of them to my side, half the day. I got better, and quite easy towards evening; but Bob (who was much bigger and older than I) did not like the idea of my going home alone, and took me under his protection. I was too proud to let him know about the prison; and after making several efforts to get rid of him, to all of which Bob Fagin in his goodness was deaf, shook hands with him on the steps of a house near Southwark Bridge on the Surrey side, making believe that I lived there. As a finishing piece of reality in case of his looking back, I knocked at the door, I recollect, and asked, when the woman opened it, if that was Mr. Robert Fagin's house."

The Saturday nights continued, as before, to be precious to him. "My usual way home was over Blackfriars Bridge, and down that turning in the Blackfriars Road which has Rowland Hill's chapel on one side, and the likeness of a golden dog licking a golden pot over a shop door on the other. There are a good many little low-browed old shops in that street, of a wretched kind; and some are unchanged now. I looked into one a few weeks ago, where I used to buy boot-laces on Saturday nights, and saw the corner where I once sat down on a stool to have a pair of ready-made half-boots fitted on. I have been seduced more than once, in that street on a Saturday night, by a show-van at a corner; and have gone in, with a very motley assemblage, to see the Fat Pig, the Wild Indian, and the Little Lady. There were two or three hat-manufactories there, then (I think they are there still); and among the things which, encountered anywhere, or under any circumstances, will instantly recall that time, is the smell of hat-making."

His father's attempts to avoid going through the court having failed, all needful ceremonies had to be undertaken to obtain the benefit of the Insolvent Debtors' Act; and in one of these little Charles had his part to play. One condition of the statute was that the wearing apparel and personal matters retained were not to exceed twenty pounds sterling in value. "It was necessary, as a matter of form, that the clothes I wore should be seen by the official appraiser. I had a half-holiday to enable me to call upon him, at his own time, at a house somewhere beyond the Obelisk. I recollect his coming out to look at me with his mouth full, and a strong smell of beer upon him, and saying good-naturedly that 'that would do,' and 'it was all right.' Certainly the hardest creditor would not have been disposed (even if he had been legally entitled) to avail himself of my poor white hat, little jacket, or corduroy trowsers. But I had a fat old silver watch in my pocket, which had been given me by my grandmother before the blacking days, and I had entertained my doubts as I went along whether that valuable possession might not bring me over the twenty pounds. So I was greatly relieved, and made him a bow of acknowledgment as I went out."

Still the want felt most by him was the companionship of boys of his own age. He had no such acquaintance. Sometimes, he remembered to have played on the coal-barges at dinner-time with Poll Green and Bob Fagin; but those were rare occasions. He generally strolled alone, about the back streets of the Adelphi; or explored the Aldephi Arches. One of his favourite localities was a little public-house by the water-side called the "Fox-under-the-Hill," approached by an underground passage which we once missed in looking for it together; and he had a vision which he has mentioned in *Copperfield* of sitting eating something on a bench outside, one fine evening, and looking at some coal-heavers dancing before the house. "I wonder what they thought of me," says David. He had himself already said the same in his fragment of autobiography.

Another characteristic little incident he made afterwards one of David's experiences, but I am able to give it here without the disguises that adapt it to the fiction. "I was such a little fellow, with my poor white hat, little jacket, and corduroy trowsers, that frequently, when I went into the bar of a strange public-house for a glass of ale or porter to wash down the saveloy and the loaf I had eaten in the street, they didn't like to give it me. I remember, one evening (I had been somewhere for my father, and was going back to the Borough over Westminster Bridge), that I went into a public-house in Parliament Street, which is still there though altered, at the corner of the short street leading into Cannon Row, and said to the landlord behind the bar, 'What is your very best—the VERY *best*—ale, a glass?' For, the occasion was a festive one, for some reason: I forget why. It may have been my birthday, or somebody else's. 'Twopence,' says he. 'Then,' says I, 'just draw me a glass of that, if you please, with a good head to it.' The landlord looked at me, in return, over the bar, from head to foot, with a strange smile on his face; and instead of drawing the beer, looked round the screen and said something to his wife, who came out from behind it, with her work in her hand, and joined him in surveying me. Here we stand, all three, before me now, in my study in Devonshire Terrace. The landlord, in his shirt-sleeves, leaning against the bar window-frame; his wife, looking over the little half-door; and I, in some confusion, looking up at them from outside the partition. They asked me a good many questions, as what my name was, how old I was, where I lived, how I was employed, etc. To all of which, that I might commit nobody, I invented appropriate answers. They served me with the ale, though I suspect it was not the strongest on the premises; and the landlord's wife, opening the little half-door and bending down, gave me a kiss that was half-admiring and half-compassionate, but all womanly and good, I am sure."

A later, and not less characteristic, occurrence of the true story of this time found also a place, three or four years after it was written, in his now famous fiction. It preceded but by a short term the discharge, from the Marshalsea, of the elder Dickens; to whom a rather considerable legacy from a relative had accrued not long before ("some hundreds," I understood), and had been paid into court during his imprisonment. The scene to be described arose on the occasion of a petition drawn up by him before he left, praying, not for the abolition of imprisonment for debt, as David Copperfield relates, but for the less dignified but more accessible boon of a bounty to the prisoners to drink His Majesty's health on His Majesty's forthcoming birthday.

"I mention the circumstance because it illustrates, to me, my early interest in observing people. When I went to the Marshal-sea of a night, I was always delighted to hear from my mother what she knew about the histories of the different debtors in the prison; and when I heard of this approaching ceremony, I was so anxious to see them all come in, one after another (though I knew the greater part of them already, to speak to, and they me), that I got leave of absence on purpose, and established myself in a corner, near the petition. It was stretched out, I recollect, on a great ironing-board, under the window, which in another part of the room made a bedstead at night. The internal regulations of the place, for cleanliness and order, and for the government of a common room in the ale-house, where hot water and some means of cooking, and a good fire, were provided for all who paid a very small subscription, were excellently administered by a governing committee of debtors, of which my father was chairman for the time being. As many of the principal officers of this body as could be got into the small room without filling it up supported him, in front of the peti-tion; and my old friend Captain Porter (who had washed himself, to do honour to so solemn an occasion) stationed himself close to it, to read it to all who were unacquainted with its contents. The door was then thrown open, and they began to come in, in a long file; several waiting on the landing outside, while one entered, affixed his signature, and went out. To everybody in succession Captain Porter said, 'Would you like to hear it read?' If he weakly showed the least disposition to hear it, Captain Porter, in a loud, sonorous voice, gave him every word of it. I remember a certain luscious roll he gave to such words as 'Majesty—gracious Majesty—your gracious Majesty's un-fortunate subjects—your Majesty's well-known munificence' —as if the words were something real in his mouth, and delicious to taste: my poor father meanwhile listening with a little of an author's vanity, and contemplating (not severely) the spikes on the opposite wall. Whatever was comical in this scene, and whatever was pathetic, I sincerely believe I perceived in my corner, whether I demonstrated or not, quite as well as I should perceive it now. I made out my own little character and story for every man who put his name to the sheet of paper. I might be able to do that now, more truly: not more earnestly, or with a closer interest. Their different peculiarities of dress, of face, of gait, of manner, were written indelibly upon my memory. I would rather have seen it than the best play ever played; and I thought about it afterwards, over the pots of paste-blacking, often and often. When I looked, with my mind's eye, into the Fleet Prison during Mr. Pickwick's incarceration, I wonder whether half a dozen men were wanting from the Marshalsea crowd that came filing in again, to the sound of Captain Porter's voice!"

When the family left the Marshalsea they all went to lodge with the lady in Little College Street, a Mrs. Roylance, who has obtained unexpected immortality as Mrs. Pipchin; and they afterwards occupied a small house in Somers Town. But, before this time, Charles was present with some of them in Tenterden Street to see his sister Fanny receive one of the prizes given to the pupils of the Royal Academy of Music. "I could not bear to think of myself—beyond the reach of all such honourable emulation and success. The tears ran down my face. I felt as if my heart were rent. I prayed, when I went to bed that night, to be lifted out of the humiliation and neglect in which I was. I never had suffered so much before. There was no envy in this." There was little need that he should say so. Extreme enjoyment in witnessing the exercise of her talents, the utmost pride in every success obtained by them, he manifested always to a degree otherwise quite unusual with him; and on the day of her funeral, which we passed together, I had most affecting proof of his tender and grateful memory of her in these childish days. A few more sentences, certainly not less touching than any that have gone before, will bring the story of them to its close. They stand here exactly as written by him.

"I am not sure that it was before this time, or after it, that the blacking warehouse was removed to Chandos Street, Covent Garden. It is no matter. Next to the shop at the corner of Bedford Street, in Chandos Street, are two rather old-fashioned houses and shops adjoining one another. They were one then, or thrown into one, for the blacking business; and had been a butter shop. Opposite to them was, and is, a public-house, where I got my ale, under these new circumstances. The stones in the street may be smoothed by my small feet going across to it at dinner-time, and back again. The establishment was larger now, and we had one or two new boys. Bob Fagin and I had attained to great dexterity in tying up the pots. I forget how many we could do in five minutes. We worked, for the light's sake, near the second window as you come from Bedford Street; and we were so brisk at it, that the people used to stop and look in. Sometimes there would be quite a little crowd there. I saw my father coming in at the door one day when we were very busy, and I wondered how he could bear it.

"Now, I generally had my dinner in the warehouse. Sometimes I brought it from home, so I was better off. I see myself coming across Russell Square from Somers Town, one morning, with some cold hotch-potch in a small basin tied up in a handkerchief. I had the same wanderings about the streets as I used to have, and was just as solitary and self-dependent as before; but I had not the same difficulty in merely living. I never, however, heard a word of being taken away, or of being otherwise than quite provided for.

"At last, one day, my father and the relative so often mentioned quarrelled; quarrelled by letter, for I took the letter from my father to him which caused the explosion, but quarrelled very fiercely. It was about me. It may have had some backward reference, in part, for anything I know, to my employment at the window. All I am certain of is that, soon after I had given him the letter, my cousin (he was a sort of cousin, by marriage) told me he was very much insulted about me; and that it was impossible to keep me, after that. I cried very much, partly because it was so sudden, and partly because in his anger he was violent about my father, though gentle to me. Thomas, the old soldier, comforted me, and said he was sure it was for the best. With a relief so strange that it was like oppression, I went home.

"My mother set herself to accommodate the quarrel, and did so next day. She brought home a request for me to return next morning, and a high character of me, which I am very sure I deserved. My father said I should go back no more, and should go to school. I do not write resentfully or angrily: for I know how all these things have worked together to make me what I am: but I never afterwards forgot, I never shall forget, I never can forget, that my mother was warm for my being sent back.

"From that hour until this at which I write, no word of that part of my childhood which I have now gladly brought to a close, has passed my lips to any human being. I have no idea how long it lasted; whether for a year, or much more, or less. From that hour, until this, my father and my mother have been stricken dumb upon it. I have never heard the least allusion to it, however far off and remote, from either of them. I have never, until I now impart it to this paper, in any burst of confidence with anyone, my own wife not excepted, raised the curtain I then dropped, thank God.

"Until old Hungerford Market was pulled down, until old Hungerford Stairs were destroyed, and the very nature of the ground changed, I never had the courage to go back to the place where my servitude began. I never saw it. I could not endure to go near it. For many years, when I came near to Robert Warrens' in the Strand, I crossed over to the opposite side of the way, to avoid a certain smell of the cement they put upon the blacking-corks, which reminded me of what I was once. It was a very long time before I liked to go up Chandos Street. My old way home by the Borough made me cry, after my eldest child could speak.

"In my walks at night I have walked there often, since then, and by degrees I have come to write this. It does not seem a tithe of what I might have written, or of what I meant to write."

The substance of some after-talk explanatory of points in the narrative, of which a note was made at the time, may be briefly added. He could hardly have been more than twelve years old when he left the place, and was still unusually small for his age; much smaller, though two years older, than his own eldest son was at the time of these confidences. His mother had been in the blacking warehouse many times; his father not more than once or twice. The rivalry of Robert Warren by Jonathan's representatives, the cousins George and James, was carried to wonderful extremes in the way of advertisement; and they were all very proud, he told me, of the cat scratching the boot, which was *their* house's device. The poets in the house's regular employ he remembered, too, and made his first study from one of them for the poet of Mrs. Jarley's waxwork. The whole enterprise, however, had the usual end of such things. The younger cousin tired of the concern; and a Mr. Wood, the proprietor who took James's share and became George's partner, sold it ultimately to Robert Warren. It continued to be his at the time Dickens and myself last spoke of it together, and he had made an excellent bargain of it.

III

SCHOOL-DAYS AND START IN LIFE

1824-30

IN what way those strange experiences of his boyhood affected him afterwards, the narrative of his life must show: but there were influences that made themselves felt even on his way to manhood.

What at once he brought out of the humiliation that had impressed him so deeply, though scarcely as yet quite consciously, was a natural dread of the hardships that might still be in store for him, sharpened by what he had gone through; and this, though in its effect for the present imperfectly understood, became by degrees a passionate resolve, even while he was yielding to circumstances, *not to be* what circumstances were conspiring to make him. All that was involved in what he had suffered and sunk into could not have been known to him at the time; but it was plain enough later, as we see; and in conversation with me after the revelation was made, he used to find, at extreme points in his life, the explanation of himself in those early trials. He had derived great good from them, but not without alloy. The fixed and eager determination, the restless and resistless energy, which opened to him opportunities of escape from many mean environments, not by turning off from any path of duty, but by resolutely rising to such excellence or distinction as might be attainable in it, brought with it some disadvantage among many noble advantages. Of this he was himself aware, but not to the full extent. What it was that in society made him often uneasy, shrinking, and over-sensitive, he knew; but all the danger he ran in bearing down and overmastering the feeling, he did not know. A too great confidence in himself, a sense that everything was possible to the will that would make it so, laid occasionally upon him self-imposed burdens greater than might be borne by anyone with safety. In that direction there was in him, at such times, something even hard and aggressive; in his determinations a something

34

that had almost the tone of fierceness; something in his nature that made his resolves insuperable, however hasty the opinions on which they had been formed. So rare were these manifestations, however, and so little did they prejudice a character as entirely open and generous as it was at all times ardent and impetuous, that only very infrequently, towards the close of the middle term of a friendship which lasted without the interruption of a day for more than three and thirty years, were they ever unfavourably presented to me. But there they were; and when I have seen strangely present, at such chance intervals, a stern and even cold isolation of self-reliance side by side with a susceptivity almost feminine and the most eager craving for sympathy, it has seemed to me as though his habitual impulses for everything kind and gentle had sunk, for the time, under a sudden hard and inexorable sense of what Fate had dealt to him in those early years. On more than one occasion indeed I had confirmation of this. "I must entreat you," he wrote to me in June 1862, "to pause for an instant, and go back to what you know of my childish days, and to ask yourself whether it is natural that something of the character formed in me then, and lost under happier circumstances, should have reappeared in the last five years. The never-to-be-forgotten misery of that old time bred a certain shrinking sensitiveness in a certain ill-clad, ill-fed child, that I have found come back in the never-to-be-forgotten misery of this later time."

One good there was, however, altogether without drawback, and which claims simply to be mentioned before my narrative is resumed. The story of his childish misery has itself sufficiently shown that he never throughout it lost his precious gift of animal spirits, or his native capacity for humorous enjoyment; and there were positive gains to him from what he underwent which were also rich and lasting. To what in the outset of his difficulties and trials gave the decisive bent to his genius, I have already made special reference; and we are to observe, of what followed, that with the very poor and unprosperous, out of whose sufferings and strugglings, and the virtues as well as vices born of them, his not least splendid successes were wrought, his childish experiences had made him actually one. They were not his clients whose cause he pleaded with such pathos and humour, and on whose side he got the laughter and tears of all the world, but in some sort his very self. Nor was it a small part of this manifest advantage that he should have obtained his experience as a child and not as a man; that only the good part, the flower and fruit of it, was plucked by him; and that nothing of the evil part, none of the earth in which the seed was planted, remained to soil him.

His next move in life can also be given in his own language. "There was a school in the Hampstead Road kept by Mr. Jones, a Welshman, to which my father dispatched me to ask for a card of terms. The boys were at dinner, and Mr. Jones was carving for them, with a pair of holland sleeves on, when I acquitted myself of this commission. He came out, and gave me what I wanted; and hoped I should become a pupil. I did. At seven o'clock one morning, very soon afterwards, I went as day scholar to Mr. Jones's establishment, which was in Mornington Place, and had its school-room sliced away by the Birmingham Railway, when that change came about. The school-room however was not threatened by directors or civil engineers then, and there was a board over the door graced with the words WELLINGTON HOUSE ACADEMY."

At Wellington House Academy he remained nearly two years, being a little over fourteen years of age when he quitted it. In his minor writings, as well as in *Copperfield*, will be found general allusions to it, and there is a paper among his pieces reprinted from *Household Words* which purports specifically to describe it. To the account therein given of himself when he went to the school, as advanced enough, so safely had his memory retained its poor fragments of early schooling, to be put into Virgil, as getting sundry prizes, and as attaining to the eminent position of its first boy, one of his two schoolfellows with whom I have had communication, makes objection; but both admit that the general features of the place are reproduced with wonderful accuracy, and more especially in those points for which the school appears to have been much more notable than for anything connected with the scholarship of its pupils.

In the reprinted piece Dickens describes it as remarkable for white mice. He says that red-polls, linnets, and even canaries, were kept by the boys in desks, drawers, hat-boxes, and other strange refuges for birds; but that white mice were the favourite stock, and that the boys trained the mice much better than the master trained the boys. He recalled in particular one white mouse who lived in the cover of a Latin dictionary, ran up ladders, drew Roman chariots, shouldered muskets, turned wheels, and even made a very creditable appearance on the stage as the Dog of Montargis, who might have achieved greater things but for having had the misfortune to mistake his way in a triumphal procession to the Capitol, when he fell into a deep inkstand, and was dyed black and drowned.

Nevertheless, he mentions the school as one also of some celebrity in its neighbourhood, though nobody could have said why; and adds that among the boys the master was supposed to know nothing, and one of the ushers was supposed to know everything. "We are still inclined to think the first named supposition perfectly correct. We went to look at the place only this last midsummer, and found that the railway had cut it up, root and branch. A great trunk line had swallowed the playground, sliced away the school-room, and pared off the corner of the house. Which, thus curtailed of its proportions, presented itself in a green stage of stucco, profile-wise towards the road, like a forlorn flat-iron without a handle, standing on end."

One who knew him in those early days, Mr. Owen P. Thomas, thus writes to me (February 1871): "I had the honour of being Mr. Dickens's schoolfellow for about two years (1824–6), both being day-scholars at Mr. Jones's 'Classical and Commercial Academy,' as then inscribed in front of the house, and which was situated at the corner of Granby Street and the Hampstead Road. The house stands now in its original state, but the school and large playground behind disappeared on the formation of the London and North-Western Railway, which at this point runs in a slanting direction from Euston Square underneath the Hampstead Road. We were all companions and playmates when out of school, as well as fellow-students therein." (Mr. Thomas includes in this remark the names of Henry Danson, now a physician in practice in London; of Daniel Tobin, whom I remember to have been frequently assisted by his old school-fellow in later years; and of Richard Bray.) "You will find a graphic sketch of the school by Mr. Dickens himself in *Household Words* of 11 October, 1851. The article is entitled 'Our School.' The names, of course, are feigned; but, allowing for slight colouring, the persons and incidents described are all true to life, and easily recognisable by anyone who attended the school at the time. The Latin master was Mr. Manville, or Mandeville, who for many years was well known at the library of the British Museum. The academy, after the railroad overthrew it, was removed to another house in the neighbourhood, but Mr. Jones and two at least of his assistant masters have long ago departed this life."

One of the latter was the usher believed to know everything,

who was writing master, mathematical master, English master,
divided the little boys with the Latin master, made out the
bills, mended the pens, and always called at parents' houses to
inquire after sick boys, because he had gentlemanly manners.
This picture, my correspondent recognised: as well as those of
the fat little dancing master who taught them hornpipes, of
the Latin master who stuffed his ears with onions for his deaf-
ness, of the gruff serving-man who nursed the boys in scarlet
fever, and of the principal himself who was always ruling
ciphering books with a bloated mahogany ruler, smiting the
palms of offenders with the same diabolical instrument, or
viciously drawing a pair of pantaloons tight with one of his
large hands and caning the wearer with the other.

"My recollection of Dickens whilst at school," Mr. Thomas
continues, "is that of a healthy-looking boy, small but well-
built, with a more than usual flow of spirits, inducing to harmless fun, seldom or ever I think to mischief, to which so many
lads at that age are prone. I cannot recall anything that then
indicated he would hereafter become a literary celebrity; but
perhaps he was too young then. He usually held his head more
erect than lads ordinarily do, and there was a general smartness about him. His week-day dress of jacket and trousers, I can
clearly remember, was what is called pepper-and-salt; and
instead of the frill that most boys of his age wore then, he had
a turn-down collar, so that he looked less youthful in consequence. He invented what we termed a 'lingo,' produced by
the addition of a few letters of the same sound to every word;
and it was our ambition, walking and talking thus along the
street, to be considered foreigners. As an alternate amusement,
the present writer well remembers extemporising tales of some
sort, and reciting them offhand, with Dickens and Danson or
Tobin walking on either side of him. I enclose you a copy of a
note I received from him when he was between thirteen and
fourteen years of age, perhaps one of the earliest productions of
his pen. The Leg referred to was the Legend of something, a
pamphlet romance I had lent him; the Clavis was of course the
Latin school book so named."

There is some underlying whim or fun in the "Leg" allusions
which Mr. Thomas appears to have overlooked, and certainly
fails to explain: but the note, which is given in facsimile on
the opposite page, may be left to speak for itself; and in the
signature the reader will be amused to see the first faint beginning
of a flourish afterwards famous.

(No date, but was written in
later part of 1825.)

Tom)

I am quite ashamed I have not returned your Leg, but you shall have it by Harry to-morrow. If you would like to purchase my Claris you shall have it of a very reduced price, a wooden leg. I have weighed your every Saturday Night—

Cheaper in comparison than a leg.

Yours &c

C Dickens.

P.S. I suppose all this time you have had

"After a lapse of years," Mr. Thomas continues, "I recognised the celebrated writer as the individual I had known so well as a boy, from having preserved this note; and upon Mr. Dickens visiting Reading in December 1854 to give one of his earliest readings for the benefit of the literary institute, of which he had become president, on Mr. Justice Talfourd's death, I took the opportunity of showing it to him, when he was much diverted therewith. On the same occasion we conversed about mutual schoolfellows, and among others Daniel Tobin was referred to, whom I remembered to have been Dickens's *most* intimate companion in the school-days (1824 to 1826). His reply was that Tobin either was then, or had previously been, assisting him in the capacity of amanuensis; but there is a subsequent mystery about Tobin, in connection with his friend and patron, which I have never been able to comprehend; for I understood shortly afterwards that there was entire separation between them, and it must have been an offence of some gravity to have sundered an acquaintance formed in early youth, and which had endured, greatly to Tobin's advantage, so long. He resided in our school-days in one of the now old and grimy-looking stone-fronted houses in George Street, Euston Road, a few doors from the "Orange Tree" tavern. It is the opinion of the other school-fellow with whom we were intimate, Doctor Danson, that upon leaving school Mr. Dickens and Tobin entered the same solicitor's office, and this he thinks was either in or near Lincoln's Inn Fields."

The offence of Tobin went no deeper than the having at last worn out even Dickens's patience and kindness. His applications for relief were so incessantly repeated, that to cut him and them adrift altogether was the only way of escape from what had become an intolerable nuisance. To Mr. Thomas's letter the reader will thank me for adding one not less interesting, with which Dr. Henry Danson has favoured me. We have here, with the same fun and animal spirits, a little of the proneness to mischief which his other schoolfellow says he was free from; but the mischief is all of the harmless kind, and might perhaps have been better described as but part of an irrepressible vivacity.

"My impression is that I was a schoolfellow of Dickens for nearly two years: he left before me, I think at about fifteen years of age. Mr. Jones's school, called the Wellington Academy, was in the Hampstead Road, at the north-east corner of Granby Street. The school-house was afterwards removed for the London and North-Western Railway. It was considered at the time a very superior sort of school, one of the best, indeed, in that part of London; but it was most shamefully mismanaged, and the boys made but very little progress. The proprietor, Mr. Jones, was a Welshman; a most ignorant fellow, and a mere tyrant; whose chief employment was to scourge the boys. Dickens has given a very lively account of this place in his paper entitled 'Our School,' but it is very mythical in many respects, and more especially in the compliment he pays in it to himself. I do not remember that Dickens distinguished himself in any way, or carried off any prizes. My belief is that he did not learn Greek or Latin there, and you will remember there is no allusion to the classics in any of his writings. He was a handsome, curly-headed lad, full of animation and animal spirits, and probably was connected with every mischievous prank in the school. I do not think he came in for any of Mr. Jones's scourging propensity: in fact, together with myself, he was only a day-pupil, and with these there was a wholesome fear of tales being carried home to the parents. His personal appearance at that time is vividly brought home to me in the portrait of him taken a few years later by Mr. Lawrence. He resided with his friends in a very small house in a street leading out of Seymour Street, north of Mr. Judkin's chapel.

"Depend on it he was quite a self-made man, and his wonderful knowledge and command of the English language must have been acquired by long and patient study after leaving his last school.

"I have no recollection of the boy you name. His chief associates were, I think, Tobin, Mr. Thomas Bray, and myself. The first-named was his chief ally, and his acquaintance with him appears to have continued many years afterwards. At about that time penny and Saturday magazines were published weekly, and were greedily read by us. We kept bees, white mice, and other living things clandestinely in our desks; and the mechanical arts were a good deal cultivated, in the shape of coach-building, and making pumps and boats, the motive power of which was the white mice.

"I think at that time Dickens took to writing small tales, and we had a sort of club for lending and circulating them. Dickens was also very strong in using a sort of lingo, which made us quite unintelligible to bystanders. We were very strong, too, in theatricals. We mounted small theatres, and got up very gorgeous scenery to illustrate the *Miller and his Men* and *Cherry and Fair Star*. I remember the present Mr. Beverley, the scene-painter, assisted us in this. Dickens was always a leader at these plays, which were occasionally presented with much solemnity before an audience of boys, and in the presence of the ushers. My brother, assisted by Dickens, got up the *Miller and his Men*, in a very gorgeous form. Master Beverley constructed the mill for us in such a way that it could tumble to pieces with the assistance of crackers. At one representation the fireworks in the last scene, ending with the destruction of the mill, were so very real that the police interfered, and knocked violently at the doors. Dickens's after-taste for theatricals might have had its origin in these small affairs.

"I quite remember Dickens on one occasion heading us in Drummond Street in pretending to be poor boys, and asking the passers-by for charity—especially old ladies; one of whom told us she 'had no money for beggar boys.' On these adventures, when the old ladies were quite staggered by the impudence of the demand, Dickens would explode with laughter and take to his heels.

"I met him one Sunday morning shortly after he left the school, and we very piously attended the morning service at Seymour Street chapel. I am sorry to say Master Dickens did not attend in the slightest degree to the service, but incited me to laughter by declaring his dinner was ready and the potatoes would be spoiled, and in fact behaved in such a manner that it was lucky for us we were not ejected from the chapel.

"I heard of him some time after from Tobin, whom I met carrying a foaming pot of London particular in Lincoln's Inn Fields, and I then understood that Dickens was in the same or some neighbouring office.

"Many years elapsed after this before I became aware, from accidentally reading 'Our School,' that the brilliant and now famous Dickens was my old schoolfellow. I didn't like to intrude myself upon him; and it was not until three or four years ago, when he presided at the University College dinner at Willis's Rooms, and made a most brilliant and effective speech, that I sent him a congratulatory note reminding him of our former fellowship. To this he sent me a kind note in reply, and which I value very much. I send you copies of these."

From Dickens himself I never heard much allusion to the school thus described; but I knew that, besides being the subject dealt with in *Household Words*, it had supplied some of the lighter traits of Salem House for *Copperfield*; and that to the fact of one of its tutors being afterwards engaged to teach a boy of Macready's, our common friend, Dickens used to point for one of the illustrations of his favourite theory as to the smallness of the world, and how things and persons apparently the most unlikely to meet were continually knocking up against each other. The employment as his amanuensis of his school-fellow Tobin dates as early as his Doctors' Commons days, but both my correspondents are mistaken in the impression they appear to have received that Tobin had been previously his fellow-clerk in the same attorney's office. I had thought him more likely to have been accompanied there by another of his boyish acquaintances, who became afterwards a solicitor, Mr. Mitton, not recollected by either of my correspondents in connection with the school, but whom I frequently met with him in later years, and for whom he had the regard arising out of such early associations. In this, however, I have since discovered my own mistake: the truth being that it was this gentleman's connection, not with the Wellington Academy, but with a school kept by Mr. Dawson in Hunter Street, Brunswick Square, where the brothers of Dickens were subsequently placed, which led to their early knowledge of each other. I fancy that they were together also, for a short time, at Mr. Molloy's in New Square, Lincoln's Inn; but, whether or not this was so, Dickens certainly had not quitted school many months before his father had made sufficient interest with an attorney of Gray's Inn, Mr. Edward Blackmore, to obtain him regular employment in his office. In this capacity of clerk, our only trustworthy glimpse of him we owe to the last-named gentleman, who has described briefly, and I do not doubt authentically, the services so rendered by him to the law. It cannot be said that they were noteworthy, though it might be difficult to find a more distinguished person who has borne the title, unless we make exception for the very father of literature himself, whom Chaucer, with amusing illustration of the way in which words change their meanings, calls "that conceited clerke Homère."

"I was well acquainted," writes Mr. Edward Blackmore of Alresford, "with his parents, and, being then in practice in Gray's Inn, they asked me if I could find employment for him. He was a bright, clever-looking youth, and I took him as a clerk. He came to me in May 1827, and left in November 1828; and I have now an account-book which he used to keep of petty disbursements in the office, in which he charged himself with the modest salary first of thirteen shillings and sixpence, and afterwards of fifteen shillings a week. Several incidents took place in the office of which he must have been a keen observer, as I recognised some of them in his *Pickwick* and *Nickleby*; and I am much mistaken if some of his characters had not their originals in persons I well remember. His taste for theatricals was much promoted by a fellow-clerk named Potter, since dead, with whom he chiefly associated. They took every opportunity, then unknown to me, of going together to a minor theatre, where (I afterwards heard) they not unfrequently engaged in parts. After he left me I saw him at times in the lord chancellor's court, taking notes of cases as a reporter. I then lost sight of him until his *Pickwick* made its appearance." This letter indicates the position he held at Mr. Blackmore's; and we have but to turn to the passage in *Pickwick* which describes the several grades of attorney's clerk, to understand it more clearly. He was very far below the articled clerk, who has paid a premium and is attorney in perspective. He was not so high as the salaried clerk, with nearly the whole of his weekly thirty shillings spent on his personal pleasures. He was not even on a level with the middle-aged copying clerk, always needy and uniformly shabby. He was simply among, however his own nature may have lifted him above, the "office-lads in their first surtouts, who feel a befitting contempt for boys at day-schools, club as they go home at night for saveloys and porter, and think there's nothing like life." Thus far, not more or less, had he now reached. He was one of the office-lads, and probably in his first surtout.

But, even thus, the process of education went on, defying what seemed to interrupt it; and in the amount of his present equipment for his needs of life, what he brought from the Wellington House Academy can have borne but the smallest proportion to his acquirement at Mr. Blackmore's. Yet to seek to identify, without help from himself, any passages in his books with those boyish law-experiences, would be idle and hopeless enough. In the earliest of his writings, and down to the very latest, he worked exhaustively the field which is opened by an attorney's office to a student of life and manners; but we have not now to deal with his numerous varieties of the *genus* clerk drawn thus for the amusement of others, but with the acquisitions which at present he was storing up for himself from the opportunities such offices opened to him. Nor would it be possible to have better illustrative comment on all these years than is furnished by his father's reply to a friend it was now hoped to interest on his behalf, which more than once I have heard him whimsically but good-humouredly imitate. "Pray, Mr. Dickens, where was your son educated?" "Why, indeed, Sir—ha! ha!—he may be said to have educated himself!" Of the two kinds of education which Gibbon says that all men who rise above the common level receive: the first that of his teachers, and the second, more personal and more important, *his own*; he had the advantage only of the last. It nevertheless sufficed for him.

Very nearly another eighteen months were now to be spent mainly in practical preparation for what he was, at this time, led finally to choose as an employment from which a fair income was certain with such talents as he possessed; his father already having taken to it, in these latter years, in aid of the family resources. In his father's house, which was at Hampstead through the first portion of the Mornington Street school-time, then in the house out of Seymour Street mentioned by Mr. Danson, and afterwards, upon the elder Dickens going into the gallery as a reporter for the *Morning Herald*, in Bentinck Street, Manchester Square, Charles had continued to live: and, influenced doubtless by the example before him, he took sudden determination to qualify himself thoroughly for what his father was lately become, a newspaper parliamentary reporter. He set resolutely therefore to the study of shorthand; and, for the additional help of such general information about books as a fairly educated youth might be expected to have, as well as to satisfy some higher personal cravings, he became an assiduous attendant in the British Museum reading-room. He would frequently refer to these days as decidedly the usefullest to himself he had ever passed; and judging from the results they must have been so. No man who knew him in later years, and talked to him familiarly of books and things, would have suspected his education in boyhood, almost entirely self-acquired as it was, to have been so rambling or haphazard as I have here described it. The secret consisted in this, that, whatever for the time he had to do, he lifted himself, there and then, to the level of, and at no time disregarded the rules that guided the hero of his novel: "Whatever I have tried to do in life, I have tried with all my heart to do well. What I have devoted myself to, I have devoted myself to completely. Never to put one hand to anything on which I could throw my whole self, and never to affect depreciation of my work, whatever it was, I find now to have been my golden rules."

Of the difficulties that beset his shorthand studies, as well as

young hero through something of the same sort of trial was also his own support. He too had his Dora, at apparently the same hopeless elevation; striven for as the one only thing to be attained, and even more unattainable, for neither did he succeed nor happily did she die; but the one idol, like the other, supplying a motive to exertion for the time, and otherwise opening out to the idolater, both in fact and fiction, a highly unsubstantial, happy, foolish time. I used to laugh and tell him I had no belief in any but the book Dora, until the incident of a sudden reappearance of the real one in his life, nearly six years after *Copperfield* was written, convinced me there had been a more actual foundation for those chapters of his book than I was ready to suppose. Still I would hardly admit it; and, that the matter could possibly affect him then, persisted in a stout refusal to believe. His reply (1855) throws a little light on this juvenile part of his career, and I therefore venture to preserve it. † 2

"I don't quite apprehend what you mean by my over-rating the strength of the feeling of five-and-twenty years ago. If you mean of my own feeling, and will only think what the desperate intensity of my nature is, and that this began when I was Charley's age; that it excluded every other idea from my mind for four years, at a time of life when four years are equal to four times four; and that I went at it with a determination to overcome all the difficulties, which fairly lifted me up into that newspaper life, and floated me away over a hundred men's heads: then you are wrong, because nothing can exaggerate that. I have positively stood amazed at myself ever since!— And so I suffered, and so worked, and so beat and hammered away at the maddest romances that ever got into any boy's head and stayed there, that to see the mere cause of it all, now, loosens my hold upon myself. Without for a moment sincerely believing that it would have been better if we had never got separated, I cannot see the occasion of so much emotion as I should see anyone else. No one can imagine in the most distant degree what pain the recollection gave me in *Copperfield*. And, just as I can never open that book as I open any other book, I cannot see the face (even at four-and-forty), or hear the voice, without going wandering away over the ashes of all that youth and hope in the wildest manner." More and more plainly seen, however, in the light of four-and-forty, the romance glided visibly away, its work being fairly done; and, at the close of the month following that in which this letter was written, during which he had very quietly made a formal call with his wife at his youthful Dora's house, and contemplated with a calm equanimity, in the hall, her stuffed favourite Jip, he began the fiction in which there was a Flora to set against its predecessor's Dora, both derived from the same original. The fancy had a comic humour in it he found it impossible to resist, but it was kindly and pleasant to the last; and if the later picture showed him plenty to laugh at in this retrospect of his youth, there was nothing he thought of more tenderly than the earlier, as long as he was conscious of anything.

IV

1831-5

DICKENS was nineteen years old when at last he entered the gallery. His father, with whom he still lived in Bentinck Street, had already, as we have seen, joined the gallery as a reporter for one of the morning papers, and was now in the more comfortable circumstances derived from the addition to his official pension which this praiseworthy labour ensured; but his own engagement on the *Chronicle* dates somewhat later. His first parliamentary service was given to the *True Sun*, a journal which had on its editorial staff some dear friends of mine, through whom I became myself a contributor to it, and afterwards, in common with all concerned, whether in its writing, reporting, printing or publishing, a sharer in its difficulties. The most formidable of these arrived one day in a general strike of the reporters; and I well remember noticing at this dread time, on the staircase of the magnificent mansion we were lodged in, a young man of my own age whose keen animation of look would have arrested attention anywhere, and whose name, upon inquiry, I then for the first time heard. It was coupled with the fact which gave it interest even then, that "young Dickens" had been spokesman for the recalcitrant reporters, and conducted their case triumphantly. He was afterwards during two sessions engaged for the *Mirror of Parliament*, which one of his uncles by the mother's side originated and conducted; and finally, in his twenty-third year, he became a reporter for the *Morning Chronicle*.

His attempt to get upon the stage dates immediately before these newspaper engagements. His Doctors' Commons reportership was a living so wearily uncertain, that a possibility of the other calling had occurred to him in quite a businesslike way. He went to theatres almost every night for a long time; studied and practised himself in parts; was so much attracted by the "At Homes" of the elder Mathews, that he resolved to make his

49

first plunge in a similar direction; and finally wrote to make offer of himself to Covent Garden. "I wrote to Bartley, who was stage-manager, and told him how young I was, and exactly what I thought I could do; and that I believed I had a strong perception of character and oddity, and a natural power of reproducing in my own person what I observed in others. This was at the time when I was at Doctors' Commons as a shorthand writer for the proctors. And I recollect I wrote the letter from a little office I had there, where the answer came also. There must have been something in my letter that struck the authorities, for Bartley wrote to me almost immediately to say that they were busy getting up the *Hunchback* (so they were), but that they would communicate with me again, in a fortnight. Punctual to the time another letter came, with an appointment to do anything of Mathews's I pleased before him and Charles Kemble, on a certain day at the theatre. My sister Fanny was in the secret, and was to go with me to play the songs. I was laid up when the day came, with a terrible bad cold and an inflammation of the face; the beginning, by the by, of that annoyance in one ear to which I am subject to this day. I wrote to say so, and added that I would resume my application next season. I made a great splash in the gallery soon afterwards; the *Chronicle* opened to me; I had a distinction in the little world of the newspaper, which made one like it; began to write; didn't want money; had never thought of the stage but as a means of getting it; gradually left off turning my thoughts that way, and never resumed the idea. I never told you this, did I? See how near I may have been to another sort of life." The letter in which he gave me this interesting detail belongs to another place; but the anticipation of so much of it here is required to complete his boyish history.

The beginning to write was a thing far more momentous to him (though then he did not know it) than his "great splash" in the gallery. In the December number for 1833 of what then was called the *Old Monthly Magazine*, his first published piece of writing had seen the light. He has described himself dropping this paper ("Mr. Minns and his Cousin," as he afterwards entitled it, but which appeared in the magazine as "A Dinner at Poplar Walk") stealthily one evening at twilight, with fear and trembling, into a dark letter-box in a dark office up a dark court in Fleet Street; and he has told his agitation when it appeared in all the glory of print. "On which occasion I walked down to Westminster Hall, and turned into it for half an hour, because my eyes were so dimmed with joy and pride that they could not bear the street, and were not fit to be seen there." He had purchased the magazine at a shop in the Strand; and exactly two years afterwards, in the younger member of a publishing firm who had called at his chambers in Furnival's Inn, to which he had moved soon after entering the gallery, with the proposal that originated *Pickwick*, he recognised the person he had bought that magazine from, and whom before or since he had never seen.

This interval of two years more than comprised what remained of his career in the gallery and the engagements connected with it; but that this occupation was of the utmost importance in its influence on his life, in the discipline of his powers as well as of his character, there can be no doubt whatever. "To the wholesome training of severe newspaper-work, when I was a very young man, I constantly refer my first successes," he said to the New York editors when he last took leave of them. It opened to him a wide and varied range of experience, which his wonderful observation, exact as it was humorous, made entirely his own. He saw the last of the old coaching days, and of the old inns that were a part of them; but it will be long before the readers of his living page see the last of the life of either. "There never was," he once wrote to me (in 1845), "anybody connected with newspapers who, in the same space of time, had so much express and post-chaise experience as I. And what gentlemen they were to serve, in such things, at the old *Morning Chronicle*! Great or small, it did not matter. I have had to charge for half a dozen break-downs in half a dozen times as many miles. I have had to charge for the damage of a great-coat from the drippings of a blazing wax-candle, in writing through the smallest hours of the night in a swift-flying carriage and pair. I have had to charge for all sorts of breakages fifty times in a journey without question, such being the ordinary results of the pace which we went at. I have charged for broken hats, broken luggage, broken chaises, broken harness—everything but a broken head, which is the only thing they would have grumbled to pay for."

Something to the same effect he said publicly twenty years later, on the occasion of his presiding, in May 1865, at the second annual dinner of the Newspaper Press Fund, when he condensed within the compass of his speech a summary of the whole of his reporting life. "I am not here," he said, "advocating the case of a mere ordinary client of whom I have little or no knowledge. I hold a brief to-night for my brothers. I went into the gallery of the House of Commons as a parliamentary reporter when I was a boy, and I left it—I can hardly believe the inexorable truth—nigh thirty years ago. I have pursued the calling of a reporter under circumstances of which many of my brethren here can form no adequate conception. I have often transcribed for the printer, from my shorthand notes, important public speeches in which the strictest accuracy was required, and a mistake in which would have been to a young man severely compromising, writing on the palm of my hand, by the light of a dark lantern, in a post-chaise and four, galloping through a wild country, and through the dead of the night, at the then surprising rate of fifteen miles an hour. The very last time I was at Exeter, I strolled into the castle-yard there to identify, for the amusement of a friend, the spot on which I once 'took,' as we used to call it, an election speech of Lord John Russell at the Devon contest, in the midst of a lively fight maintained by all the vagabonds in that division of the county, and under such a pelting rain, that I remember two good-natured colleagues who chanced to be at leisure held a pocket-handkerchief over my note-book, after the manner of a state canopy in an ecclesiastical procession. I have worn my knees by writing on them on the old back-row of the old gallery of the old House of Commons; and I have worn my feet by standing to write in a preposterous pen in the old House of Lords, where we used to be huddled together like so many sheep—kept in waiting, say, until the Woolsack might want re-stuffing. Returning home from exciting political meetings in the country to the waiting press in London, I do verily believe I have been upset in almost every description of vehicle known in this country. I have been, in my time, belated on miry by-roads, towards the small hours, forty or fifty miles from London, in a wheelless carriage, with exhausted horses and drunken post-boys, and have got back in time for publication, to be received with never-forgotten compliments by the late Mr. Black, coming in the broadest of Scotch from the broadest of hearts I ever knew. These trivial things I mention as an assurance to you that I never have forgotten the fascination of that old pursuit. The pleasure that I used to feel in the rapidity and dexterity of its exercise has never faded out of my breast. Whatever little cunning of hand or head I took to it, or acquired in it, I have so retained that I fully believe I could resume it to-morrow, very little the worse from long disuse. To this present year of my life, when I sit in this hall, or where not, hearing a dull speech (the phenomenon does occur), I sometimes beguile the tedium of the moment by mentally following the speaker in the old, old way; and sometimes, if you can believe me, I even find my hand going on the tablecloth, taking an imaginary note of it all." The latter I have known him do frequently. It was indeed a quite ordinary habit with him.

Mr. James Grant, a writer who was himself in the gallery with Dickens, and who states that among its eighty or ninety reporters he occupied the very highest rank, not merely for accuracy in reporting, but for marvellous quickness in transcribing, has lately also told us that while there he was exceedingly reserved in his manners, and that, though showing the usual courtesies to all he was concerned with in his duties, the only personal intimacy he formed was with Mr. Thomas Beard, then too reporting for the *Morning Chronicle*. I have already mentioned the friendly and familiar relations maintained with this gentleman to the close of his life; and, in confirmation of Mr. Grant's statement, I can further say that the only other associate of these early reporting days to whom I ever heard him refer with special regard was the late Mr. Vincent Dowling, many years editor of *Bell's Life*, with whom he did not continue much personal intercourse, but of whose character as well as talents he had formed a very high opinion. Nor is there anything to add to the notice of this time which the reader's fancy may not easily supply. A letter has been kept as written by him while engaged on one of his "expresses"; but it is less for its saying anything new, than for its confirming with a pleasant vividness what has been said already, that its contents will justify mention here.

He writes, on a "Tuesday morning" in May 1835, from the Bush Inn, Bristol; the occasion that has taken him to the west, connected with a reporting party, being Lord John Russell's Devonshire contest above-named, and his associate-chief being Mr. Beard, entrusted with command for the *Chronicle* in this particular express. He expects to forward "the conclusion of Russell's dinner" by Cooper's company's coach leaving the Bush at half-past six next morning; and by the first Ball's coach on Thursday morning he will forward the report of the Bath dinner, endorsing the parcel for immediate delivery, with extra rewards for the porter. Beard is to go over to Bath next morning. He is himself to come back by the mail from Marlborough; he has no doubt, if Lord John makes a speech of any

ordinary dimensions, it can be done by the time Marlborough
is reached; "and taking into consideration the immense importance of having the addition of saddle-horses from thence,
it is, beyond all doubt, worth an effort. . . . I need not say,"
he continues, "that it will be sharp work and will require two
of us; for we shall both be up the whole of the previous night,
and shall have to sit up all night again to get it off in time."
He adds that as soon as they have had a little sleep they will
return to town as quickly as they can; but they have, if the
express succeeds, to stop at sundry places along the road to
pay money and notify satisfaction. And so, for himself and
Beard, he is his editor's very sincerely.

Another anecdote of his reporting days, with its sequel, may
be added from his own alleged relation, in which, however,
mistakes occur that it seems strange he should have made.
The story, as told, is that the late Lord Derby, when Mr. Stanley,
had on some important occasion made a speech which all the
reporters found it necessary greatly to abridge; that its essential
points had nevertheless been so well given in the *Chronicle* that
Mr. Stanley, having need of it for himself in greater detail, had
sent a request to the reporter to meet him in Carlton House
Terrace and take down the entire speech; that Dickens attended
and did the work accordingly, much to Mr. Stanley's satisfaction; and that, on his dining with Mr. Gladstone in recent years,
and finding the aspect of the dining-room strangely familiar,
he discovered afterwards on inquiry that it was there he had
taken the speech. The story, as it actually occurred, is connected with the brief life of the *Mirror of Parliament*. It was
not at any special desire of Mr. Stanley's, but for the new record
of the debates, which had been started by one of the uncles of
Dickens and professed to excel *Hansard* in giving verbatim
reports, that the famous speech against O'Connell was taken
as described. The young reporter went to the room in Carlton
Terrace because the work of his uncle Barrow's publication
required to be done there; and if, in later years, the great
author was in the same room as the guest of the prime minister,
it must have been but a month or two before he died, when for
the first time he visited and breakfasted with Mr. Gladstone.

The mention of his career in the gallery may close with the
incident. I will only add that his observation while there had
not led him to form any high opinion of the House of Commons
or its heroes; and that, of the Pickwickian sense which so often
takes the place of common sense in our legislature, he omitted

no opportunity of declaring his contempt at every part of his life.

The other occupation had meanwhile not been lost sight of, and for this we are to go back a little. Since the first sketch appeared in the *Monthly Magazine*, nine others have enlivened the pages of later numbers of the same magazine, the last in February 1835, and that which appeared in the preceding August having first had the signature of Boz. This was the nickname of a pet child, his youngest brother Augustus, whom in honour of the *Vicar of Wakefield* he had dubbed Moses, which being facetiously pronounced through the nose became Boses, and being shortened became Boz. "Boz was a very familiar household word to me, long before I was an author, and so I came to adopt it." Thus had he fully invented his sketches by Boz before they were even so called, or anyone was ready to give much attention to them; and the next invention needful to himself was some kind of payment in return for them. The magazine was owned as well as conducted at this time by a Mr. Holland, who had come back from Bolivar's South American campaigns with the rank of captain, and had hoped to make it a popular mouthpiece for his ardent liberalism. But this hope, as well as his own health, quite failed; and he had sorrowfully to decline receiving any more of the sketches when they had to cease as voluntary offerings. I do not think that either he or the magazine lived many weeks after an evening I passed with him in Doughty Street, in 1837, when he spoke in a very touching way of the failure of this and other enterprises of his life, and of the help that Dickens had been to him.

Nothing thus being forthcoming from the *Monthly*, it was of course but natural that the sketches too should cease to be forthcoming; and, even before the above-named February number appeared, a new opening had been found for them. An evening off-shoot to the *Morning Chronicle* had been lately in hand; and to a countryman of Black's engaged in the preparations for it, Mr. George Hogarth, Dickens was communicating from his rooms in Furnival's Inn, on the evening of Tuesday the 20th of January, 1835, certain hopes and fancies he had formed. This was the beginning of his knowledge of an accomplished and kindly man, with whose family his relations were soon to become so intimate as to have an influence on all his future career. Mr. Hogarth had asked him, as a favour to himself, to write an original sketch for the first number of the

*c 781

enterprise, and in writing back to say with what readiness he should comply, and how anxiously he should desire to do his best for the person who had made the request, he mentioned what had arisen in his mind. It had occurred to him that he might not be unreasonably or improperly trespassing farther on Mr. Hogarth if, trusting to his kindness to refer the application to the proper quarter, he begged to ask whether it was probable, if he commenced a regular series of articles under some attractive title for the *Evening Chronicle*, its conductors would think he had any claim to *some* additional remuneration (of course, of no great amount) for doing so. In short, he wished to put it to the proprietors—first, whether a continuation of some chapters of light papers in the style of his street-sketches would be considered of use to the new journal; and secondly, if so, whether they would not think it fair and reasonable that, taking his share of the ordinary reporting business of the *Chronicle* besides, he should receive something for the papers beyond his ordinary salary as a reporter? The request was thought fair, he began the sketches, and his salary was raised from five to seven guineas a week.

They went on, with undiminished spirit and freshness, throughout the year; and much as they were talked of outside as well as in the world of newspapers, nothing in connection with them delighted the writer half so much as the hearty praise of his own editor. Mr. Black is one of the men who have passed without recognition out of a world their labours largely benefited, but with those who knew him no man was so popular, as well for his broad, kindly humour, as for his honest great-hearted enjoyment of whatever was excellent in others. Dickens to the last remembered, that it was most of all the cordial help of this good old mirth-loving man, which had started him joyfully on his career of letters. It was John Black that flung the slipper after me, he would often say, "Dear old Black! my first hearty out-and-out appreciator," is an expression in one of his letters written to me in the year he died.

THE opening of 1836 found him collecting into two volumes the first series of *Sketches by Boz*, of which he had sold the copyright for a conditional payment of (I think) a hundred and fifty pounds to a young publisher named Macrone, whose acquaintance he had made through Mr. Ainsworth a few weeks before. * 5 At this time also, we are told in a letter before quoted, the editorship of the *Monthly Magazine* having come into Mr. James Grant's hands, this gentleman, applying to him through its previous editor to know if he would again contribute to it, learnt two things: the first that he was going to be married, and the second that, having entered into an arrangement to write a monthly serial, his duties in future would leave him small spare time. Both pieces of news were soon confirmed. *The Times* of 26 March, 1836, gave notice that on the 31st would be published the first shilling number of the *Posthumous Papers of the Pickwick Club, edited by Boz*; and the same journal of a few days later announced that on 2 April Mr Charles Dickens had married Catherine, the eldest daughter of Mr. George Hogarth, whom already we have met as his fellow-worker on the *Chronicle*. The honeymoon was passed in the neighbourhood to which at all times of interest in his life he turned with a strange recurring fondness; and while the young couple are at the quiet little village of Chalk, on the road between Gravesend and Rochester, I will relate exactly the origin of the ever-memorable Mr. Pickwick.

A new publishing house had started recently, among other enterprises ingenious rather than important, a Library of Fiction; among the authors they wished to enlist in it was the writer of the sketches in the *Monthly*; and, to the extent of one paper during the past year, they had effected this through their editor, Mr. Charles Whitehead, a very ingenious and a very unfortunate man. "I was not aware," wrote the elder member of the firm to Dickens, thirteen years later, in a letter to which reference was made [1] in the preface to *Pickwick* in one of his later editions, "that you were writing in the *Chronicle*, or what your name was; but Whitehead, who was an old *Monthly* man, recollected it, and got you to write 'The Tuggs's at Ramsgate.'"

And now comes another person on the scene. "In November 1835," continues Mr. Chapman, "we published a little book called the *Squib Annual*, with plates by Seymour; and it was during my visit to him, to see after them, that he said he should like to do a series of cockney sporting-plates of a superior sort to those he had already published. I said I thought they might do, if accompanied by letterpress and published in monthly parts; and this being agreed to, we wrote to the author of *Three Courses and a Dessert* and proposed it; but receiving no answer, the scheme dropped for some months, till Seymour said he wished us to decide, as another job had offered which would fully occupy his time; and it was on this we decided to ask you to do it. Having opened already a connection with you for our Library of Fiction, we naturally applied to you to do the *Pickwick*; but I do not think we even mentioned our intention to Mr. Seymour, and I am quite sure that from the beginning to the end nobody but yourself had anything whatever to do with it. Our prospectus was out at the end of February, and it had all been arranged before that date."

The member of the firm who carried the application to him in Furnival's Inn was not the writer of this letter, but Mr. Hall, who had sold him two years before, not knowing that he was the purchaser, the magazine in which his first effusion was printed; and he has himself described what passed at the interview. "The idea propounded to me was that the monthly something should be a vehicle for certain plates to be executed by Mr. Seymour; and there was a notion, either on the part of that admirable humorous artist, or of my visitor, that a NIMROD CLUB, the members of which were to go out shooting, fishing, and so forth, and getting themselves into difficulties through their want of dexterity, would be the best means of introducing

---

[1] Not quoted in detail, on that or any other occasion; though referred to. It was, however, placed in my hands, for use if occasion should arise, when Dickens went to America in 1867. The letter bears date 7 July, 1849, and was Mr. Chapman's answer to the question Dickens had asked him, whether the account of the origin of *Pickwick* which he had given in the preface to the cheap edition in 1847 was not strictly correct. "It is *so* correctly described," was Mr. Chapman's opening remark, "that I can throw but little additional light on it." The name of his hero, I may add, Dickens took from that of a celebrated coach-proprietor of Bath.

these. I objected, on consideration, that although born and partly bred in the country I was no great sportsman, except in regard to all kinds of locomotion; that the idea was not novel, and had already been much used; that it would be infinitely better for the plates to arise naturally out of the text; and that I would like to take my own way, with a freer range of English scenes and people, and was afraid I should ultimately do so in any case, whatever course I might prescribe to myself at starting. My views being deferred to, I thought of Mr. Pickwick, and wrote the first number; from the proof-sheets of which Mr. Seymour made his drawing of the club and his happy portrait of its founder. I connected Mr. Pickwick with a club, because of the original suggestion; and I put in Mr. Winkle expressly for the use of Mr. Seymour."

Mr. Hall was dead when this statement was first made, in the preface to the cheap edition in 1847; but Mr. Chapman clearly recollected his partner's account of the interview, and confirmed every part of it, in his letter of 1849,[1] with one exception. In giving Mr. Seymour credit for the figure by which all the habitable globe knows Mr. Pickwick, and which certainly at the outset helped to make him a reality, it had given the artist too much. The reader will hardly be so startled as I was on coming to the closing line of Mr. Chapman's confirmatory letter. "As this letter is to be historical, I may as well claim what little belongs to me in the matter, and that is the figure of Pickwick. Seymour's first sketch was of a long, thin man. The present immortal one he made from my description of a friend of mine at Richmond, a fat old beau who would wear, in spite of the ladies' protests, drab tights and black gaiters. His name was John Foster."

On the coincidences, resemblances and surprises of life Dickens liked especially to dwell, and few things moved his fancy so pleasantly. The world, he would say, was so much smaller than we thought it; we were all so connected by fate without knowing it; people supposed to be far apart were so constantly elbowing each other; and to-morrow bore so close a resemblance to nothing half so much as to yesterday. Here were the only two leading incidents of his own life before I knew

---

[1] The appeal was then made to him because of recent foolish statements by members of Mr. Seymour's family, which Dickens formally contradicted. The "written testimony" to which on this occasion he referred in support of his averments, he placed in my hands on quitting England for his last visit to America; and it remains in my possession.

him: his marriage and the first appearance of his Pickwick; and it turned out after all that I had some shadowy association with both. He was married on the anniversary of my birthday, and the original of the figure of Mr. Pickwick bore my name.

* 7

The first number had not yet appeared when his *Sketches by Boz, Illustrative of Every-day Life and Every-day People*, came forth in two duodecimos with some capital cuts by Cruikshank, and with a preface in which he spoke of the nervousness he should have had in venturing alone before the public, and of his delight in getting the help of Cruikshank, who had frequently contributed to the success, though his well-earned reputation rendered it impossible for him ever to have shared the hazard, of similar undertakings. It very soon became apparent that there was no hazard here. The *Sketches* were much more talked about than the first two or three numbers of *Pickwick*, and I remember still with what hearty praise the book was first named to me by my dear friend Albany Fonblanque, as keen and clear a judge as ever lived either of books or men. Richly did it merit all the praise it had, and more, I will add, than he was ever disposed to give to it himself. He decidedly under-rated it. He gave, in subsequent writings, so much more perfect form and fullness to everything it contained, that he did not care to credit himself with the marvel of having yet so early anticipated so much. But the first sprightly runnings of his genius are undoubtedly here. Mr. Bumble is in the parish sketches, and Mr. Dawkins the dodger in the Old Bailey scenes. There is laughter and fun to excess, never misapplied; there are the minute points and shades of character, with all the discrimination and nicety of detail afterwards so famous; there is everywhere the most perfect ease and skill of handling. The observation shown throughout is nothing short of wonderful. Things are painted literally as they are; and, whatever the picture, whether of every-day vulgar, shabby genteel, or down-right low, with neither the condescending air which is affectation, nor the too familiar one which is slang. The book altogether is a perfectly unaffected, unpretentious, honest performance. Under its manly, sensible straightforward vein of talk there is running at the same time a natural flow of sentiment never sentimental, of humour always easy and unforced, and of pathos for the most part dramatic or picturesque, under which lay the germ of what his mature genius took afterwards most delight in. Of course there are inequalities in it, and some things that would have been better away: but it is a book that might have stood its ground, even if it had stood alone, as containing unusually truthful observation of a sort of life between the middle class and the low, which, having few attractions for bookish observers, was quite unhackneyed ground. It had otherwise also the very special merit of being in no respect bookish or commonplace in its descriptions of the old city with which its writer was so familiar. It was a picture of every-day London at its best and worst, in its humours and enjoyments as well as its sufferings and sins, pervaded everywhere not only with the absolute reality of the things depicted, but also with that subtle sense and mastery of feeling which gives to the reader's sympathies invariably right direction, and awakens consideration, tenderness and kindness precisely for those who most need such help.

Between the first and the second numbers of *Pickwick*, the artist, Mr. Seymour, died by his own hand; and the number came out with three instead of four illustrations. Dickens had seen the unhappy man only once, forty-eight hours before his death; when he went to Furnival's Inn with an etching for the "stroller's-tale" in that number, which, altered at Dickens's suggestion, he brought away again for the few further touches that occupied him to a late hour of the night before he destroyed himself. A notice attached to the number informed the public of this latter fact. There was at first a little difficulty in replacing him, and for a single number Mr. Buss was interposed. But before the fourth number a choice had been made, which as time went on was so thoroughly justified that, through the greater part of the wonderful career which was then beginning, the connection was kept up, and Mr. Hablot Browne's name is not unworthily associated with the masterpieces of Dickens's genius. An incident which I heard related by Mr. Thackeray at one of the Royal Academy dinners belongs to this time. "I can remember when Mr. Dickens was a very young man, and had commenced delighting the world with some charming humorous works in covers which were coloured light green and came out once a month, that this young man wanted an artist to illustrate his writings; and I recollect walking up to his chambers in Furnival's Inn, with two or three drawings in my hand which, strange to say, he did not find suitable." Dickens has himself described another change now made in the publication. "We started with a number of twenty-four pages and four illustrations. Mr. Seymour's sudden and lamented death before the second number was published brought about a quick decision upon a point already in agitation; the number became one of thirty-two pages with only two illustrations, and remained so to the end."

The Session of 1836 terminated his connection with the gallery, and some fruits of his increased leisure showed themselves before the close of the year. His eldest sister's musical attainments and connections had introduced him to many cultivators and professors of that art; he was led to take much interest in Mr. Braham's enterprise at the St. James's Theatre; and in aid of it he wrote a farce for Mr. Harley, founded upon one of his sketches, and the story and songs for an opera composed by his friend Mr. Hullah. Both the *Strange Gentleman*, acted in September, and the *Village Coquettes*, produced in December 1836, had a good success; and the last is memorable to me for having brought me first into personal communication with Dickens.

BOOK SECOND

FIRST FIVE YEARS OF FAME

1836–41. ÆT. 24–9

I

WRITING THE "PICKWICK PAPERS"

1837

THE first letter I had from him was at the close of 1836 from Furnival's Inn, when he sent me the book of his opera of the *Village Coquettes*, which had been published by Mr. Bentley; and this was followed, two months later, by his collected *Sketches*, both first and second series; which he desired me to receive "as a very small testimony of the donor's regard and obligations, as well as of his desire to cultivate and avail himself of a friendship which has been so pleasantly thrown in his way. . . . In short, if you will receive them for my sake and not for their own, you will greatly oblige me." I had met him in the interval at the house of our common friend Mr. Ainsworth, and I remember vividly the impression then made upon me.

Very different was his face in those days from that which photography has made familiar to the present generation. A look of youthfulness first attracted you, and then a candour and openness of expression which made you sure of the qualities within. The features were very good. He had a capital forehead, a firm nose with full wide nostrils, eyes wonderfully beaming with intellect and running over with humour and cheerfulness, and a rather prominent mouth strongly marked with sensibility. The head was altogether well formed and symmetrical, and the air and carriage of it were extremely spirited. The hair so scant and grizzled in later days was then of a rich brown and most luxuriant abundance, and the bearded face of his last two decades had hardly a vestige of hair or whisker; but there was that in the face as I first recollect it which no time could change, and which remained implanted on it unalterably to the last. This was the quickness, keenness, and practical power, the eager, restless, energetic outlook on each several feature, that seemed to tell so little of a student or writer of books, and so much of a man of action and business in the world. Light and motion flashed from every part of it. "It was as if made of steel," was said of it, four or five years after the time to which I am referring, by a most original and delicate observer, the late Mrs. Carlyle. "What a face is his to meet in a drawing-room!" wrote Leigh Hunt to me, the morning after I made them known to each other. "It has the life and soul in it of fifty human beings." In such sayings are expressed not alone the restless and resistless vivacity and force of which I have spoken, but that also which lay beneath them of steadiness and hard endurance.

Several unsuccessful efforts were made by each to get the other to his house before the door of either was opened at last. A son had been born to him on Twelfth-day (6 January, 1837), and before the close of the following month he and his wife were in the lodgings at Chalk they had occupied after their marriage. Early in March there is a letter from him accounting for the failure of a promise to call on me because of "a crew of house agents and attornies," through whom he had nearly missed his conveyance to Chalk, and been made "more than half wild besides." This was his last letter from Furnival's Inn. In that same month he went to 48 Doughty Street; and in his first letter to me from that address, dated at the close of the month, there is this passage: "We only called upon you a second time in the hope of getting you to dine with us, and were much disappointed not to find you. I have delayed writing a reply to your note, meaning to call upon you. I have been so much engaged, however, in the pleasant occupation of 'moving' that I have not had time; and I am obliged at last to write and say that I have been long engaged to the *Pickwick* publishers to a dinner in honour of that hero which comes off to-morrow. I am consequently unable to accept your kind invite, which I frankly own I should have liked much better."

That Saturday's celebration of his twelfth number, the anniversary of the birth of *Pickwick*, preceded by but a few weeks a personal sorrow which profoundly moved him. His wife's next youngest sister, Mary, who lived with them, and by sweetness of nature even more than by graces of person had made herself the ideal of his life, died with a terrible suddenness that for the time completely bore him down.[1] His grief and suffering were intense, and affected him, as will be seen, through many

†3

---

[1] Her epitaph, written by him, remains upon a gravestone in the cemetery at Kensal Green: "Young, beautiful, and good, God numbered her among his angels at the early age of seventeen."

after years. The publication of *Pickwick* was interrupted for two months, the effort of writing it not being possible to him. He moved for change of scene to Hampstead, and here, at the close of May, I visited him, and became first his guest. More than ordinarily susceptible at the moment to all kindliest impressions, his heart opened itself to mine. I left him as much his friend, and as entirely in his confidence, as if I had known him for years. Nor had many weeks passed before he addressed to me from Doughty Street words which it is my sorrowful pride to remember have had literal fulfilment. "I look back with unmingled pleasure to every link which each ensuing week has added to the chain of our attachment. It shall go hard, I hope, ere anything but Death impairs the toughness of a bond now so firmly riveted." It remained unweakened till death came.

There were circumstances that drew us at once into frequent and close communication. What the sudden popularity of his writings implied was known to others some time before it was known to himself; and he was only now becoming gradually conscious of all the disadvantage this had placed him at. He would have laughed if, at this outset of his wonderful fortune in literature, his genius acknowledged by all without misgiving, young, popular and prosperous, anyone had compared him to the luckless men of letters of former days, whose common fate was to be sold into a slavery which their later lives were passed in vain endeavours to escape from. Not so was his fate to be, yet something of it he was doomed to experience. He had unwittingly sold himself into a quasi-bondage, and had to purchase his liberty at a heavy cost, after considerable suffering.

It was not until the fourth or fifth number of *Pickwick* (in the latter Sam Weller made his first appearance) that its importance began to be understood by "the trade," and on the eve of the issue of its sixth number, 22 August, 1836, he had signed an agreement with Mr. Bentley to undertake the editorship of a monthly magazine to be started the following January, to which he was to supply a serial story; and soon afterwards he had agreed with the same publisher to write two other tales, the first at a specified early date; the expressed remuneration in each case being certainly inadequate to the claims of a writer of any marked popularity. Under these Bentley agreements he was now writing, month by month, the first half of *Oliver Twist*, and, under his Chapman and Hall agreement, the last half of *Pickwick*, not even by a week in advance of the printer with either, when a circumstance became known to him of which he thus wrote to me.

"I heard half an hour ago, on authority which leaves me in no doubt about the matter (from the binder of *Pickwick* in fact), that Macrone intends publishing a new issue of my *Sketches* in monthly parts of nearly the same size and in just the same form as the *Pickwick Papers*. I need not tell you that this is calculated to injure me most seriously, or that I have a very natural and most decided objection to being supposed to presume upon the success of the *Pickwick*, and thus foist this old work upon the public in its new dress for the mere purpose of putting money in my own pocket. Neither need I say that the fact of my name being before the town, attached to three publications at the same time, must prove seriously prejudicial to my reputation. As you are acquainted with the circumstances under which these copyrights were disposed of, and as I know I may rely on your kind help, may I beg you to see Macrone, and to state in the strongest and most emphatic manner my feeling on this point. I wish him to be reminded of the sums he paid for those books; of the sale he has had for them; of the extent to which he has already pushed them; and of the very great profits he must necessarily have acquired from them. I wish him also to be reminded that no intention of publishing them in this form was in the remotest manner hinted to me, by him or on his behalf, when he obtained possession of the copyright. I then wish you to put it to his feelings of common honesty and fair-dealing whether after this communication he will persevere in his intention." What else the letter contained need not be quoted, but it strongly moved me to do my best.

I found Mr. Macrone inaccessible to all arguments of persuasion, however. That he had bought the book for a small sum at a time when the smallest was not unimportant to the writer, shortly before his marriage, and that he had since made very considerable profits by it, in no way disturbed his position that he had a right to make as much as he could of what was his, without regard to how it had become so. There was nothing for it but to change front, and, admitting it might be a less evil to the unlucky author to repurchase than to let the monthly issue proceed, to ask what further gain was looked for: but so wide a mouth was opened at this that I would have no part in the costly process of filling it. I told Dickens so, and strongly counselled him to keep quiet for a time.

But the worry and vexation were too great with all the work

he had in hand, and I was hardly surprised next day to receive
the letter sent me; which yet should be prefaced with the remark that suspense of any kind was at all times intolerable to
the writer. The interval between the accomplishment of anything, and "its first motion," Dickens never could endure, and
he was too ready to make any sacrifice to abridge or end it.
This did not belong to the strong side of his character, and
advantage was frequently taken of the fact. "I sent down just
now to know whether you were at home (two o'clock), as
Chapman and Hall were with me, and, the case being urgent,
I wished to have the further benefit of your kind advice and
assistance. Macrone and his friend (arcades ambo) waited on
them this morning, and after a long discussion peremptorily
refused to take one farthing less than the two thousand pounds.
The friend repeated the statement of figures which he made
to you yesterday, and put it to Hall whether he could say from
his knowledge of such matters that the estimate of probable
profit was exorbitant. Hall, whose judgment may be relied on
in such matters, could not dispute the justice of the calculation. And so the matter stood. In this dilemma it occurred to
them (my *Pickwick* men), whether, if the *Sketches* MUST appear
in monthly numbers, it would not be better for them to appear
for their benefit and mine conjointly, than for Macrone's sole
use and behoof; whether they, having all the *Pickwick* machinery
in full operation, could not obtain for them a much larger sale
than Macrone could ever get; and whether, even at this large
price of two thousand pounds, we might not, besides retaining
the copyright, reasonably hope for a good profit on the outlay.
These suggestions having presented themselves, they came
straight to me (having obtained a few hours' respite), and proposed that we should purchase the copyrights between us for
the two thousand pounds, and publish them in monthly parts.
I need not say that no other form of publication would repay
the expenditure; and they wish me to explain by an address
that *they*, who may be fairly put forward as the parties, have
been driven into that mode of publication, or the copyright
would have been lost. I considered the matter in every possible
way. I sent for you, but you were out. I thought of" (what,
need not be repeated, now that all is past and gone) "and
consented. Was I right? I think you will say yes." I could not
say no, though I was glad to have been no party to a price so
exorbitant; which yet profited extremely little the person who
received it. He died in hardly more than two years; and if

Dickens had enjoyed the most liberal treatment at his hands,
† 4 he could not have exerted himself more generously for the
widow and children.

His new story was now beginning largely to share attention
with his *Pickwick Papers*, and it was delightful to see how real
all its people became to him. What I had most indeed to notice
in him, at the very outset of his career, was his indifference to
any praise of his performances on the merely literary side,
compared with the higher recognition of them as bits of actual
life, with the meaning and purpose on their part, and the responsibility on his, of realities rather than creatures of fancy.
The exception that might be drawn from *Pickwick* is rather
in seeming than substance. A first book has its immunities, and
the distinction of this from the rest of the writings appears in
what has been said of its origin. The plan of it was simply to
amuse. It was to string together whimsical sketches of the pencil
by entertaining sketches of the pen; and, at its beginning, where
or how it was to end was as little known to himself as to any of
its readers. But genius is a master as well as a servant, and
when the laughter and fun were at their highest something
graver made its appearance. He had to defend himself for this;
and he said that, though the mere oddity of a new acquaintance
was apt to impress one at first, the more serious qualities were
discovered when we became friends with the man. In other
words, he might have said that the change was become necessary
for his own satisfaction. The book itself, in teaching him what
his power was, had made him more conscious of what would be
expected from its use; and this never afterwards quitted him.
In what he was to do hereafter, as in all he was doing now, with
Pickwick still to finish and *Oliver* only beginning, it constantly
attended him. Nor could it well be otherwise, with all those
fanciful creations so real, to a nature in itself so practical and
earnest; and in this spirit I had well understood the letter
accompanying what had been published of *Oliver* since its
commencement the preceding February, which reached me the
day after I visited him. Something to the effect of what has
just been said, I had remarked publicly of the portion of the
story sent to me; and his instant warm-hearted acknowledgment,
of which I permit myself to quote a line or two, showed me in
what perfect agreement we were. "How can I thank you? Can
I do better than by saying that the sense of poor Oliver's reality,
which I know you have had from the first, has been the highest
of all praise to me. None that has been lavished upon me have

I felt half so much as that appreciation of my intent and meaning. You know I have ever done so, for it was your feeling for me and mine for you that first brought us together, and I hope will keep us so, till death do us part. Your notices make me grateful but very proud; so have a care of them."

There was nothing written by him after this date which I did not see before the world did, either in manuscript or proofs; and in connection with the latter I shortly began to give him the help which he publicly mentioned twenty years later in dedicating his collected writings to me. One of his letters reminds me when these corrections began, and they were continued very nearly to the last. They lightened for him a labour of which he had more than enough imposed upon him at this time by others, and they were never anything but an enjoyment to me. "I have," he wrote, "so many sheets of the *Miscellany* to correct before I can begin *Oliver*, that I fear I shall not be able to leave home this morning. I therefore send your revise of the *Pickwick* by Fred, who is on his way with it to the printers. You will see that my alterations are very slight, but I think for the better." This was the fourteenth number of the *Pickwick Papers*. Fred was his next younger brother, who lived with him at the time.

The number following this was the famous one in which the hero finds himself in the Fleet, and another of his letters will show what enjoyment the writing of it had given to himself. I had sent to ask him where we were to meet for a proposed ride that day. "HERE," was his reply. "I am slippered and jacketted, and, like that same starling who is so very seldom quoted, can't get out. I am getting on, thank Heaven, 'like a house o' fire,' and think the next *Pickwick* will bang all the others. I shall expect you at one, and we will walk to the stable together. If you know anybody at Saint Paul's, I wish you'd send round and ask them not to ring the bell so. I can hardly hear my own ideas as they come into my head, and say what they mean."

The exulting tone of confidence in what he had thus been writing was indeed well justified. He had as yet done nothing so remarkable, in blending humour with tragedy, as his picture of what the poor side of a debtors' prison was in the days of which we have seen that he had himself had bitter experience; and we have but to recall, as it rises sharply to the memory, what is contained in this portion of a work that was not only among his earliest but his least considered as to plan, to understand what it was that not alone had given him his fame so early, but which in itself held the germ of the future that awaited him. Every point was a telling one, and the truthfulness of the whole unerring. The dreadful restlessness of the place, undefined yet unceasing, unsatisfying and terrible, was pictured throughout with Defoe's minute reality; while points of character were handled in that greater style which connects with the richest oddities of humour an insight into principles of character universal as nature itself. When he resolved that Sam Weller should be occupant of the prison with Mr. Pickwick, he was perhaps thinking of his favourite Smollett, and how, when Peregrine Pickle was inmate of the Fleet, Hatchway and Pipes refused to leave him; but Fielding himself might have envied his way of setting about it. Nor is any portion of his picture less admirable than this. The comedy gradually deepening into tragedy; the shabby vagabonds who are the growth of debtors' prisons, contrasting with the poor simple creatures who are their sacrifices and victims; Mr. Mivins and Mr. Smangle, side by side with the cobbler ruined by his legacy, who sleeps under the table to remind himself of his old four-poster; Mr. Pickwick's first night in the marshal's room, Sam Weller entertaining Stiggins in the snuggery, Jingle in decline, and the chancery prisoner dying; in all these scenes there was writing of the first order, a deep feeling of character, that delicate form of humour which has a quaintly pathetic turn in it as well, comedy of the richest and broadest kind, and the easy handling throughout of a master in his art. We place the picture by the side of those of the great writers of this style of fiction in our language, and it does not fall by the comparison.

Of what the reception of the book had been up to this time, and of the popularity Dickens had won as its author, this also will be the proper place to speak. For its kind, its extent, and the absence of everything unreal or factitious in the causes that contributed to it, it is unexampled in literature. Here was a series of sketches, without the pretence to such interest as attends a well-constructed story; put forth in a form apparently ephemeral as its purpose; having none that seemed higher than to exhibit some studies of cockney manners with help from a comic artist; and after four or five parts had appeared, without newspaper notice or puffing, and itself not subserving in the public anything false or unworthy, it sprang into a popularity that each part carried higher and higher, until people at this time talked of nothing else, tradesmen recommended their goods by using its name, and its sale, outstripping at a bound that of all the most famous books of the century, had reached to an almost fabulous number. Of part one, the binder prepared four hundred; and of part fifteen, his order was for more than forty thousand. Every class, the high equally with the low, were attracted to it. The charm of its gaiety and good humour, its inexhaustible fun, its riotous overflow of animal spirits, its brightness and keenness of observation, and, above all, the incomparable ease of its many varieties of enjoyment, fascinated everybody. Judges on the bench and boys in the street, gravity and folly, the young and the old, those who were entering life and those who were quitting it, alike found it to be irresistible. "An archdeacon," wrote Mr. Carlyle afterwards to me, "with his own venerable lips, repeated to me, the other night, a strange profane story: of a solemn clergyman who had been administering ghostly consolation to a sick person; having finished, satisfactorily as he thought, and got out of the room, he heard the sick person ejaculate: 'Well, thank God, *Pickwick* will be out in ten days anyway!'—This is dreadful."

Let me add that there was something more in it all than the gratification of mere fun and laughter, or even than the rarer pleasure that underlies the outbreak of all forms of genuine humour. Another chord had been struck. Over and above the lively painting of manners which at first had been so attractive, there was something that left deeper mark. Genial and irrepressible enjoyment, affectionate heartiness of tone, unrestrained exuberance of mirth, these are not more delightful than they are fleeting and perishable qualities; but the attention eagerly excited by the charm of them in *Pickwick* found itself retained by something more permanent. We had all become suddenly conscious, in the very thick of the extravaganza of adventure and fun set before us, that here were real people. It was not somebody talking humorously about them, but they were there themselves. That a number of persons belonging to the middle and lower ranks of life (Wardles, Winkles, Wellers, Tupmans, Bardells, Snubbinses, Perkers, Bob Sawyers, Dodsons and Foggs) had been somehow added to his intimate and familiar acquaintance, the ordinary reader knew before half a dozen numbers were out; and it took not many more to make clear to the intelligent reader that a new and original genius in the walk of Smollett and Fielding had arisen in England.

I do not, for reasons to be hereafter stated, think the *Pickwick Papers* comparable to the later books; but, apart from the new vein of humour it opened, its wonderful freshness and its un-flagging animal spirits, it has two characters that will probably continue to attract to it an unfading popularity. Its pre-eminent achievement is of course Sam Weller; one of those people that take their place among the supreme successes of fiction, as one that nobody ever saw but everybody recognises, at once perfectly natural and intensely original. Who is there that has ever thought him tedious? Who is so familiar with him as not still to be finding something new in him? Who is so amazed by his inexhaustible resources, or so amused by his inextinguishable laughter, as to doubt of his being as ordinary and perfect a reality, nevertheless, as anything in the London streets? When indeed the relish has been dulled that makes such humour natural and appreciable, and not his native fun only, his ready and rich illustration, his imperturbable self-possession, but his devotion to his master, his chivalry and his gallantry, are no longer discovered, or believed no longer to exist, in the ranks of life to which he belongs, it will be worse for all of us than for the fame of his creator. Nor, when faith is lost in that possible combination of eccentricities and benevolences, shrewdness and simplicity, good sense and folly, all that suggests the ludicrous and nothing that suggests contempt for it, which form the delightful oddity of Pickwick, will the mistake committed be one merely of critical misjudgment. But of this there is small fear. Sam Weller and Mr. Pickwick are the Sancho and the Quixote of Londoners, and as little likely to pass away as the old city itself.

Dickens was very fond of riding in these early years, and there was no recreation he so much indulged, or with such profit to himself, in the intervals of his hardest work. I was his companion oftener than I could well afford the time for, the distances being great and nothing else to be done for the day; but when a note would unexpectedly arrive while I knew him to be hunted hard by one of his printers, telling me he had been sticking to work so closely that he must have rest, and, by way of getting it, proposing we should start together that morning at eleven o'clock for "a fifteen mile ride out, ditto in, and a lunch on the road," with a wind-up of six o'clock dinner in Doughty Street, I could not resist the good fellowship. His notion of finding rest from mental exertion in as much bodily exertion of equal severity continued with him to the last; taking in the later years what I always thought the too great strain of as many miles in walking as he now took in the saddle, and too often

indulging it at night: for, though he was always passionately
fond of walking, he observed as yet a moderation in it, even
accepting as sufficient my seven or eight miles' companionship.
"What a brilliant morning for a country walk!" he would
write, with not another word in his dispatch. Or, "Is it possible
that you can't, oughtn't, shouldn't, mustn't, *won't* be tempted,
this gorgeous day!" Or, "I start precisely—precisely mind—at
half-past one. Come, come, *come*, and walk in the green lanes.
You will work the better for it all the week. COME! I shall
expect you." Or, "You don't feel disposed, do you, to muffle
yourself up, and start off with me for a good brisk walk, over
Hampstead Heath? I knows a good 'ous there where we can
have a red-hot chop for dinner, and a glass of good wine":
which led to our first experience of Jack Straw's Castle, memorable for many happy meetings in coming years. But the rides
were most popular and frequent. "I think," he would write,
"Richmond and Twickenham, thro' the park, out at Knights-
bridge, and over Barnes Common—would make a beautiful
ride." Or, "Do you know, I shouldn't object to an early chop at
some village inn?" Or, "Not knowing whether my head was off
or on, it became so addled with work, I have gone riding the
old road, and should be truly delighted to meet or be overtaken
by you." Or, "Where shall it be—*oh where*—Hampstead,
Greenwich, Windsor? WHERE?????? while the day is bright,
not when it has dwindled away to nothing! For who can be of
any use whatsomdever such a day as this, excepting out of
doors?" Or it might be interrogatory summons to "A hard
trot of three hours?" or intimation as laconic "To be heard of
at Eel Pie House, Twickenham!" When first I knew him, I may
add, his carriage for his wife's use was a small chaise with a
smaller pair of ponies, which, having a habit of making sudden
rushes up by-streets in the day and peremptory standstills in
ditches by night, were changed in the following year for a more
suitable equipage.

To this mention of his habits while at work when our friendship began, I have to add what will complete the relation already
given, in connection with his *Sketches*, of the uneasy sense
accompanying his labour that it was yielding insufficient for
himself while it enriched others, which is a needful part of his
story at this time. At Midsummer 1837, replying to some
inquiries, and sending his agreement with Mr. Bentley for the
Miscellany under which he was writing *Oliver*, he went on: "It
is a very extraordinary fact (I forgot it on Sunday) that I have

NEVER HAD from him a copy of the agreement respecting the novel, which I never saw before or since I signed it at his house one morning long ago. Shall I ask him for a copy, or no? I have looked at some memoranda I made at the time, and I *fear* he has my second novel on the same terms, under the same agreement. This is a bad look-out, but we must try and mend it. You will tell me you are very much surprised at my doing business in this way. So am I, for in most matters of labour and application I am punctuality itself. The truth is (though you do not need I should explain the matter to you, my dear fellow) that, if I had allowed myself to be worried by these things, I could never have done as much as I have. But I much fear, in my desire to avoid present vexations, I have laid up a bitter store for the future." The second novel, which he had promised in a complete form for a very early date, and had already selected subject and title for, was published four years later as *Barnaby Rudge*; but of the third he at present knew nothing but that he was expected to begin it, if not in the magazine, somewhere or other independently within a specified time.

The first appeal made, in taking action upon his letter, had reference to the immediate pressure of the *Barnaby* novel; but it also opened up the question of the great change of circumstances since these various agreements had been precipitately signed by him, the very different situation brought about by the extraordinary increase in the popularity of his writings, and the advantage it would be, to both Mr. Bentley and himself, to make more equitable adjustment of their relations. Some misunderstandings followed, but were closed by a compromise in September 1837; by which the third novel was abandoned [1] on certain conditions, and *Barnaby* was undertaken to be finished by November 1838. This involved a completion of the new story during the progress of *Oliver*, whatever might be required to follow on the close of *Pickwick*; and I doubted its wisdom. But it was accepted for the time.

He had meanwhile taken his wife abroad for a ten days' summer holiday, accompanied by the shrewd observant young artist Mr. Hablot Browne, whose admirable illustrations to *Pickwick* had more than supplied Mr. Seymour's loss; and I had a letter from him on their landing at Calais on 2 July.

---

[1] I have a memorandum in Dickens's writing that £500 was to have been given for it, and an additional £250 on its sale reaching 3000 copies: but he had no ground of objection to the terms that accompanied its surrender, which were favourable.

"We have arranged for a post-coach to take us to Ghent, Brussels, Antwerp, and a hundred other places, that I cannot recollect now and couldn't spell if I did. We went this afternoon in a barouche to some gardens where the people dance, and where they were footing it most heartily—especially the women, who in their short petticoats and light caps look uncommonly agreeable. A gentleman in a blue surtout and silken berlins accompanied us from the hotel, and acted as curator. He even waltzed with a very smart lady (just to show us, condescendingly, how it ought to be done), and waltzed elegantly, too. We rang for slippers after we came back, and it turned out that this gentleman was the Boots."

His later seaside holiday was passed at Broadstairs, as were those of many subsequent years, and the little watering-place has been made memorable by his pleasant sketch of it. From his letters to myself a few lines may be given of his first doings and impressions there.

Writing on 3 September, he reports himself just risen from an attack of illness. "I am much better, and hope to begin *Pickwick* No. 18 to-morrow. You will imagine how queer I must have been when I tell you that I have been compelled for four-and-twenty mortal hours to abstain from porter or other malt liquor!!! I done it though—really. . . . I have discovered that the landlord of the Albion has delicious hollands (but what is that to *you*, for you cannot sympathise with my feelings), and that a cobbler who lives opposite to my bedroom window is a Roman Catholic, and gives an hour and a half to his devotions every morning behind his counter. I have walked upon the sands at low-water from this place to Ramsgate, and sat upon the same at high-ditto till I have been flayed with the cold. I have seen ladies and gentlemen walking upon the earth in slippers of buff, and pickling themselves in the sea in complete suits of the same. I have seen stout gentlemen looking at nothing through powerful telescopes for hours, and, when at last they saw a cloud of smoke, fancying a steamer behind it, and going home comfortable and happy. I have found out that our next neighbour has a wife and something else under the same roof with the rest of his furniture—the wife deaf and blind, and the something else given to drinking. And if you ever get to the end of this letter *you* will find out that I subscribe myself on paper as on everything else (some atonement perhaps for its length and absurdity)," etc.

In his next letter (from 12 High Street, Broadstairs, on the

7th) there is allusion to one of the many piracies of *Pickwick*, which had distinguished itself beyond the rest by a preface abusive of the writer plundered. "I recollect this 'member of the dramatic-authors'-society' bringing an action once against Chapman, who rented the City Theatre, in which it was proved that he had undertaken to write under special agreement seven melodramas for five pounds, to enable him to do which a room had been hired in a gin-shop close by. The defendant's plea was that the plaintiff was always drunk, and had not fulfilled his contract. Well; if the *Pickwick* has been the means of putting a few shillings in the vermin-eaten pockets of so miserable a creature, and has saved him from a workhouse or a jail, let him empty out his little pot of filth and welcome. I am quite content to have been the means of relieving him. Besides, he seems to have suffered by agreements!"

His own troubles in that way were compromised for the time, as already hinted, at the close of this September month; and at the end of the month following, after finishing *Pickwick* and resuming *Oliver*, the latter having been suspended by him during the recent disputes, he made his first visit to Brighton. The opening of his letter of Friday, 3 November, is full of friendly regrets that I had not joined them there. "It is a beautiful day and we have been taking advantage of it, but the wind until to-day has been so high and the weather so stormy that Kate has been scarcely able to peep out of doors. On Wednesday it blew a perfect hurricane, breaking windows, knocking down shutters, carrying people off their legs, blowing the fires out, and causing universal consternation. The air was for some hours darkened with a shower of black hats (second-hand) which are supposed to have been blown off the heads of unwary passengers in remote parts of the town, and have been industriously picked up by the fishermen. Charles Kean was advertised for *Othello*, 'for the benefit of Mrs. Sefton, having most kindly postponed for this one day his departure for London.' I have not heard whether he got to the theatre, but I am sure nobody else did. They do *The Honeymoon* to-night, on which occasion I mean to patronise the drayma. We have a beautiful bay-windowed sitting-room here, fronting the sea, but I have seen nothing of B.'s brother who was to have shown me the lions, and my notions of the place are consequently somewhat confined: being limited to the Pavilion, the Chain Pier, and the sea. The last is quite enough for me, and, unless I am joined by some male companion (do you think I shall be?), is most probably all I shall make acquaintance with. I am glad you like *Oliver* this month: especially glad that you particularise the first chapter. I hope to do great things with Nancy. If I can only work out the idea I have formed of her, and of the female who is to contrast with her, I think I may defy Mr. —— and all his works. I have had * 8 great difficulty in keeping my hands off Fagin and the rest of them in the evenings; but, as I came down for rest, I have resisted the temptation, and steadily applied myself to the labour of being idle. Did you ever read (of course you have, though) Defoe's *History of the Devil*? What a capital thing it is! I bought it for a couple of shillings yesterday morning, and have been quite absorbed in it ever since. We must have been jolter-headed geniuses not to have anticipated M.'s reply. My best remembrances to him. I see H. at this moment. I must be present at a rehearsal of that opera. It will be better than any comedy that was ever played. Talking of comedies, I still see No Thoroughfare staring me in the face, every time I look down that road. I have taken places for Tuesday next. We shall be at home at six o'clock, and I shall hope at least to see you that evening. I am afraid you will find this letter extremely dear at eightpence, but if the warmest assurances of friendship and attachment, and anxious lookings-forward to the pleasure of your society, be worth anything, throw them into the balance, together with a hundred good wishes and one hearty assurance that I am," etc., "Charles Dickens. No room for the flourish—I'll finish it the next time I write to you."

The flourish that accompanied his signature is familiar to everyone. The allusion to the comedy expresses a fancy he at this time had of being able to contribute some such achievement in aid of Macready's gallant efforts at Covent Garden to bring back to the stage its higher associations of good literature and intellectual enjoyment. It connects curiously now that un-realised hope with the exact title of the only story he ever took part himself in dramatising, and which Mr. Fechter played at the Adelphi three years before his death.

II

NOT remotely bearing on the stage, nevertheless, was the employment on which I found him busy at his return from Brighton; one result of his more satisfactory relations with Mr. Bentley having led to a promise to edit for him a Life of the celebrated clown, Grimaldi. The manuscript had been prepared from autobiographical notes by a Mr. Egerton Wilks, and contained one or two stories told so badly, and so well worth better telling, that the hope of enlivening their dullness at the cost of very little labour constituted a sort of attraction for him. Except the preface, he did not write a line of this biography, such modifications or additions as he made having been dictated by him to his father; whom I found often in exalted enjoyment of the office of amanuensis. He had also a most indifferent opinion of the mass of material which Mr. Wilks had raked together, describing it as "twaddle"; and his own modest estimate of the book, on its completion, may be guessed from the number of notes of admiration (no less than thirty) which accompanied his written mention to me of the sale with which it started in the first week of its publication. "Seventeen hundred *Grimaldis* have been already sold, and the demand increases daily!!!!!!!!!!!!!!!!!!!!!!!!!!!!!!"

It was not to have all its own way, however. A great many critical faults were found; and one point in particular was urged against his handling such a subject, that he could never himself even have seen Grimaldi. To this last objection he was moved to reply, and had prepared a letter for the *Miscellany*, "from editor to sub-editor," which it was thought best to suppress, but of which the opening remark may now be not unamusing. "I understand that a gentleman unknown is going about this town privately informing all ladies and gentlemen of discontented natures that, on a comparison of dates and putting together of many little circumstances which occur to his great sagacity, he has made the profound discovery that I can never have seen Grimaldi, whose Life I have edited, and that the book must therefore of necessity be bad. Now, sir, although I was brought up from remote country parts in the dark ages of 1819 and 1820 to behold the splendour of Christmas pantomimes and the humour of Joe, in whose honour I am informed I clapped my hands with great precocity, and although I even saw him act in the remote times of 1823; yet, as I had not then aspired to the dignity of a tail-coat, though forced by a relentless parent into my first pair of boots, I am willing, with the view of saving this honest gentleman further time and trouble, to concede that I had not arrived at man's estate when Grimaldi left the stage, and that my recollections of his acting are, to my loss, but shadowy and imperfect. Which confession I now make publicly, and without mental qualification or reserve, to all whom it may concern. But the deduction of this pleasant gentleman that therefore the Grimaldi book must be bad, I must take leave to doubt. I don't think that to edit a man's biography from his own notes it is essential you should have known him, and I don't believe that Lord Braybrooke had more than the very slightest acquaintance with Mr. Pepys, whose memoirs he edited two centuries after he died."

Enormous meanwhile, and without objection audible on any side, had been the success of the completed *Pickwick*, which we celebrated by a dinner, with himself in the chair and Talfourd in the vice-chair, everybody in hearty good humour with every other body; and a copy of which I received from him on 11 December in the most luxurious of Hayday's bindings, with a note worth preserving for its closing allusion. The passage referred to in it was a comment, in delicately chosen words, that Leigh Hunt had made on the inscription at the grave in Kensal Green. "Chapman and Hall have just sent me, with a copy of our deed, three 'extra-super' bound copies of *Pickwick*, as per specimen enclosed. The first I forward to you, the second I have presented to our good friend Ainsworth, and the third Kate has retained for herself. Accept your copy with one sincere and most comprehensive expression of my warmest friendship and esteem; and a hearty renewal, if there need be any renewal when there has been no interruption, of all those assurances of affectionate regard which our close friendship and communion for a long time back has every day implied. . . . That beautiful passage you were so kind and considerate as to send me has given me the only feeling akin to pleasure (sorrowful pleasure it is) that I have yet had connected with the loss of my dear young friend and companion; for whom my love and attachment will never diminish, and by whose side, if it please God to leave me in possession of sense to signify my wishes, my bones, whenever or wherever I die, will one day be laid. Tell Leigh Hunt when you have an opportunity how much he has affected me, and how deeply I thank him for what he has done. You cannot say it too strongly."

The "deed" mentioned was one executed in the previous month to restore to him a third ownership in the book which had thus far enriched all concerned but himself. The original understanding respecting it Mr. Edwin Chapman thus describes for me. "There was no agreement about *Pickwick* except a verbal one. Each number was to consist of a sheet and a half, for which we were to pay fifteen guineas; and we paid him for the first two numbers at once, as he required the money to go and get married with. We were also to pay more according to the sale, and I think *Pickwick* altogether cost us three thousand pounds." Adjustment to the sale would have cost four times as much, and of the actual payments I have myself no note; but, as far as my memory serves, they are overstated by Mr. Chapman. My impression is that, above and beyond the first sum due for each of the twenty numbers (making no allowance for their extension after the first to thirty-two pages), successive cheques were given, as the work went steadily on to the enormous sale it reached, which brought up the entire sum received to two thousand five hundred pounds. I had, however, always pressed so strongly the importance to him of some share in the copyright, that this at last was conceded in the deed above-mentioned, though five years were to elapse before the right should accrue; and it was only yielded as part consideration for a further agreement entered into at the same date (19 November, 1837) whereby Dickens engaged to "write a new work the title whereof shall be determined by him, of a similar character and of the same extent as the *Posthumous Papers of the Pickwick Club*," the first number of which was to be delivered on the fifteenth of the following March, and each of the numbers on the same day of each of the successive nineteen months; which was also to be the date of the payment to him, by Messrs. Chapman and Hall, of twenty several sums of one hundred and fifty pounds each for five years' use of the copyright, the entire ownership in which was then to revert to Dickens. The name of this new book, as all the world knows, was *The Life and Adventures of Nicholas Nickleby*; and between April 1838 and October 1839 it was begun and finished accordingly.

All through the interval of these arrangements *Oliver Twist* had been steadily continued. Month by month, for many months, it had run its opening course with the close of *Pickwick*, as we shall see it close with the opening of *Nickleby*; and the expectations of those who had built most confidently on the young novelist were more than confirmed. Here was the interest of a story simply but well constructed; and characters with the same impress of reality upon them, but more carefully and skilfully drawn. Nothing could be meaner than the subject, the progress of a parish or workhouse boy, nothing less so than its treatment. As each number appeared, his readers generally became more and more conscious of what already, as we have seen, had revealed itself and even the riotous fun of *Pickwick*, that the purpose was not solely to amuse; and, far more decisively than its predecessor, the new story further showed what were the not least potent elements in the still-increasing popularity that was gathering around the writer. His qualities could be appreciated as well as felt in an almost equal degree by all classes of his various readers. Thousands were attracted to him, because he placed them in the midst of scenes and characters with which they were already themselves acquainted; and thousands were reading him with no less avidity because he introduced them to passages of nature and life of which they before knew nothing, but of the truth of which their own habits and senses sufficed to assure them. Only to genius are so revealed the affinities and sympathies of high and low, in regard to the customs and usages of life; and only a writer of the first rank can bear the application of such a test. For it is by the alliance of common habits, quite as much as by the bonds of a common humanity, that we are all of us linked together; and the result of being above the necessity of depending on other people's opinions, and that of being below it, are pretty much the same. It would equally startle both high and low to be conscious of the whole that is implied in this close approximation; but for the common enjoyment of which I speak such consciousness is not required; and for the present Fagin may be left undisturbed in his school of practical ethics with only the Dodger, Charley Bates and his other promising scholars.

With such work as this in hand, it will hardly seem surprising that, as the time for beginning *Nickleby* came on, and as he thought of his promise for November, he should have the sense of "something hanging over him like a hideous nightmare." He felt that he could not complete the *Barnaby Rudge* novel by the November of that year as promised, and that the engagement he would have to break was unfitting him for engagements he might otherwise fulfil. He had undertaken what in truth was impossible. The labour of at once editing the *Miscellany*, and supplying it with monthly portions of *Oliver*, more than occupied all the time left him by other labours absolutely necessary. "I no sooner get myself up," he wrote, "high and dry, to attack *Oliver* manfully, than up come the waves of each month's work, and drive me back again into a sea of manuscript." There was nothing for it but that he should make further appeal to Mr. Bentley. "I have recently," he wrote to him on 11 February, 1838, "been thinking a great deal about *Barnaby Rudge. Grimaldi* has occupied so much of the short interval I had between the completion of the *Pickwick* and the commencement of the new work, that I see it will be wholly impossible for me to produce it by the time I had hoped, with justice to myself or profit to you. What I wish you to consider is this: would it not be far more to your interest, as well as within the scope of my ability, if *Barnaby Rudge* began in the *Miscellany* immediately on the conclusion of *Oliver Twist*, and were continued there for the same time, and then published in three volumes? Take these simple facts into consideration. If the *Miscellany* is to keep its ground, it *must* have some continuous tale from me when *Oliver* stops. If I sat down to *Barnaby Rudge*, writing a little of it when I could (and with all my other engagements it would necessarily be a very long time before I could hope to finish it that way), it would be clearly impossible for me to begin a new series of papers in the *Miscellany*. The conduct of three different stories at the same time, and the production of a large portion of each, every month, would have been beyond Scott himself. Whereas, having *Barnaby* for the *Miscellany*, we could at once supply the gap which the cessation of *Oliver* must create, and you would have all the advantage of that prestige in favour of the work which is certain to enhance the value of *Oliver Twist* considerably. Just think of this at your leisure. I am really anxious to do the best I can for you as well as for myself, and in this case the pecuniary advantage must be all on your side." This letter nevertheless, which had also requested an overdue account of the sales of the *Miscellany*, led to differences which were only adjusted after six months' wrangling; and I was party to the understanding then arrived at by which, among other things, *Barnaby* was placed upon the footing desired, and was to begin when *Oliver* closed.

Of the progress of his *Oliver*, and his habits of writing at the time, it may perhaps be worth giving some additional glimpses from his letters of 1838. "I was thinking about *Oliver* till dinner-time yesterday," he wrote on 9 March, "and, just as * 9 I had fallen upon him tooth and nail, was called away to sit with Kate. I did eight slips, however, and hope to make them fifteen this morning." Three days before a daughter had been born to him, who became a god-daughter to me; on which occasion (having closed his announcement with a postscript of "I can do nothing this morning. What time will you ride? The sooner the better for a good long spell"), we rode out fifteen miles on the Great North Road, and, after dining at the Red Lion in Barnet on our way home, distinguished the already memorable day by bringing in both hacks dead lame.

On that day week, Monday the 13th, after describing himself "sitting patiently at home waiting for *Oliver Twist*, who has not yet arrived," which was his agreeable form of saying that his fancy had fallen into sluggishness that morning, he made remark in as pleasant phrase on some piece of painful news I had sent him, now forgotten. "I have not yet seen the paper, and you throw me into a fever. The comfort is, that all the strange and terrible things come uppermost, and that the good and pleasant things are mixed up with every moment of our existence so plentifully that we scarcely heed them." At the close of the month Mrs. Dickens was well enough to accompany him to Richmond, for now the time was come to start *Nickleby*; and having been away from town when *Pickwick's* first number came out, he made it a superstition to be absent at many future similar times. The magazine-day of that April month, I remember, fell upon a Saturday, and the previous evening had brought me a peremptory summons: "Meet me at the Shakespeare on Saturday night at eight; order your horse at midnight, and ride back with me": which was duly complied with. The smallest hour was sounding into the night from St. Paul's before we started, and the night was none of the pleasantest; but we carried news that lightened every part of the road, for the sale of *Nickleby* had reached that day the astonishing number of nearly fifty thousand! I left him working with unusual cheerfulness at *Oliver Twist* when I quitted the "Star and Garter" on the next day but one, after celebrating with both friends on the previous evening an anniversary which concerned us all (their second and my twenty-sixth); and which we kept always in future at the same place, except when they were living out of England, for twenty successive years. It was a part of his love of regularity and order, as well as of his kindliness of nature, to place such friendly meetings as these under rules of habit and continuance.

III

"OLIVER TWIST"

1838

THE whole of his time not occupied with *Nickleby* was now given to *Oliver*, and as the story shaped itself to its close it took extraordinary hold of him. I never knew him work so frequently after dinner, or to such late hours (a practice he afterwards abhorred), as during the final months of this task; which it was now his hope to complete before October, though its close in the magazine would not be due until the following March. "I worked pretty well last night," he writes, referring to it in May, "very well indeed; but although I did eleven close slips before half-past twelve I have four to write to close the chapter; and, as I foolishly left them till this morning, have the steam to get up afresh." A month later he writes: "I got to the sixteenth slip last night, and shall try hard to get to the thirtieth before I go to bed." Then, on a "Tuesday night" at the opening of * 10 August, he wrote: "Hard at work still. Nancy is no more. I showed what I have done to Kate last night, who was in an unspeakable '*state*': from which and my own impression I augur well. When I have sent Sikes to the devil, I must have yours." "No, no," he wrote, in the following month: "don't, don't let us ride till to-morrow, not having yet disposed of the Jew, who is such an out and outer that I don't know what to make of him." No small difficulty to an inventor, where the creatures of his invention are found to be as real as himself; but this also was mastered; and then there remained but the closing quiet chapter to tell the fortunes of those who had figured in the tale. To this he summoned me in the first week of September, replying to a request of mine that he'd give me a call that day. "Come and give *me* a call, and let us have 'a bit o' talk' before we have a bit o' som'at else. My missis is going out to dinner, and I ought to go, but I have got a bad cold. So do you come, and sit here, and read, or work, or do something, while I write the LAST chapter of *Oliver*, which will be arter a lamb chop."

How well I remember that evening! and our talk of what should be the fate of Charley Bates, on behalf of whom (as indeed for the Dodger, too) Talfourd had pleaded as earnestly in mitigation of judgment as ever at the bar for any client he most respected.

The publication had been announced for October, but the third volume illustrations intercepted it a little. This part of the story, as we have seen, had been written in anticipation of the magazine, and the designs for it, having to be executed "in a lump," were necessarily done somewhat hastily. The matter supplied in advance of the monthly portions in the magazine formed the bulk of the last volume as published in the book; and for this the plates had to be prepared by Cruikshank also in advance of the magazine, to furnish them in time for the separate publication: Sikes and his dog, Fagin in the cell, and Rose Maylie and Oliver, being the three last. None of these Dickens had seen until he saw them in the book on the eve of its publication; when he so strongly objected to one of them that it had to be cancelled. "I returned suddenly to town yesterday afternoon," he wrote to the artist at the end of October, "to look at the latter pages of *Oliver Twist* before it was delivered to the booksellers, when I saw the majority of the plates in the last volume for the first time. With reference to the last one—Rose Maylie and Oliver—without entering into the question of great haste, or any other cause, which may have led to its being what it is, I am quite sure there can be little difference of opinion between us with respect to the result. May I ask you whether you will object to designing this plate afresh, and doing so *at once*, in order that as few impressions as possible of the present one may go forth? I feel confident you know me too well to feel hurt by this inquiry, and with equal confidence in you I have lost no time in preferring it." This letter, printed from a copy in Dickens's handwriting fortunately committed to my keeping, entirely disposes of a wonderful story [1] originally pro-

---

[1] Reproduced as below, in large type, and without a word of contradiction or even doubt, in a biography of Mr. Dickens put forth by Mr. Hotten. "Dr. Shelton McKenzie, in the American *Round Table*, relates this anecdote of *Oliver Twist*: In London I was intimate with the brothers Cruikshank, Robert and George, but more particularly with the latter. Having called upon him one day at his house (it was then in Myddleton Terrace, Pentonville), I had to wait while he was finishing an etching, for which a printer's boy was waiting. To while away the time, I gladly complied with his suggestion that I should look over a portfolio crowded with etchings, proofs and drawings which lay upon the sofa. Among these, carelessly tied together in a wrap of brown paper, was a series of some twenty-five or thirty drawings, very carefully finished, through most of which were

mulgated in America, with a minute particularity of detail that might have raised the reputation of Sir Benjamin Backbite himself. Whether all Sir Benjamin's laurels, however, should fall to the person by whom the tale is told, or whether any part belongs to the authority alleged for it, is unfortunately not quite clear. There would hardly have been a doubt, if the fable had been confined to the other side of the Atlantic; but it has been reproduced and widely circulated on this side also, and the distinguished artist whom it calumniates by attributing the invention to him has been left undefended from its slander. Dickens's letter spares me the necessity of characterising, by the only word which would have been applicable to it, a tale of such incredible and monstrous absurdity as that one of the masterpieces of its author's genius had been merely an illustration of etchings by Mr. Cruikshank!

The completed *Oliver Twist* found a circle of admirers, not so wide in its range as those of others of his books, but of a character and mark that made their honest liking for it, and steady advocacy of it, important to his fame; and the story has held its ground in the first class of his writings. It deserves that place. The admitted exaggerations in *Pickwick* are incident to its club's extravaganza of adventure of which they are part, and are easily separable from the reality of its wit and humour, and its incomparable freshness; but no such allowances were needed here. Make what deduction the too scrupulous reader of *Oliver* might please for "lowness" in the subject, the precision and the unexaggerated force of the delineation were not to be disputed. The art of copying from nature as it really exists in the common walks had not been carried by anyone to greater

carried the well-known portraits of Fagin, Bill Sikes and his dog, Nancy, the Artful Dodger, and Master Charles Bates—all well known to the readers of *Oliver Twist*. There was no mistake about it; and when Cruikshank turned round, his work finished, I said as much. He told me that it had long been in his mind to show the life of a London thief by a series of drawings engraved by himself, in which, without a single line of letterpress, the story would be strikingly and clearly told. 'Dickens,' he continued, 'dropped in here one day, just as you have done, and, while waiting until I could speak with him, took up that identical portfolio, and ferreted out that bundle of drawings. When he came to that one which represents Fagin in the condemned cell, he studied it for half an hour, and told me that he was tempted to change the whole plot of his story; not to carry Oliver Twist through adventures in the country, but to take him up into the thieves' den in London, show what their life was, and bring Oliver through it without sin or shame. I consented to let him write up to as many of the designs as he thought would suit his purpose; and that was the way in which Fagin, Sikes, and Nancy were created. My drawings suggested them, rather than his strong individuality suggested my drawings.'

perfection, or to better results in the way of combination. Such was his handling of the piece of solid, existing, everyday life, which he made here the groundwork of his wit and tenderness, that the book which did much to help out of the world the social evils it portrayed, will probably preserve longest the picture of them as they then were. Thus far indeed he had written nothing to which in a greater or less degree this felicity did not belong. At the time of which I am speaking, the debtors' prisons described in *Pickwick*, the parochial management denounced in *Oliver*, and the Yorkshire schools exposed in *Nickleby*, were all actual existences; which now have no vivider existence than in the forms he thus gave to them. With wiser purposes, he superseded the old petrifying process of the magician in the Arabian tale, and struck the prisons and parish practices of his country, and its schools of neglect and crime, into palpable life for ever. A portion of the truth of the past, of the character and very history of the moral abuses of his time, will thus remain always in his writings; and it will be remembered that with only the light arms of humour and laughter, and the gentle ones of pathos and sadness, he carried cleansing and reform into those Augean stables.

Not that such intentions are in any degree ever intruded by this least didactic of writers. It is the fact that teaches, and not any sermonising drawn from it. *Oliver Twist* is the history of a child born in a workhouse and brought up by parish overseers, and there is nothing introduced that is out of keeping with the design. It is a series of pictures from the tragi-comedy of lower life, worked out by perfectly natural agencies, from the dying mother and the starved wretches of the first volume, through the scenes and gradations of crime, careless or deliberate, which have a frightful consummation in the last volume, but are never without the reliefs and self-assertions of humanity even in scenes and among characters so debased. It is indeed the primary purpose of the tale to show its little hero, jostled as he is in the miserable crowd, preserved everywhere from the vice of its pollution by an exquisite delicacy of natural sentiment which clings to him under every disadvantage. There is not a more masterly touch in fiction (and it is by such that this delightful fancy is consistently worked out to the last) than Oliver's agony of childish grief on being brought away from the branch workhouse, the wretched home associated only with suffering and starvation, and with no kind word or look, but containing still his little companions in misery

Of the figures the book has made familiar to everyone it is not my purpose to speak. To name one or two will be enough. Bumble and his wife; Charley Bates and the Artful Dodger; the cowardly charity boy, Noah Claypole, whose *Such agony please sir* puts a school-life into a single phrase; the so-called merry old Jew, supple and blackhearted Fagin; and Bill Sikes, the bolder-faced bulky-legged ruffian, with his white hat and white shaggy dog,—who does not know them all, even to the least points of dress, look and walk, and all the small peculiarities that express great points of character? I have omitted poor wretched Nancy; yet it is to be said of her, with such honest truthfulness her strength and weakness are shown, in the virtue that lies neighboured in her nature so closely by vice, that the people meant to be entirely virtuous show poorly beside her. But, though Rose and her lover are trivial enough beside Bill and his mistress, being indeed the weak part of the story, it is the book's pre-eminent merit that vice is nowhere made attractive in it. Crime is not more intensely odious, all through, than it is also most unhappy. Not merely when its exposure comes, when guilt's latent recesses are laid bare, and the agonies of remorse are witnessed; not in the great scenes only, but in lighter and apparently careless passages; this is emphatically so. Terror and retribution dog closely at the heels both of the comedy and the tragedy of crime. They are as plainly visible when Fagin is first shown in his den, boiling the coffee in the saucepan and stopping every now and then to listen when there is the least noise below,—the villainous confidence of habit never extinguishing in him the anxious watchings and listenings of crime,—as when we see him at the last in the condemned cell, like a poisoned human rat in a hole.

A word may be added upon the attacks directed against the subject of the book, to which Dickens made reply in one of his later editions; declaring his belief that he had tried to do a service to society, and had certainly done no disservice, in depicting a knot of such associates in crime in all their deformity and squalid wretchedness, skulking uneasily through a miserable life to a painful and shameful death. It is indeed never the subject that can be objectionable, if the treatment is not so, as we may see by much popular writing since, where subjects unimpeachably high are brought low by degrading sensualism. When the object of a writer is to exhibit the vulgarity of vice, and not its pretensions to heroism or cravings for sympathy, he may measure his subject with the highest. Swindlers and thieves are our associates in *Gil Blas*; we shake hands with highwaymen and housebreakers all round in the *Beggars' Opera*; we pack cards with La Ruse or pick pockets with Jonathan in Fielding's *Mr. Wild the Great*; cruelty and vice attend us in the prints of Hogarth; but our morals stand none the looser for any of them. As the spirit of the Frenchman was pure enjoyment, the strength of the Englishmen lay in wisdom and satire. The low was set forth to pull down the false pretensions of the high. They differ in design from Dickens, because they desire less to discover the soul of goodness in things evil than to brand the stamp of evil on things apt to pass for good, but their objects and results are substantially the same. Familiar with the lowest kind of abasement of life, the knowledge is used, by both him and them, to teach what constitutes its essential elevation; and, by the very coarseness and vulgarity of the materials employed, we measure the gentlemanliness and beauty of the work that is done. The quack in morality will always call such writing immoral, and the impostors will continue to complain of its treatment of imposture; but for the rest of the world it will teach still the invaluable lesson of what men ought to be from what they are. We cannot learn it more than enough. We cannot too often be told that, as the pride and grandeur of mere external circumstance is the falsest of earthly things, so the truth of virtue in the heart is the most lovely and lasting; and from the pages of *Oliver Twist* this teaching is once again to be taken by all who will look for it there.

And now, while *Oliver* was running a great career of popularity and success, the shadow of the tale of *Barnaby Rudge*, which he was to write on similar terms and to begin in the *Miscellany* when the other should have ended, began to darken everything around him. We had much discussion respecting it, and I had no small difficulty in restraining him from throwing up the agreement altogether; but the real hardship of his position, and the considerate construction to be placed on every effort made by him to escape from obligations incurred in ignorance of the sacrifices implied by them, will be best understood from his own frank statement. On 21 January, 1839, enclosing me the copy of a letter which he proposed to send to Mr. Bentley the following morning, he thus wrote: "From what I have already said to you, you will have been led to expect that I entertained some such intention. I know you will not endeavour to dissuade me from sending it. Go it must. It is no fiction to say that at present I cannot write this

tale. The immense profits which *Oliver* has realised to its publisher, and is still realising; the paltry, wretched, miserable sum
it brought to me (not equal to what is every day paid for a
novel that sells fifteen hundred copies at most); the recollection of this, and the consciousness that I have still the slavery
and drudgery of another work on the same journeyman-terms;
the consciousness that my books are enriching everybody connected with them but myself, and that I, with such a popularity
as I have acquired, am struggling in old toils, and wasting my
energies in the very height and freshness of my fame, and the
best part of my life, to fill the pockets of others, while for those
who are nearest and dearest to me I can realise little more than
a genteel subsistence: all this puts me out of heart and spirits:
and I cannot—cannot and will not—under such circumstances
that keep me down with an iron hand, distress myself by beginning this tale until I have had time to breathe; and until the
intervention of the summer, and some cheerful days in the
country, shall have restored me to a more genial and composed
state of feeling. There—for six months *Barnaby Rudge* stands
over. And but for you, it should stand over altogether. For
I do most solemnly declare that morally, before God and man,
I hold myself released from such hard bargains as these, after
I have done so much for those who drove them. This net that
has been wound about me so chafes me, so exasperates and
irritates my mind, that to break it at whatever cost—*that* I
should care nothing for—is my constant impulse. But I have
not yielded to it. I merely declare that I must have a postpone-
ment very common in all literary agreements; and for the time
I have mentioned—six months from the conclusion of *Oliver* in
the *Miscellany*—I wash my hands of any fresh accumulation of
labour, and resolve to proceed as cheerfully as I can with that
which already presses upon me."   * 11

To describe what followed upon this is not necessary. It will
suffice to state the results. Upon the appearance in the *Miscellany*,
in the early months of 1839, of the last portion of *Oliver Twist*,
its author, having been relieved altogether from his engagement
to the magazine, handed over, in a familiar epistle from a parent
to his child, the editorship to Mr. Ainsworth; and the still sub- † 5
sisting agreement to write *Barnaby Rudge* was, upon the over-
ture of Mr. Bentley himself, in June of the following year, 1840,
also put an end to, on payment by Dickens, for the copyright
of *Oliver Twist* and such printed stock as remained of the
edition then on hand, of two thousand two hundred and fifty

pounds. What was further incident to this transaction will be told hereafter; and a few words may meanwhile be taken, not without significance in regard to it, from the parent's familiar epistle. It describes the child as aged two years and two months (so long had he watched over it); gives sundry pieces of advice concerning its circulation, and the importance thereto of light and pleasant articles of food; and concludes, after some general moralising on the shiftings and changes of this world having taken so wonderful a turn that mail-coach guards were become no longer judges of horse-flesh: "I reap no gain or profit by parting from you, nor will any conveyance of your property be required, for in this respect you have always been literally Bentley's *Miscellany* and never mine."

IV

"NICHOLAS NICKLEBY"

1838 and 1839

I WELL recollect the doubt there was, mixed with the eager expectation which the announcement of his second serial story had awakened, whether the event would justify all that interest; and if indeed it were possible that the young writer could continue to walk steadily under the burthen of the popularity laid upon him. The first number dispersed this cloud of a question in a burst of sunshine; and as much of the gaiety of nations as had been eclipsed by old Mr. Pickwick's voluntary exile to Dulwich was restored by the cheerful confidence with which young Mr. Nicholas Nickleby stepped into his shoes. Everything that had given charm to the first book was here, with more attention to the important requisite of a story, and more wealth as well as truth of character.

How this was poured forth in each successive number, it hardly needs that I should tell. To recall it now is to talk of what since has so interwoven itself with common speech and thought, as to have become almost part of the daily life of us all. It was well said of him, soon after his death, in mentioning how largely his compositions had furnished one of the chief sources of intellectual enjoyment to this generation, that his language had become part of the language of every class and rank of his countrymen, and his characters were a portion of our contemporaries. "It seems scarcely possible," continued this otherwise not too indulgent commentator, "to believe that there never were any such persons as Mr. Pickwick and Mrs. Nickleby and Mrs. Gamp. They are to us not only types of English life, but types actually existing. They at once revealed the existence of such people, and made them thoroughly comprehensible. They were not studies of persons, but persons. And yet they were idealised in the sense that the reader did not think that they were drawn from the life. They were alive; they were themselves." The writer might have added that this is proper to all true masters of fiction who work in the higher regions of their calling.

Nothing certainly could express better what the new book was at this time making manifest to its thousands of readers; not simply an astonishing variety in the creations of character, but what it was that made these creations so real; not merely the writer's wealth of genius, but the secret and form of his art. There never was anyone who had less need to talk about his characters, because never were characters so surely revealed by themselves; and it was thus their reality made itself felt at once. They talked so well that everybody took to repeating what they said, as the writer just quoted has pointed out; and the sayings being the constituent elements of the characters, these also of themselves became part of the public. This, which must always be a novelist's highest achievement, was the art carried to exquisite perfection on a more limited stage by Miss Austen; and, under widely different conditions both of art and work, it was pre-eminently that of Dickens. I told him, on reading the first dialogue of Mrs. Nickleby and Miss Knag, that he had been lately reading Miss Bates in *Emma*, but I found that he had not at this time made the acquaintance of that fine writer.

Who that recollects the numbers of *Nickleby* as they appeared can have forgotten how each number added to the general enjoyment? All that had given *Pickwick* its vast popularity, the overflowing mirth, hearty exuberance of humour, and genial kindliness of satire, had here the advantage of a better-laid design, more connected incidents, and greater precision of character. Everybody seemed immediately to know the Nickleby family as well as his own. Dotheboys, with all that rendered it, like a piece by Hogarth, both ludicrous and terrible, became a household word. Successive groups of Mantalinis, Kenwigses, Crummleses, introduced each its little world of reality, lighted up everywhere with truth and life, with capital observation, the quaintest drollery, and quite boundless mirth and fun. The brothers Cheeryble brought with them all the charities. With Smike came the first of those pathetic pictures that filled the world with pity for what cruelty, ignorance or neglect may inflict upon the young. And Newman Noggs ushered in that class of the creatures of his fancy in which he took himself perhaps the most delight, and which the oftener he dealt with the more he seemed to know how to vary and render attractive; gentlemen by nature, however shocking bad their hats or ungenteel their dialects; philosophers of modest endurance, and needy but most respectable coats; a sort of humble angels of sympathy and self-denial, though without a particle of splendour or even good looks about them, except what an eye as fine as their own feelings might discern. "My friends," wrote Sydney Smith, describing to Dickens the anxiety of some ladies of his acquaintance to meet him at dinner, "have not the smallest objection to be put into a number, but on the contrary would be proud of the distinction; and Lady Charlotte, in particular, you may marry to Newman Noggs." Lady Charlotte was not a more real person to Sydney than Newman Noggs; and all the world whom Dickens attracted to his books could draw from them the same advantage as the man of wit and genius. It has been lately objected that humanity is not seen in them in its highest or noblest types, and the assertion may hereafter be worth considering; but what is very certain is, that they have inculcated humanity in familiar and engaging forms to thousands and tens of thousands of their readers, who can hardly have failed each to make his little world around him somewhat the better for their teaching. From first to last they were never for a moment alien to either the sympathies or the understandings of any class; and there were crowds of people at this time that could not have told you what imagination meant, who were adding month by month to their limited stores the boundless gains of imagination.

One other kindliest product of humour in *Nickleby* not to be passed over in even thus briefly recalling a few first impressions of it, was the good little miniature-painter Miss La Creevy, living by herself, overflowing with affections she has no one to enrich by, but always cheerful by dint of industry and good-heartedness. When she is disappointed in the character of a woman she has been to see, she eases her mind by saying a very cutting thing at her expense *in a soliloquy*: and thereby illustrates one of the advantages of having lived alone so long, that she always made a confidante of herself; was as sarcastic as she could be, by herself, on people who offended her; pleased herself, and did no harm. Here was one of those touches, made afterwards familiar to the readers of Dickens by innumerable similar fancies, which added affection to their admiration for the writer, and enabled them to anticipate the feeling with which posterity would regard him as indeed the worthy companion of the Goldsmiths and Fieldings. There was a piece of writing, too, within not many pages of it, of which Leigh Hunt exclaimed on reading it that it surpassed the best things of the kind in Smollett that he was able to call to mind. This was the letter of Miss Squeers to Ralph Nickleby, giving him her version of the chastisement inflicted by Nicholas on the schoolmaster. "My pa requests me to write to you, the doctors considering it doubtful whether he will ever recuvver the use of his legs which prevents his holding a pen. We are in a state of mind beyond everything, and my pa is one mask of brooses both blue and green likewise two forms are steepled in his Goar. . . . Me and my brother were then the victims of his feury since which we have suffered very much which leads us to the arrowing belief that we have received some injury in our insides, especially as no marks of violence are visible externally. I am screaming out loud all the time I write and so is my brother which takes off my attention rather and I hope will excuse mistakes. . . ."

Thus rapidly may be indicated some elements that contributed to the sudden and astonishingly wide popularity of these books. I purposely reserve from my present notices of them, which are biographical rather than critical, any statement of the reasons for which I think them inferior in imagination and fancy to some of the later works; but there was increasing and steady growth in them on the side of humour, observation and character, while freshness and raciness of style continued to be an important help. There are faults of occasional exaggeration in the writing, but none that do not spring from animal spirits and good humour, or a pardonable excess, here and there, on the side of earnestness; and it has the rare virtue, whether gay or grave, of being always thoroughly intelligible and for the most part thoroughly natural, of suiting itself without effort to every change of mood, as quick, warm and comprehensive as the sympathies it is taxed to express. The tone also is excellent. We are never repelled by egotism or conceit, and misplaced ridicule never disgusts us. When good is going on, we are sure to see all the beauty of it; and when there is evil, we are in no danger of mistaking it for good. No one can paint more picturesquely by an apposite epithet, or illustrate more happily by a choice allusion. Whatever he knows or feels, too, is always at his fingers' ends, and is present through whatever he is doing. What Rebecca says to Ivanhoe of the black knight's mode of fighting would not be wholly inapplicable to Dickens's manner of writing. "There is more than mere strength, there seems as if the whole soul and spirit of the champion were given to every blow he deals." This, when a man deals his blows with a pen, is the sort of handling that freshens with new life the oldest facts, and breathes into thoughts the most familiar an emotion not felt before. There seemed to be not much to add to our knowledge of London until his books came upon us, but each in this respect outstripped the other in its marvels. In *Nickleby* the old city reappears under every aspect; and whether warmth and light are playing over what is good and cheerful in it, or the veil is uplifted from its darker scenes, it is at all times our privilege to see and feel it as it absolutely is. Its interior hidden life becomes familiar as its commonest outward forms, and we discover that we hardly knew anything of the places we supposed that we knew the best.

Of such notices as his letters give of his progress with *Nickleby*, which occupied him from February 1838 to October 1839, something may now be said. Soon after the agreement for it was signed, before the Christmas of 1837 was over, he went down into Yorkshire with Mr. Hablot Browne to look up the Cheap Schools in that county to which public attention had been painfully drawn by a law case in the previous year; which had before been notorious for cruelties committed in them, whereof he had heard as early as in his childish days; and which he was bent upon destroying if he could. I soon heard the result of his journey; and the substance of that letter, returned to him for the purpose, is in his preface to the story written for the collected edition. He came back confirmed in his design, and in February set to work upon his first chapter. On his birthday he wrote to me. "I *have* begun! I wrote four slips last night, so you see the beginning is made. And what is more, I can go on: so I hope the book is in training at last." "The first chapter of *Nicholas* is done," he wrote two days later. "It took time, but I think answers the purpose as well as it could." Then, after a dozen days more: "I wrote twenty slips of *Nicholas* yesterday, left only four to do this morning (up at 8 o'clock, too!), and have ordered my horse at one." I joined him as he expected, and we read together at dinner that day the first number of *Nicholas Nickleby*.

In the following number there was a difficulty which it was marvellous should not oftener have occurred to him in this form of publication. "I could not write a line till three o'clock," he says, describing the close of that number, "and have yet five slips to finish, and don't know what to put in them, for I have reached the point I meant to leave off with." He found easy remedy for such a miscalculation at his outset, and it was

    * 12

nearly his last as well as first misadventure of the kind: his constant difficulty in *Pickwick*, as he said repeatedly, having been not the running short but the running over: not the whip but the drag that was wanted. *Sufflaminandus erat*, as Ben Jonson said of Shakespeare. And in future works, with such marvellous nicety could he do always what he had planned, strictly within the space available, that I can only remember two other similar instances. The third number introduced the school; and "I remain dissatisfied until you have seen and read number three," was his way of announcing to me his own satisfaction with that first handling of Dotheboys Hall. Nor had it the least part in my admiration of his powers at this time, that he never wrote without the printer at his heels; that, always in his latest works two or three numbers in advance, he was never a single number in advance with this story; that the more urgent the call upon him the more readily he rose to it; and that his astonishing animal spirits never failed him. As late as the 20th in the November month of 1838, he thus wrote to me: "I have just begun my second chapter; cannot go out to-night; must get on; think there *will* be a *Nickleby* at the end of this month now (I doubted it before); and want to make a start towards it if I possibly can." That was on Tuesday; and on Friday morning in the same week, explaining the sudden failure of something that had been promised the previous day, he says: "I was writing incessantly until it was time to dress; and have not yet got the subject of my last chapter, which *must be* finished to-night."

But this was not all. Between that Tuesday and Friday an indecent assault had been committed on his book by a theatrical adapter named Stirling, who seized upon it without leave while yet only a third of it was written; hacked, cut and garbled its dialogue to the shape of one or two favourite actors; invented for it a plot and an ending of his own, and produced it at the Adelphi; where the outraged author, hard pressed as he was with an unfinished number, had seen it in the interval between the two letters I have quoted. He would not have run such a risk in later years, but he threw off lightly at present even such offences to his art; and though I was with him at a representation of his *Oliver Twist* the following month at the Surrey Theatre, when in the middle of the first scene he laid himself down upon the floor in a corner of the box and never rose from it until the drop-scene fell, he had been able to sit through *Nickleby*, and to see a merit in parts of the representation. Mr. Yates had a sufficiently humorous meaning in his wildest extravagance, and Mr. O. Smith could put into his queer angular oddities enough of a hard dry pathos to conjure up shadows at least of Mantalini and Newman Noggs; of Ralph Nickleby there was only a wig, a spencer and a pair of boots, but a quaint actor named Wilkinson proved equal to the drollery, though not to the fierce brutality of Squeers; and even Dickens, in the letter that amazed me by telling me of his visit to the theatre, was able to praise "the skilful management and dressing of the boys, the capital manner and speech of Fanny Squeers, the dramatic representation of her card-party in Squeers's parlour, the careful making-up of all the people, and the exceedingly good tableaux formed from Browne's sketches. . . . Mrs. Keeley's first appearance beside the fire (see wollum), and all the rest of Smike, was excellent; bating sundry choice sentiments and rubbish regarding the little robins in the fields which have been put in the boy's mouth by Mr. Stirling the adapter." His toleration could hardly be extended to the robins, and their author he properly punished by introducing and denouncing him at Mr. Crummles's farewell supper.

The story was well in hand at the next letter to be quoted, for I limit myself to those only with allusions that are characteristic or illustrative. "I must be alone in my glory to-day," he wrote, "and see what I can do. I perpetrated a great amount of work yesterday, and have every day indeed since Monday, but I must buckle-to again and endeavour to get the steam up. If this were to go on long, I should 'bust' the boiler. I think Mrs. Nickleby's love-scene will come out rather unique." The steam doubtless rose dangerously high when such happy inspiration came. It was but a few numbers earlier than this, while that eccentric lady was imparting her confidences to Miss Knag, that Sydney Smith confessed himself vanquished by a humour against which his own had long striven to hold out. "*Nickleby* is *very good*," he wrote to Sir George Phillips after the sixth number. "I stood out against Mr. Dickens as long as I could, but he has conquered me." * 13

The close of the story was written at Broadstairs, from which (he had taken a house "two doors from the Albion Hotel, where we had that merry night two years ago") he wrote to me on 9 September, 1839. "I am hard at it, but these windings-up wind slowly, and I shall think I have done great things if I have entirely finished by the 20th. Chapman and Hall came down yesterday with Browne's sketches and dined here. They imparted their intentions as to a Nicklebeian fête which will make you laugh heartily—so I reserve them till you come. It has been blowing great guns for the last three days, and last night (I wish you could have seen it!) there was such a sea! I staggered down to the pier and, creeping under the lee of a large boat which was high and dry, watched it breaking for nearly an hour. Of course I came back wet through." On the afternoon of Wednesday the 18th he wrote again. "I shall not finish entirely before Friday, sending Hicks the last twenty pages of manuscript by the night coach. I have had pretty stiff work as you may suppose, and I have taken great pains. The discovery is made, Ralph is dead, the loves have come all right, Tim Linkinwater has proposed, and I have now only to break up Dotheboys and the book together. I am very anxious that you should see this conclusion before it leaves my hands, and I plainly see therefore that I must come to town myself on Saturday if I would not endanger the appearance of the number. So I have written to Hicks to send proofs to your chambers as soon as he can that evening; and if you don't object I will dine with you any time after five, and we will devote the night to a careful reading. I have not written to Macready, for they have not yet sent me the title-page of dedication, which is merely 'To W. C. Macready Esq. the following pages are inscribed, as a slight token of admiration and regard, by his friend the Author.' Meanwhile will you let him know that I have fixed the Nickleby dinner for Saturday, the 5th of October. Place, the Albion in Aldersgate Street. Time, six for half-past exactly. . . . I shall be more glad than I can tell you to see you again, and I look forward to Saturday, and the evenings that are to follow it, with the most joyful anticipation. I have had a good notion for *Barnaby*, of which more anon."

The shadow from the old quarter, we see, the unwritten *Barnaby* tale, intrudes itself still; though hardly, as of old, making other pleasanter anticipations less joyful. Such indeed at this time was his buoyancy of spirit that it cost him little, compared with the suffering it gave him at subsequent similar times, to separate from the people who for twenty months had been a part of himself. The increased success they had achieved left no present room but for gladness and well-won pride; and so, to welcome them into the immortal family of the English novel, and open cheerily to their author "fresh woods and pastures new," we had the dinner-celebration. But there is small need now to speak of what has left, to one of the few

survivors, only the sadness of remembering that all who made
the happiness of it are passed away. There was Talfourd, facile
and fluent of kindliest speech, with whom we were in constant
and cordial intercourse, and to whom, grateful for his copyright
exertions in the House of Commons, he had dedicated *Pickwick*;
there was Maclise, dear and familiar friend to us both, whose
lately painted portrait of Dickens hung in the room; and there   * 14
was the painter of the "Rent Day," who made a speech as good   † 6
as his pictures, rich in colour and quaint with homely allusion,
all about the reality of Dickens's genius, and how there had been
nothing like him issuing his novels part by part since Richardson
issued his novels volume by volume, and how in both cases
people talked about the characters as if they were next-door
neighbours or friends, and how as many letters were written to
the author of *Nickleby* to implore him not to kill poor Smike
as had been sent by young ladies to the author of *Clarissa* to
"save Lovelace's soul alive." These and others are gone. Of
those who survive only three arise to my memory—Macready,[1]
who spoke his sense of the honour done him by the dedication
in English as good as his delivery of it, Mr. Edward Chapman,
and Mr. Thomas Beard.

[1] Since, alas, also gone.

V

DURING AND AFTER "NICKLEBY"

1838 and 1839

The name of his old gallery companion may carry me back from the days to which the close of *Nickleby* had led me, to those when it was only beginning. "This snow will take away the cold weather," he had written, in that birthday-letter of 1838 already quoted, "and then for Twickenham." Here a cottage was taken, nearly all the summer was passed, and a familiar face there was Mr. Beard's. There too, with Talfourd and with Thackeray and Jerrold, we had many friendly days; and the social charm of Maclise was seldom wanting. Nor was there anything that exercised a greater fascination over Dickens than the grand enjoyment of idleness, the ready self-abandonment to the luxury of laziness, which we both so laughed at in Maclise, under whose easy swing of indifference, always the most amusing at the most aggravating events and times, we knew that there was artist-work as eager, energy as unwearying, and observation almost as penetrating as Dickens's own. A greater enjoyment than the fellowship of Maclise at this period it would indeed be difficult to imagine. Dickens hardly saw more than he did, while yet he seemed to be seeing nothing; and the small esteem in which this rare faculty was held by himself, a quaint oddity that in him gave to shrewdness itself an air of Irish simplicity, his unquestionable turn for literature, and a varied knowledge of books not always connected with such intense love and such unwearied practice of one special and absorbing art, combined to render him attractive far beyond the common. His fine genius and his handsome person, of neither of which at any time he seemed himself to be in the slightest degree conscious, completed the charm. Edwin Landseer, all the world's favourite, and the excellent Stanfield, came a few months later, in the Devonshire Terrace days; but another painter-friend was George Cattermole, who had then enough and to spare of fun as well as fancy to supply ordinary artists and humorists by the dozen, and wanted only a little more ballast and steadiness to possess all that could give attraction to good-fellowship. A friend now especially welcome, also, was the novelist Mr. Ainsworth, who shared with us incessantly for the three following years in the companionship which began at his house; with whom we visited, during two of those years, friends of art and letters in his native Manchester, from among whom Dickens brought away his Brothers Cheeryble; and to whose sympathy in tastes and pursuits, accomplishments in literature, open-hearted generous ways, and cordial hospitality, many of the pleasures of later years were due. Frederick Dickens, to whom soon after this a treasury-clerkship was handsomely given, on Dickens's application, by Mr. Stanley of Alderley, known in and before those Manchester days, was for the present again living with his father, but passed much time in his brother's home; and another familiar face was that of Mr. Thomas Mitton, who had known him when himself a law-clerk in Lincoln's Inn, through whom there was introduction of the relatives of a friend and partner, Mr. Smithson, the gentleman connected with Yorkshire, mentioned in his preface to *Nickleby*, who became very intimate in his house. These, his father and mother and their two younger sons, with members of his wife's family, and his married sisters and their husbands, Mr. and Mrs. Burnett and Mr. and Mrs. Austin, are figures that all associate themselves prominently with the days of Doughty Street and the cottages of Twickenham and Petersham as remembered by me in the summers of 1838 and 1839.

In the former of these years the sports were necessarily * 15 quieter than at Petersham, where extensive garden-grounds admitted of much athletic competition, from the more difficult forms of which I in general modestly retired, but where Dickens for the most part held his own against even such accomplished athletes as Maclise and Mr. Beard. Bar-leaping, bowling and quoits were among the games carried on with the greatest ardour; and in sustained energy, or what is called keeping it up, Dickens certainly distanced every competitor. Even the lighter recreations of battledore and bagatelle were pursued with relentless activity; and at such amusements as the Petersham races, in those days rather celebrated, and which he visited daily while they lasted, he worked much harder himself than the running horses did.

What else his letters of these years enable me to recall that could possess any interest now may be told in a dozen sentences.

He wrote a farce by way of helping the Covent Garden manager which the actors could not agree about, and which he turned afterwards into a story called *The Lamplighter*. He read the piece at the theatre, before the same stage-manager to whom he had written to request a very different audience in the same green-room a few years before; and Dickens could not but fancy that into Mr. Bartley's face, as he listened to the humorous reading, there crept some strange bewildered half-consciousness that in the famous writer he saw again the youthful would-be actor. He entered his name among the students at the inn of the Middle Temple, though he did not eat dinners there until many years later. We made together a circuit of nearly all the London prisons; and, in coming to the prisoners under remand while going over Newgate, accompanied by Macready and Mr. Hablot Browne, were startled by a sudden tragic cry of "My God! there's Wainewright!" In the shabby-genteel creature, with sandy disordered hair and dirty moustache, who had turned quickly round with a defiant stare at our entrance, looking at once mean and fierce, and quite capable of the cowardly murders he had committed, Macready had been horrified to recognise a man familiarly known to him in former years, and at whose table he had dined. Between the completion of *Oliver* and its publication, Dickens went to see something of North Wales; and, joining him at Liverpool, I returned with him. Soon after his arrival he had pleasant communication with Lockhart, dining with him at Cruikshank's a little later; and this was the prelude to a *Quarterly* review of *Oliver* by Mr. Ford, written at the instance of Lockhart, but without the raciness he would have put into it, in which amends were made for previous less favourable notice in that review. Dickens had not, however, waited for this to express publicly his hearty sympathy with Lockhart's handling of some passages in his admirable *Life of Scott* that had drawn down upon him the wrath of the Ballantynes. This he did in the *Examiner*; where also I find him noticing a book by Thomas Hood: "rather poor, but I have not said so, because Hood is too, and ill besides." In the course of the year he was taken into Devonshire to select a home for his father, on the removal of the latter (who had long given up his reporting duties) from his London residence; and this he found in a cottage at Alphington, near Exeter, where he placed the elder Dickens with his wife and their youngest son. The same year closed Macready's Covent Garden management; and at the dinner to the retiring manager, when the Duke of Cambridge took the chair, Dickens spoke with that wonderful instinct of knowing what to abstain from saying as well as what to say which made his after-dinner speeches unique. Nor should mention be omitted of the Shakespeare Society, now diligently attended, of which Procter, Talfourd, Macready, Thackeray, Henry Davison, Blanchard, Charles Knight, John Bell, Douglas Jerrold, Maclise, Stanfield, George Cattermole, Charles and Tom Landseer, Frank Stone and other old friends were members, and where, out of much enjoyment and many disputings, there * 17 arose, from Dickens and all of us, plenty of after-dinner oratory. The closing months of this year of 1839 had special interest for him. At the end of October another daughter was born to him, who bears the name of that dear friend of his and mine, Macready, whom he asked to be her godfather; and before the close of the year he had moved out of Doughty Street into Devonshire † 7 Terrace, a handsome house with a garden of considerable size, shut out from the New Road by a high brick-wall facing the York gate into Regent's Park. These various matters, and his attempts at the *Barnaby* novel on the conclusion of *Nickleby*, are the subjects of his letters between October and December.

"Thank God, all goes famously. I have worked at *Barnaby* all day, and moreover seen a beautiful (and reasonable) house in Kent Terrace, where Macready once lived, but larger than his." Again (this having gone off): "*Barnaby* has suffered so much from the house-hunting, that I mustn't chop to-day." Then (for the matter of the Middle Temple) "I return the form. It's the right Temple, I take for granted. *Barnaby* moves, not at race-horse speed, but yet as fast (I think) as under these unsettled circumstances could possibly be expected." Or again: "All well. *Barnaby* has reached his tenth page. I have just turned lazy, and have passed into *Christabel*, and thence to *Wallenstern*." At last the choice was made. "A house of great promise (and great premium), 'undeniable' situation and excessive splendour, is in view. Mitton is in treaty, and I am in ecstatic restlessness. Kate wants to know whether you have any books to send her, so please to shoot here any literary rubbish on hand." To these I will only add a couple of extracts from his letters while in Exeter arranging his father's and mother's new home. They are pleasantly written; and the vividness with which everything, once seen, was photographed in his mind and memory, is humorously shown in them.

"I took a little house for them this morning" (5 March, 1839: from the New London Inn), "and if they are not pleased with it I shall be grievously disappointed. Exactly a mile beyond the city on the Plymouth road there are two white cottages: one is theirs and the other belongs to their landlady. I almost forget the number of rooms; but there is an excellent parlour with two other rooms on the ground floor, there is really a beautiful little room over the parlour which I am furnishing as a drawing-room, and there is a splendid garden. The paint and paper throughout are new and fresh and cheerful-looking, the place is clean beyond all description, and the neighbourhood I suppose the most beautiful in this most beautiful of English counties. Of the landlady, a Devonshire widow with whom I had the honour of taking lunch to-day, I must make most especial mention. She is a fat, infirm, splendidly fresh-faced country dame, rising sixty and recovering from an attack 'on the nerves' —I thought they never went off the stones, but I find they try country air with the best of us. In the event of my mother's being ill at any time, I really think the vicinity of this good dame, the very picture of respectability and good humour, will be the greatest possible comfort. *Her* furniture and domestic arrangements are a capital picture, but that I reserve till I see you, when I anticipate a hearty laugh. She bears the highest character with the bankers and the clergyman (who formerly lived in *my* cottage himself), and is a kind-hearted worthy capital specimen of the sort of life, or I have no eye for the real and no idea of finding it out.

"This good lady's brother and his wife live in the next nearest cottage, and the brother transacts the good lady's business, the nerves not admitting of her transacting it herself, although they leave her in her debilitated state something sharper than the finest lancet. Now the brother, having coughed all night till he coughed himself into such a perspiration that you might have 'wringed his hair,' according to the asseveration of eye-witnesses, his wife was sent for to negotiate with me; and if you could have seen me sitting in the kitchen with the two old women, endeavouring to make them comprehend that I had no evil intentions or covert designs, and that I had come down all that way to take some cottage and had *happened* to walk down that road and see that particular one, you would never have forgotten it. Then, to see the servant-girl run backwards and forgotten it. Then, to see the servant-girl run backwards and forwards to the sick man, and when the sick man had signed one agreement which I drew up and the old woman instantly put away in a disused tea-caddy, to see the trouble and the number of messages it took before the sick man could be brought to sign another (a duplicate) that we might have one apiece, was one of the richest scraps of genuine drollery I ever saw in all my days. How, when the business was over, we became conversational; how I was facetious, and at the same time virtuous and domestic; how I drank toasts in the beer, and stated on interrogatory that I was a married man and the father of two blessed infants; how the ladies marvelled thereat; how one of the ladies, having been in London, inquired where I lived, and, being told, remembered that Doughty Street and the Foundling Hospital were in the Old Kent Road, which I didn't contradict —all this and a great deal more must make us laugh when I return, as it makes me laugh now to think of. Of my subsequent visit to the upholsterer recommended by the landlady; of the absence of the upholsterer's wife, and the timidity of the upholsterer fearful of acting in her absence; of my sitting behind a high desk in a little dark shop, calling over the articles in requisition and checking off the prices as the upholsterer exhibited the goods and called them out; of my coming over the upholsterer's daughter, with many virtuous endearments, to propitiate the establishment and reduce the bill; of these matters I say nothing, either, for the same reason as that just mentioned. The discovery of the cottage I seriously regard as a blessing (not to speak it profanely) upon our efforts in this cause. I had heard nothing from the bank, and walked straight there, by some strange impulse, directly after breakfast. I am sure they may be happy there; for if I were older, and my course of activity were run, I am sure *I* could, with God's blessing, for many and many a year. . . ."

"The theatre is open here, and Charles Kean is to-night playing for his last night. If it had been the 'rig'lar' drama I should have gone, but I was afraid Sir Giles Overreach might upset me, so I stayed away. My quarters are excellent, and the head waiter is *such* a waiter! Knowles (not Sheridan Knowles, but Knowles of the Cheetham Hill Road) is an ass to him. This * 18 sounds bold, but truth is stranger than fiction. By the by, not the least comical thing that has occurred was the visit of the upholsterer (with some further calculations) since I began this letter. I think they took me here at the New-London for the Wonderful Being I am; they were amazingly sedulous; and no doubt they looked for my being visited by the nobility and gentry of the neighbourhood. My first and only visitor came to-night: A ruddy-faced man in faded black, with extracts from a feather-bed all over him; an extraordinary and quite miraculously dirty face; a thick stick; and the personal appearance altogether of an amiable bailiff in a green old age. I have not seen the proper waiter since, and more than suspect I shall not recover this blow. He was announced (by *the* waiter) as a 'person.' I expect my bill every minute. . . .

"The waiter is laughing outside the door with another waiter —this is the latest intelligence of my condition."

VI

NEW LITERARY PROJECT

1839

The time was now come for him seriously to busy himself with a successor to *Pickwick* and *Nickleby*, which he had not, however, waited thus long before turning over thoroughly in his mind. *Nickleby's* success had so far outgone even the expectation raised by *Pickwick's*, that, without some handsome practical admission of this fact at the close, its publishers could hardly hope to retain him. This had been frequently discussed by us, and was well understood. But, apart from the question of his resuming with them at all, he had persuaded himself it might be unsafe to resume in the old way, believing the public likely to tire of the same twenty numbers over again. There was also another and more sufficient reason for change, which naturally had great weight with him; and this was the hope that, by invention of a new mode as well as kind of serial publication, he might be able for a time to discontinue the writing of a long story with all its strain on his fancy, or in any case to shorten and vary the length of the stories written by himself, and perhaps ultimately to retain all the profits of a continuous publication, without necessarily himself contributing every line that was to be written for it. These considerations had been discussed still more anxiously; and for several months some such project had been taking form in his thoughts.

While he was at Petersham (July 1839) he thus wrote to me: "I have been thinking that subject over. Indeed I have been doing so to the great stoppage of *Nickleby* and the great worrying and fidgetting of myself. I have been thinking that if Chapman and Hall were to admit you into their confidence with respect to what they mean to do at the conclusion of *Nickleby*, without admitting me, it would help us very much. You know that I am well-disposed towards them, and that if they do something handsome, even handsomer perhaps than they dreamt of doing, they will find it their interest, and will find me tractable. You know also that I have had straightforward offers from responsible men to publish anything for me at a percentage on the profits, and take all the risk; but that I am unwilling to leave them, and have declared to you that if they behave with liberality to me I will not on any consideration, although to a certain extent I certainly and surely must gain by it. Knowing all this, I feel sure that if you were to put before them the glories of our new project, and, reminding them that when *Barnaby* is published I am clear of all engagements, were to tell them that, if they wish to secure me and perpetuate our connection, now is the time for them to step gallantly forward and make such proposals as will produce that result—I feel quite sure that if this should be done by you, as you only can do it, the result will be of the most vital importance to me and mine, and that a great deal may be effected, thus, to recompense your friend for very small profits and very large work as yet. I shall see you, please God, on Tuesday night; and if they wait upon you on Wednesday, I shall remain in town until that evening."

They came; and the tenor of the interview was so favourable that I wished him to put in writing what from time to time had been discussed in connection with the new project. This led to the very interesting letter I shall now quote, written also in the same month from Petersham. I did not remember, until I lately read it, that the notion of a possible visit to America had been in his thoughts so early.

"I should be willing to commence on the thirty-first of March, 1840, a new publication consisting entirely of original matter, of which one number price threepence should be published every week, and of which a certain amount of numbers should form a volume, to be published at regular intervals. The best general idea of the plan of the work might be given perhaps by reference to *The Tatler, The Spectator,* and Goldsmith's *Bee*; but it would be far more popular both in the subjects of which it treats and its mode of treating them.

"I should propose to start, as *The Spectator* does, with some pleasant fiction relative to the origin of the publication; to introduce a little club or knot of characters and to carry their personal histories and proceedings through the work; to introduce fresh characters constantly; to reintroduce Mr. Pickwick and Sam Weller, the latter of whom might furnish an occasional communication with great effect; to write amusing essays on the various foibles of the day as they arise; to take advantage of all passing events; and to vary the form of the papers by throwing them into sketches, essays, tales, adventures, letters from imaginary correspondents and so forth, so as to diversify the contents as much as possible.

"In addition to this general design, I may add that under particular heads I should strive to establish certain features in the work, which should be so many veins of interest and amusement running through the whole. Thus the Chapters on Chambers which I have long thought and spoken of, might be very well incorporated with it; and a series of papers has occurred to me containing stories and descriptions of London as it was many years ago, as it is now, and as it will be many years hence, to which I would give some such title as The Relaxations of Gog and Magog, dividing them into portions like the *Arabian Nights*, and supposing Gog and Magog to entertain each other with such narrations in Guildhall all night long, and to break off every morning at daylight. An almost inexhaustible field of fun, raillery, and interest, would be laid open by pursuing this idea.

"I would also commence, and continue from time to time, a series of satirical papers purporting to be translated from some Savage Chronicles, and to describe the administration of justice in some country that never existed, and record the proceedings of its wise men. The object of this series (which if I can compare it with anything would be something between *Gulliver's Travels* and the *Citizen of the World*) would be to keep a special look-out upon the magistrates in town and country, and never to leave those worthies alone.

"The quantity of each number that should be written by myself would be a matter for discussion and arrangement. Of course I should pledge and bind myself upon that head. Nobody but myself would ever pursue *these ideas*, but I must have assistance of course, and there must be some contents of a different kind. Their general nature might be agreed upon beforehand, but I should stipulate that this assistance is chosen solely by me, and that the contents of every number are as much under my own control, and subject to as little interference, as those of a number of *Pickwick* or *Nickleby*.

"In order to give fresh novelty and interest to this undertaking, I should be ready to contract to go at any specified time (say in the midsummer or autumn of the year, when a sufficient quantity of matter in advance should have been prepared, or earlier if it were thought fit) either to Ireland or to America, and to write from thence a series of papers descriptive of the places and people I see, introducing local tales, traditions, and legends, something after the plan of Washington Irving's *Alhambra*. I should wish the republication of these papers in a separate form, with others to render the subject complete (if we should deem it advisable), to form part of the arrangement for the work; and I should wish the same provision to be made for the republication of the Gog and Magog series, or indeed any that I undertook.

"This is a very rough and slight outline of the project I have in view. I am ready to talk the matter over, to give any further explanations, to consider any suggestions, or to go into the details of the subject immediately. I say nothing of the novelty of such a publication now-a-days or its chances of success. Of course I think them great, very great; indeed, almost beyond calculation, or I should not seek to bind myself to anything so extensive.

"The heads of the terms upon which I should be prepared to go into the undertaking would be—That I be made a proprietor in the work and a sharer in the profits. That when I bind myself to write a certain portion of every number, I am ensured, *for* that writing, in every number a certain sum of money. That those who assist me, and contribute the remainder of every number, shall be paid by the publishers immediately after its appearance, according to a scale to be calculated and agreed upon, on presenting my order for the amount to which they may be respectively entitled. Or, if the publishers prefer it, that they agree to pay me a certain sum for the *whole* of every number, and leave me to make such arrangements for that part which I may not write, as I think best. Of course I should require that for these payments, or any other outlay connected with the work, I am not held accountable in any way; and that no portion of them is to be considered as received by me on account of the profits. I need not add that some arrangement would have to be made, if I undertake my Travels, relative to the expenses of travelling.

"Now I want our publishing friends to take these things into consideration, and to give me the views and proposals they would be disposed to entertain when they have maturely considered the matter."

The result of their consideration was on the whole satisfactory. An additional fifteen hundred pounds was to be paid at the close of *Nickleby*, the new adventure was to be undertaken, and Cattermole was to be joined with Browne as its illustrator. Nor was its plan much modified before starting, though it was felt by us all that, for the opening numbers at least, Dickens would have to be sole contributor; and that, whatever otherwise might be its attraction, or the success of the detached papers proposed by him, some reinforcement of them from time to time, by means of a story with his name continued at reasonable if not regular intervals, would be found absolutely necessary. Without any such planned story, however, the work did actually begin; its course afterwards being determined by circumstances stronger than any project he had formed. The agreement, drawn up in contemplation of a mere miscellany of detached papers or essays, and in which no mention of any story appeared, was signed at the end of March; and its terms were such as to place him in his only proper and legitimate position in regard to all such contracts, of being necessarily a gainer in any case, and, in the event of success, the greatest gainer of all concerned in the undertaking. All the risk of every kind was to be undergone by the publishers; and, as part of the expenses to be defrayed by them of each weekly number, he was to receive fifty pounds. Whatever the success or failure, this was always to be paid. The numbers were then to be accounted for separately, and half the realised profits paid to him, the other half going to the publishers; each number being held strictly responsible for itself, and the loss upon it, supposing any, not carried to the general account. The work was to be continued for twelve months certain, with leave to the publishers then to close it; but if they elected to go on, he was himself bound to the enterprise for five years, and the ultimate copyright as well as profit was to be equally divided.

Six weeks before signature of this agreement, while a title was still undetermined, I had this letter from him. "I will dine with you. I intended to spend the evening in strict meditation (as I did last night); but perhaps I had better go out, lest all work and no play should make me a dull boy. *I* have a list of titles too, but the final title I have determined on—or something very near it. I have a notion of this old file in the queer house, opening the book by an account of himself, and, among other peculiarities, of his affection for an old quaint queer-cased clock; showing how that when they have sat alone together in the long evenings, he has got accustomed to its voice, and come to consider it as the voice of a friend; how its striking, in the night, has seemed like an assurance to him that it was still a cheerful watcher at his chamber-door; and how its very face has seemed to have something of welcome in its dusty features, and to relax from its grimness when he has looked at it from his chimney-corner. Then I mean to tell how that he has kept odd manuscripts in the old, deep, dark, silent closet where the weights are; and taken them from thence to read (mixing up his enjoyments with some notion of his clock); and how, when the club came to be formed, they, by reason of their punctuality and his regard for his dumb servant, took their name from it. And thus I shall call the book either *Old Humphrey's Clock*, or *Master Humphrey's Clock*; beginning with a woodcut of old Humphrey and his clock, and explaining the why and wherefore. All Humphrey's own papers will then be dated From my clock-side, and I have divers thoughts about the best means of introducing the others. I thought about this all day yesterday and all last night till I went to bed. I am sure I can make a good thing of this opening, which I have thoroughly warmed up to in consequence."

A few days later: "I incline rather more to *Master Humphrey's Clock* than *Old Humphrey's*—if so be that there is no danger of the Pensive confounding master with a boy." After two days more: "I was thinking all yesterday, and have begun at *Master Humphrey* to-day." Then, a week later: "I have finished the first number, but have not been able to do more in the space than lead up to the Giants, who are just on the scene."

VII

"OLD CURIOSITY SHOP"

1840 *and* 1841

A DAY or two after the date of the last letter quoted, Dickens and his wife, with Maclise and myself, visited Landor in Bath, and it was during three happy days passed together there that the fancy which was shortly to take the form of little Nell first occurred to its author. But as yet with the intention only of * 19 making out of it a tale of a few chapters. On 1 March we returned from Bath; and on the 4th I had this letter: "If you can manage to give me a call in the course of the day or evening, I wish you would. I am laboriously turning over in my mind how I can best effect the improvement we spoke of last night, which I will certainly make by hook or by crook, and which I would like you to see *before* it goes finally to the printer's. I have determined not to put that witch-story into number 3, for I am by no means satisfied of the effect of its contrast with Humphrey. I think of lengthening Humphrey, finishing the description of the society, and closing with the little child-story, which is SURE to be effective, especially after the old man's quiet way." Then there came hard upon this: "What do you think of the following double title for the beginning of that little tale? 'PERSONAL ADVENTURES OF MASTER HUMPHREY: *The Old Curiosity Shop*.' I have thought of *Master Humphrey's Tale, Master Humphrey's Narrative, A Passage in Master Humphrey's Life*—but I don't think any does as well as this. I have also thought of *The Old Curiosity Dealer and the Child* instead of *The Old Curiosity Shop*. Perpend. Topping waits."—And thus was taking gradual form, with less direct consciousness of design on his own part than I can remember in any other instance throughout his career, a story which was to add largely to his popularity, more than any other of his works to make the bond between himself and his readers one of personal attachment, and very widely to increase the sense entertained of his powers as a pathetic as well as humorous writer.

117

He had not written more than two or three chapters, when the capability of the subject for more extended treatment than he had at first proposed to give to it pressed itself upon him, and he resolved to throw everything else aside, devoting himself to the one story only. There were other strong reasons for this. Of the first number of the *Clock* nearly seventy thousand were sold; but with the discovery that there was no continuous tale the orders at once diminished, and a change must have been made even if the material and means for it had not been ready. There had been an interval of three numbers between the first and second chapters, which the society of Mr. Pickwick and the two Wellers made pleasant enough; but after the introduction of Dick Swiveller there were three consecutive chapters; and in the continued progress of the tale to its close there were only two more breaks, one between the fourth and fifth chapters and one between the eighth and ninth, pardonable and enjoyable now for the sake of Sam and his father. The re-introduction of those old favourites, it will have been seen, formed part of his original plan; of his abandonment of which his own description may be added, from his preface to the collected edition. "The first chapter of this tale appeared in the fourth number of *Master Humphrey's Clock*, when I had already been made uneasy by the desultory character of that work, and when, I believe, my readers had thoroughly participated in the feeling. The commencement of a story was a great satisfaction to me, and I had reason to believe that my readers participated in this feeling too. Hence, being pledged to some interruptions and some pursuit of the original design, I set cheerfully about disentangling myself from those impediments as fast as I could; and, this done, from that time until its completion *The Old Curiosity Shop* was written and published from week to week, in weekly parts."

He had very early himself become greatly taken with it. "I am very glad indeed," he wrote to me after the first half-dozen chapters, "that you think so well of the *Curiosity Shop*, and especially that what may be got out of Dick strikes you. I *mean* to make much of him. I feel the story extremely myself, which I take to be a good sign; and am already warmly interested in it. I shall run it on now for four whole numbers together, to give it a fair chance." Every step lightened the road, as it became more and more real with each character that appeared in it; and I still recall the glee with which he told me what he intended to do not only with Dick Swiveller, but with Septimus Brass, changed afterwards to Sampson. Undoubtedly, however, Dick was his favourite. "Dick's behaviour in the matter of Miss Wackles will, I hope, give you satisfaction," is the remark of another of his letters. "I cannot yet discover that his aunt has any belief in him, or is in the least degree likely to send him a remittance, so that he will probably continue to be the sport of destiny." His difficulties were the quickly recurring times of publication, the confined space in each number that yet had to contribute its individual effect, and (from the suddenness with which he had begun) the impossibility of getting in advance. "I was obliged to cramp most dreadfully what I thought a pretty idea in the last chapter. I hadn't room to turn": to this or a similar effect his complaints are frequent, and of the vexations named it was by far the worst. But he steadily bore up against all, and made a triumph of the little story.

To help his work he went twice to Broadstairs, in June and in September; and at his first visit (17 June) thus wrote: "It's now four o'clock and I have been at work since half-past eight. I have really dried myself up into a condition which would almost justify me in pitching off the cliff, head first—but I must get richer before I indulge in a crowning luxury. Number 15, which I began to-day, I anticipate great things from. There is a description of getting gradually out of town, and passing through neighbourhoods of distinct and various characters, with which, if I had read it as anybody else's writing, I think I should have been very much struck. The child and the old man are on their journey of course, and the subject is a very pretty one." Between the two Broadstairs visits he informed me: "I intended calling on you this morning on my way back from Bevis Marks, whither I went to look at a house for Sampson Brass. But I got mingled up in a kind of social paste with the Jews of Houndsditch, and roamed about among them till I came out in Moorfields, quite unexpectedly. So I got into a cab, and came home again, very tired, by way of the City Road." At the opening of September he was again at the little watering-place. The residence he most desired there, Fort House, stood prominently at the top of a breezy hill on the road to Kingsgate, with a cornfield between it and the sea, and this in many subsequent years he always occupied; but he was fain to be content, as yet, with Lawn House, a smaller villa between the hill and the cornfield, from which he now wrote of his attentions to Mr. Sampson Brass's sister. "I have been at work of course" (2 September) "and have just finished a number. I have effected a reform by virtue of which we breakfast at a quarter before eight, so that I get to work at half-past, and am commonly free by one o'clock or so, which is a great happiness. Dick is now Sampson's clerk, and I have touched Miss Brass in Number 25, lightly, but effectively I hope."

At this point it became necessary to close the first volume of the *Clock*, which was issued accordingly with a dedication to Samuel Rogers, and a preface to which allusion will be made hereafter. "I have opened the second volume," he wrote on 9 September, "with Kit; and I saw this morning looking out at the sea, as if a veil had been lifted up, an affecting thing that I can do with him bye and bye. *Nous verrons.*" "I am glad you like that Kit number," he wrote twelve days later, "I thought you would. I have altered that about the opera-going. Of course I had no intention to delude the many-headed into a false belief concerning opera nights, but merely to specify a class of senators. I needn't have done it, however, for God knows they're pretty well all alike." This referred to an objection made by me to something he had written of "opera-going senators on Wednesday nights"; and, of another change made in compliance with some other objection, he wrote on 4 October: "You will receive the proof herewith. I have altered it. You must let it stand now. I really think the dead mankind a million fathoms deep, the best thing in the sentence. I have a notion of the dreadful silence down there, and of the stars shining through upon their drowned eyes—the fruit, let me tell you, of a solitary walk by starlight on the cliffs. As to the child-image I have made a note of it for alteration. In number thirty there will be some cutting needed, I think. I have, however, something in my eye near the beginning which I can easily take out. You will recognise a description of the road we travelled between Birmingham and Wolverhampton: but I had conceived it so well in my mind that the execution doesn't please me quite as well as I expected. I shall be curious to know whether you think there's anything in the notion of the man and his furnace-fire. It would have been a good thing to have opened a new story with, I have been thinking since."

In the middle of October he returned to town, and by the end of the month he had so far advanced that the close of the story began to be not far distant. "Tell me what you think," he had written just before his return, "of 36 and 37 ? The way is clear for Kit now, and for a great effect at the last with the Marchioness." The last allusion I could not in the least understand, until I found, in the numbers just sent me, those exquisite chapters of the tale, the fifty-seventh and fifty-eighth, in which Dick Swiveller realises his threat to Miss Wackles, discovers the small creature whom his destiny is expressly saving up for him, dubs her Marchioness, and teaches her the delights of hot purl and cribbage. This is comedy of the purest kind; its great charm being the good-hearted fellow's kindness to the poor desolate child hiding itself under cover of what seems only mirth and fun. Altogether, and because of rather than in spite of his weaknesses, Dick is a captivating person. His gaiety and good humour survive such accumulations of "staggerers," he makes such discoveries of the "rosy" in the very smallest of drinks, and becomes himself by his solacements of verse such a "perpetual grand Apollo," that his failings are all forgiven; and hearts resolutely shut against victims of destiny in general, open themselves freely to Dick Swiveller.

At the opening of November, there seems to have been a wish on Maclise's part to try his hand at an illustration for the story; but I do not remember that it bore other fruit than a very pleasant day at Jack Straw's Castle, where Dickens read one of the later numbers to us. "Maclise and myself (alone in the carriage)," he wrote, "will be with you at two exactly. We propose driving out to Hampstead and walking there, if it don't rain in buckets'-full. I shan't send Bradburys' the MS. of next number till to-morrow, for it contains the shadow of the number after that, and I want to read it to Mac, as, if he likes the subject, it will furnish him with one, I think. You can't imagine (gravely I write and speak) how exhausted I am to-day with yesterday's labours. I went to bed last night utterly dispirited and done up. All night I have been pursued by the child; and this morning I am unrefreshed and miserable. I don't know what to do with myself. . . . I think the close of the story will be great." Connected with the same design on Maclise's part, there was a subsequent reading at my house of the number shadowed forth by what had been read at Hampstead. "I will bring the MS.," he writes on 12 November, "and, for Mac's information if needful, the number before it. I have only this moment put the finishing touch to it. The difficulty has been tremendous—the anguish unspeakable. I didn't say six. Therefore dine at half-past five like a Christian. I shall bring Mac at that hour."

He had sent me, shortly before, the chapters in which the Marchioness nurses Dick in his fever, and puts his favourite philosophy to the hard test of asking him whether he has ever put pieces of orange-peel into cold water and made believe it was wine. "If you make believe very much it's quite nice; but if you don't, you know, it hasn't much flavour": so it stood originally, and to the latter word in the little creature's mouth objection seems to have been made. Replying (on 16 December) he writes: "'If you make believe very much it's quite nice; but if you don't, you know, it seems as if it would bear a little more seasoning, certainly.' I think that's better. Flavour is a common word in cookery, and among cooks, and so I used it. The part you cut out in the other number, which was sent me this morning, I had put in with a view to Quilp's last appearance on any stage, which is casting its shadow upon my mind; but it will come well enough without such a preparation, so I made no change. I mean to shirk Sir Robert Inglis, and work to-night. I have been solemnly revolving the general story all this morning. The forty-fifth number will certainly be the close. Perhaps this forty-first which I am now at work on, had better contain the announcement of *Barnaby*? I am glad you like Dick and the Marchioness in that sixty-fourth chapter—I thought you would."

Fast shortening as the life of little Nell was now, the dying year might have seen it pass away; but I never knew him wind up any tale with such a sorrowful reluctance as this. He caught at any excuse to hold his hand from it, and stretched to the utmost limit the time left to complete it in. Christmas interposed its delays too, so that twelfth-night had come and gone when I wrote to him in the belief that he was nearly done. "Done!" he wrote back to me on Friday the 7th, "done!!! Why bless you, I shall not be done till Wednesday night. I only began yesterday, and this part of the story is not to be galloped over, I can tell you. I think it will come famously—but I am the wretchedest of the wretched. It casts the most horrible shadow upon me, and it is as much as I can do to keep moving at all. I tremble to approach the place a great deal more than Kit; a great deal more than Mr. Garland; a great deal more than the Single Gentleman. I shan't recover it for a long time. Nobody will miss her like I shall. It is such a very painful thing to me, that I really cannot express my sorrow. Old wounds bleed afresh when I only think of the way of doing it: what the actual doing it will be, God knows. I can't preach to myself the schoolmaster's consolation, though I try. Dear Mary died yesterday, when I think of this sad story. I don't know what to say about dining to-morrow—perhaps you'll send up to-morrow

morning for news? That'll be the best way. I have refused
several invitations for this week and next, determining to go
nowhere till I had done. I am afraid of disturbing the state
I have been trying to get into, and having to fetch it all back
again." He had finished, all but the last chapter, on the Wednesday named; that was 12 January; and on the following
night he read to me the two chapters of Nell's death, the seventy-
first and seventy-second, with the result described in a letter of
the following Monday, 17 January, 1841.

"I can't help letting you know how much your yesterday's
letter pleased me. I felt sure you liked the chapters when we read
them on Thursday night, but it was a great delight to have my
impression so strongly and heartily confirmed. You know how
little value I should set on what I had done, if all the world
cried out that it was good, and those whose good opinion and
approbation I value most were silent. The assurance that this
little closing of the scene touches and is felt by you so strongly,
is better to me than a thousand most sweet voices out of doors.
When I first began, *on your valued suggestion*, to keep my
thoughts upon this ending of the tale, I resolved to try and do
something which might be read by people about whom Death
had been, with a softened feeling, and with consolation. . . .
After you left last night, I took my desk upstairs; and writing
until four o'clock this morning, finished the old story. It makes
me very melancholy to think that all these people are lost to me
for ever, and I feel as if I never could become attached to any
new set of characters." The words printed in italics, as underlined by himself, give me my share in the story which had gone
so closely to his heart. I was responsible for its tragic ending.
He had not thought of killing her, when, about half-way through,
I asked him to consider whether it did not necessarily belong
even to his own conception, after taking so mere a child through
such a tragedy of sorrow, to lift her also out of the commonplace of ordinary happy endings, so that the gentle pure little
figure and form should never change to the fancy. All that
I meant he seized at once, and never turned aside from it again.

The published book was an extraordinary success, and, in
America more especially, very greatly increased the writer's
fame. The pathetic vein it had opened was perhaps mainly the
cause of this, but opinion at home continued still to turn on
the old characteristics; the freshness of humour of which the
pathos was but another form or product, the grasp of reality
with which character had again been seized, the discernment

of good under its least attractive forms and of evil in its most captivating disguises, the cordial wisdom and sound heart, the enjoyment and fun, luxuriant yet under proper control. No falling-off was found in these, and I doubt if any of his people have been more widely liked than Dick Swiveller and the Marchioness. The characters generally indeed work out their share in the purpose of the tale; the extravagances of some of them help to intensify its meaning; and the sayings and doings of the worst and the best alike have their point and applicability. Many an over-suspicious person will find advantage in remembering what a too liberal application of Foxey's principle of suspecting everybody brought Mr. Brass to; and many an over-hasty judgment of poor human nature will unconsciously be checked, when it is remembered that Mr. Nubbles *did* come back to work out that shilling.

But the main idea and chief figure of the piece constitute its interest for most people, and give it rank upon the whole with the most attractive productions of English fiction. I am not acquainted with any story in the language more adapted to strengthen in the heart what most needs help and encouragement, to sustain kindly and innocent impulses, to awaken everywhere the sleeping germs of good. It includes necessarily much pain, much uninterrupted sadness; but the brightness and the sunshine are not lost in the gloom. The humour is so benevolent; the view of errors that have no depravity in them is so indulgent; the quiet courage under calamity, the purity that nothing impure can soil, are so full of tender teaching. Its effect as a mere piece of art, too, considering the circumstances in which I have shown it to be written, I think noteworthy. It began with a plan for but a short half-dozen chapters; it grew into a full-proportioned story under the warmth of the feeling it had inspired its writer with; its very incidents created a necessity at first not seen; and it was carried to a close only contemplated after a full half of it had been written. Yet, from the opening of the tale to that undesigned ending; from the image of little Nell asleep amid the quaint grotesque figures of the old curiosity warehouse, to that other final sleep she takes among the grim forms and carvings of the old church aisle; the main purpose seems to be always present. The characters and incidents that at first appear most foreign to it, are found to have had with it a close relation. The hideous lumber and rottenness that surround the child in her grandfather's home, take shape again in Quilp and his filthy gang. In the first still picture of Nell's innocence in the midst of strange and alien forms, we have the forecast of her after-wanderings, her patient miseries, her sad maturity of experience before its time. Without the show-people and their blended fictions and realities, their waxworks, dwarfs, giants, and performing dogs, the picture would have wanted some part of its significance. Nor could the genius of Hogarth himself have given it higher expression than in the scenes by the cottage door, the furnace fire, and the burial-place of the old church, over whose tombs and gravestones hang the puppets of Mr. Punch's show while the exhibitors are mending and repairing them. And when, at last, Nell sits within the quiet old church where all her wanderings end, and gazes on those silent monumental groups of warriors, with helmets, swords, and gauntlets wasting away around them; the associations among which her life had opened seem to have come crowding on the scene again, to be present at its close. But, stripped of their strangeness; deepened into solemn shapes by the suffering she has undergone; gently fusing every feeling of a life past into hopeful and familiar anticipation of a life to come; and already imperceptibly lifting her, without grief or pain, from the earth she loves, yet whose grosser paths her light steps only touched to show the track through them to Heaven. This is genuine art, and such as all cannot fail to recognise who read the book in a right sympathy with the conception that pervades it. Nor, great as the discomfort was of reading it in brief weekly snatches, can I be wholly certain that the discomfort of so writing it involved nothing but disadvantage. With so much in every portion to do, and so little space to do it in, the opportunities to a writer for mere self-indulgence were necessarily rare.

Of the innumerable tributes the story has received, and to none other by Dickens have more or more various been paid, there is one, the very last, which has much affected me. Not many months before my friend's death, he had sent me two *Overland Monthlies* containing two sketches by a young American writer far away in California, "The Luck of Roaring Camp," and "The Outcasts of Poker Flat," in which he had found such subtle strokes of character as he had not anywhere else in late years discovered; the manner resembling himself, but the matter fresh to a degree that had surprised him; the painting in all respects masterly; and the wild rude thing painted, a quite wonderful reality. I have rarely known him more honestly moved. A few months passed; telegraph wires flashed over the world that he had passed away on 9 June; and the young writer of whom he had then written to me, all unconscious of that praise, put his tribute of gratefulness and sorrow into the form of a poem called *Dickens in Camp*.[1] It embodies the same kind of incident which had so affected the "master" himself, in the papers to which I have referred; it shows the gentler influences, which, in even those Californian wilds, can restore outlawed "roaring camps" to silence and humanity; and there is hardly any form of posthumous tribute which I can imagine likely to have better satisfied his desire of fame, than one which should thus connect with the special favourite among all his heroines, the restraints and authority exerted by his genius over the rudest and least civilised of competitors in that far fierce race for wealth.

> Above the pines the moon was slowly drifting,
>   The river sang below;
> The dim Sierras, far beyond, uplifting
>   Their minarets of snow:
>
> The roaring camp-fire, with rude humour, painted
>   The ruddy tints of health
> On haggard face and form that drooped and fainted
>   In the fierce race for wealth;
>
> Till one arose, and from his pack's scant treasure
>   A hoarded volume drew,
> And cards were dropped from hands of listless leisure
>   To hear the tale anew;
>
> And then, while round them shadows gathered faster,
>   And as the fire-light fell,
> He read aloud the book wherein the Master
>   Had writ of "Little Nell":
>
> Perhaps 'twas boyish fancy,—for the reader
>   Was youngest of them all,—
> But, as he read, from clustering pine and cedar
>   A silence seemed to fall;
>
> The fir-trees gathering closer in the shadows,
>   Listened in every spray,
> While the whole camp, with "Nell" on English meadows,
>   Wandered and lost their way:
>
> And so in mountain solitudes—o'ertaken
>   As by some spell divine—
> Their cares dropped from them like the needles shaken
>   From out the gusty pine.
>
> Lost is that camp, and wasted all its fire;
>   And he who wrought that spell?—
> Ah, towering pine and stately Kentish spire,
>   Ye have one tale to tell!

[1] *Poems*, by Bret Harte.

Lost is that camp! but let its fragrant story
    Blend with the breath that thrills
With hop-vines' incense all the pensive glory
    That fills the Kentish hills.

And on that grave where English oak and holly
    And laurel wreaths entwine,
Deem it not all a too presumptuous folly,—
    This spray of Western pine!

July, 1870.

VIII

It was an excellent saying of the first Lord Shaftesbury, that, seeing every man of any capacity holds within himself two men, the wise and the foolish, each of them ought freely to be allowed his turn; and it was one of the secrets of Dickens's social charm that he could, in strict accordance with this saying, allow each part of him its turn; could afford thoroughly to give rest and relief to what was serious in him, and, when the time came to play his gambols, could surrender himself wholly to the enjoyment of the time, and become the very genius and embodiment of one of his own most whimsical fancies.

Turning back from the narrative of his last piece of writing to recall a few occurrences of the year during which it had occupied him, I find him at its opening in one of these humorous moods, and another friend, with myself, enslaved by its influence. "What on earth does it all mean!" wrote poor puzzled Mr. Landor to me, enclosing a letter from him of the date 11 February, the day after the royal nuptials of that year. In this he had related to our old friend a wonderful hallucination arising out of that event, which had then taken entire possession of him. "Society is unhinged here," thus ran the letter, "by her majesty's marriage, and I am sorry to add that I have fallen hopelessly in love with the Queen, and wander up and down with vague and dismal thoughts of running away to some uninhabited island with a maid of honour, to be entrapped by conspiracy for that purpose. Can you suggest any particular young person, serving in such a capacity, who would suit me? It is too much perhaps to ask you to join the band of noble youths (Forster is in it, and Maclise) who are to assist me in this great enterprise, but a man of your energy would be invaluable. I have my eye upon Lady . . ., principally because she is very beautiful, and has no strong brothers. Upon this, and other points of the scheme, however, we will confer more at large when we meet; and meanwhile burn this document, that no suspicion may arise or rumour get abroad."

The maid of honour and the uninhabited island were flights of fancy, but the other daring delusion was for a time encouraged to such whimsical lengths, not alone by him but (under his influence) by the two friends named, that it took the wildest forms of humorous extravagance; and of the private confidences much interchanged, as well as of his own style of open speech in which the joke of a despairing unfitness for any further use or enjoyment of life was unflaggingly kept up, to the amazement of bystanders knowing nothing of what it meant and believing he had half lost his senses, I permit myself to give from his letters one further illustration. "I am utterly lost in misery," he writes on 12 February, "and can do nothing. I have been reading *Oliver*, *Pickwick*, and *Nickleby* to get my thoughts together for the new effort, but all in vain:

> My heart is at Windsor,
> My heart isn't here;
> My heart is at Windsor,
> A following my dear.

I saw the Responsibilities this morning, and burst into tears. The presence of my wife aggravates me. I loathe my parents. I detest my house. I begin to have thoughts of the Serpentine, of the Regent's Canal, of the razors upstairs, of the chemist's down the street, of poisoning myself at Mrs. ——'s table, of hanging myself upon the pear-tree in the garden, of abstaining from food and starving myself to death, of being bled for my cold and tearing off the bandage, of falling under the feet of cab-horses in the New Road, of murdering Chapman and Hall and becoming great in story (SHE must hear something of me then—perhaps sign the warrant: or is that a fable?), of turning Chartist, of heading some bloody assault upon the palace and saving Her by my single hand——of being anything but what I have been, and doing anything but what I have done. Your distracted friend, C. D." The wild derangement of asterisks in every shape and form, with which this incoherence closed, cannot be given.

Some ailments which dated from an earlier period in his life made themselves felt in the spring of the year, as I remember, and increased horse exercise was strongly recommended to him. "I find it will be positively necessary to go, for five days in the week at least," he wrote in March, "on a perfect regimen of diet and exercise, and am anxious not to delay treating for a horse." We were now, therefore, when he was not at the seaside, much on horseback in suburban lanes and roads; and the spacious garden of his new house was also turned to healthful use at even his busiest working times. I mark this, too, as the time when the first of his ravens took up residence; and as the beginning of disputes with two of his neighbours about the smoking of the stable chimney, which his groom Topping, a highly absurd little man with flaming red hair, so complicated by secret devices of his own, meant to conciliate each complainant alternately and having the effect of aggravating both, that law proceedings were only barely avoided. "I shall give you," he writes, "my latest report of the chimney in the form of an address from Topping, made to me on our way from little Hall's at Norwood the other night, where he and Chapman and I had been walking all day, while Topping drove Kate, Mrs. Hall, and her sisters, to Dulwich. Topping had been regaled upon the premises, and was just drunk enough to be confidential. 'Beggin' your pardon, sir, but the genelman next door sir, seems to be gettin' quite comfortable and pleasant about the chimley.'—'I don't think he is, Topping.'—'Yes he is sir I think. He comes out in the yard this morning and says *Coachman* he says' (observe the vision of a great large fat man called up by the word) '*is that your raven* he says *Coachman ? or is it Mr. Dickens's raven ?* he says. My master's sir, I says. *Well*, he says, *it's a fine bird. I think the chimley 'ill do now Coachman,—now the jint's taken off the pipe* he says. I hope it will sir, I says; my master's a genelman as wouldn't annoy no genelman if he could help it, I'm sure; and my own missis is so afraid of havin' a bit o' fire that o' Sundays our little bit o' weal or what not, goes to the baker's a purpose.—*Damn the chimley Coachman,* he says, *it's a smokin' now.*—It an't a smokin' your way sir, I says; *Well,* he says, *no more it is, Coachman, and as long as it smokes anybody else's way, it's all right and I'm agreeable.*' Of course I shall now have the man from the other side upon me, and very likely with an action of nuisance for smoking into his conservatory."

A graver incident, which occurred to him also among his earliest experiences as tenant of Devonshire Terrace, illustrates too well the practical turn of his kindness and humanity not to deserve relation. He has himself described it, in one of his minor writings, in setting down what he remembered as the only good that ever came of a beadle. "Of that great parish functionary," he remarks, "having newly taken the lease of a house in a certain distinguished metropolitan parish, a house which then appeared to me to be a frightfully first-class family mansion involving awful responsibilities, I became the prey." In other words he was summoned, and obliged to sit, as juryman at an inquest on the body of a little child alleged to have been murdered by its mother; of which the result was, that, by his persevering exertion, seconded by the humane help of the coroner, Mr. Wakley, the verdict of himself and his fellow-jurymen charged her only with the concealment of birth. "The poor desolate creature dropped upon her knees before us with protestations that we were right (protestations among the most affecting that I have ever heard in my life), and was carried away insensible. I caused some extra care to be taken of her in the prison, and counsel to be retained for her defence when she was tried at the Old Bailey; and her sentence was lenient, and her history and conduct proved that it was right." How much he felt the little incident, at the actual time of its occurrence, may be judged from the few lines written next morning: "Whether it was the poor baby, or its poor mother, or the coffin, or my fellow-jurymen, or what not, I can't say, but last night I had a most violent attack of sickness and indigestion, which not only prevented me from sleeping, but even from lying down. Accordingly Kate and I sat up through the dreary watches."

The day of the first publication of *Master Humphrey* (Saturday, 4 April) had by this time come, and, according to the rule observed in his two other great ventures, he left town with Mrs. Dickens on Friday the 3rd. With Maclise we had been together at Richmond the previous night; and I joined him at Birmingham the day following, with news of the sale of the whole sixty thousand copies to which the first working had been limited, and of orders already in hand for ten thousand more! The excitement of the success somewhat lengthened our holiday; and, after visiting Shakespeare's house at Stratford, and Johnson's at Lichfield, we found our resources so straitened in returning, that, employing as our messenger of need his younger brother Alfred, who had joined us from Tamworth where he was a student-engineer, we had to pawn our gold watches at Birmingham.

At the end of the following month he went to Broadstairs, and not many days before (on 20 May) a note from Mr. Jerdan on behalf of Mr. Bentley opened the negotiations formerly referred to, which transferred to Messrs. Chapman and Hall the agreement for *Barnaby Rudge*. I was myself absent when he left, and in a letter announcing his departure he had written:

"I don't know of a word of news in all London, but there will be plenty next week, for I am going away, and I hope you'll send me an account of it. I am doubtful whether it will be a murder, a fire, a vast robbery, or the escape of Gould, but it will be something remarkable no doubt. I almost blame myself for the death of that poor girl who leaped off the monument upon my leaving town last year. She would not have done it if I had remained, neither would the two men have found the skeleton in the sewers." His prediction was quite accurate, for I had to tell him, after not many days, of the potboy who shot at the queen. "It's a great pity they couldn't suffocate that boy, Master Oxford," he replied very sensibly, "and say no more about it. To have put him quietly between two feather-beds would have stopped his heroic speeches, and dulled the sound of his glory very much. As it is, she will have to run the gauntlet of many a fool and madman, some of whom may perchance be better shots and use other than Brummagem firearms." How much of this actually came to pass, the reader knows.

From the letters of his present Broadstairs visit, there is little more to add to the account of his progress with his story; but a sentence may be given for its characteristic expression of his invariable habit upon entering any new abode, whether to stay in it for days or for years. On a Monday night he arrived, and on the Tuesday (2 June) wrote: "Before I tasted bit or drop yesterday, I set out my writing-table with extreme taste and neatness, and improved the disposition of the furniture generally." He stayed till the end of June; when Maclise and myself joined him for the pleasure of posting back home by way of his favourite Chatham, Rochester, and Cobham, where we passed two agreeable days in revisiting well-remembered scenes. Meanwhile there had been brought to a close the treaty for repurchase of *Oliver* and surrender of *Barnaby*, upon terms which are succinctly stated in a letter written by him to Messrs. Chapman and Hall on 2 July, the day after our return.

"The terms upon which you advance the money to-day for * 20 the purchase of the copyright and stock of *Oliver* on my behalf, are understood between us to be these. That this £2250 is to be deducted from the purchase-money of a work by me entitled *Barnaby Rudge*, of which two chapters are now in your hands, and of which the whole is to be written within some convenient time to be agreed upon between us. But if it should not be written (which God forbid!) within five years, you are to have a lien to this amount on the property belonging to me that is now in your hands, namely, my shares in the stock and copyright of *Sketches by Boz, The Pickwick Papers, Nicholas Nickleby, Oliver Twist,* and *Master Humphrey's Clock*; in which we do not include any share of the current profits of the last-named work, which I shall remain at liberty to draw at the times stated in our agreement. Your purchase of *Barnaby Rudge* is made upon the following terms. It is to consist of matter sufficient for ten monthly numbers of the size of *Pickwick* and *Nickleby*, which you are however at liberty to divide and publish in fifteen smaller numbers if you think fit. The terms for the purchase of this edition in numbers, and for the copyright of the whole book for six months after the publication of the last number, are £3000. At the expiration of the six months the whole copyright reverts to me." The sequel was, as all the world knows, that Barnaby became successor to little Nell, the money being repaid by the profits of the *Clock*; but I ought also to mention the generous sequel that was given to the small service thus rendered to him, by the gift, after not many days, of an antique silver-mounted jug of great beauty of form and workmanship, and with a wealth far beyond artist's design or jeweller's chasing in written words that accompanied it.[1] They were accepted to commemorate, not the help they would have far overpaid, but the gladness of his own escape from the last of the agreements that had hampered the opening of his career, and the better future which was now before him.

At the opening of August he was with Mrs. Dickens for some days in Devonshire, on a visit to his father, but he had to take his work with him; and they had only one real holiday, when Dawlish, Teignmouth, Babbicombe, and Torquay were explored, returning to Exeter at night. In the beginning of September he was again at Broadstairs.

"I was just going to work," he wrote on the 9th, "when I got

[1] "Accept from me" (8 July, 1840), "as a slight memorial of your attached companion, the poor keepsake which accompanies this. My heart is not an eloquent one on matters which touch it most, but suppose this claret jug the urn in which it lies, and believe that its warmest and truest blood is yours. This was the object of my fruitless search, and your curiosity, on Friday. At first I scarcely knew what trifle (you will deem it valuable, I know, for the giver's sake) to send you; but I thought it would be pleasant to connect it with our jovial moments, and to let it add, to the wine we shall drink from it together, a flavour which the choicest vintage could never impart. Take it from my hand—filled to the brim and running over with truth and earnestness. I have just taken one parting look at it, and it seems the most elegant thing in the world to me, for I lose sight of the vase in the crowd of welcome associations that are clustering and wreathing themselves about it."

this letter, and the story of the man who went to Chapman and Hall's knocked me down flat. I wrote until now (a quarter to one) against the grain, and have at last given it up for one day. Upon my word it is intolerable. I have been grinding my teeth all the morning. I think I could say in two lines something about the general report with propriety. I'll add them to the proof" (the preface to the first volume of the *Clock* was at this time in preparation), "giving you full power to cut them out if you should think differently from me, and from C and H, who in such a matter must be admitted judges." He refers here to a report, rather extensively circulated at the time, and which through various channels had reached his publishers, that he was suffering from loss of reason and was under treatment in an asylum.[1] I would have withheld it from him, as an absurdity that must quickly be forgotten—but he had been told of it, and there was a difficulty in keeping within judicious bounds his not unnatural wrath.

A few days later (the 15th) he wrote: "I have been rather surprised of late to have applications from Roman Catholic clergymen, demanding (rather pastorally and with a kind of grave authority) assistance, literary employment, and so forth. At length it struck me, that, through some channel or other, I must have been represented as belonging to that religion. Would you believe, that in a letter from Lamert at Cork, to my mother, which I saw last night, he says, 'What do the papers mean by saying that Charles is demented, and further, *that he has turned Roman Catholic ?*'!" Of the begging-letter writers, hinted at here, I ought earlier to have said something. In one of his detached essays he has described, without a particle of exaggeration, the extent to which he was made a victim by this class of swindler, and the extravagance of the devices practised on him; but he had not confessed, as he might, that for much of what he suffered he was himself responsible, by giving so largely, as at first he did, to almost everyone who applied to him. What at last brought him to his senses in this

[1] Already he had been the subject of similar reports on the occasion of the family sorrow which compelled him to suspend the publication of *Pickwick* for two months when, upon issuing a brief address in resuming his work (30 June, 1837), he said: "By one set of intimate acquaintances, especially well-informed, he has been killed outright; by another, driven mad; by a third, imprisoned for debt; by a fourth, sent per steamer to the United States; by a fifth, rendered incapable of mental exertion for evermore; by all, in short, represented as doing anything but seeking in a few weeks' retirement the restoration of that cheerfulness and peace of which a sad bereavement had temporarily deprived him."

respect, I think, was the request made by the adventurer who had exhausted every other expedient, and who desired finally, after describing himself reduced to the condition of a travelling Cheap Jack in the smallest way of crockery, that a donkey might be left out for him next day, which he would duly call for. This I perfectly remember, and I much fear that the applicant was the Daniel Tobin before mentioned.

Many and delightful were other letters written from Broadstairs at this date, filled with whimsical talk and humorous description, relating chiefly to an eccentric friend who stayed with him most of the time, and is sketched in one of his published papers as Mr. Kindheart; but all too private for reproduction now. He returned in the middle of October, when we resumed our almost daily ridings, foregatherings with Maclise at Hampstead and elsewhere, and social entertainments with Macready, Talfourd, Procter, Stanfield, Fonblanque, Elliotson, Tennent, d'Orsay, Quin, Harness, Wilkie, Edwin Landseer, Rogers, Sydney Smith, and Bulwer. Of the genius of the author of *Pelham* and *Eugene Aram* he had, early and late, the highest admiration, and he took occasion to express it during the present year in a new preface which he published to *Oliver Twist*. Other friends became familiar in later years; but, disinclined as he was to the dinner invitations that reached him from every quarter, all such meetings with those whom I have named, and in an especial manner the marked attentions shown him by Miss Coutts, which began with the very beginning of his career, were invariably welcome.

To speak here of the pleasure his society afforded, would anticipate the fitter mention to be made hereafter. But what in this respect distinguishes nearly all original men, he possessed eminently. His place was not to be filled up by any other. To the most trivial talk he gave the attraction of his own character. It might be a small matter; something he had read or observed during the day, some quaint odd fancy from a book, a vivid little outdoor picture, the laughing exposure of some imposture, or a burst of sheer mirthful enjoyment; but of its kind it would be something unique, because genuinely part of himself. This, and his unwearying animal spirits, made him the most delightful of companions; no claim on good-fellowship ever found him wanting; and no one so constantly recalled to his friends the description Johnson gave of Garrick, as " the cheerfullest man of his age."

Of what occupied him in the way of literary labour in the

autumn and winter months of the year, some description has been given; and, apart from what has already thus been said of his work at the closing chapters of *The Old Curiosity Shop*, nothing now calls for more special allusion, except that in his town-walks in November, impelled thereto by specimens recently discovered in his country walks between Broadstairs and Ramsgate, he thoroughly explored the ballad literature of Seven Dials, and would occasionally sing, with an effect that justified his reputation for comic singing in his childhood, not a few of those wonderful productions. His last successful labour of the year was the reconciliation of two friends: and his motive, as well as the principle that guided him, as they are described by himself, I think worth preserving. For the first: "In the midst of this child's death, I, over whom something of the bitterness of death has passed, not lightly perhaps, was reminded of many old kindnesses, and was sorry in my heart that men who really liked each other should waste life at arm's length." For the last: "I have laid it down as a rule in my judgment of men, to observe narrowly whether some (of whom one is disposed to think badly) don't carry all their faults upon the surface, and others (of whom one is disposed to think well) don't carry many more beneath it. I have long ago made sure that our friend is in the first class; and when I know all the foibles a man has, with little trouble in the discovery, I begin to think he is worth liking." His latest letter of the year, dated the day following, closed with the hope that we might, he and I, enjoy together "fifty more Christmases, at least, in this world, and eternal summers in another." Alas!

IX

"BARNABY RUDGE"

1841

THE letters of 1841 yield similar fruit as to his doings and sayings, and may in like manner first be consulted for the literary work he had in hand.

He had the advantage of beginning *Barnaby Rudge* with a fair amount of story in advance, which he had only to make suitable, by occasional readjustment of chapters, to publication in weekly portions; and on this he was engaged before the end of January. "I am at present" (22 January, 1841) "in what Leigh Hunt would call a kind of impossible state—thinking what on earth Master Humphrey can think of through four mortal pages. I added here and there to the last chapter of the *Curiosity Shop* yesterday, and it leaves me only four pages to write." (They were filled by a paper from Humphrey introductory of the new tale, in which will be found a striking picture of London, from midnight to the break of day.) "I also made up, and wrote the needful insertions for, the second number of *Barnaby*—so that I came back to the mill a little." Hardly yet: for after four days he writes, having meanwhile done nothing: "I have been looking (three o'clock) with an appearance of extraordinary interest and study at *one leaf* of the *Curiosities of Literature* ever since half-past ten this morning—I haven't the heart to turn over." Then, on Friday the 29th, better news came. "I didn't stir out yesterday, but sat and *thought* all day; not writing a line; not so much as the cross of a *t* or dot of an *i*. I imaged forth a good deal of *Barnaby* by keeping my mind steadily upon him; and am happy to say I have gone to work this morning in good twig, strong hope, and cheerful spirits. Last night I was unutterably and impossible-to-form-an-idea-of-ably miserable. . . . By the by don't engage yourself otherwise than to me for Sunday week, because it's my birthday. I have no doubt we shall have got over our troubles here by that time, and I purpose having a snug dinner in the study." We had the dinner, though the troubles were not over; but the

137

next day another son was born to him. "Thank God," he wrote on the 9th, "quite well. I am thinking hard, and have just written to Browne inquiring when he will come and confer about the raven." He had by this time resolved to make that bird, whose accomplishments had been daily ripening and enlarging for the last twelve months to the increasing mirth and delight of all of us, a prominent figure in *Barnaby*; and the invitation to the artist was for a conference how best to introduce him graphically.

The next letter mentioning *Barnaby* was from Brighton (25 February), whither he had flown for a week's quiet labour. "I have (it's four o'clock) done a very fair morning's work, at which I have sat very close, and been blessed besides with a clear view of the end of the volume. As the contents of one number usually require a day's thought at the very least, and often more, this puts me in great spirits. I think—that is, I hope —the story takes a great stride at this point, and takes it WELL. *Nous verrons.* Grip will be strong, and I build greatly on the Varden household."

Upon his return he had to lament a domestic calamity, which, for its connection with a famous personage in *Barnaby*, must be mentioned here. The raven had for some days been ailing, and Topping had reported of him, as Hamlet declares of himself, that he had lost his mirth and foregone all custom of exercises: but Dickens paid no great heed, remembering his recovery from an illness of the previous summer when he swallowed some white paint; so that the graver report which led him to send for the doctor came upon him unexpectedly, and nothing but his own language can worthily describe the result. Unable from the state of his feelings to write two letters, he sent the narrative to Maclise under an enormous black seal, for transmission to me.

"You will be greatly shocked" (the letter is dated Friday evening, 12 March, 1841) "and grieved to hear that the Raven is no more. He expired to-day at a few minutes after twelve o'clock at noon. He had been ailing for a few days, but we anticipated no serious result, conjecturing that a portion of the white paint he swallowed last summer might be lingering about his vitals without having any serious effect upon his constitution. Yesterday afternoon he was taken so much worse that I sent an express for the medical gentleman (Mr. Herring), who promptly attended, and administered a powerful dose of castor oil. Under the influence of this medicine, he recovered so far as to be able at eight o'clock p.m. to bite Topping. His night was peaceful. This morning at daybreak he appeared better; received (agreeably to the doctor's directions) another dose of castor oil; and partook plentifully of some warm gruel, the flavour of which he appeared to relish. Towards eleven o'clock he was so much worse that it was found necessary to muffle the stable-knocker. At half-past, or thereabouts, he was heard talking to himself about the horse and Topping's family, and to add some incoherent expressions which are supposed to have been either a foreboding of his approaching dissolution, or some wishes relative to the disposal of his little property: consisting chiefly of half-pence which he had buried in different parts of the garden. On the clock striking twelve he appeared slightly agitated, but he soon recovered, walked twice or thrice along the coach-house, stopped to bark, staggered, exclaimed *Halloa old girl !* (his favourite expression), and died.

"He behaved throughout with a decent fortitude, equanimity, and self-possession, which cannot be too much admired. I deeply regret that being in ignorance of his danger I did not attend to receive his last instructions. Something remarkable about his eyes occasioned Topping to run for the doctor at twelve. When they returned together our friend was gone. It was the medical gentleman who informed me of his decease. He did it with great caution and delicacy, preparing me by the remark that 'a jolly queer start had taken place'; but the shock was very great notwithstanding. I am not wholly free from suspicions of poison. A malicious butcher has been heard to say that he would 'do' for him: his plea was that he would not be molested in taking orders down the mews, by any bird that wore a tail. Other persons have also been heard to threaten: among others, Charles Knight, who has just started a weekly publication price fourpence: *Barnaby* being, as you know, threepence. I have directed a post-mortem examination, and the body has been removed to Mr. Herring's school of anatomy for that purpose.

"I could wish, if you can take the trouble, that you could enclose this to Forster immediately after you have read it. I cannot discharge the painful task of communication more than once. Were they ravens who took manna to somebody in the wilderness? At times I hope they were, and at others I fear they were not, or they would certainly have stolen it by the way. In profound sorrow, I am ever your bereaved friend C. D. Kate is as well as can be expected, but terribly low as you may suppose. The children seem rather glad of it. He bit their ankles. But that was play."

In what way the loss was replaced, so that *Barnaby* should have the fruit of continued study of the habits of the family of birds which Grip had so nobly represented, Dickens has told in the preface to the story; and another, older, and larger Grip, obtained through Mr. Smithson, was installed in the stable, almost before the stuffed remains of his honoured predecessor had been sent home in a glass case, by way of ornament to his bereaved master's study.

I resume our correspondence on what he was writing. "I see there is yet room for a few lines" (25 March), "and you are quite right in wishing what I cut out to be restored. I did not want Joe to be so short about Dolly, and really wrote his references to that young lady carefully—as natural things with a meaning in them. Chigwell, my dear fellow, is the greatest place in the world. Name your day for going. Such a delicious old inn opposite the churchyard—such a lovely ride—such beautiful forest scenery—such an out of the way, rural place—such a sexton! I say again, name your day." The day was named at once; and the whitest of stones marks it now in sorrowful memory. His promise was exceeded by our enjoyment; and his delight in the double recognition, of himself and of *Barnaby*, by the landlord of the nice old inn, far exceeded any pride he would have taken in what the world thinks the highest sort of honour.

"I have shut myself up" (26 March) "by myself to-day, and mean to try and 'go it' at the *Clock*; Kate being out, and the house peacefully dismal. I don't remember altering the exact part you object to, but if there be anything here you object to, knock it out ruthlessly." "Don't fail" (5 April) "to erase anything that seems to you too strong. It is difficult for me to judge what tells too much, and what does not. I am trying a very quiet number to set against this necessary one. I hope it will be good, but I am in very sad condition for work. Glad you think this powerful. What I have put in is more relief, from the raven." Two days later: "I have done that number, and am now going to work on another. I am bent (please Heaven) on finishing the first chapter by Friday night. I hope to look in upon you to-night, when we'll dispose of the toasts for Saturday. Still bilious—but a good number, I hope, notwithstanding. Jeffrey has come to town, and was here yesterday." The toasts to be disposed of were those to be given at the dinner on the 10th to celebrate the second volume of *Master Humphrey*; when Talfourd presided, and there was much jollity. According to the memorandum drawn up that Saturday night now lying before me, we all in the greatest good humour glorified each other: Talfourd proposing the *Clock*, Macready Mrs. Dickens, Dickens the publishers, and myself the artists; Macready giving Talfourd, Talfourd Macready, Dickens myself, and myself the comedian Mr. Harley, whose humorous songs had been no inconsiderable element in the mirth of the evening.

Five days later he writes: "I finished the number yesterday, and, although I dined with Jeffrey, and was obliged to go to Lord Denman's afterwards (which made me late), have done eight slips of the *Lamplighter* for Mrs. Macrone, this morning. When I have got that off my mind I shall try to go on steadily, fetching up the *Clock* lee-way." The *Lamplighter* was his old farce, which he now turned into a comic tale; and this, with other contributions given him by friends and edited by him as *Pic Nic Papers*, enabled him to help the widow of his old publisher in her straitened means by a gift of £300. He had finished his work of charity before he next wrote of *Barnaby Rudge*, but he was fetching up his lee-way lazily. "I am getting on" (29 April) "very slowly. I want to stick to the story; and the fear of committing myself, because of the impossibility of trying back or altering a syllable, makes it much harder than it looks. It was too bad of me to give you the trouble of cutting the number, but I knew so well you would do it in the right places. For what Harley would call the 'onward work' I really think I have some famous thoughts." There is an interval of a month before the next allusion. "Solomon's expression" (3 June) "I meant to be one of those strong ones to which strong circumstances give birth in the commonest minds. Deal with it as you like. . . . Say what you please of Gordon" (I had objected to some points in his view of this madman, stated much too favourably as I thought), "he must have been at heart a kind man, and a lover of the despised and rejected, after his own fashion. He lived upon a small income, and always within it; was known to relieve the necessities of many people; exposed in his place the corrupt attempt of a minister to buy him out of Parliament; and did great charities in Newgate. He always spoke on the people's side, and tried against his muddled brains to expose the profligacy of both parties. He never got anything by his madness, and never sought it. The wildest and most raging attacks of the time, allow him these merits; and not to let him have 'em in their full extent, remembering in what a (politically) wicked time he lived, would lie upon my conscience heavily. The libel he was imprisoned for when he died, was on the queen of France; and the French government interested themselves warmly to procure his release—which I think they might have done, but for Lord Grenville." I was more successful in the counsel I gave against a fancy he had at this part of the story, that he should introduce as actors in the Gordon Riots three splendid fellows who should order, lead, control, and be obeyed as natural guides of the crowd in that delirious time, and who should turn out, when all was over, to have broken out from Bedlam: but though he saw the unsoundness of this, he could not so readily see, in Gordon's case, the danger of taxing ingenuity to ascribe a reasonable motive to acts of sheer insanity. The feeblest parts of the book are those in which Lord George and his secretary appear.

He left for Scotland after the middle of June, but he took work with him. "You may suppose," he wrote from Edinburgh on the 30th, "I have not done much work—but by Friday night's post from here I hope to send the first long chapter of a number and both the illustrations; from Loch Earn on Tuesday night, the closing chapter of that number; from the same place on Thursday night, the first long chapter of another, with both the illustrations; and, from some place which no man ever spelt, but which sounds like Ballyhoolish, on Saturday, the closing chapter of that number, which will leave us all safe till I return to town." Nine days later he wrote from "Ballechelish": "I have done all I can or need do in the way of *Barnaby* until I come home, and the story is progressing (I hope you will think) to good strong interest. I have left it, I think, at an exciting point, with a good dawning of the riots. In the first of the two numbers I have written since I have been away, I forget whether the blind man, in speaking to Barnaby about riches, tells him they are to be found in *crowds*. If I have not actually used that word, will you introduce it? A perusal of the proof of the following number (70) will show you how, and why." "Have you," he wrote, shortly after his return (29 July), "seen no. 71? I thought there was a good glimpse of a crowd, from a window, eh?" He had now taken thoroughly to the interest of his closing chapters, and felt more than ever the constraints of his form of publication. "I am warming up very much" (on 5 August from Broadstairs) "about *Barnaby*. Oh! If I only had him, from this time to the end, in monthly numbers. *N'importe!* I hope the interest will be pretty strong —and, in every number, stronger." Six days later, from the same place: "I was always sure I could make a good thing of

Barnaby, and I think you'll find that it comes out strong to the last word. I have another number ready, all but two slips. Don't fear for young Chester. The time hasn't come—there we go again, you see, with the weekly delays. I am in great heart and spirits with the story, and with the prospect of having time to think before I go on again." A month's interval followed, and what occupied it will be described shortly. On 11 September he wrote: "I have just burnt into Newgate, and am going in the next number to tear the prisoners out by the hair of their heads. The number which gets into the jail you'll have in proof by Tuesday." This was followed up a week later: "I have let all the prisoners out of Newgate, burnt down Lord Mansfield's, and played the very devil. Another number will finish the fires, and help us on towards the end. I feel quite smoky when I am at work. I want elbow-room terribly." To this trouble, graver supervened at his return, a serious personal sickness not the least; but he bore up gallantly, and I had never better occasion than now to observe his quiet endurance of pain, how little he thought of himself where the sense of self is commonly supreme, and the manful duty with which everything was done that, ailing as he was, he felt it necessary to do. He was still in his sick-room (22 October) when he wrote: "I hope I shan't leave off any more, now, until I have finished *Barnaby*." Three days after that, he was busying himself eagerly for others; and on 2 November the printers received the close of *Barnaby Rudge*.

This tale was Dickens's first attempt out of the sphere of the life of the day and its actual manners. Begun during the progress of *Oliver Twist*, it had been for some time laid aside; the form it ultimately took had been comprised only partially within its first design; and the story in its finished shape presented strongly a special purpose, the characteristic of all but his very earliest writings. Its scene is laid at the time when the incessant execution of men and women, comparatively innocent, disgraced every part of the country; demoralising thousands, whom it also prepared for the scaffold. In those days the theft of a few rags from a bleaching-ground, or the abstraction of a roll of ribbons from a counter, was visited with the penalty of blood; and such laws brutalised both their ministers and victims. It was the time, too, when a false religious outcry brought with it appalling guilt and misery. Such vices leave more behind them than the first forms assumed, and involve a lesson sufficiently required to justify a writer in dealing with them. There were also others grafted on them. In Barnaby himself it was desired to show what sources of comfort there might be, for the patient and cheerful heart, in even the worst of all human afflictions; and in the hunted life of the outcast father, whose crime had entailed not that affliction only, but other more fearful wretchedness, we have as powerful a picture as any in his writings of the inevitable and unfathomable consequences of sin. It was the late Lord Lytton's opinion that Dickens had done nothing finer in point of art than this. But, as the story went on, it was incident to such designs that what had been accomplished in its predecessor could hardly be attained here, in singleness of purpose, unity of idea, or harmony of treatment; and other defects supervened in the management of the plot. The interest with which the tale begins, has ceased to be its interest before the close; and what has chiefly taken the reader's fancy at the outset, almost wholly disappears in the power and passion with which, in the later chapters, the great riots are described. So admirable is this description, however, that it would be hard to have to surrender it even for a more perfect structure of fable.

There are few things more masterly in any of his books. From the first low mutterings of the storm to its last terrible explosion, the frantic outbreak of popular ignorance and rage is depicted with unabated power. The aimlessness of idle mischief by which the ranks of the rioters are swelled at the beginning; the recklessness induced by the monstrous impunity allowed to the early excesses; the sudden spread of drunken guilt into every haunt of poverty, ignorance, or mischief in the wicked old city, where such rich materials of crime lie festering; the wild action of its poison on all, without scheme or plan of any kind, who come within its reach; the horrors that are more bewildering for so complete an absence of purpose in them; and, when all is done, the misery found to have been self-inflicted in every cranny and corner of London, as if a plague had swept over the streets: these are features in the picture of an actual occurrence, to which the manner of the treatment gives extraordinary force and meaning. Nor, in the sequel, is there anything displayed with more profitable vividness, than the law's indiscriminate cruelty at last in contrast with its cowardly indifference at first; while, among the casual touches lighting up the scene with flashes of reality that illumine every part of it, may be instanced the discovery, in the quarter from which screams for succour are loudest when Newgate is supposed to be accidentally on fire, of four men who were certain in any case to have perished on the drop next day.

The story, which has unusually careful writing in it, and much manly upright thinking, has not so many people eagerly adopted as of kin by everybody, as its predecessors are famous for; but it has yet a fair proportion of such as take solid form within the mind, and keep hold of the memory. To these belong in an especial degree Gabriel Varden and his household, on whom are lavished all the writer's fondness, and not a little of his keenest humour. The honest locksmith with his jovial jug, and the tink-tink-tink of his pleasant nature making cheerful music out of steel and iron; the buxom wife, with her plaguy tongue that makes everyone wretched whom her kindly disposition would desire to make happy; the good-hearted plump little Dolly, coquettish minx of a daughter, with all she suffers and inflicts by her fickle winning ways, and her small self-admiring vanities; and Miggs the vicious and slippery, acid, amatory, and of uncomfortable figure, sower of family discontents and discords, who swears all the while she wouldn't make or meddle with 'em "not for a annual gold mine and found in tea and sugar";—there is not much social painting anywhere with a better domestic moral, than in all these; and a nice propriety of feeling and thought regulates the use of such satire throughout. No one knows more exactly how far to go with that formidable weapon; or understands better that what satirises everything, in effect satirises nothing.

Another excellent group is that which the story opens with, in the quaint old kitchen of the "Maypole"; John Willett and his friends, genuinely comic creations all of them. Then we have Barnaby and his raven: the light-hearted idiot, as unconscious of guilt as of suffering, and happy with no sense but of the influences of nature; and the grave sly bird, with sufficient sense to make himself as unhappy as rascally habits will make the human animal. There is poor brutish Hugh, too, loitering lazily outside the "Maypole" door, with a storm of passions in him raging to be let loose; already the scaffold's withered fruit, as he is doomed to be its ripe offering; and though with all the worst instincts of the savage, yet not without also some of the best. Still farther out of kindly nature's pitying reach lurks the worst villain of the scene: with this sole claim to consideration, that it was by constant contact with the filthiest instrument of law and state he had become the mass of moral filth he is. Mr. Dennis the hangman is a portrait that Hogarth would have painted with the same wholesome severity of satire employed upon it in *Barnaby Rudge*.

X

IN EDINBURGH

1841

AMONG the occurrences of the year, apart from the tale he was writing, the birth of his fourth child and second son has been briefly mentioned. "I mean to call the boy Edgar," he wrote the day after he was born (9 February), "a good honest Saxon name, I think." He changed his mind in a few days, however, on resolving to ask Landor to be godfather. This intention, as soon as formed, he announced to our excellent old friend; telling him it would give the child something to boast of, to be called Walter Landor, and that to call him so would do his own heart good. For, as to himself, whatever realities had gone out of the ceremony of christening, the meaning still remained in it of enabling him to form a relationship with friends he most loved: and as to the boy, he held that to give him a name to be proud of was to give him also another reason for doing nothing unworthy or untrue when he came to be a man. Walter, alas! only lived to manhood. He obtained a military cadetship through the kindness of Miss Coutts, and died at Calcutta on the last day of 1863, in his twenty-third year.

The interest taken by this distinguished lady in Dickens and his family began, as I have said, at an earlier date than even this; and I remember his pleasure, while *Oliver Twist* was going on, at her father's mention of him in a speech at Birmingham, for his advocacy of the cause of the poor. Whether to the new poor-law Sir Francis Burdett objected as strongly as we have seen that Dickens did, as well as many other excellent men, who forgot the atrocities of the system it displaced in their indignation at the needless harshness with which it was worked at the outset, I have not at hand the means of knowing. But certainly this continued to be strongly the feeling of Dickens, who exulted at nothing so much as at any misadventure to the Whigs in connection with it. "How often used Black and I," he wrote to me in April, "to quarrel about the effect of the poor-law bill! Walter comes in upon the cry. See whether the Whigs go out upon it." It was the strong desire he had to make himself heard upon it, even in parliament, that led him not immediately to turn aside from a proposal, now privately made by some of the magnates of Reading, to bring him in for that † 8 borough; but the notion was soon dismissed, as, on its revival more than once in later times, it continued very wisely to be. His opinions otherwise were extremely radical at present, as will be apparent shortly; and he did not at all relish Peel's majority of one when it came soon after, and unseated the Whigs. It was just now, I may add, he greatly enjoyed a quiet setting-down of Moore by Rogers at Sir Francis Burdett's table, for talking exaggerated Toryism. So debased was the House of Commons by reform, said Moore, that a Burke, if you could find him, would not be listened to. "No such thing, Tommy," said Rogers; "*find yourself*, and they'd listen even to you."

This was not many days before he hinted to me an intention soon to be carried out in a rather memorable manner. "I have done nothing to-day" (18 March: we had bought books together, the day before, at Tom Hill's sale) "but cut the *Swift*, looking into it with a delicious laziness in all manner of delightful places, and put poor Tom's books away. I had a letter from Edinburgh this morning, announcing that Jeffrey's visit to London will be the week after next; telling me that he drives about Edinburgh declaring there has been 'nothing so good as Nell since Cordelia,' which he writes also to all manner of people; and informing me of a desire in that romantic town to give me greeting and welcome. For this and other reasons I am disposed to make Scotland my destination in June rather than Ireland. Think, *do* think, meantime (here are ten good weeks), whether you couldn't, by some effort worthy of the owner of the gigantic helmet, go with us. Think of such a fortnight—York, Carlisle, Berwick, your own Borders, Edinburgh, Rob Roy's country, railroads, cathedrals, country inns, Arthur's Seat, lochs, glens, and home by sea. DO think of this seriously, at leisure." It was very tempting, but not to be.

Early in April Jeffrey came, many feasts and entertainments welcoming him, oi which he very sparingly partook; and before he left, the visit to Scotland in June was all duly arranged, to be initiated by the splendid welcome of a public dinner in Edinburgh, with Lord Jeffrey himself in the chair. "Willy Allan," the celebrated artist, had come up meanwhile, with increasing note of preparation; and it was while we were all regretting Wilkie's absence abroad, and Dickens with warrantable pride was saying how surely the great painter would have gone to this dinner, that the shock of his sudden death [1] came, and there was left but the sorrowful satisfaction of honouring his memory. There was one other change before the day. "I heard from Edinburgh this morning," he wrote on 15 June. "Jeffrey is not well enough to take the chair, so Wilson does. I think under all circumstances of politics, acquaintance, and *Edinburgh Review*, that it's much better as it is—Don't you?"

His first letter from Edinburgh, where he and Mrs. Dickens had taken up quarters at the Royal Hotel on their arrival the previous night, is dated 23 June. "I have been this morning to the Parliament House, and am now introduced (I hope) to everybody in Edinburgh. The hotel is perfectly besieged, and I have been forced to take refuge in a sequestered apartment at the end of a long passage, wherein I write this letter. They talk of 300 at the dinner. We are very well off in point of rooms, having a handsome sitting-room, another next to it for *Clock* purposes, a spacious bedroom, and large dressing-room adjoining. The castle is in front of the windows, and the view noble. There was a supper ready last night which would have been a dinner anywhere." This was his first practical experience of the honours his fame had won for him, and it found him as eager to receive as all were eager to give. Very interesting still, too, are those who took leading part in the celebration; and, in his pleasant sketches of them, there are some once famous and familiar figures not so well known to the present generation. Here, among the first, are Wilson and Robertson.

"The renowned Peter Robertson is a large, portly, full-faced man with a merry eye, and a queer way of looking under his spectacles which is characteristic and pleasant. He seems a very warm-hearted earnest man too, and I felt quite at home with him forthwith. Walking up and down the hall of the courts of law (which was full of advocates, writers to the signet, clerks, and idlers) was a tall, burly, handsome man of eight and fifty, with a gait like O'Connell's, the bluest eye you can imagine, and long hair—longer than mine—falling down in a wild way under the broad brim of his hat. He had on a surtout coat, a blue checked shirt; the collar standing up, and kept in its place with a wisp of black neckerchief; no waistcoat; and a

---

[1] Dickens refused to believe it at first. "My heart assures me Wilkie liveth," he wrote. "He is the sort of man who will be VERY old when he dies"—and certainly one would have said so.

large pocket-handkerchief thrust into his breast, which was all broad and open. At his heels followed a wiry, sharp-eyed, shaggy devil of a terrier, dogging his steps as he went slashing up and down, now with one man beside him, now with another, and now quite alone, but always at a fast, rolling pace, with his head in the air, and his eyes as wide open as he could get them. I guessed it was Wilson, and it was. A bright, clear-complexioned, mountain-looking fellow, he looks as though he had just come down from the Highlands, and had never in his life taken pen in hand. But he has had an attack of paralysis in his right arm, within this month. He winced when I shook hands with him; and once or twice when we were walking up and down, slipped as if he had stumbled on a piece of orange-peel. He is a great fellow to look at, and to talk to; and, if you could divest your mind of the actual Scott, is just the figure you would put in his place."

Nor have the most ordinary incidents of the visit any lack of interest for us now, in so far as they help to complete the picture of himself. "Allan has been squiring me about, all the morning. He and Fletcher have gone to a meeting of the dinner-stewards, and I take the opportunity of writing to you. They dine with us to-day, and we are going to-night to the theatre. M'Ian is playing there. I mean to leave a card for him before evening. We are engaged for every day of our stay, already; but the people I have seen are so very hearty and warm in their manner that much of the horror of lionization gives way before it. I am glad to find that they propose giving me for a toast on Friday the Memory of Wilkie. I should have liked it better than anything, if I could have made my choice. Communicate all particulars to Mac. I would to God you were both here. Do dine together at the Gray's Inn on Friday, and think of me. If I don't drink my first glass of wine to you, may my pistols miss fire, and my mare slip her shoulder. All sorts of regard from Kate. She has gone with Miss Allan to see the house she was born in, etc. Write me soon, and long, etc."

His next letter was written the morning after the dinner, on Saturday, 26 June. "The great event is over; and being gone, I am a man again. It was the most brilliant affair you can conceive; the completest success possible, from first to last. The room was crammed, and more than seventy applicants for tickets were of necessity refused yesterday. Wilson was ill, but plucked up like a lion, and spoke famously. I send you a paper herewith, but the report is dismal in the extreme. They say there will be a better one—I don't know where or when. Should there be, I will send it to you. I *think* (ahem!) that I spoke rather well. It was an excellent room, and both the subjects (Wilson and Scottish Literature, and the Memory of Wilkie) were good to go upon. There were nearly two hundred ladies present. The place is so contrived that the cross table is raised enormously: much above the heads of people sitting below: and the effect on first coming in (on me, I mean) was rather tremendous. I was quite self-possessed, however, and, notwithstanding the enthoosemoosy, which was very startling, as cool as a cucumber. I wish to God you had been there, as it is impossible for the 'distinguished guest' to describe the scene. It beat all natur'. . . ."

Here was the close of his letter. "I have been expecting every day to hear from you, and not hearing mean to make this the briefest epistle possible. We start next Sunday (that's to-morrow week). We are going out to Jeffrey's to-day (he is very unwell), and return here to-morrow evening. If I don't find a letter from you when I come back, expect no Lights and Shadows of Scottish Life from your indignant correspondent. Murray the manager made very excellent, tasteful, and gentlemanly mention of Macready, about whom Wilson had been asking me divers questions during dinner." "A hundred thanks for your letter," he writes four days later. "I read it this morning with the greatest pleasure and delight, and answer it with ditto, ditto. Where shall I begin—about my darlings? I am delighted with Charley's precocity. He takes arter his father, he does. God bless them, you can't imagine (*you !* how can you?) how much I long to see them. It makes me quite sorrowful to think of them. . . . Yesterday, sir, the Lord Provost, council, and magistrates voted me by acclamation the freedom of the city, in testimony (I quote the letter just received from 'James Forrest, Lord Provost') 'of the sense entertained by them of your distinguished abilities as an author.' I acknowledged this morning in appropriate terms the honour they had done me, and through me the pursuit to which I was devoted. It *is* handsome, is it not?"

The parchment scroll of the city-freedom, recording the grounds on which it was voted, hung framed in his study to the last, and was one of his valued possessions. Answering some question of mine, he told me further as to the speakers, and gave some amusing glimpses of the party-spirit which still at that time ran high in the capital of the north.

"The men who spoke at the dinner were all the most rising men here, and chiefly at the Bar. They were all, alternately, Whigs and Tories; with some few Radicals, such as Gordon, who gave the memory of Burns. He is Wilson's son-in-law and the Lord Advocate's nephew—a very masterly speaker indeed, who ought to become a distinguished man. Neaves, who gave the other poets, a *little* too lawyer-like for my taste, is a great gun in the courts. Mr. Primrose is Lord Rosebery's son. Adam Black, the publisher as you know. Dr. Alison, a very popular friend of the poor. Robertson you know. Allan you know. Colquhoun is an advocate. All these men were selected for the toasts as being crack speakers, known men, and opposed to each other very strongly in politics. For this reason, the professors and so forth who sat upon the platform about me made no speeches and had none assigned them. I felt it was very remarkable to see such a number of grey-headed men gathered about my brown flowing locks; and it struck most of those who were present very forcibly. The judges, Solicitor-General, Lord Advocate, and so forth, were all here to call, the day after our arrival. The judges never go to public dinners in Scotland. Lord Meadowbank alone broke through the custom, and none of his successors have imitated him. It will give you a good notion of *party* to hear that the Solicitor-General and Lord-Advocate refused to go, though they had previously engaged, unless the croupier or the chairman were a Whig. Both (Wilson and Robertson) were Tories, simply because, Jeffrey excepted, no Whig could be found who was adapted to the office. The solicitor laid strict injunctions on Napier not to go if a Whig were not in office. No Whig was, and he stayed away. I think this is good—bearing in mind that all the old Whigs of Edinburgh were cracking their throats in the room. They give out that they were ill, and the Lord Advocate did actually lie in bed all the afternoon; but this is the real truth, and one of the judges told it me with great glee. It seems they couldn't quite trust Wilson or Robertson, as they thought; and feared some Tory demonstration. Nothing of the kind took place; and ever since, these men have been the loudest in their praises of the whole affair."

The close of his letter tells us all his engagements, and completes his grateful picture of the hearty Scottish welcome. It has also some personal touches worth preserving. "A threat reached me last night (they have been hammering at it in their papers, it seems, for some time) of a dinner at Glasgow. But

*F 781

I hope, having circulated false rumours of my movements, to get away before they send to me; and only to stop there on my way home, to change horses and send to the post-office. . . . You will like to know how we have been living. Here's a list of engagements, past and present. Wednesday we dined at home, and went incog. to the theatre at night, to Murray's box: the pieces admirably done, and M'Ian in the *Two Drovers* quite wonderful, and most affecting. Thursday, to Lord Murray's; dinner and evening party. Friday, *the* dinner. Saturday, to Jeffrey's, a beautiful place about three miles off" (Craig Crook, which at Lord Jeffrey's invitation I afterwards visited with him), "stop there all night, dine on Sunday, and home at eleven. Monday, dine at Dr. Alison's, four miles off. Tuesday, dinner and evening party at Allan's. Wednesday, breakfast with Napier, dine with Blackwoods seven miles off, evening party at the treasurer's of the Town Council, supper with all the artists (! !). Thursday, lunch at the Solicitor-General's, dine at Lord Gillies's, evening party at Joseph Gordon's, one of Brougham's earliest supporters. Friday, dinner and evening party at Robertson's. Saturday, dine again at Jeffrey's; back to the theatre, at half-past nine to the moment, for public appearance; places all let, etc., etc., etc. Sunday, off at seven o'clock in the morning to Stirling, and then to Callender, a stage further. Next day, to Loch Earn, and pull up there for three days, to rest and work. The moral of all this is, that there is no place like home; and that I thank God most heartily for having given me a quiet spirit, and a heart that won't hold many people. I sigh for Devonshire Terrace and Broadstairs, for battledore and shuttlecock; I want to dine in a blouse with you and Mac; and I feel Topping's merits more acutely than I have ever done in my life. On Sunday evening, 17 July, I shall revisit my household gods, please Heaven. I wish the day were here. For God's sake be in waiting. I wish you and Mac would dine in Devonshire Terrace that day with Fred. He has the key of the cellar. *Do.* We shall be at Inverary in the Highlands on Tuesday week, getting to it through the pass of Glencoe, of which you may have heard! On Thursday following we shall be at Glasgow, where I shall hope to receive your last letter before we meet. At Inverary, too, I shall make sure of finding at least one, at the post-office. . . . Little Allan is trying hard for the post of queen's limner for Scotland, vacant by poor Wilkie's death. Everyone is in his favour but —— who is jobbing for someone else. Appoint him, will you, and I'll give up the

* 21

premiership.—How I breakfasted to-day in the house where Scott lived seven and twenty years; how I have made solemn pledges to write about missing children in the *Edinburgh Review*, and will do my best to keep them; how I have declined to be brought in, free gratis for nothing and qualified to boot, for a Scotch county that's going a-begging, lest I should be thought to have dined on Friday under false pretences; these, with other marvels, shall be yours anon. . . . I must leave off sharp, to get dressed and off upon the seven miles dinner trip. Kate's affectionate regards. My hearty loves to Mac and Grim." Grim was another great artist having the same beginning to his name, whose tragic studies had suggested an epithet quite inapplicable to any of his personal qualities.

The narrative of the trip to the Highlands must have a chapter to itself, and its incidents of adventure and comedy. The latter chiefly were due to the guide who accompanied him, a quasi-highlander himself, named a few pages back as Mr. Kindheart, whose real name was Mr. Angus Fletcher, and to whom it hardly needs that I should give other mention than will be supplied by such future notices of him as his friend's letters may contain. He had much talent, but too fitful and wayward to concentrate on a settled pursuit; and though at the time we knew him first he had taken up the profession of a sculptor, he abandoned it soon afterwards. His mother, a woman distinguished by many remarkable qualities, lived now in the English lake-country; and it was no fault of hers that her son preferred a wandering life to that of home. His unfitness for an ordinary career was, perhaps, the secret of such liking for him as Dickens had. Fletcher's eccentricity and absurdities, divided often by the thinnest partition from a foolish extravagance, but occasionally clever, and always the genuine though whimsical outgrowth of the life he led, had a curious charm for Dickens. He enjoyed the oddity and humour; tolerated all the rest; and to none more freely than to Kindheart during the next few years, both in Italy and in England, opened his house and hospitality.

XI

IN THE HIGHLANDS

1841

FROM Loch Earn Head Dickens wrote on Monday, 5 July, having reached it, "wet through," at four that afternoon. "Having had a great deal to do in a crowded house on Saturday night at the theatre, we left Edinburgh yesterday morning at half-past seven, and travelled, with Fletcher for our guide, to a place called Stewart's Hotel, nine miles further than Callender. We had neglected to order rooms, and were obliged to make a sitting-room of our own bed-chamber; in which my genius for stowing furniture away was of the very greatest service. Fletcher slept in a kennel with three panes of glass in it, which formed part and parcel of a window; the other three panes whereof belonged to a man who slept on the other side of the partition. He told me this morning that he had had a nightmare all night, and had screamed horribly, he knew. The stranger, as you may suppose, hired a gig and went off at full gallop with the first

* 22   glimpse of daylight. Being very tired (for we had not had more than three hours' sleep on the previous night) we lay till ten this morning; and at half-past eleven went through the Trossachs to Loch Katrine, where I walked from the hotel after tea last night. It is impossible to say what a glorious scene it was. It rained as it never does rain anywhere but here. We conveyed Kate up a rocky pass to go and see the island of the Lady of the Lake, but she gave in after the first five minutes, and we left her, very picturesque and uncomfortable, with Tom" (the servant they had brought with them from Devonshire Terrace) "holding an umbrella over her head, while we climbed on. When we came back, she had gone into the carriage. We were wet through to the skin, and came on in that state four and twenty miles. Fletcher is very good-natured, and of extraordinary use in these outlandish parts. His habit of going into kitchens and bars, disconcerting at Broadstairs, is here of great service. Not expecting us till six, they hadn't lighted our fires when we

arrived here; and if you had seen him (with whom the responsibility of the omission rested) running in and out of the sitting-room and the two bedrooms with a great pair of bellows, with which he distractedly blew each of the fires out in turn, you would have died of laughing. He had on his head a great highland cap, on his back a white coat, and cut such a figure as even the Inimitable can't depicter. . . .

"The inns, inside and out, are the queerest places imaginable. From the road, this one," at Loch Earn Head, "looks like a white wall, with windows in it by mistake. We have a good sitting-room though, on the first floor: as large (but not as lofty) as my study. The bedrooms are of that size which renders it impossible for you to move, after you have taken your boots off, without chipping pieces out of your legs. There isn't a basin in the Highlands which will hold my face; not a drawer which will open after you have put your clothes in it; not a water-bottle capacious enough to wet your toothbrush. The huts are wretched and miserable beyond all description. The food (for those who can pay for it) 'not bad,' as M. would say: oatcake, mutton, hotchpotch, trout from the loch, small beer bottled, marmalade, and whisky. Of the last-named article I have taken about a pint to-day. The weather is what they call 'soft'—which means that the sky is a vast waterspout that never leaves off emptying itself; and the liquor has no more effect than water. . . . (I am going to work to-morrow, and hope before leaving here to write you again. The elections have been sad work indeed. That they should return Sibthorp and reject Bulwer, is, by Heaven, a national disgrace. . . . I don't wonder the devil flew over Lincoln. The people were far too addle-headed, even for him.) . . . I don't bore you with accounts of Ben this and that, and Lochs of all sorts of names, but this is a wonderful region. The way the mists were stalking about to-day, and the clouds lying down upon the hills; the deep glens, the high rocks, the rushing waterfalls, and the roaring rivers down in deep gulfs below; were all stupendous. This house is wedged round by great heights that are lost in the clouds; and the loch, twelve miles long, stretches out its dreary length before the windows. In my next I shall soar to the sublime, perhaps; in this here present writing I confine myself to the ridiculous. But I am always," etc., etc.

His next letter bore the date of "Ballechelish, Friday evening, ninth July, 1841, half-past nine, P.M." and described what we had often longed to see together, the Pass of Glencoe. ". . . I can't go to bed without writing to you from here, though the post will not leave this place until we have left it, and arrived at another. On looking over the route which Lord Murray made out for me, I found he had put down Thursday next for Abbotsford and Dryburgh Abbey, and a journey of seventy miles besides! Therefore, and as I was happily able to steal a march upon myself at Loch Earn Head, and to finish in two days what I thought would take me three, we shall leave here tomorrow morning; and, by being a day earlier than we intended at all the places between this and Melrose (which we propose to reach by Wednesday night), we shall have a whole day for Scott's house and tomb, and still be at York on Saturday evening, and home, God willing, on Sunday. . . . We left Loch Earn Head last night, and went to a place called Killin, eight miles from it, where we slept. I walked some six miles with Fletcher after we got there, to see a waterfall; and truly it was a magnificent sight, foaming and crashing down three great steeps of riven rock; leaping over the first as far off as you could carry your eye, and rumbling and foaming down into a dizzy pool below you, with a deafening roar. To-day we have had a journey of between fifty and sixty miles, through the bleakest and most desolate part of Scotland, where the hill-tops are still covered with great patches of snow, and the road winds over steep mountain passes and on the brink of deep brooks and precipices. The cold all day has been *intense*, and the rain sometimes most violent. It has been impossible to keep warm, by any means; even whisky failed; the wind was too piercing even for that. One stage of ten miles, over a place called the Black Mount, took us two hours and a half to do; and when we came to a lone public called the 'King's House,' at the entrance to Glencoe—this was about three o'clock—we were wellnigh frozen. We got a fire directly, and in twenty minutes they served us up some famous kippered salmon, broiled; a broiled fowl; hot mutton, ham and poached eggs; pancakes; oatcakes; wheaten bread; butter; bottled porter; hot water, lump sugar, and whisky; of which we made a very hearty meal. All the way, the road had been among moors and mountains with huge masses of rock, which fell down God knows where, sprinkling the ground in every direction, and giving it the aspect of the burial-place of a race of giants. Now and then we passed a hut or two, with neither window nor chimney, and the smoke of the peat fire rolling out at the door. But there were not six of these dwellings in a dozen miles; and anything so bleak and wild, and mighty in its loneliness, as the whole country, it is impossible to conceive. Glencoe itself is perfectly *terrible*. The pass is an awful place. It is shut in on each side by enormous rocks from which great torrents come rushing down in all directions. In amongst these rocks on one side of the pass (the left as we came) there are scores of glens, high up, which form such haunts as you might imagine yourself wandering in, in the very height and madness of a fever. They will live in my dreams for years—I was going to say as long as I live, and I seriously think so. The very recollection of them makes me shudder. . . . Well, I will not bore you with my impressions of these tremendous wilds, but they really are fearful in their grandeur and amazing solitude. Wales is a mere toy compared with them."

The further mention of his guide's whimsical ways may stand, since it cannot now be the possible occasion of pain or annoyance, or of anything but very innocent laughter.

"We are here in a bare white house on the banks of Loch Leven, but in a comfortably furnished room on the top of the house — that is, on the first floor — with the rain pattering against the window as though it were December, the wind howling dismally, a cold damp mist on everything without, a blazing fire within halfway up the chimney, and a most infernal piper practising under the window for a competition of pipers which is to come off shortly. . . . The store of anecdotes of Fletcher with which we shall return, will last a long time. It seems that the F.'s are an extensive clan, and that his father was a highlander. Accordingly, wherever he goes, he finds out some cotter or small farmer who is his cousin. I wish you could see him walking into his cousins' curds and cream and into their dairies generally! Yesterday morning between eight and nine, I was sitting writing at the open window, when the postman came to the inn (which at Loch Earn Head is the post office) for the letters. He is going away, when Fletcher, who has been writing somewhere below stairs, rushes out and cries 'Holloa there! Is that the Post?' 'Yes!' somebody answers. 'Call him back!' says Fletcher. 'Just sit down till I've done, *and don't go away till I tell you.*'—Fancy! The General Post, with the letters of forty villages in a leathern bag! . . . To-morrow at Oban. Sunday at Inverary. Monday at Tarbet. Tuesday at Glasgow (and that night at Hamilton). Wednesday at Melrose. Thursday at Ditto. Friday I don't know where. Saturday at York. Sunday —how glad I shall be to shake hands with you. My love to Mac. I thought he'd have written once. Ditto to Macready. I had a very nice and welcome letter from him, and a most hearty one from Elliotson. . . . P.S. Half asleep. So, excuse drowsiness of matter and composition. I shall be full of joy to meet another letter from you! . . . P.P.S. They speak Gaelic here, of course, and many of the common people understand very little English. Since I wrote this letter, I rang the girl upstairs, and gave elaborate directions (you know my way) for a pint of sherry to be made into boiling negus; mentioning all the ingredients one by one, and particularly nutmeg. When I had quite finished, seeing her obviously bewildered, I said, with great gravity, 'Now you know what you're going to order?' 'Oh yes. Sure.' 'What?'—a pause—'Just'—another pause—'Just plenty of *nutbergs*'!"

The impression made upon him by the Pass of Glencoe was not overstated in this letter. It continued with him; and, even where he expected to find Nature in her most desolate grandeur, on the dreary waste of an American prairie, his imagination went back with a higher satisfaction to Glencoe. But his experience of it is not yet completely told. The sequel was in a letter of two days later date from "Dalmally, Sunday, July the eleventh, 1841."

"As there was no place of this name in our route, you will be surprised to see it at the head of this present writing. But our being here is a part of such moving accidents by flood and field as will astonish you. If you should happen to have your hat on, take it off, that your hair may stand on end without any interruption. To get from Ballyhoolish (as I am obliged to spell it when Fletcher is not in the way; and he is out at this moment) to Oban, it is necessary to cross two ferries, one of which is an arm of the sea, eight or ten miles broad. Into this ferry-boat, passengers, carriages, horses, and all, get bodily, and are got across by hook or by crook if the weather be reasonably fine. Yesterday morning, however, it blew such a strong gale that the landlord of the inn, where we had paid for horses all the way to Oban (thirty miles), honestly came upstairs just as we were starting, with the money in his hand, and told us it would be impossible to cross. There was nothing to be done but to come back five and thirty miles, through Glencoe and Inverouran, to a place called Tyndrum, whence a road twelve miles long crosses to Dalmally, which is sixteen miles from Inverary. Accordingly we turned back, and in a great storm of wind and rain began to retrace the dreary road we had come the day before. . . . I was not at all ill-pleased to have to come again through that awful Glencoe. If it had been tremendous on the previous day, yesterday it was perfectly horrific. It had rained all night, and was raining then, as it only does in these parts. Through the whole glen, which is ten miles long, torrents were boiling and foaming, and sending up in every direction spray like the smoke of great fires. They were rushing down every hill and mountain side, and tearing like devils across the path, and down into the depths of the rocks. Some of the hills looked as if they were full of silver, and had cracked in a hundred places. Others as if they were frightened, and had broken out into a deadly sweat. In others there was no compromise or division of streams, but one great torrent came roaring down with a deafening noise, and a rushing of water that was quite appalling. Such a *spaet*, in short (that's the country word), has not been known for many years, and the sights and sounds were beyond description. The postboy was not at all at his ease, and the horses were very much frightened (as well they might be) by the perpetual raging and roaring; one of them started as we came down a steep place, and we were within that much (——) of tumbling over a precipice; just then, too, the drag broke, and we were obliged to go on as we best could without it: getting out every now and then, and hanging on at the back of the carriage to prevent its rolling down too fast, and going Heaven knows where. Well, in this pleasant state of things we came to 'King's House' again, having been four hours doing the sixteen miles. The rumble where Tom sat was by this time so full of water, that he was obliged to borrow a gimlet, and bore holes in the bottom to let it run out. The horses that were to take us on, were out upon the hills, somewhere within ten miles round; and three or four bare-legged fellows went out to look for 'em, while we sat by the fire and tried to dry ourselves. At last we got off again (without the drag and with a broken spring, no smith living within ten miles), and went limping on to Inverouran. In the first three miles we were in a ditch and out again, and lost a horse's shoe. All this time it never once left off raining; and was very windy, very cold, very misty, and most intensely dismal. So we crossed the Black Mount, and came to a place we had passed the day before, where a rapid river runs over a bed of broken rock. Now this river, sir, had a bridge last winter, but the bridge broke down when the thaw came, and has never since been mended; so travellers cross upon a little platform, made of rough deal planks stretching from rock to rock; and carriages and horses ford the water at a certain point. As the platform is the reverse of steady (we had proved this the day before), is very slippery, and affords anything but a pleasant footing, having only a trembling little rail on one side, and on the other nothing between it and the foaming stream, Kate decided to remain in the carriage, and trust herself to the wheels rather than to her feet. Fletcher and I got out, and it was going away, when I advised her, as I had done several times before, to come with us; for I saw that the water was very high, the current being greatly swollen by the rain, and that the postboy had been eyeing it in a very disconcerted manner for the last half-hour. This decided her to come out; and Fletcher, she, Tom, and I, began to cross, while the carriage went about a quarter of a mile down the bank, in search of a shallow place. The platform shook so much that we could only come across two at a time, and then it felt as if it were hung on springs. As to the wind and rain! . . . well, put into one gust all the wind and rain you ever saw and heard, and you'll have some faint notion of it! When we got safely to the opposite bank, there came riding up a wild highlander in a great plaid, whom we recognised as the landlord of the inn, and who, without taking the least notice of us, went dashing on, with the plaid he was wrapped in streaming in the wind, screeching in Gaelic to the postboy on the opposite bank, and making the most frantic gestures you ever saw, in which he was joined by some other wild men on foot, who had come across by a short cut, knee deep in mire and water. As we began to see what this meant, we (that is, Fletcher and I) scrambled on after them, while the boy, horses, and carriage were plunging in the water, which left only the horses' heads and the boy's body visible. By the time we got up to them, the man on horseback and the men on foot were perfectly mad with pantomime; for as to any of their shouts being heard by the boy, the water made such a great noise that they might as well have been dumb. It made me quite sick to think how I should have felt if Kate had been inside. The carriage went round and round like a great stone, the boy was as pale as death, the horses were struggling and plashing and snorting like sea-animals, and we were all roaring to the driver to throw himself off, and let them and the coach go to the devil, when suddenly it came all right (having got into shallow water), and, all tumbling and dripping and jogging from side to side, climbed up to the dry land. I assure you we looked rather queer, as we wiped our faces and stared at each other in a little cluster round about it. It seemed that the man on horseback had been looking at us through a telescope as we came to the track, and knowing that the place was very dangerous, and seeing that we meant to bring the carriage, had come on at a great gallop to show the driver the only place where he could cross. By the time he came up, the man had taken the water at a wrong place, and in a word was as nearly drowned (with carriage, horses, luggage, and all) as ever man was. Was *this* a good adventure?

"We all went on to the inn—the wild man galloping on first, to get a fire lighted—and there we dined on eggs and bacon, oatcake, and whisky; and changed and dried ourselves. The place was a mere knot of little outhouses, and in one of these there were fifty highlanders *all drunk*. . . . Some were drovers, some pipers, and some workmen engaged to build a hunting-lodge for Lord Breadalbane hard by, who had been driven in by stress of weather. One was a paperhanger. He had come out three days before to paper the inn's best room, a chamber almost large enough to keep a Newfoundland dog in; and, from the first half-hour after his arrival to that moment, had been hopelessly and irreclaimably drunk. They were lying about in all directions: on forms, on the ground, about a loft overhead, round the turf-fire wrapped in plaids, on the tables, and under them. We paid our bill, thanked our host very heartily, gave some money to his children, and after an hour's rest came on again. At ten o'clock at night, we reached this place, and were overjoyed to find quite an English inn, with good beds (those we have slept on, yet, have always been of straw), and every possible comfort. We breakfasted this morning at half-past ten, and at three go on to Inverary to dinner. I believe the very rough part of the journey is over, and I am really glad of it. Kate sends all kinds of regards. I shall hope to find a letter from you at Inverary when the post reaches there, to-morrow. I wrote to Oban yesterday, desiring the post-office keeper to send any he might have for us, over to that place. Love to Mac."

One more letter, brief, but overflowing at every word with his generous nature, must close the delightful series written from Scotland. It was dated from Inverary the day following his exciting adventure; promised me another from Melrose (which has unfortunately not been kept with the rest); and enclosed the invitation to a public dinner at Glasgow. "I have returned for answer that I am on my way home, on pressing business connected with my weekly publication, and can't stop. But I have offered to come down any day in September or October, and accept the honour then. Now, I shall come and return per mail; and if this suits them, enter into a solemn league and covenant to come with me. *Do.* You must. I am sure you will. . . . Till my next, and always afterwards, God bless you. I got your welcome letter this morning, and have read it a hundred times. What a pleasure it is. Kate's best regards. I am dying for Sunday, and wouldn't stop now for twenty dinners of twenty thousand each.

always your affectionate friend

CD.

"Will Lord John meet the parliament, or resign first?" I agreed to accompany him to Glasgow; but illness intercepted that celebration.

XII

AGAIN AT BROADSTAIRS

1841

SOON after his return, at the opening of August, he went to Broadstairs; and the direction in which that last question shows his thoughts to have been busy, was that to which he turned his first holiday leisure. He sent me some rhymed squibs as his anonymous contribution to the fight the Liberals were then making, against what was believed to be intended by the return to office of the Tories; ignorant as we were how much wiser than his party the statesman then at the head of it was, or how greatly what we all most desired would be advanced by the very success that had been most disheartening. There will be no harm now in giving extracts from one or two of these pieces, which will sufficiently show the tone of all of them, and with what relish they were written. A celebrated address had been delivered at Tamworth, in which the orator, though in those days big with nothing much larger or graver than a sliding-scale, had made a mystery of it as an infallible specific for public affairs, which he refused to prescribe till regularly called in; and this was good-humouredly laughed at in a quack-doctor's proclamation, to the tune of "A Cobbler there was."

> He's a famous corn-doctor, of wonderful skill—
> No cutting, no rooting up, purging, or pill—
> You're merely to take, 'stead of walking or riding,
> The light schoolboy exercise, innocent sliding.
> > Tol de rol, etc.
>
> There's no advice gratis. If high ladies send
> His legitimate fee, he's their soft-spoken friend.
> At the great public counter, with one hand behind him
> And one in his waistcoat, they're certain to find him.
> > Tol de rol, etc.
>
> He has only to add he's the true Doctor Flam,
> All others being purely fictitious and sham;
> The house is a large one, tall, slated, and white,
> With a lobby, and lights in the passage at night.
> > Tol de rol, diddle doll, etc.

I doubt if he ever enjoyed anything more than the power of thus taking part occasionally, unknown to outsiders, in the sharp conflict the press was waging at the time. "By Jove, how radical I am getting!" he wrote to me (13 August). "I wax stronger and stronger in the true principles every day. I don't know whether it's the sea, or no, but so it is." He would at times even talk, in moments of sudden indignation at the political outlook, of carrying off himself and his household gods, like Coriolanus, to a world elsewhere! "Thank God there is a Van Diemen's Land. That's my comfort. Now, I wonder if I should make a good settler! I wonder, if I went to a new colony with my head, hands, legs, and health, I should force myself to the top of the social milk-pot, and live upon the cream! What do you think? Upon my word I believe I should."

Among his political squibs during the Tory interregnum were some subjects for pictures after the manner of Peter Pindar, of which one or two stanzas will show the tone and spirit.

> To you, Maclise, who Eve's fair daughters paint
> With Nature's hand, and want the maudlin taint
> Of the sweet Chalon school of silk and ermine:
> To you, O Landseer, who from year to year
> Delight in beasts and birds, and dogs and deer,
> And seldom give us any human vermin—
>
> To all who practise art, or make-believe,
> I offer subjects they may take or leave.
>
> .   .   .   .   .   .
>
> Paint, squandering the Club's election gold,
> Fierce lovers of the Constitution old,
> Our Lords, that sacred lady's greatest debtors;
> And let the Law forbidding any voice
> Or act of Peer to influence the choice
> Of English people, flourish in bright letters.
>
> Paint that same dear old lady ill at ease,
> Weak in her second childhood, hard to please,
> Unknowing what she ails or what she wishes;
> With all her Carlton nephews at the door,
> Deaf'ning both aunt and nurses with their roar—
> Fighting, already, for the loaves and fishes!

The last of these rhymes I will give entire. This had no touch of personal satire in it, and he would himself, for that reason, have least objected to its revival. Thus ran his new version of "The Fine Old English Gentleman, to be said or sung at all Conservative dinners":

> I'll sing you a new ballad, and I'll warrant it first-rate,
> Of the days of that old gentleman who had that old estate;

When they spent the public money at a bountiful old rate
On ev'ry mistress, pimp, and scamp, at ev'ry noble gate,
    In the fine old English Tory times;
    Soon may they come again!

The good old laws were garnished well with gibbets, whips, and chains,
With fine old English penalties, and fine old English pains,
With rebel heads and seas of blood once hot in rebel veins;
For all these things were requisite to guard the rich old gains
    Of the fine old English Tory times;
    Soon may they come again!

This brave old code, like Argus, had a hundred watchful eyes,
And ev'ry English peasant had his good old English spies,
To tempt his starving discontent with fine old English lies,
Then call the good old Yeomanry to stop his peevish cries,
    In the fine old English Tory times;
    Soon may they come again.

The good old times for cutting throats that cried out in their need,
The good old times for hunting men who held their fathers' creed,
The good old times when William Pitt, as all good men agreed,
Came down direct from Paradise at more than railroad speed. . . .
    Oh the fine old English Tory times;
    When will they come again!

In those rare days, the press was seldom known to snarl or bark,
But sweetly sang of men in pow'r, like any tuneful lark;
Grave judges, too, to all their evil deeds were in the dark;
And not a man in twenty score knew how to make his mark.
    Oh the fine old English Tory times;
    Soon may they come again! . . .

But Tolerance, though slow in flight, is strong-wing'd in the main;
That night must come on these fine days, in course of time was plain;
The pure old spirit struggled, but its struggles were in vain;
A nation's grip was on it, and it died in choking pain,
    With the fine old English Tory days,
    All of the olden time.

The bright old day now dawns again; the cry runs through the land,
In England there shall be—dear bread! In Ireland—sword and brand!
And poverty, and ignorance, shall swell the rich and grand,
So, rally round the rulers with the gentle iron hand,
    Of the fine old English Tory days;
    Hail to the coming time!

Of matters in which he had been specially interested before
he quitted London, one or two may properly be named. He had
always sympathised, almost as strongly as Archbishop Whately
did, with Doctor Elliotson's mesmeric investigations; and, rein-
forced as these were in the present year by the displays of a
Belgian youth whom another friend, Mr. Chauncy Hare Towns-
hend, brought over to England, the subject, which to the last
had an attraction for him, was for the time rather ardently
followed up. The improvement during the last few years in the

London prisons was another matter of eager and pleased inquiry with him; and he took frequent means of stating what in this respect had been done, since even the date when his *Sketches* were written, by two most efficient public officers at Clerkenwell and Tothill Fields, Mr. Chesterton and Lieutenant Tracey, whom the course of these inquiries turned into private friends. His last letter to me before he quitted town sufficiently explains itself. "Slow rises worth by poverty deprest" was the thought in his mind at every part of his career, and he never for a moment was unmindful of the duty it imposed upon him. "I subscribed for a couple of copies" (31 July) "of this little book. I knew nothing of the man, but he wrote me a very modest letter of two lines, some weeks ago. I have been much affected by the little biography at the beginning, and I thought you would like to share the emotion it had raised in me. I wish we were all in Eden again—for the sake of these toiling creatures."

In the middle of August (Monday, 16th) I had announcement that he was coming up for special purposes. "I sit down to write to you without an atom of news to communicate. Yes, I have—something that will surprise you, who are pent up in dark and dismal Lincoln's Inn Fields. It is the brightest day you ever saw. The sun is sparkling on the water so that I can hardly bear to look at it. The tide is in, and the fishing-boats are dancing like mad. Upon the green-topped cliffs the corn is cut and piled in shocks; and thousands of butterflies are fluttering about, taking the bright little red flags at the mast-heads for flowers, and panting with delight accordingly. [Here the Inimitable, unable to resist the brilliancy out of doors, breaketh off, rusheth to the machines, and plungeth into the sea. Returning, he proceedeth:] Jeffrey is just as he was when he wrote the letter I sent you. No better, and no worse. I had a letter from Napier on Saturday, urging the children's labour subject upon me. But, as I hear from Southwood Smith that the report cannot be printed until the new parliament has sat at the least six weeks, it will be impossible to produce it before the January number. I shall be in town on Saturday morning, and go straight to you. A letter has come from little Hall, begging that when I *do* come to town I will dine there, as they wish to talk about the new story. I have written to say that I will do so on Saturday, and we will go together; but I shall be by no means good company. . . . I have more than half a mind to start a bookseller of my own. I could; with good capital too, as you know; and ready to spend it *G. Varden beware!*"

Small causes of displeasure had been growing out of the *Clock*, and were almost unavoidably incident to the position in which he found himself respecting it. Its discontinuance had become necessary, the strain upon himself being too great without the help from others which experience had shown to be impracticable; but I thought he had not met the difficulty wisely by undertaking, which already he had done, to begin a new story so early as the following March. On his arrival therefore we decided on another plan, with which we went armed that Saturday afternoon to his publishers; and of which the result will be best told by himself. He had returned to Broadstairs the following morning, and next day (Monday, 23 August) he wrote to me in very enthusiastic terms of the share I had taken in what he calls "the development on Saturday afternoon; when I thought Chapman very manly and sensible, Hall morally and physically feeble though perfectly well-intentioned, and both the statement and reception of the project quite triumphant. Didn't you think so too?" A fortnight later, Tuesday, 7 September, the agreement was signed in my chambers, and its terms were to the effect following. The *Clock* was to cease with the close of *Barnaby Rudge*, the respective ownerships continuing as provided; and the new work in twenty numbers, similar to those of *Pickwick* and *Nickleby*, was not to begin until after an interval of twelve months, in November 1842. During its publication he was to receive £200 monthly, to be accounted as part of the expenses; for all which, and all risks incident, the publishers made themselves responsible, under conditions the same as in the *Clock* agreement; except that, out of the profits of each number, they were to have only a fourth, three-fourths going to him, and this arrangement was to hold good until the termination of six months from the completed book, when, upon payment to him of a fourth of the value of all existing stock, they were to have half the future interest. During the twelve months' interval before the book began, he was to be paid £150 each month; but this was to be drawn from his three-fourths of the profits, and in no way to interfere with the monthly payments of £200 while the publication was going on. Such was the * 23 "project," excepting only a provision to be mentioned hereafter against the improbable event of the profits being inadequate to the repayment: and some fear as to the use he was likely to make of the leisure it afforded him seemed to me its only drawback.

That this fear was not ill-founded appears at the close of his next letter. "There's no news" (13 September) "since my last. We are going to dine with Rogers to-day, and with Lady Essex, who is also here. Rogers is much pleased with Lord Ashley, who was offered by Peel a post in the government, but resolutely refused to take office unless Peel pledged himself to factory improvement. Peel 'hadn't made up his mind'; and Lord Ashley was deaf to all other inducements, though they must have been very tempting. Much do I honour him for it. I am in an exquisitely lazy state, bathing, walking, reading, lying in the sun, doing everything but working. This frame of mind is super-induced by the prospect of rest, and the promising arrangements which I owe to you. I am still haunted by visions of America, night and day. To miss this opportunity would be a sad thing. Kate cries dismally if I mention the subject. But, God willing, I think it *must* be managed somehow!"

BOOK THIRD

AMERICA

1841–2. ÆT. 29–30

I

EVE OF THE VISIT

1841

THE notion of America was in his mind, as we have seen, when he first projected the *Clock*, and a very hearty letter from Washington Irving about little Nell and the *Curiosity Shop*, expressing the delight with his writings and the yearnings for himself which had indeed been pouring in upon him for some time from every part of the States, had very strongly revived it. He answered Irving with more than his own warmth: unable to thank him enough for his cordial and generous praise, or to tell him what lasting gratification it had given. "I wish I could find in your welcome letter," he added, "some hint of an intention to visit England. I should love to go with you, as I have gone, God knows how often, into Little Britain, and East Cheap, and Green Arbour Court, and Westminster Abbey. . . . It would gladden my heart to compare notes with you about all those delightful places and people that I used to walk about and dream of in the daytime, when a very small and not-over-particularly-taken-care-of boy." After interchange of these letters the subject was frequently revived; upon his return from Scotland it began to take shape as a thing that somehow or other, at no very distant date, *must be*; and at last, near the end of a letter filled with many unimportant things, the announcement, doubly underlined, came to me.

The decision once taken, he was in his usual fever until its difficulties were disposed of. The objections to separation from the children led at first to the notion of taking them, but this was as quickly abandoned; and what remained to be overcome yielded readily to the kind offices of Macready, the offer of whose home to the little ones during the time of absence, though not accepted to the full extent, gave yet the assurance needed to quiet natural apprehensions. All this, including an arrangement for publication of such notes as might occur to him on the journey, took but a few days; and I was reading in my chambers

a letter he had written the previous day from Broadstairs, when
a note from him reached me, written that morning in London,
to tell me he was on his way to take share of my breakfast. He
had come overland by Canterbury after posting his first letter;
had seen Macready the previous night; and had completed some
part of the arrangements. This mode of rapid procedure was
characteristic of him at all similar times, and will appear in the
few following extracts from his letters.

"Now" (19 September) "to astonish you. After balancing,
considering, and weighing the matter in every point of view,
I HAVE MADE UP MY MIND (WITH GOD'S LEAVE) TO GO TO AMERICA
—AND TO START AS SOON AFTER CHRISTMAS AS IT WILL BE SAFE
TO GO." Further information was promised immediately; and a
request followed, characteristic as any he could have added to
his design of travelling so far away, that we should visit once
more together the scenes of his boyhood. "On the ninth of
October we leave here. It's a Saturday. If it should be fine dry
weather, or anything like it, will you meet us at Rochester, and
stop there two or three days to see all the lions in the surrounding country? Think of this. . . . If you'll arrange to come, I'll
have the carriage down, and Topping; and, supposing news from
Glasgow don't interfere with us, which I fervently hope it will
not, I will ensure that we have much enjoyment."

Three days later than that which announced his resolve, the
subject was resumed. "I wrote to Chapman and Hall, asking
them what they thought of it, and saying I meant to keep a
notebook, and publish it for half a guinea or thereabouts, on
my return. They instantly sent the warmest possible reply, and
said they had taken it for granted I would go, and had been
speaking of it only the day before. I have begged them to make
every inquiry about the fares, cabins, berths, and times of
sailing; and I shall make a great effort to take Kate *and* the children. In that case I shall try to let the house furnished, for six
months (for I shall remain that time in America); and if I succeed,
the rent will nearly pay the expenses out and home. I have
heard of family cabins at £100; and I think one of these is large
enough to hold us all. A single fare, I think, is forty guineas.
I fear I could not be happy if we had the Atlantic between us;
but leaving them in New York while I ran off a thousand miles
or so, would be quite another thing. If I can arrange all my
plans before publishing the *Clock* address, I shall state therein
that I am going: which will be no unimportant consideration,
as affording the best possible reason for a long delay. How I am

to get on without you for seven or eight months, I cannot, upon my soul, conceive. I dread to think of breaking up all our old happy habits for so long a time. The advantages of going, however, appear by steady looking-at so great, that I have come to persuade myself it is a matter of imperative necessity. Kate weeps whenever it is spoken of. Washington Irving has got a nasty low fever. I heard from him a day or two ago."

His next letter was the unexpected arrival which came by hand from Devonshire Terrace, when I thought him still by the sea. "This is to give you notice that I am coming to break-fast with you this morning on my way to Broadstairs. I repeat it, sir,—on my way *to* Broadstairs. For, directly I got Macready's note yesterday, I went to Canterbury, and came on by day-coach for the express purpose of talking with him; which I did between eleven and twelve last night in Clarence Terrace. The American preliminaries are necessarily startling, and, to a gentleman of my temperament, destroy rest, sleep, appetite, and work, unless definitely arranged. Macready has quite decided me in respect of time and so forth. The instant I have wrung a reluctant consent from Kate, I shall take our joint passage in the mail-packet for next January. I never loved my friends so well as now." We had all discountenanced his first thought of taking the children; and, upon this and other points, the experience of our friend, who had himself travelled over the States, was very valuable. His next letter, two days later from Broadstairs, informed me of the result of the Macready conference. "Only a word. Kate is quite reconciled. Anne" (her maid) "goes, and is amazingly cheerful and light of heart upon it. And I think, at present, that it's a greater trial to me than anybody. The 4th of January is the day. Macready's note to Kate was received and acted upon with a perfect response. She talks about it quite gaily, and is satisfied to have nobody in the house but Fred, of whom, as you know, they are all fond. He has got his promotion, and they give him the increased salary from the day on which the minute was made by Baring. I feel so amiable, so meek, so fond of people, so full of gratitudes and reliances, that I am like a sick man. And I am already counting the days between this and coming home again."

He was soon, alas! to be what he compared himself to. I met him at Rochester at the end of September, as arranged; we passed a day and night there; a day and night in Cobham and its neighbourhood, sleeping at the "Leather Bottle"; and a day and night at Gravesend. But we were hardly returned when some slight symptoms of bodily trouble took suddenly graver form, and an illness followed involving the necessity of surgical attendance. This, which, with mention of the helpful courage displayed by him, has before been alluded to, put off necessarily the Glasgow dinner; and he had scarcely left his bedroom when a trouble arose near home which touched him to the depths of the greatest sorrow of his life, and, in the need of exerting himself for others, what remained of his own illness seemed to pass away.

His wife's younger brother had died with the same unexpected suddenness that attended her younger sister's death; and the event had followed close upon the decease of Mrs. Hogarth's mother while on a visit to her daughter and Mr. Hogarth. "As no steps had been taken towards the funeral," he wrote (25 October) in reply to my offer of such service as I could render, "I thought it best at once to bestir myself; and not even you could have saved my going to the cemetery. It is a great trial to me to give up Mary's grave; greater than I can possibly express. I thought of moving her to the catacombs, and saying nothing about it; but then I remembered that the poor old lady is buried next her at her own desire, and could not find it in my heart, directly she is laid in the earth, to take her grandchild away. The desire to be buried next her is as strong upon me now, as it was five years ago; and I *know* (for I don't think there ever was love like that I bear her) that it will never diminish. I fear I can do nothing. Do you think I can? They would move her on Wednesday, if I resolved to have it done. I cannot bear the thought of being excluded from her dust; and yet I feel that her brothers and sisters, and her mother, have a better right than I to be placed beside her. It is but an idea. I neither think nor hope (God forbid!) that our spirits would ever mingle *there*. I ought to get the better of it, but it is very hard. I never contemplated this—and coming so suddenly, and after being ill, it disturbs me more than it ought. It seems like losing her a second time. . . ." "No," he wrote the morning after, "I tried that. No, there is no ground on either side to be had. I must give it up. I shall drive over there, please God, on Thursday morning, before they get there; and look at her coffin."

He suffered more than he let anyone perceive, and was obliged again to keep his room for some days. On 2 November he reported himself as progressing and ordered to Richmond, which, after a week or so, he changed to the "White Hart" at Windsor, where I passed some days with him and Mrs. Dickens, and her

younger sister Georgina; but it was not till near the close of
that month he could describe himself as thoroughly on his legs
again, in the ordinary state on which he was wont to pride himself, bolt upright, staunch at the knees, a deep sleeper, a hearty
eater, a good laugher; and nowhere a bit the worse, "'bating a
little weakness now and then, and a slight nervousness at times."

We had some days of much enjoyment at the end of the year,
when Landor came up from Bath for the christening of his
godson; and the *Britannia*, which was to take the travellers
from us in January, brought over to them in December all
sorts of cordialities, anticipations, and stretchings-forth of
hands, in token of the welcome awaiting them. On New Year's
Eve they dined with me, and I with them on New Year's Day;
when (his house having been taken for the period of his absence
by General Sir John Wilson) we sealed up his wine-cellar, after
opening therein some sparkling Moselle in honour of the ceremony, and drinking it then and there to his happy return. Next
morning (it was a Sunday) I accompanied them to Liverpool,
Maclise having been suddenly stayed by his mother's death;
the intervening day and its occupations have been humorously
sketched in his American book; and on the fourth they sailed.
I never saw the *Britannia* after I stepped from her deck back
to the small steamer that had taken us to her. "How little
I thought" (were the last lines of his first American letter), "the
first time you mounted the shapeless coat, that I should have
such a sad association with its back as when I saw it by the
paddle-box of that small steamer."

II

THE first lines of that letter were written as soon as he got sight of earth again, from the banks of Newfoundland, on Monday, 17 January, the fourteenth day from their departure: even then so far from Halifax that they could not expect to make it before Wednesday night, or to reach Boston until Saturday or Sunday. They had not been fortunate in the passage. During the whole voyage, the weather had been unprecedentedly bad, the wind for the most part dead against them, the wet intolerable, the sea horribly disturbed, the days dark, and the nights fearful. On the previous Monday night it had blown a hurricane, beginning at five in the afternoon and raging all night. His description of the storm is published, and the peculiarities of a steamer's behaviour in such circumstances are hit off as if he had been all his life a sailor. Any but so extraordinary an observer would have described a steamer in a storm as he would have described a sailing-ship in a storm. But any description of the latter would be as inapplicable to my friend's account of the other as the ways of a jackass to those of a mad bull. In the letter from which it was taken, however, there were some things addressed to myself alone. "For two or three hours we gave it up as a lost thing; and with many thoughts of you, and the children, and those others who are dearest to us, waited quietly for the worst. I never expected to see the day again, and resigned myself to God as well as I could. It was a great comfort to think of the earnest and devoted friends we had left behind, and to know that the darlings would not want."

This was not an exaggerated apprehension of a landsman merely. The head engineer, who had been in one or other of the Cunard vessels since they began running, had never seen such stress of weather; and I heard Captain Hewitt himself say afterwards that nothing but a steamer, and one of that strength, could have kept her course and stood it out. A sailing vessel must have beaten off and driven where she could; while through all the fury of that gale they actually made fifty-four miles headlong through the tempest, straight on end, not varying their track in the least.

He stood out against sickness only for the day following that on which they sailed. For the three following days he kept his bed; miserable enough; and had not, until the eighth day of the voyage, six days before the date of his letter, been able to get to work at the dinner-table. What he then observed of his fellow-travellers, and had to tell of their life on board, has been set forth in his *Notes* with delightful humour; but in its first freshness I received it in this letter, and some whimsical passages, then suppressed, there will be no harm in printing now.

"We have 86 passengers; and such a strange collection of beasts never was got together upon the sea, since the days of the Ark. I have never been in the saloon since the first day; the noise, the smell, and the closeness being quite intolerable. I have only been on deck *once*!—and then I was surprised and disappointed at the smallness of the panorama. The sea, running as it does and has done, is very stupendous, and viewed from the air or some great height would be grand no doubt. But seen from the wet and rolling decks, in this weather and these circumstances, it only impresses one giddily and painfully. I was very glad to turn away, and come below again.

"I have established myself, from the first, in the ladies' cabin —you remember it? I'll describe its other occupants, and our way of passing the time, to you.

"First, for the occupants. Kate and I, and Anne—when she is out of bed, which is not often. A queer little Scotch body, a Mrs. P——,[1] whose husband is a silversmith in New York. He married her at Glasgow three years ago, and bolted the day after the wedding; being (which he had not told her) heavily in debt. Since then she has been living with her mother; and she is now going out under the protection of a male cousin, to give him a year's trial. If she is not comfortable at the expiration of that time, she means to go back to Scotland again. A Mrs. B——, about twenty years old, whose husband is on board with her. He is a young Englishman domiciled in New York, and by trade (as well as I can make out) a woollen-draper. They have been married a fortnight. A Mr. and

[1] The initials used here are in no case those of the real names, being employed in every case for the express purpose of disguising the names. Generally the remark is applicable to all initials used in the letters printed in the course of this work. The exceptions are unimportant.

Mrs. C——, marvellously fond of each other, complete the catalogue. Mrs. C——, I have settled, is a publican's daughter, and Mr. C—— is running away with her, the till, the time-piece off the bar mantel-shelf, the mother's gold watch from the pocket at the head of the bed, and other miscellaneous property. The women are all pretty; unusually pretty. I never saw such good faces together, anywhere."

Their "way of passing the time" will be found in the *Notes* much as it was written to me; except that there was one point connected with the card-playing which he feared might overtax the credulity of his readers, but which he protested had occurred more than once. "Apropos of rolling, I have forgotten to mention that in playing whist we are obliged to put the tricks in our pockets, to keep them from disappearing altogether; and that five or six times in the course of every rubber we are all flung from our seats, roll out at different doors, and keep on rolling until we are picked up by stewards. This has become such a matter of course, that we go through it with perfect gravity: and, when we are bolstered up on our sofas again, resume our conversation or our game at the point where it was interrupted." The news that excited them from day to day, too, of which little more than a hint appears in the *Notes*, is worth giving as originally written.

"As for news, we have more of that than you would think for. One man lost fourteen pounds at *vingt-un* in the saloon yesterday, or another got drunk before dinner was over, or another was blinded with lobster sauce spilt over him by the steward, or another had a fall on deck and fainted. The ship's cook was drunk yesterday morning (having got at some salt-water-damaged whisky), and the captain ordered the boatswain to play upon him with the hose of the fire-engine until he roared for mercy—which he didn't get; for he was sentenced to look out, for four hours at a stretch for four nights running, without a greatcoat, and to have his grog stopped. Four dozen plates were broken at dinner. One steward fell down the cabin stairs with a round of beef, and injured his foot severely. Another steward fell down after him, and cut his eye open. The baker's taken ill: so is the pastry-cook. A new man, sick to death, has been required to fill the place of the latter officer, and has been dragged out of bed and propped up in a little house upon deck, between two casks, and ordered (the captain standing over him) to make and roll out pie-crust; which he protests, with tears in his eyes, it is death to him in his bilious state to look at. Twelve dozen of bottled porter has got loose upon deck, and the bottles are rolling about distractedly, overhead. Lord Mulgrave (a handsome fellow, by the by, to look at, and nothing but a good 'un to go) laid a wager with twenty-five other men last night, whose berths, like his, are in the fore-cabin which can only be got at by crossing the deck, that he would reach his cabin first. Watches were set by the captain's, and they sallied forth, wrapped up in coats and storm caps. The sea broke over the ship so violently, that they were *five and twenty minutes* holding on by the hand-rail at the starboard paddle-box, drenched to the skin by every wave, and not daring to go on or come back, lest they should be washed overboard. News! A dozen murders in town wouldn't interest us half as much."

Nevertheless their excitements were not over. At the very end of the voyage came an incident very lightly touched in the *Notes*, but more freely told to me under date of 21 January. "We were running into Halifax Harbour on Wednesday night, with little wind and a bright moon; had made the light at its outer entrance, and given the ship in charge to the pilot; were playing our rubber, all in good spirits (for it had been comparatively smooth for some days, with tolerably dry decks and other unusual comforts), when suddenly the ship STRUCK! A rush upon deck followed of course. The men (I mean the crew! think of this) were kicking off their shoes and throwing off their jackets preparatory to swimming ashore; the pilot was beside himself; the passengers dismayed; and everything in the most intolerable confusion and hurry. Breakers were roaring ahead; the land within a couple of hundred yards; and the vessel driving upon the surf, although her paddles were worked backwards, and everything done to stay her course. It is not the custom of steamers, it seems, to have an anchor ready. An accident occurred in getting ours over the sides; and for half an hour we were throwing up rockets, burning blue lights, and firing signals of distress, all of which remained unanswered, though we were so close to the shore that we could see the waving branches of the trees. All this time, as we veered about, a man was heaving the lead every two minutes; the depths of water constantly decreasing; and nobody self-possessed but Hewitt. They let go the anchor at last, got out a boat, and sent her ashore with the fourth officer, the pilot, and four men aboard, to try and find out where we were. The pilot had no idea; but Hewitt put his little finger upon a certain part of the chart, and was as confident of the exact spot (though he had never been there in his life) as if he had lived there from infancy. The boat's return about an hour afterwards proved him to be quite right. We had got into a place called the Eastern Passage, in a sudden fog and through the pilot's folly. We had struck upon a mud-bank, and driven into a perfect little pond, surrounded by banks and rocks and shoals of all kinds: the only safe speck in the place. Eased by this report, and the assurance that the tide was past the ebb, we turned in at three o'clock in the morning, to lie there all night.''

The next day's landing at Halifax, and delivery of the mails, are sketched in the *Notes*; but not his personal part in what followed. "Then, sir, comes a breathless man who has been already into the ship and out again, shouting my name as he tears along. I stop, arm in arm with the little doctor whom I have taken ashore for oysters. The breathless man introduces himself as The Speaker of the House of Assembly; *will* drag me away to his house; and *will* have a carriage and his wife sent down for Kate, who is laid up with a hideously swollen face. Then he drags me up to the Governor's house (Lord Falkland is the Governor), and then Heaven knows where; concluding with both Houses of Parliament, which happen to meet for the session that very day, and are opened by a mock speech from the throne delivered by the Governor, with one of Lord Grey's sons for his aide-de-camp, and a great host of officers about him. I wish you could have seen the crowds cheering the Inimitable in the streets. I wish you could have seen judges, law-officers, bishops, and law-makers welcoming the Inimitable. I wish you could have seen the Inimitable shown to a great elbow-chair by the Speaker's throne, and sitting alone in the middle of the floor of the House of Commons, the observed of all observers, listening with exemplary gravity to the queerest speaking possible, and breaking in spite of himself into a smile as he thought of this commencement to the Thousand and One stories in reserve for home and Lincoln's Inn Fields and Jack Straw's Castle.—Ah, Forster! when I *do* come back again!——''

He resumed his letter at Tremont House on Saturday, 28 January, having reached Boston that day week at five in the afternoon; and as his first American experience is very lightly glanced at in the *Notes*, a fuller picture will perhaps be welcome. "As the Cunard boats have a wharf of their own at the Custom House, and that a narrow one, we were a long time (an hour at least) working in. I was standing in full fig on the

* 24

paddle-box beside the captain, staring about me, when suddenly, long before we were moored to the wharf, a dozen men came leaping on board at the peril of their lives, with great bundles of newspapers under their arms; worsted comforters (very much the worse for wear) round their necks; and so forth. 'Aha!' says I, 'this is like our London Bridge': believing of course that these visitors were newsboys. But what do you think of their being EDITORS? And what do you think of their tearing violently up to me and beginning to shake hands like madmen? Oh! If you could have seen how I wrung their wrists! And if you could but know how I hated one man in very dirty gaiters, and with very protruding upper teeth, who said to all comers after him, 'So you've been introduced to our friend Dickens—eh?' There was one among them, though, who really was of use; a Doctor S——, editor of the ——. He ran off here (two miles at least), and ordered rooms and dinner. And in course of time Kate and I and Lord Mulgrave (who was going back to his regiment at Montreal on Monday, and had agreed to live with us in the meanwhile) sat down in a spacious and handsome room to a very handsome dinner, 'bating peculiarities of putting on table, and had forgotten the ship entirely. A Mr. Alexander, to whom I had written from England, promising to sit for a portrait, was on board directly we touched the land, and brought us here in his carriage. Then, after sending a present of most beautiful flowers, he left us to ourselves, and we thanked him for it."

What further he had to say of that week's experience, finds its first public utterance here. "How can I tell you," he continues, "what has happened since that first day? How can I give you the faintest notion of my reception here; of the crowds that pour in and out the whole day; of the people that line the streets when I go out; of the cheering when I went to the theatre; of the copies of verses, letters of congratulation, welcomes of all kinds, balls, dinners, assemblies without end? There is to be a public dinner to me here in Boston, next Tuesday, and great dissatisfaction has been given to the many by the high price (three pounds sterling each) of the tickets. There is to be a ball next Monday week at New York, and 150 names appear on the list of the committee. There is to be a dinner in the same place, in the same week, to which I have had an invitation with every known name in America appended to it. But what can I tell you about any of these things which will give you the slightest notion of the enthusiastic greeting they give me, or the cry that runs through the whole country! I have had deputations from the Far West, who have come from more than two thousand miles distance: from the lakes, the rivers, the backwoods, the log-houses, the cities, factories, villages, and towns. Authorities from nearly all the States have written to me. I have heard from the universities, congress, senate, and bodies, public and private, of every sort and kind. 'It is no nonsense, and no common feeling,' wrote Dr. Channing to me yesterday. 'It is all heart. There never was, and never will be, such a triumph.' And it is a good thing, is it not, . . . to find those fancies it has given me and you the greatest satisfaction to think of, at the core of it all? It makes my heart quieter, and me a more retiring, sober, tranquil man to watch the effect of those thoughts in all this noise and hurry, even than if I sat, pen in hand, to put them down for the first time. I feel, in the best aspects of this welcome, something of the presence and influence of that spirit which directs my life, and through a heavy sorrow has pointed upward with unchanging finger for more than four years past. And if I know my heart, not twenty times this praise would move me to an act of folly. . . ."

There were but two days more before the post left for England, and the close of this part of his letter sketched the engagements that awaited him on leaving Boston. "We leave here next Saturday. We go to a place called Worcester, about 75 miles off, to the house of the governor of this place; and stay with him all Sunday. On Monday we go on by railroad about 50 miles farther to a town called Springfield, where I am met by a 'reception committee' from Hartford 20 miles farther, and carried on by the multitude: I am sure I don't know how, but I shouldn't wonder if they appear with a triumphal car. On Wednesday I have a public dinner there. On Friday I shall be obliged to present myself in public again, at a place called Newhaven, about 30 miles farther. On Saturday evening I hope to be at New York; and there I shall stay ten days or a fortnight. You will suppose that I have enough to do. I am sitting for a portrait and for a bust. I have the correspondence of a secretary of state, and the engagements of a fashionable physician. I have a secretary whom I take on with me. He is a young man of the name of Q——; was strongly recommended to me; is most modest, obliging, silent, and willing; and does his work *well*. He boards and lodges at my expense when we travel; and his salary is ten dollars per month—about two pounds five of our English money. There will be dinners and balls at Washington, Philadelphia, Baltimore, and I believe everywhere. In

Canada, I have promised to *play* at the theatre with the officers, for the benefit of a charity. We are already weary, at times, past all expression; and I finish this by means of a pious fraud. We were engaged to a party, and have written to say we are both desperately ill. . . . 'Well,' I can fancy you saying, 'but about his impressions of Boston and the Americans?'—Of the latter, I will not say a word until I have seen more of them, and have gone into the interior. I will only say, now, that we have never yet been required to dine at a table d'hôte; that, thus far, our rooms are as much our own here, as they would be at the 'Clarendon'; but that for an odd phrase now and then—such as *Snap of cold weather;* a *tongue-y man* for a talkative fellow; *Possible ?* as a solitary interrogation; and *Yes ?* for indeed—I should have marked, so far, no difference whatever between the parties here and those I have left behind. The women are very beautiful, but they soon fade; the general breeding is neither stiff nor forward; the good nature, universal. If you ask the way to a place—of some common waterside man, who don't know you from Adam—he turns and goes with you. Universal deference is paid to ladies; and they walk about at all seasons, wholly unprotected. . . . This hotel is a trifle smaller than Finsbury Square; and is made so infernally hot (I use the expression advisedly), by means of a furnace with pipes running through the passages, that we can hardly bear it. There are no curtains to the beds, or to the bedroom windows. I am told there never are, hardly, all through America. The bedrooms are indeed very bare of furniture. Ours is nearly as large as your great room, and has a wardrobe in it of painted wood not larger (I appeal to K) than an English watch-box. I slept in this room for two nights, quite satisfied with the belief that it was a shower bath."

The last addition made to this letter, from which many most vivid pages of the *Notes* (among them the bright quaint picture of Boston streets) were taken with small alteration, bore date 29 January. "I hardly know what to add to all this long and unconnected history. Dana, the author of that *Two Years before the Mast*" (a book which I had praised much to him, thinking it like De Foe), "is a very nice fellow indeed; and in appearance not at all the man you would expect. He is short, mild-looking, and has a care-worn face. His father is exactly like George Cruikshank after a night's jollity—only shorter. The professors at the Cambridge University, Longfellow, Felton, Jared Sparks, are noble fellows. So is Kenyon's friend, Ticknor. Bancroft is a famous man; a straightforward, manly, earnest heart; and talks much of you, which is a great comfort. Doctor Channing I will tell you more of, after I have breakfasted alone with him next Wednesday. . . . Sumner is of great service to me. . . . The president of the Senate here presides at my dinner on Tuesday. Lord Mulgrave lingered with us till last Tuesday (we had our little captain to dinner on the Monday), and then went on to Canada. Kate is quite well, and so is Anne, whose smartness surpasses belief. They yearn for home, and so do I.

"Of course you will not see in the papers any true account of our voyage, for they keep the dangers of the passage, when there are any, very quiet. I observed so many perils peculiar to steamers that I am still undecided whether we shall not return by one of the New York liners. On the night of the storm I was wondering within myself where we should be, if the chimney were blown overboard: in which case, it needs no great observation to discover that the vessel must be instantly on fire from stem to stern. When I went on deck next day, I saw that it was held up by a perfect forest of chains and ropes, which had been rigged in the night. Hewitt told me (when we were on shore, not before) that they had men lashed, hoisted up, and swinging there, all through the gale, getting these stays about it. This is not agreeable—is it?

"I wonder whether you will remember that next Tuesday is my birthday! This letter will leave here that morning.

"On looking back through these sheets, I am astonished to find how little I have told you, and how much I have, even now, in store which shall be yours by word of mouth. The American poor, the American factories, the institutions of all kinds— I have a book, already. There is no man in this town, or in this State of New England, who has not a blazing fire and a meat dinner every day of his life. A flaming sword in the air would not attract so much attention as a beggar in the streets. There are no charity uniforms, no wearisome repetition of the same dull ugly dress, in that blind school. All are attired after their own tastes, and every boy and girl has his or her individuality as distinct and unimpaired as you would find it in their own homes. At the theatres, all the ladies sit in the fronts of the boxes. The gallery are as quiet as the dress circle at dear Drury Lane. A man with seven heads would be no sight at all, compared with one who couldn't read and write.

"I won't speak (I say 'speak'! I wish I could) about the dear precious children, because I know how much we shall hear

* 25

about them when we receive those letters from home for which we long so ardently."

Unmistakably to be seen, in this earliest of his letters, is the quite fresh and unalloyed impression first received by him at this memorable visit; and it is due, as well to himself as to the country which welcomed him, that this should be considered independently of any modification or change it afterwards underwent. Of the fervency and universality of the welcome there could be no doubt, and as little that it sprang from feelings honourable both to giver and receiver. The sources of Dickens's popularity in England were in truth multiplied many-fold in America. The hearty, cordial, and humane side of his genius had fascinated them quite as much; but there was also something beyond this. The cheerful temper that had given new beauty to the commonest forms of life, the abounding humour which had added largely to all innocent enjoyment, the honourable and in those days rare distinction of America which left no home in the Union inaccessible to such advantages, had made Dickens the object everywhere of grateful admiration, for the most part of personal affection. But even this was not all. I do not say it either to lessen or increase the value of the tribute, but to express simply what it was; and there cannot be a question that the young English author, whom by his language the Americans claimed equally for their own, was almost universally regarded by them as a kind of embodied protest against what was believed to be worst in the institutions of England, depressing and overshadowing in a social sense, and adverse to purely intellectual influences. In all their newspapers of every grade at the time, the feeling of triumph over the Mother Country in this particular is predominant. You worship titles, they said, and military heroes, and millionaires, and we of the New World want to show you, by extending the kind of homage that the Old World reserves for kings and conquerors to a young man with nothing to distinguish him but his heart and his genius, what it is we think in these parts worthier of honour than birth or wealth, a title or a sword. Well, there was something in this, too, apart from a mere crowing over the Mother Country. The Americans had honestly more than a common share in the triumphs of a genius, which in more than one sense had made the deserts and wildernesses of life to blossom like the rose. They were entitled to select for a welcome, as emphatic as they might please to render it, the writer who pre-eminently in his generation had busied himself to "detect and save," in human creatures, such sparks of virtue as misery or vice had not availed to extinguish; to discover what is beautiful and comely, under what commonly passes for the ungainly and deformed; to draw happiness and hopefulness from despair itself; and, above all, so to have made known to his own countrymen the wants and sufferings of the poor, the ignorant, and the neglected, that they could be left in absolute neglect no more. "A triumph has been prepared for him," wrote Mr. Ticknor to our dear friend Kenyon, "in which the whole country will join. He will have a progress through the States unequalled since Lafayette's." Daniel Webster told the Americans that Dickens had done more already to ameliorate the condition of the English poor than all the statesmen Great Britain had sent into Parliament. His sympathies are such, exclaimed Doctor Channing, as to recommend him in an especial manner to us. He seeks out that class, in order to benefit them, with whom American institutions and laws sympathise most strongly; and it is in the passions, sufferings, and virtues of the mass that he has found his subjects of most thrilling interest. "He shows that life in its rudest form may wear a tragic grandeur that amidst follies and excesses, provoking laughter or scorn, the moral feelings do not wholly die; and that the haunts of the blackest crime are sometimes lighted up by the presence and influence of the noblest souls. His pictures have a tendency to awaken sympathy with our race, and to change the unfeeling indifference which has prevailed towards the depressed multitude, into a sorrowful and indignant sensibility to their wrongs and woes."

Whatever may be the turn which we are to see the welcome take, by dissatisfaction that arose on both sides, it is well that we should thus understand what in its first manifestations was honourable to both. Dickens had his disappointments, and the Americans theirs; but what was really genuine in the first enthusiasm remained without grave alloy from either; and the letters, as I proceed to give them, will so naturally explain and illustrate the misunderstanding as to require little further comment. I place here on record two letters of invitation to public entertainments in New York which reached him before he quitted Boston. The mere signatures suffice to show how universal was the welcome from that great city of the Union.

"NEW YORK, 24 *January*, 1842.

"*To* CHARLES DICKENS, Esq.

"DEAR SIR,

"The undersigned, for themselves and in behalf of a

wide circle of their fellow-citizens, desire to congratulate you on your safe arrival, and tender to you a sincere and hearty *Welcome*.

"Tho' *personally* unknown, still we can assure you that you will find yourself no stranger among us; that genius with which you have been so signally gifted, and which your pen has directed with such consummate skill in delineating every passion and sympathy and peculiarity of the human mind, has secured to you a passport to all hearts; whilst your happy personifications, and apt illustrations, pointing at every turn a practical and fruitful moral, have rendered your name as familiar to us as household words.

"In testimony of our respect and high regard, and as a slight, tho' thankful, tribute to your genius, we request that you will name as early a day as may suit your convenience, to meet us in this city at a public dinner, where, as elsewhere, it will be our pride and pleasure to express our gratitude to you for the many such intellectual feasts you have so often spread before us.

"We are very truly and cordially your friends,

"S. JONES.
W. T. McCOSEN.
SAM. R. BETTS.
JNO. DUCK.
THEODORE SEDGWICK.
WM. SAML. JOHNSON.
D. S. KENNEDY.
JAMES G. KING.
HENRY BREVOORT.
CHARLES MARCH.
ANTH. BARCLAY.
J. PRESCOTT HALL.
JAS. GALLATIN.
JOHN A. KING.
WILLIAM KENT.
DAVID C. COLDEN.
G. G. HOWLAND.
JAMES J. JONES.
JACOB B. LE ROY.
M. C. PATERSON.

"WASHINGTON IRVING.
PHILIP HONE.
DANL. B. TALLMADGE.
H. S. JONES.
MURRAY HOFFMAN.
HENRY CARY.
CH. KING.
W. C. BRYANT.
W. B. ASTOR.
MATURIN LIVINGSTON.
HAMILTON FISK.
JAS. D. OGDEN.
M. H. GRINNELL.
WM. H. ASPINNALL.
EDWARD CURTIS.
EDWARD JONES.
WM. C. RHINELANDER.
ABM. SCHIRMERSTRONG.
THO. M. LUDLOW.
FITZGREENE HALLECK.
C. W. AUGTS. DAVIS."

"NEW YORK, *January 26, 1842.*

"SIR,

"The citizens of New York having received the agreeable intelligence of your arrival in the United States, and appreciating the value of your labours in the cause of humanity, and the eminently successful exercise of your literary talents, are ambitious to be among the foremost in tendering to you and your lady the hearty welcome which they are persuaded is in reserve for you in all parts of our country. With this object in view we have been appointed a committee in behalf of a large meeting of gentlemen convened for the purpose, to request your attendance at a public ball to be given in this city.

"Mr. Colden, one of our number, will have the honor of presenting this invitation, and is charged with the agreeable duty of presenting their congratulations on your arrival. We shall expect thro' *him* your kind acceptance of this invitation, and your designation of the day when it may suit your convenience to attend.

"We are, Sir,
"With great respect,
"Yr. obt. servants,

"ROBT. H. MORRIS.	"WM. STARR MILLER.
PHILIP HONE.	F. A. TALLMADGE.
JOHN W. FRANCIS.	CHAS. W. SANAFORE.
J. W. EDMONDS.	GEO. P. MORRIS.
DANL. B. TALLMADGE.	SAML. P. LYMAN.
C. W. AUGTS. DAVIS.	WM. TURNER.
JOHN C. CHEESMAN.	H. INMAN.
WM. H. MAXWELL	A. G. WONG.
DUNCAN C. PELL.	R. FAYERWEATHER.
PROSPER M. WETMORE.	W. R. NORTHALL.
A. M. COUZENS.	MARTIN HOFFMAN.
JOHN R. LIVINGSTON, JR.	J. BECKMAN FISH.
WM. B. DEAR.	JAMES PHALEN.
JAMES M. SMITH, JR.	W. H. APPLETON.
WM. GRANDIN.	S. DRAPER, JR.
WADDELL.	F. W. EDMONDS.
D. G. GREGORY.	JNO. S. BARTLETT.
M. H. GRINNELL.	JNO. INMAN.

"*To* CHARLES DICKENS, Esq., etc."

III

SECOND IMPRESSIONS

1842

His second letter, radiant with the same kindly warmth that gave always charm to his genius, was dated from the Carlton Hotel, New York, on 14 February, but its only allusion of any public interest was to the beginning of his agitation of the question of international copyright. He went to America with no express intention of starting this question in any way; and certainly with no belief that such remark upon it as a person in his position could alone be expected to make, would be resented strongly by any sections of the American people. But he was not long left in doubt on this head. He had spoken upon it twice publicly, "to the great indignation of some of the editors here, who are attacking me for so doing, right and left." On the other hand all the best men had assured him, that, if only at once followed up in England, the blow struck might bring about a change in the law; and, yielding to the agreeable delusion that the best men could be a match for the worst in such a matter, he urged me to enlist on his side what force was obtainable, and in particular, as he had made Scott's claim his war-cry, to bring Lockhart into the field. I could not do much, but what I could was done.

Three days later he began another letter; and, as this will be entirely new to the reader, I shall print it as it reached me, with only such omission of matter concerning myself as I think it my duty, however reluctantly, to make throughout these extracts. There was nothing in its personal details, or in those relating to international copyright, available for his *Notes*; from which they were excluded by the two rules he observed in that book, the first to be altogether silent as to the copyright discussion, and the second to abstain from all mention of individuals. But there can be no harm here in violating either rule, for, as Sydney Smith said with his humorous sadness, "we are all dead now."

"Carlton House, New York: Thursday, February Seventeenth,

1842. . . . As there is a sailing-packet from here to England to-morrow which is warranted (by the owners) to be a marvellous fast sailer, and as it appears most probable that she will reach home (I write the word with a pang) before the Cunard steamer of next month, I indite this letter. And lest this letter should reach you before another letter which I despatched from here last Monday, let me say in the first place that I *did* despatch a brief epistle to you on that day, together with a newspaper, and a pamphlet touching the Boz ball; and that I put in the post-office at Boston another newspaper for you containing an account of the dinner, which was just about to come off, you remember, when I wrote to you from that city.

"It was a most superb affair; and the speaking *admirable*. Indeed, the general talent for public speaking here, is one of the most striking of the things that force themselves upon an Englishman's notice. As every man looks on to being a member of Congress, every man prepares himself for it; and the result is quite surprising. You will observe one odd custom—the drinking of sentiments. It is quite extinct with us, but here everybody is expected to be prepared with an epigram as a matter of course.

"We left Boston on the fifth, and went away with the governor of the city to stay till Monday at his house at Worcester. He married a sister of Bancroft's, and another sister of Bancroft's went down with us. The village of Worcester is one of the prettiest in New England. . . . On Monday morning at nine o'clock we started again by railroad and went on to Springfield, where a deputation of two were waiting, and everything was in readiness that the utmost attention could suggest. Owing to the mildness of the weather, the Connecticut River was 'open,' *videlicet* not frozen, and they had a steamboat ready to carry us on to Hartford; thus saving a land-journey of only twenty-five miles, but on such roads at this time of year that it takes nearly twelve hours to accomplish! The boat was very small, the river full of floating blocks of ice, and the depth where we went (to avoid the ice and the current) not more than a few inches. After two hours and a half of this queer travelling we got to Hartford. There, there was quite an English inn; except in respect of the bedrooms, which are always uncomfortable; and the best committee of management that has yet presented itself. They kept us more quiet, and were more considerate and thoughtful, even to their own exclusion, than any I have yet had to deal with. Kate's face being horribly bad, I determined to give her a rest here; and accordingly wrote to get rid of my engagement at Newhaven, on that plea. We remained in this town until the eleventh: holding a formal levee every day for two hours, and receiving on each from two hundred to three hundred people. At five o'clock on the afternoon of the eleventh, we set off (still by railroad) for Newhaven, which we reached about eight o'clock. The moment we had had tea, we were forced to open another levee for the students and professors of the college (the largest in the States), and the townspeople. I suppose we shook hands, before going to bed, with considerably more than five hundred people; and I stood, as a matter of course, the whole time. . . .

"Now, the deputation of two had come on with us from Hartford; and at Newhaven there was another committee; and the immense fatigue and worry of all this, no words can exaggerate. We had been in the morning over jails and deaf and dumb asylums; had stopped on the journey at a place called Wallingford, where a whole town had turned out to see me, and to gratify whose curiosity the train stopped expressly; had had a day of great excitement and exertion on the Thursday (this being Friday); and were inexpressibly worn out. And when at last we got to bed and were 'going' to fall asleep, the choristers of the college turned out in a body, under the window, and serenaded us! We had had, by the by, another serenade at Hartford, from a Mr. Adams (a nephew of John Quincey Adams) and a German friend. *They* were most beautiful singers: and when they began, in the dead of the night, in a long, musical, echoing passage outside our chamber door; singing, in low voices to guitars, about home and absent friends and other topics that they knew would interest us; we were more moved than I can tell you. In the midst of my sentimentality though, a thought occurred to me which made me laugh so immoderately that I was obliged to cover my face with the bedclothes. 'Good Heavens!' I said to Kate, 'what a monstrously ridiculous and commonplace appearance my boots must have, outside the door!' I never *was* so impressed with a sense of the absurdity of boots, in all my life.

"The Newhaven serenade was not so good; though there were a great many voices, and a 'reg'lar' band. It hadn't the heart of the other. Before it was six hours old, we were dressing with might and main, and making ready for our departure: it being a drive of twenty minutes to the steamboat, and the hour of sailing nine o'clock. After a hasty breakfast we started off; and after another levee on the deck (actually on the deck), and 'three times three for Dickens,' moved towards New York.

"I was delighted to find on board a Mr. Felton whom I had known at Boston. He is the Greek Professor at Cambridge, and was going on to the ball and dinner. Like most men of his class whom I have seen, he is a most delightful fellow—unaffected, hearty, genial, jolly; quite an Englishman of the best sort. We drank all the porter on board, ate all the cold pork and cheese, and were very merry indeed. I should have told you, in its proper place, that both at Hartford and Newhaven a regular bank was subscribed, by these committees, for *all* my expenses. No bill was to be got at the bar, and everything was paid for. But as I would on no account suffer this to be done, I stoutly and positively refused to budge an inch until Mr. Q—— should have received the bills from the landlord's own hands, and paid them to the last farthing. Finding it impossible to move me, they suffered me, most unwillingly, to carry the point.

"About half-past 2, we arrived here. In half an hour more, we reached this hotel, where a very splendid suite of rooms was prepared for us; and where everything is very comfortable, and no doubt (as at Boston) *enormously* dear. Just as we sat down to dinner, David Colden made his appearance; and when he had gone, and we were taking our wine, Washington Irving came in alone, with open arms. And here he stopped until ten o'clock at night." (Through Lord Jeffrey, with whom he was connected by marriage, and Macready, of whom he was the cordial friend, we already knew Mr. Colden; and his subsequent visits to Europe led to many years' intimate and much enjoyed intercourse.) "Having got so far, I shall divide my discourse into four points. First, the ball. Secondly, some slight specimens of a certain phase of character in the Americans. Thirdly, international copyright. Fourthly, my life here, and projects to be carried out while I remain.

"Firstly, the ball. It came off last Monday (*vide* pamphlet).

"At a quarter-past 9, exactly" (I quote the printed order of proceeding), "we were waited upon by 'David Colden, Esquire, and General George Morris'; habited, the former, in full ball costume, the latter in the full-dress uniform of Heaven knows what regiment of militia. The general took Kate, Colden gave his arm to me, and we proceeded downstairs to a carriage at the door, which took us to the stage door of the theatre: greatly to the disappointment of an enormous crowd who were besetting the main door, and making a most tremendous hullaballoo. The scene on our entrance was very striking. There were three thousand people present in full dress; from the roof to the floor, the theatre was decorated magnificently; and the light, glitter, glare, show, noise, and cheering, baffle my descriptive powers. We were walked in through the centre of the centre dress-box, the front whereof was taken out for the occasion; so to the back of the stage, where the mayor and other dignitaries received us; and we were then paraded all round the enormous ballroom, twice, for the gratification of the many-headed. That done, we began to dance—Heaven knows how we did it, for there was no room. And we continued dancing until, being no longer able even to stand, we slipped away quietly, and came back to the hotel. All the documents connected with this extraordinary festival (quite unparalleled here) we have preserved; so you may suppose that on this head alone we shall have enough to show you when we come home. The bill of fare for supper is, in its amount and extent, quite a curiosity.

"Now, the phase of character in the Americans which amuses me most, was put before me in its most amusing shape by the circumstances attending this affair. I had noticed it before, and have since, but I cannot better illustrate it than by reference to this theme. Of course I can do nothing but in some shape or other it gets into the newspapers. All manner of lies get there, and occasionally a truth so twisted and distorted that it has as much resemblance to the real fact as Quilp's leg to Taglioni's. But with this ball to come off, the newspapers were if possible unusually loquacious; and in their accounts of me, and my seeings, sayings, and doings on the Saturday night and Sunday before, they describe my manner, mode of speaking, dressing, and so forth. In doing this, they report that I am a very charming fellow (of course), and have a very free and easy way with me; 'which,' say they, 'at first amused a few fashionables'; but soon pleased them exceedingly. Another paper, coming after the ball, dwells upon its splendour and brilliancy; hugs itself and its readers upon all that Dickens saw; and winds up by gravely expressing its conviction, that Dickens was never in such society in England as he has seen in New York, and that its high and striking tone cannot fail to make an indelible impression on his mind! For the same reason I am always represented, whenever I appear in public, as being 'very pale'; 'apparently thunderstruck'; and utterly confounded by all I see. . . . You recognise the queer vanity which is at the root of all this? I have plenty of stories in connection with it to amuse you with when I return.

"Twenty-fourth February.

"It is unnecessary to say . . . that this letter *didn't* come by the sailing-packet, and *will* come by the Cunard boat. After the ball I was laid up with a very bad sore throat, which confined me to the house four whole days; and as I was unable to write, or indeed to do anything but doze and drink lemonade, I missed the ship. . . . I have still a horrible cold, and so has Kate, but in other respects we are all right. I proceed to my third head: the international copyright question.

"I believe there is no country, on the face of the earth, where there is less freedom of opinion on any subject in reference to which there is a broad difference of opinion than in this. . . . There!—I write the words with reluctance, disappointment, and sorrow; but I believe it from the bottom of my soul. I spoke, as you know, of international copyright at Boston; and I spoke of it again at Hartford. My friends were paralysed with wonder at such audacious daring. The notion that I, a man alone by himself, in America, should venture to suggest to the Americans that there was one point on which they were neither just to their own countrymen nor to us, actually struck the boldest dumb! Washington Irving, Prescott, Hoffman, Bryant, Halleck, Dana, Washington Allston—every man who writes in this country is devoted to the question, and not one of them *dares* to raise his voice and complain of the atrocious state of the law. It is nothing that of all men living, I am the greatest loser by it. It is nothing that I have a claim to speak and be heard. The wonder is that a breathing man can be found with temerity enough to suggest to the Americans the possibility of their having done wrong. I wish you could have seen the faces that I saw, down both sides of the table at Hartford, when I began to talk about Scott. I wish you could have heard how I gave it out. My blood so boiled as I thought of the monstrous injustice that I felt as if I were twelve feet high when I thrust it down their throats.

"I had no sooner made that second speech than such an outcry began (for the purpose of deterring me from doing the like in this city) as an Englishman can form no notion of. Anonymous letters; verbal dissuasions; newspaper attacks making Colt (a murderer who is attracting great attention here) an angel by comparison with me; assertions that I was no gentleman, but a mere mercenary scoundrel; coupled with the most monstrous misrepresentations relative to my design and purpose in visiting the United States; came pouring in upon me every day. The dinner committee here (composed of the first gentlemen in America, remember that) were so dismayed, that they besought me not to pursue the subject, *although they every one agreed with me.* I answered that I would. That nothing should deter me. . . . That the shame was theirs, not mine; and that as I would not spare them when I got home, I would not be silenced here. Accordingly, when the night came, I asserted my right, with all the means I could command to give it dignity, in face, manner, or words; and I believe that if you could have seen and heard me, you would have loved me better for it than ever you did in your life.

"The *New York Herald*, which you will receive with this, is the *Satirist* of America; but having a great circulation (on account of its commercial intelligence and early news), it can afford to secure the best reporters. . . . My speech is done, upon the whole, with remarkable accuracy. There are a great many typographical errors in it; and by the omission of one or two words, or the substitution of one word for another, it is often materially weakened. Thus I did not say that I 'claimed' my right, but that I 'asserted' it; and I did not say that I had 'some claim,' but that I had 'a most righteous claim' to speak. But altogether it is very correct."

Washington Irving was chairman of this dinner, and having from the first a dread that he should break down in his speech, the catastrophe came accordingly. Near him sat the Cambridge professor who had come with Dickens by boat from Newhaven, with whom already a warm friendship had been formed that lasted for life, and who has pleasantly sketched what happened. Mr. Felton saw Irving constantly in the interval of preparation, and could not but despond at his daily iterated foreboding of "I shall certainly break down": though, besides the real dread, there was a sly humour which heightened its whimsical horror with an irresistible drollery. But the professor plucked up hope a little when the night came, and he saw that Irving had laid under his plate the manuscript of his speech. During dinner, nevertheless, his old foreboding cry was still heard, and "at last the moment arrived; Mr. Irving rose; and the deafening and long-continued applause by no means lessened his apprehension. He began in his pleasant voice; got through two or three sentences pretty easily, but in the next hesitated; and, after one or two attempts to go on, gave it up, with a graceful allusion to the tournament and the troop of knights all armed and eager for the fray; and ended with the toast CHARLES DICKENS, THE GUEST OF THE NATION. 'There!' said he, as he resumed his seat amid applause as great as had greeted his rising, 'There! I told you I should break down, and I've done it!'" He was in London a few months later, on his way to Spain; and I heard Thomas Moore describe at Rogers's table the difficulty there had been to overcome his reluctance, because of this breakdown, to go to the dinner of the Literary Fund on the occasion of Prince Albert's presiding. "However," said Moore, "I told him only to attempt a few words, and I suggested what they should be, and he said he'd never thought of anything so easy, and he went and did famously." I knew very well, as I listened, that this had *not* been the result; but as the distinguished American had found himself, on this second occasion, not among orators as in New York, but among men as unable as himself to speak in public, and equally able to do better things, he was doubtless more reconciled to his own failure. I have been led to this digression by Dickens's silence on his friend's breakdown. He had so great a love for Irving that it was painful to speak of him as at any disadvantage, and of the New York dinner he wrote only in its connection with his own copyright speeches.

"The effect of all this copyright agitation at least has been to awaken a great sensation on both sides of the subject; the respectable newspapers and reviews taking up the cudgels as strongly in my favour, as the others have done against me. Some of the vagabonds take great credit to themselves (grant us patience!) for having made me popular by publishing my books in newspapers: as if there were no England, no Scotland, no Germany, no place but America in the whole world. A splendid satire upon this kind of trash has just occurred. A man came here yesterday, and demanded, not besought, but demanded, pecuniary assistance; and fairly bullied Mr. Q—— for money. When I came home, I dictated a letter to this effect—that such applications reached me in vast numbers every day; that if I were a man of fortune, I could not render assistance to all who sought it; and that, depending on my own exertion for all the help I could give, I regretted to say I could afford him none. Upon this, my gentleman sits down and writes me that he is an itinerant bookseller; that he is the first man who sold my books in New York; that he is distressed in the city where I am revelling in luxury, that he thinks it rather strange that the man who wrote *Nickleby* should be utterly destitute of feeling; and that he would have me 'take care I don't repent it.' What do you think of *that*?—as Mac would say. I thought it such a good commentary, that I dispatched the letter to the editor of the only English newspaper here, and told him he might print it if he liked.

"I will tell you what *I* should like, my dear friend, always supposing that your judgment concurs with mine; and that you would take the trouble to get such a document. I should like to have a short letter addressed to me, by the principal English authors who signed the international copyright petition, expressive of their sense that I have done my duty to the cause. I am sure I deserve it, but I don't wish it on that ground. It is because its publication in the best journals here would unquestionably do great good. As the gauntlet is down, let us go on. Clay has already sent a gentleman to me express from Washington (where I shall be on the 6th or 7th of next month) to declare his strong interest in the matter, his cordial approval of the 'manly' course I have held in reference to it, and his desire to stir in it if possible. I have lighted up such a blaze that a meeting of the foremost people on the other side (very respectfully and properly conducted in reference to me, personally, I am bound to say) was held in this town t'other night. And it would be a thousand pities if we did not strike as hard as we can, now that the iron is so hot.

"I have come at last, and it is time I did, to my life here, and intentions for the future. I can do nothing that I want to do, go nowhere where I want to go, and see nothing that I want to see. If I turn into the street, I am followed by a multitude. If I stay at home, the house becomes, with callers, like a fair. If I visit a public institution, with only one friend, the directors come down incontinently, waylay me in the yard, and address me in a long speech. I go to a party in the evening, and am so enclosed and hemmed about by people, stand where I will, that I am exhausted for want of air. I dine out, and have to talk about everything and everybody. I go to church for quiet, and there is a violent rush to the neighbourhood of the pew I sit in, and the clergyman preaches *at* me. I take my seat in a railroad car, and the very conductor won't leave me alone. I get out at a station, and can't drink a glass of water, without having a hundred people looking down my throat when I open my mouth to swallow. Conceive what all this is! Then by every post, letters on letters arrive, all about nothing, and all demanding an immediate answer. This man is offended because I won't live in his house; and that man is thoroughly disgusted because I won't go out more than four times in one evening. I have no rest or peace, and am in a perpetual worry.

"Under these febrile circumstances, which this climate especially favours, I have come to the resolution that I will not (so far as my will has anything to do with the matter) accept any more public entertainments or public recognitions of any kind, during my stay in the United States; and in pursuance of this determination I have refused invitations from Philadelphia, Baltimore, Washington, Virginia, Albany, and Providence. Heaven knows whether this will be effectual, but I shall soon see, for on Monday morning the 28th we leave for Philadelphia. There I shall only stay three days. Thence we go to Baltimore, and *there* I shall only stay three days. Thence to Washington, where we may stay perhaps ten days; perhaps not so long. Thence to Virginia, where we may halt for one day; and thence to Charleston, where we may pass a week perhaps; and where we shall very likely remain until your March letters reach us, through David Colden. I had a design of going from Charleston to Columbia in South Carolina, and there engaging a carriage, a baggage-tender and negro boy to guard the same, and a saddle-horse for myself—with which caravan I intended going 'right away,' as they say here, into the West, through the wilds of Kentucky and Tennessee, across the Alleghany Mountains, and so on until we should strike the lakes and could get to Canada. But it has been represented to me that this is a track only known to travelling merchants; that the roads are bad, the country a tremendous waste, the inns log-houses, and the journey one that would play the very devil with Kate. I am staggered, but not deterred. If I find it possible to be done in the time, I mean to do it; being quite satisfied that without some such dash, I can never be a free agent, or see anything worth the telling.

"We mean to return home in a packet-ship—not a steamer. Her name is the *George Washington*, and she will sail from here, for Liverpool, on the seventh of June. At that season of the year, they are seldom more than three weeks making the voyage; and I never will trust myself upon the wide ocean, if it please Heaven, in a steamer again. When I tell you all that I observed on board that *Britannia*, I shall astonish you. Meanwhile, consider two of their dangers. First, that if the funnel were blown overboard, the vessel must instantly be on fire, from stem to stern: to comprehend which consequence, you have only to understand that the funnel is more than 40 feet high, and that at night you see the solid fire two or three feet above its top. Imagine this swept down by a strong wind, and picture to yourself the amount of flame on deck; and that a strong wind is likely to sweep it down you soon learn, from the precautions taken to keep it up in a storm, when it is the first thing thought of. Secondly, each of these boats consumes between London and Halifax 700 tons of coals; and it is pretty clear, from this enormous difference of weight in a ship of only 1200 tons burden in all, that she must be either too heavy when she comes out of port, or too light when she goes in. The daily difference in her rolling, as she burns the coals out, is something absolutely fearful. Add to all this, that by day and night she is full of fire and people, that she has no boats, and that the struggling of that enormous machinery in a heavy sea seems as though it would rend her into fragments—and you may have a pretty considerable damned good sort of a feeble notion that it don't fit nohow; and that it an't calculated to make you smart, overmuch; and that you don't feel special bright; and by no means first-rate; and not at all tonguey (or disposed for conversation); and that however rowdy you may be by natur', it does use you up com-plete, and that's a fact; and makes you quake considerable, and disposed toe damn the ĕngīne!—All of which phrases, I beg to add, are pure Americanisms of the first water.

"When we reach Baltimore, we are in the regions of slavery. It exists there, in its least shocking and most mitigated form; but there it is. They whisper, here (they dare only whisper, you know, and that below their breaths), that on that place, and all through the South, there is a dull gloomy cloud on which the very word seems written. I shall be able to say, one of these days, that I accepted no public mark of respect in any place where slavery was;—and that's something.

"The ladies of America are decidedly and unquestionably beautiful. Their complexions are not so good as those of English-women; their beauty does not last so long; and their figures are very inferior. But they are most beautiful. I still reserve my opinion of the national character—just whispering that I tremble for a Radical coming here, unless he is a Radical on principle, by reason and reflection, and from the sense of right. I fear that if he were anything else, he would return home a Tory. . . . I say no more on that head for two months from this time, save that I do fear that the heaviest blow ever dealt at liberty will be dealt by this country, in the failure of its example to the earth. The scenes that are passing in Congress now, all tending to the separation of the States, fill one with such a deep disgust that I dislike the very name of Washington (meaning the place, not the man), and am repelled by the mere thought of approaching it.

"Twenty-seventh February. Sunday.

"There begins to be great consternation here. in reference to the Cunard packet which (we suppose) left Liverpool on the fourth. She has not yet arrived. We scarcely know what to do with ourselves in our extreme anxiety to get letters from home. I have really had serious thoughts of going back to Boston, alone, to be nearer news. We have determined to remain here until Tuesday afternoon, if she should not arrive before, and to send Mr. Q—— and the luggage on to Philadelphia to-morrow morning. God grant she may not have gone down: but every ship that comes in brings intelligence of a terrible gale (which indeed was felt ashore here) on the night of the fourteenth; and the sea-captains swear (not without some prejudice, of course) that no steamer could have lived through it, supposing her to have been in its full fury. As there is no steam packet to go to England, supposing the *Caledonia* not to arrive, we are obliged to send our letters by the Garrick ship, which sails early to-morrow morning. Consequently I must huddle this up, and dispatch it to the post-office with all speed. I have so much to say that I could fill quires of paper, which renders this sudden pull-up the more provoking.

"I have in my portmanteau a petition for an international copyright law, signed by all the best American writers with Washington Irving at their head. They have requested me to hand it to Clay for presentation, and to back it with any remarks I may think proper to offer. So 'Hoo-roar for the principle, as the moneylender said, ven he vouldn't renoo the bill.'

"God bless you. . . . You know what I would say about home and the darlings. A hundred times God bless you. . . . Fears are entertained for Lord Ashburton also. Nothing has been heard of him."

A brief letter, sent me next day by the minister's bag, was in effect a postscript to the foregoing; and expressed still more strongly the apprehensions his voyage out had impressed him with and which, though he afterwards saw reason greatly to modify them, were not so strange at that time as they appear to us now.

"Carlton House, New York, February twenty-eighth, 1842. . . . The *Caledonia*, I grieve and regret to say, has not arrived. If she left England to her time, she has been four and twenty days at sea. There is no news of her; and on the nights of the fourteenth and eighteenth it blew a terrible gale, which almost justifies the worst suspicions. For myself, I have hardly any hope of her; having seen enough, in our passage out, to convince me that steaming across the ocean in heavy weather is as yet an experiment of the utmost hazard.

"As it was supposed that there would be no steamer whatever for England this month (since in ordinary course the *Caledonia* would have returned with the mails on the 2nd of March) I hastily got the letters ready yesterday and sent them by the *Garrick*; which may perhaps be three weeks out, but is not very likely to be longer. But belonging to the Cunard Company is a boat called the *Unicorn*, which in the summer time plies up the St. Lawrence, and brings passengers from Canada to join the British and North American steamers at Halifax. In the winter she lies at the last-mentioned place; from which news has come this morning that they have sent her on to Boston for the mails; and, rather than interrupt the communication, mean to dispatch her to England in lieu of the poor *Caledonia*. This in itself, by the way, is a daring deed; for she was originally built to run between Liverpool and Glasgow, and is no more designed for the Atlantic than a Calais packet-boat; though she once crossed it, in the summer season.

"You may judge, therefore, what the owners think of the probability of the *Caledonia's* arrival. How slight an alteration in our plans would have made us passengers on board of her!

"It would be difficult to tell you, my dear fellow, what an impression this has made upon our minds, or with what intense anxiety and suspense we have been waiting for your letters from home. We were to have gone South to-day, but linger here until to-morrow afternoon (having sent the secretary and luggage forward) for one more chance of news. Love to dear Macready, and to dear Mac, and every one we care for. It's useless to speak of the dear children. It seems now as though we should never hear of them. . . .

"P.S. Washington Irving is a *great* fellow. We have laughed most heartily together. He is just the man he ought to be. So is Doctor Channing, with whom I have had an interesting correspondence since I saw him last at Boston. Halleck is a merry little man. Bryant a sad one, and very reserved. Washington Allston the painter (who wrote *Monaldi*) is a fine specimen of a glorious old genius. Longfellow, whose volume of poems I have got for you, is a frank accomplished man as well as a fine writer, and will be in town 'next fall.' Tell Macready that I suspect prices here must have rather altered since his time. I paid our fortnight's bill here, last night. We have dined out every day (except when I was laid up with a sore throat), and only had in all four bottles of wine. The bill was £70 English!!!

"You will see, by my other letter, how we have been fêted and feasted; and how there is war to the knife about the international copyright; and how I *will* speak about it, and decline to be put down. . . .

"Oh for news from home! I think of your letters so full of heart and friendship, with perhaps a little scrawl of Charley's or Mamey's, lying at the bottom of the deep sea; and am as full of sorrow as if they had once been living creatures.—Well! they *may* come, yet."

They did reach him, but not by the *Caledonia*. His fears as to that vessel were but too well founded. On the very day when she was due in Boston (18 February) it was learnt in London that she had undergone misadventure; that, her decks having been swept and her rudder torn away, though happily no lives were lost, she had returned disabled to Cork; and that the *Arcadia*, having received her passengers and mails, was to sail with them from Liverpool next day.

Of the main subject of that letter written on the day preceding; of the quite unpremeditated impulse, out of which sprang his advocacy of claims which he felt to be represented in his person; of the injustice done by his entertainers to their guest in ascribing such advocacy to selfishness; and of the graver wrong done by them to their own highest interests, nay, even to their commonest and most vulgar interests, in continuing to reject those claims; I will add nothing now to what all those years ago I laboured very hard to lay before many readers. It will be enough if I here print, from the author's letters I sent out to him by the next following mail in compliance with his wish, this which follows from a very dear friend of his and mine. I fortunately had it transcribed before I posted it to him; Mr. Carlyle having in some haste written from "Templand, 26 March, 1842," and taken no copy.

"We learn by the newspapers that you everywhere in America stir up the question of international copyright, and thereby awaken huge dissonance where all else were triumphant unison for you. I am asked my opinion of the matter, and requested to write it down in words.

"Several years ago, if memory err not, I was one of many English writers, who, under the auspices of Miss Martineau, did already sign a petition to congress praying for an international copyright between the two Nations,—which properly are not two Nations, but one; *indivisible* by parliament, congress, or any kind of human law or diplomacy, being already *united* by Heaven's Act of Parliament, and the everlasting law of Nature and Fact. To that opinion I still adhere, and am like to continue adhering.

"In discussion of the matter before any congress or parliament manifold considerations and argumentations will necessarily arise; which to me are not interesting, nor essential for helping me to a decision. They respect the time and manner in which the thing should be; not at all whether the thing should be or not. In an ancient book, reverenced I should hope on both sides of the Ocean, it was thousands of years ago written down in the most decisive and explicit manner, 'Thou *shalt not* steal.' That thou belongest to a different 'Nation,' and canst steal without being certainly hanged for it, gives thee no permission to steal! Thou shalt *not* in anywise steal at all! So it is written down, for Nations and for Men, in the Law-Book of the Maker of this Universe. Nay, poor Jeremy Bentham and others step in here, and will demonstrate that it is actually our true convenience and expediency not to steal; which I for my share, on the great scale and on the small, and in all conceivable scales and shapes, do also firmly believe it to be. For example, if Nations abstained from stealing, what need were there of fighting,—with its butcherings and burnings, decidedly the most expensive thing in this world? How much more two Nations, which, as I said, are but one Nation; knit in a thousand ways by Nature and Practical Intercourse; indivisible brother elements of the same great SAXONDOM, to which in all honourable ways be long life!

"When Mr. Robert Roy M'Gregor lived in the district of Menteith on the Highland border two centuries ago, he for his part found it more convenient to supply himself with beef by stealing it alive from the adjacent glens, than by buying it killed in the Stirling butchers'-market. It was Mr. Roy's plan of supplying himself with beef in those days, this of stealing it. In many a little 'Congress' in the district of Menteith, there was debating, doubt it not, and much specious argumentation this way and that, before they could ascertain that, really and truly, buying was the best way to get your beef; which however in the long run they did with one assent find it indisputably to be: and accordingly they hold by it to this day."

This brave letter was an important service rendered at a critical time, and Dickens was very grateful for it. But, as time went on, he had other and higher causes for gratitude to its writer. Admiration of Carlyle increased with his years; and there was no one whom in later life he honoured so much, or had a more profound regard for.

IV

PHILADELPHIA AND THE SOUTH

1842

DICKENS's next letter was begun in the "United States Hotel, Philadelphia," and bore date "Sunday, sixth March, 1842." It treated of much dealt with afterwards at greater length in the *Notes*, but the freshness and vivacity of the first impressions in it have surprised me. I do not, however, print any passage here which has not its own interest independently of anything contained in that book. The rule will be continued, as in the portions of letters already given, of not transcribing anything before printed, or anything having even but a near resemblance to descriptions that appear in the *Notes*.

". . . As this is likely to be the only quiet day I shall have for a long time, I devote it to writing to you. We have heard nothing from you yet, and only have for our consolation the reflection that the *Columbia* is now on her way out. No news * 26A had been heard of the *Caledonia* yesterday afternoon, when we left New York. We *were* to have quitted that place last Tuesday, but have been detained there all the week by Kate having so bad a sore throat that she was obliged to keep her bed. We left yesterday afternoon at five o'clock, and arrived here at eleven last night. Let me say, by the way, that this is a very trying climate.

"I have often asked Americans in London which were the better railroads—ours or theirs? They have taken time for reflection, and generally replied, on mature consideration, that they rather thought we excelled; in respect of the punctuality with which we arrived at our stations, and the smoothness of our travelling. I wish you could see what an American railroad is, in some parts where I now have seen them. I won't say I wish you could feel what it is, because that would be an unchristian and savage aspiration. It is never enclosed, or warded off. You walk down the main street of a large town: and, slap-dash, headlong, pell-mell, down the middle of the street; with pigs burrowing, and boys flying kites and playing marbles, and men smoking, and women talking, and children crawling, close to the very rails; there comes tearing along a mad locomotive with its train of cars, scattering a red-hot shower of sparks (from its *wood* fire) in all directions; screeching, hissing, yelling, and panting; and nobody one atom more concerned than if it were a hundred miles away. You cross a turnpike-road; and there is no gate, no policeman, no signal—nothing to keep the way-farer or quiet traveller out of the way, but a wooden arch on which is written in great letters 'Look out for the locomotive.' And if any man, woman, or child, don't look out, why it's his or her fault, and there's an end of it.

"The cars are like very shabby omnibuses—only larger; holding sixty or seventy people. The seats, instead of being placed long-ways, are put crosswise, back to front. Each holds two. There is a long row of these on each side of the caravan, and a narrow passage up the centre. The windows are usually all closed, and there is very often, in addition, a hot, close, most intolerable charcoal stove in a red-hot glow. The heat and close-ness are quite insupportable. But this is the characteristic of all American houses, of all the public institutions, chapels, theatres, and prisons. From the constant use of the hard anthra-cite coal in these beastly furnaces, a perfectly new class of diseases is springing up in the country. Their effect upon an Englishman is briefly told. He is always very sick and very faint; and has an intolerable headache, morning, noon, and night.

"In the ladies' car, there is no smoking of tobacco allowed. All gentlemen who have ladies with them, sit in this car; and it is usually very full. Before it, is the gentlemen's car; which is something narrower. As I had a window close to me yesterday which commanded this gentlemen's car, I looked at it pretty often, perforce. The flashes of saliva flew so perpetually and incessantly out of the windows all the way, that it looked as though they were ripping open feather-beds inside, and letting the wind dispose of the feathers. But this spitting is universal. In the courts of law, the judge has his spittoon on the bench, the counsel have theirs, the witness has his, the prisoner his, and the crier his. The jury are accommodated at the rate of three men to a spittoon (or spit-box as they call it here); and the spectators in the gallery are provided for, as so many men who in the course of nature expectorate without cessation. There are spit-boxes in every steamboat, bar-room, public dining-room, house of office, and place of general resort; no matter what it be. In the hospitals, the students are requested, by placard, to use the boxes provided for them, and not to spit upon the stairs. I have twice seen gentlemen, at evening parties in New York, turn aside when they were not engaged in conversation, and spit upon the drawing-room carpet. And in every bar-room and hotel passage the stone floor looks as if it were paved with open oysters—from the quantity of this kind of deposit which tessellates it all over. . . .

"The institutions at Boston, and at Hartford, are most admirable. It would be very difficult indeed to improve upon them. But this is not so at New York; where there is an ill-managed lunatic-asylum, a bad jail, a dismal workhouse, and a perfectly intolerable place of police-imprisonment. A man is found drunk in the streets, and is thrown into a cell below the surface of the earth; profoundly dark; so full of noisome vapours that when you enter it with a candle you see a ring about the light, like that which surrounds the moon in wet and cloudy weather; and so offensive and disgusting in its filthy odours, that you *cannot bear* its stench. He is shut up within an iron door, in a series of vaulted passages where no one stays; has no drop of water, or ray of light, or visitor, or help of any kind; and there he remains until the magistrate's arrival. If he die (as one man did not long ago) he is half eaten by the rats in an hour's time (as this man was). I expressed, on seeing these places the other night, the disgust I felt, and which it would be impossible to repress. 'Well; I don't know,' said the night constable—that's a national answer by the by—'Well; I don't know. I've had six and twenty young women locked up here together, and beautiful ones too, and that's a fact.' The cell was certainly no larger than the wine-cellar in Devonshire Terrace; at least three feet lower; and stunk like a common sewer. There was one woman in it then. The magistrate begins his examinations at five o'clock in the morning; the watch is set at seven at night; if the prisoners have been given in charge by an officer, they are not taken out before nine or ten; and in the interval they remain in these places, where they could no more be heard to cry for help, in case of a fit or swoon among them, than a man's voice could be heard after he was coffined up in his grave.

"There is a prison in the same city, and indeed in the same building, where prisoners for grave offences await their trial, and to which they are sent back when under remand. It sometimes happens that a man or woman will remain here for twelve months, waiting the result of motions for new trial, and in arrest of judgment, and what not. I went into it the other day: without any notice of preparation, otherwise I find it difficult to catch them in their work-a-day aspect. I stood in a long, high, narrow building, consisting of four galleries one above the other, with a bridge across each, on which sat a turnkey, sleeping or reading as the case might be. From the roof, a couple of wind-sails dangled and drooped, limp and useless; the sky-light being fast closed, and they only designed for summer use. In the centre of the building was the eternal stove; and along both sides of every gallery was a long row of iron doors—looking like furnace doors, being very small, but black and cold as if the fires within had gone out.

"A man with keys appears, to show us round. A good-looking fellow, and, in his way, civil and obliging." (I omit a dialogue of which the substance has been printed, and give only that which appears for the first time here.)

"'Suppose a man's here for twelve months. Do you mean to say he never comes out at that little iron door?'

"'He *may* walk some, perhaps—not much.'

"'Will you show me a few of them?'

"'Ah! All, if you like.'

"He threw open a door, and I looked in. An old man was sitting on his bed, reading. The light came in through a small chink, very high up in the wall. Across the room ran a thick iron pipe to carry off filth; this was bored for the reception of something like a big funnel in shape; and over the funnel was a water-cock. This was his washing-apparatus and water-closet. It was not savoury, but not very offensive. He looked up at me; gave himself an odd, dogged kind of shake; and fixed his eyes on his book again. I came out, and the door was shut and locked. He had been there a month, and would have to wait another month for his trial. 'Has he ever walked out now, for instance?' 'No.' . . .

"'In England, if a man is under sentence of death even, he has a yard to walk in at certain times.'

"'Possible?'

"Making me this answer with a coolness which is perfectly untranslatable and inexpressible, and which is quite peculiar to the soil, he took me to the women's side; telling me, upon the way, all about this man, who, it seems, murdered his wife, and will certainly be hanged. The women's doors have a small square aperture in them; I looked through one, and saw a pretty boy about ten or twelve years old, who seemed lonely and miserable

enough—as well he might. 'What's *he* been doing?' says I.
'Nothing,' says my friend. 'Nothing!' says I. 'No,' says he.
'He's here for safe keeping. He saw his father kill his mother,
and is detained to give evidence against him—that was his
father you saw just now.' 'But that's rather hard treatment for
a witness, isn't it?' 'Well! I don't know. It an't a very rowdy
life, and *that's* a fact.' So my friend, who was an excellent fellow
in his way, and very obliging, and a handsome young man to
boot, took me off to show me some more curiosities; and I was
very much obliged to him, for the place was so hot, and I so
giddy, that I could scarcely stand. . . .

"When a man is hanged in New York, he is walked out of
one of these cells, without any condemned sermon or other
religious formalities, straight into the narrow jail yard, which
may be about the width of Cranbourn Alley. There, a gibbet
is erected, which is of curious construction; for the culprit
stands on the earth with the rope about his neck, which passes
through a pulley in the top of the 'Tree' (see *Newgate Calendar
passim*), and is attached to a weight something heavier than the
man. This weight, being suddenly let go, drags the rope down
with it, and sends the criminal flying up fourteen feet into the
air; while the judge, and jury, and five and twenty citizens
(whose presence is required by the law), stand by, that they may
afterwards certify to the fact. This yard is a very dismal place;
and when I looked at it, I thought the practice infinitely
superior to ours: much more solemn, and far less degrading
and indecent.

"There is another prison near New York which is a house of
correction. The convicts labour in stone quarries near at hand,
but the jail has no covered yards or shops, so that when the
weather is wet (as it was when I was there) each man is shut
up in his own little cell, all the live-long day. These cells, in
all the correction-houses I have seen, are on one uniform plan
—thus:

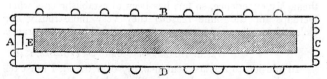

A, B, C, and D, are the walls of the building with windows in
them, high up in the wall. The shaded place in the centre

represents four tiers of cells, one above the other, with doors of grated iron, and a light grated gallery to each tier. Four tiers front to B, and four to D, so that by this means you may be said, in walking round, to see eight tiers in all. The intermediate blank space you walk in, looking up at these galleries; so that, coming in at the door E, and going either to the right or left till you come back to the door again, you see all the cells under one roof and in one high room. Imagine them in number 400, and in every one a man locked up; this one with his hands through the bars of his grate, this one in bed (in the middle of the day, remember), and this one flung down in a heap upon the ground with his head against the bars like a wild beast. Make the rain pour down in torrents outside. Put the everlasting stove in the midst; hot, suffocating, and vaporous, as a witch's cauldron. Add a smell like that of a thousand old mildewed umbrellas wet through, and a thousand dirty clothesbags, musty, moist, and fusty, and you will have some idea—a very feeble one, my dear friend, on my word—of this place yesterday week. You know of course that we adopted our improvements in prison-discipline from the American pattern; but I am confident that the writers who have the most lustily lauded the American prisons, have never seen Chesterton's domain or Tracey's. There is no more comparison between those two prisons of ours, and any I have seen here YET, than there is between the keepers here, and those two gentlemen. Putting out of sight the difficulty we have in England of finding *useful* labour for the prisoners (which of course arises from our being an older country, and having vast numbers of artisans unemployed), our system is more complete, more impressive, and more satisfactory in every respect. It is very possible that I have not come to the best, not having yet seen Mount Auburn. I will tell you when I have. And also when I have come to those inns, mentioned—vaguely rather—by Miss Martineau, where they undercharge literary people for the love the landlords bear them. My experience, so far, has been of establishments where (perhaps for the same reason) they very monstrously and violently overcharge a man whose position forbids remonstrance.

"WASHINGTON, *Sunday, March the Thirteenth*, 1842.

"In allusion to the last sentence, my dear friend, I must tell you a slight experience I had in Philadelphia. My rooms had been ordered for a week, but, in consequence of Kate's illness, only Mr Q——— and the luggage had gone on. Mr Q——— always lives at the table d'hôte, so that while we were in New York our rooms were empty. The landlord not only charged me half the full rent for the time during which the rooms were reserved for us (which was quite right), but charged me also *for board for myself and Kate and Anne, at the rate of nine dollars per day* for the same period, when we were actually living, at the same expense, in New York!!! I *did* remonstrate upon this head; but was coolly told it was the custom (which I have since been assured is a lie), and had nothing for it but to pay the amount. What else could I do? I was going away by the steamboat at five o'clock in the morning; and the landlord knew perfectly well that my disputing an item of his bill would draw down upon me the sacred wrath of the newspapers, which would one and all demand in capitals if THIS was the gratitude of the man whom America had received as she had never received any other man but La Fayette?

"I went last Tuesday to the Eastern Penitentiary near Philadelphia, which is the only prison in the States, or I believe, in the world, on the principle of hopeless, strict, and unrelaxed solitary confinement, during the whole term of the sentence. It is wonderfully kept, but a most dreadful, fearful place. The inspectors, immediately on my arrival in Philadelphia, invited me to pass the day in the jail, and to dine with them when I had finished my inspection, that they might hear my opinion of the system. Accordingly I passed the whole day in going from cell to cell, and conversing with the prisoners. Every facility was given me, and no constraint whatever imposed upon any man's free speech. If I were to write you a letter of twenty sheets, I could not tell you this one day's work; so I will reserve it until that happy time when we shall sit round the table at Jack Straw's—you, and I, and Mac—and go over my diary. I never shall be able to dismiss from my mind the impressions of that day. Making notes of them, as I have done, is an absurdity, for they are written, beyond all power of erasure, in my brain. I saw men who had been there five years, six years, eleven years, two years, two months, two days; some whose term was nearly over, and some whose term had only just begun. Women too, under the same variety of circumstances. Every prisoner who comes into the jail, comes at night; is put into a bath, and dressed in the prison garb; and then a black hood is drawn over his face and head, and he is led to the cell from which he never stirs again until his whole period of confinement has expired. I looked at some of them with the same awe as

I should have looked at men who had been buried alive, and dug up again.

"We dined in the jail: and I told them after dinner how much the sight had affected me, and what an awful punishment it was. I dwelt upon this; for, although the inspectors are extremely kind and benevolent men, I question whether they are sufficiently acquainted with the human mind to know what it is they are doing. Indeed, I am sure they do not know. I bore testimony, as every one who sees it must, to the admirable government of the institution (Stanfield is the keeper: grown a little younger, that's all); and added that nothing could justify such a punishment, but its working a reformation in the prisoners. That for short terms—say two years for the maximum—I conceived, especially after what they had told me of its good effects in certain cases, it might perhaps be highly beneficial; but that, carried to so great an extent, I thought it cruel and unjustifiable; and further, that their sentences for small offences were very rigorous, not to say savage. All this they took like men who were really anxious to have one's free opinion, and to do right. And we were very much pleased with each other, and parted in the friendliest way.

"They sent me back to Philadelphia in a carriage they had sent for me in the morning; and then I had to dress in a hurry, and follow Kate to Cary's the bookseller's where there was a party. He married a sister of Leslie's. There are three Miss Leslies here, very accomplished; and one of them has copied all her brother's principal pictures. These copies hang about the room. We got away from this as soon as we could; and next morning had to turn out at five. In the morning I had received and shaken hands with five hundred people, so you may suppose that I was pretty well tired. Indeed I am obliged to be very careful of myself; to avoid smoking and drinking; to get to bed soon; and to be particular in respect of what I eat. . . . You cannot think how bilious and trying the climate is. One day it is hot summer, without a breath of air; the next, twenty degrees below freezing, with a wind blowing that cuts your skin like steel. These changes have occurred here several times since last Wednesday night.

"I have altered my route, and don't mean to go to Charleston. The country, all the way from here, is nothing but a dismal swamp; there is a bad night of sea-coasting in the journey; the equinoctial gales are blowing hard; and Clay (a most charming fellow, by the by), whom I have consulted, strongly dissuades me. The weather is intensely hot there; the spring fever is coming on; and there is very little to see, after all. We therefore go next Wednesday night to Richmond, which we shall reach on Thursday. There, we shall stop three days; my object being to see some tobacco plantations. Then we shall go by James River back to Baltimore, which we have already passed through, and where we shall stay two days. Then we shall go West at once, straight through the most gigantic part of this continent: across the Alleghany Mountains, and over a prairie.

"STILL AT WASHINGTON, Fifteenth March, 1842. . . . It is impossible, my dear friend, to tell you what we felt, when Mr. Q—— (who is a fearfully sentimental genius, but heartily interested in all that concerns us) came to where we were dining last Sunday, and sent in a note to the effect that the *Caledonia* had arrived! Being really assured of her safety, we felt as if the distance between us and home were diminished by at least one-half. There was great joy everywhere here, for she had been quite despaired of, but *our* joy was beyond all telling. This news came on by express. Last night your letters reached us. I was dining with a club (for I can't avoid a dinner of that sort, now and then), and Kate sent me a note about nine o'clock to say they were here. But she didn't open them—which I consider heroic—until I came home. That was about half-past ten; and we read them until nearly two in the morning.

"I won't say a word about your letters; except that Kate and I have come to a conclusion which makes me tremble in my shoes, for we decide that humorous narrative is your forte, and not statesmen of the Commonwealth. I won't say a word about your news; for how could I in that case, while you want to hear what we are doing, resist the temptation of expending pages on those darling children! . . .

"I have the privilege of appearing on the floor of both houses here, and go to them every day. They are very handsome and commodious. There is a great deal of bad speaking, but there are a great many very remarkable men, in the legislature: such as John Quincey Adams, Clay, Preston, Calhoun, and others: with whom I need scarcely add I have been placed in the friendliest relations. Adams is a fine old fellow—seventy-six years old, but with most surprising vigour, memory, readiness, and pluck. Clay is perfectly enchanting; an irresistible man. There are some very noble specimens, too, out of the West. Splendid men to look at, hard to deceive, prompt to act, lions in energy, Crichtons in varied accomplishments, Indians in quickness of eye and gesture, Americans in affectionate and generous impulse. It would be difficult to exaggerate the nobility of some of these glorious fellows.

"When Clay retires, as he does this month, Preston will become the leader of the Whig party. He so solemnly assures me that the international copyright shall and will be passed, that I almost begin to hope; and I shall be entitled to say, if it be, that I have brought it about. You have no idea how universal the discussion of its merits and demerits has become; or how eager for the change I have made a portion of the people.

"You remember what Webster was, in England. If you *could* but see him here! If you could only have seen him when he called on us the other day—feigning abstraction in the dreadful pressure of affairs of state; rubbing his forehead as one who was a-weary of the world; and exhibiting a sublime caricature of Lord Burleigh. He is the only thoroughly unreal man I have seen on this side of the ocean. Heaven help the President! All parties are against him, and he appears truly wretched. We go to a levee at his house to-night. He has invited me to dinner on Friday, but I am obliged to decline; for we leave, per steamboat, to-morrow night.

"I said I wouldn't write anything more concerning the American people, for two months. Second thoughts are best. I shall not change, and may as well speak out—to *you*. They are friendly, earnest, hospitable, kind, frank, very often accomplished, far less prejudiced than you would suppose, warm-hearted, fervent, and enthusiastic. They are chivalrous in their universal politeness to women, courteous, obliging, disinterested; and, when they conceive a perfect affection for a man (as I may venture to say of myself), entirely devoted to him. I have received thousands of people of all ranks and grades, and have never once been asked an offensive or unpolite question—except by Englishmen, who, when they have been 'located' here for some years, are worse than the devil in his blackest painting. The State is a parent to its people: has a parental care and watch over all poor children, women labouring of child, sick persons, and captives. The common men render you assistance in the streets, and would revolt from the offer of a piece of money. The desire to oblige is universal; and I have never once travelled in a public conveyance, without making some generous acquaintance whom I have been sorry to part from, and who has in many cases come on miles, to see us again. But I don't like the country. I would not live here on any consideration. It goes against the grain with me. It would with you. I think it impossible, utterly impossible, for any Englishman to live here and be happy. I have a confidence that I must be right, because I have everything, God knows, to lead me to the opposite conclusion: and yet I cannot resist coming to this one. As to the causes, they are too many to enter upon here. . . .

"One of two petitions for an international copyright which I brought here from American authors, with Irving at their head, has been presented to the House of Representatives. Clay retains the other for presentation to the Senate after I have left Washington. The presented one has been referred to a committee; the Speaker has nominated as its chairman Mr. Kennedy, member for Baltimore, who is himself an author and notoriously favourable to such a law; and I am going to assist him in his report.

"RICHMOND, IN VIRGINIA. *Thursday Night, March* 17.

"Irving was with me at Washington yesterday, and *wept heartily* at parting. He is a fine fellow, when you know him well; and you would relish him, my dear friend, of all things. We have laughed together at some absurdities we have encountered in company, quite in my vociferous Devonshire Terrace style. The 'Merrikin' government have treated him, he says, most liberally and handsomely in every respect. He thinks of sailing for Liverpool on the 7th of April; passing a short time in London; and then going to Paris. Perhaps you may meet him. If you do, he will know that you are my dearest friend, and will open his whole heart to you at once. His secretary of legation, Mr. Coggleswell, is a man of very remarkable information, a great traveller, a good talker, and a scholar.

"I am going to sketch you our trip here from Washington, as it involves nine miles of a 'Virginny Road.' That done, I must be brief, good brother. . . ."

The reader of the *American Notes* will remember the humorous descriptions of the night steamer on the Potomac, and of the black driver over the Virginia Road. Both were in this letter; which, after three days, he resumed "At Washington again, Monday, March the twenty-first.

"We had intended to go to Baltimore from Richmond, by a place called Norfolk: but one of the boats being under repair, I found we should probably be detained at this Norfolk two days. Therefore we came back here yesterday, by the road we had travelled before; lay here last night; and go on to Baltimore this afternoon, at four o'clock. It is a journey of only two hours and a half. Richmond is a prettily situated town; but, like other towns in slave districts (as the planters themselves admit), has an aspect of decay and gloom which to an unaccustomed eye is *most* distressing. In the black car (for they don't let them sit with the whites) on the railroad as we went there, were a mother and family whom the steamer was conveying away, to sell; retaining the man (the husband and father I mean) on his plantation. The children cried the whole way. Yesterday, on board the boat, a slave owner and two constables were our fellow-passengers. They were coming here in search of two negroes who had run away on the previous day. On the bridge at Richmond there is a notice against fast driving over it, as it is rotten and crazy: penalty—for whites, five dollars; for slaves, fifteen stripes. My heart is lightened as if a great load had been taken from it, when I think that we are turning our backs on this accursed and detested system. I really don't think I could have borne it any longer. It is all very well to say 'be silent on the subject.' They won't let you be silent. They *will* ask you what you think of it; and *will* expatiate on slavery as if it were one of the greatest blessings of mankind. 'It's not,' said a hard, bad-looking fellow to me the other day, 'it's not the interest of a man to use his slaves ill. It's damned nonsense that you hear in England.'—I told him quietly that it was not a man's interest to get drunk, or to steal, or to game, or to indulge in any other vice, but he *did* indulge in it for all that. That cruelty, and the abuse of irresponsible power, were two of the bad passions of human nature, with the gratification of which, considerations of interest or of ruin had nothing whatever to do; and that, while every candid man must admit that even a slave might be happy enough with a good master, all human beings knew that bad masters, cruel masters, and masters who disgraced the form they bore, were matters of experience and history, whose existence was as undisputed as that of slaves themselves. He was a little taken aback by this, and asked me if I believed in the Bible. Yes, I said, but if any man could prove to me that it sanctioned slavery, I would place no further credence in it. 'Well, then,' he said, 'by God, sir, the niggers must be kept down, and the whites have put down the coloured people wherever they have found them.' 'That's the whole question,' said I. 'Yes, and by God,' says he, 'the British had better not stand out on that point when Lord Ashburton comes over, for I never felt so warlike as I do now, and that's a fact.'

I was obliged to accept a public supper in this Richmond, and I saw plainly enough, there, that the hatred which these Southern States bear to us as a nation has been fanned up and revived again by this Creole business, and can scarcely be exaggerated. . . . We were desperately tired at Richmond, as we went to a great many places, and received a very great number of visitors. We appoint usually two hours in every day for this latter purpose, and have our room so full at that period that it is difficult to move or breathe. Before we left Richmond, a gentleman told me, when I really was so exhausted that I could hardly stand, that 'three people of great fashion' were much offended by having been told, when they called last evening, that I was tired and not visible, then, but would be 'at home' from twelve to two next day! Another gentleman (no doubt of great fashion also) sent a letter to me two hours after I had gone to bed preparatory to rising at four next morning, with instructions to the slave who brought it to knock me up and wait for an answer!

"I am going to break my resolution of accepting no more public entertainments, in favour of the originators of the printed document overleaf. They live upon the confines of the Indian territory, some two thousand miles or more west of New York! Think of my dining there! And yet, please God, the festival will come off—I should say about the 12th or 15th of next month. . . ."

The printed document was a series of resolutions, moved at a public meeting attended by all the principal citizens, judges, professors, and doctors of St. Louis, urgently inviting, to that city of the Far West, the distinguished writer, then the guest of America, eulogising his genius, and tendering to him their warmest hospitalities. He was at Baltimore when he closed his letter.

"BALTIMORE. *Tuesday, March 22nd.*

"I have a great diffidence in running counter to any impression formed by a man of Maclise's genius, on a subject he has fully considered." (Referring apparently to some remark by myself on the picture of the Play-scene in *Hamlet* exhibited this year.) "But I quite agree with you about the King in *Hamlet*. Talking of Hamlet, I constantly carry in my great-coat pocket the *Shakespeare* you bought for me in Liverpool. What an unspeakable source of delight that book is to me!

"Your Ontario letter I found here to-night: sent on by the vigilant and faithful Colden, who makes everything having reference to us, or our affairs, a labour of the heartiest love. We devoured its contents, greedily. Good Heaven, my dear fellow, how I miss you! and how I count the time 'twixt this and coming home again. Shall I ever forget the day of our parting at Liverpool! when even —— became jolly and radiant in his sympathy with our separation! Never, never shall I forget that time. Ah! how seriously I thought then, and how seriously I have thought many, many times since, of the terrible folly of ever quarrelling with a true friend, on good for nothing trifles! Every little hasty word that has ever passed between us rose up before me like a reproachful ghost. At this great distance, I seem to look back upon any miserable small interruption of our affectionate intercourse, though only for the instant it has never outlived, with a sort of pity for myself as if I were another creature.

"I have bought another accordion. The steward lent me one, on the passage out, and I regaled the ladies' cabin with my performances. You can't think with what feeling I play *Home Sweet Home* every night, or how pleasantly sad it makes us. . . . And so God bless you. . . . I leave space for a short postscript before sealing this, but it will probably contain nothing. The dear, dear children! what a happiness it is to know that they are in such hands.

"P.S. Twenty-third March, 1842. Nothing new. And all well. I have not heard that the *Columbia* is in, but she is hourly expected. Washington Irving has come on for another leave-taking, and dines with me to-day. We start for the West, at half after eight to-morrow morning. I send you a newspaper, the most respectable in the States, with a very just copyright article."

V

CANAL AND STEAM BOAT JOURNEYS

1842

IT would not be possible that a more vivid or exact impression, than that which is derivable from these letters, could be given of either the genius or the character of the writer. The whole man is here in the supreme hour of his life, and in all the enjoyment of its highest sensations. Inexpressibly sad to me has been the task of going over them, but the surprise has equalled the sadness. I had forgotten what was in them. That they contained, in their first vividness, all the most prominent descriptions of the published book, I knew. But the reproduction of any part of these was not permissible here; and believing that the substance of them had been thus almost wholly embodied in the *American Notes*, when they were lent to assist in its composition, I turned to them with very small expectation of finding anything available for present use. Yet the difficulty has been, not to find but to reject; and the rejection when most unavoidable has not been most easy. Even where the subjects recur that are in the printed volume, there is a freshness of first impressions in the letters that renders it no small trial to act strictly on the rule adhered to in these extracts from them. In the *Notes* there is of course very much, masterly in observation and description, of which there is elsewhere no trace; but the passages amplified from the letters have not been improved, and the manly force and directness of some of their views and reflections, conveyed by touches of a picturesque completeness that no elaboration could give, have here and there not been strengthened by rhetorical additions in the printed work. There is also a charm in the letters which the plan adopted in the book necessarily excluded from it. It will always of course have value as a deliberate expression of the results gathered from the American experiences, but the *personal narrative* of this famous visit to America is in the letters alone. In what way his experiences arose, the desire at the outset to see nothing that was not favourable, the slowness with which adverse impressions were formed, and the eager recognition of every better quality that arose and remained above the fault-finding, are discoverable only in the letters.

Already it is manifest from them that the before-named disappointments, as well of the guest in his entertainers as of the entertainers in their guest, had their beginning in the copyright differences; but it is not less plain that the social dissatisfactions on his side were of even earlier date, and had certainly nothing to do with the country itself. It was objected to him, I well remember, that in making such unfavourable remarks as his published book did on many points, he was assailing the democratic institutions that had formed the character of the nation: but the answer is obvious, that, democratic institutions being universal in America, they were as fully entitled to share in the good as in the bad; and in what he praised, of which there is here abundant testimony, he must be held to have exalted those institutions as much, as he could be held to depreciate them in what he blamed. He never sets himself up in judgment on the entire people. As we see, from the way in which the letters show us that the opinions he afterwards published were formed, he does not draw conclusions upon only half-finished observation; and he refrains throughout from the example too strongly set him, even in the terms of his welcome by the writers of America, of flinging one nation in the other's face. He leaves each upon its own ground. His object in his publication, as in the first impressions recorded here, is to exhibit social influences at work as he saw them himself; and it would surely have been of all bad compliments the worst, when resolving, in the tone and with the purpose of a friend, to make public what he had observed in America, if he had supposed that such a country would take truth amiss.

There is, however, one thing to be especially remembered, as well in reading the letters as in judging of the book which was founded on them. It is a point to which I believe Mr. Emerson directed the attention of his countrymen. Everything of an objectionable kind, whether the author would have it so or not, stands out more prominently and distinctly than matter of the opposite description. The social sin is a more tangible thing than the social virtue. Pertinaciously to insist upon the charities and graces of life, is to outrage their quiet and unobtrusive character; but we incur the danger of extending the vulgarities and indecencies, if we countenance by omitting to expose them. And if this is only kept in view in reading what is here given, the proportion of censure will be found not to overbalance unfairly the admiration and praise.

Apart from such considerations, it is to be also said, the letters, from which I am now printing exactly as they were written, have claims, as mere literature, of an unusual kind. Unrivalled quickness of observation, the rare faculty of seizing out of a multitude of things the thing that is essential, the irresistible play of humour, such pathos as only humorists of this high order possess, and the unwearied unforced vivacity of ever fresh, buoyant, bounding animal spirits, never found more natural, variously easy, or picturesque expression. Written amid such distraction, fatigue, and weariness as they describe, amid the jarring noises of hotels and streets, aboard steamers, on canal boats, and in log huts, there is not an erasure in them. Not external objects only, but feelings, reflections, and thoughts, are photographed into visible forms with the same unexampled ease. They borrow no help from the matters of which they treat. They would have given, to the subjects described, old acquaintance and engrossing interest if they had been about a people in the moon. Of the personal character at the same time self-portrayed, others, whose emotions it less vividly awakens, will judge more calmly and clearly than myself. Yet to myself only can it be known how small were the services of friendship that sufficed to rouse all the sensibilities of this beautiful and noble nature. Throughout our life-long intercourse it was the same. His keenness of discrimination failed him never excepting here, when it was lost in the limitless extent of his appreciation of all kindly things; and never did he receive what was meant for a benefit that he was not eager to return it a hundredfold. No man more truly generous ever lived.

His next letter was begun from "On board the canal boat. Going to Pittsburgh. Monday, March twenty-eighth, 1842"; and the difficulties of rejection, to which reference has just been made, have been nowhere felt by me so much. Several of the descriptive masterpieces of the book are in it, with such touches of original freshness as might fairly have justified a reproduction of them in their first form. Among these are the Harrisburgh coach on its way through the Susquehanah Valley; the railroad across the mountain; the brown-forester of the Mississippi, the interrogative man in pepper-and-salt, and the affecting scene of the emigrants put ashore as the steamer passes up the Ohio. But all that I may here give, bearing any resemblance to what is given in the *Notes*, are, the opening sketch of the small creature on the top of the queer stage coach, to which the printed version fails to do adequate justice; and an experience to which the interest belongs of having suggested the settlement of Eden in *Martin Chuzzlewit*. " . . . We left Baltimore last Thursday the twenty-fourth at half-past eight in the morning, by railroad; and got to a place called York, about twelve. There we dined, and took a stage-coach for Harrisburgh; twenty-five miles further. This stage-coach was like nothing so much as the body of one of the swings you see at a fair set upon four wheels and roofed and covered at the sides with painted canvas. There were twelve *inside*! I, thank my stars, was on the box. The luggage was on the roof; among it, a good-sized dining-table, and a big rocking-chair. We also took up an intoxicated gentleman, who sat for ten miles between me and the coachman; and another intoxicated gentleman who got up behind, but in the course of a mile or two fell off without hurting himself, and was seen in the distant perspective reeling back to the grog-shop where we had found him. There were four horses to this land-ark, of course; but we did not perform the journey until half-past six o'clock that night. . . . The first half of the journey was tame enough, but the second lay through the valley of the Susquehanah (I think I spell it right, but I haven't that *American Geography* at hand) which is very beautiful. . . .

"I think I formerly made a casual remark to you touching the precocity of the youth of this country. When we changed horses on this journey I got down to stretch my legs, refresh myself with a glass of whisky and water, and shake the wet off my great-coat—for it was raining very heavily, and continued to do so, all night. Mounting on my seat again, I observed something lying on the roof of the coach, which I took to be a rather large fiddle in a brown bag. In the course of ten miles or so, however, I discovered that it had a pair of dirty shoes at one end, and a glazed cap at the other; and further observation demonstrated it to be a small boy, in a snuff-coloured coat, with his arms quite pinioned to his sides by deep forcing into his pockets. He was, I presume, a relative or friend of the coachman's, as he lay a-top of the luggage, with his face towards the rain; and, except when a change of position brought his shoes in contact with my hat, he appeared to be asleep. Sir, when we stopped to water the horses, about two miles from Harrisburgh, this thing slowly upreared itself to the height of three foot eight, and fixing its eyes on me with a mingled expression of complacency, patronage, national independence, and sympathy for all outer barbarians and foreigners, said, in shrill piping accents, 'Well now, stranger, I guess you find this a-most like an English a'ternoon,—hey?' It is unnecessary to add that I thirsted for his blood. . . .

"We had all next morning in Harrisburgh, as the canal boat was not to start until three o'clock in the afternoon. The officials called upon me before I had finished breakfast; and as the town is the seat of the Pennsylvanian legislature, I went up to the Capitol. I was very much interested in looking over a number of treaties made with the poor Indians, their signatures being rough drawings of the creatures or weapons they are called after; and the extraordinary drawing of these emblems, showing the queer, unused, shaky manner in which each man has held the pen, struck me very much.

"You know my small respect for our House of Commons. These local legislatures are too insufferably apish of mighty legislation, to be seen without bile: for which reason, and because a great crowd of senators and ladies had assembled in both houses to behold the Inimitable, and had already begun to pour in upon him even in the secretary's private room, I went back to the hotel, with all speed. The members of both branches of the legislature followed me there, however, so we had to hold the usual levee before our half-past one o'clock dinner. We received a great number of them. Pretty nearly every man spat upon the carpet, as usual; and one blew his nose—with his fingers—also on the carpet, which was a very neat one, the room given up to us being the private parlour of the land-lord's wife. This has become so common since, however, that it scarcely seems worth mentioning. Please to observe that the gentleman in question was a member of the Senate, which answers (as they very often tell me) to our House of Lords.

"The innkeeper was the most attentive, civil, and obliging person I ever saw in my life. On being asked for his bill, he said there was no bill: the honour and pleasure, etc., being more than sufficient. I did not permit this, of course; and begged Mr. Q—— to explain to him, that, travelling four strong, I could not hear of it on any account.

"And now I come to the Canal Boat. Bless your heart and soul, my dear fellow,—if you could only see us on board the canal boat! Let me think, for a moment, at what time of the day or night I should best like you to see us. In the morning?

Between five and six in the morning, shall I say? Well! you *would* like to see me, standing on the deck, fishing the dirty water out of the canal with a tin ladle chained to the boat by a long chain; pouring the same into a tin basin (also chained up in like manner); and scrubbing my face with the jack-towel. At night, shall I say? I don't know that you *would* like to look into the cabin at night, only to see me lying on a temporary shelf exactly the width of this sheet of paper when it's open (*I measured it this morning*), with one man above me, and another below; and, in all, eight and twenty in a low cabin, which you can't stand upright in with your hat on. I don't think you would like to look in at breakfast time either, for then these shelves have only just been taken down and put away, and the atmosphere of the place is, as you may suppose, by no means fresh; though there *are* upon the table tea and coffee, and bread and butter, and salmon, and shad, and liver, and steak, and potatoes, and pickles, and ham, and pudding, and sausages; and three and thirty people sitting round it, eating and drinking; and savoury bottles of gin, and whisky, and brandy, and rum, in the bar hard by; and seven and twenty out of the eight and twenty men, in foul linen, with yellow streams from half-chewed tobacco trickling down their chins. Perhaps the best time for you to take a peep would be the present: eleven o'clock in the forenoon: when the barber is at his shaving, and the gentlemen are lounging about the stove waiting for their turns, and not more than seventeen are spitting in concert, and two or three are walking overhead (lying down on the luggage every time the man at the helm calls 'Bridge!'), and I am writing this in the ladies' cabin, which is a part of the gentlemen's, and only screened off by a red curtain. Indeed it exactly resembles the dwarf's private apartment in a caravan at a fair; and the gentlemen, generally, represent the spectators at a penny-a-head. The place is just as clean and just as large as that caravan you and I were in at Greenwich Fair last past. Outside, it is exactly like any canal boat you have seen near the Regent's Park, or elsewhere.

"You never can conceive what the hawking and spitting is, the whole night through. Last night was the worst. *Upon my honour and word* I was obliged, this morning, to lay my fur-coat on the deck, and wipe the half-dried flakes of spittle from it with my handkerchief: and the only surprise seemed to be, that I should consider it necessary to do so. When I turned in last night I put it on a stool beside me, and there it lay, under a cross fire from five men—three opposite; one above; and one below. I make no complaints, and show no disgust. I am looked upon as highly facetious at night, for I crack jokes with everybody near me until we fall asleep. I am considered very hardy in the morning, for I run up, bare-necked, and plunge my head into the half-frozen water, by half-past five o'clock. I am respected for my activity, inasmuch as I jump from the boat to the towing-path, and walk five or six miles before breakfast; keeping up with the horses all the time. In a word, they are quite astonished to find a sedentary Englishman roughing it so well, and taking so much exercise; and question me very much on that head. The greater part of the men will sit and shiver round the stove all day, rather than put one foot before the other. As to having a window open, that's not to be thought of.

"We expect to reach Pittsburgh to-night, between eight and nine o'clock; and there we ardently hope to find your March letters awaiting us. We have had, with the exception of Friday afternoon, exquisite weather, but cold. Clear starlight and moonlight nights. The canal has run, for the most part, by the side of the Susquehanah and Iwanata rivers; and has been carried through tremendous obstacles. Yesterday, we crossed the mountain. This is done *by railroad*. . . . You dine at an inn upon the mountain; and, including the half-hour allowed for the meal, are rather more than five hours performing this strange part of the journey. The people north and 'down east' have terrible legends of its danger; but they appear to be exceedingly careful, and don't go to work at all wildly. There are some queer precipices close to the rails, certainly; but every precaution is taken, I am inclined to think, that such difficulties, and such a vast work, will admit of.

"The scenery, before you reach the mountains, and when you are on them, and after you have left them, is very fine and grand; and the canal winds its way through some deep, sullen gorges, which, seen by moonlight, are very impressive: though immeasurably inferior to Glencoe, to whose terrors I have not seen the smallest *approach*. We have passed, both in the mountains and elsewhere, a great number of new settlements, and detached log-houses. Their utterly forlorn and miserable appearance baffles all description. I have not seen six cabins out of six hundred, where the windows have been whole. Old hats, old clothes, old boards, old fragments of blanket and paper, are stuffed into the broken glass; and their air is misery and desolation. It pains the eye to see the stumps of great trees thickly strewed in every field of wheat; and never to lose the eternal swamp and dull morass, with hundreds of rotten trunks, of elm and pine and sycamore and logwood, steeped in its unwholesome water; where the frogs so croak at night that after dark there is an incessant sound as if millions of phantom teams, with bells, were travelling through the upper air, at an enormous distance off. It is quite an oppressive circumstance, too, to *come* upon great tracks, where settlers have been burning down the trees; and where their wounded bodies lie about, like those of murdered creatures; while here and there some charred and blackened giant rears two bare arms aloft, and seems to curse his enemies. The prettiest sight I have seen was yesterday, when we—on the heights of the mountain, and in a keen wind —looked down into a valley full of light and softness: catching glimpses of scattered cabins; children running to the doors; dogs bursting out to bark; pigs scampering home, like so many prodigal sons; families sitting out in their gardens; cows gazing upward, with a stupid indifference; men in their shirt-sleeves looking on at their unfinished houses, and planning work for to-morrow;—and the train riding on, high above them, like a storm. But I know this is beautiful—very—very beautiful!

". . . I wonder whether you and Mac mean to go to Greenwich Fair! Perhaps you dine at the 'Crown and Sceptre' to-day, for it's Easter Monday—who knows! I wish you drank punch, dear Forster. It's a shabby thing, not to be able to picture you with that cool green glass. . . .

"I told you of the many uses of the word 'fix.' I ask Mr. Q—— on board a steam-boat if breakfast be nearly ready, and he tells me yes he should think so, for when he was last below the steward was 'fixing the tables'—in other words, laying the cloth. When we have been writing, and I beg him (do you remember anything of my love of order, at this distance of time?) to collect our papers, he answers that he'll 'fix 'em presently.' So when a man's dressing he's 'fixing' himself, and when you put yourself under a doctor he 'fixes' you in no time. T'other night, before we came on board here, when I had ordered a bottle of mulled claret and waited some time for it, it was put on table with an apology from the landlord (a lieutenant-colonel) that 'he fear'd it wasn't fixed properly.' And here, on Saturday morning, a Western man, handing the potatoes to Mr. Q—— at breakfast, inquired if he wouldn't take some of 'these fixings' with his meat. I remained as grave as a judge. I catch them looking at me sometimes, and feel that they think I don't take any notice. Politics are very high here; dreadfully strong; handbills, denunciations, invectives, threats, and quarrels. The question is, who shall be the next president. The election comes off in *three years and a-half* from this time."

He resumed his letter, "On board the steam-boat from Pittsburgh to Cincinnati, April the first, 1842. A very tremulous steam-boat, which makes my hand shake. This morning, my dear friend, this very morning, which, passing by without bringing news from England, would have seen us on our way to St. Louis (via Cincinnati and Louisville) with sad hearts and dejected countenances, and the prospect of remaining for at least three weeks longer without any intelligence of those so inexpressibly dear to us—this very morning, bright and lucky morning that it was, a great packet was brought to our bedroom door, from HOME. How I have read and re-read your affectionate, hearty, interesting, funny, serious, delightful, and thoroughly Forsterian Columbia letter, I will not attempt to tell you; or how glad I am that you liked my first; or how afraid I am that my second was not written in such good spirits as it should have been; or how glad I am again to think that my third *was*; or how I hope you will find some amusement from my fourth: this present missive. All this, and more affectionate and earnest words than the post-office would convey at any price, though they have no sharp edges to hurt the stamping-clerk—you will understand, I know, without expression, or attempt at expression. So having got over the first agitation of so much pleasure; and having walked the deck; and being now in the cabin, where one party are playing at chess, and another party are asleep, and another are talking round the stove, and all are spitting; and a persevering bore of a horrible New Englander with a droning voice like a gigantic bee *will* sit down beside me, though I am writing, and talk incessantly, in my very ear, to Kate;—here goes again.

"Let me see. I should tell you, first, that we got to Pittsburgh between eight and nine o'clock of the evening of the day on which I left off at the top of this sheet; and were there received by a little man (a very little man) whom I knew years ago in London. He rejoiceth in the name of D—— G——; and, when I knew him, was in partnership with his father on the Stock Exchange, and lived handsomely at Dalston. They failed in business soon afterwards, and then this little man began to turn to account what had previously been his amusement and accomplishment, by painting little subjects for the fancy shops. So I lost sight of him, nearly ten years ago; and here he turned up t'other day, as a portrait painter in Pittsburgh! He had previously written me a letter which moved me a good deal, by a kind of quiet independence and contentment it breathed, and still a painful sense of being alone, so very far from home. I received it in Philadelphia, and answered it. He dined with us every day of our stay in Pittsburgh (they were only three), and was truly gratified and delighted to find me unchanged—more so than I can tell you. I am very glad to-night to think how much happiness we have fortunately been able to give him.

"Pittsburgh is like Birmingham—at least its townsfolks say so; and I didn't contradict them. It is, in one respect. There is a great deal of smoke in it. I quite offended a man at our yesterday's levee, who supposed I was 'now quite at home,' by telling him that the notion of London being so dark a place was a popular mistake. We had very queer customers at our receptions, I do assure you. Not least among them, a gentleman with his inexpressibles imperfectly buttoned and his waistband resting on his thighs, who stood behind the half-opened door, and could by no temptation or inducement be prevailed upon to come out. There was also another gentleman, with one eye and one fixed gooseberry, who stood in a corner motionless like an eight-day clock, and glared upon me, as I courteously received the Pittsburgians. There were also two red-headed brothers—boys—young dragons rather—who hovered about Kate, and wouldn't go. A great crowd they were, for three days; and a very queer one.

"STILL IN THE SAME BOAT. *April the Second*, 1842.

"Many, many, happy returns of the day. It's only eight o'clock in the morning now, but we mean to drink your health after dinner, in a bumper; and scores of Richmond dinners to us! We have some wine (a present sent on board by our Pittsburgh landlord) in our own cabin; and we shall tap it to good purpose, I assure you; wishing you all manner and kinds of happiness, and a long life to ourselves that we may be partakers of it. We have wondered a hundred times already, whether you and Mac will dine anywhere together, in honour of the day. I say yes, but Kate says no. She predicts that you'll ask Mac, and he won't go. I have not yet heard from him.

"We have a better cabin here, than we had on board the *Britannia*; the berths being much wider, and the den having two doors: one opening on the ladies' cabin, and one upon a little gallery in the stern of the boat. We expect to be at Cincinnati some time on Monday morning, and we carry about fifty passengers. The cabin for meals goes right through the boat, from the prow to the stern, and is very long; only a small portion of it being divided off, by a partition of wood and ground-glass, for the ladies. We breakfast at half after seven, dine at one, and sup at six. Nobody will sit down to any one of these meals, though the dishes are smoking on the board, until the ladies have appeared, and taken their chairs. It was the same in the canal boat.

"The washing department is a little more civilised than it was on the canal, but bad is the best. Indeed the Americans when they are travelling, as Miss Martineau seems disposed to admit, are exceedingly negligent: not to say dirty. To the best of my making out, the ladies, under most circumstances, are content with smearing their hands and faces in a very small quantity of water. So are the men; who superadd to that mode of ablution a hasty use of the common brush and comb. It is quite a practice, too, to wear but one cotton shirt a week, and three or four fine linen *fronts*. Anne reports that this is Mr. Q——'s course of proceeding: and my portrait-painting friend told me that it was the case with pretty nearly all his sitters; so that when he bought a piece of cloth not long ago and instructed the sempstress to make it *all* into shirts, not fronts, she thought him deranged.

"My friend the New Englander, of whom I wrote last night, is perhaps the most intolerable bore on this vast continent. He drones, and snuffles, and writes poems, and talks small philosophy and metaphysics, and never *will* be quiet, under any circumstances. He is going to a great temperance convention at Cincinnati; along with a doctor of whom I saw something at Pittsburgh. The doctor, in addition to being everything that the New Englander is, is a phrenologist besides. I dodge them about the boat. Whenever I appear on deck, I see them bearing down upon me—and fly. The New Englander was very anxious last night that he and I should 'form a magnetic chain,' and magnetise the doctor, for the benefit of all incredulous passengers; but I declined, on the plea of tremendous occupation in the way of letter-writing.

"And speaking of magnetism, let me tell you that the other night at Pittsburgh, there being present only Mr. Q—— and the portrait-painter, Kate sat down, laughing, for me to try my hand upon her. I had been holding forth upon the subject rather luminously, and asserting that I thought I could exercise the influence, but had never tried. In six minutes, I magnetised her into hysterics, and then into the magnetic sleep. I tried again next night, and she fell into the slumber in little more than two minutes. . . . I can wake her with perfect ease; but I confess (not being prepared for anything so sudden and complete) I was on the first occasion rather alarmed. . . . The Western parts being sometimes hazardous, I have fitted out the whole of my little company with LIFE PRESERVERS, which I inflate with great solemnity when we get aboard any boat, and keep, as Mrs. Cluppins did her umbrella in the court of common pleas, ready for use upon a moment's notice. . . ."

He resumed his letter, on "Sunday, April the third," with allusion to a general who had called upon him in Washington with two literary ladies, and had written to him next day for an immediate interview, as "the two LL's" were ambitious of the honour of a personal introduction. "Besides the doctor and the dread New Englander, we have on board that valiant general who wrote to me about the 'two LL's.' He is an old, old man with a weazen face, and the remains of a pigeon-breast in his military surtout. He is acutely gentlemanly and officer-like. The breast has so subsided, and the face has become so strongly marked, that he seems, like a pigeon pie, to show only the feet of the bird outside, and to keep the rest to himself. He is perhaps *the* most horrible bore in this country. And I am quite serious when I say that I do not believe there are, on the whole earth besides, so many intensified bores as in these United States. No man can form an adequate idea of the real meaning of the word, without coming here. There are no particular characters on board with these three exceptions. Indeed I seldom see the passengers but at meal times, as I read and write in our own little state room. . . . I have smuggled two chairs into our crib; and write this on a book upon my knee. Everything is in the neatest order, of course; and my shaving tackle, dressing case, brushes, books, and papers, are arranged with as much precision as if we were going to remain here a month. Thank God we are not.

"The average width of the river rather exceeds that of the Thames at Greenwich. In parts it is much broader; and then there is usually a green island, covered with trees, dividing it into two streams. Occasionally we stop for a few minutes at a small town, or village (I ought to say city, everything is a city here); but the banks are for the most part deep solitudes, overgrown with trees, which, in these western latitudes, are already in leaf and very green. . . .

"All this I see as I write, from the little door into the stern-gallery which I mentioned just now. It don't happen six times in a day that any other passenger comes near it; and, as the weather is amply warm enough to admit of our sitting with it open, here we remain from morning until night: reading, writing, talking. What our theme of conversation is, I need not tell you. No beauty or variety makes us weary less for home. We count the days, and say, 'When May comes, and we can say—*next month*—the time will seem almost gone.' We are never tired of imagining what you are all about. I allow of no calculation for the difference of clocks, but insist on a corresponding minute in London. It is much the shortest way, and best. . . . Yesterday, we drank your health and many happy returns—in wine, after dinner; in a small milk-pot jug of gin-punch, at night. And when I made a temporary table, to hold the little candlestick, of one of my dressing-case trays; cunningly inserted under the mattress of my berth with a weight a-top of it to keep it in its place, so that it made a perfectly exquisite bracket; we agreed, that, please God, this should be a joke at the 'Star and Garter' on the second of April eighteen hundred and forty-three. If your blank *can* be surpassed . . . believe me ours transcends it. My heart gets, sometimes, SORE for home.

"At Pittsburgh I saw another solitary confinement prison: Pittsburgh being also in Pennsylvania. A horrible thought occurred to me when I was recalling all I had seen, that night. *What if ghosts be one of the terrors of the jails?* I have pondered on it often, since then. The utter solitude by day and night; the many hours of darkness; the silence of death; the mind for ever brooding on melancholy themes, and having no relief; sometimes an evil conscience very busy: imagine a prisoner covering up his head in the bedclothes and looking out from time to time, with a ghastly dread of some inexplicable silent figure that always sits upon his bed, or stands (if a thing can be said to stand, that never walks as men do) in the same corner of his cell. The more I think of it, the more certain I feel that not a few of these men (during a portion of their imprisonment at least) are nightly visited by spectres. I did ask one man in this last jail, if he dreamed much. He gave me a most

extraordinary look, and said—under his breath—in a whisper
—'No.' . . .

"CINCINNATI. *Fourth April*, 1842.

"We arrived here this morning: about three o'clock, I believe,
but I was fast asleep in my berth. I turned out soon after six,
dressed, and breakfasted on board. About half after eight, we
came ashore and drove to the hotel, to which we had written on
from Pittsburgh ordering rooms; and which is within a stone's
throw of the boat wharf. Before I had issued an official notifica-
tion that we were 'not at home,' two judges called, on the part
of the inhabitants, to know when we would receive the townspeople. We appointed to-morrow morning, from half-past eleven
to one; arranged to go out with these two gentlemen, to see the
town *at* one; and were fixed for an evening party to-morrow
night at the house of one of them. On Wednesday morning we
go on by the mail-boat to Louisville, a trip of fourteen hours;
and from that place proceed in the next good boat to St. Louis,
which is a voyage of four days. Finding from my judicial friends
(well-informed and most agreeable gentlemen) this morning,
that the prairie travel to Chicago is a very fatiguing one, and
that the lakes are stormy, sea-sicky, and not over-safe at this
season, I wrote by our captain to St. Louis (for the boat that
brought us here goes on there), to the effect that I should not
take the lake route, but should come back here; and should
visit the prairies, which are within thirty miles of St. Louis,
immediately on my arrival there. . . .

"I have walked to the window, since I turned this page, to
see what aspect the town wears. We are in a wide street: paved
in the carriage-way with small white stones, and in the footway
with small red tiles. The houses are for the most part one story
high; some are of wood; others of a clean white brick. Nearly
all have green blinds outside every window. The principal shops
over the way, are, according to the inscriptions over them, a
Large Bread Bakery; a Book Bindery; a Dry Goods Store; and
a Carriage Repository; the last-named establishment looking
very like an exceedingly small retail coal-shed. On the pavement
under our window, a black man is chopping wood; and another
black man is talking (confidentially) to a pig. The public table,
at this hotel, and at the hotel opposite, has just now finished
dinner. The diners are collected on the pavement, on both sides
of the way, picking their teeth, and talking. The day being
warm, some of them have brought chairs into the street. Some

are on three chairs; some on two; and some, in defiance of all
known laws of gravity, are sitting quite comfortably on one:
with three of the chair's legs, and their own two, high up in the
air. The loungers, underneath our window, are talking of a
great Temperance convention which comes off here to-morrow.
Others, about me. Others, about England. Sir Robert Peel is
popular here, with everybody. . . ."

VI

FAR WEST: TO NIAGARA FALLS

1842

THE next letter described his experiences in the Far West, his stay in St. Louis, his visit to a Prairie, the return to Cincinnati, and, after a stage-coach ride from that city to Columbus, the travel thence to Sandusky, and so, by Lake Erie, to the Falls of Niagara. All these subjects appear in the *Notes*, but nothing printed there is repeated in the extracts now to be given. Of the closing passages of his journey, when he turned from Columbus in the direction of home, the story, here for the first time told, is in his most characteristic vein; the account that will be found on the prairie will probably be preferred to what is given in the *Notes*; the Cincinnati sketches are very pleasant; and even such a description as that of the Niagara Falls, of which so much is made in the book, has here an independent novelty and freshness. The first vividness is in his letter. The naturalness of associating, with a grandeur so mighty and resistless, no image or sense but of repose, is best presented suddenly; and, in a few words, we have the material as well as moral beauty of a scene unrivalled in its kind upon the earth. The instant impression we find to be worth more than the eloquent recollection.

The captain of the boat that had dropped them at Cincinnati and gone to St. Louis, had stayed in the latter place until they were able to join and return with him; this letter bears date accordingly, "On board the *Messenger* again. Going from St. Louis back to Cincinnati. Friday, fifteenth April, 1842"; and its first paragraph is an outline of the movements which it afterwards describes in detail. "We remained in Cincinnati one whole day after the date of my last, and left on Wednesday morning the 6th. We reached Louisville soon after midnight on the same night; and slept there. Next day at one o'clock we put ourselves on board another steamer, and travelled on until last Sunday evening the tenth; when we reached St. Louis at about nine o'clock. The next day we devoted to seeing the city. Next day, Tuesday the twelfth, I started off with a party of men (we were fourteen in all) to see a prairie; returned to St. Louis about noon on the thirteenth; attended a soirée and ball—not a dinner—given in my honour that night; and yesterday afternoon at four o'clock we turned our faces homewards. Thank Heaven!

"Cincinnati is only fifty years old, but it is a very beautiful city: I think the prettiest place I have seen here, except Boston. It has risen out of the forest like an Arabian Night city; is well laid out; ornamented in the suburbs with pretty villas; and above all, for this is a very rare feature in America, has smooth turf-plots and well-kept gardens. There happened to be a great temperance festival; and the procession mustered under, and passed, our windows early in the morning. I suppose they were twenty thousand strong, at least. Some of the banners were quaint and odd enough. The ship-carpenters, for instance, displayed on one side of their flag, the good Ship Temperance in full sail; on the other, the Steamer Alcohol blowing up sky-high. The Irishmen had a portrait of Father Mathew, you may be sure. And Washington's broad lower jaw (by the by, Washington had not a pleasant face) figured in all parts of the ranks. In a kind of square at one outskirt of the city, they divided into bodies, and were addressed by different speakers. Drier speaking I never heard. I own that I felt quite uncomfortable to think they could take the taste of it out of their mouths with nothing better than water.

"In the evening we went to a party at Judge Walker's, and were introduced to at least one hundred and fifty first-rate bores, separate and singly. I was required to sit down by the greater part of them, and talk! In the night we were serenaded (as we * 28 usually are in every place we come to), and very well serenaded, I assure you. But we were very much knocked up. I really think my face has acquired a fixed expression of sadness from the constant and unmitigated boring I endure. The 'LL's' have carried away all my cheerfulness. There is a line in my chin (on the right side of the under-lip), indelibly fixed there by the New Englander I told you of in my last. I have the print of a crow's foot on the outside of my left eye, which I attribute to the literary characters of small towns. A dimple has vanished from my cheek, which I felt myself robbed of at the time by a wise legislator. But on the other hand I am really indebted for a good broad grin to P— E—, literary critic of Philadelphia, and sole proprietor of the English language in its grammatical and idiomatical purity; to P— E—, with the shiny straight hair and turned-down shirt collar, who taketh all of us English men of letters to task in print, roundly and uncompromisingly, but told me at the same time that I had 'awakened a new era' in his mind.

"The last 200 miles of the voyage from Cincinnati to St. Louis are upon the Mississippi, for you come down the Ohio to its mouth. It is well for society that this Mississippi, the renowned father of waters, had no children who take after him. It is the beastliest river in the world. . . ." (His description is in the *Notes*.)

"Conceive the pleasure of rushing down this stream by night (as we did last night) at the rate of fifteen miles an hour; striking against floating blocks of timber every instant; and dreading some infernal blow at every bump. The helmsman in these boats is in a little glass-house upon the roof. In the Mississippi, another man stands in the very head of the vessel, listening and watching intently; listening, because they can tell in dark nights by the noise when any great obstruction is at hand. This man holds the rope of a large bell which hangs close to the wheel-house, and whenever he pulls it, the engine is to stop directly, and not to stir until he rings again. Last night, this bell rang at least once in every five minutes; and at each alarm there was a concussion which nearly flung one out of bed. . . . While I have been writing this account, we have shot out of that hideous river, thanks be to God; never to see it again, I hope, but in a nightmare. We are now on the smooth Ohio, and the change is like the transition from pain to perfect ease.

"We had a very crowded levee in St. Louis. Of course the paper had an account of it. If I were to drop a letter in the street, it would be in the newspaper next day, and nobody would think its publication an outrage. The editor objected to my hair, as not curling sufficiently. He admitted an eye; but objected again to dress, as being somewhat foppish, 'and indeed perhaps rather flash.—But such,' he benevolently adds, 'are the differences between American and English taste—rendered more apparent, perhaps, by all the other gentlemen present being dressed in black.' Oh, that you could have seen the other gentlemen! . . .

"A St. Louis lady complimented Kate upon her voice and manner of speaking, assuring her that she should never have suspected her of being Scotch, or even English. She was so obliging as to add that she would have taken her for an American anywhere: which she (Kate) was no doubt aware was a very great compliment, as the Americans were admitted on all hands to have greatly refined upon the English language! I need not tell you that out of Boston and New York a nasal drawl is universal, but I may as well hint that the prevailing grammar is also more than doubtful; that the oddest vulgarisms are received idioms; that all the women who have been bred in slave-states speak more or less like negroes, from having been constantly in their childhood with black nurses; and that the most fashionable and aristocratic (these are two words in great use), instead of asking you in what place you were born, inquire where you 'hail from'!!

"Lord Ashburton arrived at Annapolis t'other day, after a voyage of forty-odd days in heavy weather. Straightway the newspapers state, on the authority of a correspondent who 'rowed round the ship' (I leave you to fancy her condition), that America need fear no superiority from England, in respect of her wooden walls. The same correspondent is 'quite pleased' with the frank manner of the English officers; and patronises them as being, for John Bulls, quite refined. My face, like Haji Baba's, turns upside down, and my liver is changed to water, when I come upon such things, and think who writes and who read them. . . .

"They won't let me alone about slavery. A certain Judge in St. Louis went so far yesterday, that I fell upon him (to the indescribable horror of the man who brought him) and told him a piece of my mind. I said that I was very averse to speaking on the subject here, and always forbore, if possible: but when he pitied our national ignorance of the truths of slavery, I must remind him that we went upon indisputable records, obtained after many years of careful investigation, and at all sorts of self-sacrifice; and that I believed we were much more competent to judge of its atrocity and horror, than he who had been brought up in the midst of it. I told him that I could sympathise with men who admitted it to be a dreadful evil, but frankly confessed their inability to devise a means of getting rid of it: but that men who spoke of it as a blessing, as a matter of course, as a state of things to be desired, were out of the pale of reason; and that for them to speak of ignorance or prejudice was an absurdity too ridiculous to be combated. . . .

"It is not six years ago, since a slave in this very same St. Louis being arrested (I forget for what), and knowing he had no chance of a fair trial be his offence what it might, drew his bowie knife and ripped the constable across the body. A scuffle ensuing, the desperate negro stabbed two others with the same weapon. The mob who gathered round (among whom were men of mark, wealth, and influence in the place) over-powered him by numbers; carried him away to a piece of open ground beyond the city; *and burned him alive*. This, I say, was done within six years in broad day; in a city with its courts, lawyers, tipstaffs, judges, jails, and hangman; and not a hair on the head of one of those men has been hurt to this day. And it is, believe me, it is the miserable, wretched independence in small things; the paltry republicanism which recoils from honest service to an honest man, but does not shrink from every trick, artifice, and knavery in business; that makes these slaves necessary, and will render them so, until the indignation of other countries sets them free.

"They say the slaves are fond of their masters. Look at this pretty vignette (part of the stock-in-trade of a newspaper), and judge how you would feel, when men, looking in your face, told you such tales with the newspaper lying on the table. In all the slave districts, advertisements for runaways are as much matters of course as the announcement of the play for the evening with us. The poor creatures themselves fairly worship English people: they would do anything for them. They are perfectly acquainted with all that takes place in reference to emancipation; and *of course* their attachment to us grows out of their deep devotion to their owners. I cut this illustration out of a newspaper which had a leader in reference to *the abominable and hellish doctrine of Abolition—repugnant alike to every law of God and Nature*. 'I know something,' said a Dr. Bartlett (a very accomplished man), late a fellow-passenger of ours: 'I know something of their fondness for their masters. I live in Kentucky; and I can assert upon my honour, that, in my neighbourhood, it is as common for a runaway slave, retaken, to draw his bowie knife and rip his owner's bowels open, as it is for you to see a drunken fight in London.'

"SAME BOAT, *Saturday, Sixteenth April*, 1842.

"Let me tell you, my dear Forster, before I forget it, a pretty little scene we had on board the boat between Louisville and St. Louis, as we were going to the latter place. It is not much to tell, but it was very pleasant and interesting to witness."

What follows has been printed in the *Notes*, and ought not, by the rule I have laid down, to be given here. But, beautiful as the printed description is, it has not profited by the alteration of some touches, and the omission of others in the first fresh version of it, which, for that reason, I here preserve—one of the most charming soul-felt pictures of character and emotion that ever warmed the heart in fact or fiction. It was, I think, Jeffrey's favourite passage in all the writings of Dickens: and certainly, if anyone would learn the secret of their popularity, it is to be read in the observation and description of this little incident.

"There was a little woman on board, with a little baby; and both little woman and little child were cheerful, good-looking, bright-eyed, and fair to see. The little woman had been passing a long time with a sick mother in New York, and had left her home in St. Louis in that condition in which ladies who truly love their lords desire to be. The baby had been born in her mother's house, and she had not seen her husband (to whom she was now returning) for twelve months: having left him a month or two after their marriage. Well, to be sure, there never was a little woman so full of hope, and tenderness, and love, and anxiety, as this little woman was: and there she was, all the livelong day, wondering whether 'he' would be at the wharf; and whether 'he' had got her letter; and whether, if she sent the baby on shore by somebody else, *'he' would know it, meeting it in the street*: which, seeing that he had never set eyes upon it in his life, was not very likely in the abstract, but was probable enough to the young mother. She was such an artless little creature; and was in such a sunny, beaming, hopeful state; and let out all this matter, clinging close about her heart, so freely; that all the other lady passengers entered into the spirit of it as much as she: and the captain (who heard all about it from his wife) was wondrous sly, I promise you: inquiring, every time we met at table, whether she expected anybody to meet her at St. Louis, and supposing she wouldn't want to go ashore the night we reached it, and cutting many other dry jokes which convulsed all his hearers, but especially the ladies. There was one little, weazen, dried-apple old woman among them, who took occasion to doubt the constancy of husbands under such circumstances of bereavement; and there was another lady (with a lap dog), old enough to moralise on the lightness of human affections, and yet not so old that she could help nursing the baby now and then, or laughing with the rest when the little woman called it by its father's name, and asked it all manner of fantastic questions concerning him, in the joy of her heart. It was something of a blow to the little woman, that when we were within twenty miles of our destination, it became clearly necessary to put the baby to bed; but she got over that with the same good humour, tied a little handkerchief over her little head, and came out into the gallery with the rest. Then, such an oracle as she became in reference to the localities! and such facetiousness as was displayed by the married ladies! and such sympathy as was shown by the single ones! and such peals of laughter as the little woman herself (who would just as soon have cried) greeted every jest with! At last, there were the lights of St. Louis—and here was the wharf—and those were the steps— and the little woman, covering her face with her hands, and laughing, or seeming to laugh, more than ever, ran into her own cabin, and shut herself up tight. I have no doubt that, in the charming inconsistency of such excitement, she stopped her ears lest she should hear 'him' asking for her; but I didn't see her do it. Then a great crowd of people rushed on board, though the boat was not yet made fast, and was staggering about among the other boats to find a landing-place; and everybody looked for the husband, and nobody saw him; when all of a sudden, right in the midst of them—God knows how she ever got there—there was the little woman hugging with both arms round the neck of a fine, good-looking, sturdy fellow! And in a moment afterwards, there she was again, dragging him through the small door of her small cabin, to look at the baby as he lay asleep!—What a good thing it is to know that so many of us would have been quite downhearted and sorry if that husband had failed to come."

He then resumes: but in what follows nothing is repeated that will be found in his printed description of the jaunt to the looking-glass prairie.

"But about the Prairie—it is not, I must confess, so good in its way as this; but I'll tell you all about that too, and leave you to judge for yourself. Tuesday the 12th was the day fixed; and we were to start at five in the morning—sharp. I turned out at four; shaved and dressed; got some bread and milk; and throwing up the window, looked down into the street. Deuce a coach was there, nor did anybody seem to be stirring in the house. I even waited until half-past five; but no preparations being visible then, I left Mr. Q—— to look out, and lay down upon the bed again. There I slept until nearly seven, when I was called. . . . Exclusive of Mr. Q—— and myself, there were twelve of my committee in the party; all lawyers except one. He was an intelligent, mild, well-informed gentleman of my own age—the unitarian minister of the place. With him, and two other companions, I got into the first coach. . . .

"We halted at so good an inn at Lebanon that we resolved to return there at night, if possible. One would scarcely find a better village alehouse of a homely kind in England. During our halt I walked into the village, and met a *dwelling-house* coming down-hill at a good round trot, drawn by some twenty oxen! We resumed our journey as soon as possible, and got upon the looking-glass prairie at sunset. We halted near a solitary log-house for the sake of its water; unpacked the baskets; formed an encampment with the carriages; and dined.

"Now, a prairie is undoubtedly worth seeing—but more that one may say one has seen it, than for any sublimity it possesses in itself. Like most things, great or small, in this country, you hear of it with considerable exaggerations. Basil Hall was really quite right in depreciating the general character of the scenery. The widely-famed Far West is not to be compared with even the tamest portions of Scotland or Wales. You stand upon the prairie, and see the unbroken horizon all round you. You are on a great plain, which is like a sea without water. I am exceedingly fond of wild and lonely scenery, and believe that I have the faculty of being as much impressed by it as any man living. But the prairie fell, by far, short of my preconceived idea. I felt no such emotions as I do in crossing Salisbury Plain. The excessive flatness of the scene makes it dreary, but tame. Grandeur is certainly not its characteristic. I retired from the rest of the party, to understand my own feelings the better; and looked all round, again and again. It was fine. It was worth the ride. The sun was going down, very red and bright; and the prospect looked like that ruddy sketch of Catlin's, which attracted our attention (you remember?); except that there was not so much ground as he represents, between the spectator and the horizon. But to say (as the fashion is, here) that the sight is a landmark in one's existence, and awakens a new set of sensations, is sheer gammon. I would say to every man who can't see a prairie—go to Salisbury Plain, Marlborough Downs, or any of the broad, high, open lands near the sea. Many of them are fully as impressive; and Salisbury Plain is *decidedly* more so.

"We had brought roast fowls, buffalo's tongue, ham, bread, cheese, butter, biscuits, sherry, champagne, lemons and sugar for punch, and abundance of ice. It was a delicious meal: and as they were most anxious that I should be pleased, I warmed

myself into a state of surpassing jollity; proposed toasts from
the coach-box (which was the chair); ate and drank with the
best; and made, I believe, an excellent companion to a very
friendly companionable party. In an hour or so, we packed up,
and drove back to the inn at Lebanon. While supper was preparing, I took a pleasant walk with my Unitarian friend; and
when it was over (we drank nothing with it but tea and coffee)
we went to bed. The clergyman and I had an exquisitely clean
little chamber of our own: and the rest of the party were
quartered overhead. . . .

"We got back to St. Louis soon after twelve at noon; and
I rested during the remainder of the day. The soirée came off at
night, in a very good ball-room at our inn—the 'Planter's
House.' The whole of the guests were introduced to us, singly.
We were glad enough, you may believe, to come away at midnight; and were very tired. Yesterday, I wore a blouse. To-day,
a fur-coat. Trying changes!

"IN THE SAME BOAT.
"*Sunday, Sixteenth April,* 1842.

"The inns in these outlandish corners of the world would
astonish you by their goodness. The 'Planter's House' is as
large as the Middlesex Hospital and built very much on our
hospital plan, with long wards abundantly ventilated, and
plain whitewashed walls. They had a famous notion of sending
up at breakfast-time large glasses of new milk with blocks of
ice in them as clear as crystal. Our table was abundantly
supplied indeed at every meal. One day when Kate and I were
dining alone together, in our own room, we counted sixteen
dishes on the table at the same time.

"The society is pretty rough, and intolerably conceited. All
the inhabitants are young. *I didn't see one grey head in St. Louis.*
There is an island close by, called Bloody Island. It is the
duelling ground of St. Louis; and is so called from the last
fatal duel which was fought there. It was a pistol duel, breast
to breast, and both parties fell dead at the same time. One of
our prairie party (a young man) had acted there as second in
several encounters. The last occasion was a duel with rifles, at
forty paces; and coming home he told us how he had bought
his man a coat of green linen to fight in, woollen being usually
fatal to rifle wounds. Prairie is variously called (on the refinement principle, I suppose) Para*a*rer; par*e*arer; and paro*a*rer.
I am afraid, my dear fellow, you will have had great difficulty
in reading all the foregoing text. I have written it, very labo-

riously, on my knee; and the engine throbs and starts as if the boat were possessed with a devil.

"We went ashore at Louisville this night week, where I left off, two lines above; and slept at the hotel, in which we had put up before. The *Messenger* being abominably slow, we got our luggage out next morning, and started on again at eleven o'clock in the *Benjamin Franklin* mail-boat: a splendid vessel with a cabin more than two hundred feet long, and little state-rooms affording proportionate conveniences. She got in at Cincinnati by one o'clock next morning, when we landed in the dark and went back to our old hotel. As we made our way on foot over the broken pavement, Anne measured her length upon the ground, but didn't hurt herself. I say nothing of Kate's troubles—but you recollect her propensity? She falls into, or out of, every coach or boat we enter; scrapes the skin off her legs; brings great sores and swellings on her feet; chips large fragments out of her ankle-bones; and makes herself blue with bruises. She really has, however, since we got over the first trial of being among circumstances so new and so fatiguing, made a *most admirable* traveller in every respect. She has never screamed or expressed alarm under circumstances that would have fully justified her in doing so, even in my eyes; has never given way to despondency or fatigue, though we have now been travelling incessantly, through a very rough country, for more than a month, and have been at times, as you may readily suppose, most thoroughly tired; has always accommodated her-self, well and cheerfully, to everything; and has pleased me very much, and proved herself perfectly game.

"We remained at Cincinnati all Tuesday the nineteenth, and all that night. At eight o'clock on Wednesday morning the twentieth, we left in the mail stage for Columbus: Anne, Kate, and Mr. Q—— inside; I on the box. The distance is a hundred and twenty miles; the road macadamised; and for an American road, very good. We were three and twenty hours performing the journey. We travelled all night; reached Columbus at seven in the morning; breakfasted; and went to bed until dinner time. At night we held a levee for half an hour, and the people poured in as they always do: each gentleman with a lady on each arm, exactly like the Chorus to *God Save the Queen*. I wish you could see them, that you might know what a splendid comparison this is. They wear their clothes precisely as the chorus people do; and stand—supposing Kate and me to be in the centre of the stage, with our backs to the footlights—just as the company would, on the first night of the season. They shake hands exactly after the manner of the guests at a ball at the Adelphi or the Haymarket; receive any facetiousness on my part, as if there were a stage direction 'all laugh'; and have rather more difficulty in 'getting off' than the last gentlemen, in white pantaloons, polished boots, and berlins, usually display, under the most trying circumstances.

"Next morning, that is to say on Friday the 22nd at seven o'clock exactly, we resumed our journey. The stage from Columbus to this place only running thrice a week, and not on that day, I bargained for an 'exclusive extra' with four horses, for which I paid forty dollars, or eight pounds English: the horses changing as they would if it were the regular stage. To ensure our getting on properly, the proprietors sent an agent on the box; and, with no other company but him and a hamper full of eatables and drinkables, we went upon our way. It is impossible to convey an adequate idea to you of the kind of road over which we travelled. I can only say that it was, at the best, but a track through the wild forest, and among the swamps, bogs, and morasses of the withered bush. A great portion of it was what is called a 'corduroy road': which is made by throwing round logs or whole trees into a swamp, and leaving them to settle there. Good Heaven! if you only felt one of the least of the jolts with which the coach falls from log to log! It is like nothing but going up a steep flight of stairs in an omnibus. Now the coach flung us in a heap on its floor, and now crushed our heads against its roof. Now one side of it was deep in the mire, and we were holding on to the other. Now it was lying on the horses' tails, and now again upon its own back. But it never, never, was in any position, attitude, or kind of motion to which we are accustomed in coaches; or made the smallest approach to our experience of the proceedings of any sort of vehicle that goes on wheels. Still, the day was beautiful, the air delicious, and we were *alone*: with no tobacco spittle, or eternal prosy conversation about dollars and politics (the only two subjects they ever converse about, or can converse upon) to bore us. We really enjoyed it; made a joke of the being knocked about; and were quite merry. At two o'clock we stopped in the wood to open our hamper and dine; and we drank to our darlings and all friends at home. Then we started again and

went on until ten o'clock at night: when we reached a place
called Lower Sandusky, sixty-two miles from our starting point.
The last three hours of the journey were not very pleasant, for
it lightened—awfully: every flash very vivid, very blue, and
very long: and, the wood being so dense that the branches on
either side of the track rattled and broke *against* the coach, it
was rather a dangerous neighbourhood for a thunderstorm.

"The inn at which we halted was a rough log-house. The
people were all abed, and we had to knock them up. We had the
queerest sleeping-room, with two doors, one opposite the other;
both opening directly on the wild black country, and neither
having any lock or bolt. The effect of these opposite doors was,
that one was always blowing the other open: an ingenuity in
the art of building, which I don't remember to have met with
before. You should have seen me, in my shirt, blockading them
with portmanteaux, and desperately endeavouring to make
the room tidy! But the blockading was really needful, for in
my dressing-case I have about £250 in gold; and for the amount
of the middle figure in that scarce metal, there are not a few
men in the West who would murder their fathers. Apropos of
this golden store, consider at your leisure the strange state of
things in this country. It has no money; really *no money*. The
bank paper won't pass; the newspapers are full of advertisements from tradesmen who sell by barter; and American gold
is not to be had, or purchased. I bought sovereigns, English
sovereigns, at first: but as I could get none of them at Cincinnati to this day, I have had to purchase French gold;
20-franc pieces; with which I am travelling as if I were
in Paris!

"But let's go back to Lower Sandusky. Mr. Q—— went to bed
up in the roof of the log-house somewhere, but was so beset by
bugs that he got up after an hour and *lay in the coach* . . .
where he was obliged to wait till breakfast time. We breakfasted,
driver and all, in the one common room. It was papered with
newspapers, and was as rough a place as need be. At half-past
seven we started again, and we reached Sandusky at six o'clock
yesterday afternoon. It is on Lake Erie, twenty-four hours'
journey by steam-boat from Buffalo. We found no boat here,
nor has there been one, since. We are waiting, with everything
packed up, ready to start on the shortest notice; and are
anxiously looking out for smoke in the distance.

"There was an old gentleman in the log inn at Lower
Sandusky who treats with the Indians on the part of the

American Government, and has just concluded a treaty with the Wyandot Indians at that place to remove next year to some land provided for them west of the Mississippi: a little way beyond St. Louis. He described his negotiation to me, and their reluctance to go, exceedingly well. They are a fine people, but degraded and broken down. If you could see any of their men and women on a racecourse in England, you would not know them from gipsies.

"We are in a small house here, but a very comfortable one, and the people are exceedingly obliging. Their demeanour in these country parts is invariably morose, sullen, clownish, and repulsive. I should think there is not, on the face of the earth, a people so entirely destitute of humour, vivacity, or the capacity of enjoyment. It is most remarkable. I am quite serious when I say that I have not heard a hearty laugh these six weeks, except my own; nor have I seen a merry face on any shoulders but a black man's. Lounging listlessly about, idling in bar-rooms; smoking; spitting; and lolling on the pavement in rocking-chairs, outside the shop doors; are the only recreations. I don't think the national shrewdness extends beyond the Yankees; that is, the Eastern men. The rest are heavy, dull, and ignorant. Our landlord here is from the East. He is a handsome, obliging, civil fellow. He comes into the room with his hat on; spits in the fire-place as he talks; sits down on the sofa with his hat on; pulls out his newspaper, and reads: but to all this I am accustomed. He is anxious to please and that is enough.

"We are wishing very much for a boat; for we hope to find our letters at Buffalo. It is half-past one; and as there is no boat in sight, we are fain (sorely against our wills) to order an early dinner.

"*Tuesday, April Twenty-sixth*, 1842.
"NIAGARA FALLS!!! (UPON THE ENGLISH SIDE).

"I don't know at what length I might have written you from Sandusky, my beloved friend, if a steamer had not come in sight just as I finished the last unintelligible sheet (oh! the ink in these parts!): whereupon I was obliged to pack up bag and baggage, to swallow a hasty apology for a dinner, and to hurry my train on board with all the speed I might. She was a fine steamship, four hundred tons burden, name the *Constitution*, had very few passengers on board, and had bountiful and handsome accommodation. It's all very fine talking about

Lake Erie, but it won't do for persons who are liable to sea-sickness. We were all sick. It's almost as bad in that respect as the Atlantic. The waves are very short, and horribly constant. We reached Buffalo at six this morning; went ashore to breakfast; sent to the post-office forthwith; and received—oh! who or what can say with how much pleasure and what unspeakable delight!—our English letters!

"We lay all Sunday night at a town (and a beautiful town too) called Cleveland; on Lake Erie. The people poured on board, in crowds, by six on Monday morning, to see me; and a party of 'gentlemen' actually planted themselves before our little cabin, and stared in at the door and windows *while I was washing, and Kate lay in bed.* I was so incensed at this, and at a certain newspaper published in that town which I had accidentally seen in Sandusky (advocating war with England to the death, saying that Britain must be 'whipped again,' and promising all true Americans that within two years they should sing *Yankee Doodle* in Hyde Park and *Hail Columbia* in the courts of Westminster), that when the mayor came on board to present himself to me, according to custom, I refused to see him, and bade Mr. Q—— tell him why and wherefore. His honour took it very coolly, and retired to the top of the wharf, with a big stick and a whittling knife, with which he worked so lustily (staring at the closed door of our cabin all the time) that long before the boat left the big stick was no bigger than a cribbage peg!

"I never in my life was in such a state of excitement as coming from Buffalo here, this morning. You come by railroad; and are nigh two hours upon the way. I looked out for the spray, and listened for the roar, as far beyond the bounds of possibility, as though, landing in Liverpool, I were to listen for the music of your pleasant voice in Lincoln's Inn Fields. At last, when the train stopped, I saw two great white clouds rising up from the depths of the earth—nothing more. They rose up slowly, gently, majestically, into the air. I dragged Kate down a deep and slippery path leading to the ferry boat; bullied Anne for not coming fast enough; perspired at every pore; and felt, it is impossible to say how, as the sound grew louder and louder in my ears, and yet nothing could be seen for the mist.

"There were two English officers with us (ah! what *gentlemen*, what noblemen of nature they seemed), and they hurried off with me; leaving Kate and Anne on a crag of ice; and clambered after me over the rocks at the foot of the small Fall, while the ferryman was getting the boat ready. I was not disappointed—

but I could make out nothing. In an instant, I was blinded by the spray, and wet to the skin. I saw the water tearing madly down from some immense height, but could get no idea of shape, or situation, or anything but vague immensity. But when we were seated in the boat, and crossing at the very foot of the cataract—then I began to feel what it was. Directly I had changed my clothes at the inn I went out again, taking Kate with me; and hurried to the Horseshoe Fall. I went down alone, into the very basin. It would be hard for a man to stand nearer God than he does there. There was a bright rainbow at my feet; and from that I looked up to—great Heaven! to *what* a fall of bright green water! The broad, deep, mighty stream seems to die in the act of falling; and, from its unfathomable grave, arises that tremendous ghost of spray and mist which is never laid, and has been haunting this place with the same dread solemnity—perhaps from the creation of the world.

"We purpose remaining here a week. In my next, I will try to give you some idea of my impressions, and to tell you how they change with every day. At present it is impossible. I can only say that the first effect of this tremendous spectacle on me, was peace of mind—tranquillity—great thoughts of eternal rest and happiness—nothing of terror. I can shudder at the recollection of Glencoe (dear friend, with Heaven's leave we must see Glencoe together), but whenever I think of Niagara, I shall think of its beauty.

"If you could hear the roar that is in my ears as I write this. Both Falls are under our windows. From our sitting-room and bedroom we look down straight upon them. There is not a soul in the house but ourselves. What would I give if you and Mac were here, to share the sensations of this time! I was going to add, what would I give if the dear girl whose ashes lie in Kensal Green, had lived to come so far along with us—but she has been here many times, I doubt not, since her sweet face faded from my earthly sight.

"One word on the precious letters before I close. You are right, my dear fellow, about the papers; and you are right (I grieve to say) about the people. *Am I right?* quoth the conjuror. *Yes!* from gallery, pit, and boxes. I *did* let out those things, at first, against my will, but when I come to tell you all—well; only wait—only wait—till the end of July. I say no more.

"I do perceive a perplexingly divided and subdivided duty, in the matter of the book of travels. Oh! the sublimated essence

of comicality that I *could* distil, from the materials I have! . . .
You are a part, and an essential part, of our home, dear friend,
and I exhaust my imagination in picturing the circumstances
under which I shall surprise you by walking into 58 Lincoln's
Inn Fields. We are truly grateful to God for the health and
happiness of our inexpressibly dear children and all our friends.
But one letter more—only one. . . . I don't seem to have been
half affectionate enough, but there *are* thoughts, you know, that
lie too deep for words.''

VII

My friend was better than his word, and two more letters reached me before his return. The opening of the first was written from Niagara on the 3rd, and its close from Montreal on the 12th, of May; from which latter city also, on the 26th of that month, the last of all was written.

Much of the first of these letters had reference to the international copyright agitation, and gave strong expression to the indignation awakened in him (nor less in some of the best men of America) by the adoption, at a public meeting in Boston itself, of a memorial against any change of the law, in the course of which it was stated, that, if English authors were invested with control over the republication of their own books, it would be no longer possible for American editors *to alter and adapt them to the American taste*. This deliberate declaration, however, unsparing as Dickens's anger at it was, in effect vanquished him. He saw the hopelessness of persevering in any present effort to bring about the change desired; and he took the determination, not only to drop any allusion to it in his proposed book, but to try what effect might be produced, when he should again be in England, by a league of English authors to suspend further intercourse with American publishers while the law should remain as it is. On his return he made accordingly a public appeal to this effect, stating his own intention for the future to forego all profit derivable from the authorised transmission of early proofs across the Atlantic; but his hopes in this particular also were doomed to disappointment. I now leave the subject, quoting only from his present letter the general remarks with which it is dismissed by himself.

> "NIAGARA FALLS.
> "*Tuesday, Third May*, 1842.

"I'll tell you what the two obstacles to the passing of an international copyright law with England, are: firstly, the national love of 'doing' a man in any bargain or matter of business; secondly, the national vanity. Both these characteristics prevail to an extent which no stranger can possibly estimate.

"With regard to the first, I seriously believe that it is an essential part of the pleasure derived from the perusal of a popular English book, that the author gets nothing for it. It is so dar-nation 'cute—so knowing in Jonathan to get his reading on those terms. He has the Englishman so regularly on the hip that his eye twinkles with slyness, cunning, and delight; and he chuckles over the humour of the page with an appreciation of it, quite inconsistent with, and apart from, its honest purchase. The raven hasn't more joy in eating a stolen piece of meat, than the American has in reading the English book which he gets for nothing.

"With regard to the second, it reconciles that better and more elevated class who are above this sort of satisfaction, with surprising ease. The man's read in America! The Americans like him! They are glad to see him when he comes here! They flock about him, and tell him that they are grateful to him for spirits in sickness; for many hours of delight in health; for a hundred fanciful associations which are constantly interchanged between themselves and their wives and children at home! It is nothing that all this takes place in countries where he is *paid*: it is nothing that he has won fame for himself elsewhere, and profit too. The Americans read him; the free, enlightened, independent Americans; and what more *would* he have? Here's reward enough for any man. The national vanity swallows up all other countries on the face of the earth, and leaves but this above the ocean. Now, mark what the real value of this American reading is. Find me in the whole range of literature one single solitary English book which becomes popular with them, before it has forced itself on their attention by going through the ordeal at home and becoming popular there—and I am content that the law should remain as it is, for ever and a day. I must make one exception. There *are* some mawkish tales of fashionable life before which crowds fall down as they were gilded calves, which at home have been snugly enshrined in circulating libraries from the date of their publication.

"As to telling them they will have no literature of their own, the universal answer (out of Boston) is, 'We don't want one. Why should we pay for one when we can get it for nothing? Our people don't think of poetry, sir. Dollars, banks, and cotton are *our* books, sir.' And they certainly are in one sense; for a lower average of general information than exists in this country on all other topics, it would be very hard to find. So much, at present, for international copyright."

The same letter kept the promise made in its predecessor that one or two more sketches of character should be sent. "One of the most amusing phrases in use all through the country, for its constant repetition, and adaptation to every emergency, is 'Yes, Sir.' Let me give you a specimen." (The specimen was the dialogue, in the *Notes*, of straw-hat and brown-hat, during the stage-coach ride to Sandusky.) "I am not joking, upon my word. This is exactly the dialogue. Nothing else occurring to me at this moment, let me give you the secretary's portrait. Shall I?

"He is of a sentimental turn—strongly sentimental; and tells Anne as June approaches that he hopes 'we shall sometimes think of him' in our own country. He wears a cloak, like Hamlet; and a very tall, big, limp, dusty black hat, which he exchanges on long journeys for a cap like Harlequin's. . . . He sings; and in some of our quarters, when his bedroom has been near ours, we have heard him grunting bass notes through the keyhole of his door, to attract our attention. His desire that I should formally ask him to sing, and his devices to make me do so, are irresistibly absurd. There was a piano in our room at Hartford (you recollect our being there, early in February?)—and he asked me one night, when we were alone, if 'Mrs. D.' played. 'Yes, Mr. Q——.' 'Oh indeed, Sir! *I* sing: so whenever you want *a little soothing*——' You may imagine how hastily I left the room, on some false pretences, without hearing more.

"He paints. . . . An enormous box of oil colours is the main part of his luggage: and with these he blazes away, in his own room, for hours together. Anne got hold of some big-headed pot-bellied sketches he made of the passengers on board the canal-boat (including me in my fur-coat), the recollection of which brings the tears into my eyes at this minute. He painted the Falls, at Niagara, superbly; and is supposed now to be engaged on a full-length representation of me: waiters having reported that chamber-maids have said that there is a picture in his room which has a great deal of hair. One girl opined that it was 'the beginning of the King's Arms'; but I am pretty sure the Lion is myself. . . .

"Sometimes, but not often, he commences a conversation. That usually occurs when we are walking the deck after dark; or when we are alone together in a coach. It is his practice at such times to relate the most notorious and patriarchal Joe Miller, as something that occurred in his own family. When travelling by coach, he is particularly fond of imitating cows and pigs; and nearly challenged a fellow-passenger the other day, who had been moved by the display of this accomplishment into telling him that he was 'a perfect calf.' He thinks it an indispensable act of politeness and attention to inquire constantly whether we're not sleepy, or, to use his own words, whether we don't 'suffer for sleep.' If we have taken a long nap of fourteen hours or so, after a long journey, he is sure to meet me at the bedroom door when I turn out in the morning, with this inquiry. But apart from the amusement he gives us, I could not by possibility have lighted on anyone who would have suited my purpose so well. I have raised his ten dollars per month to twenty; and mean to make it up for six months."

The conclusion of this letter was dated from "Montreal, Thursday, twelfth May"; and was little more than an eager yearning for home. "This will be a very short and stupid letter, my dear friend; for the post leaves here much earlier than I expected, and all my grand designs for being unusually brilliant fall to the ground. I will write you *one line* by the next Cunard boat—reserving all else until our happy and long long looked-for meeting.

"We have been to Toronto and Kingston; experiencing attentions at each which I should have difficulty in describing. The wild and rabid Toryism of Toronto, is, I speak seriously, *appalling*. English kindness is very different from American. People send their horses and carriages for your use, but they don't exact as payment the right of being always under your nose. We had no less than *five* carriages at Kingston waiting our pleasure at one time; not to mention the commodore's barge and crew, and a beautiful government steamer. We dined with Sir Charles Bagot last Sunday. Lord Mulgrave was to have met us yesterday at Lachine; but as he was wind-bound in his yacht and couldn't get in, Sir Richard Jackson sent his drag four-in-hand, with two other young fellows who are also his aides, and in we came in grand style.

"The Theatricals (I think I told you I have been invited to play with the officers of the Coldstream Guards here) are, *A Roland for an Oliver; Two o'clock in the Morning;* and either the *Young Widow*, or *Deaf as a Post*. Ladies (unprofessional) are going to play, for the first time. I wrote to Mitchell at New York for a wig for Mr. Snobbington, which has arrived, and is brilliant. If they had done *Love, Law, and Physick,* as at first proposed, I was already 'up' in Flexible, having played it of old, before my authorship days; but if it should be Splash in the *Young Widow,* you will have to do me the favor to imagine me in a smart livery-coat, shiny black hat and cockade, white knee-cords, white top-boots, blue stock, small whip, red cheeks and dark eyebrows. Conceive Topping's state of mind if I bring this dress home and put it on unexpectedly! . . . God bless you, dear friend. I can say nothing about the seventh, the day on which we sail. It is impossible. Words cannot express what we feel now that the time is so near. . . ."

His last letter, dated from "Peasco's Hotel, Montreal, Canada, twenty-sixth of May," described the private theatricals, and enclosed me a bill of the play.

"This, like my last, will be a stupid letter, because both Kate and I are thrown into such a state of excitement by the near approach of the seventh of June, that we can do nothing, and think of nothing.

"The play came off last night. The audience, between five and six hundred strong, were invited as to a party; a regular table with refreshments being spread in the lobby and saloon. We had the band of the Twenty-Third (one of the finest in the service) in the orchestra, the theatre was lighted with gas, the scenery was excellent, and the properties were all brought from private houses. Sir Charles Bagot, Sir Richard Jackson, and their staffs were present; and as the military portion of the audience were all in full uniform, it was really a splendid scene.

"We 'went' also splendidly; though with nothing very remarkable in the acting way. We had for Sir Mark Chase a genuine odd fish, with plenty of humour; but our Tristram Sappy was not up to the marvellous reputation he has somehow or other acquired here. I am not, however, let me tell you, placarded as a stage-manager for nothing. Everybody was told they would have to submit to the most iron despotism; and didn't I come Macready over them? Oh, no. By no means. Certainly not. The pains I have taken with them, and the perspiration I have expended, during the last ten days, exceed in amount anything you can imagine. I had regular plots of the scenery made out, and lists of the properties wanted; and had them nailed up by the prompter's chair. Every letter that was to be delivered was written; every piece of money that had to be given, provided; and not a single thing lost sight of. I prompted, myself, when I was not on; when I was, I made the regular prompter of the

Private Theatricals.

COMMITTEE.

Mrs. TORRENS.
W. C. ERMATINGER, Esq. | Mrs. PERRY.
| Captain TORRENS.
THE EARL OF MULGRAVE.

STAGE MANAGER—MR. CHARLES DICKENS.

QUEEN'S THEATRE, MONTREAL.

ON WEDNESDAY EVENING, MAY 25TH, 1842,
WILL BE PERFORMED,

A ROLAND FOR AN OLIVER.

MRS. SELBORNE.	*Mrs Torrens*
MARIA DARLINGTON.	*Miss Griffin*
MRS. FIXTURE.	*Miss Ermatinger*
MR. SELBORNE.	*Lord Mulgrave*
ALFRED HIGHFLYER.	*Mr. Charles Dickens*
SIR MARK CHASE.	*Honnable Mr. McMurren*
FIXTURE.	*Captain Willoughby.*
GAMEKEEPER.	*Captain Granville*

AFTER WHICH, AN INTERLUDE IN ONE SCENE, (FROM THE FRENCH,) CALLED

Past Two o'Clock in the Morning.

THE STRANGER.	*Captain Granville*
MR. SNOBBINGTON.	*Mr. Charles Dickens*

TO CONCLUDE WITH THE FARCE, IN ONE ACT, ENTITLED

DEAF AS A POST.

MRS. PLUMPLEY.	*Mrs Torrens*
AMY TEMPLETON.	*Mrs Charles Dickens !!!!!!!*
SOPHY WALTON.	*Mrs Perry.*
SALLY MAGGS.	*Miss Griffin*
CAPTAIN TEMPLETON.	*Captain Torrens*
MR. WALTON.	*Captain Willoughby.*
TRISTRAM SAPPY.	*Doctor Griffin*
CRUPPER.	*Lord Mulgrave*
GALLOP.	*Mr. Charles Dickens.*

MONTREAL, May 24, 1842.   GAZETTE OFFICE.

theatre my deputy; and I never saw anything so perfectly touch and go, as the first two pieces. The bedroom scene in the interlude was as well furnished as Vestris had it; with a 'practicable' fireplace blazing away like mad, and everything in a concatenation accordingly. I really do believe that I was very funny: at least I know that I laughed heartily at myself, and made the part a character, such as you and I know very well: a mixture of T——, Harley, Yates, Keeley, and Jerry Sneak. It went with a roar, all through; and as I am closing this, they have told me I was so well made up that Sir Charles Bagot, who sat in the stage-box, had no idea who played Mr. Snobbington, until the piece was over.

"But only think of Kate playing! and playing devilish well, I assure you! All the ladies were capital, and we had no wait or hitch for an instant. You may suppose this, when I tell you that we began at eight, and had the curtain down at eleven. It is their custom here, to prevent heartburnings in a very heartburning town, whenever they have played in private, to repeat the performances in public. So, on Saturday (substituting, of course, real actresses for the ladies), we repeat the two first pieces to a paying audience, for the manager's benefit. . . .

"I send you a bill, to which I have appended a key.

"I have not told you half enough. But I promise you I shall make you shake your sides about this play. Wasn't it worthy of Crummles that when Lord Mulgrave and I went to the door to receive the Governor-General, the regular prompter followed us in agony with four tall candlesticks with wax candles in them, and besought us with a bleeding heart to carry two apiece, in accordance with all the precedents? . . .

"I have hardly spoken of our letters, which reached us yesterday, shortly before the play began. A hundred thousand thanks for your delightful mainsail of that gallant little packet I read it again and again; and had it all over again at breakfast time this morning. I heard also, by the same ship, from Talfourd, Miss Coutts, Brougham, Rogers, and others. A delicious letter from Mac too, as good as his painting I swear. Give my hearty love to him. . . . God bless you, my dear friend. As the time draws nearer, we get FEVERED with anxiety for home. . . . Kiss our darlings for us. We shall soon meet, please God, and be happier and merrier than ever we were, in all our lives. . . . Oh home—home—home—home—home—home—HOME!!!!!!!!!!!"

VIII

"AMERICAN NOTES"

1842

THE reality did not fall short of the anticipation of home. His return was the occasion of unbounded enjoyment; and what he had planned before sailing as the way we should meet, received literal fulfilment. By the sound of his cheery voice I first knew that he was come; and from my house we went together to Maclise, also "without a moment's warning." A Greenwich dinner in which several friends (Talfourd, Milnes, Procter, Maclise, Stanfield, Marryat, Barham, Hood, and Cruikshank among them) took part, and other immediate greetings, followed; but the most special celebration was reserved for autumn, when, by way of challenge to what he had seen while abroad, a home-journey was arranged with Stanfield, Maclise, and myself for his companions, into such of the most striking scenes of a picturesque English county as the majority of us might not before have visited: Cornwall being ultimately chosen.

Before our departure he was occupied by his preparation of the *American Notes*; and to the same interval belongs the arrival in London of Mr. Longfellow, who became his guest, and (for both of us I am privileged to add) our attached friend. Longfellow's name was not then the familiar word it has since been in England; but he had already written several of his most felicitous pieces, and he possessed all the qualities of delightful companionship, the culture and the charm, which have no higher type than the accomplished and genial American. He reminded me, when lately again in England, of two experiences out of many we had enjoyed together this quarter of a century before. One of them was a day at Rochester, when, met by one of those prohibitions which are the wonder of visitors and the shame of Englishmen, we overleapt gates and barriers, and, setting at defiance repeated threats of all the terrors of law coarsely expressed to us by the custodian of the place, explored minutely the castle ruins. The other was a night among those portions of the population which outrage law and defy its terrors all the days of their lives, the tramps and thieves of London; when, under guidance and protection of the most trusted officers of the two great metropolitan prisons afforded to us by Mr. Chesterton and Lieut. Tracy, we went over the worst haunts of the most dangerous classes. Nor will it be unworthy of remark, in proof that attention is not drawn vainly to such scenes, that, upon Dickens going over them a dozen years later when he wrote a paper about them for his *Household Words,* he found important changes effected whereby these human dens, if not less dangerous, were become certainly more decent. On the night of our earlier visit, Maclise, who accompanied us, was struck with such sickness on entering the first of the Mint lodging-houses in the Borough, that he had to remain, for the time we were in them, under guardianship of the police outside. Longfellow returned home by the *Great Western* from Bristol on 21 October, enjoying as he passed through Bath the hospitality of Landor; and at the end of the following week we started on our Cornish travel.

But what before this had occupied Dickens in the writing way must now be told. Not long after his reappearance amongst us, his house being still in the occupation of Sir John Wilson, he went to Broadstairs, taking with him the letters from which I have quoted so largely to help him in preparing his *American Notes*; and one of his first announcements to me (18 July) shows not only this labour in progress, but the story he was under engagement to begin in November working in his mind. "The subjects at the beginning of the book are of that kind that I can't *dash* at them, and now and then they fret me in consequence. When I come to Washington, I am all right. The solitary prison at Philadelphia is a good subject, though; I forgot that for the moment. Have you seen the Boston chapter yet? . . . I have never been in Cornwall either. A mine certainly; and a letter for that purpose shall be got from Southwood Smith. I have some notion of opening the new book in the lantern of a lighthouse!" A letter a couple of months later (16 September) recurs to that proposed opening of his story which after all he laid aside; and shows how rapidly he was getting his *American Notes* into shape. "At the Isle of Thanet races yesterday I saw—oh! who shall say what an immense amount of character in the way of inconceivable villainy and blackguardism! I even got some new wrinkles in the way of showmen, conjurors, pea-and-thimblers, and trampers generally. I think of opening my new book on the coast of Cornwall, in some terrible dreary iron-bound spot. I hope to have finished the American book before the end of next month; and we will then together fly down into that desolate region." Our friends having Academy engagements to detain them, we had to delay a little; and I meanwhile turn back to his letters to observe his progress with his *Notes*, and other employments or enjoyments of the interval. They require no illustration that they will not themselves supply: but I may remark that the then collected *Poems* of Tennyson had become very favourite reading with him; and that while in America Mr. Mitchell the comedian had given him a small white shaggy terrier, who bore at first the imposing name of Timber Doodle, and became a domestic pet and companion.

"I have been reading" (7 August) "Tennyson all this morning on the seashore. Among other trifling effects, the waters have dried up as they did of old, and shown me all the mermen and mermaids, at the bottom of the ocean; together with millions of queer creatures, half-fish and half-fungus, looking down into all manner of coral caves and seaweed conservatories; and staring in with their great dull eyes at every open nook and loophole. Who else, too, could conjure up such a close to the extraordinary and as Landor would say 'most woonderful' series of pictures in the 'dream of fair women,' as:

> Squadrons and squares of men in brazen plates,
> Scaffolds, still sheets of water, divers woes,
> Ranges of glimmering vaults with iron grates,
> And hushed seraglios!

I am getting on pretty well, but it was so glittering and sunshiny yesterday that I was forced to make holiday." Four days later: "I have not written a word this blessed day. I got to New York yesterday, and think it goes as it should. . . . Little doggy improves rapidly, and now jumps over my stick at the word of command. I have changed his name to Snittle Timbery, as more sonorous and expressive. He unites with the rest of the family in cordial regards and loves. *Nota Bene*. The Margate theatre is open every evening, and the Four Patagonians (see Goldsmith's *Essays*) are performing thrice a week at Ranelagh. . . ."

A visit from me was at this time due, to which these were held out as inducements; and there followed what it was supposed I could not resist, a transformation into the broadest farce of a deep tragedy by a dear friend of ours. "Now you really must come. Seeing only is believing, very often isn't that, and even Being the thing falls a long way short of believing it. Mrs. Nickleby herself once asked me, as you know, if I really believed there ever was such a woman; but there'll be no more belief, either in me or my descriptions, after what I have to tell of our excellent friend's tragedy, if you don't come and have it played again for yourself 'by particular desire.' We saw it last night, and oh! if you had but been with us! Young Betty, doing what the mind of man without my help never *can* conceive, with his legs like padded boot-trees wrapped up in faded yellow drawers, was the hero. The comic man of the company enveloped in a white sheet, with his head tied with red tape like a brief and greeted with yells of laughter whenever he appeared, was the venerable priest. A poor toothless old idiot at whom the very gallery roared with contempt when he was called a tyrant, was the remorseless and aged Creon. And Ismene being arrayed in spangled muslin trousers very loose in the legs and very tight in the ankles such as Fatima would wear in *Blue Beard*, was at her appearance immediately called upon for a song. After this can you longer . . . .?"

With the opening of September I had renewed report of his book, and of other matters. "The Philadelphia chapter I think very good, but I am sorry to say it has not made as much in print as I hoped. . . . In America they have forged a letter with my signature, which they coolly declare appeared in the *Chronicle* with the copyright circular; and in which I express myself in such terms as you may imagine, in reference to the dinners and so forth. It has been widely distributed all over the States; and the felon who invented it is a 'smart man' of course. You are to understand that it is not done as a joke, and is scurrilously reviewed. Mr. Park Benjamin begins a lucubration upon it with these capitals, DICKENS IS A FOOL, AND A LIAR. . . . I have a new protégé, in the person of a wretched deaf and dumb boy whom I found upon the sands the other day, half dead, and have got (for the present) into the union infirmary at Minster. A most deplorable case."

On the 14th he told me: "I have pleased myself very much to-day in the matter of Niagara. I have made the description very brief (as it should be), but I fancy it is good. I am beginning to think over the introductory chapter, and it has meanwhile occurred to me that I should like, at the beginning of the volumes, to put what follows on a blank page. *I dedicate this Book to those friends of mine in America, who, loving their country, can bear the truth, when it is written good humouredly and in a kind spirit* What do you think? Do you see any objection?" My reply is to be inferred from what he sent back on the 20th

"I don't quite see my way towards an expression in the dedication of any feeling in reference to the American reception. Of course I have always intended to glance at it, gratefully, in the end of the book; and it will have its place in the introductory chapter, if we decide for that. Would it do to put in, after 'friends in America,' *who giving me a welcome I must ever gratefully and proudly remember, left my judgment free, and* who, loving, etc. If so, so be it."

Before the end of the month he wrote: "For the last two or three days I have been rather slack in point of work; not being in the vein. To-day I had not written twenty lines before I rushed out (the weather being gorgeous) to bathe. And when I have done that, it is all up with me in the way of authorship until to-morrow. The little dog is in the highest spirits; and jumps, as Mr. Kenwigs would say, perpetivally. I have had letters by the *Britannia* from Felton, Prescott, Mr. Q—— and others, all very earnest and kind. I think you will like what I have written on the poor emigrants and their ways as I literally and truly saw them on the boat from Quebec to Montreal."

This was a passage, which, besides being in itself as attractive as any in his writings, gives such perfect expression to a feeling that underlies them all that I subjoin it in a note.[1] On board

[1] "Cant as we may, and as we shall to the end of all things, it is very much harder for the poor to be virtuous than it is for the rich; and the good that is in them, shines the brighter for it. In many a noble mansion lives a man, the best of husbands and of fathers, whose private worth in both capacities is justly lauded to the skies. But bring him here, upon this crowded deck. Strip from his fair young wife her silken dress and jewels, unbind her braided hair, stamp early wrinkles on her brow, pinch her pale cheek with care and much privation, array her faded form in coarsely patched attire, let there be nothing but his love to set her forth or deck her out, and you shall put it to the proof indeed. So change his station in the world that he shall see in those young things who climb about his knee, not records of his wealth and name, but little wrestlers with him for his daily bread; so many poachers on his scanty meal; so many units to divide his every sum of comfort, and farther to reduce its small amount. In lieu of the endearments of childhood in its sweetest aspect, heap upon him all its pains and wants, its sicknesses and ills, its fretfulness, caprice and querulous endurance: let its prattle be, not of engaging infant fancies, but of cold, and thirst, and hunger: and if his fatherly affection outlive all this, and he be patient, watchful, tender; careful of his children's lives, and mindful always of their joys and sorrows; then send him back to parliament, and pulpit, and to quarter sessions, and when he hears fine talk of the depravity of those who live from hand to mouth, and labour hard to do it, let him speak up, as one who knows, and tell those holders-forth that they, by parallel with such a class, should be high angels in their daily lives, and lay but humble siege to heaven at last. . . . Which of us shall say what he would be, if such realities, with small relief or change all through his days, were his! Looking round upon these people: far from home, houseless, indigent, wandering, weary with travel and hard living: and seeing how

this Canadian steamboat he encountered crowds of poor emigrants and their children; and such was their patient kindness and cheerful endurance, in circumstances where the easy-living rich could hardly fail to be monsters of impatience and selfishness, that it suggested to him a reflection than which it was not possible to have written anything more worthy of observation, or more absolutely true. Jeremy Taylor has the same philosophy in his lesson on opportunities, but here it was beautified by the example with all its fine touches. It made us read Rich and Poor by new translation.

The printers were now hard at work, and in the last week of September he wrote: "I send you proofs as far as Niagara. . . . I am rather holiday-making this week . . . taking principal part in a regatta here yesterday, very pretty and gay indeed. We think of coming up in time for Macready's opening, when perhaps you will give us a chop; and of course you and Mac will dine with *us* the next day? I shall leave nothing of the book to do after coming home, please God, but the two chapters on slavery and the people which I could manage easily in a week, if need were. . . . The policeman who supposed the Duke of Brunswick to be one of the swell mob, ought instantly to be made an inspector. The suspicion reflects the highest credit (I seriously think) on his penetration and judgment." Three days later: "For the last two days we have had gales blowing from the north-east, and seas rolling on us that drown the pier. To-day it is tremendous. Such a sea was never known here at this season, and it is running in at this moment in waves of twelve feet high. You would hardly know the place. But we shall be punctual to your dinner hour on Saturday. If the wind should hold in the same quarter, we may be obliged to come up by land; and in that case I should start the caravan at six in the morning. . . . What do you think of this for my title—*American Notes for General Circulation*; and of this motto?

"In reply to a question from the Bench, the Solicitor for the Bank observed, that this kind of notes circulated the most extensively, in those parts of the world where they were stolen and forged.

Old Bailey Report."

---

patiently they nursed and tended their young children: how they consulted ever their wants first, then half supplied their own; what gentle ministers of hope and faith the women were; how the men profited by their example; and how very, very seldom even a moment's petulance or harsh complaint broke out among them: I felt a stronger love and honour of my kind come glowing on my heart, and wished to God there had been many atheists in the better part of human nature there, to read this simple lesson in the book of life."

The motto was omitted, objection being made to it; and on the last day of the month I had the last of his letters during this Broadstairs visit. "Strange as it may appear to you" (25 September), "the sea is running so high that we have no choice but to return by land. No steamer can come out of Ramsgate, and the Margate boat lay out all night on Wednesday with all her passengers on board. You may be sure of us therefore on Saturday at 5, for I have determined to leave here to-morrow, as we could not otherwise manage it in time; and have engaged an omnibus to bring the whole caravan by the overland route. . . . We cannot open a window, or a door; legs are of no use on the terrace; and the Margate boats can only take people aboard at Herne Bay!" He brought with him all that remained to be done of his second volume except the last two chapters, including that to which he has referred as "introductory"; and on the following Wednesday (5 October) he told me that the first of these was done. "I want you very much to come and dine to-day that we may repair to Drury Lane together; and let us say half-past four, or there is no time to be comfortable. I am going out to Tottenham this morning, on a cheerless mission I would willingly have avoided. Hone, of the *Every Day Book*, is dying; and sent Cruikshank yesterday to beg me to go and see him, as, having read no books but mine of late, he wanted to see and shake hands with me before (as George said) 'he went.' There is no help for it, of course; so to Tottenham I repair, this morning. I worked all day, and till midnight; and finished the slavery chapter yesterday." The cheerless visit had its mournful sequel before the next month closed, when he went with the same companion to poor Hone's funeral.

On 10 October I heard from him that the chapter intended to be introductory to the *Notes* was written, and waiting our conference whether or not it should be printed. We decided against it; on his part so reluctantly, that I had to undertake for its publication when a more fitting time should come. This in my judgment has arrived, and the chapter first sees the light on this page. There is no danger at present, as there would have been when it was written, that its proper self-assertion should be mistaken for an apprehension of hostile judgments which he was anxious to deprecate or avoid. He is out of reach of all that now; and reveals to us here, as one whom fear or censure can touch no more, his honest purpose in the use of satire even where his humorous temptations were strongest. What he says will on other grounds also be read with unusual interest, for it will be found to connect itself impressively not with his first experiences only, but with his second visit to America at the close of his life. He held always the same high opinion of what was best in that country, and always the same contempt for what was worst in it.

"INTRODUCTORY, AND NECESSARY TO BE READ

"I have placed the foregoing title at the head of this page, because I challenge and deny the right of any person to pass judgment on this book, or to arrive at any reasonable conclusion in reference to it, without first being at the trouble of becoming acquainted with its design and purpose.

"It is not statistical. Figures of arithmetic have already been heaped upon America's devoted head, almost as lavishly as figures of speech have been piled above Shakespeare's grave.

"It comprehends no small talk concerning individuals, and no violation of the social confidences of private life. The very prevalent practice of kidnapping live ladies and gentlemen, forcing them into cabinets, and labelling and ticketing them whether they will or no, for the gratification of the idle and the curious, is not to my taste. Therefore I have avoided it.

"It has not a grain of any political ingredient in its whole composition.

"Neither does it contain, nor have I intended that it should contain, any lengthened and minute account of my personal reception in the United States; not because I am, or ever was, insensible to that spontaneous effusion of affection and generosity of heart, in a most affectionate and generous-hearted people; but because I conceive that it would ill become me to flourish matter necessarily involving so much of my own praises, in the eyes of my unhappy readers.

"This book is simply what it claims to be—a record of the impressions I received from day to day, during my hasty travels in America, and sometimes (but not always) of the conclusions to which they, and after-reflection on them, have led me; a description of the country I passed through; of the institutions I visited; of the kind of people among whom I journeyed; and of the manners and customs that came within my observation. Very many works having just the same scope and range, have been already published, but I think that these two volumes stand in need of no apology on that account. The interest of such productions, if they have any, lies in the varying impressions made by the same novel things on different minds; and not in new discoveries or extraordinary adventures.

"I can scarcely be supposed to be ignorant of the hazard I run in writing of America at all. I know perfectly well that there is, in that country, a numerous class of well-intentioned persons prone to be dissatisfied with all accounts of the Republic whose citizens they are, which are not couched in terms of exalted and extravagant praise. I know perfectly well that there is in America, as in most other places laid down in maps of the great world, a numerous class of persons so tenderly and delicately constituted, that they cannot bear the truth in any form. And I do not need the gift of prophecy to discern afar off, that they who will be aptest to detect malice, ill-will, and all uncharitableness in these pages, and to show, beyond any doubt, that they are perfectly inconsistent with that grateful and enduring recollection which I profess to entertain of the welcome I found awaiting me beyond the Atlantic—will be certain native journalists, veracious and gentlemanly, who were at great pains to prove to me, on all occasions during my stay there, that the aforesaid welcome was utterly worthless.

"But, venturing to dissent even from these high authorities, I formed my own opinion of its value in the outset, and retain it to this hour; and in asserting (as I invariably did on all public occasions) my liberty and freedom of speech while I was among the Americans, and in maintaining it at home, I believe that I best show my sense of the high worth of that welcome, and of the honourable singleness of purpose with which it was extended to me. From first to last I saw, in the friends who crowded round me in America, old readers, over-grateful and over-partial perhaps, to whom I had happily been the means of furnishing pleasure and entertainment; not a vulgar herd who would flatter and cajole a stranger into turning with closed eyes from all the blemishes of the nation, and into chaunting its praises with the discrimination of a street ballad-singer. From first to last I saw, in those hospitable hands, a home-made wreath of laurel; and not an iron muzzle disguised beneath a flower or two.

"Therefore I take—and hold myself not only justified in taking, but bound to take—the plain course of saying what I think, and noting what I saw; and as it is not my custom to exalt what in my judgment are foibles and abuses at home, so

I have no intention of softening down, or glozing over, those that I have observed abroad.

"If this book should fall into the hands of any sensitive American who cannot bear to be told that the working of the institutions of his country is far from perfect; that in spite of the advantage she has over all other nations in the elastic freshness and vigour of her youth, she is far from being a model for the earth to copy; and that even in those pictures of the national manners with which he quarrels most, there is still (after the lapse of several years, each of which may be fairly supposed to have had its stride in improvement) much that is just and true at this hour; let him lay it down, now, for I shall not please him. Of the intelligent, reflecting, and educated among his countrymen, I have no fear; for I have ample reason to believe, after many delightful conversations not easily to be forgotten, that there are very few topics (if any) on which their sentiments differ materially from mine.

"I may be asked—'If you have been in any respect disappointed in America, and are assured beforehand that the expression of your disappointment will give offence to any class, why do you write at all?' My answer is, that I went there expecting greater things than I found, and resolved as far as in me lay to do justice to the country, at the expense of any (in my view) mistaken or prejudiced statements that might have been made to its disparagement. Coming home with a corrected and sobered judgment, I consider myself no less bound to do justice to what, according to my best means of judgment, I found to be the truth."

Of the book for whose opening page this matter introductory was written it will be enough merely to add that it appeared on 18 October; that before the close of the year four large editions had been sold; and that in my opinion it thoroughly deserved the estimate formed of it by one connected with America by the strongest social affections, and otherwise in all respects an honourable, high-minded, upright judge. "You have been very tender," wrote Lord Jeffrey, "to our sensitive friends beyond sea, and my whole heart goes along with every word you have written. I think that you have perfectly accomplished all that you profess or undertake to do, and that the world has never yet seen a more faithful, graphic, amusing, kind-hearted narrative."

I permit myself so far to anticipate a later page as to print here a brief extract from one of the letters of the last American visit. Without impairing the interest with which the narrative of that time will be read in its proper place, I shall thus indicate the extent to which present impressions were modified by the experience of twenty-six years later. He is writing from Philadelphia on the fourteenth of January, 1868.

"I see *great changes* for the better, socially. Politically, no. England governed by the Marylebone vestry and the penny papers, and England as she would be after years of such governing, is what I make of *that*. Socially, the change in manners is remarkable. There is much greater politeness and forbearance in all ways. . . . On the other hand there are still provincial oddities wonderfully quizzical; and the newspapers are constantly expressing the popular amazement at 'Mr. Dickens's extraordinary composure.' They seem to take it ill that I don't stagger on to the platform overpowered by the spectacle before me, and the national greatness. They are all so accustomed to do public things with a flourish of trumpets, that the notion of my coming in to read without somebody first flying up and delivering an 'Oration' about me, and flying down again and leading me in, is so very unaccountable to them, that sometimes they have no idea until I open my lips that it can possibly be Charles Dickens."

BOOK FOURTH

LONDON AND GENOA

1843–5. ÆT. 31–3

I

FIRST YEAR OF "MARTIN CHUZZLEWIT"

1843

THE Cornish trip had come off, meanwhile, with such unexpected and continued attraction for us that we were well into the third week of absence before we turned our faces homeward. Railways helped us then not much; but where the roads were inaccessible to post-horses, we walked. Tintagel was visited, and no part of mountain or sea consecrated by the legends of Arthur was left unexplored. We ascended to the cradle of the highest tower of Mount St. Michael, and descended into several mines. Land and sea yielded each its marvels to us; but of all the impressions brought away, of which some afterwards took forms as lasting as they could receive from the most delightful art, I doubt if any were the source of such deep emotion to us all as a sunset we saw at Land's End. Stanfield knew the wonders of the Continent, the glories of Ireland were native to Maclise, I was familiar from boyhood with Border and Scottish scenery, and Dickens was fresh from Niagara; but there was something in the sinking of the sun behind the Atlantic that autumn afternoon, as we viewed it together from the top of the rock projecting farthest into the sea, which each in his turn declared to have no parallel in memory.

But with the varied and overflowing gladness of those three memorable weeks it would be unworthy now to associate only the saddened recollection of the sole survivor. "Blessed star of morning!" wrote Dickens to Felton while yet the glow of its enjoyment was upon him. "Such a trip as we had into Cornwall just after Longfellow went away! . . . Sometimes we travelled all night, sometimes all day, sometimes both. . . . Heavens! If you could have seen the necks of bottles, distracting in their immense varieties of shape, peering out of the carriage pockets! If you could have witnessed the deep devotion of the post-boys, the wild attachment of the hostlers, the maniac glee of the waiters! If you could have followed us into the earthy old

K 781   271

churches we visited, and into the strange caverns on the gloomy sea-shore, and down into the depths of mines, and up to the tops of giddy heights where the unspeakably green water was roaring, I don't know how many hundred feet below! If you could have seen but one gleam of the bright fires by which we sat in the big rooms of the ancient inns at night, until long after the small hours had come and gone. . . . I never laughed in my life as I did on this journey. It would have done you good to hear me. I was choking and gasping and bursting the buckle off the back of my stock, all the way. And Stanfield got into such apoplectic entanglements that we were often obliged to beat him on the back with portmanteaus before we could recover him. Seriously, I do believe there never was such a trip. And they made such sketches, those two men, in the most romantic of our halting-places, that you would have sworn we had the Spirit of Beauty with us, as well as the Spirit of Fun."

*30

The Logan Stone, by Stanfield, was one of them; and it laughingly sketched both the charm of what was seen, and the mirth of what was done, for it perched me on the top of the stone. It is historical, however, the ascent having been made; and of this and other examples of steadiness at heights which deterred the rest, as well as of a subject suggested for a painting of which Dickens became the unknown purchaser, Maclise reminded me in some pleasant allusions many years later, which, notwithstanding their tribute to my athletic achievements, the good-natured reader must forgive my printing. They complete the little picture of our trip. Something I had written to him of recent travel among the mountain scenery of the wilder coasts of Donegal had touched the chord of these old remembrances. "As to your clambering," he replied, "don't I know what happened of old? Don't I still see the Logan Stone, and you perched on the giddy top, while we, rocking it on its pivot, shrank from all that lay concealed below! Should I ever have blundered on the waterfall of St. Wighton, if you had not piloted the way? And when we got to Land's End, with the green sea far under us lapping into solitary rocky nooks where the mermaids live, who but you only had the courage to stretch over, to see those diamond jets of brightness that I swore then, and believe still, were the flappings of their tails! And don't I recall you again, sitting on the tip-top stone of the cradle-turret over the highest battlement of the castle of St. Michael's Mount, with not a ledge or coigne of vantage 'twixt you and the fathomless ocean under you, distant three thousand feet!

Last, do I forget you clambering up the goat-path to King Arthur's castle of Tintagel, when, in my vain wish to follow, I grovelled and clung to the soil like a Caliban, and you, in the manner of a tricksy spirit and stout Ariel, actually danced up and down before me!"

The waterfall I led him to was among the records of the famous holiday, celebrated also by Thackeray in one of his pen-and-ink pleasantries, which were sent by both painters to the next year's Academy; and so eager was Dickens to possess this landscape by Maclise which included the likeness of a member of his family, yet so anxious that our friend should be spared the sacrifice which he knew would follow an avowal of his wish, that he bought it under a feigned name before the Academy opened, and steadily refused to take back the money which on discovery of the artifice Maclise pressed upon him. Our friend, who already had munificently given him a charming drawing of his four children to accompany him and his wife to America, had his generous way nevertheless; and as a voluntary offering four years later, painted Mrs. Dickens on a canvas the same size as the picture of her husband in 1839.

"Behold finally, the title of the new book," was the first note I had from Dickens (12 November) after our return; "don't lose it, for I have no copy." Title and even story had been undetermined while we travelled, from the lingering wish he still had to begin it among those Cornish scenes; but this intention had now been finally abandoned, and the reader lost nothing by his substitution, for the lighthouse or mine in Cornwall, of the Wiltshire village forge on the windy autumn evening which opens the tale of *Martin Chuzzlewit*. Into that name he finally settled, but only after much deliberation, as a mention of his changes will show. Martin was the prefix to all, but the surname varied from its first form of Sweezleden, Sweezleback, and Sweezlewag, to those of Chuzzletoe, Chuzzleboy, Chubblewig, and Chuzzlewig; nor was Chuzzlewit chosen at last until after more hesitation and discussion. What he had sent me in his letter as finally adopted, ran thus: "The Life and Adventures of Martin Chuzzlewig, his family, friends, and enemies. Comprising all his wills and his ways. With an historical record of what he did and what he didn't. The whole forming a complete key to the house of Chuzzlewig." All which latter portion of the title was of course dropped as the work became modified, in its progress, by changes at first not contemplated; but as early as the third number he drew up the plan of "old Martin's plot to degrade and punish Pecksniff," and the difficulties he encountered in departing from other portions of his scheme were such as to render him, in his subsequent stories, more bent upon constructive care at the outset, and on adherence as far as might be to any design he had formed.

The first number, which appeared in January 1843, had not been quite finished when he wrote to me on 8 December: "The *Chuzzlewit* copy makes so much more than I supposed, that the number is nearly done. Thank God!" Beginning so hurriedly as at last he did, altering his course at the opening and seeing little as yet of the main track of his design, perhaps no story was ever begun by him with stronger heart or confidence. Illness kept me to my rooms for some days, and he was so eager to try the effect of Pecksniff and Pinch that he came down with the ink hardly dry on the last slip to read the manuscript to me. Well did Sydney Smith, on writing to say how very much the number had pleased him, foresee the promise there was in those characters. "Pecksniff and his daughters, and Pinch, are admirable—quite first-rate painting, such as no one but yourself can execute!" And let me here at once remark that the notion of taking Pecksniff for a type of character was really the origin of the book; the design being to show, more or less by every person introduced, the number and variety of humours and vices that have their root in selfishness.

Another piece of his writing that claims mention at the close of 1842 was a prologue contributed to the *Patrician's Daughter*, Mr. Westland Marston's first dramatic effort, which had attracted him by the beauty of its composition less than by the courage with which its subject had been chosen from the actual life of the time.

> Not light its import, and not poor its mien;
> Yourselves the actors, and your homes the scene.

This was the date, too, of Mr. Browning's tragedy of the *Blot on the 'Scutcheon*, which I took upon myself, after reading it in the manuscript, privately to impart to Dickens; and I was not mistaken in the belief that it would profoundly touch him. "Browning's play," he wrote (25 November), "has thrown me into a perfect passion of sorrow. To say that there is anything in its subject save what is lovely, true, deeply affecting, full of the best emotion, the most earnest feeling, and the most true and tender source of interest, is to say that there is no light in the sun, and no heat in blood. It is full of genius, natural and great thoughts, profound and yet simple and beautiful in its vigour. I know nothing that is so affecting, nothing in any book I have ever read, as Mildred's recurrence to that 'I was so young—I had no mother.' I know no love like it, no passion like it, no moulding of a splendid thing after its conception, like it. And I swear it is a tragedy that MUST be played; and must be played, moreover, by Macready. There are some things I would have changed if I could (they are very slight, mostly broken lines); and I assuredly would have the old servant *begin his tale upon the scene*; and be taken by the throat, or drawn upon, by his master, in its commencement. But the tragedy I never shall forget, or less vividly remember than I do now. And if you tell Browning that I have seen it, tell him that I believe from my soul there is no man living (and not many dead) who could produce such a work.—Macready likes the altered prologue very much. . . ." There will come a more convenient time to speak of his general literary likings, or special regard for contemporary books; but I will say now that nothing interested him more than successes won honestly in his own field, and that in his large and open nature there was no hiding-place for little jealousies. An instance occurs to me which may be named at once, when, many years after the present date, he called my attention very earnestly to two tales then in course of publication in *Blackwood's Magazine*, and afterwards collected under the title of *Scenes of Clerical Life*. "Do read them," he wrote. "They are the best things I have seen since I began my course."

Eighteen hundred and forty-three opened with the most *31 vigorous prosecution of his *Chuzzlewit* labour. "I hope the number will be very good," he wrote to me of number two (8 January). "I have been hammering away, and at home all day. Ditto yesterday; except for two hours in the afternoon, when I ploughed through snow half a foot deep, round about the wilds of Willesden." For the present, however, I shall glance only briefly from time to time at his progress with the earlier portions of the story on which he was thus engaged until the midsummer of 1844. Disappointments arose in connection with it, unexpected and strange, which had important influence upon him: but I reserve the mention of these for awhile, that I may speak of the leading incidents of 1843.

"I am in a difficulty," he wrote (12 February), "and am coming down to you sometime to-day or to-night. I couldn't write a line yesterday; not a word, though I really tried hard. In a kind of despair I started off at half-past two with my pair of petticoats to Richmond; and dined there!! Oh what a lovely day it was in those parts." His pair of petticoats were Mrs. Dickens and her sister Georgina: the latter, since his return from America, having become part of his household, of which she remained a member until his death; and he had just reason to be proud of the steadiness, depth, and devotion of her friendship. In a note-book begun by him in January 1855, where for the first time in his life he jotted down hints and fancies proposed to be made available in future writings, I find a character sketched of which the most part was applicable to his sister-in-law, if the whole was not suggested by her. "She—sacrificed to children, and sufficiently rewarded. From a child herself, always 'the children' (of somebody else) to engross her. And so it comes to pass that she is never married; never herself has a child; is always devoted 'to the children' (of somebody else); and they love her; and she has always youth dependent on her till her death—and dies quite happily." Not many days after that holiday at Richmond, a slight unstudied outline in pencil was made by Maclise of the three who formed the party there, as we all sat together; and never did a touch so light carry with it more truth of observation. The likenesses of all are excellent. Nothing ever done of Dickens has conveyed more vividly his look and bearing at this yet youthful time. He is in his most pleasing aspect; flattered, if you will; but nothing that is known to me gives a general impression so lifelike and true of the then frank, eager, handsome face.

It was a year of much illness with me, which had ever helpful and active sympathy from him. "Send me word how you are," he wrote, two days later. "But not so much for that I now write, as to tell you, peremptorily, that I insist on your wrapping yourself up and coming here in a hackney-coach, with a big portmanteau, to-morrow. It surely is better to be unwell with a Quick and Cheerful (and Co.) in the neighbourhood, than in the dreary vastness of Lincoln's Inn Fields. Here is the snuggest tent-bedstead in the world, and there you are with the drawing-room for your workshop, the Q and C for your pal, and 'everythink in a concatenation accordingly.' I begin to have hopes of the regeneration of mankind after the reception of Gregory last night, though I have none of the *Chronicle* for not denouncing the villain. Have you seen the note touching my *Notes* in the blue and yellow?"

The first of these closing allusions was to the editor of the infamous *Satirist* having been hissed from the Covent Garden stage, on which he had presented himself in the character of Hamlet; and I remember with what infinite pleasure I afterwards heard Chief Justice Tindal in court, charging the jury in an action brought by this malefactor, and referring to a publican of St. Giles's as having paid men to take part in hissing him, avow the pride felt in "living in the same parish with a man of that humble station of life," who was capable of paying money out of his pocket to punish what he believed to be an outrage to decency. The second allusion was to a statement of the reviewer of the *American Notes* in the *Edinburgh* to the effect, that, if he had been rightly informed, Dickens had gone to America as a kind of missionary in the cause of international copyright; to which a prompt contradiction had been given in *The Times*. "I deny it," wrote Dickens, "wholly. He is wrongly informed; and reports, without inquiry, a piece of information which I could only characterise by using one of the shortest and strongest words in the language."

The disputes that had arisen out of his work on America, I may add, stretched over great part of the year. It will quite suffice, however, to say here that the ground taken by him in his letters written on the spot, and printed in the present volume, which in all the more material statements his book invited public judgment upon and which he was moved to reopen in *Chuzzlewit*, was so kept by him against all comers, that none of the counter-statements or arguments dislodged him from a square inch of it. But the controversy is dead now; and he took occasion, on his later visit to America, to write its epitaph.

Though I did not, to revert to his February letter, obey its cordial bidding by immediately taking up quarters with him, I soon after joined him at a cottage he rented in Finchley; and here, walking and talking in the green lanes as the midsummer months were coming on, his introduction of Mrs. Gamp, and the uses to which he should apply that remarkable personage, first occurred to him. In his preface to the book he speaks of her as a fair representation, at the time it was published, of the hired attendant on the poor in sickness: but he might have added that the rich were no better off, for Mrs. Gamp's original was in reality a person hired by a most distinguished friend of his own, a lady, to take charge of an invalid very dear to her; and the common habit of this nurse in the sick-room, among other Gampish peculiarities, was to rub her nose along the top of the tall fender. Whether or not, on that first mention of her, I had any doubts whether such a character could be made a central figure in his story, I do not now remember; but if there were any at the time, they did not outlive the contents of the packet which introduced her to me in the flesh a few weeks after our return. "Tell me," he wrote from Yorkshire, where he had been meanwhile passing a pleasant holiday with a friend, "what you think of Mrs. Gamp? You'll not find it easy to get through the hundreds of misprints in her conversation, but I want your opinion at once. I think you know already something of mine. I mean to make a mark with her." The same letter enclosed me a clever and pointed parable in verse which he had written for an annual edited by Lady Blessington.[1]

[1] "I have heard, as you have, from Lady Blessington, for whose behoof I have this morning penned the lines I send you herewith. But I have only done so to excuse myself, for I have not the least idea of their suiting her; and I hope she will send them back to you for the *Ex*." July 1843. The lines are quite worth preserving.

A WORD IN SEASON

They have a superstition in the East,
    That Allah, written on a piece of paper,
Is better unction than can come of priest,
    Of rolling incense, and of lighted taper:
Holding, that any scrap which bears that name
    In any characters its front impress'd on,
Shall help the finder thro' the purging flame,
    And give his toasted feet a place to rest on.

Accordingly, they make a mighty fuss
    With every wretched tract and fierce oration,
And hoard the leaves—for they are not, like us,
    A highly civilised and thinking nation:
And, always stooping in the miry ways
    To look for matter of this earthly leaven,
They seldom, in their dust-exploring days,
    Have any leisure to look up to Heaven.

So have I known a country on the earth
    Where darkness sat upon the living waters,
And brutal ignorance, and toil, and dearth
    Were the hard portion of its sons and daughters:
And yet, where they who should have oped the door
    Of charity and light, for all men's finding,
Squabbled for words upon the altar-floor,
    And rent The Book, in struggles for the binding.

The gentlest man among those pious Turks
    God's living image ruthlessly defaces;
Their best High Churchman, with no faith in works
    Bowstrings the Virtues in the market-places.
The Christian Pariah, whom both sects curse
    (They curse all other men, and curse each other),
Walks thro' the world, not very much the worse,
    Does all the good he can, and loves his brother

Another allusion in the February letter reminds me of the interest which his old work for the *Chronicle* gave him in everything affecting its credit, and that this was the year when Mr. John Black ceased to be the editor, in circumstances reviving strongly all Dickens's sympathies. "I am deeply grieved" (3 May, 1843) "about Black. Sorry from my heart's core. If I could find him out, I would go and comfort him this moment." He did find him out; and he and a certain number of us did also comfort this excellent man after a fashion extremely English, by giving him a Greenwich dinner on 20 May; when Dickens had arranged and ordered all to perfection, and the dinner succeeded in its purpose, as in other ways, quite wonderfully. Among the entertainers were Sheil and Thackeray, Fonblanque and Charles Buller, Southwood Smith and William Johnson Fox, Macready and Maclise, as well as myself and Dickens.

There followed another similar celebration, in which one of those entertainers was the guest and that owed hardly less to Dickens's exertions, when, at the "Star and Garter" at Richmond in the autumn, we wished Macready good-speed on his way to America. Dickens took the chair at that dinner; and with Stanfield, Maclise, and myself, was in the following week to have accompanied the great actor to Liverpool to say good-bye to him on board the Cunard ship, and bring his wife back to London after their leave-taking; when a word from our excellent friend Captain Marryat, startling to all of us except Dickens himself, struck him out of our party. Marryat thought that Macready might suffer in the States by any public mention of his having been attended on his way by the author of the *American Notes* and *Martin Chuzzlewit*, and our friend at once agreed with him. "Your main and foremost reason," he wrote to me, "for doubting Marryat's judgment, I can at once destroy. It has occurred to me many times; I have mentioned the thing to Kate more than once; and I had intended *not* to go on board, charging Radley to let nothing be said of my being in his house. I have been prevented from giving any expression to my fears by a misgiving that I should seem to attach, if I did so, too much importance to my own doings. But now that I have Marryat at my back, I have not the least hesitation in saying that I am certain he is right. I have very great apprehensions that the *Nickleby* dedication will damage Macready. Marryat is wrong in supposing it is not printed in the American editions, for I have myself seen it in the shop windows of several cities. If I were to go on board with him, I have not the least doubt

*K 781

that the fact would be placarded all over New York before he had shaved himself in Boston. And that there are thousands of men in America who would pick a quarrel with him on the mere statement of his being my friend, I have no more doubt than I have of my existence. You have only doubted Marryat because it is impossible for *any man* to know what they are in their own country who has not seen them there."

This letter was written from Broadstairs, whither he had gone in August, after such help as he only could give, and never took such delight as in giving, to a work of practical humanity. Earlier in the year he had presided at a dinner for the Printers' Pension Fund, which Thomas Hood, Douglas Jerrold, and myself attended with him; and upon the terrible summer-evening accident at sea by which Mr. Elton the actor lost his life, it was mainly by Dickens's unremitting exertions, seconded admirably by Mr. Serle and warmly taken up by Mr. Elton's own profession (the most generous in the world), that ample provision was made for the many children. At the close of August I had news of him from his favourite watering-place, too characteristic to be omitted. The day before had been a day of "terrific heat," yet this had not deterred him from doing what he was too often suddenly prone to do in the midst of his hardest work. "I performed an insane match against time of eighteen miles by the milestones in four hours and a half, under a burning sun the whole way. I could get" (he is writing next morning) "no sleep at night, and really began to be afraid I was going to have a fever. You may judge in what kind of authorship-training I am to-day. I could as soon eat the cliff as write about anything." A few days later, however, all was well again; and a sketch of himself for his friend Professor Felton will show his seaside life in ordinary. "In a bay-window in a one-pair sits, from nine o'clock to one, a gentleman with rather long hair and no neckcloth, who writes and grins, as if he thought he were very funny indeed. At one he disappears, presently emerges from a bathing-machine, and may be seen, a kind of salmon-coloured porpoise, splashing about in the ocean. After that he may be viewed in another bay-window on the ground floor, eating a strong lunch; and after that, walking a dozen miles or so, or lying on his back in the sand reading a book. Nobody bothers him unless they know he is disposed to be talked to; and I am told he is very comfortable indeed. He's as brown as a berry, and they *do* say is a small fortune to the innkeeper who sells beer and cold punch. But this is mere rumour. Sometimes he goes up to London (eighty miles or so away), and then I'm told there is a sound in Lincoln's Inn Fields at night, as of men laughing, together with a clinking of knives and forks and wine-glasses."

* 31A

He returned to town "for good" on Monday, 2 October, and from the Wednesday to the Friday of that week was at Manchester, presiding at the opening of its great Athenæum, when Mr. Cobden and Mr. Disraeli also "assisted." Here he spoke mainly on a matter always nearest his heart, the education of the very poor. He protested against the danger of calling a little learning dangerous; declared his preference for the very least of the little over none at all; proposed to substitute for the old a new doggerel,

> Though house and lands be never got,
> Learning can give what they can *not;*

told his listeners of the real and paramount danger we had lately taken Longfellow to see in the nightly refuges of London, "thousands of immortal creatures condemned without alternative or choice to tread, not what our great poet calls the primrose path to the everlasting bonfire, but one of jagged flints and stones laid down by brutal ignorance"; and contrasted this with the unspeakable consolation and blessings that a little knowledge had shed on men of the lowest estate and most hopeless means, "watching the stars with Ferguson the shepherd's boy, walking the streets with Crabbe, a poor barber here in Lancashire with Arkwright, a tallow-chandler's son with Franklin, shoe-making with Bloomfield in his garret, following the plough with Burns, and high above the noise of loom and hammer, whispering courage in the ears of workers I could this day name in Sheffield and in Manchester."

The same spirit impelled him to give eager welcome to the remarkable institution of Ragged Schools, which, begun by a shoemaker of Portsmouth and a chimney-sweep of Windsor and carried on by a peer of the realm, has had results of incalculable importance to society. The year of which I am writing was its first, as this in which I write is its last; and in the interval, out of three hundred thousand children to whom it has given some sort of education, it is computed also to have given to a third of that number the means of honest employment.[1] "I sent

"After a period of twenty-seven years, from a single school of five small infants, the work has grown into a cluster of some 300 schools, an aggregate of nearly 30,000 children, and a body of 3,000 voluntary teachers, most of them the sons and daughters of toil. . . . Of more than 300,000

Miss Coutts," he had written (24 September), "a sledge-hammer account of the Ragged Schools; and as I saw her name for two hundred pounds in the clergy education subscription list, took pains to show her that religious mysteries and difficult creeds wouldn't do for such pupils. I told her, too, that it was of immense importance they should be *washed*. She writes back to know what the rent of some large airy premises would be, and what the expense of erecting a regular bathing or purifying place; touching which points I am in correspondence with the authorities. I have no doubt she will do whatever I ask her in the matter. She is a most excellent creature, I protest to God, and I have a most perfect affection and respect for her."

One of the last things he did at the close of the year, in the like spirit, was to offer to describe the Ragged Schools for the *Edinburgh Review.* "I have told Napier," he wrote to me, "I will give a description of them in a paper on education, if the *Review* is not afraid to take ground against the Church Catechism and other mere formularies and subtleties, in reference to the education of the young and ignorant. I fear it is extremely improbable it will consent to commit itself so far." His fears were well-founded; but the statements then made by him give me opportunity to add that it was his impatience of differences on this point with clergymen of the Established Church that had led him, for the past year or two, to take sittings in the Little Portland Street Unitarian chapel; for whose officiating minister, Mr. Edward Tagart, he had a friendly regard which continued long after he had ceased to be a member of his congregation. That he did so cease, after two or three years, I can distinctly state; and of the frequent agitation of his mind and thoughts in connection with this all-important theme, there will be other occasions to speak. But upon essential points he had never any sympathy so strong as with the leading doctrines of the Church of England; to these, as time went on, he found himself able to accommodate all minor differences; and the unswerving

children which, on the most moderate calculation, we have a right to conclude have passed through these schools since their commencement, I venture to affirm that more than 100,000 of both sexes have been placed out in various ways, in emigration, in the marine, in trades, and in domestic service. For many consecutive years I have contributed prizes to thousands of the scholars; and let no one omit to call to mind what these children were, whence they came, and whither they were going without this merciful intervention. They would have been added to the perilous swarm of the wild, the lawless, the wretched, and the ignorant, instead of being, as by God's blessing they are, decent and comfortable, earning an honest livelihood, and adorning the community to which they belong."—Letter of Lord Shaftesbury in *The Times* of 13 November, 1871.

faith in Christianity itself, apart from sects and schisms, which had never failed him at any period of his life, found expression at its close in the language of his will. Twelve months before his death, these words were written: "I direct that my name be inscribed in plain English letters on my tomb. . . . I conjure my friends on no account to make me the subject of any monument, memorial, or testimonial whatever. I rest my claim to the remembrance of my country on my published works, and to the remembrance of my friends upon their experience of me in addition thereto. I commit my soul to the mercy of God, through our Lord and Saviour Jesus Christ; and I exhort my dear children humbly to try to guide themselves by the teaching of the New Testament in its broad spirit, and to put no faith in any man's narrow construction of its letter here or there."

Active as he had been in the now ending year, and great as were its varieties of employment; his genius in its highest mood, his energy unwearied in good work, and his capacity for enjoyment without limit; he was able to signalise its closing months by an achievement supremely fortunate, which but for disappointments the year had also brought might never have been thought of. He had not begun until a week after his return from Manchester, where the fancy first occurred to him, and before the end of November he had finished, his memorable *Christmas Carol*. It was the work of such odd moments of leisure as were left him out of the time taken up by two numbers of his *Chuzzlewit*; and though begun with but the special design of adding something to the *Chuzzlewit* balance, I can testify to the accuracy of his own account of what befell him in its composition, with what a strange mastery it seized him for itself, how he wept over it, and laughed, and wept again, and excited himself to an extraordinary degree, and how he walked thinking of it fifteen and twenty miles about the black streets of London, many and many a night after all sober folks had gone to bed. And when it was done, as he told our American friend Mr. Felton, he let himself loose like a madman. "Forster is out again," he added, by way of illustrating our practical comments on his book-celebration of the jovial old season, "and if he don't go in again after the manner in which we have been keeping Christmas, he must be very strong indeed. Such dinings, such dancings, such conjurings, such blind-man's buffings, such theatre-goings, such kissings-out of old years and kissings-in of new ones, never took place in these parts before."

Yet had it been to him, this closing year, a time also of much anxiety and strange disappointments of which I am now to speak; and before, with that view, we go back for a while to its earlier months, one step into the new year may be taken for what marked it with interest and importance to him. Eighteen hundred and forty-four was but fifteen days old when a third son (his fifth child, which received the name of its godfather Francis Jeffrey) was born; and here is an answer sent by him, two days later, to an invitation from Maclise, Stanfield, and myself to dine with us at Richmond: "DEVONSHIRE LODGE, *Seventeenth of January*, 1844. FELLOW COUNTRYMEN! The appeal with which you have honoured me, awakens within my breast emotions that are more easily to be imagined than described. Heaven bless you. I shall indeed be proud, my friends, to respond to such a requisition. I had withdrawn from Public Life—I fondly thought for ever—to pass the evening of my days in hydropathical pursuits, and the contemplation of virtue. For which latter purpose, I had bought a looking-glass.—But, my friends, private feeling must ever yield to a stern sense of public duty. The Man is lost in the Invited Guest, and I comply. Nurses, wet and dry; apothecaries; mothers-in-law; babies; with all the sweet (and chaste) delights of private life; these, my countrymen, are hard to leave. But you have called me forth, and I will come. Fellow countrymen, your friend and faithful servant, CHARLES DICKENS."

II

"CHUZZLEWIT" had fallen short of all the expectations formed of it in regard to sale. By much the most masterly of his writings hitherto, the public had rallied to it in far less numbers than to any of its predecessors. The primary cause of this, there is little doubt, had been the change to weekly issues in the form of publication of his last two stories; for into everything in this world mere habit enters more largely than we are apt to suppose. Nor had the temporary withdrawal to America been favourable to an immediate resumption by his readers of their old and intimate relations. This also is to be added, that the excitement by which a popular reputation is kept up to the highest selling mark will always be subject to lulls too capricious for explanation. But whatever the causes, here was the undeniable fact of a grave depreciation of sale in his writings, unaccompanied by any falling off either in themselves or in the writer's reputation. It was very temporary; but it was present, and to be dealt with accordingly. The forty and fifty thousand purchasers of *Pickwick* and *Nickleby*, the sixty and seventy thousand of the early numbers of the enterprise in which the *Old Curiosity Shop* and *Barnaby Rudge* appeared, had fallen to little over twenty thousand. They rose somewhat on Martin's ominous announcement, at the end of the fourth number, that he'd *go to America*; but though it was believed that this resolve, which Dickens adopted as suddenly as his hero, might increase the number of his readers, that reason influenced him less than the challenge to make good his *Notes* which every mail had been bringing him from unsparing assailants beyond the Atlantic. The substantial effect of the American episode upon the sale was yet by no means great. A couple of thousand additional purchasers were added, but the highest number at any time reached before the story closed was twenty-three thousand. Its sale, since, has ranked next after *Pickwick* and *Copperfield*.

We were now, however, to have a truth brought home to us which few that have had real or varied experience in such matters can have failed to be impressed by—that publishers are bitter bad judges of an author, and are seldom safe persons to consult in regard to the fate or fortunes that may probably await him. Describing the agreement for this book in September 1841, I spoke of a provision against the improbable event of its profits proving inadequate to certain necessary repayments. In this unlikely case, which was to be ascertained by the proceeds of the first five numbers, the publishers were to have power to appropriate fifty pounds a month out of the two hundred pounds payable for authorship in the expenses of each number; but though this had been introduced with my knowledge, I knew also too much of the antecedent relations of the parties to regard it as other than a mere form to satisfy the attorneys in the case. The fifth number, which landed Martin and Mark in America, and the sixth, which described their first experiences, were published; and on the eve of the seventh, in which Mrs. Gamp was to make her first appearance, I heard with infinite pain that from Mr. Hall, the younger partner of the firm which had enriched itself by *Pickwick* and *Nickleby*, and a very kind well-disposed man, there had dropped an inconsiderate hint to the writer of those books that it might be desirable to put the clause in force. It had escaped him without his thinking of all that it involved; certainly the senior partner, whatever amount of as thoughtless sanction he had at the moment given to it, always much regretted it, and made endeavours to exhibit his regret; but the mischief was done, and for the time was irreparable.

"I am so irritated," Dickens wrote to me on 28 June, "so rubbed in the tenderest part of my eyelids with bay-salt, by what I told you yesterday, that a wrong kind of fire is burning in my head, and I don't think I *can* write. Nevertheless, I am trying. In case I should succeed, and should not come down to you this morning, shall you be at the club or elsewhere after dinner? I am bent on paying the money. And before going into the matter with anybody I should like you to propound from me the one preliminary question to Bradbury and Evans. It is more than a year and a half since Clowes wrote to urge me to give him a hearing, in case I should ever think of altering my plans. A printer is better than a bookseller, and it is quite as much the interest of one (if not more) to join me. But whoever it is, or whatever, I am bent upon paying Chapman and Hall *down*. And when I have done that, Mr. Hall shall have a piece of my mind."

What he meant by the proposed repayment will be understood by what formerly was said of his arrangements with those gentlemen on the repurchase of his early copyrights. Feeling no surprise at this announcement, I yet prevailed with him to suspend proceedings until his return from Broadstairs in October; and what then I had to say led to memorable resolves. The communication he had desired me to make to his printers had taken them too much by surprise to enable them to form a clear judgment respecting it; and they replied by suggestions which were in effect a confession of that want of confidence in themselves. They enlarged upon the great results that would follow a re-issue of his writings in a cheap form; they strongly urged such an undertaking; and they offered to invest to any desired amount in the establishment of a magazine or other periodical to be edited by him. The possible dangers, in short, incident to their assuming the position of publishers as well as printers of new works from his pen, seemed at first to be so much greater than on closer examination they were found to be, that at the outset they shrank from encountering them. And hence the remarkable letter I shall now quote (1 November, 1843).

"Don't be startled by the novelty and extent of my project. Both startled *me* at first; but I am well assured of its wisdom and necessity. I am afraid of a magazine—just now. I don't think the time a good one, or the chances favourable. I am afraid of putting myself before the town as writing tooth and nail for bread, headlong, after the close of a book taking so much out of one as *Chuzzlewit*. I am afraid I could not do it, with justice to myself. I know that whatever we may say at first, a new magazine, or a new anything, would require so much propping, that I should be *forced* (as in the *Clock*) to put myself into it, in my old shape. I am afraid of Bradbury and Evans's desire to force on the cheap issue of my books, or any of them, prematurely. I am sure if it took place yet awhile, it would damage me and damage the property, *enormously*. It is very natural in them to want it; but, since they do want it, I have no faith in their regarding me in any other respect than they would regard any other man in a speculation. I see that this is really your opinion as well; and I don't see what I gain, in such a case, by leaving Chapman and Hall. If I had made money, I should unquestionably fade away from the public eye for a year, and enlarge my stock of description and observation by seeing countries new to me; which it is most necessary to me that I should see, and which with an increasing family I can scarcely hope to see at all, unless I see them now. Already for some time I have had this hope and intention before me; and, though not having yet made money, I find or fancy that I can put myself in the position to accomplish it. And this is the course I have before me. At the close of *Chuzzlewit* (by which time the debt will have been materially reduced) I purpose drawing from Chapman and Hall my share of the subscription—bills, or money, will do equally well. I design to tell them that it is not likely I shall do anything for a year; that, in the meantime, I make no arrangement whatever with anyone; and our business matters rest *in statu quo*. The same to Bradbury and Evans. I shall let the house if I can; if not, leave it to be let. I shall take all the family, and two servants —three at most—to some place which I know beforehand to be CHEAP and in a delightful climate, in Normandy or Brittany, to which I shall go over, first, and where I shall rent some house for six or eight months. During that time, I shall walk through Switzerland, cross the Alps, travel through France and Italy; take Kate perhaps to Rome and Venice, but not elsewhere; and in short see everything that is to be seen. I shall write my descriptions to you from time to time, exactly as I did in America; and you will be able to judge whether or not a new and attractive book may not be made on such ground. At the same time I shall be able to turn over the story I have in my mind, and which I have a strong notion might be published with great advantage, *first in Paris*—but that's another matter to be talked over. And of course I have not yet settled, either, whether any book about the travel, or this, should be the first. 'All very well,' you say, 'if you had money enough.' Well, but if I can see my way to what would be necessary without binding myself in any form to anything; without paying interest, or giving any security but one of my Eagle five thousand pounds; you would give up that objection. And I stand committed to no bookseller, printer, moneylender, banker, or patron whatever; and decidedly strengthen my position with my readers, instead of weakening it, drop by drop, as I otherwise must. Is it not so? and is not the way before me, plainly this? I infer that in reality you do yourself think that what I first thought of is *not* the way? I have told you my scheme very baldly, as I said I would. I see its great points, against many prepossessions the other way—as, leaving England, home, friends, everything I am fond of—but it seems to me, at a critical time, *the* step to set me right. A blessing on Mr. Mariotti my Italian master, and his pupil! . . . If you have any breath left, tell Topping how you are."

I had certainly not much after reading this letter, written amid all the distractions of his work, with both the *Carol* and *Chuzzlewit* in hand; but such insufficient breath as was left to me I spent against the project, and in favour of far more consideration than he had given to it before anything should be settled. "I expected you," he wrote next day (2 November), "to be startled. If I was startled myself, when I first got this project of foreign travel into my head, MONTHS AGO, how much more must you be, on whom it comes fresh: numbering only hours! Still, I am very resolute upon it—very. I am convinced that my expenses abroad would not be more than half of my expenses here; the influence of change and nature upon me, enormous. You know, as well as I, that I think *Chuzzlewit* in a hundred points immeasurably the best of my stories. That I feel my power now, more than I ever did. That I have a greater confidence in myself than I ever had. That I *know*, if I have health, I could sustain my place in the minds of thinking men, though fifty writers started up to-morrow. But how many readers do *not* think! How many take it upon trust from knaves and idiots, that one writes too fast, or runs a thing to death! How coldly did this very book go on for months, until it forced itself up in people's opinion, without forcing itself up in sale! If I wrote for forty thousand Forsters, or for forty thousand people who know I write because I can't help it, I should have no need to leave the scene. But this very book warns me that if I *can* leave it for a time, I had better do so, and must do so. Apart from that again, I feel that longer rest after this story would do me good. You say two or three months, because you have been used to see me for eight years never leaving off. But it is not rest enough. It is impossible to go on working the brain to that extent for ever. The very spirit of the thing, in doing it, leaves a horrible despondency behind, when it is done; which must be prejudicial to the mind, so soon renewed and so seldom let alone. What would poor Scott have given to have gone abroad, of his own free will, a young man, instead of creeping there, a driveller, in his miserable decay! I said myself in my note to you—anticipating what you put to me—that it was a question *what* I should come out with, first. The travel-book, if to be done at all, would cost me very little trouble; and surely would go very far to pay charges, whenever published. We have spoken of the baby, and of leaving it here with Catherine's mother. Moving the children into France could not, in any ordinary course of things, do them anything but good. And the question is, what it would do to that by which they live: not what it would do to them. . . . I had forgotten that point in the B. and E. negotiation; but they certainly suggested instant publication of the reprints, or at all events of some of them; by which of course I know, and as you point out, I could provide of myself what is wanted. I take this as putting the thing distinctly as a matter of trade, and feeling it so. And, as a matter of trade with them or anybody else, as a matter of trade between me and the public, should I not be better off a year hence, with the reputation of having seen so much in the meantime? The reason which induces you to look upon this scheme with dislike —separation for so long a time—surely has equal weight with me. I see very little pleasure in it, beyond the natural desire to have been in those great scenes; I anticipate no enjoyment at the time. I have come to look upon it as a matter of policy and duty. I have a thousand other reasons, but shall very soon myself be with you."

There were difficulties, still to be strongly urged, against taking any present step to a final resolve; and he gave way a little. But the pressure was soon renewed. "I have been," he wrote (10 November), "all day in *Chuzzlewit* agonies—conceiving only. I hope to bring forth to-morrow. Will you come here at six? I want to say a word or two about the cover of the *Carol* and the advertising, and to consult you on a nice point in the tale. It will come wonderfully I think. Mac will call here soon after, and we can then all three go to Bulwer's together. And do, my dear fellow, do for God's sake turn over about Chapman and Hall, and look upon my project as *a settled thing*. If you object to see them, I must write to them." My reluctance to any present change in his publishing arrangements was connected with the little story, which, amid all his troubles and "*Chuzzlewit* agonies," he was steadily carrying to its close; and which remains a splendid proof of the consciousness of power felt by him, and of his confidence that it had never been greater than when his readers were thus falling off from him. He had entrusted the *Carol* for publication on his own account, under the usual terms of commission, to the firm he had been so long associated with; and at such a moment to tell them, short of absolute necessity, his intention to quit them altogether, I thought a needless putting in peril of the little book's chances.

He yielded to this argument; but the issue, as will be found, was less fortunate than I hoped.

Let disappointments, or annoyances, however, beset him as they might, once heartily in his work and all was forgotten. His temperament of course coloured everything, cheerful or sad, and his present outlook was disturbed by imaginary fears: but it was very certain that his labours and successes thus far had enriched others more than himself, and while he knew that his mode of living had been scrupulously governed by what he believed to be his means, the first suspicion that these might be inadequate made a change necessary to so upright a nature. It was the turning-point of his career; and the issue, though not immediately, ultimately justified him. Much of his present restlessness I was too ready myself to ascribe to that love of change which was always arising from his passionate desire to vary and extend his observation; but even as to this the result showed him right in believing that he should obtain intellectual advantage from the effects of such further travel. Here indeed he spoke from experience, for already he had returned from America with wider views than when he started, and with more maturity of mind. The money difficulties on which he dwelt were also, it is now to be admitted, unquestionable. Beyond his own domestic expenses necessarily increasing, there were many, never-satisfied, constantly-recurring claims from family quarters, not the more easily avoidable because unreasonable and unjust; and it was after describing to me one such with great bitterness, a few days following the letter last quoted, that he thus replied on the following day (19 November) to the comment I had made upon it: "I was most horribly put out for a little while; for I had got up early to go to work, and was full of interest in what I had to do. But having eased my mind by that note to you, and taken a turn or two up and down the room, I went at it again, and soon got so interested that I blazed away till 9 last night; only stopping ten minutes for dinner! I suppose I wrote eight printed pages of *Chuzzlewit* yesterday. The consequence is that I *could* finish to-day, but am taking it easy, and making myself laugh very much." The very next day, unhappily, there came to himself a repetition of precisely similar trouble in exaggerated form, and to me a fresh reminder of what was gradually settling into a fixed resolve. "I am quite serious and sober when I say, that I have very grave thoughts of keeping my whole menagerie in Italy three years."

Of the book which awoke such varied feelings and was the

occasion of such vicissitudes of fortune, some notice is now
due; and this, following still my former rule, will be not so
much critical as biographical. He had left for Italy before the
completed tale was published, and its reception for a time was
exactly what his just-quoted letter prefigures. It had forced
itself up in public opinion without forcing itself up in sale. It
was felt generally to be an advance upon his previous stories,
and his own opinion is not to be questioned that it was in a
hundred points immeasurably the best of them thus far; less
upon the surface, and going deeper into springs of character.
Nor would it be difficult to say, in a single word, where the
excellence lay that gave it this superiority. It had brought the
highest faculty into play: over and above other qualities it
had given scope to the imagination; and it first expressed the
distinction in this respect between his earlier and his later books.
Apart wholly from this, too, his letters will have confirmed a
remark already made upon the degree to which his mental
power had been enlarged by the effect of his visit to America.

In construction and conduct of story *Martin Chuzzlewit* is
defective, character and description constituting the chief part
of its strength. But what it lost as a story by the American
episode it gained in the other direction; young Martin, by
happy use of a bitter experience, casting off his slough of selfishness in the poisonous swamp of Eden. Dickens often confessed,
however, the difficulty it had been to him to have to deal with
this gap in the main course of his narrative; and I will give an
instance from a letter he wrote to me when engaged upon the
number in which Jonas brings his wife to her miserable home.
"I write in haste" (28 July, 1843), "for I have been at work
all day; and, it being against the grain with me to go back to
America when my interest is strong in the other parts of the
tale, have got on but slowly. I have a great notion to work out
* 32 with Sydney's favourite,[1] and long to be at him again." But
obstructions of this kind with Dickens measured only and always
the degree of readiness and resource with which he rose to
meet them, and never had his handling of character been so
masterly as in *Chuzzlewit*. The persons delineated in former
books had been more agreeable, but never so interpenetrated
with meanings brought out with a grasp so large, easy, and firm.
As well in this as in the passionate vividness of its descriptions,
the imaginative power makes itself felt. The windy autumn
night, with the mad desperation of the hunted leaves and the

[1] Chuffey.

roaring mirth of the blazing village forge; the market-day at Salisbury; the winter walk, and the coach journey to London by night; the ship voyage over the Atlantic; the stormy midnight travel before the murder, the stealthy enterprise and cowardly return of the murderer; these are instances of first-rate description, original in the design, imaginative in all the detail, and very complete in the execution. But the higher power to which I direct attention is even better discerned in the persons and dialogue. With nothing absent or abated in its sharp impressions of reality, there are more of the subtle requisites which satisfy reflection and thought. We have in this book for the most part, not only observation, but the outcome of it, the knowledge as well as the fact. While we witness as vividly the life immediately passing, we are more conscious of the permanent life above and beyond it. Nothing nearly so effective therefore had yet been achieved by him. He had scrutinised as truly and satirised as keenly; but had never shown the imaginative insight with which he now sent his humour and his art into the core of the vices of the time.

Sending me the second chapter of his eighth number on 15 August, he gave me the latest tidings from America. "I gather from a letter I have had this morning that Martin has made them all stark staring raving mad across the water. I wish you would consider this. Don't you think the time has come when I ought to state that such public entertainments as I received in the States were either accepted before I went out, or in the first week after my arrival there; and that as soon as I began to have any acquaintance with the country, I set my face against any public recognition whatever but that which was forced upon me to the destruction of my peace and comfort—and made no secret of my real sentiments." We did not agree as to this, and the notion was abandoned; though his correspondent had not overstated the violence of the outbreak in the States when those chapters exploded upon them. But though an excitable they are a good-humoured and placable people; and, as time moved on a little, the laughter on that side of the Atlantic became quite as great as our amusement on this side, at the astonishing fun and comicality of these scenes. With a little reflection the Americans had doubtless begun to find out that the advantage was not all with us, nor the laughter wholly against them.

They had no Pecksniff at any rate. Bred in a more poisonous swamp than their Eden, of greatly older standing and much

harder to be drained, Pecksniff was all our own. The confession
is not encouraging to national pride, but this character is so
far English, that though our countrymen as a rule are by no
means Pecksniffs the ruling weakness is to countenance and
encourage the race. When people call the character exaggerated,
and protest that the lines are too broad to deceive anyone, they
only refuse, naturally enough, to sanction in a book what half
their lives is passed in tolerating if not in worshipping. Dickens,
illustrating his never-failing experience of being obliged to subdue
in his books what he knew to be real for fear it should be deemed
impossible, had already made the remark in his preface to
Nickleby, that the world, which is so very credulous in what
professes to be truth, is most incredulous in what professes to
be imaginary. They agree to be deceived in a reality, and reward
themselves by refusing to be deceived in a fiction. That a great
many people who might have sat for Pecksniff should condemn
him for a grotesque impossibility, as Dickens averred to be the
case, was no more than might be expected. A greater danger he
has exposed more usefully in showing the larger numbers, who,
desiring to be thought better than they are, support eagerly
pretensions that keep their own in countenance, and without
being Pecksniffs, render Pecksniffs possible. All impostures
would have something suspicious or too forbidding in their
look if we were not prepared to meet them halfway.

There is one thing favourable to us, however, even in this view,
which a French critic has lately suggested. Informing us that
there are no Pecksniffs to be found in France, Mr. Taine explains
this by the fact that his countrymen have ceased to affect
virtue, and pretend only to vice; that a charlatan setting up
morality would have no sort of following; that religion and the
domestic virtues have gone so utterly to rags as not to be worth
putting on for a deceitful garment; and that, no principles being
left to parade, the only chance for the French modern Tartuffe
is to confess and exaggerate weaknesses. We seem to have something of an advantage here. We require at least that the respectable homage of vice to virtue should not be omitted. "Charity,
my dear," says our English Tartuffe, upon being bluntly called
what he really is, "when I take my chamber-candlestick to-
night, remind me to be more than usually particular in praying
for Mr. Anthony Chuzzlewit, who has done me an injustice."
No amount of self-indulgence weakens or lowers his pious and
reflective tone. "Those are her daughters," he remarks, making
maudlin overtures to Mrs. Todgers in memory of his deceased

wife. "Mercy and Charity, Charity and Mercy, not unholy names I hope. She was beautiful. She had a small property." When his condition is such that his friends have to put him to bed, they are only half down the staircase when he is seen to be "fluttering" on the top landing, desiring to collect their sentiments on the nature of human life. "Let us be moral. Let us contemplate existence." He turns his old pupil out of doors in the attitude of blessing him, and when he has discharged that social duty, sheds a few tears in the back garden. No conceivable position, action, or utterance finds him without the vice in which his being is wholly steeped and saturated. In his own house with his daughters he continues it to keep his hand in; and from the mere habit of keeping up appearances to himself falls into the trap of Jonas. Thackeray used to say that there was nothing finer in rascaldom than this ruin of Pecksniff by his son-in-law at the very moment when the oily hypocrite believes himself to be achieving his masterpiece of dissembling over the more vulgar avowed ruffian. "'Jonas!' cried Mr. Pecksniff much affected, 'I am not a diplomatical character; my heart is in my hand. By far the greater part of the inconsiderable savings I have accumulated in the course of—I hope—a not dishonourable or useless career, is already given, devised, or bequeathed (correct me, my dear Jonas, if I am technically wrong), with expressions of confidence which I will not repeat; and in securities which it is unnecessary to mention; to a person whom I cannot, whom I will not, whom I need not name.' Here he gave the hand of his son-in-law a fervent squeeze, as if he would have added, 'God bless you: be very careful of it when you get it!'"

Certainly Dickens thus far had done nothing of which, as in this novel, the details were filled in with such incomparable skill; where the wealth of comic circumstance was lavished in such overflowing abundance on single types of character; or where generally, as throughout the story, the intensity of his observation of individual humours and vices had taken so many varieties of imaginative form. Everything in *Chuzzlewit* indeed had grown under treatment, as will be commonly the case in the handling of a man of genius, who never knows where any given conception may lead him, out of the wealth of resource in development and incident which it has itself created. "As to the way," he wrote to me of its two most prominent figures, as soon as all their capabilities were revealed to him, "as to the way in which these characters have opened out, that is to me

one of the most surprising processes of the mind in this sort of
invention. Given what one knows, what one does not know
springs up; and I am as absolutely certain of its being true, as
I am of the law of gravitation—if such a thing be possible,
more so." The remark displays exactly what in all his important
characters was the very process of creation with him.

Nor was it in the treatment only of his present fiction, but
also in its subject to design, that he had gone higher than in
preceding efforts. Broadly what he aimed at, he would have
expressed on the title-page if I had not dissuaded him, by
printing there as its motto a verse altered from that prologue
of his own composition to which I have formerly referred:
"Your homes the scene, yourselves the actors, here!" Debtors'
prisons, parish Bumbledoms, Yorkshire schools, were vile
enough, but something much more pestiferous was now the
aim of his satire; and he had not before so decisively shown
vigour, daring, or discernment of what lay within reach of his
art, as in taking such a person as Pecksniff for the central
figure in a tale of existing life. Setting him up as the glass
through which to view the groups around him, we are not the
less moved to a hearty detestation of the social vices they
exhibit, and pre-eminently of selfishness in all its forms, because
we see more plainly than ever that there is but one vice which
is quite irremediable. The elder Chuzzlewits are bad enough,
but they bring their self-inflicted punishments; the Jonases and
Tigg Montagues are execrable, but the law has its halter and its
penal servitude; the Moulds and Gamps have plague-bearing
breaths, from which sanitary wisdom may clear us; but from
the sleek, smiling, crawling abomination of a Pecksniff, there is
no help but self-help. Every man's hand should be against
him, for his is against every man; and, as Mr. Taine very wisely
warns us, the virtues have most need to be careful that they
do not make themselves panders to his vice. It is an amiable
weakness to put the best face on the worst things, but there is
none more dangerous. There is nothing so common as the mistake of Tom Pinch, and nothing so rare as his excuses.

The art with which that delightful character is placed at
Mr. Pecksniff's elbow at the beginning of the story, and the
help he gives to set fairly afloat the falsehood he innocently
believes, contribute to an excellent management of this part
of the design; and the same prodigal wealth of invention and
circumstance which gives its higher imaginative stamp to the
book, appears as vividly in its lesser as in its leading figures,

There are wonderfully suggestive touches in the household of Mould the undertaker; and in the vivid picture presented to us by one of Mrs. Gamp's recollections, we are transported to the youthful games of his children. "The sweet creeturs! playing at berryins down in the shop, and follerin' the order-book to its long home in the iron safe!" The American scenes themselves are not more full of life and fun and freshness, and do not contribute more to the general hilarity, than the cockney group at Todgers's; which is itself a little world of the qualities and humours that make up the interest of human life, whether high or low, vulgar or fine, filled in with a master's hand. Here, in a mere byestroke as it were, are the finest things of the earlier books superadded to the new and higher achievement that distinguished the later productions. No part indeed of the execution of this remarkable novel is inferior. Young Bailey and Sweedlepipes are in the front rank of his humorous creations; and poor Mrs. Todgers, worn but not depraved by the cares of gravy and solicitudes of her establishment, with calculation shining out of one eye but with kindliness and good-heartedness still beaming in the other, is quite as perfect a picture in her way as even the portentous Mrs. Gamp with her grim grotesqueness, her filthy habits and foul enjoyments, her thick and damp but most amazing utterances, her moist clammy functions, her pattens, her bonnet, her bundle, and her umbrella. But such prodigious claims must have a particular mention.

This world-famous personage has passed into and become one with the language, which her own parts of speech have certainly not exalted or refined. To none even of Dickens's characters has there been such a run of popularity; and she will remain among the everlasting triumphs of fiction, a superb masterpiece of English humour. What Mr. Mould says of her in his enthusiasm, that she's the sort of woman one would bury for nothing, and do it neatly too, every one feels to be an appropriate tribute; and this, by a most happy inspiration, is exactly what the genius to whom she owes her existence did, when he called her into life, to the foul original she was taken from. That which enduringly stamped upon his page its most mirth-moving figure, had stamped out of English life for ever one of its disgraces. The mortal Mrs. Gamp was handsomely put into her grave, and only the immortal Mrs. Gamp survived. Age will not wither this one, nor custom stale her variety; for here she has a special advantage over even Mr. Pecksniff himself. She has a friend, an *alter ego*, whose kind of service to her is expressed by her first utterance in the story; and with this, which introduces her, we may leave her most fitly. "'Mrs. Harris,' I says, at the very last case as ever I acted in, which it was but a young person, 'Mrs. Harris,' I says, 'leave the bottle on the chimley-piece, and don't ask me to take none, but let me put my lips to it when I am so dispoged.' 'Mrs. Gamp,' she says in answer, 'if ever there was a sober creetur to be got at eighteen-pence a day for working people, and three and six for gentle-folks—night watching,' said Mrs. Gamp with emphasis, 'being a extra charge—you are that inwallable person.' 'Mrs. Harris,' I says to her, 'don't name the charge, for if I could afford to lay all my fellow-creeturs out for nothink, I would gladly do it, sich is the love I bears 'em.'" To this there is nothing to be added, except that in the person of that astonishing friend every phase of fun and comedy in the character is repeated, under fresh conditions of increased appreciation and enjoyment. By the exuberance of comic invention which gives his distinc-tion to Mr. Pecksniff, Mrs. Gamp profits quite as much; the same wealth of laughable incident which surrounds that worthy man is upon her heaped to overflowing; but over and above this, by the additional invention of Mrs. Harris, it is all reproduced, acted over with renewed spirit, and doubled and quadrupled in her favour. This on the whole is the happiest stroke of humorous art in all the writings of Dickens.

But this is a chapter of disappointments, and I have now to state, that as *Martin Chuzzlewit's* success was to seem to him at first only distant and problematical, so even the prodigious immediate success of the *Christmas Carol* itself was not to be an unmitigated pleasure. Never had little book an outset so full of brilliancy of promise. Published but a few days before Christmas, it was hailed on every side with enthusiastic greeting. The first edition of six thousand copies was sold the first day, and on 3 January, 1844, he wrote to me that "two thousand of the three printed for second and third editions are already taken by the trade." But a very few weeks were to pass before the darker side of the picture came. "Such a night as I have passed!" he wrote to me on Saturday morning, 10 February. "I really believed I should never get up again, until I had passed through all the horrors of a fever. I found the *Carol* accounts awaiting me, and they were the cause of it. The first six thousand copies show a profit of £230! And the last four will yield as much more. I had set my heart and soul upon a

Thousand, clear. What a wonderful thing it is, that such a great success should occasion me such intolerable anxiety and disappointment! My year's bills, unpaid, are so terrific, that all the energy and determination I can possibly exert will be required to clear me before I go abroad; which, if next June come and find me alive, I shall do. Good Heaven, if I had only taken heart a year ago! Do come soon, as I am very anxious to talk with you. We can send round to Mac after you arrive, and tell him to join us at Hampstead or elsewhere. I was so utterly knocked down last night, that I came up to the contemplation of all these things quite bold this morning. If I can let the house for this season, I will be off to some seaside place as soon as a tenant offers. I am not afraid, if I reduce my expenses; but if I do not, I shall be ruined past all mortal hope of redemption."

The ultimate result was that his publishers were changed, and the immediate result that his departure for Italy became a settled thing; but a word may be said on these *Carol* accounts before mention is made of his new publishing arrangements. * 33 Want of judgment had been shown in not adjusting the expenses of production with a more equable regard to the selling price, but even as it was, before the close of the year, he had received £726 from a sale of fifteen thousand copies; and the difference between this and the amount realised by the same proportion of the sale of the successor to the *Carol*, undoubtedly justified him in the discontent now expressed. Of that second sale, as well as of the third and fourth, more than double the numbers of the *Carol* were at once sold, and of course there was no complaint of any want of success; but the truth really was, as to all the Christmas stories issued in this form, that the price charged, while too large for the public addressed by them, was too little to remunerate their outlay; and when in later years he put forth similar fancies for Christmas, charging for them fewer pence than the shillings required for these, he counted his purchasers, with fairly corresponding gains to himself, not by tens but by hundreds of thousands. The sale of one of those pieces, five years before his death, went up in its first week to 250,000.

It was necessary now that negotiations should be resumed with his printers, but before any step was taken Messrs. Chapman and Hall were informed of his intention not to open fresh publishing relations with them after *Chuzzlewit* should have closed. Then followed deliberations and discussions, many and grave, which settled themselves at last into the form of an agreement with Messrs. Bradbury and Evans executed on 1 June 1844; by which upon advance made to him of £2800, he assigned to them a fourth share in whatever he might write during the next ensuing eight years, to which the agreement was to be strictly limited. There were the usual protecting clauses, but no interest was to be paid, and no obligations were imposed as to what works should be written, if any, or the form of them; the only farther stipulation having reference to the event of a periodical being undertaken whereof Dickens might be only partially editor or author, in which case his proprietorship of copyright and profits was to be two-thirds instead of three-fourths. There was an understanding, at the time this agreement was signed, that a successor to the *Carol* would be ready for the Christmas of 1844; but no other promise was asked or made in regard to any other book, nor had he himself decided what form to give to his experiences of Italy, if he should even finally determine to publish them at all.

Between this agreement and his journey six weeks elapsed, and there were one or two characteristic incidents before his departure: but mention must first be interposed of the success quite without alloy that also attended the little book, and carried off in excitement and delight every trace of doubt or misgiving. "Blessings on your kind heart," wrote Jeffrey to the author of the *Carol*. "You should be happy yourself, for you may be sure you have done more good by this little publication, fostered more kindly feelings, and prompted more positive acts of beneficence, than can be traced to all the pulpits and confessionals in Christendom since Christmas 1842." "Who can listen," exclaimed Thackeray, "to objections regarding such a book as this? It seems to me a national benefit, and to every man or woman who reads it a personal kindness." Such praise expressed what men of genius felt and said: but the small volume had other tributes, less usual and not less genuine. There poured upon its author daily, all through that Christmas time, letters from complete strangers to him which I remember reading with a wonder of pleasure; not literary at all, but of the simplest domestic kind; of which the general burden was to tell him, amid many confidences, about their homes, how the *Carol* had come to be read aloud there, and was to be kept upon a little shelf by itself, and was to do them no end of good. Anything more to be said of it will not add much to this.

There was indeed nobody that had not some interest in the

message of the *Christmas Carol*. It told the selfish man to rid
himself of selfishness; the just man to make himself generous;
and the good-natured man to enlarge the sphere of his good
nature. Its cheery voice of faith and hope, ringing from one
end of the island to the other, carried pleasant warning alike
to all, that if the duties of Christmas were wanting no good
could come of its outward observances; that it must shine
upon the cold hearth and warm it, and into the sorrowful heart
and comfort it; that it must be kindness, benevolence, charity,
mercy, and forbearance, or its plum pudding would turn to
bile, and its roast beef be indigestible. Nor could any man * 34
have said it with the same appropriateness as Dickens. What
was marked in him to the last was manifest now. He had
identified himself with Christmas fancies. Its life and spirits,
its humour in riotous abundance, of right belonged to him. Its
imaginations, as well as its kindly thoughts, were his; and its
privilege to light up with some sort of comfort the squalidest
places, he had made his own. Christmas Day was not more
social or welcome: New Year's Day not more new: Twelfth
Night not more full of characters. The duty of diffusing enjoyment had never been taught by a more abundant, mirthful,
thoughtful, ever-seasonable writer.

Something also is to be said of the spirit of the book, and of
others like it that followed, which will not anticipate special
allusions to be made hereafter. No one was more intensely fond
than Dickens of old nursery tales, and he had a secret delight
in feeling that he was here only giving them a higher form. The
social and manly virtues he desired to teach, were to him not
less the charm of the ghost, the goblin, and the fairy fancies
of his childhood; however rudely set forth in those earlier days.
What now were to be conquered were the more formidable
dragons and giants that had their places at our own hearths,
and the weapons to be used were of a finer than the "ice-
brook's temper." With brave and strong restraints, what is
evil in ourselves was to be subdued; with warm and gentle
sympathies, what is bad or unreclaimed in others was to be
redeemed; the Beauty was to embrace the Beast, as in the
divinest of all those fables; the star was to rise out of the ashes,
as in our much-loved Cinderella; and we were to play the
Valentine with our wilder brothers, and bring them back with
brotherly care to civilisation and happiness. Nor is it to be
doubted, I think, that, in that largest sense of benefit, great
public and private service was done; positive, earnest, practical

good; by the extraordinary popularity, and nearly universal acceptance, which attended these little holiday volumes. They carried to countless firesides, with new enjoyment of the season, better apprehension of its claims and obligations; they mingled grave with glad thoughts, much to the advantage of both; what seemed almost too remote to meddle with they brought within reach of the charities, and what was near they touched with a dearer tenderness; they comforted the generous, rebuked the sordid, cured folly by kindly ridicule and comic humour, and, saying to their readers, *Thus you have done, but it were better Thus*, may for some have realised the philosopher's famous experience, and by a single fortunate thought revised the whole manner of a life. Literary criticism here is a second-rate thing, and the reader may be spared such discoveries as it might have made in regard to the *Christmas Carol*.

III

YEAR OF DEPARTURE FOR ITALY

1844

AND now, before accompanying Dickens on his Italian travel, one or two parting incidents will receive illustration from his letters. A thoughtful little poem written during the past summer for Lady Blessington has been quoted on a previous page: and it may remind me to say here what warmth of regard he had for her, and for all the inmates of Gore House; how uninterruptedly joyous and pleasurable were his associations with them; and what valued help they now gave in his preparations for Italy. The poem, as we have seen, was written during a visit made in Yorkshire to the house of Mr. Smithson, already named as the partner of his early companion, Mr. Mitton; and this visit he repeated in sadder circumstances during the present year, when (April 1844) he attended Mr. Smithson's funeral. With members or connections of the family of this friend, h' intercourse long continued.

In the previous February, on the 26th and 28th respectiv' he had taken the chair at two great meetings, in Liverpo' the Mechanics' Institution, and in Birmingham of the technic Institution, to which reference is made by hi' letter of the 21st. I quote the allusion because it sh early the sensitive regard to his position as a man and his scrupulous consideration for the feelings interest of the class, which he manifested in many often greatly self-sacrificing ways all through his me on the following point. And as I must write to already lost a post, advise me by bearer. This Li' tion, which is wealthy and has a high grammar s' of which receive in salaries upwards of £2000 extent horrifies me; I am struggling throu' morning), writes me yesterday by its secret' about the order of the proceedings on M' thus. 'I beg to send you proflxtd, with t'

committee, a bank order for twenty pounds in payment of the expenses contingent on your visit to Liverpool.'—And there, sure enough, it is. Now my impulse was, *and is*, decidedly to return it. Twenty pounds is not of moment to me; and any sacrifice of independence is worth it twenty times twenty times told. But haggling in my mind is a doubt whether that would be proper, and not boastful (in an inexplicable way); and whether as an author, I have a right to put myself on a basis which the professors of literature in other forms *connected with the Institution* cannot afford to occupy. Don't you see? But of course you do. The case stands thus. The Manchester Institution, being in debt, appeals to me as it were *in formâ pauperis*, and makes no such provision as I have named. The Birmingham Institution, just struggling into life with great difficulty, applies to me on the same grounds. But the Leeds people (thriving) write to me, making the expenses a distinct matter of business; and the Liverpool, as a point of delicacy, say nothing about it to the last minute, and then send the money. Now, what in the name of goodness ought I to do?—I am as much puzzled with the cheque as Colonel Jack was with his gold. If it would have settled the matter to put it in the fire yesterday, I should certainly have done it. Your opinion is requested. I think I shall have grounds for a very good speech at Brummagem; but I am not sure about Liverpool; having misgivings of over-gentility." My opinion was clearly for sending the money back, which accordingly was done.

Both speeches, duly delivered to enthusiastic listeners at the places named, were good, and both, with suitable variations, had the same theme: telling his popular audience in Birmingham that the principle of their institute, education comprehensive and unsectarian, was the only safe one, for that without danger no society could go on punishing men for preferring vice to virtue without giving them the means of knowing what virtue was; and reminding his genteeler audience in Liverpool, that if happily they had been themselves well taught, so much the more should they seek to extend the benefit to all, since, whatever the precedence due to rank, wealth, or intellect, there yet a nobility beyond them, expressed unaffectedly by the 's verse and in the power of education to confer.

> Howe'er it be, it seems to me,
>   'Tis only noble to be good:
> True hearts are more than coronets,
>   And simple faith than Norman blood.

He underwent some suffering, which he might have spared himself, at his return. "I saw the *Carol* last night," he wrote to me of a dramatic performance of the little story at the Adelphi. "Better than usual, and Wright seems to enjoy Bob Cratchit, but *heart-breaking* to me. Oh Heaven! if any forecast of *this* was ever in my mind! Yet O. Smith was drearily better than I expected. It is a great comfort to have that kind of meat underdone; and his face is quite perfect." Of what he suffered from these adaptations of his books, multiplied remorselessly at every theatre, I have forborne to speak, but it was the subject of complaint with him incessantly; and more or less satisfied as he was with individual performances, such as Mr. Yates's Quilp or Mantalini and Mrs. Keeley's Smike or Dot, there was only one, that of Barnaby Rudge by the Miss Fortescue who became afterwards Lady Gardner, on which I ever heard him dwell with a thorough liking. It is true that to the dramatisations of his next and other following Christmas stories he gave help himself; but, even then, all such efforts to assist special representations were mere attempts to render more tolerable what he had no power to prevent, and, with a few rare exceptions, they were never very successful. Another and graver wrong was the piracy of his writings, every one of which had been reproduced with merely such colourable changes of title, incidents, and names of characters, as were believed to be sufficient to evade the law and adapt them to "penny" purchasers. So shamelessly had this been going on ever since the days of *Pickwick*, in so many outrageous ways and with all but impunity, that a course * 35 repeatedly urged by Talfourd and myself was at last taken in the present year with the *Christmas Carol* and the *Chuzzlewit* pirates. Upon a case of such peculiar flagrancy, however, that the vice-chancellor would not even hear Dickens's counsel; and what it cost our dear friend Talfourd to suppress his speech exceeded by very much the labour and pains with which he had prepared it. "The pirates," wrote Dickens to me, after leaving the court on 18 January, "are beaten flat. They are bruised, bloody, battered, smashed, squelched, and utterly undone. Knight Bruce would not hear Talfourd, but instantly gave judgment. He had interrupted Anderton constantly by asking him to produce a passage which was not an expanded or contracted idea from my book. And at every successive passage he cried out, 'That is Mr. Dickens's case. Find another!' He said that there was not a shadow of doubt upon the matter. That there was no authority which would bear a construction in their favour; the piracy going beyond all previous instances. They might mention it again in a week, he said, if they liked, and might have an issue if they pleased; but they would probably consider it unnecessary after that strong expression of his opinion. Of course I will stand by what we have agreed as to the only terms of compromise with the printers. I am determined that I will have an apology for their affidavits. The other men may pay their costs and get out of it, but I will stick to my friend the author." Two days later he wrote: "The further affidavits put in by way of extenuation by the printing rascals *are* rather strong, and give one a pretty correct idea of what the men must be who hold on by the heels of literature. Oh! the agony of Talfourd at Knight Bruce's not hearing him! He had sat up till three in the morning, he says, preparing his speech; and would have done all kinds of things with the affidavits. It certainly was a splendid subject. We have heard nothing from the vagabonds yet. I once thought of printing the affidavits without a word of comment, and sewing them up with *Chuzzlewit*. Talfourd is strongly disinclined to compromise with the printers on any terms. In which case it would be referred to the master to ascertain what profits had been made by the piracy, and to order the same to be paid to me. But wear and tear of law is my consideration." The undertaking to which he had at last to submit was, that upon ample public apology, and payment of all costs, the offenders should be let go: but the real result was that, after infinite vexation and trouble, he had himself to pay all the costs incurred on his own behalf; and, a couple of years later, upon repetition of the wrong he had suffered in so gross a form that proceedings were again advised by Talfourd and others, he wrote to me from Switzerland the condition of mind to which his experience had brought him. "My feeling about the —— is the feeling common, I suppose, to three-fourths of the reflecting part of the community in our happiest of all possible countries; and that is, that it is better to suffer a great wrong than to have recourse to the much greater wrong of the law. I shall not easily forget the expense, and anxiety, and horrible injustice of the *Carol* case, wherein, in asserting the plainest right on earth, I was really treated as if I were the robber instead of the robbed. Upon the whole, I certainly would much rather NOT proceed. What do you think of sending in a grave protest against what has been done in this case, on account of the immense amount of piracy to which I am daily exposed, and because I have been already met in the Court of

Chancery with the legal doctrine that silence under such wrongs
barred my remedy: to which Talfourd's written opinion might
be appended as proof that we stopped under no discouragement.
It is useless to affect that I don't know I have a morbid sus-
ceptibility of exasperation, to which the meanness and badness
of the law in such a matter would be stinging in the last degree.
And I know of nothing that *could* come, even of a successful
action, which would be worth the mental trouble and disturbance it would cost." [1]

A few notes of besetting temptations during his busiest days
at *Chuzzlewit*, one taken from each of the first four months of
the year when he was working at its masterly closing scenes,
will amusingly exhibit, side by side, his powers of resistance
and capacities of enjoyment. "I had written you a line" (16
January), "pleading Jonas and Mrs. Gamp, but this frosty day
tempts me sorely. I am distractingly late, but I look at the sky,
think of Hampstead, and feel hideously tempted. Don't come
with Mac, and fetch me. I couldn't resist if you did." In the
next (18 February), he is not the tempted, but the tempter.
"Stanfield and Mac have come in, and we are going to Hampstead to dinner. I leave Betsy Prig as you know, so don't you

[1] The reader may be amused if I add in a note what he said of the pirates
in those earlier days when grave matters touched him less gravely. On the
eve of the first number of *Nickleby* he had issued a proclamation. "Whereas
we are the only true and lawful Boz. And whereas it hath been reported
to us, who are commencing a new work, that some dishonest dullards
resident in the by-streets and cellars of this town impose upon the unwary
and credulous, by producing cheap and wretched imitations of our delect-
able works. And whereas we derive but small comfort under this injury
from the knowledge that the dishonest dullards aforesaid cannot, by
reason of their mental smallness, follow near our heels, but are constrained
to creep along by dirty and little-frequented ways, at a most respectful
and humble distance behind. An whereas, in like manner, as some other
vermin are not worth the killing for the sake of their carcasses, so these
kennel pirates are not worth the powder and shot of the law, inasmuch
as whatever damages they may commit they are in no condition to pay
any. This is to give notice, that we have at length devised a mode of
execution for them, so summary and terrible, that if any gang or gangs
thereof presume to hoist but one shred of the colours of the good ship
Nickleby, we will hang them on gibbets so lofty and enduring that their
remains shall be a monument of our just vengeance to all succeeding ages;
and it shall not lie in the power of any lord high admiral, on earth, t cause
them to be taken down again." The last paragraph of the proclamation
informed the potentates of Paternoster Row, that from the then ensuing
day of the thirtieth of March, until further notice, "we s all hold our Levees,
as heretofore, on the last evening but one of every month, between the
hours of seven and nine, at our Board of Trade, number one hundred and
eighty-six in the Strand, London; where we again request the attendance
(in vast crowds) of their accredited agents and ambassadors. Gentlemen
to wear knots upon their shoulders; and patent cabs to draw up with their
doors towards the grand entrance, for the convenience of loading."

make a scruple about leaving Mrs. Harris. We shall stroll lei-
surely up, to give you time to join us, and dinner will be on
the table at ' Jack Straw's' at four. . . . In the very improbable
(surely impossible?) case of your not coming, we will call on
you at a quarter before eight, to go to the ragged school." The
next (5 March) shows him in yielding mood, and pitying himself
for his infirmity of compliance. "Sir, I will—he—he—he—he—
he—he—I will NOT eat with you, either at your own house or
the club. But the morning looks bright, and a walk to Hampstead would suit me marvellously. If you should present yourself at my gate (bringing the R. A.'s along with you) I shall
not be sapparized. So no more at this writing from poor
MR. DICKENS." But again the tables are turned, and he is
tempter in the last; written on that Shakespeare day (23
April) which we kept always as a festival, and signed in character expressive of his then present unfitness for any of the
practical affairs of life, including the very pressing business
which at the moment ought to have occupied him, namely,
attention to the long-deferred nuptials of Miss Charity Pecksniff.
"November blasts! Why it's the warmest, most genial, most
intensely bland, delicious, growing, springy, songster-of-the-
grovy, bursting-forth-of-the-buddy, day as ever was. At half-
past four I shall expect you. Ever, MODDLE."

Moddle, the sentimental noodle hooked by Miss Pecksniff who
flies on his proposed wedding-day from the frightful prospect
before him, the reader of course knows; and has perhaps admired for his last superb outbreak of common sense. It was a
rather favourite bit of humour with Dickens: and I find it
pleasant to think that he never saw the description given of it
by a trained and skilful French critic, who has been able to pass
under his review the whole of English literature without any
apparent sense or understanding of one of its most important
as well as richest elements. A man without the perception of
humour taking English prose literature in hand, can of course
set about it only in one way. Accordingly, in Mr. Taine's decisive
judgments of our last great humorist, which proceed upon a
principle of psychological analysis which it is only fair to say
he applies impartially to everybody, *Pickwick*, *Oliver Twist*,
and *The Old Curiosity Shop* are not in any manner even named
or alluded to; Mrs. Gamp is only once mentioned as always
talking of Mrs. Harris, and Mr. Micawber also only once as
using always the same emphatic phrases; the largest extracts
are taken from the two books in all the Dickens series that are

weakest on the humorous side, *Hard Times* and the *Chimes*; *Nickleby*, with its many laughter-moving figures, is dismissed in a line and a half; Mr. Toots, Captain Cuttle, Susan Nipper, Toodles, and the rest have no place in what is said of *Dombey*; and, to close with what has caused and must excuse my digression, Mr. Augustus Moddle is introduced as a gloomy maniac who makes us laugh and makes us shudder, and as drawn so truly for a madman, that though at first sight agreeable he is in reality horrible!

A month before the letter subscribed by Dickens in the character, so happily unknown to himself, of this gloomy maniac, he had written to me from amidst his famous chapter in which the tables are turned on Pecksniff; but here I quote the letter chiefly for noticeable words at its close. "I heard from Macready by the *Hibernia*. I have been slaving away regularly, but the weather is against rapid progress. I altered the verbal error, and substituted for the action you didn't like some words expressive of the hurry of the scene. Macready sums up slavery in New Orleans in the way of a gentle doubting on the subject, by a 'but' and a dash. I believe it is in New Orleans that the man is lying under sentence of death, who, not having the fear of God before his eyes, did not deliver up a captive slave to the torture? The largest gun in that country has not burst yet— *but it will*. Heaven help us, too, from explosions nearer home! I declare I never go into what is called 'society' that I am not aweary of it, despise it, hate it, and reject it. The more I see of its extraordinary conceit, and its stupendous ignorance of what is passing out of doors, the more certain I am that it is approaching the period when, being incapable of reforming itself, it will have to submit to be reformed by others off the face of the earth." Thus we see that the old radical leanings were again rather strong in him at present, and I may add that he had found occasional recent vent for them by writing in the *Morning Chronicle*.

Some articles thus contributed by him having set people talking, the proprietors of the paper rather eagerly mooted the question what payment he would ask for contributing regularly; and ten guineas an article was named. Very sensibly, however, the editor who had succeeded his old friend Black pointed out to him, that though even that sum would not be refused in the heat of the successful articles just contributed, yet (I quote his own account in a letter of 7 March, 1844) so much would hardly be paid continuously; and thereupon an understanding was come to, that he would write as a volunteer and leave his payment to be adjusted to the results. "Then said the editor—and this I particularly want you to turn over in your mind, at leisure—supposing me to go abroad, could I contemplate such a thing as the writing of a letter a week under any signature I chose, with such scraps of descriptions and impressions as suggested themselves to my mind? If so, would I do it for the *Chronicle*? And if so again, what would I do it for? He thought for such contributions Easthope would pay anything. I told him that the idea had never occurred to me; but that I was afraid he did not know what the value of such contributions would be. He repeated what he had said before; and I promised to consider whether I could reconcile it to myself to write such letters at all. The pros and cons need to be very carefully weighed. I will not tell you to which side I incline, but if we should disagree, or waver on the same points, we will call Bradbury and Evans to the council. I think it more than probable that we shall be of exactly the same mind, but I want you to be in possession of the facts and therefore send you this rigmarole." The rigmarole is not unimportant; because, though we did not differ on the wisdom of saying No to the *Chronicle*, the "council" spoken of was nevertheless held, and in it lay the germ of another newspaper enterprise he permitted himself to engage in twelve months later, to which he would have done more wisely to have also answered No.

The preparation for departure was now actively going forward, and especially his inquiries for two important adjuncts thereto, a courier and a carriage. As to the latter it occurred to him that he might perhaps get for little money "some good old shabby devil of a coach—one of those vast phantoms that hide themselves in a corner of the Pantechnicon"; and exactly such a one he found there; sitting himself inside it, a perfect Sentimental Traveller, while the managing man told him its history. "As for comfort—let me see—it is about the size of your library; with night-lamps and day-lamps and pockets and imperials and leathern cellars, and the most extraordinary contrivances. Joking apart, it is a wonderful machine. And when you see it (if you *do* see it) you will roar at first, and will then proclaim it to be 'perfectly brilliant, my dear fellow.'" It was marked sixty pounds; he got it for five-and-forty; and my own emotions respecting it he had described by anticipation quite correctly. In finding a courier he was even more fortunate; and these successes were followed by a third apparently very promising, but in the result less satisfactory. His house was let to not very careful people.

The tenant having offered herself for Devonshire Terrace unexpectedly, during the last week or two of his stay in England he went into temporary quarters in Osnaburgh Terrace: and here a domestic difficulty befell of which the mention may be amusing, when I have disposed of an incident that preceded it too characteristic for omission. The Mendicity Society's officers had caught a notorious begging-letter writer, had identified him as an old offender against Dickens of which proofs were found on his person, and had put matters in train for his proper punishment; when the wretched creature's wife made such appeal before the case was heard at the police-court, that Dickens broke down in his character of prosecutor, and at the last moment, finding what was said of the man's distress at the time to be true, relented. "When the Mendicity officers themselves told me the man was in distress, I desired them to suppress what they knew about him, and slipped out of the bundle (in the police-office) his first letter, which was the greatest lie of all. For he looked wretched, and his wife had been waiting about the street to see me, all the morning. It was an exceedingly bad case however, and the imposition, all through, very great indeed. Insomuch that I could not *say* anything in his favour, even when I saw him. Yet I was not sorry that the creature found the loophole for escape. The officers had taken him illegally without any warrant; and really they messed it all through, quite facetiously."

He will himself also best relate the small domestic difficulty into which he fell in his temporary dwelling, upon his unexpectedly discovering it to be unequal to the strain of a dinner party for which invitations had gone out just before the sudden "let" of Devonshire Terrace. The letter is characteristic in other ways, or I should hardly have gone so far into domesticities here; and it enables me to add that with the last on its list of guests, Mr. Thomas Chapman, the chairman of Lloyd's, he held frequent kindly intercourse, and that few things more absurd or unfounded have been invented, even of Dickens, than that he found any part of the original of Mr. Dombey in the nature, the appearance, or the manners of this excellent and much-valued friend. "Advise, advise," he wrote (9 Osnaburgh Terrace, 28 May, 1844), "advise with a distracted man. Investigation below stairs renders it, as my father would say, 'manifest to any person of ordinary intelligence, if the term may be considered allowable,' that the Saturday's dinner cannot come off here with safety. It would be a toss-up, and might come down heads, but it would put us into an agony with that kind of people. . . . Now, I feel a difficulty in dropping it altogether, and really fear that this might have an indefinably suspicious and odd appearance. Then said I at breakfast this morning, I'll send down to the Clarendon. Then says Kate, have it at Richmond. Then I say that might be inconvenient to the people. Then she says, how could it be if we dine late enough? Then I am very much offended without exactly knowing why; and come up here, in a state of hopeless mystification. . . . What do you think? Ellis would be quite as dear as anybody else; and unless the weather changes, the place is objectionable. I must make up my mind to do one thing or other, for we shall meet Lord Denman at dinner to-day. Could it be dropped decently? That, I think very doubtful. Could it be done for a couple of guineas apiece at the Clarendon? . . . In a matter of more importance I could make up my mind. But in a matter of this kind I bother and bewilder myself, and come to no conclusion whatever. Advise! Advise! . . . List of the invited. There's Lord Normanby. And there's Lord Denman. There's Easthope, wife, and sister. There's Sydney Smith. There's you and Mac. There's Babbage. There's a Lady Osborne and her daughter. There's Southwood Smith. And there's Quin. And there are Thomas Chapman and his wife. So many of these people have never dined with us, that the fix is particularly tight. Advise! Advise!" My advice was for throwing over the party altogether, but additional help was obtained and the dinner went off very pleasantly. It was the last time we saw Sydney Smith.

Of one other characteristic occurrence he wrote before he left; and the very legible epigraph round the seal of his letter, "It is particularly requested that if Sir James Graham should open this, he will not trouble himself to seal it again," expresses both its date and its writer's opinion of a notorious transaction of the time. "I wish" (28 June) "you would read this, and give it me again when we meet at Stanfield's to-day. Newby has written to me to say that he hopes to be able to give Overs more money than was agreed on." The enclosure was the proof-sheet of a preface written by him to a small collection of stories by a poor carpenter dying of consumption, who hoped by their publication, under protection of such a name, to leave behind

him some small provision for his ailing wife and little children.[1]
The book was dedicated to the kind physician, Doctor Elliotson,
whose name was for nearly thirty years a synonym with us all
for unwearied, self-sacrificing, beneficent service to every one
in need.

The last incident before Dickens's departure was a farewell
dinner to him at Greenwich, which took also the form of a
celebration for the completion of *Chuzzlewit*, or, as the Ballantynes used to call it in Scott's case, a christening dinner; when
Lord Normanby took the chair, and I remember sitting next
the great painter Turner, who had come with Stanfield, and
had enveloped his throat, that sultry summer day, in a huge
red belcher-handkerchief, which nothing would induce him to
remove. He was not otherwise demonstrative, but enjoyed himself in a quiet silent way, less perhaps at the speeches than at
the changing lights on the river. Carlyle did not come; telling
me in his reply to the invitation that he truly loved Dickens,
having discerned in the inner man of him a real music of the
genuine kind, but that he'd rather testify to this in some other
form than that of dining out in the dog-days.

[1] He wrote from Marseilles (17 December, 1844): "When poor Overs
was dying he suddenly asked for a pen and ink and some paper, and made
up a little parcel for me which it was his last conscious act to direct. She
(his wife) told me this and gave it me. I opened it last night. It was a
copy of his little book in which he had written my name, 'With his devotion.' I thought it simple and affecting of the poor fellow." From a later
letter a few lines may be added. "Mrs. Overs tells me" (Monte Vacchi,
30 March, 1845) "that Miss Coutts has sent her, at different times, sixteen
pounds, has sent a doctor to her children, and has got one of the girls
into the Orphan School. When I wrote her a word in the poor woman's
behalf, she wrote me back to the effect that it was a kindness to herself
to have done so, 'for what is the use of my means but to try and do some
good with them?'"

IV

IDLENESS AT ALBARO: VILLA BAGNERELLO

1844

THE travelling party arrived at Marseilles on the evening of Sunday, 14 July. Not being able to get *vetturino* horses in Paris, they had come on post; paying for nine horses but bringing only four, and thereby saving a shilling a mile out of what the four would have cost in England. So great thus far, however, had been the cost of travel, that "what with distance, caravan, sight-seeing, and everything," two hundred pounds would be nearly swallowed up before they were at their destination. The success otherwise had been complete. The children had not cried in their worst troubles, the carriage had gone lightly over abominable roads, and the courier had proved himself a perfect gem. "Surrounded by strange and perfectly novel circumstances," Dickens wrote to me from Marseilles, "I feel as if I had a new head on side by side with my old one."

To what shrewd and kindly observation the old one had helped him at every stage of his journey, his published book of travel tells, and of all that there will be nothing here; but a couple of experiences at his outset, of which he told me afterwards, have enough character in them to be worth mention.

Shortly before there had been some public interest about the captain of a Boulogne steamer apprehended on a suspicion of having stolen specie, but reinstated by his owners after a public apology to him on their behalf; and Dickens had hardly set foot on the boat that was to carry them across, when he was attracted by the look of its captain, and discovered him after a minute's talk to be that very man. "Such an honest, simple, good fellow, I never saw," said Dickens, as he imitated for me the homely speech in which his confidences were related. The Boulogne people, he said, had given him a piece of plate, "but Lord bless us! it took a deal more than that to get him round again in his own mind; and for weeks and weeks he was un-

common low to be sure. Newgate, you see! What a place for a
seafaring man as had held up his head afore the best on 'em,
and had more friends, I mean to say, and I do tell you the daylight truth, than any man on this station—ah! or any other,
I don't care where!"

His first experience in a foreign tongue he made immediately
on landing, when he had gone to the bank for money, and after
delivering with most laborious distinctness a rather long address
in French to the clerk behind the counter, was disconcerted
by that functionary's cool inquiry in the native-born Lombard
Street manner, "How would you like to take it, sir?" He took
it, as everybody must, in five-franc pieces, and a most inconvenient coinage he found it; for he required so much that he
had to carry it in a couple of small sacks, and was always
"turning hot about suddenly" taking it into his head that he
had lost them.

The evening of Tuesday, 16 July, saw him in a villa at
Albaro, the suburb of Genoa in which, upon the advice of our
Gore House friends, he had resolved to pass the summer months
before taking up his quarters in the city. His wish was to have
had Lord Byron's house there, but it had fallen into neglect
and become the refuge of a third-rate wineshop. The matter
had then been left to Angus Fletcher who just now lived near
Genoa, and he had taken at a rent absurdly above its value an * 36
unpicturesque and uninteresting dwelling, which at once impressed its new tenant with its likeness to a pink jail. "It is,"
he said to me, "the most perfectly lonely, rusty, stagnant old
staggerer of a domain that you can possibly imagine. What
would I give if you could only look round the courtyard! *I* look
down into it, whenever I am near that side of the house, for
the stable is so full of 'vermin and swarmers' (pardon the
quotation from my inimitable friend) that I always expect to
see the carriage going out bodily, with legions of industrious
fleas harnessed to and drawing it off, on their own account. We
have a couple of Italian work-people in our establishment; and
to hear one or other of them talking away to our servants with
the utmost violence and volubility in Genoese, and our servants
answering with great fluency in English (very loud: as if the
others were only deaf, not Italian), is one of the most ridiculous
things possible. The effect is greatly enhanced by the Genoese
manner, which is exceedingly animated and pantomimic; so
that two friends of the lower class conversing pleasantly in
the street, always seem on the eve of stabbing each other

forthwith. And a stranger is immensely astonished at their not doing it."

The heat tried him less than he expected, excepting always the sirocco, which, near the sea as they were, and right in the course of the wind as it blew against the house, made everything hotter than if there had been no wind. "One feels it most, on first getting up. Then, it is really so oppressive that a strong determination is necessary to enable one to go on dressing; one's tendency being to tumble down anywhere and lie there." It seemed to hit him, he said, behind the knee, and make his legs so shake that he could not walk or stand. He had unfortunately a whole week of this without intermission, soon after his arrival; but then came a storm, with wind from the mountains, and he could bear the ordinary heat very well. What at first had been a home-discomfort, the bare walls, lofty ceilings, icy floors, and lattice blinds, soon became agreeable; there were regular afternoon breezes from the sea; in his courtyard was a well of very pure and very cold water; there were new milk and eggs by the bucketful, and, to protect from the summer insects these and other dainties, there were fresh vine-leaves by the thousand; and he satisfied himself, by the experience of a day or two in the city, that he had done well to come first to its suburb by the sea. What startled and disappointed him most were the frequent cloudy days. He opened his third letter (3 August) by telling me there was a thick November fog, that rain was pouring incessantly, and that he did not remember to have seen in his life, at that time of year, such cloudy weather as he had seen beneath Italian skies.

"The story goes that it is in autumn and winter, when other countries are dark and foggy, that the beauty and clearness of this are most observable. I hope it may prove so; for I have postponed going round the hills which encircle the city, or seeing any of the sights, until the weather is more favourable. I have never yet seen it so clear, for any long time of the day together, as on a bright, lark-singing, coast-of-France, discerning day at Broadstairs; nor have I ever seen so fine a sunset *throughout*, as is very common there. But the scenery is exquisite, and at certain periods of the evening and the morning the blue of the Mediterranean surpasses all conception or description. It is the most intense and wonderful colour, I do believe, in all nature."

In his second letter from Albaro there was more of this subject; and an outbreak of whimsical enthusiasm in it, meant especially for Maclise, is followed by some capital description. "I address you, my friend," he wrote, "with something of the lofty spirit of an exile, a banished commoner, a sort of Anglo-Pole. I don't exactly know what I have done for my country in coming away from it, but I feel it is something; something great; something virtuous and heroic. Lofty emotions rise within me, when I see the sun set on the blue Mediterranean. I am the limpet on the rock: my father's name is Turner, and my boots are green. . . . Apropos of blue. In a certain picture called the 'Serenade' for which Browning wrote that verse [1] in Lincoln's Inn Fields, you, O Mac, painted a sky. If you ever have occasion to paint the Mediterranean, let it be exactly of that colour. It lies before me now, as deeply and intensely blue. But no such colour is above me. Nothing like it. In the south of France, at Avignon, at Aix, at Marseilles, I saw deep blue skies; and also in America. But the sky above me is familiar to my sight. Is it heresy to say that I have seen its twin brother shining through the window of Jack Straw's? that down in Devonshire Terrace I have seen a better sky? I dare say it is; but like a great many other heresies, it is true. . . . But such green, green, green, as flutters in the vineyard down below the windows, *that* I never saw; nor yet such lilac and such purple as float between me and the distant hills; nor yet in anything, picture, book, or vestal boredom, such awful, solemn, impenetrable blue, as in that same sea. It has such an absorbing, silent, deep, profound effect, that I can't help thinking it suggested the idea of Styx. It looks as if a draught of it, only so much as you could scoop up on the beach in the hollow of your hand, would wash out everything else, and make a great blue blank of your intellect. . . . When the sun sets clearly, by Heaven, it is majestic. From any one of eleven windows here, or from a terrace overgrown with grapes, you may behold the broad sea, villas, houses, mountains, forts, strewn with rose leaves. Strewn with them? Steeped in them! Dyed, through and through and through. For a moment. No more. The sun is impatient and fierce (like everything else in these parts), and goes down headlong. Run to fetch your

---

[1] I send my heart up to thee, all my heart,
In this my singing!
For the stars help me, and the sea bears part;
The very night is clinging
Closer to Venice' streets to leave one space
Above me, whence thy face
May light my joyous heart to thee its dwelling-place.

Written to express Maclise's subject in the Academy catalogue.

hat—and it's night. Wink at the right time of black night—and it's morning. Everything is in extremes. There is an insect here that chirps all day. There is one outside the window now. The chirp is very loud: something like a Brobdingnagian grasshopper. The creature is born to chirp; to progress in chirping; chirp louder, louder, louder, till it gives one tremendous chirp and bursts itself. That is its life and death. Everything is 'in a concatenation accordingly.' The day gets brighter, brighter, brighter, till it's night. The summer gets hotter, hotter, hotter, till it explodes. The fruit gets riper, riper, riper, till it tumbles down and rots. . . . Ask me a question or two about fresco: will you be so good? All the houses are painted in fresco, hereabout (the outside walls I mean, the fronts, backs, and sides), and all the colour has run into damp and green seediness, and the very design has straggled away into the component atoms of the plaster. Beware of fresco! Sometimes (but not often) I can make out a Virgin with a mildewed glory round her head, holding nothing in an undiscernible lap with invisible arms; and occasionally the leg or arm of a cherub. But it is very melancholy and dim. There are two old fresco-painted vases outside my own gate, one on either hand, which are so faint that I never saw them till last night; and only then, because I was looking over the wall after a lizard who had come upon me while I was smoking a cigar above, and crawled over one of these embellishments in his retreat. . . ."

That letter sketched for me the story of his travel through France, and I may at once say that I thus received, from week to week, the "first sprightly runnings" of every description in his *Pictures from Italy*. But my rule as to the American letters must be here observed yet more strictly; and nothing resembling his printed book, however distantly, can be admitted into these pages. Even so my difficulty of rejection will not be less; for as he had not actually decided, until the very last, to publish his present experiences at all, a larger number of the letters were left unrifled by him. He had no settled plan from the first, as in the other case.

His most valued acquaintance at Albaro was the French consul-general, a student of our literature who had written on his books in one of the French reviews, and who with his English wife lived in the very next villa, though so oddly shut away by its vineyard that to get from the one adjoining house to the other was a mile's journey. Describing, in that August letter, his first call from this new friend thus pleasantly self-recom-

mended, he makes the visit his excuse for breaking off from a
facetious description of French inns to introduce to me a sketch,
from a pencil outline by Fletcher, of what bore the imposing
name of the Villa di Bella Vista, but which he called by the
homelier one of its proprietor, Bagnerello. "This, my friend, is
quite accurate. Allow me to explain it. You are standing, sir,
in our vineyard, among the grapes and figs. The Mediterranean
is at your back as you look at the house: of which two sides,
out of four, are here depicted. The lower story (nearly concealed
by the vines) consists of the hall, a wine-cellar, and some store-
rooms. The three windows on the left of the first floor belong to

the sala, lofty and whitewashed, which has two more windows
round the corner. The fourth window *did* belong to the dining-
room, but I have changed one of the nurseries for better air;
and it now appertains to that branch of the establishment. The
fifth and sixth, or two right-hand windows, sir, admit the light
to the Inimitable's (and uxor's) chamber; to which the first
window round the right-hand corner, which you perceive in
shadow, also belongs. The next window in shadow, young sir, is
the bower of Miss H——. The next, a nursery window; the same
having two more round the corner again. The bowery-looking
place stretching out upon the left of the house is the terrace,
which opens out from a French window in the drawing-room
on the same floor of which you see nothing, and forms one side
of the courtyard. The upper windows belong to some of those

uncounted chambers upstairs; the fourth one, longer than the rest, being in Fletcher's bedroom. There is a kitchen or two up there besides, and my dressing-room; which you can't see from this point of view. The kitchens and other offices in use are down below, under that part of the house where the roof is longest. On your left, beyond the Bay of Genoa, about two miles off, the Alps stretch out into the far horizon; on your right, at three or four miles distance, are mountains crowned with forts. The intervening space on both sides is dotted with villas, some green, some red, some yellow, some blue, some (and ours among the number) pink. At your back, as I have said, sir, is the ocean; with the slim Italian tower of the ruined church of St. John the Baptist rising up before it, on the top of a pile of savage rocks. You go through the courtyard, and out at the gate, and down a narrow lane to the sea. Note. The sala goes sheer up to the top of the house; the ceiling being conical, and the little bedrooms built round the spring of its arch. You will observe that we make no pretension to architectural magnificence, but that we have abundance of room. And here I am beholding only vines and the sea for days together. . . . Good Heavens! How I wish you'd come for a week or two, and taste the white wine at a penny farthing the pint. It is excellent. . . ." Then, after seven days: "I have got my paper and inkstand and figures now (the box from Osnaburgh Terrace only came last Thursday), and can think—I have begun to do so every morning—with a business-like air, of the Christmas book. My paper is arranged, and my pens are spread out, in the usual form. I think you know the form—don't you? My books have not passed the custom-house yet, and I tremble for some volumes of Voltaire. . . . I write in the best bedroom. The sun is off the corner window at the side of the house by a very little after twelve; and I can then throw the blinds open, and look up from my paper, at the sea, the mountains, the washed-out villas, the vineyards, at the blistering white-hot fort with a sentry on the drawbridge standing in a bit of shadow no broader than his own musket, and at the sky, as often as I like. It is a very peaceful view, and yet a very cheerful one. Quiet as quiet can be."

Not yet, however, had the time for writing come. A sharp attack of illness befell his youngest little daughter, Kate, and troubled him much. Then, after beginning the Italian grammar himself, he had to call in the help of a master; and this learning of the language took up time. But he had an aptitude for it, and after a month's application told me (24 August) that he could ask in Italian for whatever he wanted in any shop or coffee-house, and could read it pretty well. "I wish you could see me" (16 September), "without my knowing it, walking about alone here. I am now as bold as a lion in the streets. The audacity with which one begins to speak when there is no help for it, is quite astonishing." The blank impossibility at the out-set, however, of getting native meanings conveyed to his English servants, he very humorously described to me; and said the spell was first broken by the cook, "being really a clever woman, and not entrenching herself in that astonishing pride of ignorance which induces the rest to oppose themselves to the receipt of any information through any channel, and which made A—— careless of looking out of window, in America, even to see the Falls of Niagara." So that he soon had to report the gain to all of them, from the fact of this enterprising woman having so primed herself with "the names of all sorts of vegetables, meats, soups, fruits, and kitchen necessaries," that she was able to order whatever was needful of the peasantry that were trotting in and out all day, basketed and barefooted. Her example became at once contagious;[1] and before the end of the second week of September news reached me that "the servants are beginning to pick up scraps of Italian; some of them go to a weekly conversazione of servants at the Governor's every Sunday night, having got over their consternation at the frequent introduction of quadrilles on these occasions: and I think they begin to like their foreigneering life."

In the tradespeople they dealt with at Albaro he found amusing points of character. Sharp as they were after money, their idleness quenched even that propensity. Order for imme-diate delivery two or three pounds of tea, and the tea-dealer would be wretched. "Won't it do to-morrow?" "I want it now," you would reply; and he would say, "No, no, there can be no hurry!" He remonstrated against the cruelty. But every-

[1] Not, however, happily for them, in another important particular, for on the eve of their return to England she declared her intention of staying behind and marrying an Italian. "She will have to go to Florence, I find" (12 May, 1845), "to be married in Lord Holland's house: and even then is only married according to the English law: having no legal rights from such a marriage, either in France or Italy. The man hasn't a penny. If there were an opening for a nice clean restaurant in Genoa—which I don't believe there is, for the Genoese have a natural enjoyment of dirt, garlic, and oil—it would still be a very hazardous venture; as the priests will certainly damage the man, if they can, for marrying a Protestant woman. However, the utmost I can do is to take care, if such a crisis should arrive, that she shall not want the means of getting home to England. As my father would observe, 'she has sown and must reap.'"

where there was deference, courtesy, more than civility. "In a café a little tumbler of ice costs something less than threepence, and if you give the waiter in addition what you would not offer to an English beggar, say, the third of a halfpenny, he is profoundly grateful." The attentions received from English residents were unremitting.[1] In moments of need at the outset, they bestirred themselves ("large merchants and grave men") as if they were the family's salaried purveyors; and there was in especial one gentleman named Curry whose untiring kindness was long remembered.

The light, eager, active figure soon made itself familiar in the streets of Genoa, and he never went into them without bringing some oddity away. I soon heard of the Strada Nuova and Strada Balbi; of the broadest of the two as narrower than Albany Street, and of the other as less wide than Drury Lane or Wych Street; but both filled with palaces of noble architecture and of such vast dimensions that as many windows as there are days in the year might be counted in one of them, and this not covering by any means the largest plot of ground. I heard too of the other streets, none with footways, and all varying in degrees of narrowness, but for the most part like Field Lane in Holborn, with little breathing-places like St. Martin's Court; and the widest only in parts wide enough to enable a carriage and pair to turn. "Imagine yourself looking down a street of Reform Clubs cramped after this odd fashion, the lofty roofs almost seeming to meet in the perspective." In the churches nothing struck him so much as the profusion of trash and tinsel in them that contrasted with their real splendours of embellishment. One only, that of the Cappucini friars, blazed every inch of it with gold, precious stones, and paintings of priceless art; the principal contrast to its radiance being the dirt of its masters, whose bare legs, corded waists, and coarse brown serge never

---

[1] He had carried with him, I may here mention, letters of introduction to residents in all parts of Italy, of which I believe he delivered hardly one. Writing to me a couple of months before he left the country he congratulated himself on this fact. "We are living very quietly; and I am now more than ever glad that I have kept myself aloof from the 'receiving' natives always, and delivered scarcely any of my letters of introduction. If I had, I should have seen nothing and known less. I have observed that the English women who have married foreigners are invariably the most audacious in the license they assume. Think of one lady married to a royal chamberlain (not here) who said at dinner to the master of the house at a place where I was dining—that she had brought back his *Satirist*, but didn't think there was quite so much 'fun' in it as there used to be. I looked at the paper afterwards, and found it crammed with such vile obscenity as positively made one's hair stand on end."

changed by night or day, proclaimed amid their corporate wealth their personal vows of poverty. He found them less pleasant to meet and look at than the country people of their suburb on *festa*-days, with the Indulgences that gave them the right to make merry stuck in their hats like turnpike-tickets. He did not think the peasant girls in general good-looking, though they carried themselves daintily and walked remarkably well: but the ugliness of the old women, begotten of hard work and a burning sun, with porters' knots of coarse grey hair grubbed up over wrinkled and cadaverous faces, he thought quite stupendous. He was never in a street a hundred yards long without getting up perfectly the witch part of *Macbeth*.

With the theatres of course he soon became acquainted, and of that of the puppets he wrote to me again and again with humorous rapture. "There are other things," he added, after giving me the account which is published in his book, "too solemnly surprising to dwell upon. They must be seen. They must be seen. The enchanter carrying off the bride is not greater than his men brandishing fiery torches and dropping their lighted spirits of wine at every shake. Also the enchanter himself, when, hunted down and overcome, he leaps into the rolling sea, and finds a watery grave. Also the second comic man, aged about 55 and like George the Third in the face, when he gives out the play for the next night. They must all be seen. They can't be told about. Quite impossible." The living performers he did not think so good, a disbelief in Italian actors having been always a heresy with him, and the deplorable length of dialogue to the small amount of action in their plays making them sadly tiresome. The first that he saw at the principal theatre was a version of Balzac's *Père Goriot*. "The domestic Lear I thought at first was going to be very clever. But he was too pitiful—perhaps the Italian reality would be. He was immensely applauded, though." He afterwards saw a version of Dumas' preposterous play of *Kean*, in which most of the representatives of English actors wore red hats with steeple crowns, and very loose blouses with broad belts and buckles round their waists. "There was a mysterious person called the Prince of Var-lees" (Wales), "the youngest and slimmest man in the company, whose badinage in Kean's dressing-room was irresistible; and the dresser wore top-boots, a Greek skull-cap, a black velvet jacket, and leather breeches. One or two of the actors looked very hard at me to see how I was touched by these English peculiarities—especially when Kean kissed his male friends on both cheeks." The arrangements of the house, which he described as larger than Drury Lane, he thought excellent. Instead of a ticket for the private box he had taken on the first tier, he received the usual key for admission which let him in as if he lived there; and for the whole set-out, "quite as comfortable and private as a box at our opera," paid only eight-and-four-pence English. The opera itself had not its regular performers until after Christmas, but in the summer there was a good comic company, and he saw the *Scaramuccia* and the *Barber of Seville* brightly and pleasantly done. There was also a day theatre, beginning at half-past four in the afternoon; but beyond the novelty of looking on at the covered stage as he sat in the fresh pleasant air, he did not find much amusement in the Goldoni comedy put before him. There came later a Russian circus, which the unusual rains of that summer prematurely extinguished.

The Religious Houses he made early and many inquiries about, and there was one that had stirred and baffled his curiosity much before he discovered what it really was. All that was visible from the street was a great high wall, apparently quite alone, no thicker than a party wall, with grated windows, to which iron screens gave further protection. At first he supposed there had been a fire; but by degrees came to know that on the other side were galleries, one above another, and nuns always pacing them to and fro. Like the wall of a racket-ground outside, it was inside a very large nunnery; and let the poor sisters walk never so much, neither they nor the passers-by could see anything of each other. It was close upon the Acqua Sola, too; a little park with still young but very pretty trees, and fresh and cheerful fountains, which the Genoese made their Sunday promenade; and underneath which was an archway with great public tanks, where, at all ordinary times, washer-women were washing away, thirty or forty together. At Albaro they were worse off in this matter: the clothes there being washed in a pond, beaten with gourds, and whitened with a preparation of lime: "so that," he wrote to me (24 August), "what between the beating and the burning they fall into holes unexpectedly, and my white trousers, after six weeks' washing, would make very good fishing-nets. It is such a serious damage that when we get into the Peschiere we mean to wash at home."

Exactly a fortnight before this date, he had hired rooms in the Peschiere from the first of the following October; and so ended the house-hunting for his winter residence, that had taken him so often to the city. The Peschiere was the largest palace in Genoa let on hire, and had the advantage of standing on a height aloof from the town, surrounded by its own gardens. The rooms taken had been occupied by an English colonel, the remainder of whose term was let to Dickens for 500 francs a month (£20); and a few days after (20 August) he described to me a fellow-tenant: "A Spanish duke has taken the room under me in the Peschiere. The duchess was his mistress many years, and bore him (I think) six daughters. He always promised her that if she gave birth to a son, he would marry her; and when at last the boy arrived, he went into her bedroom, saying— 'Duchess, I am charmed to salute you!' And he married her in good earnest, and legitimatised (as by the Spanish law he could) all the other children." The beauty of the new abode will justify a little description when he takes up his quarters there. One or two incidents may be related, meanwhile, of the closing weeks of his residence at Albaro.

In the middle of August he dined with the French consul-general, and there will now be no impropriety in printing his agreeable sketch of the dinner. "There was present, among other Genoese, the Marquis di Negri: a very fat and much older Jerdan, with the same thickness of speech and size of tongue. He was Byron's friend, keeps open house here, writes poetry, improvises, and is a very good old Blunderbore; just the sort of instrument to make an artesian well with, anywhere. Well, sir, after dinner, the consul proposed my health, with a little French conceit to the effect that I had come to Italy to have personal experience of its lovely climate, and that there was this similarity between the Italian sun and its visitor, that the sun shone into the darkest places and made them bright and happy with its benignant influence, and that my books had done the like with the breasts of men, and so forth. Upon which Blunderbore gives his bright-buttoned blue coat a great rap on the breast, turns up his fishy eyes, stretches out his arm like the living statue defying the lightning at Astley's, and delivers four impromptu verses in my honour, at which every-body is enchanted, and I more than anybody—perhaps with the best reason, for I didn't understand a word of them. The consul then takes from his breast a roll of paper, and says, 'I shall read them!' Blunderbore then says, 'Don't!' But the consul does, and Blunderbore beats time to the music of the verse with his knuckles on the table; and perpetually ducks forward to look round the cap of a lady sitting between himself and me to see what I think of them. I exhibit lively emotion. The verses are in French—short line—on the taking of Tangiers by the Prince de Joinville; and are received with great applause; especially by a nobleman present who is reported to be unable to read and write. They end in my mind (rapidly translating them into prose) thus:

The cannon of France	Rendering thanks
Shake the foundation	To Heaven.
Of the wondering sea,	The King
The artillery on the shore	And all the Royal Family
Is put to silence.	Are bathed
Honour to Joinville	In tears.
And the Brave!	They call upon the name
The Great Intelligence	Of Joinville!
Is borne	France also
Upon the wings of Fame	Weeps, and echoes it.
To Paris.	Joinville is crowned
Her national citizens	With Immortality;
Exchange caresses	And Peace and Joinville,
In the streets!	And the Glory of France,
The temples are crowded	Diffuse themselves
With religious patriots	Conjointly.

If you can figure to yourself the choice absurdity of receiving anything into one's mind in this way, you can imagine the labour I underwent in my attempts to keep the lower part of my face square, and to lift up one eye gently, as with admiring attention. But I am bound to add that this is really pretty literal; for I read them afterwards." At his French friend's house he afterwards made the acquaintance of Lamartine.

This was the year of several uncomfortable glories incident to France in the last three years of her Orleans dynasty; among them the Tahiti business, as politicians may remember; and so hot became rumours of war with England at the opening of September that Dickens had serious thoughts of at once striking his tent. One of his letters was filled with the conflicting doubts in which they lived for nigh a fortnight, every day's arrival contradicting the arrival of the day before: so that, as he told me, you met a man in the street to-day, who told you there would certainly be war in a week; and you met the same man in the street to-morrow, and he swore he always knew there would be nothing but peace; and you met him again the day after, and he said it all depended *now* on something perfectly new and unheard of before, which somebody else said had just come to the knowledge of some consul in some dispatch which said something about some telegraph which had been at work somewhere, signalising some prodigious intelligence. However, it all passed harmlessly away, leaving him undisturbed opportunity to avail himself of a pleasure that arose out of the consul-general's dinner party, and to be present at a great reception given shortly after by the good "old Blunderbore" just mentioned, on the occasion of his daughter's birthday.

The marquis had a splendid house, but Dickens found the grounds so carved into grottoes and fanciful walks as to remind him of nothing so much as our old White Conduit House, except that he would have been well pleased, on the present occasion, to have discovered a waiter crying, "Give your orders, gents!" it being not easy to him at any time to keep up, the whole night through, on ices and variegated lamps merely. But the scene for awhile was amusing enough, and not rendered less so by the delight of the marquis himself, "who was constantly diving out into dark corners and then among the lattice-work and flower pots, rubbing his hands and going round and round with explosive chuckles in his huge satisfaction with the entertainment." With horror it occurred to Dickens, however, that four more hours of this kind of entertainment would be too much; that the Genoa gates closed at twelve; and that as the carriage had not been ordered till the dancing was expected to be over and the gates to reopen, he must make a sudden bolt if he would himself get back to Albaro. "I had barely time," he told me, "to reach the gate before midnight; and was running as hard as I could go, downhill, over uneven ground, along a new street, called the Strada Sevra, when I came to a pole fastened straight across the street, nearly breast-high, without any light or watchman—quite in the Italian style. I went over it, headlong, with such force that I rolled myself completely white in the dust; but although I tore my clothes to shreds, I hardly scratched myself except in one place on the knee. I had no time to think of it then, for I was up directly and off again to save the gate: but when I got outside the wall and saw the state I was in, I wondered I had not broken my neck. I 'took it easy' after this, and walked home, by lonely ways enough, without meeting a single soul. But there is nothing to be feared, I believe, from midnight walks in this part of Italy. In other places you incur the danger of being stabbed by mistake; whereas the people here are quiet and good-tempered, and very rarely commit any outrage."

Such adventures, nevertheless, are seldom without consequences, and there followed in this case a short but sharp attack of illness. It came on with the old "unspeakable and agonising pain in the side," for which Bob Fagin had prepared and applied the hot bottles in the old warehouse time; and it yielded quickly to powerful remedies. But for a few days he had to content himself with the minor sights of Albaro. He sat daily in the shade of the ruined chapel on the seashore. He looked in at the *festa* in the small country church, consisting mainly of a tenor singer, a seraphine, and four priests sitting gaping in a row on one side of the altar, "in flowered satin dresses and little cloth caps, looking exactly like the band at a wild-beast caravan." He was interested in the wine-making, and in seeing the country tenants preparing their annual presents for their landlords, of baskets of grapes and other fruit prettily dressed with flowers. The season of the grapes, too, brought out after dusk strong parties of rats to eat them as they ripened, and so many shooting parties of peasants to get rid of these despoilers, that as he first listened to the uproar of the firing and the echoes he half fancied it a siege of Albaro. The flies mustered strong, too, and the mosquitoes;[1] so that at night he had to lie covered up with gauze, like cold meat in a safe.

Of course all news from England, and especially visits paid him by English friends who might be travelling in Italy, were a great delight. This was the year when O'Connell was released from prison by the judgment of the Lords on appeal. "I have no faith in O'Connell taking the great position he might upon this: being beleaguered by vanity always. Denman delights me. I am glad to think I have always liked him so well. I am sure that whenever he makes a mistake it *is* a mistake; and that no man lives who has a grander and nobler scorn of every mean and dastard action. I would to Heaven it were decorous to pay him some public tribute of respect. . . . O'Connell's speeches are the old thing: fretty, boastful, frothy, waspish at the voices in the crowd, and all that: but with no true greatness. . . . What a relief to turn to that noble letter of Carlyle's" (in which a timely testimony had been borne to the truthfulness

[1] What his poor little dog suffered should not be omitted from the troubles of the master who was so fond of him. "Timber has had every hair upon his body cut off because of the fleas, and he looks like the ghost of a drowned dog come out of a pond after a week or so. It is very awful to see him slide into a room. He knows the change upon him, and is always turning round and round to look for himself. I think he'll die of grief." Three weeks later: "Timber's hair is growing again, so that you can dimly perceive him to be a dog. The fleas only keep three of his legs off the ground now, and he sometimes moves of his own accord towards some place where they don't want to go." His improvement was slow, but after this continuous

and honour of Mazzini), "which I think above all praise. My love to him." Among his English visitors were Mr. Tagart's family, on their way from a scientific congress at Milan; and Peter (now become Lord) Robertson from Rome, of whose talk he wrote pleasantly. The sons of Burns had been entertained during the autumn in Ayrshire at what was called a Burns Festival, of which, through Jerrold who was present, no very favourable account had been sent him; and this was now confirmed by Robertson. "There was one man who spoke a quarter of an hour or so, to the toast of the navy; and could say nothing more than 'the—British—Navy—always appreciates—' which remarkable sentiment he repeated over and over again for that space of time; and then sat down. Robertson told me also that Wilson's allusion to, or I should rather say expatiation upon, the 'vices' of Burns, excited but one sentiment: and added, very sensibly, 'By God! I want to know *what Burns did*! I never heard of his doing anything that need be strange or unaccountable to the Professor's mind.' In short he fully confirmed Jerrold in all respects." The same letter told, too, something of his reading. Jerrold's *Story of a Feather* he had derived much enjoyment from. "Gauntwolf's sickness and the career of that snuffbox, masterly. I have been deep in Voyages and Travels, and in De Foe. Tennyson I have also been reading, again and again. What a great creature he is. . . . What about the *Goldsmith*? Apropos, I am all eagerness to write a story about the length of his most delightful of all stories."

In the second week of September he went to meet his brother Frederick at Marseilles, and bring him back over the Cornice road to pass a fortnight's holiday at Genoa: and his description of the first inn upon the Alps they slept in is too good to be lost. "We lay last night," he wrote (9 September), "at the first halting-place on this journey, in an inn which is not entitled, as it ought to be, The house of call for fleas and vermin in general, but is entitled The grand hotel of the Post! I hardly know what to compare it to. It seemed something like a house in Somers Town originally built for a wine-vaults and never finished, but grown very old. There was nothing to eat in it and nothing to drink. They had lost the teapot; and when they found it, they couldn't make out what had become of the lid, which, turning up at last and being fixed on to the teapot, couldn't be got off again for the pouring-in of more water. Fleas of elephantine dimensions were gambolling boldly in the dirty beds; and the mosquitoes!—But here let me draw a curtain (as I would have

* 37

done if there had been any). We had scarcely any sleep, and rose up with hands and arms hardly human."

In four days they were at Albaro, and the morning after their arrival Dickens underwent the terrible shock of seeing his brother very nearly drowned in the bay. He swam out into * 38 too strong a current, and was only narrowly saved by the accident of a fishing-boat preparing to leave the harbour at the time. "It was a world of horror and anguish," Dickens wrote to me, "crowded into four or five minutes of dreadful agitation; and to complete the terror of it, Georgy, Charlotte" (the nurse), "and the children were on a rock in full view of it all, crying, as you may suppose, like mad creatures." His own bathing was from the rock, and, as he had already told me, of the most primitive kind. He went in whenever he pleased, broke his head against sharp stones if he went in with that end foremost, floundered about till he was all over bruises, and then climbed and staggered out again. "Everybody wears a dress. Mine extremely theatrical: Masaniello to the life: shall be preserved for your inspection in Devonshire Terrace." I will add another personal touch, also Masaniello-like, which marks the beginning of a change which, though confined for the present to his foreign residence and removed when he came to England, was resumed somewhat later, and in a few more years wholly altered the aspect of his face. "The moustaches are glorious, glorious. I have cut them shorter, and trimmed them a little at the ends to improve the shape. They are charming, charming. Without them, life would be a blank."

V

WORK IN GENOA: PALAZZO PESCHIERE

1844

In the last week of September they moved from Albaro into Genoa, amid a violent storm of wind and wet, "great guns blowing," the lightning incessant, and the rain driving down in a dense thick cloud. But the worst of the storm was over when they reached the Peschiere. As they passed into it along the stately old terraces, flanked on either side with antique sculptured figures, all the seven fountains were playing in its gardens, and the sun was shining brightly on its groves of camellias and orange-trees.

It was a wonderful place, and I soon became familiar with the several rooms that were to form their home for the rest of their stay in Italy. In the centre was the grand sala, fifty feet high, of an area larger than "the dining-room of the Academy," and painted, walls and ceiling, with frescoes three hundred years old, "as fresh as if the colours had been laid on yesterday." On the same floor as this great hall were a drawing-room and a dining-room,[1] both covered also with frescoes still bright enough to make them thoroughly cheerful, and both so nicely proportioned as to give to their bigness all the effect of snugness.[2] Out of these opened three other chambers that were turned into sleeping-rooms and nurseries. Adjoining the sala, right and left, were the two best bedrooms; "in size and shape like those

[1] "Into which we might put your large room—I wish we could!—away in one corner, and dine without knowing it."

[2] "Very vast you will say, and very dreary; but it is not so really. The paintings are so fresh, and the proportions so agreeable to the eye, that the effect is not only cheerful, but snug. . . . We are a little incommoded by applications from strangers to go over the interior. The paintings were designed by Michael Angelo, and have a great reputation. . . . Certain of these frescoes were reported officially to the Fine Art Commissioners by Wilson as the best in Italy. . . . I allowed a party of priests to be shown the great hall yesterday. . . . It is in perfect repair, and the doors almost shut—which is quite a miraculous circumstance. I wish you could see it, my dear F. Gracious Heavens! if you could only *come back* with me, wouldn't I soon flash on your astonished sight." (6 October.)

at Windsor Castle but greatly higher"; both having altars, a range of three windows with stone balconies, floors tessellated in patterns of black and white stone, and walls painted every inch: on the left, nymphs pursued by satyrs "as large as life and as wicked"; on the right, "Phaeton larger than life, with horses bigger than Meux and Co.'s, tumbling headlong down into the best bed." The right-hand room he occupied with his wife, and of the left took possession as a study; writing behind a big screen he had lugged into it, and placed by one of the windows, from which he could see over the city, as he wrote, as far as the lighthouse in its harbour. Distant little over a mile as the crow flew, flashing five times in four minutes, and on dark nights, as if by magic, illuminating brightly the whole palace-front every time it shone, this lighthouse was one of the wonders of Genoa.

When it had all become more familiar to him, he was fond of dilating on its beauties; and even the dreary sound of the chaunting from neighbouring mass-performances, as it floated in at all the open windows, which at first was a sad trouble, came to have its charm for him. I remember a vivid account he gave me of a great *festa* on the hill behind the house, when the people alternately danced under tents in the open air, and rushed to say a prayer or two in an adjoining church bright with red and gold and blue and silver; so many minutes of dancing, and of praying, in regular turns of each. But the view over into Genoa, on clear bright days, was a never-failing enjoyment. The whole city then, without an atom of smoke, and with every possible variety of tower and steeple pointing up into the sky, lay stretched out below his windows. To the right and left were lofty hills, with every indentation in their rugged sides sharply discernible; and on one side of the harbour stretched away into the dim bright distance the whole of the Cornice, its first highest range of mountains hoary with snow. Sitting down one spring day to write to me, he thus spoke of the sea and of the garden: "Beyond the town is the wide expanse of the Mediterranean, as blue, at this moment, as the most pure and vivid prussian blue on Mac's palette when it is newly set; and on the horizon there is a red flush, seen nowhere as it is here. Immediately below the windows are the gardens of the house, with goldfish swimming and diving in the fountains; and below them, at the foot of a steep slope, the public garden and drive, where the walks are marked out by hedges of pink roses, which blush and shine through the green trees and vines, close up to the balconies of these windows. No custom can impair, and no description enhance, the beauty of the scene."

All these and other glories and beauties, however, did not come to him at once. They counted for little indeed when he first set himself seriously to write. "Never did I stagger so upon a threshold before. I seem as if I had plucked myself out of my proper soil when I left Devonshire Terrace; and could take root no more until I return to it. . . . Did I tell you how many fountains we have here? No matter. If they played nectar, they wouldn't please me half so well as the West Middlesex waterworks at Devonshire Terrace." The subject for his new Christmas story he had chosen, but he had not found a title for it, or the machinery to work it with; when, at the moment of what seemed to be his greatest trouble, both reliefs came. Sitting down one morning resolute for work, though against the grain, his hand being out and everything inviting to idleness, such a peal of chimes arose from the city as he found to be "maddening." All Genoa lay beneath him, and up from it, with some sudden set of the wind, came in one fell sound the clang and clash of all its steeples, pouring into his ears, again and again, in a tuneless, grating, discordant, jerking, hideous vibration that made his ideas "spin round and round till they lost themselves in a whirl of vexation and giddiness, and dropped down dead." He had never before so suffered, nor did he again; but this was his description to me next day, and his excuse for having failed in a promise to send me his title. Only two days later, however, came a letter in which not a syllable was written but "We have heard THE CHIMES at midnight, Master Shallow!" and I knew he had discovered what he wanted.

Other difficulties were still to be got over. He craved for the London streets. He so missed his long night-walks before beginning anything that he seemed, as he said, dumbfounded without them. "I can't help thinking of the boy in the school-class whose button was cut off by Walter Scott and his friends. Put me down on Waterloo Bridge at eight o'clock in the evening, with leave to roam about as long as I like, and I would come home, as you know, panting to go on. I am sadly strange as it is, and can't settle. You will have lots of hasty notes from me while I am at work: but you know your man; and whatever strikes me, I shall let off upon you as if I were in Devonshire Terrace. It's a great thing to have my title, and see my way how to work the bells. Let them clash upon me now from all the churches and convents in Genoa, I see nothing but the old London belfry

I have set them in. In my mind's eye, Horatio, I like more and more my notion of making, in this little book, a great blow for the poor. Something powerful, I think I can do, but I want to be tender too, and cheerful; as like the *Carol* in that respect as may be, and as unlike it as such a thing can be. The duration of the action will resemble it a little, but I trust to the novelty of the machinery to carry that off; and if my design be anything at all, it has a grip upon the very throat of the time." (8 October.)

Thus bent upon his work, for which he never had been in more earnest mood, he was disturbed by hearing that he must attend the levee of the governor, who had unexpectedly arrived in the city, and who would take it as an affront, his eccentric friend Fletcher told him, if that courtesy were not immediately paid. "It was the morning on which I was going to begin, so I wrote round to our consul,"—praying, of course, that excuse should be made for him. Don't bother yourself, replied that sensible functionary, for all the consuls and governors alive; but shut yourself up by all means. "So," continues Dickens, telling me the tale, "he went next morning in great state and full costume, to present two English gentlemen. 'Where's the great poet?' said the Governor. 'I want to see the great poet.' 'The great poet, your excellency,' said the consul, 'is at work, writing a book, and begged me to make his excuses.' 'Excuses!' said the Governor, 'I wouldn't interfere with such an occupation for all the world. Pray tell him that my house is open to the honour of his presence when it is perfectly convenient for him; but not otherwise. And let no gentleman,' said the Governor, a surweyin' of his suite with a majestic eye, 'call upon Signor Dickens till he is understood to be disengaged.' And he sent somebody with his own cards next day. Now I *do* seriously call this, real politeness and pleasant consideration—not positively American, but still gentlemanly and polished. The same spirit pervades the inferior departments; and I have not been required to observe the usual police regulations, or to put myself to the slightest trouble about anything." (18 October.)

The picture I am now to give of him at work should be prefaced by a word or two that may throw light on the design he was working at. It was a large theme for so small an instrument; and the disproportion was not more characteristic of the man, than the throes of suffering and passion to be presently undergone by him for results that many men would smile at. He was bent, as he says, on striking a blow for the poor. They had always been his clients, they had never been forgotten in any of his books, but here nothing else was to be remembered. He had become, in short, terribly earnest in the matter. Several months before he left England I had noticed in him the habit of more gravely regarding many things before passed lightly enough; the hopelessness of any true solution of either political or social problems by the ordinary Downing Street methods had been startlingly impressed on him in Carlyle's writings; and in the parliamentary talk of that day he had come to have as little faith for the putting down of any serious evil, as in a then notorious city alderman's gabble for the putting down of suicide. The latter had stirred his indignation to its depths just before he came to Italy, and his increased opportunities of solitary reflection since had strengthened and extended it. When he came therefore to think of his new story for Christmas time, he resolved to make it a plea for the poor. He did not want it to resemble his *Carol*, but the same kind of moral was in his mind. He was to try and convert Society, as he had converted Scrooge, by showing that its happiness rested on the same foundations as those of the individual, which are mercy and charity not less than justice. Whether right or wrong in these assumptions, need not be questioned here, where facts are merely stated to render intelligible what will follow; he had not made politics at any time a study, and they were always an instinct with him rather than a science; but the instinct was wholesome and sound, and to set class against class he never ceased to think as odious as he thought it righteous at all times to help each to a kindlier knowledge of the other. And so, here in Italy, amid the grand surroundings of this Palazzo Peschiere, the hero of his imagination was to be a sorry old drudge of a London ticket-porter, who in his anxiety not to distrust or think hardly of the rich, has fallen into the opposite extreme of distrusting the poor. From such distrust it is the object of the story to reclaim him; and, to the writer of it, the tale became itself of less moment than what he thus intended it to enforce. Far beyond mere vanity in authorship went the passionate zeal with which he began, and the exultation with which he finished, this task. When we met at its close, he was fresh from Venice, which had impressed him as "the wonder" and "the new sensation" of the world: but well do I remember how high above it all arose the hope that filled his mind. "Ah!" he said to me, "when I saw those places, how I thought that to leave one's hand upon the time, lastingly upon the time, with one tender touch for the mass of toiling people that nothing could obliterate, would be to lift oneself above the dust of all the Doges in their graves, and stand upon a giant's staircase that Samson couldn't overthrow!" In varying forms this ambition was in all his life.

Another incident of these days will exhibit aspirations of a more solemn import that were not less part of his nature. It was depth of sentiment rather than clearness of faith which kept safe the belief on which they rested against all doubt or question of its sacredness, but every year seemed to strengthen it in him. This was told me in his second letter after reaching the Peschiere; the first having sent me some such commissions in regard to his wife's family as his kindly care for all connected with him frequently led to. "Let me tell you," he wrote (30 September), "of a curious dream I had, last Monday night; and of the fragments of reality I can collect, which helped to make it up. I have had a return of rheumatism in my back, and knotted round my waist like a girdle of pain; and had laid awake nearly all that night under the infliction, when I fell asleep and dreamed this dream. Observe that throughout I was as real, animated, and full of passion as Macready (God bless him!) in the last scene of *Macbeth*. In an indistinct place, which was quite sublime in its indistinctness, I was visited by a Spirit. I could not make out the face, nor do I recollect that I desired to do so. It wore a blue drapery, as the Madonna might in a picture by Raphael; and bore no resemblance to any one I have known except in stature. I think (but I am not sure) that I recognised the voice. Anyway, I knew it was poor Mary's spirit. I was not at all afraid, but in a great delight, so that I wept very much, and stretching out my arms to it called it 'Dear.' At this, I thought it recoiled; and I felt immediately, that not being of my gross nature, I ought not to have addressed it so familiarly. 'Forgive me!' I said. 'We poor living creatures are only able to express ourselves by looks and words. I have used the word most natural to *our* affections; and you know my heart.' It was so full of compassion and sorrow for me—which I knew spiritually, for, as I have said, I didn't perceive its emotions by its face— that it cut me to the heart; and I said, sobbing, 'Oh! give me some token that you have really visited me!' 'Form a wish,' it said. I thought, reasoning with myself: 'If I form a selfish wish, it will vanish.' So I hastily discarded such hopes and anxieties of my own as came into my mind, and said, 'Mrs. Hogarth is surrounded with great distresses'—observe, I never thought of saying 'your mother' as to a mortal creature—'will you extricate her?' 'Yes.' 'And her extrication is to be a certainty to me, that this has really happened?' 'Yes.' 'But answer me one other question!' I said, in an agony of entreaty lest it should leave me. 'What is the True religion?' As it paused a moment without replying, I said—Good God, in such an agony of haste, lest it should go away!—'You think, as I do, that the Form of religion does not so greatly matter, if we try to do good?—or,' I said, observing that it still hesitated, and was moved with the greatest compassion for me, 'perhaps the Roman Catholic is the best? perhaps it makes one think of God oftener, and believe in him more steadily?' 'For *you*,' said the Spirit, full of such heavenly tenderness for me, that I felt as if my heart would break; 'for *you*, it is the best!' Then I awoke, with the tears running down my face, and myself in exactly the condition of the dream. It was just dawn. I called up Kate, and repeated it three or four times over, that I might not unconsciously make it plainer or stronger afterwards. It was exactly this. Free from all hurry, nonsense, or confusion, whatever. Now, the strings I can gather up, leading to this, were three. The first you know, from the main subject of my last letter. The second was, that there is a great altar in our bedroom, at which some family who once inhabited this palace had mass performed in old time: and I had observed within myself, before going to bed, that there was a mark in the wall, above the sanctuary, where a religious picture used to be; and I had wondered within myself what the subject might have been, *and what the face was like*. Thirdly, I had been listening to the convent bells (which ring at intervals in the night), and so had thought, no doubt, of Roman Catholic services. And yet, for all this, put the case of that wish being fulfilled by any agency in which I had no hand; and I wonder whether I should regard it as a dream, or an actual Vision!" It was perhaps natural that he should omit, from his own considerations awakened by the dream, the very first that would have risen in any mind to which his was intimately known—that it strengthens other evidences, of which there are many in his life, of his not having escaped those trying regions of reflection which most men of thought and all men of genius have at some time to pass through. In such disturbing fancies during the next year or two I may add that the book which helped him most was the *Life of Arnold*. "I respect and reverence his memory," he wrote to me in the middle of October, in reply to my mention of what had most attracted myself in it, "beyond all expression. I must have that book. Every sentence that you quote from it is the text-book of my faith."

He kept his promise that I should hear from him while writing, and I had frequent letters when he was fairly in his work. "With my steam very much up, I find it a great trial to be so far off from you, and consequently to have no one (always excepting Kate and Georgy) to whom to expatiate on my day's work. And I want a crowded street to plunge into at night. And I want to be 'on the spot' as it were. But apart from such things, the life I lead is favourable to work." In his next letter: "I am in regular, ferocious excitement with the *Chimes*; get up at seven; have a cold bath before breakfast; and blaze away, wrathful and red-hot, until three o'clock or so: when I usually knock off (unless it rains) for the day. . . . I am fierce to finish in a spirit bearing some affinity to those of truth and mercy, and to shame the cruel and the canting. I have not forgotten my catechism. 'Yes, verily, and with God's help, so I will!'"

Within a week he had completed his first part, or quarter. "I send you to-day" (18 October), "by mail, the first and longest of the four divisions. This is great for the first week, which is usually uphill. I have kept a copy in shorthand in case of accidents. I hope to send you a parcel every Monday until the whole is done. I do not wish to influence you, but it has a great hold upon me, and has affected me, in the doing, in divers strong ways, deeply, forcibly. To give you better means of judgment I will sketch for you the general idea, but pray don't read it until you have read this first part of the MS." I print it here. It is a good illustration of his method in all his writing. His idea is in it so thoroughly, that, by comparison with the tale as printed, we see the strength of its mastery over his first design. Thus always, whether his tale was to be written in one or in twenty numbers, his fancies controlled him. He never, in any of his books, accomplished what he had wholly preconceived, often as he attempted it. Few men of genius ever did. Once at the sacred heat that opens regions beyond ordinary vision, imagination has its own laws; and where characters are so real as to be treated as existences, their creator himself cannot help them having their own wills and ways. Fern the farm-labourer is not here, nor yet his niece the little Lilian (at first called Jessie) who is to give to the tale its most tragical scene; and there are intimations of poetic fancy at the close of my sketch which the published story fell short of. Altogether the comparison is worth observing.

"The general notion is this. That what happens to poor Trotty in the first part, and what will happen to him in the second (when he takes the letter to a punctual and a great man of business, who is balancing his books and making up his accounts, and complacently expatiating on the necessity of clearing off every liability and obligation, and turning over a new leaf and starting fresh with the new year), so dispirits him, who can't do this, that he comes to the conclusion that his class and order have no business with a new year, and really are 'intruding.' And though he will pluck up for an hour or so, at the christening (I think) of a neighbour's child, that evening: still, when he goes home, Mr. Filer's precepts will come into his mind, and he will say to himself, 'we are a long way past the proper average of children, and it has no business to be born': and will be wretched again. And going home, and sitting there alone, he will take that newspaper out of his pocket, and reading of the crimes and offences of the poor, especially of those whom Alderman Cute is going to put down, will be quite confirmed in his misgiving that they are bad; irredeemably bad. In this state of mind he will fancy that the Chimes are calling to him; and saying to himself 'God help me. Let me go up to 'em. I feel as if I were going to die in despair—of a broken heart; let me die among the bells that have been a comfort to me!'—will grope his way up into the tower; and fall down in a kind of swoon among them. Then the third quarter, or in other words the beginning of the second half of the book, will open with the Goblin part of the thing: the bells ringing, and innumerable spirits (the sound or vibration of them) flitting and tearing in and out of the church-steeple, and bearing all sorts of missions and commissions and reminders and reproaches, and comfortable recollections and what not, to all sorts of people and places. Some bearing scourges; and others flowers, and birds, and music; and others pleasant faces in mirrors, and others ugly ones; the bells haunting people in the night (especially the last of the old year) according to their deeds. And the bells themselves, who have a goblin likeness to humanity in the midst of their proper shapes, and who shine in a light of their own, will say (the Great Bell being the chief spokesman) 'Who is he that being of the poor doubts the right of poor men to the inheritance which Time reserves for them, and echoes an unmeaning cry against his fellows?' Toby, all aghast, will tell him it is he, and why it is. Then the spirits of the bells will bear him through the air to various scenes, charged with this trust: That they show him how the poor and wretched, at the worst—yes, even in the crimes that aldermen put down, and he has thought so horrible—have some deformed and hunchbacked goodness clinging to them; and how they have their right and share in Time. Following out the history of Meg, the bells will show her, that marriage broken off and all friends dead, with an infant child; reduced so low, and made so miserable, as to be brought at last to wander out at night. And in Toby's sight, her father's, she will resolve to drown herself and the child together. But before she goes down to the water, Toby will see how she covers it with a part of her own wretched dress, and adjusts its rags so as to make it pretty in its sleep, and hangs over it, and smooths its little limbs, and loves it with the dearest love that God ever gave to mortal creatures; and when she runs down to the water, Toby will cry, 'Oh spare her! Chimes, have mercy on her! Stop her!'—and the bells will say, 'Why stop her? She is bad at heart—let the bad die.' And Toby on his knees will beg and pray for mercy: and in the end the bells will stop her, by their voices, just in time. Toby will see, too, what great things the punctual man has left undone on the close of the old year, and what accounts he has left unsettled: punctual as he is. And he will see a great many things about Richard, once so near being his son-in-law, and about a great many people. And the moral of it all will be, that he has his portion in the new year no less than any other man, and that the poor require a deal of beating out of shape before their human shape is gone; that even in their frantic wickedness there may be good in their hearts triumphantly asserting itself, though all the aldermen alive say 'No,' as he has learnt from the agony of his own child; and that the truth is Trustfulness in them, not doubt, nor putting down, nor filing them away. And when at last a great sea rises, and this sea of Time comes sweeping down, bearing the alderman and such mudworms of the earth away to nothing, dashing them to fragments in its fury—Toby will climb a rock and hear the bells (now faded from his sight) pealing out upon the waters. And as he hears them, and looks round for help, he will wake up and find himself with the newspaper lying at his foot; and Meg sitting opposite to him at the table, making up the ribbons for her wedding to-morrow; and the window open, that the sound of the bells ringing the old year out and the new year in may enter. They will just have broken out, joyfully; and Richard will dash in to kiss Meg before Toby, and have the first kiss of the new year (he'll get it too); and the neighbours will crowd round with good wishes; and a band will strike up gaily (Toby knows a Drum in private); and the altered circumstances, and the ringing of the bells, and the jolly music, will so transport the old fellow that he will lead off a country dance forthwith in an entirely new step, consisting of his old familiar trot. Then quoth the inimitable—Was it a dream of Toby's after all? Or is Toby but a dream? and Meg a dream? and all a dream! In reference to which, and the realities of which dreams are born, the inimitable will be wiser than he can be now, writing for dear life, with the post just going and, the brave C—— booted. . . . Ah how I hate myself, my dear fellow, for this lame and halting outline of the Vision I have in my mind. But it must go to you. . . . You will say what is best for the frontispiece. . . ."

With the second part or quarter, after a week's interval, came announcement of the enlargement of his plan, by which he hoped better to carry out the scheme of the story, and to get, for its following part, an effect for his heroine that would increase the tragic interest. "I am still in stout heart with the tale. I think it well-timed and a good thought; and as you know I wouldn't say so to anybody else, I don't mind saying freely thus much. It has great possession of me every moment in the day; and drags me where it will. . . . If you only could have read it all at once!—But you never would have done that, anyway, for I never should have been able to keep it to myself; so that's nonsense. I hope you'll like it. I would give a hundred pounds (and think it cheap) to see you read it. . . . Never mind."

That was the first hint of an intention of which I was soon to hear again; but meanwhile, after eight more days, the third part came, with the scene from which he expected so much, and with a mention of what the writing of it had cost him. "This book (whether in the Hajji Baba sense or not I can't say, but certainly in the literal one) has made my face white in a foreign land. My cheeks, which were beginning to fill out, have sunk again; my eyes have grown immensely large; my hair is very lank; and the head inside the hair is hot and giddy. Read the scene at the end of the third part, twice. I wouldn't write it twice for something. . . . You will see that I have substituted the name of Lilian for Jessie. It is prettier in sound, and suits my music better. I mention this, lest you should wonder who and what I mean by that name. To-morrow I shall begin afresh (starting the next part with a broad grin, and ending it with the very soul of jollity and happiness); and I hope to finish by next Monday at latest. Perhaps on Saturday. I hope you will like the little book. Since I conceived, at the beginning of the second part, what must happen in the third, I have undergone as much sorrow and agitation as if the thing were real; and have wakened up with it at night. I was obliged to lock myself in when I finished it yesterday, for my face was swollen for the time to twice its proper size, and was hugely ridiculous. . . ." His letter ended abruptly. "I am going for a long walk, to clear my head. I feel that I am very shaky from work, and throw down my pen for the day. There! (That's where it fell)." A huge blot represented it, and, as Hamlet says, the rest was silence.

Two days later, answering a letter from me that had reached him in the interval, he gave sprightlier account of himself, and described a happy change in the weather. Up to this time, he protested, they had not had more than four or five clear days. All the time he had been writing they had been wild and stormy. "Wind, hail, rain, thunder and lightning. To-day," just before he sent me his last manuscript, "has been November slack-baked, the sirocco having come back; and to-night it blows great guns with a raging storm." "Weather worse," he wrote after three Mondays, "than any November English weather I have ever beheld, or any weather I have had experience of anywhere. So horrible to-day that all power has been rained and gloomed out of me. Yesterday, in pure determination to get the better of it, I walked twelve miles in mountain rain. You never saw it rain. Scotland and America are nothing to it." But now all this was over. "The weather changed on Saturday night, and has been glorious ever since. I am afraid to say more in its favour, lest it should change again." It did not. I think there were no more complainings. I heard now of autumn days, with the mountain wind, lovely, enjoyable, exquisite past expression. I heard of mountain walks behind the Peschiere, most beautiful and fresh, among which, and along the beds of dry rivers and torrents, he could "pelt away," in any dress, without encountering a soul but the *contadini*. I heard of his starting off one day after finishing work, "fifteen miles to dinner—oh my stars! at such an inn!!!" On another day, of a party to dinner at their pleasant little banker's at Quinto six miles off, to which, while the ladies drove, he was able "to walk in the sun of the middle of the day and to walk home again at night." On another, of an expedition up the mountain on mules. And on another of a memorable tavern-dinner with their merchant friend Mr. Curry, in which there were such successions of surprising dishes of genuine native cookery that they took two hours in the serving, but of the component parts of not one of which was he able to form the remotest conception: the site of the tavern being on the city wall, its name in Italian sounding very romantic and meaning "the Whistle," and its bill of fare kept for an experiment to which, before another month should be over, he challenged my cookery in Lincoln's Inn.

A visit from him to London was to be expected almost immediately! That all remonstrance would be idle, under the restless excitement his work had awakened, I well knew. It was not merely the wish he had, natural enough, to see the last proofs and the woodcuts before the day of publication, which he could not otherwise do; but it was the stronger and more eager wish, before that final launch, to have a vivider sense than letters could give him of the effect of what he had been doing. "If I come, I shall put up at Cuttris's" (then the Piazza Hotel in Covent Garden), "that I may be close to you. Don't say to anybody, except our immediate friends, that I am coming. Then I shall not be bothered. If I should preserve my present fierce writing humour, in any pass I may run to Venice, Bologna, and Florence, before I turn my face towards Lincoln's Inn Fields; and come to England by Milan and Turin. But this of course depends in a great measure on your reply." My reply, dwelling on the fatigue and cost, had the reception I foresaw. "Notwithstanding what you say, I am still in the same mind about coming to London. Not because the proofs concern me at all (I should be an ass as well as a thankless vagabond if they did), but because of that unspeakable restless something which would render it almost as impossible for me to remain here and not see the thing complete, as it would be for a full balloon, left to itself, not to go up. I do not intend coming from *here*, but by way of Milan and Turin (previously going to Venice), and so, across the wildest pass of the Alps that may be open, to Strasbourg. . . . As you dislike the Young England gentleman I shall knock him out, and replace him by a man (I can dash him in at your rooms in an hour) who recognises no virtue in anything but the good old times, and talks of them, parrot-like, whatever the matter is. A real good old city Tory, in a blue coat and bright buttons and a white cravat, and with a tendency of blood to the head. File away at Filer, as you please; but bear in mind that the *Westminster Review* considered Scrooge's presentation of the turkey to Bob Cratchit as grossly incompatible with political economy. I don't care at all for the skittle-playing." These were among things I had objected to.

But the close of his letter revealed more than its opening of the reason, not at once so frankly confessed, for the long winter-journey he was about to make; and if it be thought that, in printing the passage, I take a liberty with my friend, it will be found that equal liberty is taken with myself, whom it good-naturedly caricatures; so that the reader can enjoy his laugh at either or both. "Shall I confess to you, I particularly want Carlyle above all to see it before the rest of the world, when it is done; and I should like to inflict the little story on him and on dear old gallant Macready with my own lips, and to have Stanny and the other Mac sitting by. Now, if you was a real gent, you'd get up a little circle for me, one wet evening, when I come to town: and would say, 'My boy (SIR, will you have the goodness to leave those books alone and go downstairs—WHAT the Devil are you doing! And mind, sir, I can see nobody—Do you hear? Nobody. I am particularly engaged with a gentleman from Asia)—My boy, would you give us that little Christmas book (a little Christmas book of Dickens's, Macready, which I'm anxious you should hear); and don't slur it, now, or be too fast, Dickens, please!'—I say, if you was a real gent, something to this effect might happen. I shall be under sailing orders the moment I have finished. And I shall produce myself (please God) in London on the very day you name. For one week: to the hour."

The wish was complied with, of course; and that night in Lincoln's Inn Fields led to rather memorable issues. His next letter told me the little tale was done. "Third of November, 1844. Half-past two, afternoon. Thank God! I have finished the *Chimes*. This moment. I take up my pen again to-day, to say only that much; and to add that I have had what women call 'a real good cry.'" Very genuine all this, it is hardly necessary to say. The little book thus completed was not one of his greater successes, and it raised him up some objectors; but there was that in it which more than repaid the suffering its writing cost him, and the enmity its opinions provoked; and in his own heart it had a cherished corner to the last. The intensity of it seemed always best to represent to himself what he hoped to be longest remembered for; and exactly what he felt as to this, his friend Jeffrey warmly expressed. "All the tribe of selfishness, and cowardice and cant, will hate you in their hearts, and cavil when they can; will accuse you of wicked exaggeration, and excitement to discontent, and what they pleasantly call disaffection! But never mind. The good and the brave are with you, and the truth also."

He resumed his letter on 4 November. "Here is the brave courier measuring bits of maps with a carving fork, and going up mountains on a teaspoon. He and I start on Wednesday for Parma, Modena, Bologna, Venice, Verona, Brescia, and Milan. Milan being within a reasonable journey from here, Kate and Georgy will come to meet me when I arrive there on my way towards England; and will bring me all letters from you. I shall be there on the 18th. . . . Now, you know my punctiwality. Frost, ice, flooded rivers, steamers, horses, passports and custom-houses may damage it. But my design is, to walk into Cuttris's coffee-room on Sunday the 1st of December, in good time for dinner. I shall look for you at the farther table by the fire—where we generally go. . . . But the party for the night following? I know you have consented to the party. Let me see. Don't have anyone, this particular night, to dinner, but let it be a summons for the special purpose at half-past 6. Carlyle, indispensable, and I should like his wife of all things: *her* judgment would be invaluable. You will ask Mac, and why not his sister? Stanny and Jerrold I should particularly wish; Edwin Landseer; Blanchard; perhaps Harness; and what say you to Fonblanque and Fox? I leave it to you. You know the effect I want to try. . . . Think the *Chimes* a letter, my dear fellow, and forgive this. I will not fail to write to you on my travels. Most probably from Venice. And when I meet you (in sound health I hope), oh Heaven! what a week we will have."

VI

ITALIAN TRAVEL

1844

So it all fell out accordingly. He parted from his disconsolate
wife, as he told me in his first letter from Ferrara, on Wednesday,
6 November: left her shut up in her palace like a baron's lady
in the time of the Crusades; and had his first real experience of
the wonders of Italy. He saw Parma, Modena, Bologna, Ferrara,
Venice, Verona, and Mantua. As to all which the impressions
conveyed to me in his letters have been more or less given in
his published *Pictures*. They are charmingly expressed. There
is a sketch of a cicerone at Bologna which will remain in his
books among the many delightful examples of his unerring
and loving perception for every gentle, heavenly, and tender
soul, under whatever conventional disguise it wanders here on
earth, whether as poorhouse orphan or lawyer's clerk, archi-
tect's pupil at Salisbury or cheerful little guide to graves at
Bologna; and there is another memorable description in his
Rembrandt sketch, in form of a dream, of the silent, unearthly,
watery wonders of Venice. This last, though not written until after
his London visit, had been prefigured so vividly in what he
wrote at once from the spot, that those passages from his letter [1]

[1] "I began this letter, my dear friend" (he wrote it from Venice on
Tuesday night the 12th of November), "with the intention of describing
my travels as I went on. But I have seen so much, and travelled so hard
(seldom dining, and being almost always up by candle-light), that I must
reserve my crayons for the greater leisure of the Peschiere after we have
met, and I have again returned to it. As soon as I have fixed a place in
my mind, I bolt—at such strange seasons and at such unexpected angles,
that the brave C. stares again. But in this way, and by insisting on having
everything shown to me whether or no, and against all precedents and
orders of proceeding, I get on wonderfully." Two days before he had
written to me from Ferrara, after the very pretty description of the vineyards between Piacenza and Parma which will be found in the *Pictures
from Italy* (pp. 203-4): "If you want an antidote to this, I may observe
that I got up, this moment, to fasten the window; and the street looked
as like some byeway in Whitechapel—or—I look again—like Wych
Street, down by the little barber's shop on the same side of the way as
Holywell Street—or—I look again—as like Holywell Street itself—as
ever street was like to street, or ever will be, in this world."

may be read still with a quite undiminished interest. "I must not," he said, "anticipate myself. But, my dear fellow, nothing in the world that ever you have heard of Venice, is equal to the magnificent and stupendous reality. The wildest visions of the *Arabian Nights* are nothing to the piazza of Saint Mark, and the first impression of the inside of the church. The gorgeous and wonderful reality of Venice is beyond the fancy of the wildest dreamer. Opium couldn't build such a place, and enchantment couldn't shadow it forth in a vision. All that I have heard of it, read of it in truth or fiction, fancied of it, is left thousands of miles behind. You know that I am liable to disappointment in such things from over-expectation, but Venice is above, beyond, out of all reach of coming near, the imagination of a man. It has never been rated high enough. It is a thing you would shed tears to see. When I came *on board* here last night (after a five miles' row in a gondola; which, somehow or other, I wasn't at all prepared for); when, from seeing the city lying, one night, upon the distant water, like a ship, I came plashing through the silent and deserted streets; I felt as if the houses were reality—the water, fever-madness. But when, in the bright, cold bracing day, I stood upon the piazza this morning, by Heaven, the glory of the place was insupportable! And diving down from that into its wickedness and gloom—its awful prisons deep below the water; its judgment chambers, secret doors, deadly nooks, where the torches you carry with you blink as if they couldn't bear the air in which the frightful scenes were acted; and coming out again into the radiant, unsubstantial Magic of the town; and diving in again, into vast churches, and old tombs—a new sensation, a new memory, a new mind came upon me. Venice is a bit of my brain from this time. My dear Forster, if you could share my transports (as you would if you were here) what would I not give! I feel cruel not to have brought Kate and Georgy; positively cruel and base. Canaletti and Stanny, miraculous in their truth. Turner, very noble. But the reality itself, beyond all pen or pencil. I never saw the thing before that I should be afraid to describe. But to tell what Venice is, I feel to be an impossibility. And here I sit alone, writing it; with nothing to urge me on, or goad me to that estimate, which, speaking of it to anyone I loved, and being spoken to in return, would lead me to form. In the sober solitude of a famous inn; with the great bell of Saint Mark ringing twelve at my elbow; with three arched windows in my room (two stories high) looking down upon the Grand Canal and away, beyond, to where the sun went down to-night in a blaze; and thinking over again those silent speaking faces of Titian and Tintoretto; I swear (uncooled by any humbug I have seen) that Venice is *the* wonder and the new sensation of the world! If you could be set down in it, never having heard of it, it would still be so. With your foot upon its stones, its pictures before you, and its history in your mind, it is something past all writing of or speaking of—almost past all thinking of. You couldn't talk to me in this room, nor I to you, without shaking hands and saying 'Good God, my dear fellow, have we lived to see this!'"

Five days later, Sunday the 17th, he was at Lodi, from which he wrote to me that he had been, like Leigh Hunt's pig, up "all manner of streets" since he left his palazzo; that with one exception he had not on any night given up more than five hours to rest; that all the days except two had been bad ("the last two foggy as Blackfriars Bridge on Lord Mayor's Day"); and that the cold had been dismal. But what cheerful, keen, observant eyes he carried everywhere; and, in the midst of new and unaccustomed scenes, and of objects and remains of art for which no previous study had prepared him, with what a delicate play of imagination and fancy the accuracy of his ordinary vision was exalted and refined, I think strikingly shown by the few unstudied passages I am preserving from these friendly letters. He saw everything for himself; and from mistakes in judging for himself which not all the learning and study in the world will save common men, the intuition of genius almost always saved him. Hence there is hardly anything uttered by him, of this much-trodden and wearisomely visited, but eternally beautiful and interesting country, that will not be found worth listening to.

"I am already brim-full of cant about pictures, and shall be happy to enlighten you on the subject of the different schools, at any length you please. It seems to me that the preposterous exaggeration in which our countrymen delight in reference to this Italy, hardly extends to the really good things.[1] Perhaps

---

[1] Four months later, after he had seen the galleries at Rome and the other great cities, he sent me a remark which has since had eloquent reinforcement from critics of undeniable authority. "The most famous of the oil paintings in the Vatican you know through the medium of the finest line-engravings in the world; and as to some of them I must doubt, if you had seen them with me, whether you might not think you had lost little in having only known them hitherto in that translation. Where the drawing is poor and meagre, or alloyed by time,—it is so, and it must be, often; though no doubt it is a heresy to hint at such a thing,—the engraving presents the forms and the idea to you, in a simple majesty which such

it is in its nature, that there it should fall short. I have never yet seen any praise of Titian's great picture of the 'Assumption of the Virgin' at Venice, which soared half as high as the beautiful and amazing reality. It is perfection. Tintoretto's picture too, of the 'Assembly of the Blest,' at Venice also, with all the lines in it (it is of immense size and the figures are countless) tending majestically and dutifully to Almighty God in the centre, is grand and noble in the extreme. There are some wonderful portraits there, besides; and some confused, and hurried, and slaughterous battle pieces, in which the surprising art that presents the generals to your eye, so that it is almost impossible you can miss them in a crowd though they are in the thick of it, is very pleasant to dwell upon. I have seen some delightful pictures; and some (at Verona and Mantua) really too absurd and ridiculous even to laugh at. Hampton Court is a fool to 'em—and oh there are some rum 'uns there, my friend. Some werry rum 'uns. . . . Two things are clear to me already. One is, that the rules of art are much too slavishly followed; making it a pain to you, when you go into galleries day after day, to be so very precisely sure where this figure will be turning round, and that figure will be lying down, and that other will have a great lot of drapery twined about him,

defects impair. Where this is not the case, and all is stately and harmonious, still it is somehow in the very grain and nature of a delicate engraving to suggest to you (I think) the utmost delicacy, finish, and refinement, as belonging to the original. Therefore, though the Picture in this latter case will greatly charm and interest you, it does not take you by surprise. You are quite prepared beforehand for the fullest excellence of which it is capable." In the same letter he wrote of what remained always a delight in his memory, the charm of the more private collections. He found magnificent portraits and paintings in the private palaces, where he thought them seen to greater advantage than in galleries; because in numbers not so large as to distract attention or confuse the eye. "There are portraits innumerable by Titian, Rubens, Rembrandt and Vandyke; heads by Guido, and Domenichino, and Carlo Dolci; subjects by Raphael, and Correggio, and Murillo, and Paul Veronese, and Salvator; which it would be difficult indeed to praise too highly, or to praise enough. It is a happiness to me to think that they cannot be felt, as they should be felt, by the profound connoisseurs who fall into fits upon the longest notice and the most unreasonable terms. Such tenderness and grace, such noble elevation, purity, and beauty so shine upon me from some well-remembered spots in the walls of these galleries, as to relieve my tortured memory from legions of whining friars and waxy holy families. I forgive, from the bottom of my soul, whole orchestras of earthly angels, and whole groves of St. Sebastians stuck as full of arrows according to pattern as a lying-in pincushion is stuck with pins. And I am in no humour to quarrel even with that priestly infatuation, or priestly doggedness of purpose, which persists in reducing every mystery of our religion to some literal development in paint and canvas, equally repugnant to the reason and the sentiment of any thinking man."

and so forth. This becomes a perfect nightmare. The second is, that these great men, who were of necessity very much in the hands of the monks and priests, painted monks and priests a vast deal too often. I constantly see, in pictures of tremendous power, heads quite below the story and the painter; and I invariably observe that those heads are of the convent stamp, and have their counterparts, exactly, in the convent inmates of this hour. I see the portraits of monks I know at Genoa, in all the lame parts of strong paintings: so I have settled with myself that in such cases the lameness was not with the painter, but with the vanity and ignorance of his employers, who *would* be apostles on canvas at all events."

In the same letter he described the Inns. "It is a great thing —quite a matter of course—with English travellers, to decry the Italian inns. Of course you have no comforts that you are used to in England; and travelling alone, you dine in your bedroom always: which is opposed to our habits. But they are immeasurably better than you would suppose. The attendants are very quick; very punctual; and so obliging, if you speak to them politely, that you would be a beast not to look cheerful, and take everything pleasantly. I am writing this in a room like a room on the two-pair front of an unfinished house in Eaton Square: the very walls make me feel as if I were a bricklayer distinguished by Mr. Cubitt with the favour of having it to take care of. The windows won't open, and the doors won't shut; and these latter (a cat could get in, between them and the floor) have a windy command of a colonnade which is open to the night, so that my slippers positively blow off my feet, and make little circuits in the room—like leaves. There is a very ashy wood-fire, burning on an immense hearth which has no fender (there is no such thing in Italy); and it only knows two extremes—an agony of heat when wood is put on, and an agony of cold when it has been on two minutes. There is also an uncomfortable stain in the wall, where the fifth door (not being strictly indispensable) was walled up a year or two ago, and never painted over. But the bed is clean; and I have had an excellent dinner; and without being obsequious or servile, which is not at all the characteristic of the people in the north of Italy, the waiters are so amiably disposed to invent little attentions which they suppose to be English, and are so lighthearted and good-natured, that it is a pleasure to have to do with them. But so it is with all the people. *Vetturino*-travelling involves a stoppage of two hours in the middle of the day, to bait the horses. At that time I always walk on. If there are many turns in the road, I necessarily have to ask my way, very often ; and the men are such gentlemen, and the women such ladies, that it is quite an interchange of courtesies."

Of the help his courier continued to be to him I had whimsical instances in almost every letter, but he appears too often in the published book to require such celebration here. He is, however, an essential figure to two little scenes sketched for me at Lodi, and I may preface them by saying that Louis Roche, a native of Avignon, justified to the close his master's high opinion. He was again engaged for nearly a year in Switzerland, and soon after, poor fellow, though with a jovial robustness of look and breadth of chest that promised unusual length of days, was killed by heart-disease. "The brave C. continues to be a prodigy. He puts out my clothes at every inn as if I were going to stay there twelve months; calls me to the instant every morning ; lights the fire before I get up; gets hold of roast fowls and produces them in coaches at a distance from all other help, in hungry moments; and is invaluable to me. He is such a good fellow, too, that little rewards don't spoil him. I always give him, after I have dined, a tumbler of Sauterne or Hermitage or whatever I may have; sometimes (as yesterday) when we have come to a public-house at about eleven o'clock, very cold, having started before daybreak and had nothing, I make him take his breakfast with me; and this renders him only more anxious than ever, by redoubling attentions, to show me that he thinks he has got a good master. . . . I didn't tell you that the day before I left Genoa, we had a dinner-party—our English consul and his wife; the banker; Sir George Crawford and his wife; the De la Rues; Mr. Curry; and some others, fourteen in all. At about nine in the morning, two men in immense paper caps inquired at the door for the brave C., who presently introduced them in triumph as the governor's cooks, his private friends, who had come to dress the dinner! Jane wouldn't stand this, however; so we were obliged to decline. Then there came, at half-hourly intervals, six gentlemen having the appearance of English clergymen, being other private friends who had come to wait. . . . We accepted *their* services; and you never saw anything so nicely and quietly done. He had asked, as a special distinction, to be allowed the supreme control of the dessert; and he had ices made like fruit, had pieces of crockery turned upside-down so as to look like other pieces of crockery non-

† 11

existent in this part of Europe, and carried a case of toothpicks in his pocket. Then his delight was, to get behind Kate at one end of the table, to look at me at the other, and to say to Georgy in a low voice whenever he handed her anything, 'What does master think of datter 'rangement? Is he cōntĕnt?' . . . If you could see what these fellows of couriers are when their families are not upon the move, you would feel what a prize he is. I can't make out whether he was ever a smuggler, but nothing will induce him to give the custom-house officers anything: in consequence of which that portmanteau of mine has been unnecessarily opened twenty times. Two of them will come to the coach-door, at the gate of a town. 'Is there anything contraband in this carriage, signore?' 'No, no. There's nothing here. I am an Englishman, and this is my servant.' 'A buono mano signore?' 'Roche' (in English), 'give him something, and get rid of him.' He sits unmoved. 'A buono mano signore?' 'Go along with you!' says the brave C. 'Signore, I am a custom-house officer!' 'Well, then, more shame for you!'—he always makes the same answer. And then he turns to me and says in English: while the custom-house officer's face is a portrait of anguish framed in the coach-window, from his intense desire to know what is being told to his disparagement: 'Datter chip,' shaking his fist at him, 'is greatest tief—and you know it you rascal—as never did en-razh me so, that I cannot bear myself!' I suppose chip to mean chap, but it may include the custom-house officer's father and have some reference to the old block, for anything I distinctly know."

He closed his Lodi letter next day at Milan, whither his wife and her sister had made an eighty miles' journey from Genoa, to pass a couple of days with him in Prospero's old dukedom before he left for London. "We shall go our several ways on Thursday morning, and I am still bent on appearing at Cuttris's on Sunday the first, as if I had walked thither from Devonshire Terrace. In the meantime I shall not write to you again . . . to enhance the pleasure (if anything *can* enhance the pleasure) of our meeting. . . . I am opening my arms so wide!" One more letter I had nevertheless; written at Strasbourg on Monday night the 25th; to tell me that I might look for him one day earlier, so rapid had been his progress. He had been in bed only once, at Fribourg for two or three hours, since he left Milan; and he had sledged through the snow on the top of the Simplon in the midst of prodigious cold. "I am sitting here *in* a wood fire, and drinking brandy and water scalding hot, with a faint idea of coming warm in time. My face is at present tingling with the frost and wind, as I suppose the cymbals may, when that turbaned Turk attached to the Life Guards' band has been newly clashing at them in St. James's Park. I am in hopes it may be the preliminary agony of returning animation."

There was certainly no want of animation when we met. I have but to write the words to bring back the eager face and figure, as they flashed upon me so suddenly this wintry Saturday night that almost before I could be conscious of his presence I felt the grasp of his hand. It is almost all I find it possible to remember of the brief, bright meeting. Hardly did he seem to have come when he was gone. But all that the visit proposed he accomplished. He saw his little book in its final form for publication; and, to a select few brought together on Monday, 2 December, at my house, had the opportunity of reading it aloud. An occasion rather memorable, in which was the germ of those readings to larger audiences by which, as much as by his books, the world knew him in his later life; but of which no detail beyond the fact remains in my memory, and all are now dead who were present at it excepting only Mr. Carlyle and myself. Among those, however, who have thus passed away was one, our excellent Maclise, who, anticipating the advice of Captain Cuttle, had "made a note of it" in pencil. The reader may be assured (with allowance for a touch of caricature to which I may claim to be considered myself as the chief and very marked victim), that in the grave attention of Carlyle, the eager interest of Stanfield and Maclise, the keen look of poor Laman Blanchard, Fox's rapt solemnity, Jerrold's skyward gaze, and the tears of Harness and Dyce, the characteristic points of the scene are sufficiently rendered. All other recollection of it is passed and gone; but that at least its principal actor was made glad and grateful, sufficient further testimony survives. Such was the report made of it, that once more, on the pressing intercession of our friend Thomas Ingoldsby (Mr. Barham), there was a second reading to which the presence and enjoyment of Fonblanque gave new zest; and when I expressed * 40 to Dickens, after he left us, my grief that he had so tempestuous a journey for such brief enjoyment, he replied that the visit had been one happiness and delight to him. "I would not recall an inch of the way to or from you, if it had been twenty times as long and twenty thousand times as wintry. It was worth any travel—anything! With the soil of the road in the very grain of my cheeks, I swear I wouldn't have missed that week, that first night of our meeting, that one evening of the reading at your rooms, aye, and the second reading too, for any easily stated or conceived consideration."

He wrote from Paris, at which he had stopped on his way back to see Macready, whom an engagement to act there with Mr. Mitchell's English company had prevented from joining us in Lincoln's Inn Fields. There had been no such frost and snow since 1829, and he gave dismal report of the city. With Macready he had gone two nights before to the Odéon to see Alexander Dumas' *Christine* played by Madame St. George, "once Napoleon's mistress; now of an immense size, from dropsy I suppose; and with little weak legs which she can't stand upon. Her age, withal, somewhere about 80 or 90. I never in my life beheld such a sight. Every stage conventionality she ever picked up (and she has them all) has got the dropsy too, and is swollen and bloated hideously. The other actors never looked at one another, but delivered all their dialogues to the pit, in a manner so egregiously unnatural and preposterous that I couldn't make up my mind whether to take it as a joke or an outrage." And then came allusion to a project we had started on the night of the reading, that a private play should be got up by us on his return from Italy. "You and I, sir, will reform this altogether." He had but to wait another night, however, when he saw it all reformed at the Italian Opera where Grisi was singing in *Il Pirato*, and "the passion and fire of a scene between her, Mario, and Fornasari, was as good and great as it is possible for anything operatic to be. They drew on one another, the two men— not like stage-players, but like Macready himself: and she, rushing in between them, now clinging to this one, now to that, now making a sheath for their naked swords with her arms, now tearing her hair in distraction as they broke away from her and plunged again at each other; was prodigious." This was the theatre at which Macready was immediately to act, and where Dickens saw him next day rehearse the scene before the doge and council in *Othello*, "not as usual facing the float but arranged on one side," with an effect that seemed to him to heighten the reality of the scene.

He left Paris on the night of the 13th with the *malle poste*, which did not reach Marseilles till fifteen hours behind its time, after three days and three nights travelling over horrible roads. Then, in a confusion between the two rival packets for Genoa, he unwillingly detained one of them more than an hour from sailing; and only managed at last to get to her just as she was moving out of harbour. As he went up the side, he saw a strange sensation among the angry travellers whom he had detained so long; heard a voice exclaim "I am blarmed if it ain't DICKENS!" and stood in the centre of a group of *Five Americans*! But the pleasantest part of the story is that they were, one and all, glad to see him; that their chief man, or leader, who had met him in New York, at once introduced them all round with the remark, "Personally our countrymen, and you, can fix it friendly, sir, I do expectuate"; and that, through the stormy passage to Genoa which followed, they were excellent friends. For the greater part of the time, it is true, Dickens had to keep to his cabin; but he contrived to get enjoyment out of them nevertheless. The member of the party who had the travelling dictionary wouldn't part with it, though he was dead sick in the cabin next to my friend's; and every now and then Dickens was conscious of his fellow-travellers coming down to him, crying out in varied tones of anxious bewilderment, "I say, what's French for a pillow?" "Is there any Italian phrase for a lump of sugar? Just look, will you?" "What the devil does echo mean? The garsong says echo to everything!" They were excessively curious to know, too, the population of every little town on the Cornice, and all its statistics; "perhaps the very last subjects within the capacity of the human intellect," remarks Dickens, "that would ever present themselves to an Italian steward's mind. He was a very willing fellow, our steward; and, having some vague idea that they would like a large number, said at hazard fifty thousand, ninety thousand, four hundred thousand, when they asked about the population of a place not larger than Lincoln's Inn Fields. And when they said, *Non Possible!* (which was the leader's invariable reply), he doubled or trebled the amount; to meet what he supposed to be their views, and make it quite satisfactory."

VII

ON 22 December he had resumed his ordinary Genoa life; and of a letter from Jeffrey, to whom he had dedicated his little book, he wrote as "most energetic and enthusiastic. Filer sticks in his throat rather, but all the rest is quivering in his heart. He is very much struck by the management of Lilian's story, and cannot help speaking of that; writing of it all indeed with the freshness and ardour of youth, and not like a man whose blue and yellow has turned grey." Some of its words have been already given. "Miss Coutts has sent Charley, with the best of letters to me, a Twelfth Cake weighing ninety pounds, magnificently decorated; and only think of the characters, Fairburn's Twelfth Night characters, being detained at the custom-house for Jesuitical surveillance! But these fellows are—— Well! never mind. Perhaps you have seen the history of the Dutch minister at Turin, and of the spiriting away of his daughter by the Jesuits? It is all true; though, like the history of our friend's servant,[1] almost incredible. But their devilry is such that I am assured by our consul that if, while we are in the south, we were to let our children go out with servants on whom we could not implicitly rely, these holy men would trot even their small feet into churches with a view to their ultimate conversion! It is tremendous even to see them in the streets, or slinking about this garden." Of his purpose to start for the south of Italy in the middle of January, taking his wife with him, his letter the following week told me; dwelling on all he had missed, in that first Italian Christmas, of our old enjoyments of the season in England; and closing its pleasant talk with a postscript at midnight. "First of January, 1845. Many many many happy

---

[1] In a previous letter he had told me that history. "Apropos of servants, I must tell you of a child-bearing handmaiden of some friends of ours, a thorough out and outer, who, by way of expiating her sins, caused herself, the other day, to be received into the bosom of the infallible Church. She had two marchionesses for her sponsors; and she is heralded in the Genoa newspapers as Miss B——, an English lady, who has repented of her errors and saved her soul alive."

returns of the day! A life of happy years! The Baby is dressed in thunder, lightning, rain, and wind. His birth is most portentous here."

It was of ill-omen to me, one of its earliest incidents being my only brother's death; but Dickens had a friend's true helpfulness in sorrow, and a portion of what he then wrote to me I permit myself to preserve in a note [1] for what it relates of his own sad experiences and solemn beliefs and hopes. The journey southward began on 20 January, and five days later I had a letter written from La Scala, at a little inn, "supported on low brick arches like a British haystack," the bed in their room "like a mangle," the ceiling without lath or plaster, nothing to speak of available for comfort or decency, and nothing particular to eat or drink. "But for all this I have become attached to the country and I don't care who knows it." They had left Pisa that morning and Carrara the day before: at the latter place an ovation awaiting him, the result of the zeal of our eccentric friend Fletcher, who happened to be staying there with an English marble-merchant. "There is a beautiful little * 41 theatre there, built of marble; and they had it illuminated that night, in my honour. There was really a very fair opera; but it is curious that the chorus has been always, time out of mind, made up of labourers in the quarries, who don't know a note of music, and sing entirely by ear. It was crammed to excess, and I had a great reception; a deputation waiting upon us in the box, and the orchestra turning out in a body afterwards and

[1] "I feel the distance between us now, indeed. I would to Heaven, my dearest friend, that I could remind you in a manner more lively and affectionate than this dull sheet of paper can put on, that you have a Brother left. One bound to you by ties as strong as ever Nature forged. By ties never to be broken, weakened, changed in any way—but to be knotted tighter up, if that be possible, until the same end comes to them as has come to these. That end but the bright beginning of a happier union, I believe; and have never more strongly and religiously believed (and oh! Forster, with what a sore heart I have thanked God for it) than when that shadow has fallen on my own hearth, and made it cold and dark as suddenly as in the home of that poor girl you tell me of. . . . When you write to me again, the pain of this will have passed. No consolation can be so certain and so lasting to you as that softened and manly sorrow which springs up from the memory of the Dead. I read your heart as easily as if I held it in my hand, this moment. And I know—I *know*, my dear friend—that before the ground is green above him, you will be content that what was capable of death in him, should lie there. . . . I am glad to think it was so easy, and full of peace. What can we hope for more, when our own time comes!—The day when he visited us in our old house is as fresh to me as if it had been yesterday. I remember him as well as I remember you. . . . I have many things to say, but cannot say them now. Your attached and loving friend for life, and far, I hope, beyond it. C. D." (8 January, 1845.)

serenading us at Mr. Walton's." Between this and Rome they
had a somewhat wild journey; and before Radicofani was reached,
there were disturbing rumours of bandits and even uncomfortable whispers as to their night's lodging-place. "I really began
to think we might have an adventure; and as I had brought
(like an ass) a bag of napoleons with me from Genoa, I called
up all the theatrical ways of letting off pistols that I could call
to mind, and was the more disposed to fire them through not
having any." It ended in no worse adventure, however, than a
somewhat exciting dialogue with an old professional beggar
at Radicofani itself, in which he was obliged to confess that
he came off second-best. It transpired at a little town hanging
on a hillside, of which the inhabitants, being all of them beggars,
had the habit of swooping down, like so many birds of prey,
upon any carriage that approached it.

"Can you imagine" (he named a first-rate bore, for whose
name I shall substitute) "M. F. G. in a very frowsy brown cloak
concealing his whole figure, and with very white hair and a
very white beard, darting out of this place with a long staff in
his hand, and begging? There he was, whether you can or not;
out of breath with the rapidity of his dive, and staying with his
staff all the Radicofani boys, that he might fight it out with
me alone. It was very wet, and so was I: for I had kept, according to custom, my box-seat. It was blowing so hard that I could
scarcely stand; and there was a custom-house on the spot,
besides. Over and above all this, I had no small money; and the
brave C. never has, when I want it for a beggar. When I had
excused myself several times, he suddenly drew himself up and
said, with a wizard look (fancy the aggravation of M. F. G. as
a wizard!), 'Do you know what you are doing, my lord? Do you
mean to go on to-day?' 'Yes,' I said, 'I do.' 'My lord,' he said,
'do you know that your *vetturino* is unacquainted with this part
of the country; that there is a wind raging on the mountain,
which will sweep you away; that the courier, the coach, and all
the passengers, were blown from the road last year; and that
the danger is great and almost certain?' 'No,' I said, 'I don't.'
'My lord, you don't understand me, I think?' 'Yes, I do, d——
you!' nettled by this (you feel it? I confess it). 'Speak to my
servant. It's his business. Not mine'—for he really was too
like M. F. G. to be borne. If you could have seen him!—'Santa
Maria, these English lords! It's not their business if they're
killed! They leave it to their servants!' He drew off the boys;
whispered them to keep away from the heretic; and ran up

the hill again, almost as fast as he had come down. He stopped at a little distance as we moved on; and pointing to Roche with his long staff cried loudly after me, 'It's *his* business if you're killed, is it, my lord? Ha! ha! ha! whose business is it when the English lords are born! Ha! ha! ha!' The boys taking it up in a shrill yell, I left the joke and them at this point. But I must confess that I thought he had the best of it. And he had so far reason for what he urged, that when we got on the mountain pass the wind became terrific, so that we were obliged to take Kate out of the carriage lest she should be blown over, carriage and all, and had ourselves to hang on to it, on the windy side, to prevent its going Heaven knows where!"

The first impression of Rome was disappointing. It was the evening of 30 January, and the cloudy sky, dull cold rain and muddy footways, he was prepared for; but he was not prepared for the long streets of commonplace shops and houses like Paris or any other capital, the busy people, the equipages, the ordinary walkers up and down. "It was no more my Rome, degraded and fallen and lying asleep in the sun among a heap of ruins, than Lincoln's Inn Fields is. So I really went to bed in a very indifferent humour." That all this yielded to later and worthier impressions I need hardly say; and he had never in his life, he told me afterwards, been so moved or overcome by any sight as by that of the Coliseum, "except perhaps by the first contemplation of the Falls of Niagara." He went to Naples for the interval before the Holy Week; and his first letter from it was to say that he had found the wonderful aspects of Rome before he left, and that for loneliness and grandeur of ruin nothing could transcend the southern side of the Campagna. But farther and farther south the weather had become worse; and for a week before his letter (11 February), the only bright sky he had seen was just as the sun was coming up across the sea at Terracina. "Of which place, a beautiful one, you can get a very good idea by imagining something as totally unlike the scenery in *Fra Diavolo* as possible." He thought the bay less striking at Naples than at Genoa, the shape of the latter being more perfect in its beauty, and the smaller size enabling you to see it all at once, and feel it more like an exquisite picture. The city he conceived the greatest dislike to.[1] "The condition of

---

[1] He makes no mention in his book of the pauper burial-place at Naples, to which the reference made in his letters is striking enough for preservation. "In Naples, the burying place of the poor people is a great paved yard with three hundred and sixty-five pits in it: every one covered by a square stone which is fastened down. One of these pits is opened every

the common people here is abject and shocking. I am afraid the conventional idea of the picturesque is associated with such misery and degradation that a new picturesque will have to be established as the world goes onward. Except Fondi there is nothing on earth that I have seen so dirty as Naples. I don't know what to liken the streets to where the mass of the *lazzaroni* live. You recollect that favourite pig-stye of mine near Broadstairs? They are more like streets of such apartments heaped up story on story, and tumbled house on house, than anything else I can think of, at this moment." In a later letter he was even less tolerant. "What would I give that you should see the *lazzaroni* as they really are—mere squalid, abject, miserable animals for vermin to batten on; slouching, slinking, ugly, shabby, scavenging scarecrows! And oh the raffish counts and more than doubtful countesses, the noodles and the blacklegs, the good society! And oh the miles of miserable streets and

* 43 wretched occupants, to which Saffron Hill or the Borough Mint is a kind of small gentility, which are found to be so picturesque by English lords and ladies; to whom the wretchedness left behind at home is lowest of the low, and vilest of the vile, and commonest of all common things. Well! well! I have often thought that one of the best chances of immortality for a writer is in the Death of his language, when he immediately becomes good company: and I often think here,—What *would* you say to these people, milady and milord, if they spoke out of the homely dictionary of your own 'lower orders!'" He was again at Rome on Sunday the second of March.

night in the year; the bodies of the pauper dead are collected in the city; brought out in a cart (like that I told you of at Rome); and flung in uncoffined. Some lime is then cast down into the pit; and it is sealed up until a year is past, and its turn again comes round. Every night there is a pit opened; and every night that same pit is sealed up again for a twelvemonth. The cart has a red lamp attached, and at about ten o'clock at night you see it glaring through the streets of Naples: stopping at the doors of hospitals and prisons, and such places, to increase its freight; and then rattling off again. Attached to the new cemetery (a very pretty one, and well-kept: immeasurably better in all respects than Père-la-Chaise) there is another similar yard, but not so large. . . ." In connection with the same subject he adds: "About Naples, the dead are borne along the street, uncovered, on an open bier; which is sometimes hoisted on a sort of palanquin, covered with a cloth of scarlet and gold. This exposure of the deceased is not peculiar to that part of Italy; for about midway between Rome and Genoa we encountered a funeral procession attendant on the body of a woman, which was presented in its usual dress, to my eyes (looking from my elevated seat on the box of a travelling carriage) as if she were alive, and resting on her bed. An attendant priest was chanting lustily—and as badly as the priests invariably do. Their noise is horrible . . ."

Sad news from me as to a common and very dear friend awaited him there; but it is a subject on which I may not dwell further than to say that there arose from it much to redeem even such a sorrow, and that this I could not indicate better than by these wise and tender words from Dickens: "No philosophy will bear these dreadful things, or make a moment's head against them, but the practical one of doing all the good we can, in thought and deed. While we can, God help us! ourselves stray from ourselves so easily; and there are all around us such frightful calamities besetting the world in which we live; nothing else will carry us through it. . . . What a comfort to reflect on what you tell me. Bulwer Lytton's conduct is that of a generous and noble-minded man, as I have ever thought him. Our dear good Procter too! And Thackeray—how earnest they have all been! I am very glad to find you making special mention of Charles Lever. I am glad over every name you write. It says something for our pursuit, in the midst of all its miserable disputes and jealousies, that the common impulse of its followers, in such an instance as this, is surely and certainly of the noblest."

After the ceremonies of the Holy Week, of which the descriptions sent to me were reproduced in his book, he went to Florence,[1] which lived always afterwards in his memory with Venice, and with Genoa. He thought these the three great Italian cities. "There are some places here,[2]—oh Heaven how

---

[1] The reader will perhaps think with me that what he noticed, on the roads in Tuscany more than in any others, of wayside crosses and religious memorials, may be worth preserving. ". . . You know that in the streets and corners of roads, there are all sorts of crosses and similar memorials to be seen in Italy. The most curious are, I think, in Tuscany. There is very seldom a figure on the cross, though there is sometimes a face; but they are remarkable for being garnished with little models in wood of every possible object that can be connected with the Saviour's death. The cock that crowed when Peter had denied his Master thrice, is generally perched on the tip-top; and an ornithological phenomenon he always is. Under him is the inscription.Then, hung on to the cross-beam, are the spear, the reed with the sponge of vinegar and water at the end, the coat without seam for which the soldiers cast lots, the dice-box with which they threw for it, the hammer that drove in the nails, the pincers that pulled them out, the ladder which was set against the cross, the crown of thorns, the instrument of flagellation, the lantern with which Mary went to the tomb —I suppose; I can think of no other—and the sword with which Peter smote the high priest's servant. A perfect toy-shop of little objects; repeated at every four or five miles all along the highway."

[2] Of his visit to Fiesole I have spoken in my *Life of Landor*. "Ten years after Landor had lost this home, an Englishman travelling in Italy, his friend and mine, visited the neighbourhood for his sake, drove out from Florence to Fiesole, and asked his coachman which was the villa in which the Landor family lived. 'He was a dull dog, and pointed to Boccaccio's. I didn't believe him. He was so deuced ready that I knew he lied. I went

fine! I wish you could see the tower of the Palazzo Vecchio as it lies before me at this moment, on the opposite bank of the Arno! But I will tell you more about it, and about all Florence, from my shady arm-chair up among the Peschiere oranges. I shall not be sorry to sit down in it again. . . . Poor Hood, poor Hood! I still look for his death, and he still lingers on. And Sydney Smith's brother gone after poor dear Sydney himself! Maltby will wither when he reads it; and poor old Rogers will contradict some young man at dinner, every day for three weeks."

Before he left Florence (on 4 April) I heard of a "very pleasant and very merry day" at Lord Holland's; and I ought to have mentioned how much he was gratified at Naples, by the attentions of the English Minister there, Mr. Temple, Lord Palmerston's brother, whom he described as a man supremely agreeable, with everything about him in perfect taste, and with that truest gentleman-manner which has its root in kindness and generosity of nature. He was back at home in the Peschiere on Wednesday, 9 April. Here he continued to write to me every week, for as long as he remained, of whatever he had seen: with no definite purpose as yet, but the pleasure of interchanging with myself the impressions and emotions undergone by him. "Seriously," he wrote to me on 13 April, "it is a great pleasure to me to find that you are really pleased with these shadows in the water, and think them worth the looking at. Writing at such odd places, and in such odd seasons, I have been half savage with myself, very often, for not doing better. But d'Orsay, from whom I had a charming letter three days since, seems to think as you do of what he has read in those shown to him, and says they remind him vividly of the real aspect of these scenes. . . . Well, if we should determine after we have sat in council,

up to the convent, which is on a height, and was leaning over a dwarf wall basking in the noble view over a vast range of hill and valley, when a little peasant girl came up and began to point out the localities. *Ecco la villa l andora!* was one of the first half-dozen sentences she spoke. My heart swelled as Landor's would have done when I looked down upon it, nestling among its olive-trees and vines, and with its upper windows (there are five above the door) open to the setting sun. Over the centre of these there is another story, set upon the house-top like a tower; and all Italy, except its sea, is melted down into the glowing landscape it commands. I plucked a leaf of ivy from the convent-garden as I looked; and here it is. For Landor. With my love.' So wrote Mr. Dickens to me from Florence on the 2nd of April, 1845; and when I turned over Landor's papers in the same month after an interval of exactly twenty years, the ivy leaf was found carefully enclosed, with the letter in which I had sent it." Dickens had asked him before leaving what he would most wish to have in remembrance of Italy. "An ivy leaf from Fiesole," said Landor.

that the experiences they relate are to be used, we will call B. and E. to their share and voice in the matter." Shortly before he left, the subject was again referred to (7 June). "I am in as great doubt as you about the letters I have written you with these Italian experiences. I cannot for the life of me devise any plan of using them to my own satisfaction, and yet think entirely with you that in some form I ought to use them." Circumstances not in his contemplation at this time settled the form they ultimately took.

Two more months were to finish his Italian holiday, and I do not think he enjoyed any part of it so much as its close. He had formed a real friendship for Genoa, was greatly attached to the social circle he had drawn round him there, and liked rest after his travel all the more for the little excitement of living its activities over again, week by week, in these letters to me. And so, from his "shady arm-chair up among the Peschiere oranges," I had at regular intervals what he called his rambling talk; went over with him again all the roads he had taken; and of the more important scenes and cities, such as Venice, Rome, and Naples, received such rich filling-in to the first out-lines sent, as fairly justified the title of *Pictures* finally chosen for them. The weather all the time too had been without a flaw. "Since our return," he wrote on 27 April, "we have had charming spring days. The garden is one grove of roses; we have left off fires; and we breakfast and dine again in the great hall, with the windows open. To-day we have rain, but rain was rather wanted I believe, so it gives offence to nobody. As far as I have had an opportunity of judging yet, the spring is the most delightful time in this country. But for all that, I am looking with eagerness to the tenth of June, impatient to renew our happy old walks and old talks in dear old home."

Of incidents during these remaining weeks there were few, but such as he mentioned had in them points of humour or character still worth remembering. Two men were hanged in the city; and two ladies of quality, he told me, agreed to keep up for a time a prayer for the souls of these two miserable creatures so incessant that Heaven should never for a moment be left alone: to which end "they relieved each other" after such wise, that, for the whole of the stated time, one of them was always on her knees in the cathedral church of San Lorenzo. From which he inferred that "a morbid sympathy for criminals is not wholly peculiar to England, though it affects more people in that country perhaps than in any other."

* 44

Of Italian usages to the dead some notices from his letters have been given, and he had an example before he left of the way in which they affected English residents. A gentleman of his friend Fletcher's acquaintance living four miles from Genoa had the misfortune to lose his wife; and no attendance on the dead beyond the city gate, nor even any decent conveyance, being practicable, the mourner, to whom Fletcher had promised nevertheless the sad satisfaction of an English funeral, which he had meanwhile taken enormous secret pains to arrange with a small Genoese upholsterer, was waited upon, on the appointed morning, by a very bright yellow hackney-coach-and-pair driven by a coachman in yet brighter scarlet knee-breeches and waistcoat, who wanted to put the husband and the body inside together. "They were obliged to leave one of the coach-doors open for the accommodation even of the coffin; the widower walked beside the carriage to the Protestant cemetery; and Fletcher followed on a big grey horse." [1]

Scarlet breeches reappear, not less characteristically, in what his next letter told of a couple of English travellers who took possession at this time (24 May) of a portion of the ground floor of the Peschiere. They had with them a meek English footman who immediately confided to Dickens's servants, among other personal grievances, the fact that he was made to do everything, even cooking, in crimson breeches; which in a hot climate, he protested, was "a grinding of him down." "He is a poor soft country fellow; and his master locks him up at night in a basement room with iron bars to the window. Between which our

[1] "It matters little now," says Dickens, after describing this incident in one of his minor writings, "for coaches of all colours are alike to poor Kindheart, and he rests far north of the little cemetery with the cypress trees, by the city walls where the Mediterranean is so beautiful." Since the first volume, I observe allusion made to Fletcher's mother, in Crabb Robinson's *Diary*, as formerly a lady of great renown in Scotland, whose husband, the friend of Jeffrey, Horner, and Brougham in their early days, had been counsel for Joseph Gerrald in 1793. "She was an English beauty and heiress. Brougham eulogises her in his collected speeches. I knew her 30 years ago at Mrs. Barbauld's. . . . She is excellent in conversation." (*Diary*, 1844, iii. 259.) Her Autobiography has been lately published by her daughter. Since my early editions I have found a letter from Dickens on Fletcher's death in 1862. "Poor Fletcher is dead. Just as I am closing my letter I hear the sad story. He had been taken suddenly ill near the railway station at Leeds, and being accidentally recognised by one of the railway men was carried to the Infirmary, where the doctor obtained his sister Lady Richardson's address, and wrote to her. She arrived to find him in a dangerous state, and after lingering four days he died. Poor Kindheart! I think of all that made him so pleasant to us, and am full of grief." From another sure source I know that every possible attention was paid to him, and that for the last three days, together with his sister, his brother-in-law Sir John Richardson was in attendance.

servants poke wine in, at midnight. His master and mistress buy old boxes at the curiosity shops, and pass their lives in lining 'em with bits of parti-coloured velvet. A droll existence, is it not? We are lucky to have had the palace to ourselves until now, but it is so large that we never see or hear these people; and I should not have known even, if they had not called upon us, that another portion of the ground floor had been taken by some friends of old Lady Holland—whom I again seem to see crying about dear Sydney Smith, behind that green screen as we last saw her together." [1]

Then came a little incident also characteristic. An English ship of war, the *Fantôme*, appeared in the harbour; and from her commander, Sir Frederick Nicolson, Dickens received, among attentions very pleasant to him, an invitation to lunch on board and bring his wife, for whom, at a time appointed, a boat was to be sent to the Ponte Reale (the royal bridge). But no boat being there at the time, Dickens sent off his servant in another boat to the ship to say he feared some mistake. "While we were walking up and down a neighbouring piazza in his absence, a brilliant fellow in a dark blue shirt with a white hem to it all round the collar, regular corkscrew curls, and a face as brown as a berry, comes up to me and says, 'Beg your pardon sir, Mr. Dickens?' 'Yes.' 'Beg your pardon sir, but I'm one of the ship's company of the *Phantom* sir, cox'en of the cap'en's gig sir, she's a-lying off the pint sir—been there half an hour.' 'Well but my good fellow,' I said, ' you're at the wrong place!' 'Beg your pardon sir, I was afeerd it was the wrong place sir, but I've asked them Genoese here, sir, twenty times if it was Port Real; and they knows no more than a dead jackass!'—Isn't it a good thing to have made a regular Portsmouth name of it?"

That was in his letter of 1 June; which began by telling me it had been twice begun and twice flung into the basket, so great was his indisposition to write as the time for departure came, and which ended thus: "The fire-flies at night now, are miraculously splendid; making another firmament among the rocks on the sea-shore, and the vines inland. They get into the bedrooms, and fly about, all night, like beautiful little lamps.[2]

[1] Sydney died on 22 February ('45), in his seventy-seventh year.
[2] A remark on this, made in my reply, elicited what follows in a letter during his travel home: "Odd enough that remark of yours. I had been wondering at Rome that Juvenal (which I have been always lugging out of a bag, on all occasions) never used the fire-flies for an illustration. But even now, they are only partially seen; and nowhere I believe in such enormous numbers as on the Mediterranean coast-road, between Genoa and Spezzia. I will ascertain for curiosity's sake, whether there are any at

. . . I have surrendered much I had fixed my heart upon, as you know, admitting you have had reason for not coming to us here: but I stand by the hope that you and Mac will come and meet us at Brussels; it being so very easy. A day or two there, and at Antwerp, would be very happy for us; and we could still dine in Lincoln's Inn Fields on the day of arrival." I had been unable to join him in Genoa, urgently as he had wished it; but what is said here was done, and Jerrold was added to the party.

His last letter from Genoa was written on 7 June, not from the Peschiere, but from a neighbouring palace, "Brignole Rosso," into which he had fled from the miseries of moving. "They are all at sixes and sevens up at the Peschiere, as you may suppose; and Roche is in a condition of tremendous excitement, engaged in settling the inventory with the house-agent, who has just told me he is the devil himself. I had been appealed to, and had contented myself with this expression of opinion, 'Signor Noli, you are an old impostor!' '*Illustrissimo*,' said Signor Noli in reply, 'your servant is the devil himself: sent on earth to torture me.' I look occasionally towards the Peschiere (it is visible from this room), expecting to see one of them flying out of a window. Another great cause of commotion is, that they have been paving the lane by which the house is approached, ever since we returned from Rome. We have not been able to get the carriage up since that time, in consequence; and unless they finish to-night, it can't be packed in the garden, but the things will have to be brought down in baskets, piecemeal, and packed in the street. To avoid this inconvenient necessity, the Brave made proposals of bribery to the paviors last night, and induced them to pledge themselves that the carriage should come up at seven this evening. The manner of doing that sort of paving work here, is to take a pick or two with an axe, and then lie down to sleep for an hour. When I came out, the Brave had issued forth to examine the ground; and was standing alone in the sun among a heap of prostrate figures: with a Great Despair depicted in his face, which it would be hard to surpass. It was like a picture—'After the Battle.' Napoleon by the Brave: Bodies by the Paviors."

He came home by the Great St. Gothard, and was quite

this time in Rome, or between it and the country-house of Mæcenas—on the ground of Horace's journey. I know there is a place on the French side of Genoa, where they begin at a particular boundary-line, and are never seen beyond it. . . . All wild to see you at Brussels! What a meeting we will have, please God!"

carried away by what he saw of Switzerland. The country was so divine that he should have wondered indeed if its sons and daughters had ever been other than a patriotic people. Yet, infinitely above the country he had left as he ranked it in its natural splendours, there was something more enchanting than these that he lost in leaving Italy; and he expressed this delightfully in the letter from Lucerne (14 June) which closes the narrative of his Italian life.

"We came over the St. Gothard, which has been open only eight days. The road is cut through the snow, and the carriage winds along a narrow path between two massive snow walls, twenty feet high or more. Vast plains of snow range up the mountain-sides above the road, itself seven thousand feet above the sea; and tremendous waterfalls, hewing out arches for themselves in the vast drifts, go thundering down from precipices into deep chasms, here and there and everywhere; the blue water tearing through the white snow with an awful beauty that is most sublime. The pass itself, the mere pass over the top, is not so fine, I think, as the Simplon; and there is no plain upon the summit, for the moment it is reached the descent begins. So that the loneliness and wildness of the Simplon are not equalled *there*. But being much higher, the ascent and the descent range over a much greater space of country; and on both sides there are places of terrible grandeur, unsurpassable, I should imagine, in the world. The Devil's Bridge, terrific! The whole descent between Andermatt (where we slept on Friday night) and Altdorf, William Tell's town, which we passed through yesterday afternoon, is the highest sublimation of all you can imagine in the way of Swiss scenery. Oh God! what a beautiful country it is! How poor and sunken, beside it, is Italy in its brightest aspect!

"I look upon the coming down from the Great St. Gothard with a carriage and four horses and only one postilion, as the most dangerous thing that a carriage and horses can do. We had two great wooden logs for drags, and snapped them both like matches. The road is like a geometrical staircase, with horrible depths beneath it; and at every turn it is a toss-up, or seems to be, whether the leaders shall go round or over. The lives of the whole party may depend upon a strap in the harness; and if we broke our rotten harness once yesterday, we broke it at least a dozen times. The difficulty of keeping the horses together in the continual and steep circle, is immense. They slip and slide, and get their legs over the traces, and are dragged up against the rocks; carriage, horses, harness, all a confused heap. The Brave, and I, and the postilion, were constantly at work, in extricating the whole concern from a tangle, like a skein of thread. We broke two thick iron chains, and crushed the box of a wheel, as it was; and the carriage is now undergoing repair, under the window, on the margin of the lake: where a woman in short petticoats, a stomacher, and two immensely long tails of black hair hanging down her back very nearly to her heels, is looking on—apparently dressed for a melodrama, but in reality a waitress at this establishment.

"If the Swiss villages looked beautiful to me in winter, their summer aspect is most charming: most fascinating: most delicious. Shut in by high mountains capped with perpetual snow; and dotting a rich carpet of the softest turf, overshadowed by great trees; they seem so many little havens of refuge from the troubles and miseries of great towns. The cleanliness of the little baby-houses of inns is wonderful to those who come from Italy. But the beautiful Italian manners, the sweet language, the quick recognition of a pleasant look or cheerful word; the captivating expression of a desire to oblige in everything; are left behind the Alps. Remembering them, I sigh for the dirt again: the brick floors, bare walls, unplastered ceilings, and broken windows."

We met at Brussels; Maclise, Jerrold, myself, and the travellers; passed a delightful week in Flanders together; and were in England at the close of June.

BOOK FIFTH

LONDON, LAUSANNE AND PARIS

1845–7. ÆT. 33–5

I

AGAIN IN ENGLAND

1845–6

His first letter after again taking possession of Devonshire Terrace revived a subject on which opinions had been from time to time interchanged during his absence, and to which there was allusion in the agreement executed before his departure. The desire was still as strong with him as when he started *Master Humphrey's Clock* to establish a periodical, that, while relieving his own pen by enabling him to receive frequent help from other writers, might yet retain always the popularity of his name. "I really think I have an idea, and not a bad one, for the periodical. I have turned it over, the last two days, very much in my mind: and think it positively good. I incline still to weekly; price three-halfpence, if possible; partly original, partly select; notices of books, notices of theatres, notices of all good things, notices of all bad ones; *Carol* philosophy, cheerful views, sharp anatomisation of humbug, jolly good temper; papers always in season, pat to the time of year; and a vein of glowing, hearty, generous, mirthful, beaming reference in everything to Home and Fireside. And I would call it, sir:

THE CRICKET

A cheerful creature that chirrups on the Hearth.

Natural History.

"Now, don't decide hastily till you've heard what I would do. I would come out, sir, with a prospectus on the subject of the Cricket that should put everybody in a good temper, and make such a dash at people's fenders and arm-chairs as hasn't been made for many a long day. I could approach them in a different mode under this name, and in a more winning and immediate way, than under any other. I would at once sit down upon their very hobs; and take a personal and confidential position with them which should separate me, instantly, from all other periodicals periodically published, and supply a distinct and sufficient reason for my coming into existence. And I would chirp, chirp, chirp away in every number until I chirped it up to——well, you shall say how many hundred thousand! . . . Seriously, I feel a capacity in this name and notion which appears to give us a tangible starting-point, and a real, defined, strong, genial drift and purpose. I seem to feel that it is an aim and name which people would readily and pleasantly connect with *me*; and that, for a good course and a clear one, instead of making circles pigeon-like at starting, here we should be safe. I think the general recognition would be likely to leap at it; and of the helpful associations that could be clustered round the idea at starting, and the pleasant tone of which the working of it is susceptible, I have not the smallest doubt. . . . But you shall determine. What do you think? And what do you say? The chances are, that it will either strike you instantly, or not strike you at all. Which is it, my dear fellow? You know I am not bigoted to the first suggestions of my own fancy: but you know also exactly how I should use such a lever, and how much power I should find in it. Which is it? What do you say? —I have not myself said half enough. Indeed I have said next to nothing; but like the parrot in the negro-story, I 'think a dam deal.'"

My objection, incident more or less to every such scheme, was the risk of losing its general advantage by making it too specially dependent on individual characteristics: but there was much in favour of the present notion, and its plan had been modified so far, in the discussions that followed, as to involve less absolute personal identification with Dickens,—when discussion, project, everything was swept away by a larger scheme, in its extent and its danger more suitable to the wild and hazardous enterprises of that prodigious year (1845) of excitement and disaster. In this more tremendous adventure, already hinted at on a previous page, we all became involved; and the chirp of the Cricket, delayed in consequence until Christmas, was heard then in circumstances quite other than those first intended. The change he thus announced to me about half-way through the summer, in the same letter which told me the success of d'Orsay's kind exertion to procure a fresh engagement for his
* 45 courier Roche. "What do you think of a notion that has occurred to me in connection with our abandoned little weekly? It would

be a delicate and beautiful fancy for a Christmas book, making the Cricket a little household god—silent in the wrong and sorrow of the tale, and loud again when all went well and happy." The reader will not need to be told that thus originated the story of the *Cricket on the Hearth*, a Fairy Tale of Home, which had a great popularity in the Christmas days of 1845. Its sale at the outset doubled that of both its predecessors.

But as yet the larger adventure had not made itself known, and the interval was occupied with the private play of which the notion had been started between us at his visit in December, and which led to his disclosure of a passage in his early career belonging to that interval between his school-days and start in life when he had to pass nearly two weary years as a reporter for one of the offices in Doctors' Commons, from which he sought relief by an attempt to get upon the stage. I had asked him, after his return to Genoa, whether he continued to think that we should have the play; and his reply began thus: "ARE we to have that play??? Have I spoken of it, ever since I came home from London, as a settled thing! I do not know if I have ever told you seriously, but I have often thought, that I should certainly have been as successful on the boards as I have been between them. I assure you, when I was on the stage at Montreal (not having played for years) I was as much astonished at the reality and ease, to myself, of what I did as if I had been another man. See how oddly things come about!"

Then came the interesting bit of autobiography the reader has had before him already; and his account of the stage practice he had previously gone through with a view to the adventure, contained in the same letter, may be added here. "This was at the time when I was at Doctors' Commons as a shorthand writer for the proctors. It wasn't a very good living (though not a *very* bad one), and was wearily uncertain; which made me think of the Theatre in quite a business-like way. I went to some theatre every night, with a very few exceptions, for at least three years: really studying the bills first, and going to where there was the best acting: and always to see Mathews whenever he played. I practised immensely (even such things as walking in and out, and sitting down in a chair): often four, five, six hours a day: shut up in my own room, or walking about in the fields. I prescribed to myself, too, a sort of Hamiltonian system for learning parts; and learnt a great number. I haven't even lost the habit now, for I knew my Canadian parts immediately, though they were new to me. I must have done a good deal: for, just as Macready found me out, they used to challenge me at Braham's: and Yates, who was knowing enough in those things, wasn't to be parried at all. It was just the same, that day at Keeley's, when they were getting up the *Chuzzlewit* last June. If you think Macready would be interested in this Strange news from the South, tell it him. Fancy Bartley or Charles Kemble *now*! And how little they suspect me!" In the later letter from Lucerne, written as he was travelling home, he adds: "*Did* I ever tell you the details of my theatrical idea, before? Strange, that I should have quite forgotten it. I had an odd fancy, when I was reading the unfortunate little farce at Covent Garden, that Bartley looked as if some struggling recollection and connection were stirring up within him—but it may only have been his doubts of that humorous composition."

What Might have Been is a history of too little profit to be worth anybody's writing, and here there is no call even to regret how great an actor was in Dickens lost. He took to a higher calling, but it included the lower. There was no character created by him into which life and reality were not thrown with such vividness, that to his readers the thing written did not seem the thing actually done, whether the form of disguise put on by the enchanter was Mrs. Gamp, Tom Pinch, Mr. Squeers, or Fagin the Jew. He had the power of projecting himself into shapes and suggestions of his fancy which is one of the marvels of creative imagination, and what he desired to express he became. The assumptions of the theatre have the same method at a lower pitch, depending greatly on personal accident; but the accident as much as the genius favoured Dickens, and another man's conception underwent in his acting the process which in writing he applied to his own. Into both he flung himself with the passionate fullness of his nature; and though the theatre had limits for him that may be named hereafter, and he was always greater in quickness of assumption than in steadiness of delineation, there was no limit to his delight and enjoyment in the adventures of our theatrical holiday.

In less than three weeks after his return we had selected our play, cast our parts, and all but engaged our theatre; as I find by a note from my friend of 22 July, in which the good-natured laugh can give no offence now, since all who might have objected to it have long gone from us. Fanny Kelly, the friend of Charles Lamb, and a genuine successor to the old school of actresses in which the Mrs. Orgers and Miss Popes were bred, was not more delightful on the stage than impracticable when off, and the

little theatre in Dean Street which the Duke of Devonshire's
munificence had enabled her to build, and which with any
ordinary good sense might handsomely have realised both its
uses, as a private school for young actresses and a place of public
amusement, was made useless for both by her mere whims and
fancies. "Heavens! such a scene as I have had with Miss Kelly
here, this morning! She wanted us put off until the theatre
should be cleaned and brushed up a bit, and she would and
she would not, for she is eager to have us and alarmed when
she thinks of us. By the foot of Pharaoh, it was a great scene!
Especially when she choked, and had the glass of water brought.
She exaggerates the importance of our occupation, dreads the
least prejudice against her establishment in the minds of any
of our company, says the place already has quite ruined her,
and with tears in her eyes protests that any jokes at her additional expense in print would drive her mad. By the body of
Cæsar, the scene was incredible! It's like a preposterous dream!"
Something of our play is disclosed by the oaths à la Bobadil,
and of our actors by "the jokes" poor Miss Kelly was afraid
of. We had chosen EVERY MAN IN HIS HUMOUR, with special
regard to the singleness and individuality of the "humours"
portrayed in it; and our company included the leaders of a
journal then in its earliest years, but already not more renowned
as the most successful joker of jokes yet known in England,
than famous for that exclusive use of its laughter and satire
for objects the highest or most harmless which makes it still
so enjoyable a companion to mirth-loving right-minded men.
Maclise took earnest part with us, and was to have acted, but
fell away on the eve of the rehearsals; and Stanfield, who went
so far as to rehearse Downright twice, then took fright and also
ran away; but Jerrold, who played Master Stephen, brought * 46
with him Lemon, who took Brainworm; Leech, to whom
Master Matthew was given; A'Beckett, who had condescended
to the small part of William; and Mr. Leigh, who had Oliver
Cob. I played Kitely, and Bobadil fell to Dickens, who took
upon him the redoubtable Captain long before he stood in his
dress at the footlights; humouring the completeness of his
assumption by talking and writing Bobadil, till the dullest of
our party were touched and stirred to something of his own
heartiness of enjoyment. One or two hints of these have been
given, and I will only add to them his refusal of my wish that
he should go and see some special performance of the *Gamester*.
"Man of the House. *Gamester!* By the foot of Pharaoh, I will

not see the *Gamester*. Man shall not force, nor horses drag, this poor gentleman-like carcass into the presence of the *Gamester*. I have said it. . . . The player Mac hath bidden me to eat and likewise drink with him, thyself, and short-necked Fox to-night. An' I go not, I am a hog, and not a soldier. But an' thou goest not—Beware, citizen! Look to it. . . . Thine as thou meritest. BOBADIL (Captain). Unto Master Kitely. These."

The play was played on 21 September with a success that outran the wildest expectation; and turned our little enterprise into one of the small sensations of the day. The applause of the theatre found so loud an echo in the press, that for the time nothing else was talked about in private circles; and after a week or two we had to yield (we did not find it difficult) to a pressure of demand for more public performance in a larger theatre, by which a useful charity received important help, and its committee showed their gratitude by an entertainment to us at the Clarendon, a month or two later, when Lord Lansdowne took the chair. There was also another performance by us at the same theatre, before the close of the year, of the *Elder Brother* by Beaumont and Fletcher. I may not further indicate the enjoyments that attended the success, and gave always to the first of our series of performances a pre-eminently pleasant place in memory.

Of the thing itself, however, it is necessary to be said that a modicum of merit goes a long way in all such matters, and it would not be safe now to assume that ours was much above the average of amateur attempts in general. Lemon certainly had most of the stuff, conventional as well as otherwise, of a regular actor in him, but this was not of a high kind; and though Dickens had the title to be called a born comedian, the turn for it being in his very nature, his strength was rather in the vividness and variety of his assumptions, than in the completeness, finish, or ideality he could give to any part of them. It is expressed exactly by what he says of his youthful preference for the representations of the elder Mathews. At the same time this was in itself so thoroughly genuine and enjoyable, and had in it such quickness and keenness of insight, that of its kind it was unrivalled; and it enabled him to present in Bobadil, after a richly coloured picture of bombastical extravagance and comic exaltation in the earlier scenes, a contrast in the later of tragical humility and abasement that had a wonderful effect. But greatly as his acting contributed to the success of the

night, this was nothing to the service he had rendered as manager. It would be difficult to describe it. He was the life and soul
of the entire affair. I never seemed till then to have known his
business capabilities. He took everything on himself, and did
the whole of it without an effort. He was stage-director, very
often stage-carpenter, scene-arranger, property-man, prompter,
and bandmaster. Without offending anyone he kept everyone in
order. For all he had useful suggestions, and the dullest of clays
under his potter's hand were transformed into little bits of
porcelain. He adjusted scenes, assisted carpenters, invented
costumes, devised playbills, wrote out calls, and enforced as
well as exhibited in his proper person everything of which he
urged the necessity on others. Such a chaos of dirt, confusion,
and noise, as the little theatre was the day we entered it, and
such a cosmos as he made it of cleanliness, order, and silence,
before the rehearsals were over! There were only two things left
as we found them, bits of humanity both, understood from the
first as among the fixtures of the place: a Man in a Straw Hat,
tall, and very fitful in his exits and entrances, of whom we
never could pierce the mystery, whether he was on guard or in
possession, or what he was; and a solitary little girl who flitted
about so silently among our actors and actresses that she might
have been deaf and dumb but for sudden small shrieks and starts
elicited by the wonders going on, which obtained for her the
name of Fireworks. There is such humorous allusion to both
in a letter of Dickens's of a year's later date, on the occasion of
the straw-hatted mystery revealing itself as a gentleman in
training for the tragic stage, that it may pleasantly close for
the present our private theatricals.

"Our straw-hatted friend from Miss Kelly's! Oh my stars!
To think of him, all that time—Macbeth in disguise; Richard
the Third grown straight; Hamlet as he appeared on his sea-
voyage to England. What an artful villain he must be, never
to have made any sign of the melodrama that was in him! What
a wicked-minded and remorseless Iago to have seen you doing
Kitely night after night! raging to murder you and seize the
part! Oh, fancy Miss Kelly 'getting him up' in Macbeth. Good
Heaven! what a mass of absurdity must be shut up sometimes
within the walls of that small theatre in Dean Street! Fireworks
will come out shortly, depend upon it, in the dumb line; and will
relate her history in profoundly unintelligible motions that will
be translated into long and complicated descriptions by a grey-
headed father, and a red-wigged countryman, his son. You

remember the dumb dodge of relating an escape from captivity? Clasping the left wrist with the right hand, and the right wrist with the left hand—alternately (to express chains)—and then going round and round the stage very fast, and coming hand over hand down an imaginary cord: at the end of which there is one stroke on the drum, and a kneeling to the chandelier? If Fireworks can't do that—and won't somewhere—I'm a Dutchman."

Graver things now claim a notice which need not be proportioned to their gravity, because, though they had an immediate effect on Dickens's fortunes, they do not otherwise form part of his story. But first let me say, he was at Broadstairs for three weeks in the autumn; [1] we had the private play on his return; and a month later, on 28 October, a sixth child and fourth son, named Alfred Tennyson after his godfathers d'Orsay and Tennyson, was born in Devonshire Terrace. A death in the family followed, the older and more gifted of his ravens having indulged the same illicit taste for putty and paint which had been fatal to his predecessor. Voracity killed him, as it killed Scott's. He died unexpectedly before the kitchen-fire. "He kept his eye to the last upon the meat as it roasted, and suddenly turned over on his back with a sepulchral cry of *Cuckoo!*" The letter which told me this (31 October) announced to me also

---

[1] Characteristic glimpse of this Broadstairs holiday is afforded by a letter of 19 August, 1845. "Perhaps it is a fair specimen of the old adventures which befall the Inimitable, that the cab in which the children and the luggage were (I and my womankind being in the other) got its shafts broken in the city, last Friday morning, through the horse stumbling on the greasy pavement; and was drawn to the wharf (about a mile) by a stout man, amid such frightful howlings and derisive yellings on the part of an infuriated populace, as I never heard before. Conceive the man in the broken shafts with his back towards the cab; all the children looking out of the windows; and the muddy portmanteaus and so forth (which were all tumbled down when the horse fell) tottering and nodding on the box! The best of it was, that *our* cabman, being an intimate friend of the damaged cabman, insisted on keeping him company; and proceeded at a solemn walk, in front of the procession; thereby securing to me a liberal share of the popular curiosity and congratulation. . . . Everything here at Broadstairs is the same as of old. I have walked 20 miles a day since I came down, and I went to a circus at Ramsgate on Saturday night, where *Mazeppa* was played in three long acts without an H in it: as if for a wager. Evven, and edds, and orrors, and ands, were as plentiful as blackberries; but the letter H was neither whispered in Evven, nor muttered in Ell, nor permitted to dwell in any form on the confines of the sawdust." With this I will couple another theatrical experience of this holiday, when he saw a Giant played by a village comedian with a quite Gargantuesque felicity, and singled out for admiration his fine manner of sitting down to a hot supper (of children), with the self-lauding exalting remark, by way of grace, "How pleasant is a quiet conscience and an approving mind!"

that he was at a deadlock in his Christmas story: "Sick, bothered and depressed. Visions of Brighton come upon me; and I have a great mind to go there to finish my second part, or to Hampstead. I have a desperate thought of 'Jack Straw's.' I never was in such bad writing cue as I am this week, in all my life." The reason was not far to seek. In the preparation for the proposed new Daily Paper to which reference has been made, he was now actively assisting, and had all but consented to the publication of his name.

I entertained at this time, for more than one powerful reason, the greatest misgiving of his intended share in the adventure. It was not fully revealed until later on what difficult terms, physical as well as mental, Dickens held the tenure of his imaginative life; but already I knew enough to doubt the wisdom of what he was at present undertaking. In all intellectual labour, his will prevailed so strongly when he fixed it on any object of desire, that what else its attainment might exact was never duly measured; and this led to frequent strain and unconscious waste of what no man could less afford to spare. To the world gladdened by his work, its production might always have seemed quite as easy as its enjoyment; but it may be doubted if ever any man's mental effort cost him more. His habits were robust, but not his health; that secret had been disclosed to me before he went to America; and to the last he decidedly refused to admit the enormous price he had paid for his triumphs and successes. The morning after his last note I heard again. "I have been so very unwell this morning, with giddiness, and headache, and botheration of one sort or other, that I didn't get up till noon: and, shunning Fleet Street" (the office of the proposed new paper), "am now going for a country walk, in the course of which you will find me, if you feel disposed to come away in the carriage that goes to you with this. It is to call for a pull of the first part of the *Cricket*, and will bring you, if you like, by way of Hampstead to me, and subsequently to dinner. There is much I should like to discuss, if you can manage it. It's the loss of my walks, I suppose; but I am as giddy as if I were drunk, and can hardly see." I gave far from sufficient importance at the time to the frequency of complaints of this kind, or to the recurrence, at almost regular periods after the year following the present, of those spasms in the side of which he has recorded an instance in the recollections of his childhood, and of which he had an attack in Genoa; but though not conscious of it to its full extent, this consideration was among those that influenced me in a determination to endeavour to turn him from what could not but be regarded as full of peril. His health, however, had no real prominence in my letter; and it is strange now to observe that it appears as an argument in his reply. I had simply put before him, in the strongest form, all the considerations drawn from his genius and fame that should deter him from the labour and responsibility of a daily paper, not less than from the party and political involvements incident to it; and here was the material part of the answer made: "Many thanks for your affectionate letter, which is full of generous truth. These considerations weigh with me, *heavily*: but I think I descry in these times, greater stimulants to such an effort; greater chance of some fair recognition of it; greater means of persevering in it, or retiring from it unscratched by any weapon one should care for; than at any other period. And most of all I have, sometimes, that possibility of failing health or fading popularity before me, which beckons me to such a venture when it comes within my reach. At the worst, I have written to little purpose, if I cannot *write myself right* in people's minds, in such a case as this."

And so it went on: but it does not fall within my plan to describe more than the issue, which was to be accounted so far at least fortunate that it established a journal which has advocated steadily improvements in the condition of all classes, rich as well as poor, and has been able, during late momentous occurrences, to give wider scope to its influence by its enterprise and liberality. To that result, the great writer whose name gave its earliest attraction to the *Daily News* was not enabled to contribute much; but from him it certainly received the first impress of the opinions it has since consistently maintained. Its prospectus is before me in his handwriting, but it bears upon itself sufficiently the character of his hand and mind. The paper would be kept free, it said, from personal influence or party bias; and would be devoted to the advocacy of all rational and honest means by which wrong might be redressed, just rights maintained, and the happiness and welfare of society promoted.

The day for the appearance of its first number was that which was to follow Peel's speech for the repeal of the Corn Laws; but, brief as my allusions to the subject are, the remark should be made that even before this day came there were interruptions to the work of preparation, at one time very grave, which threw such "changes of vexation" on Dickens's personal relations to the venture as went for to destroy both his faith and his pleasure in it. No opinion need be offered as to where most of the blame lay, and it would be useless now to apportion the share that might possibly have belonged to himself; but, owing to this cause, his editorial work began with such diminished ardour that its brief continuance could not but be looked for. A little note written "before going home" at six o'clock in the morning of Wednesday, 21 January, 1846, to tell me they had "been at press three-quarters of an hour, and were out before *The Times*," marks the beginning; and a note written in the night of Monday, 9 February, "tired to death and quite worn out," to say that he had just resigned his editorial functions, describes the end. I had not been unprepared. A week before (Friday, 30 January) he had written: "I want a long talk with you. I was obliged to come down here in a hurry to give out a travelling letter I meant to have given out last night, and could not call upon you. Will you dine with us to-morrow at six sharp? I have been revolving plans in my mind this morning for quitting the paper and going abroad again to write a new book in shilling numbers. Shall we go to Rochester to-morrow week (my birthday) if the weather be, as it surely must be, better?" To Rochester accordingly we had gone, he and Mrs. Dickens and her sister, with Maclise and Jerrold and myself; going over the old Castle, Watts's Charity, and Chatham fortifications on the Saturday, passing Sunday in Cobham church and Cobham Park; having our quarters both days at the "Bull" Inn made famous in *Pickwick*; and thus, by indulgence of the desire which was always strangely urgent in him, associating his new resolve in life with those earliest scenes of his youthful time. On one point our feeling had been in thorough agreement. If long continuance with the paper was not likely, the earliest possible departure from it was desirable. But as the letters descriptive of his Italian travel (turned afterwards into *Pictures from Italy*) had begun with its first number, his name could not at once be withdrawn; and, for the time during which they were still to appear, he consented to contribute other occasional letters on important social questions. Public executions and Ragged Schools were among the subjects chosen by him, and all were handled with conspicuous ability. But the interval they covered was a short one.

To the supreme control which he had quitted, I succeeded, retaining it very reluctantly for the greater part of that weary, anxious, laborious year; but in little more than four months from the day the paper started, the whole of Dickens's connection with the *Daily News*, even that of contributing letters with his signature, had ceased. As he said in the preface to the republished *Pictures*, it was a mistake, in so departing from his old pursuits, to have disturbed the old relations between himself and his readers. It had, however, been "a brief mistake"; the departure had been only "for a moment"; and now those pursuits were "joyfully" to be resumed in Switzerland. Upon the latter point we had much discussion; but he was bent on again removing himself from London, and his glimpse of the Swiss mountains on his coming from Italy had given him a passion to visit them again. "I don't think," he wrote to me, "I *could* shut out the paper sufficiently, here, to write well. No. . . . I will write my book in Lausanne and in Genoa, and forget everything else if I can; and by living in Switzerland for the summer, and in Italy or France for the winter, I shall be saving money while I write." So therefore it was finally determined.

There is not much that calls for mention before he left. The first conceiving of a new book was always a restless time, and other subjects beside the characters that were growing in his mind would persistently intrude themselves into his night-wanderings. With some surprise I heard from him afterwards, for example, of a communication opened with a leading member of the government to ascertain what chances there might be for his appointment, upon due qualification, to the paid magistracy of London: the reply not giving him encouragement to entertain the notion further. It was of course but an outbreak of momentary discontent; and if the answer had been as hopeful, as, for others' sake rather than his own, one could have wished it to be, the result would have been the same. Just upon the eve of his departure, I may add, he took much interest in the establishment of the General Theatrical Fund, of which he remained a trustee until his death. It had originated in the fact that the funds of the two large theatres, themselves then disused for theatrical performances, were no longer available for the ordinary members of the profession; and on the occasion of his presiding at its first dinner in April, he said, very happily, that now the statue of Shakespeare outside the door of Drury Lane, as emphatically as his bust inside the church of Stratford-on-Avon, *pointed out his grave*. I am tempted also to mention as felicitous a word which I heard fall from him at one of the many private dinners that were got up in those days of parting to give him friendliest farewell. "Nothing is ever so good as it is

thought," said Lord Melbourne. "And nothing so bad," interposed Dickens.

The last incidents were that he again obtained Roche for his
travelling servant, and that he let his Devonshire Terrace house
to Sir James Duke for twelve months, the entire proposed term
of his absence. On 30 May they all dined with me, and on the
following day left England.

II

1846

HALTING at Ostend, Verviers, Coblentz, and Mannheim, they reached Strasburg on 7 June: the beauty of the weather showing them the Rhine at its best. At Mayence there had come aboard their boat a German, who soon after accosted Mrs. Dickens on deck in excellent English: "Your countryman Mr. Dickens is travelling this way just now, our papers say. Do you know him, or have you passed him anywhere?" Explanations ensuing, it turned out, by one of the odd chances my friend thought himself always singled out for, that he had with him a letter of introduction to the brother of this gentleman; who then spoke to him of the popularity of his books in Germany, and of the many persons he had seen reading them in the steamboats as he came along. Dickens remarking at this how great his own vexation was not to be able himself to speak a word of German, "Oh dear! that needn't trouble you," rejoined the other; "for even in so small a town as ours, where we are mostly primitive people and have few travellers, I could make a party of at least forty people who understand and speak English as well as I do, and of at least as many more who could manage to read you in the original." His town was Worms, which Dickens afterwards saw, ". . . a fine old place, though greatly shrunken and decayed in respect of its population; with a picturesque old cathedral standing on the brink of the Rhine, and some brave old churches shut up, and so hemmed in and overgrown with vineyards that they look as if they were turning into leaves and grapes."

He had no other adventure on the Rhine. But, on the same steamer, a not unfamiliar bit of character greeted him in the well-known lineaments, moral and physical, of two travelling Englishmen who had got an immense barouche on board with them, and had no plan whatever of going anywhere in it. One of them wanted to have this barouche wheeled ashore at every little town and village they came to. The other was bent upon "seeing it out," as he said—meaning, Dickens supposed, the river; though neither of them seemed to have the slightest interest in it. "The locomotive one would have gone ashore without the carriage, and would have been delighted to get rid of it; but they had a joint courier, and neither of them would part with *him* for a moment; so they went growling and grumbling on together, and seemed to have no satisfaction but in asking for impossible viands on board the boat, and having a grim delight in the steward's excuses."

From Strasburg they went by rail on the 8th to Basle, from which they started for Lausanne next day, in three coaches, two horses to each, taking three days for the journey: its only enlivening incident being an uproar between the landlord of an inn on the road, and one of the *voituriers* who had libelled Boniface's establishment by complaining of the food. "After various defiances on both sides, the landlord said, 'Scélérat! Mécréant! Je vous boaxerai!' to which the *voiturier* replied, 'Aha! Comment dites-vous? Voulez-vous boaxer? Eh? Voulez-vous? Ah! Boaxez-moi donc! Boaxez-moi!'—at the same time accompanying these retorts with gestures of violent significance, which explained that this new verb-active was founded on the well-known English verb to boax, or box. If they used it once, they used it at least a hundred times, and goaded each other to madness with it always." The travellers reached the Hôtel Gibbon at Lausanne on the evening of Thursday, 11 June; having been tempted as they came along to rest somewhat short of it, by a delightful glimpse of Neuchâtel. "On consideration however I thought it best to come on here, in case I should find, when I begin to write, that I want streets sometimes. In which case, Geneva (which I hope would answer the purpose) is only four and twenty miles away."

He at once began house-hunting, and had two days' hard work of it. He found the greater part of those let to the English like small villas in the Regent's Park, with verandahs, glass doors opening on lawns, and alcoves overlooking lake and mountains. One he was tempted by, higher up the hill, "poised above the town like a ship on a high wave"; but the possible fury of its winter winds deterred him. Greater still was the temptation to him of "L'Elysée," more a mansion than a villa; with splendid grounds overlooking the lake, and in its corridors and staircases as well as furniture like an old-fashioned country house in England; which he could have got for twelve months for £160. "But when I came to consider its vastness, I was rather dismayed at the prospect of windy nights in the autumn, with nobody staying in the house to make it gay." And so he again fell back upon the very first place he had seen, Rosemont, quite a doll's house; with two pretty little *salons*, a dining-room, hall, and kitchen, on the ground floor; and with just enough bedrooms upstairs to leave the family one to spare. "It is beautifully situated on the hill that rises from the lake, within ten minutes' walk of this hotel, and furnished, though scantily as all here are, better than others except Elysée, on account of its having been built and fitted up (the little *salons* in the Parisian way) by the landlady and her husband for themselves. They live now in a smaller house like a porter's lodge, just within the gate. A portion of the grounds is farmed by a farmer, and *he* lives close by; so that, while it is secluded, it is not at all lonely." The rent was to be ten pounds a month for half a year, with reduction to eight for the second half, if he should stay so long; and the rooms and furniture were to be described to me, so that according to custom I should be quite at home there, as soon as, also according to a custom well known, his own ingenious rearrangements and improvements in the chairs and tables should be completed. "I shall merely observe at present therefore, that my little study is upstairs, and looks out, from two French windows opening into a balcony, on the lake and mountains; and that there are roses enough to smother the whole establishment of the *Daily News* in. Likewise, there is a pavilion in the garden, which has but two rooms in it; in one of which I think you shall do your work when you come. As to bowers for reading and smoking, there are as many scattered about the grounds as there are in Chalk Farm tea-gardens. But the Rosemont bowers are really beautiful. Will you come to the bowers . . .?"

Very pleasant were the earliest impressions of Switzerland with which this first letter closed. "The country is delightful in the extreme—as leafy, green, and shady, as England; full of deep glens, and branchy places (rather a Leigh Huntish expression), and bright with all sorts of flowers in profusion. It abounds in singing birds besides—very pleasant after Italy; and the moonlight on the lake is noble. Prodigious mountains rise up from its opposite shore (it is eight or nine miles across, at this point), and the Simplon, the St. Gothard, Mont Blanc and all the Alpine wonders are piled there, in tremendous grandeur. The cultivation is uncommonly rich and profuse. There are all manner of walks, vineyard, green lanes, cornfields, and pastures full of hay. The general neatness is as remarkable as in England. There are no priests or monks in the streets, and the people appear to be industrious and thriving. French (and very intelligible and pleasant French) seems to be the universal language. I never saw so many booksellers' shops crammed within the same space, as in the steep up-and-down streets of Lausanne."

Of the little town he spoke in his next letter as having its natural dullness increased by that fact of its streets going up and down hill abruptly and steeply, like the streets in a dream; and the consequent difficulty of getting about it. "There are some suppressed churches in it, now used as packers' warehouses: with cranes and pulleys growing out of steeple-towers; little doors for lowering goods through, fitted into blocked-up oriel windows; and cart-horses stabled in crypts. These also help it to give a deserted and disused appearance. On the other hand, as it is a perfectly free place subject to no prohibitions or restrictions of any kind, there are all sorts of new French books and publications in it, and all sorts of fresh intelligence from the world beyond the Jura Mountains. It contains only one Roman Catholic church, which is mainly for the use of the Savoyards and Piedmontese who come trading over the Alps. As for the country, it cannot be praised too highly, or reported too beautiful. There are no great waterfalls, or walks through mountain-gorges, *close* at hand, as in some other parts of Switzerland; but there is a charming variety of enchanting scenery. There is the shore of the lake, where you may dip your feet, as you walk, in the deep blue water, if you choose. There are the hills to climb up, leading to the great heights above the town; or to stagger down, leading to the lake. There is every possible variety of deep green lanes, vineyard, cornfield, pasture-land, and wood. There are excellent country roads that might be in Kent or Devonshire; and, closing up every view and vista, is an eternally changing range of prodigious mountains—sometimes red, sometimes grey, sometimes purple, sometimes black, sometimes white with snow; sometimes close at hand; and sometimes very ghosts in the clouds and mist."

In the heart of these things he was now to live and work for at least six months; and, as the love of nature was as much a passion with him in his intervals of leisure, as the craving for crowds and streets when he was busy with the creatures of his fancy, no man was better qualified to enjoy what was thus open to him from his little farm.

The view from each side of it was different in character, and from one there was visible the liveliest aspect of Lausanne itself, close at hand, and seeming, as he said, to be always coming down the hill with its steeples and towers, not able to stop itself. "From a fine long broad balcony on which the windows of my little study on the first floor (where I am now writing) open, the lake is seen to wonderful advantage,—losing itself by degrees in the solemn gorge of mountains leading to the Simplon pass. Under the balcony is a stone colonnade, on which the six French windows of the drawing-room open; and quantities of plants are clustered about the pillars and seats, very prettily. One of these drawing-rooms is furnished (like a French hotel) with red velvet, and the other with green; in both, plenty of mirrors and nice white muslin curtains; and for the larger one in cold weather there is a carpet, the floors being bare now, but inlaid in squares with different coloured woods." His description did not close until, in every nook and corner inhabited by the several members of the family, I was made to feel myself at home; but only the final sentence need be added. "Walking out into the balcony as I write, I am suddenly reminded, by the sight of the Castle of Chillon glittering in the sunlight on the lake, that I omitted to mention that object in my catalogue of the Rosemont beauties. Please to put it, like George Robins, in a line by itself."

Regular evening walks of nine or ten miles were named in the same letter (22 June) as having been begun; and thoughts of his books were already stirring in him. "An odd shadowy undefined idea is at work within me, that I could connect a great battlefield somehow with my little Christmas story. Shapeless visions of the repose and peace pervading it in after-time; with the corn and grass growing over the slain, and people singing at the plough; are so perpetually floating before me, that I cannot but think there may turn out to be something good in them when I see them more plainly. . . . I want to get Four Numbers of the monthly book done here, and the Christmas book. If all goes well, and nothing changes, and I can accomplish this by the end of November, I shall run over to you in England for a few days with a light heart, and leave Roche to move the caravan to Paris in the meanwhile. It will be just the very point in the story when the life and crowd of that extraordinary place will come vividly to my assistance in writing." Such was his design; and, though difficulties not now seen started up which he had a hard fight to get through, he managed to accom-

plish it. His letter ended with a promise to tell me, when next
he wrote, of the small colony of English who seemed ready to
give him even more than the usual welcome. Two visits had thus
early been paid him by Mr. Haldimand, formerly a member of
the English parliament, an accomplished man, who, with his
sister Mrs. Marcet (the well-known authoress), had long made
Lausanne his home. He had a very fine seat just below Rosemont, and his character and station had made him quite the
little sovereign of the place. "He has founded and endowed all
sorts of hospitals and institutions here, and he gives a dinner
to-morrow to introduce our neighbours, whoever they are."

He found them to be happily the kind of people who rendered
entirely pleasant those frank and cordial hospitalities which
the charm of his personal intercourse made everyone so eager
to offer him. The dinner at Mr. Haldimand's was followed by
dinners from the guests he met there; from an English lady * 49
married to a Swiss, Mr. and Mrs. Cerjat, clever and agreeable
both, far beyond the common; from her sister wedded to an
Englishman, Mr. and Mrs. Goff; and from Mr. and Mrs. Watson
of Rockingham Castle in Northamptonshire, who had taken
the Elysée on Dickens giving it up, and with whom, as with
Mr. Haldimand, his relations continued to be very intimate
long after he left Lausanne. In his drive to Mr. Cerjat's dinner
a whimsical difficulty presented itself. He had set up, for use
of his wife and children, an odd little one-horse carriage; made
to hold three persons sideways, so that they should avoid the
wind always blowing up or down the valley; and he found it
attended with one of the drollest consequences conceivable.
"It can't be easily turned; and as you face to the side, all sorts
of evolutions are necessary to bring you 'broad-side to' before
the door of the house where you are going. The country houses
here are very like those upon the Thames between Richmond
and Kingston (this, particularly), with grounds all round. At
Mr. Cerjat's we were obliged to be carried, like the child's riddle,
round the house and round the house, without touching the
house; and we were presented in the most alarming manner
three of a row, first to all the people in the kitchen, then to the
governess who was dressing in her bedroom, then to the drawing-
room where the company were waiting for us, then to the
dining-room where they were spreading the table, and finally
to the hall where we were got out—scraping the windows of
each apartment as we glared slowly into it."

A dinner party of his own followed of course; and a sad

occurrence, of which he and his guests were unconscious, sig-
nalised the evening (15 July). "While we were sitting at dinner,
one of the prettiest girls in Lausanne was drowned in the lake—
in the most peaceful water, reflecting the steep mountains, and
crimson with the setting sun. She was bathing in one of the
nooks set apart for women, and seems somehow to have en-
tangled her feet in the skirts of her dress. She was an accomplished swimmer, as many of the girls are here, and drifted,
suddenly, out of only five-feet water. Three or four friends who
were with her, *ran away*, screaming. Our children's governess
was on the lake in a boat with M. Verdeil (my prison-doctor)
and his family. They ran inshore immediately; the body was
quickly got out; and M. Verdeil, with three or four other doctors,
laboured for some hours to restore animation; but she only
sighed once. After all that time, she was obliged to be borne,
stiff and stark, to her father's house. She was his only child,
and but 17 years old. He has been nearly dead since, and all
Lausanne has been full of the story. I was down by the lake,
near the place, last night; and a boatman *acted* to me the whole
scene: depositing himself finally on a heap of stones, to represent
the body."

With M. Verdeil, physician to the prison and vice-president
of the council of health, introduced by Mr. Haldimand, there
had already been much communication; and I could give
nothing more characteristic of Dickens than his reference to
this, and other similar matters in which his interest was strongly
* 50 moved during his first weeks at Lausanne.

'Some years ago, when they set about reforming the prison
at Lausanne, they turned their attention, in a correspondence
of republican feeling, to America; and taking the Philadelphian
system for granted, adopted it. Terrible fits, new phases of
mental affection, and horrible madness, among the prisoners,
were very soon the result; and attained to such an alarming
height, that M. Verdeil, in his public capacity, began to report
against the system, and went on reporting and working against
it until he formed a party who were determined not to have it,
and caused it to be abolished—except in cases where the imprisonment does not exceed ten months in the whole. It is
remarkable that in his notes of the different cases, there is
every effect I mentioned as having observed myself at Philadelphia; even down to those contained in the description of
the man who had been there thirteen years, and who *picked
his hands* so much as he talked. He has only recently, he says,

read the *American Notes*; but he is so much struck by the perfect coincidence that he intends to republish some extracts from his own notes, side by side with these passages of mine translated into French. I went with him over the prison the other day. It is wonderfully well arranged for a continental jail, and in perfect order. The sentences however, or some of them, are very terrible. I saw one man sent there for murder under circumstances of mitigation—for 30 years. Upon the silent social system all the time! They weave, and plait straw, and make shoes, small articles of turnery and carpentry, and little common wooden clocks. But the sentences are too long for that monotonous and hopeless life; and, though they are well-fed and cared for, they generally break down utterly after two or three years. One delusion seems to become common to three-fourths of them after a certain time of imprisonment. Under the impression that there is something destructive put into their food 'pour les guérir de crime' (says M. Verdeil), they refuse to eat!"

It was at the Blind Institution, however, of which Mr. Haldimand was the president and great benefactor, that Dickens's attention was most deeply arrested; and there were two cases in especial of which the detail may be read with as much interest now as when my friend's letters were written, and as to which his own suggestions open up still rather startling trains of thought. The first, which in its attraction for him he found equal even to Laura Bridgman's, was that of a young man of eighteen: "born deaf and dumb, and stricken blind by an accident when he was about five years old. The Director of the institution, M. Hertzel, is a young German of great ability, and most uncommonly prepossessing appearance. He propounded to the scientific bodies of Geneva, a year ago (when this young man was under education in the asylum), the possibility of teaching him to speak—in other words, to play with his tongue upon his teeth and palate as if on an instrument, and connect particular performances with particular words conveyed to him in the finger-language. They unanimously agreed that it was quite impossible. The German set to work, and the young man now speaks very plainly and distinctly: without the least modulation, of course, but with comparatively little hesitation; expressing the words aloud as they are struck, so to speak, upon his hands; and showing the most intense and wonderful delight in doing it. This is commonly acquired, as you know, by the deaf and dumb who learn by sight; but it has never been before achieved in the case of a deaf, dumb, and blind subject. He is an extremely lively, intelligent, good-natured fellow; an excellent carpenter; a first-rate turner; and runs about the building with a certainty and confidence which none of the merely blind pupils acquire. He has a great many ideas, and an instinctive dread of death. He knows of God, as of Thought enthroned somewhere; and one told, on nature's prompting (the devil's of course), a lie. He was sitting at dinner, and the Director asked him whether he had had anything to drink; to which he instantly replied 'No,' in order that he might get some more, though he had been served in his turn. It was explained to him that this was a wrong thing, and wouldn't do, and that he was to be locked up in a room for it: which was done. Soon after this, he had a dream of being bitten in the shoulder by some strange animal. As it left a great impression on his mind, he told M. the Director that he had told another lie in the night. In proof of it he related his dream, and added, 'it must be a lie you know, because there is no strange animal here, and I never was bitten.' Being informed that this sort of lie was a harmless one, and was called a dream, he asked whether dead people ever dreamed[1] while they were lying in the ground. He is one of the most curious and interesting studies possible."

The second case had come in on the very day that Dickens visited the place. "When I was there (8th of July) there had come in, that morning, a girl of ten years old, born deaf and dumb and blind, and so perfectly untaught that she has not learnt to have the least control even over the performance of the common natural functions. . . . And yet she *laughs sometimes* (good God! conceive what at!)—and is dreadfully sensitive from head to foot, and very much alarmed, for some hours before the coming on of a thunderstorm. Mr. Haldimand has been long trying to induce her parents to send her to the asylum. At last they have consented; and when I saw her, some of the little blind girls were trying to make friends with her, and to lead her gently about. She was dressed in just a loose robe from the necessity of changing her frequently, but had been in a bath, and had had her nails cut (which were previously very long and dirty), and was not at all ill-looking—quite the reverse; with a remarkably good and pretty little mouth, but a low and undeveloped head of course. It was pointed out to me, as very singular, that the moment she is left alone, or freed from any-

---

[1] ". . . Ay, there's the rub;
For in that sleep of death what dreams may come,
When we have shuffled off this mortal coil . . ."

body's touch (which is the same thing to her), she instantly crouches down with her hands up to her ears, in exactly the position of a child before its birth; and so remains. I thought this such a strange coincidence with the utter want of advancement in her moral being, that it made a great impression on me; and conning it over and over, I began to think that this is surely the invariable action of savages too, and that I have seen it over and over again described in books of voyages and travels. Not having any of these with me, I turned to *Robinson Crusoe*; and I find Defoe says, describing the savages who came on the island after Will Atkins began to change for the better and commanded under the grave Spaniard for the common defence, 'their posture was generally sitting upon the ground, with their knees up towards their mouth, and the head put between the two hands, leaning down upon the knees'—exactly the same attitude!" In his next week's letter he reported further: "I have not been to the Blind Asylum again yet, but they tell me that the deaf and dumb and blind child's *face* is improving obviously, and that she takes great delight in the first effort made by the Director to connect himself with an occupation of her time. He gives her, every day, two smooth round pebbles to roll over and over between her two hands. She appears to have an idea that it is to lead to something; distinctly recognises the hand that gives them to her, as a friendly and protecting one; and sits for hours quite busy."

To one part of his thoughtful suggestion I objected, and would have attributed to a mere desire for warmth, in her as in the savage, what he supposed to be part of an undeveloped or embryo state explaining also the absence of sentient and moral being. To this he replied (25 July): "I do not think that there is reason for supposing that the savage attitude originates in the desire of warmth, because all naked savages inhabit hot climates; and their instinctive attitude, if it had reference to heat or cold, would probably be the coolest possible; like their delight in water, and swimming. I do not think there is any race of savage men, however low in grade, inhabiting cold climates, who do not kill beasts and wear their skins. The girl decidedly improves in face, and, if one can yet use the word as applied to her, in manner too. No communication by the speech of touch has yet been established with her, but the time has not been long enough." In a later letter he tells me (24 August): "The deaf, dumb, and blind girl is decidedly improved, and very much improved, in this short time. No communication is yet established with her, but that is not to be expected. They have got her out of that strange, crouching position; dressed her neatly; and accustomed her to have a pleasure in society. She laughs frequently, and also claps her hands and jumps; having, God knows how, some inward satisfaction. I never saw a more tremendous thing in its way, in my life, than when they stood her, t'other day, in the centre of a group of blind children who sang a chorus to the piano; and brought her hand, and kept it, in contact with the instrument. A shudder pervaded her whole being, her breath quickened, her colour deepened,—and I can compare it to nothing but returning animation in a person nearly dead. It was really awful to see how the sensation of the music fluttered and stirred the locked-up soul within her." The same letter spoke again of the youth: "The male subject is well and jolly as possible. He is very fond of smoking. I have arranged to supply him with cigars during our stay here; so he and I are in amazing sympathy. I don't know whether he thinks I grow them, or make them, or produce them by winking, or what. But it gives him a notion that the world in general belongs to me. . . ." Before his kind friend left Lausanne the poor fellow had been taught to say, "Monsieur Dickens m'a donné les cigares," and at their leave-taking his gratitude was expressed by incessant repetition of these words for a full half-hour.

Certainly by no man was gratitude more persistently earned than by Dickens, from all to whom nature or the world had been churlish or unfair. Not to those only made desolate by poverty or the temptations incident to it, but to those whom natural defects or infirmities had placed at a disadvantage with their kind, he gave his first consideration; helping them personally where he could, sympathising and sorrowing with them always, but above all applying himself to the investigation of such alleviation or cure as philosophy or science might be able to apply to their condition. This was a desire so eager as properly to be called one of the passions of his life, visible in him to the last hour of it.

Only a couple of weeks, themselves not idle ones, had passed over him at Rosemont when he made a dash at the beginning of his work; from which indeed he had only been detained so long by the non-arrival of a box despatched from London before his own departure, containing not his proper writing materials only, but certain quaint little bronze figures that thus early stood upon his desk, and were as much needed for the easy flow of his writing as blue ink or quill pens. "I have not been idle (28th of June) since I have been here, though at first I was 'kept out' of the big box as you know. I had a good deal to write for Lord John about the Ragged Schools. I set to work and did that. A good deal for Miss Coutts, in reference to her charitable projects. I set to work and did *that*. Half of the children's New Testament to write, or pretty nearly. I set to work and * 51 did *that*. Next I cleared off the greater part of such correspond- † 12 ence as I had rashly pledged myself to; and then . . .

BEGAN DOMBEY!

I performed this feat yesterday—only wrote the first slip—but there it is, and it is a plunge straight over head and ears into the story. . . . Besides all this, I have really gone with great vigour at the French, where I find myself greatly assisted by the Italian; and am subject to two descriptions of mental fits in reference to the Christmas book: one, of the suddenest and wildest enthusiasm; one, of solitary and anxious consideration. . . . By the way, as I was unpacking the big box I took hold of a book, and said to 'Them,'—'Now, whatever passage my thumb rests on, I shall take as having reference to my work.' It was TRISTRAM SHANDY, and opened at these words, 'What a work it is likely to turn out! Let us begin it!'"

The same letter told me that he still inclined strongly to "the field of battle notion" for his Christmas volume, but was not as yet advanced in it; being curious first to see whether its capacity seemed to strike me at all. My only objection was to his adventure of opening two stories at once, of which he did not yet see the full danger; but for the moment the Christmas fancy was laid aside, and not resumed, except in passing allusions, until after the close of August, when the first two numbers of *Dombey* were done. The interval supplied fresh illustration of his life in his new home, not without much interest; and as I have shown what a pleasant social circle, "wonderfully friendly and hospitable" to the last, already had grouped * 52 itself round him in Lausanne, and how full of matter to be heard and learned he found such institutions as its prison and blind school, the picture will receive attractive touches if I borrow from his letters written during this outset of *Dombey* some further notices as well of the general progress of his work, as of what was specially interesting or amusing to him at the time, and of how the country and the people impressed him. In all of these character will be found strongly marked.

III

SWISS PEOPLE AND SCENERY

1846

WHAT at once had struck him as the wonderful feature in the mountain scenery was its ever-changing and yet unchanging aspect. It was never twice like the same thing to him. Shifting and altering, advancing and retreating, fifty times a day, it was unalterable only in its grandeur. The lake itself too had every kind of varying beauty for him. By moonlight it was indescribably solemn; and before the coming of a storm had a strange property in it of being disturbed, while yet the sky remained clear and the evening bright, which he found to be very mysterious and impressive. Such a storm had come among his earliest and most grateful experiences; a degree of heat worse even than in Italy [1] having disabled him at the outset for all exertion until the lightning, thunder, and rain arrived. The letter telling me this (5 July) described the fruit as so abundant in the little farm, that the trees of the orchard in front of his house were bending beneath it; spoke of a field of wheat sloping down to the side window of his dining-room as already cut and carried; and said that the roses, which the hurricane of rain had swept away, were come back lovelier and in greater numbers than ever.

Of the ordinary Swiss people he formed from the first a high opinion which everything during his stay among them confirmed. He thought it the greatest injustice to call them "the

[1] "When it is very hot, it is hotter than in Italy. The overhanging roofs of the houses, and the quantity of wood employed in their construction (where they use tile and brick in Italy), render them perfect forcing-houses. The walls and floors, hot to the hand all the night through, interfere with sleep; and thunder is almost always booming and rumbling among the mountains." Besides this, though there were no mosquitoes as in Genoa, there was at first a plague of flies, more distressing even than at Albaro. "They cover everything eatable, fall into everything drinkable, stagger into the wet ink of newly-written words and make tracks on the writing-paper, clog their legs in the lather on your chin while you are shaving in the morning, and drive you frantic at any time when there is daylight if you fall asleep."

Americans of the Continent." In his first letters he said of the peasantry all about Lausanne that they were as pleasant a people as need be. He never passed, on any of the roads, man, woman, or child, without a salutation; and anything churlish or disagreeable he never noticed in them. "They have not," he continued, "the sweetness and grace of the Italians, or the agreeable manners of the better specimens of French peasantry, but they are admirably educated (the schools of this canton are extraordinarily good, in every little village), and always prepared to give a civil and pleasant answer. There is no greater mistake. I was talking to my landlord [1] about it the other day, and he said he could not conceive how it had ever arisen, but that when he returned from his eighteen years' service in the English Navy he shunned the people, and had no interest in them until they gradually forced their real character upon his observation. We have a cook and a coachman here, taken at hazard from the people of the town; and I never saw more obliging servants, or people who did their work so truly *with a will*. And in point of cleanliness, order, and punctuality to the moment, they are unrivalled. . . ."

The first great gathering of the Swiss peasantry which he saw was in the third week after his arrival, when a country fête was held at a place called The Signal; a deep green wood, on the sides and summit of a very high hill overlooking the town and all the country round; and he gave me a pleasant account of it. "There were various booths for eating and drinking, and the selling of trinkets and sweetmeats; and in one place there was a great circle cleared, in which the common people waltzed and polka'd, without cessation, to the music of a band. There was a great roundabout for children (oh my stars what a family were proprietors of it! A sunburnt father and mother, a hump-backed boy, a great poodle-dog possessed of all sorts of accomplishments, and a young murderer of seventeen who turned the machinery); and there were some games of chance and skill established under trees. It was very pretty. In some of the drinking booths there were parties of

[1] His preceding letter had sketched his landlord for me. ". . . There was an annual child's fête at the Signal the other night: given by the town. It was beautiful to see perhaps a hundred couple of children dancing in an immense ring in a green wood. Our three eldest were among them, presided over by my landlord, who was 18 years in the English Navy, and is the Sous Préfet of the town—a very good fellow indeed; quite an Englishman. Our landlady, nearly twice his age, used to keep the Inn (a famous one) at Zurich; and having made £50,000 bestowed it on a young husband. She might have done worse."

German peasants, twenty together perhaps, singing national drinking-songs, and making a most exhilarating and musical chorus by rattling their cups and glasses on the table and clinking them against each other, to a regular tune. You know it as a stage dodge, but the real thing is splendid. Further down the hill, other peasants were rifle-shooting for prizes, at targets set on the other side of a deep ravine, from two to three hundred yards off. It was quite fearful to see the astonishing accuracy of their aim, and how, every time a rifle awakened the ten thousand echoes of the green glen, some men crouching behind a little wall immediately in front of the targets, sprung up with large numbers in their hands denoting where the ball had struck the bull's eyes — and then in a moment disappeared again. Standing in a ring near these shooters was another party of Germans singing hunting-songs, in parts, most melodiously. And down in the distance was Lausanne, with all sorts of haunted-looking old towers rising up before the smooth water of the lake, and an evening sky all red, and gold, and bright green. When it closed in quite dark, all the booths were lighted up; and the twinkling of the lamps among the forest of trees was beautiful. . . ." To this pretty picture, a letter of a little later date, describing a marriage on the farm, added further comical illustration of the rifle-firing propensities of the Swiss, and had otherwise also whimsical touches of character. "One of the farmer's people—a sister, I think—was married from here the other day. It is wonderful to see how naturally the smallest girls are interested in marriages. Katey and Mamey were as excited as if they were eighteen. The fondness of the Swiss for gunpowder on interesting occasions, is one of the drollest things. For three days before, the farmer himself, in the midst of his various agricultural duties, plunged out of a little door near my windows, about once in every hour, and fired off a rifle. I thought he was shooting rats who were spoiling the vines; but he was merely relieving his mind, it seemed, on the subject of the approaching nuptials. All night afterwards, he and a small circle of friends kept perpetually letting off guns under the casement of the bridal chamber. A Bride is always drest here in black silk; but this bride wore merino of that colour, observing to her mother when she bought it (the old lady is 82, and works on the farm), 'You know, mother, I am sure to want mourning for you, soon; and the same gown will do.'"

* 53

Meanwhile, day by day, he was steadily moving on with his

first number; feeling sometimes the want of streets in an "extraordinary nervousness it would be hardly possible to describe," that would come upon him after he had been writing all day; but all other times finding the repose of the place very favourable to industry. "I am writing slowly at first, of course" (5 July), "but I hope I shall have finished the first number in the course of a fortnight at furthest. I have done the first chapter, and begun another. I say nothing of the merits thus far, or of the idea beyond what is known to you; because I prefer that you should come as fresh as may be upon them. I shall certainly have a great surprise for people at the end of the fourth number; and I think there is a new and peculiar sort of interest, involving the necessity of a little bit of delicate treatment whereof I will expound my idea to you by and by. When I have done this number, I may take a run to Chamonix perhaps. My thoughts have necessarily been called away from the Christmas book. The first Dombey done, I think I should fly off to that, whenever the idea presented itself vividly before me. I still cherish the Battle fancy, though it is nothing but a fancy as yet." A week later he told me that he hoped to finish the first number by that day week or thereabouts, when he should then run and look for his Christmas book in the glaciers at Chamonix. His progress to this point had been pleasing him. "I think Dombey very strong—with great capacity in its leading idea; plenty of character that is likely to tell; and some rollicking facetiousness, to say nothing of pathos. I hope you will soon judge of it for yourself, however; and I know you will say what you think. I have been very constantly at work." Six days later I heard that he had still eight slips to write, and for a week had put off Chamonix.

But though the fourth chapter yet was incomplete, he could repress no longer the desire to write to me of what he was doing (18 July). "I think the general idea of Dombey is interesting and new, and has great material in it. But I don't like to discuss it with you till you have read number one, for fear I should spoil its effect. When done—about Wednesday or Thursday, please God—I will send it in two days' posts, seven letters each day. If you have it set at once (I am afraid you couldn't read it, otherwise than in print) I know you will impress on B. & E. the necessity of the closest secrecy. The very name getting out, would be ruinous. The points for illustration, and the enormous care required, make me excessively anxious. The man for Dombey, if Browne could see him, the class man to a T, is

Sir A—— E——, of D——'s. Great pains will be necessary with Miss Tox. The Toodle Family should not be too much caricatured, because of Polly. I should like Browne to think of Susan Nipper, who will not be wanted in the first number. After the second number, they will all be nine or ten years older; but this will not involve much change in the characters, except in the children and Miss Nipper. What a brilliant thing to be telling you all these names so familiarly, when you know nothing about 'em! I quite enjoy it. By the by, I hope you may like the introduction of Solomon Gills. I think he lives in a good sort of house. . . . One word more. What do you think, as a name for the Christmas book, of THE BATTLE OF LIFE? It is not a name I have conned at all, but has just occurred to me in connection with that foggy idea. If I can see my way, I think I will take it next, and clear it off. If you knew how it hangs about me, I am sure you would say so too. It would be an immense relief to have it done, and nothing standing in the way of *Dombey*."

Within the time left for it the opening number was done, but two little incidents preceded still the trip to Chamonix. The first was a visit from Hallam to Mr. Haldimand. "Heavens! how Hallam did talk yesterday! I don't think I ever saw him so tremendous. Very good-natured and pleasant, in his way, but Good Heavens! how he did talk. That famous day you and I remember was nothing to it. His son was with him, and his daughter (who has an impediment in her speech, as if nature were determined to balance that faculty in the family), and his niece, a pretty woman, the wife of a clergyman and a friend of Thackeray's. It strikes me that she must be 'the little woman' he proposed to take us to drink tea with, once, in Golden Square. Don't you remember? His great favourite? She is quite a charming person anyhow." I hope to be pardoned for preserving an opinion which more familiar later acquaintance confirmed, and which can hardly now give anything but pleasure to the lady of whom it is expressed. To the second incident he alludes more briefly. "As Haldimand and Mrs. Marcet and the Cerjats had devised a small mountain expedition for us to-morrow, I didn't like to allow Chamonix to stand in the way. So we go with them first, and start on our own account on Tuesday. We are extremely pleasant with these people." The close of the same letter (25 July), mentioning two pieces of local news, gives intimation of the dangers incident to all Swiss travelling, and of such special precautions as were necessary for the holiday among the mountains he was now about to take. "My first news is that a crocodile is said to have escaped from the Zoological Gardens at Geneva, and to be now 'zigzag-zigging' about the lake. But I can't make out whether this is a great fact, or whether it is a pious fraud to prevent too much bathing and liability to accidents. The other piece of news is more serious. An English family whose name I don't know, consisting of a father, mother, and daughter, arrived at the Hôtel Gibbon here last Monday, and started off on some mountain expedition in one of the carriages of the country. It was a mere track, the road, and ought to have been travelled only by mules, but the Englishman persisted (as Englishmen do) in going on in the carriage; and in answer to all the representations of the driver that no carriage had ever gone up there, said he needn't be afraid he wasn't going to be paid for it, and so forth. Accordingly, the coachman got down and walked by the horses' heads. It was fiery hot; and after much tugging and rearing, the horses began to back, and went down bodily, carriage and all, into a deep ravine. The mother was killed on the spot; and the father and daughter are lying at some house hard by, not expected to recover."

His next letter (written on 2 August) described his own first real experience of mountain travel. "I begin my letter to-night, but only begin, for we returned from Chamonix in time for dinner just now, and are pretty considerably done up. We went by a mountain pass not often crossed by ladies, called the Col de Balme, where your imagination may picture Kate and Georgy on mules *for ten hours at a stretch* riding up and down the most frightful precipices. We returned by the pass of the Tête Noire, which Talfourd knows, and which is of a different character, but astonishingly fine too. Mont Blanc, and the Valley of Chamonix, and the Mer de Glace, and all the wonders of that most wonderful place, are above and beyond one's wildest expectations. I cannot imagine anything in nature more stupendous or sublime. If I were to write about it now, I should quite rave—such prodigious impressions are rampant within me. . . . You may suppose that the mule-travelling is pretty primitive. Each person takes a carpet-bag strapped on the mule behind himself or herself: and that is all the baggage that can be carried. A guide, a thorough-bred mountaineer, walks all the way, leading the lady's mule; I say lady's *par excellence*, in compliment to Kate; and all the rest struggle on as they please. The cavalcade stops at a lone hut for an hour and a half in the middle of the day, and lunches brilliantly on whatever it can get. Going by that Col de Balme pass, you climb up and up and up for five hours and more, and look—from a mere unguarded ledge of path on the side of the precipice—into such awful valleys, that at last you are firm in the belief that you have got above everything in the world, and that there can be nothing earthly overhead. Just as you arrive at this conclusion, a different (and O! Heaven! what a free and wonderful) air comes blowing on your face; you cross a ridge of snow; and lying before you (wholly unseen till then), towering up into the distant sky, is the vast range of Mont Blanc, with attendant mountains diminished by its majestic side into mere dwarfs tapering up into innumerable rude Gothic pinnacles; deserts of ice and snow; forests of firs on mountain sides, of no account at all in the enormous scene; villages down in the hollow, that you can shut out with a finger; waterfalls, avalanches, pyramids and towers of ice, torrents, bridges; mountain upon mountain until the very sky is blocked away, and you must look up, overhead, to see it. Good God, what a country Switzerland is, and what a concentration of it is to be beheld from that one spot! And (think of this in Whitefriars and in Lincoln's Inn!) at noon on the second day from here, the first day being but half a one by the by and full of uncommon beauty, you lie down on that ridge and see it all! . . . I think I must go back again (whether you come or not!) and see it again before the bad weather arrives. We have had sunlight, moonlight, a perfectly transparent atmosphere with not a cloud, and the grand plateau on the very summit of Mont Blanc so clear by day and night that it was difficult to believe in intervening chasms and precipices, and almost impossible to resist the idea that one might sally forth and climb up easily. I went into all sorts of places; armed with a great pole with a spike at the end of it, like a leaping-pole, and with pointed irons buckled on to my shoes; and am all but knocked up. I was very anxious to make the expedition to what is called 'The Garden': a green spot covered with wild flowers, lying across the Mer de Glace, and among the most awful mountains: but I could find no Englishman at the hotels who was similarly disposed, and the Brave *wouldn't* go. No, sir! He gave in point blank (having been horribly blown in a climbing excursion the day before), and couldn't stand it. He is too heavy for such work, unquestionably. In all other respects, I think he has exceeded himself on this journey: and if you could have seen him riding a very small mule up a road exactly like the broken stairs of Rochester Castle, with a brandy

* 54

bottle slung over his shoulder, a small pie in his hat, a roast fowl looking out of his pocket, and a mountain staff of six feet long carried crosswise on the saddle before him, you'd have said so. He was (next to me) the admiration of Chamonix, but he utterly quenched me on the road.''

On the road as they returned there had been a small adventure, the day before this letter was written. Dickens was jingling slowly up the Tête Noire pass (his mule having thirty-seven bells on its head), riding at the moment quite alone, when—" an Englishman came bolting out of a little chaletain, a most inaccessible and extraordinary place, and said with great glee, 'There has been an accident here, sir!' I had been thinking of anything else you please! and, having no reason to suppose him an Englishman except his language, which went for nothing in the confusion, stammered out a reply in French and stared at him, in a very damp shirt and trousers, as he stared at me in a similar costume. On his repeating the announcement, I began to have a glimmering of common sense; and so arrived at a knowledge of the fact that a German lady had been thrown from her mule and had broken her leg, at a short distance off, and had found her way in great pain to that cottage, where the Englishman, a Prussian, and a Frenchman, had presently come up; and the Frenchman, by extraordinary good fortune, was a surgeon! They were all from Chamonix, and the three latter were walking in company. It was quite charming to see how attentive they were. The lady was from Lausanne; where she had come from Frankfort to make excursions with her two boys, who are at the college here, during the vacation. She had no other attendants, and the boys were crying and very frightened. The Englishman was in the full glee of having just cut up one white dress, two chemises, and three pocket-handkerchiefs, for bandages; the Frenchman had set the leg skilfully; the Prussian had scoured a neighbouring wood for some men to carry her forward; and they were all at it, behind the hut, making a sort of hand-barrow on which to bear her. When it was constructed, she was strapped upon it; had her poor head covered over with a handkerchief, and was carried away; and we all went on in company: Kate and Georgy consoling and tending the sufferer, who was very cheerful, but had lost her husband only a year." With the same delightful observation, and missing no touch of kindly character that might give each actor his place in the little scene, the sequel is described; but it does not need to add more. It was hoped that by means of relays of men at

Martigny the poor lady might have been carried on some twenty miles, in the cooler evening, to the head of the lake, and so have been got into the steamer; but she was too exhausted to be borne beyond the inn, and there she had to remain until joined by relatives from Frankfort.

A few days' rest after his return were interposed, before he began his second number; and until the latter had been completed, and the Christmas story taken in hand, I do not admit the reader to his full confidence about his writing. But there were other subjects that amused and engaged him up to that date, as well when he was idle as when again he was at work, to which expression so full of character is given in his letters that they properly find mention here.

Early in August he visited Chillon, when the aspect of the lake, five minutes after sunset, the sky at the time being covered with sullen black clouds reflected in the deep water, much impressed him. The Castle itself he thought the best deserving and least exaggerated in its repute, of all the places he had seen. 'The unsupportable solitude and dreariness of the white walls and towers, the sluggish moat and drawbridge, and the lonely ramparts, I never saw the like of. But there is a courtyard inside; surrounded by prisons, *oubliettes*, and old chambers of torture; so terrifically sad, that death itself is not more sorrowful. And Oh! a wicked old Grand Duke's bedchamber upstairs in the tower, with a secret staircase down into the chapel where the bats were wheeling about; and Bonnivard's dungeon; and a horrible trap whence prisoners were cast out into the lake; and a stake all burnt and crackled up, that still stands in the torture-ante-chamber to the saloon of justice (!)—what tremendous places! Good God, the greatest mystery in all the earth, to me, is how or why the world was tolerated by its Creator through the good old times, and wasn't dashed to fragments."

On 9 August he wrote to me that there was to be a prodigious fête that day in Lausanne, in honour of the first anniversary
* 55 of the proclamation of the New Constitution: "beginning at sunrise with the firing of great guns, and twice two thousand rounds of rifles by two thousand men; proceeding at eleven o'clock with a great service, and some speechifying, in the church; and ending to-night with a great ball in the public promenade, and a general illumination of the town." The authorities had invited him to a place of honour in the ceremony; and though he did not go ("having been up till three o'clock in the morning, and being fast asleep at the appointed time"), the

reply that sent his thanks expressed also his sympathy. He was
the readier with this from having discovered, in the "old" or
"gentlemanly" party of the place ("including of course the
sprinkling of English who are always Tory, hang 'em!"), so
wonderfully sore a feeling about the revolution thus celebrated,
that to avoid its fête the majority had gone off by steamer the
day before, and those who remained were prophesying assaults
on the unilluminated houses, and other excesses. Dickens had
no faith in such predictions. "The people are as perfectly good-
tempered and quiet always, as people can be. I don't know what
the last government may have been, but they seem to me to do
very well with this, and to be rationally and cheaply provided
for. If you believe what the discontented assert, you wouldn't
believe in one solitary man or woman with a grain of goodness or
civility. I find nothing *but* civility; and I walk about in all sorts
of out-of-the-way places, where they live rough lives enough,
in solitary cottages." The issue was told in two postscripts
to his letter, and showed him to be so far right. "P.S. 6 o'clock
afternoon. The fête going on, in great force. Not one of 'the
old party' to be seen. I went down with one to the ground
before dinner, and nothing would induce him to go within the
barrier with me. Yet what they call a revolution was nothing
but a change of government. Thirty-six thousand people, in
this small canton, petitioned against the Jesuits—God knows
with good reason. The government chose to call them 'a mob.'
So, to prove that they were not, they turned the government
out. I honour them for it. They are a genuine people, these
Swiss. There is better metal in them than in all the stars and
stripes of all the fustian banners of the so-called, and falsely-
called, U-nited States. They are a thorn in the sides of European
despots, and a good wholesome people to live near Jesuit-ridden
Kings on the brighter side of the mountains." "P.P.S. August
10th. . . . The fête went off as quietly as I supposed it would;
and they danced all night."

These views had forcible illustration in a subsequent letter,
where he describes a similar revolution that occurred at Geneva
before he left the country; and nothing could better show his
practical good sense in a matter of this kind. The description
will be given shortly; and meanwhile I subjoin a comment made
by him, not less worthy of attention, upon my reply to his
account of the anti-Jesuit celebration at Lausanne. "I don't
know whether I have mentioned before, that in the valley of
the Simplon hard by here, where (at the bridge of St. Maurice,

over the Rhone) this Protestant canton ends and a Catholic canton begins, you might separate two perfectly distinct and different conditions of humanity by drawing a line with your stick in the dust on the ground. On the Protestant side, neatness; cheerfulness; industry; education; continual aspiration, at least, after better things. On the Catholic side, dirt, disease, ignorance, squalor, and misery. I have so constantly observed the like of this, since I first came abroad, that I have a sad misgiving that the religion of Ireland lies as deep at the root of all its sorrows, even as English misgovernment and Tory villainy." Almost the counterpart of this remark is to be found in one of the later writings of Macaulay.

IV

SKETCHES CHIEFLY PERSONAL

1846

SOME sketches from the life in his pleasantest vein now claim to be taken from the same series of letters; and I will prefix one or two less important notices, for the most part personal also, that have characteristic mention of his opinions in them.

Home-politics he criticised, in what he wrote on 24 August, much in the spirit of his last excellent remark on the Protestant and Catholic cantons; having no sympathy with the course taken by the Whigs in regard to Ireland after they had defeated Peel on his coercion bill and resumed the government. "I am perfectly appalled by the hesitation and cowardice of the Whi7s. To bring in that arms bill, bear the brunt of the attack upon it, take out the obnoxious clauses, still retain the bill, and finally withdraw it, seems to me the meanest and most halting way of going to work that ever was taken. I cannot believe in them. Lord John must be helpless among them. They seem somehow or other never to know what cards they hold in their hands, and to play them out blindfold. The contrast with Peel (as he was last) is, I agree with you, certainly not favourable. I don't believe now they ever would have carried the repeal of the corn law, if they could." Referring in the same letter [1] to the reluctance of public men of all parties to give the needful help to schemes of emigration, he ascribed it to a secret belief in "the gentle politico-economical principle that a surplus

[1] Where he makes remark also on a class of offences which are still most inadequately punished: "I hope you will follow up your idea about the defective state of the law in reference to women, by some remarks on the inadequate punishment of that ruffian flippantly called by the liners the Wholesale Matrimonial Speculator. My opinion is, that in any well-ordered state of society, and advanced spirit of social jurisprudence, he would have been flogged more than once (privately), and certainly sentenced to transportation for no less a term than the rest of his life. Surely the man who threw the woman out of window was no worse, if so bad."

population must and ought to starve"; in which, for himself, he never could see anything but disaster for all who trusted to it. "I am convinced that its philosophers would sink any government, any cause, any doctrine, even the most righteous. There is a sense and humanity in the mass, in the long run, that will not bear them; and they will wreck their friends always, as they wrecked them in the working of the Poor Law Bill. Not all the figures that Babbage's calculating machine could turn up in twenty generations, would stand in the long run against the general heart."

Of other topics in his letters, one or two have the additional attractiveness derivable from touches of personal interest when these may with propriety be printed. "I am very sorry to hear of Haydon's death. If any subscription be proposed, put me down for five pounds." An unfortunate son of Leigh Hunt died also just at this time, and I preserve the allusion to him for the opportunity of explaining it. "I quite shuddered at John Hunt's having applied to that generous duke. It went against the grain with me, sorely, after the story of the two hundred pounds. I don't know what I should have done, if I had been Hunt." The duke was the late Duke of Devonshire; and the story was this. During the delay of the promised production of Leigh Hunt's first play, he asked the duke for £200 as a loan for two years; and the duke replied by taking the money himself to Hunt's house in Edwardes Square. On the last day of the second year within which repayment was promised, Hunt sent back the £200; and was startled, the morning after, by another visit from the duke, who pressed upon him its reacceptance as a gift. He added that there would be no obligation, for he was himself Hunt's debtor. He was ill when asked for the loan, and it had done him good to comply with the request. Never but once before had borrowed money ever come back to him, and he should always retain the sense of pleasure which its return had occasioned. "He remained grateful." It is a charming story, and hard to say who shows in it to the greatest advantage, Hunt or the duke.

The letter goes on to speak of Hood. "I have been reading poor Hood's *Tylney Hall*: the most extraordinary jumble of impossible extravagance, and especial cleverness, I ever saw. The man drawn to the life from the pirate bookseller, is wonderfully good; and his recommendation to a reduced gentleman from the university, to rise from nothing as he, the pirate, did, and go round to the churches and see whether there's an opening, and begin by being a beadle, is one of the finest things I ever read, in its way." The same letter has a gentle little trait of the great duke, touching in its simplicity, and worth preserving. "I had a letter from Tagart the day before yesterday, with a curious little anecdote of the Duke of Wellington in it. They have had a small cottage at Walmer; and one day—the other day only—the old man met their little daughter Lucy, a child about Mamey's age, near the garden; and having kissed her, and asked her what was her name, and who and what her parents were, tied a small silver medal round her neck with a bit of pink ribbon, and asked the child to keep it in remembrance of him. There is something good, and aged, and odd in it. Is there not?"

Another of his personal references was to Lord Grey, to whose style of speaking and general character of mind he had always a strongly-expressed dislike, drawn not impartially or quite justly from the days of reaction that followed the Reform debates, when the Whig leader's least attractive traits were presented to the young reporter. "He is a very intelligent agreeable fellow, the said Watson, by the by" (he is speaking of the member of the Lausanne circle with whom he established friendliest after-intercourse); 'he sat for Northamptonshire in the Reform Bill time, and is high sheriff of his county and all the rest of it; but has not the least nonsense about him, and is a thorough good liberal. He has a charming wife, who draws well, and is making a sketch of Rosemont for us that shall be yours in Paris. . . ."

". . . He was giving me some good recollections of Lord Grey the other evening when we were playing at battledore (old Lord Grey I mean), and of the constitutional impossibility he and Lord Lansdowne and the rest laboured under, of ever personally attaching a single young man, in all the excitement of that exciting time, to the leaders of the party. It was quite a delight to me, as I listened, to recall my own dislike of his style of speaking. . . . The shape of his head (I see it now) was misery to me, and weighed down my youth. . . ."

It was now the opening of the second week in August; and before he finally addressed himself to the second number of *Dombey*, he had again turned a lingering look in the direction of his Christmas tale. "It would be such a great relief to me to get that small story out of the way." Wisely, however, again he refrained, and went on with *Dombey*; at which he had been working for a little time when he described to me (24 August) a

visit from two English travellers, of one of whom with the
slightest possible touch he gives a speaking likeness.

* 56

'Not having your letter as usual, I sat down to write to you
on speculation yesterday, but lapsed in my uncertainty into
Dombey, and worked at it all day. It was, as it has been since
last Tuesday morning, incessantly raining regular mountain
rain. After dinner, at a little after seven o'clock, I was walking
up and down under the little colonnade in the garden, racking
my brain about *Dombeys* and *Battles of Lives*, when two travel-
stained-looking men approached, of whom one, in a very limp
and melancholy straw hat, ducked perpetually to me as he
came up the walk. I couldn't make them out at all; and it wasn't
till I got close up to them that I recognized A—— and (in the
straw hat) N——. They had come from Geneva by the steamer,
and taken a scrambling dinner on board. I gave them some
fine Rhine wine, and cigars innumerable. A—— enjoyed himself and was quite at home. N—— (an odd companion for a
man of genius) was snobbish, but pleased and good-natured.
A—— had a five-pound note in his pocket which he had worn
down, by careless carrying about, to some two-thirds of its
original size, and which was so ragged in its remains that when
he took it out bits of it flew about the table. 'Oh Lor you know
—now really—like Goldsmith you know—or any of those great
men!' said N——, with the very 'snatches in his voice and burst
of speaking' that reminded Leigh Hunt of Cloten. . . . The
clouds were lying, as they do in such weather here, on the
earth, and our friends saw no more of Lake Leman than of
Battersea. Nor had they, it might appear, seen more of the Mer
de Glace, on their way here; their talk about it bearing much
resemblance to that of the man who had been to Niagara and
said it was nothing but water."

His next letter described a day's party of the Cerjats, Watsons,
and Haldimands, among the neighbouring hills, which, contrary to his custom while at work, he had been unable to resist
the temptation of joining. They went to a mountain-lake
twelve miles off, had dinner at the public-house on the lake,
and returned home by Vevey at which they rested for tea;
and where pleasant talk with Mr. Cerjat led to anecdotes of an
excellent friend of ours, formerly resident at Lausanne, with
which the letter closed. Our friend was a distinguished writer,
and a man of many sterling fine qualities, but with a habit of
occasional free indulgence in coarseness of speech, which,
though his earlier life had made it as easy to acquire as difficult

to drop, did always less than justice to a very manly, honest, and really gentle nature. He had as much genuinely admirable stuff in him as any favourite hero of Smollett or Fielding, and I never knew anyone who reminded me of those characters so much. "It would seem, Mr. Cerjat tells me, that he was, when here, infinitely worse in his general style of conversation, than now—sermuchser, as Toodle says, that Cerjat describes himself as having always been in unspeakable agony when he was at his table, lest he should forget himself (or remember himself, as I suggested) and break out before the ladies. There happened to be living here at that time a stately English baronet and his wife, who had two sons concerning whom they cherished the idea of accomplishing their education into manhood coexistently with such perfect purity and innocence, that they were hardly to know their own sex. Accordingly, they were sent to no school or college, but had masters of all sorts at home, and thus reached eighteen years or so, in what Falstaff calls a kind of male green-sickness. At this crisis of their innocent existence, our ogre friend encountered these lambs at dinner, with their father, at Cerjat's house; and, as if possessed by a devil, launched out into such frightful and appalling impropriety that years of education in Newgate would have been as nothing compared with their experience of that one afternoon. After turning paler and paler, and more and more stony, the baronet, with a half-suppressed cry, rose and fled. But the sons—intent on the ogre—remained instead of following. . . . Isn't it a good story? I can SEE our friend and his pupils now. . . . Poor fellow! He seems to have a hard time of it in his home . . . and to have been himself, in all good-natured easy-going ways, just what we know him now."

There were at this date some fresh arrivals of travelling English at Lausanne, outside their own little circle, and among them another baronet and his family made amusing appearance. "We have another English family here, one Sir Joseph and his lady, and ten children. Sir Joseph, a large baronet something in the Graham style, with a little, loquacious, flat-faced, damaged-featured, *old young* wife. They are fond of society, and couldn't well have less. They delight in a view, and live in a close street at Ouchy down among the drunken boatmen and the drays and omnibuses, where nothing whatever is to be seen but the locked wheels of carts scraping down the uneven, steep, stone pavement. The baronet plays double-dummy all day long, with an unhappy Swiss whom he has entrapped for that purpose; the baronet's lady pays visits; and the baronet's daughters play a Lausanne piano, which must be heard to be appreciated. . . ."

Another sketch in the same letter touches little more than the eccentricities (but all in good taste and good humour) of the subject of it, who is still gratefully remembered by English residents in Italy for his scholarly munificence, and for very valuable service conferred by it on Italian literature. "Another curious man is backwards and forwards here—a Lord Vernon, who is well-informed, a great Italian scholar deep in Dante, and a very good-humoured gentleman, but who has fallen into the strange infatuation of attending every rifle-match that takes place in Switzerland, accompanied by two men who load rifles for him, one after another, which he has been frequently known to fire off, two a minute, for fourteen hours at a stretch, without once changing his position or leaving the ground. He wins all kinds of prizes; gold watches, flags, teaspoons, teaboards, and so forth; and is constantly travelling about with them, from place to place, in an extraordinary carriage, where you touch a spring and a chair flies out, touch another spring and a bed appears, touch another spring and a closet of pickles opens, touch another spring and disclose a pantry! while Lady Vernon (said to be handsome and accomplished) is continually cutting across this or that Alpine pass in the night, to meet him on the road for a minute or two, on one of his excursions; these being the only times at which she can catch him. The last time he saw her was five or six months ago, when they met and supped together on the St. Gothard! It is a monomania with him, of course. He is a man of some note; seconded one of Lord Melbourne's addresses; and had forty thousand a year, now reduced to ten, but nursing and improving every day. He was with us last Monday, and comes back from some out-of-the-way place to join another small picnic next Friday. As I have said, he is the very soul of good nature and cheerfulness, but one can't help being melancholy to see a man wasting his life in such a singular delusion. Isn't it odd? He knows my books very well, and seems interested in everything concerning them; being indeed accomplished in books generally, and attached to many elegant tastes."

But the most agreeable addition to their own special circle was referred to in his first September letter, just when he was coming to the close of his second number of *Dombey*. "There are two nice girls here, the Ladies Taylor, daughters of Lord

Headfort. Their mother was daughter (I think) of Sir John Stevenson, and Moore dedicated one part of the *Irish Melodies* to her. They inherit the musical taste, and sing very well. A proposal is on foot for our all bundling off on Tuesday (sixteen strong) to the top of the Great St. Bernard. But the weather seems to have broken, and the autumn rains to have set in; which I devoutly hope will break up the party. It would be a most serious hindrance to me, just now; but I have rashly promised. Do you know young Romilly? He is coming over from Geneva when 'the reading' comes off, and is a fine fellow, I am told. There is not a bad little theatre here; and by way of an artificial crowd, I should certainly have got it open with an amateur company, if we were not so few that the only thing we want is the audience. . . ." The "reading" named by him was that of his first number, which was to "come off" as soon as I could get the proofs out to him; but which the changes needful to be made, and to be mentioned hereafter, still delayed. The St. Bernard holiday, which within sight of his Christmas-book labour he would fain have thrown over, came off as proposed, very fortunately for the reader, who might otherwise have lost one of his pleasantest descriptions. But before giving it, one more little sketch of character may be interposed; as delicately done as anything in his writings. Steele's observation is in the outline, and Charles Lamb's humour in its touch of colouring.

". . . There are two old ladies (English) living here who may serve me for a few lines of gossip—as I have intended they should, over and over again, but I have always forgotten it. There were originally four old ladies, sisters, but two of them have faded away in the course of eighteen years, and withered by the side of John Kemble in the cemetery. They are very little and very skinny; and each of them wears a row of false curls, like little rolling-pins, so low upon her brow, that there is no forehead; nothing above the eyebrows but a deep horizontal wrinkle, and then the curls. They live upon some small annuity. For thirteen years they have wanted very much to move to Italy, as the eldest old lady says the climate of this part of Switzerland doesn't agree with her, and preys upon her spirits; but they have never been able to go, because of the difficulty of moving 'the books.' This tremendous library belonged once upon a time to the father of these old ladies, and comprises about fifty volumes. I have never been able to see what they are, because one of the old ladies always sits before them; but they look, outside, like very old backgammon boards.

The two deceased sisters died in the firm persuasion that this precious property could never be got over the Simplon without some gigantic effort to which the united family was unequal. The two remaining sisters live, and will die also, in the same belief. I met the eldest (evidently drooping) yesterday, and recommended her to try Genoa. She looked shrewdly at the snow that closes up the mountain prospect just now, and said when the spring was quite set in, and the avalanches were down, and the passes well open, she would certainly try that place, if they could devise any plan, in the course of the winter, for moving 'the books.' The whole library will be sold by auction here, when they are both dead, for about a napoleon; and some young woman will carry it home in two journeys with a basket."

The last letter sent me before he fell upon his self-appointed task for Christmas, contained a delightful account of the trip to the Great St. Bernard. It was dated on 6 September.

"The weather obstinately clearing, we started off last Tuesday for the Great St. Bernard, returning here on Friday afternoon. The party consisted of eleven people and two servants—Haldimand, Mr. and Mrs. Cerjat and one daughter, Mr. and Mrs. Watson, two Ladies Taylor, Kate, Georgy, and I. We were wonderfully unanimous and cheerful; went away from here by the steamer; found at its destination a whole omnibus provided by the Brave (who went on in advance everywhere); rode therein to Bex; found two large carriages ready to take us to Martigny; slept there; and proceeded up the mountain on mules next day. Although the St. Bernard convent is, as I dare say you know, the highest inhabited spot but one in the world, the ascent is extremely gradual and uncommonly easy: really presenting no difficulties at all until within the last league, when the ascent, lying through a place called the valley of desolation, is very awful and tremendous, and the road is rendered toilsome by scattered rocks and melting snow. The convent is a most extraordinary place, full of great vaulted passages, divided from each other with iron gratings; and presenting a series of the most astonishing little dormitories, where the windows are so small (on account of the cold and snow), that it is as much as one can do to get one's head out of them. Here we slept: supping, thirty strong, in a rambling room with a great wood-fire in it set apart for that purpose; with a grim monk, in a high black sugar-loaf hat with a great knob at the top of it, carving the dishes. At five o'clock in the morning the chapel bell rang in the dismallest way for matins: and I,

lying in bed close to the chapel, and being awakened by the
solemn organ and the chaunting, thought for a moment I had
died in the night and passed into the unknown world.

"I wish to God you could see that place. A great hollow on the
top of a range of dreadful mountains, fenced in by riven rocks
of every shape and colour: and in the midst, a black lake, with
phantom clouds perpetually stalking over it. Peaks, and points,
and plains of eternal ice and snow, bounding the view, and
shutting out the world on every side: the lake reflecting
nothing: and no human figure in the scene. The air so fine,
that it is difficult to breathe without feeling out of breath; and
the cold so exquisitely thin and sharp that it is not to be described. Nothing of life or living interest in the picture, but the
grey dull walls of the convent. No vegetation of any sort or
kind. Nothing growing, nothing stirring. Everything iron-bound,
and frozen up. Beside the convent, in a little outhouse with a
grated iron door which you may unbolt for yourself, are the
bodies of people found in the snow who have never been claimed
and are withering away—not laid down, or stretched out, but
standing up, in corners and against walls; some erect and horribly human, with distinct expressions on the faces; some sunk
down on their knees; some dropping over on one side; some
tumbled down altogether, and presenting a heap of skulls and
fibrous dust. There is no other decay in that atmosphere; and
there they remain during the short days and the long nights,
the only human company out of doors, withering away by grains,
and holding ghastly possession of the mountain where they died.

'It is the most distinct and individual place I have seen, even
in this transcendent country. But, for the Saint Bernard holy
fathers and convent in themselves, I am sorry to say that they
are a piece of as sheer humbug as we ever learnt to believe in,
in our young days. Trashy French sentiment and the dogs (of
which, by the by, there are only three remaining) have done it
all. They are a lazy set of fellows; not over fond of going out
themselves; employing servants to clear the road (which has
not been important or much used as a pass these hundred
years); rich; and driving a good trade in Innkeeping: the convent
being a common tavern in everything but the sign. No charge
is made for their hospitality, to be sure; but you are shown to
a box in the chapel, where everybody puts in more than could,
with any show of face, be charged for the entertainment; and
from this the establishment derives a right good income. As
to the self-sacrifice of living up there, they are obliged to go

there young, it is true, to be inured to the climate: but it is an infinitely more exciting and various life than any other convent can offer; with constant change and company through the whole summer; with a hospital for invalids down in the valley, which affords another change; and with an annual begging-journey to Geneva and this place and all the places round for one brother or other, which affords further change. The brother who carved at our supper could speak some English, and had just had *Pickwick* given him!—what a humbug he will think me when he tries to understand it! If I had had any other book of mine with me, I would have given it him, that I might have had some chance of being intelligible. . . ."

V

LITERARY LABOUR AT LAUSANNE

1846

SOMETHING of the other side of the medal has now to be presented. His letters enable us to see him amid his troubles and difficulties of writing, as faithfully as in his leisure and enjoyments; and when, to the picture thus given of Dickens's home life in Switzerland, some account has been added of the vicissitudes of literary labour undergone in the interval, as complete a representation of the man will be afforded as could be taken from any period of his career. Of the larger life whereof it is part, the Lausanne life is indeed a perfect microcosm, wanting only the London streets. This was his chief present want, as will shortly be perceived: but as yet the reader does not feel it, and he sees otherwise in all respects at his best the great observer and humorist; interested in everything that commended itself to a thoroughly earnest and eagerly inquiring nature; popular beyond measure with all having intercourse with him; the centre, and very soul, of social enjoyment; letting nothing escape a vision that was not more keen than kindly; and even when apparently most idle, never idle in the sense of his art, but adding day by day to experiences that widened its range, and gave freer and healthier play to an imagination always busily at work, alert and active in a singular degree, and that seemed to be quite untiring. At his heart there was a genuine love of nature at all times; and strange as it may seem to connect this with such forms of humorous delineation as are most identified with his genius, it is yet the literal truth that the impressions of this noble Swiss scenery were with him during the work of many subsequent years: a present and actual, though it might be seldom a directly conscious, influence. When he said afterwards, that, while writing the book on which he is now engaged, he had not seen less clearly each step of the wooden midshipman's staircase, each pew of the church in which Florence was married, or each bed in the dormitory of

417

Dr. Blimber's establishment, because he was himself at the time by the Lake of Geneva, he might as truly have said that he saw them all the more clearly even because of that circumstance. He worked his humour to its greatest results by the freedom and force of his imagination; and while the smallest or commonest objects around him were food for the one, the other might have pined or perished without additional higher aliment. Dickens had little love for Wordsworth, but he was himself an example of the truth the great poet never tired of enforcing, that Nature has subtle helps for all who are admitted to become free of her wonders and mysteries.

Another noticeable thing in him is impressed upon these letters, as upon many also heretofore quoted, for indeed all of them are marvellously exact in the reproduction of his nature. He did not think lightly of his work; and the work that occupied him at the time was for the time paramount with him. But the sense he entertained, whether right or wrong, of the importance of what he had to do, of the degree to which it concerned others that the power he held should be exercised successfully, and of the estimate he was justified in forming as the fair measure of its worth, does not carry with it of necessity presumption or self-conceit. Few men have had less of either. It was part of the intense individuality by which he effected so much, to set the high value which in general he did upon what he was striving to accomplish; he could not otherwise have mastered one-half of what he designed; and we are able to form an opinion, more just now for ourselves than it might have seemed to us than from others, of the correctness of such self-judgment. The fussy pretension of small men in great places, and the resolute self-assertion of great men in small places, are things essentially different. *Respice finem.* The exact relative importance of all our pursuits is to be arrived at by nicer adjustments of the Now and the Hereafter than are possible to contemporary judgments; and there have been some indications since his death confirmatory of the belief, that the estimate which he thought himself entitled to form of the labours to which his life was devoted, will be strengthened, not lessened, by time.

Dickens proposed to himself, it will be remembered, to write at Lausanne not only the first four numbers of his larger book, but the Christmas book suggested to him by his fancy of a battle-field; and reserving what is to be said of *Dombey* to a later chapter, this and its successes will deal only with what he finished as well as began in Switzerland, and will show at what cost even so much was achieved amid his other and larger engagements.

He had restless fancies and misgivings before he settled to his first notion. "I have been thinking this last day or two," he wrote on 25 July, "that good Christmas characters might be grown out of the idea of a man imprisoned for ten or fifteen years: his imprisonment being the gap between the people and circumstances of the first part and the altered people and circumstances of the second, and his own changed mind. Though I shall probably proceed with the Battle idea, I should like to know what you think of this one?" It was afterwards used in a modified shape for the *Tale of Two Cities*. "I shall begin the little story straightway," he wrote, a few weeks later; "but I have been dimly conceiving a very ghostly and wild idea, which I suppose I must now reserve for the *next* Christmas book. *Nous verrons*. It will mature in the streets of Paris by night, as well as in London." This took ultimately the form of the *Haunted Man*, which was not written until the winter of 1848. At last I knew that his first slip was done, and that even his eager busy fancy would not turn him back again.

But other unsatisfied wants and cravings had meanwhile broken out in him, of which I heard near the close of the second number of *Dombey*. The first he had finished at the end of July; and the second, which he began on 8 August, he was still at work upon in the first week of September, when this remarkable announcement came to me. It was his first detailed confession of what he felt so continuously, and if that were possible even more strongly as the years went on, that there is no single passage in any of his letters which throws such a flood of illuminative light into the portions of his life which will always awaken the greatest interest. Very much that is to follow must be read by it. "You can hardly imagine," he wrote on 30 August, "what infinite pains I take, or what extraordinary difficulty I find in getting on FAST. Invention, thank God, seems the easiest thing in the world; and I seem to have such a preposterous sense of the ridiculous, after this long rest" (it was now over two years since the close of *Chuzzlewit*), "as to be constantly requiring to restrain myself from launching into extravagances in the height of my enjoyment. But the difficulty of going at what I call a rapid pace, is prodigious: it is almost an impossibility. I suppose this is partly the effect of two years' ease, and partly of the absence of streets and numbers of figures. I can't express how much I want these. It seems as if they supplied something to my brain, which it cannot bear, when busy, to lose. For a week or a fortnight I can write prodigiously in a retired place (as at Broadstairs), and a day in London sets me up again and starts me. But the toil and labour of writing, day after day, without that magic lantern, is IMMENSE!! I don't say this at all in low spirits, for we are perfectly comfortable here, and I like the place very much indeed, and the people are even more friendly and fond of me than they were in Genoa. I only mention it as a curious fact, which I have never had an opportunity of finding out before. *My* figures seem disposed to stagnate without crowds about them. I wrote very little in Genoa (only the *Chimes*), and fancied myself conscious of some such influence there—but Lord! I had two miles of streets at least, lighted at night, to walk about in; and a great theatre to repair to, every night." At the close of the letter he told me that he had pretty well matured the general idea of the Christmas book, and was burning to get to work on it. He thought it would be all the better, for a change, to have no fairies or spirits in it, but to make it a simple domestic tale.

* 58

In less than a week from this date his second number was finished, his first slip of the little book done, and his confidence greater. They had had wonderful weather, so clear that he could see from the Neuchâtel road the outline of Mont Blanc, sixty miles off, as plainly as if he were standing close under it in the courtyard of the little inn at Chamonix; and, though again it was raining when he wrote, his "nailed shoes" were by him and his "great waterproof cloak" in preparation for a "fourteen-mile walk" before dinner. Then, after three days more, came something of a sequel to the confession before made, which will be read with equal interest. "The absence of any accessible streets continues to worry me, now that I have so much to do, in a most singular manner. It is quite a little mental phenomenon. I should not walk in them in the daytime, if they were here, I dare say: but at night I want them beyond description. I don't seem able to get rid of my spectres unless I can lose them in crowds. However, as you say, there are streets in Paris, and good suggestive streets too: and trips to London will be nothing then. WHEN I have finished the Christmas book, I shall fly to Geneva for a day or two, before taking up with *Dombey* again. I like this place better and better; and never saw, I think, more agreeable people than our little circle is made up of. It is so little, that one is not 'bothered' in the least; and their interest in the Inimitable seems to strengthen daily. I read them

* 59

the first number, last night 'was a' week, with unrelatable success; and old Mrs. Marcet, who is devilish 'cute, guessed directly (but I didn't tell her she was right) that little Paul would die. They were all so apprehensive that it was a great pleasure to read it; and I shall leave here, if all goes well, in a brilliant shower of sparks struck out of them by the promised reading of the Christmas book." Little did either of us then imagine to what these readings were to lead, but even thus early they were taking in his mind the shape of a sort of jest that the smallest opportunity of favour might have turned into earnest. In his very next letter he wrote to me: "I was thinking the other day that in these days of lecturings and readings, a great deal of money might possibly be made (if it were not *infra dig.*) by one's having Readings of one's own books. It would be an *odd* thing. I think it would take immensely. What do you say? Will you step to Dean Street, and see how Miss Kelly's engagement-book (it must be an immense volume!) stands? Or shall I take the St. James's?" My answer is to be inferred from his rejoinder: but even at this time, while heightening and carrying forward his jest, I suspected him of graver desires than he cared to avow; and the time was to come, after a dozen years, when with earnestness equal to his own I continued to oppose, for reasons to be stated in their place, that which he had set his heart upon too strongly to abandon, and which I still can only wish he had preferred to surrender with all that seemed to be its enormous gains! "I don't think you have exercised your usual judgment in taking Covent Garden for me. I doubt it is too large for my purpose. However, I shall stand by whatever you propose to the proprietors."

Soon came the changes of trouble and vexation I had too surely seen. "You remember," he wrote, "your objection about the two stories. I made over-light of it. I ought to have considered that I have never before really tried the opening of two together—having always had one pretty far ahead when I have been driving a pair of them. I know it all now. The apparent impossibility of getting each into its place, coupled with that craving for streets, so thoroughly put me off the track, that, up to Wednesday or Thursday last, I really contemplated, at times, the total abandonment of the Christmas book this year, and the limitation of my labours to *Dombey and Son!* I cancelled the beginning of a first scene—which I have never done before—and, with a notion in my head, ran wildly about and about it, and could not get the idea into any natural socket. At length, thank Heaven, I nailed it all at once; and after going on comfortably up to yesterday, and working yesterday from half-past nine to six, I was last night in such a state of enthusiasm about it that I think I was an inch or two taller. I am a little cooler to-day, with a headache to boot; but I really begin to hope you will think it a pretty story, with some delicate notions in it agreeably presented, and with a good human Christmas groundwork. I fancy I see a great domestic effect in the last part."

That was written on 20 September; but six days later changed the picture, and surprised me not a little. I might grudge the space thus given to one of the least important of his books but that the illustration goes farther than the little tale it refers to, and is a picture of him in his moods of writing, with their weakness as well as strength upon him, of a perfect truth and applicability to every period of his life. Movement and change while he was working were not mere restlessness, as we have seen; it was no impatience of labour, or desire of pleasure, that led at such times to his eager craving for the fresh crowds and faces in which he might lose or find the creatures of his fancy; and recollecting this, much hereafter will be understood that might else be very far from clear, in regard to the sensitive conditions under which otherwise he carried on these exertions of his brain. "I am going to write you" (26 September) "a most startling piece of intelligence. I fear there may be NO CHRISTMAS BOOK! I would give the world to be on the spot to tell you this. Indeed I once thought of starting for London to-night. I have written nearly a third of it. It promises to be pretty; quite a new idea in the story, I hope; but to manage it without the supernatural agency now impossible of introduction, and yet to move it naturally within the required space, or with any shorter limit than a *Vicar of Wakefield*, I find to be a difficulty so perplexing—the past *Dombey* work taken into account—that I am fearful of wearing myself out if I go on, and not being able to come back to the greater undertaking with the necessary freshness and spirit. If I had nothing but the Christmas book to do, I WOULD do it; but I get horrified and distressed beyond conception at the prospect of being jaded when I come back to the other, and making it a mere race against time. I have written the first part; I know the end and upshot of the second; and the whole of the third (there are only three in all). I know the purport of each character, and the plain idea that each is to work out; and I have the principal effects sketched on paper. It cannot end *quite* happily, but will end cheerfully and pleasantly. But

my soul sinks before the commencement of the second part—
the longest—and the introduction of the under-idea. (The main
one already developed, with interest.) I don't know how it is.
I suppose it is the having been almost constantly at work in
this quiet place; and the dread for the *Dombey*; and the not
being able to get rid of it, in noise and bustle. The beginning
two books together is also, no doubt, a fruitful source of the
difficulty; for I am now sure I could not have invented the *Carol*
at the commencement of the *Chuzzlewit*, or gone to a new book
from the *Chimes*. But this is certain. I am sick, giddy, and capri-
ciously despondent. I have had nights; am full of disquietude
and anxiety; and am constantly haunted by the idea that I
am wasting the marrow of the larger book, and ought to be at
rest. One letter that I wrote you before this, I have torn up.
In that the Christmas book was wholly given up for this year:
but I now resolved to make one effort more. I will go to Geneva
to-morrow, and try on Monday and Tuesday whether I can
get on at all bravely, in the changed scene. If I cannot, I am convinced that I had best hold my hand at once; and not fritter
my spirits and hope away, with that long book before me. You
may suppose that the matter is very grave when I can so nearly
abandon anything in which I am deeply interested, and fourteen
or fifteen close MS. pages of which, that have made me laugh
and cry, are lying in my desk. Writing this letter at all, I have
a great misgiving that the letter I shall write you on Tuesday
night will not make it better. Take it, for Heaven's sake, as
an extremely serious thing, and not a fancy of the moment.
Last Saturday after a very long day's work, and last Wednesday after finishing the first part, I was full of eagerness and
pleasure. At all other times since I began, I have been brooding
and brooding over the idea that it was a wild thing to dream of,
ever: and that I ought to be at rest for the *Dombey*."

The letter came, written on Wednesday not Tuesday night,
and it left the question still unsettled. "When I came here"
(Geneva, 30 September) "I had a bloodshot eye; and my
head was so bad, with a pain across the brow, that I thought
I must have got cupped. I have become a great deal better,
however, and feel quite myself again to-day. . . . I still have
not made up my mind as to what I CAN do with the Christmas
book. I would give any money that it were possible to consult
with you. I have begun the second part this morning, and have
done a very fair morning's work at it, but I do not feel it *in
hand* within the necessary space and divisions: and I have a

great uneasiness in the prospect of falling behindhand with the other labour, which is so transcendently important. I feel quite sure that unless I (being in reasonably good state and spirits) like the Christmas book myself, I had better not go on with it; but had best keep my strength for *Dombey*, and keep my number in advance. On the other hand I am dreadfully averse to abandoning it, and am so torn between the two things that I know not what to do. It is impossible to express the wish I have that I could take counsel with you. Having begun the second part I will go on here, to-morrow and Friday (Saturday, the Talfourds come to us at Lausanne, leaving on Monday morning), unless I see new reason to give it up in the meanwhile. Let it stand thus—that my next Monday's letter shall finally decide the question. But if you have not already told Bradbury and Evans of my last letter I think it will now be best to do so. . . . This non-publication of a Christmas book, if it must be, I try to think light of with the greater story just begun, and with this *Battle of Life* story (of which I really think the leading idea is very pretty) lying by me, for future use. But I would like you to consider, in the event of my not going on, how best, by timely announcement, in November's or December's *Dombey*, I may seem to hold the ground prospectively. . . . Heaven send me a good deliverance! If I don't do it, it will be the first time I ever abandoned anything I had once taken in hand; and I shall not have abandoned it until after a most desperate fight. I could do it, but for the *Dombey*, as easily as I did last year or the year before. But I cannot help falling back on that continually: and this, combined with the peculiar difficulties of the story for a Christmas book, and my being out of sorts, discourages me sadly. . . . Kate is here, and sends her love. . . ." A postscript was added on the following day. "Georgy has come over from Lausanne, and joins with Kate, etc. My head remains greatly better. My eye is recovering its old hue of beautiful white, tinged with celestial blue. If I hadn't come here, I think I should have had some bad low fever. The sight of the rushing Rhone seemed to stir my blood again. I don't think I shall want to be cupped, this bout; but it looked, at one time, worse than I have confessed to you. If I have any return, I will have it done immediately."

He stayed two days longer at Geneva, which he found to be a very good place; pleasantly reporting himself as quite dismayed at first by the sight of gas in it, and as trembling at the noise in its streets, which he pronounced to be fully equal to the uproar of Richmond in Surrey; but deriving from it some sort of benefit both in health and in writing. So far his trip had been successful, though he had to leave the place hurriedly to welcome his English visitors to Rosemont.

One social and very novel experience he had in his hotel, however, the night before he left, which may be told before he hastens back to Lausanne; for it could hardly now offend anyone even if the names were given. "And now, sir, I will describe, modestly, tamely, literally, the visit to the small select circle which I promised should make your hair stand on end. In our hotel were a Mother and a Daughter, who came to the Peschiere shortly before we left it, and who have a deep admiration for your humble servant the inimitable B. They are both very clever. Daughter, extremely well-informed in languages living and dead, books, and gossip; very pretty; with two little children, and not yet five and twenty. Mother, plump, fresh, and rosy; matronly, but full of spirits and good looks. Nothing would serve them but we *must* dine with them; and accordingly, on Friday at six, we went down to their room. I knew them to be rather odd. For instance, I have known the Mother, *full dressed*, walk alone through the streets of Genoa, the squalid Italian by-streets, to the Governor's soirée; and announce herself at the palace of state, by knocking at the door. I have also met the Daughter full dressed, without any cap or bonnet, walking a mile to the opera, with all sorts of jingling jewels about her, beside a sedan chair in which sat enthroned her mama. Consequently, I was not surprised at such little sparkles in the conversation (from the young lady) as 'Oh God what a sermon we had here, last Sunday!' 'And did you ever read such infernal trash as Mrs. Gore's?'—and the like. Still, but for Kate and Georgy (who were decidedly in the way, as we agreed afterwards), I should have thought it all very funny; and, as it was, I threw the ball back again, was mighty free and easy, made some rather broad jokes, and was highly applauded. 'You smoke, don't you?' said the young lady, in a pause of this kind of conversation. 'Yes,' I said, 'I generally take a cigar after dinner when I am alone.' 'I'll give you a good 'un,' said she, 'when we go upstairs.' Well, sir, in due course we went upstairs, and there we were joined by an American lady residing in the same hotel, who looked like what we call in old England 'a reg'lar Bunter'—fluffy face (rouged); considerable development of figure; one groggy eye; blue satin dress made low with short sleeves, and shoes of the same. Also a daughter; face likewise fluffy; figure likewise developed; dress likewise low, with short sleeves, and shoes of the same; and one eye not yet actually groggy, but going to be. American lady married at sixteen; American daughter sixteen now, often mistaken for sisters, etc. When that was over, the younger of our entertainers brought out a cigar box, and gave me a cigar, made of negrohead she said, which would quell an elephant in six whiffs. The box was full of cigarettes—good large ones, made of pretty strong tobacco; I always smoke them here, and used to smoke them at Genoa, and I knew them well. When I lighted my cigar, Daughter lighted hers at mine; leaned against the mantelpiece, in conversation with me; put out her stomach, folded her arms, and with her pretty face cocked up sideways and her cigarette smoking away like a Manchester cotton mill, laughed, and talked, and smoked, in the most gentlemanly manner I ever beheld. Mother immediately lighted her cigar; American lady immediately lighted hers; and in five minutes the room was a cloud of smoke, with us four in the centre pulling away bravely, while American lady related stories of her 'Hookah' upstairs, and described different kinds of pipes. But even this was not all. For presently two Frenchmen came in, with whom, and the American lady, Daughter sat down to whist. The Frenchmen smoked of course (they were really modest gentlemen and seemed dismayed), and Daughter played for the next hour or two with a cigar continually in her mouth —never out of it. She certainly smoked six or eight. Mother gave in soon—I think she only did it out of vanity. American lady had been smoking all the morning. I took no more; and Daughter and the Frenchmen had it all to themselves.

"Conceive this in a great hotel, with not only their own servants, but half a dozen waiters coming constantly in and out! I showed no atom of surprise, but I never *was* so surprised, so ridiculously taken aback, in my life; for in all my experience of 'ladies' of one kind and another, I never saw a woman— not a basket woman or a gipsy—smoke, before!" He lived to have larger and wider experience, but there was enough to startle as well as amuse him in the scene described.

But now Saturday is come; he has hurried back for the friends who are on their way to his cottage; and on his arrival, even before they have appeared, he writes to tell me his better news of himself and his work.

"In the breathless interval" (Rosemont, 3 October) "between our return from Genoa and the arrival of the Talfourds (expected in an hour or two), I cannot do better than write to you. For I think you will be well pleased if I anticipate my promise, and Monday, at the same time. I have been greatly better at Geneva, though I am still made uneasy by occasional giddiness and headache: attributable, I have not the least doubt, to the absence of streets. There is an idea here, too, that people are occasionally made despondent and sluggish in their spirits by this great mass of still water, Lake Leman. At any rate I have been very uncomfortable: at any rate I am, I hope, greatly better: and (lastly) at any rate I hope and trust, *now*, the Christmas book will come in due course!! I have had three very good days' work at Geneva, and trust I may finish the second part (the third is the shortest) by this day week. Whenever I finish it, I will send you the first two together. I do not think they can begin to illustrate it, until the third arrives; for it is a single-minded story, as it were, and an artist should know the end: which I don't think very likely, unless he reads it." Then, after relating a superhuman effort he was making to lodge his visitors in his doll's house ("I didn't like the idea of turning them out at night. It is so dark in these lanes and groves, when the moon's not bright"), he sketched for me what he possibly might, and really did, accomplish. He would by great effort finish the small book on the 20th; would fly to Geneva for a week to work a little at *Dombey*, if he felt "pretty sound;" in any case would finish his number three by the 10th of November; and on that day would start for Paris: "so that, instead of resting unprofitably here, I shall be using my interval of idleness to make the journey and get into a new house, and shall hope so to put a pinch of salt on the tail of the sliding number in advance. . . . I am horrified at the idea of getting the blues (and bloodshots) again." Though I did not then know how gravely ill he had been, I was fain to remind him that it was bad economy to make business out of rest itself; but I received prompt confirmation that all was falling out as he wished. The Talfourds stayed two days: "and I think they were very happy. He was in his best aspect; the manner so well known to us, not the less lovable for being laughable; and if you could have seen him going round and round the coach that brought them, as a preliminary to paying the *voiturier* to whom he couldn't speak, in a currency he didn't understand, you never would have forgotten it." His friends left Lausanne on the 5th; and five days later he sent me two-thirds of the manuscript of his Christmas book.

VI

GENEVESE REVOLUTION AND "BATTLE OF LIFE"

1846

"I SEND you in twelve letters, counting this as one, the first two parts (thirty-five slips) of the Christmas book. I have two present anxieties respecting it. One to know that you have received it safely; and the second to know how it strikes you. Be sure you read the first and second parts together. . . . There seems to me to be interest in it, and a pretty idea; and it is unlike the others. . . . There will be some minor points for consideration: as, the necessity for some slight alteration in one or two of the Doctor's speeches in the first part; and whether it should be called 'The Battle of Life. A Love Story'—to express both a love story in the common acceptation of the phrase, and also a story of love; with one or two other things of that sort. We can moot these by and by. I made a tremendous day's work of it yesterday and was horribly excited—so I am going to rush out, as fast as I can: being a little used up, and sick. . . . But never say die! I have been to the glass to look at my eye. Pretty bright!"

I made it brighter next day by telling him that the first number of *Dombey* had outstripped in sale the first of *Chuzzlewit* by more than twelve thousand copies; and his next letter, sending the close of his little tale, showed his need of the comfort my pleasant news had given him. "I really do not know what this story is worth. I am so floored: wanting sleep, and never having had my head free from it for this month past. I think there are some places in this last part which I may bring better together in the proof, and where a touch or two may be of service; particularly in the scene between Craggs and Michael Warden, where as it stands, the interest seems anticipated. But I shall have the benefit of your suggestions, and my own then cooler head, I hope; and I will be very careful with the proofs, and keep them by me as long as I can. . . . Mr. Britain must have another Christian name, then? 'Aunt Martha' is

428

the Sally of whom the Doctor speaks in the first part. Martha is a better name. What do you think of the concluding paragraph? Would you leave it for happiness' sake? It is merely experimental. . . . I am flying to Geneva to-morrow morning." (That was on 18 October; and on the 20th he wrote from Geneva.) "We came here yesterday, and we shall probably remain until Katey's birthday, which is next Thursday week. I shall fall to work on number three of *Dombey* as soon as I can. At present I am the worse for wear, but nothing like as much so as I expected to be on Sunday last. I had not been able to sleep for some time, and had been hammering away, morning, noon, and night. A bottle of hock on Monday, when Elliotson dined with us (he went away homeward yesterday morning), did me a world of good; the change comes in the very nick of time; and I feel in Dombeian spirits already. . . . But I have still rather a damaged head, aching a good deal occasionally, as it is doing now, though I have not been cupped—yet. . . . I dreamed all last week that the *Battle of Life* was a series of chambers impossible to be got to rights or got out of, through which I wandered drearily all night. On Saturday night I don't think I slept an hour. I was perpetually roaming through the story, and endeavouring to dovetail the revolution here into the plot. The mental distress quite horrible."

Of the "revolution" he had written to me a week before, from Lausanne; where the news had just reached them, that, upon the Federal Diet decreeing the expulsion of the Jesuits, the Roman Catholic cantons had risen against the decree, the result being that the Protestants had deposed the grand council and established a provisional government, dissolving the Catholic league. His interest in this, and prompt seizure of what really was brought into issues by the conflict, is every way characteristic of Dickens. "You will know," he had written from Lausanne on 11 October, "long before you get this, all about the revolution at Geneva. There were stories of plots against the Government when I was there, but I didn't believe them; for all sorts of lies are always afloat against the radicals, and wherever there is a consul from a Catholic Power the most monstrous fictions are in perpetual circulation against them: as in this very place, where the Sardinian consul was gravely whispering the other day that a society called the Homicides had been formed, whereof the president of the council of state, the O'Connell of Switzerland and a clever fellow, was a member; who were sworn on skulls and cross-bones to exterminate men of property and so forth. There was a great stir here in Lausanne, on the day of the fight in Geneva. We heard the guns (they shook this house) all day; and seven hundred men marched out of the town to go and help the radical party—arriving at Geneva just after it was all over. There is no doubt they had received secret help from Lausanne; for a powder barrel, found by some of the Genevese populace with 'Canton de Vaud' painted on it, was carried on a pole about the streets as a standard, to show that they were sympathised with by friends outside. It was a poor mean fight enough, I am told by Lord Vernon, who was present and who was with us last night. The Government was afraid; having no confidence whatever, I dare say, in its own soldiers; and the cannon were fired everywhere except at the opposite party, who (I mean the revolutionists) had barricaded a bridge with an omnibus only, and certainly in the beginning might have been turned with ease. The precision of the common men with the rifle was especially shown by a small party of *five*, who waited on the ramparts near one of the gates of the town, to turn a body of soldiery who were coming in to the Government assistance. They picked out every officer and struck him down instantly, the moment the party appeared; there were three or four of them; upon which the soldiers gravely turned round and walked off. I dare say there are not fifty men in Lausanne who wouldn't click your card off a target a hundred and fifty yards away, at least. I have seen them, time after time, fire across a great ravine as wide as the ornamental ground in St. James's Park, and never miss the bull's-eye.

"It is a horribly ungentlemanly thing to say here, though I *do* say it without the least reserve—but my sympathy is all with the radicals. I don't know any subject on which this indomitable people have so good a right to a strong feeling as Catholicity—if not as a religion, clearly as a means of social degradation. They know what it is. They live close to it. They have Italy beyond their mountain. They can compare the effect of the two systems at any time in their own valleys; and their dread of it, and their horror of the introduction of Catholic priests and emissaries into their towns, seem to me the most rational feeling in the world. Apart from this, you have no conception of the preposterous, insolent little aristocracy of Geneva: the most ridiculous caricature the fancy can suggest of what we know in England. I was talking to two famous gentlemen (very intelligent men) of that place, not long ago, who came over to invite me to a sort of reception there—which I declined. Really their talk about 'the people' and 'the masses,' and the necessity they would shortly be under of shooting a few of them as an example for the rest, was a kind of monstrosity one might have heard at Genoa. The audacious insolence and contempt of the people by their newspapers, too, is quite absurd. It is difficult to believe that men of sense can be such donkeys politically. It was precisely such a state of things that brought about the change in Lausanne. There was a most respectful petition presented on the Jesuit question, signed by its tens of thousands of small farmers; the regular peasants of the canton, all splendidly taught in public schools, and intellectually as well as physically a most remarkable body of labouring men. This document is treated by the gentlemanly party with the most sublime contempt, and the signatures are said to be the signatures of 'the rabble.' Upon which, each man of the rabble shoulders his rifle, and walks in upon a given day agreed upon among them to Lausanne; and the gentlemanly party walk out without striking a blow."

Such traces of the "revolution" as he found upon his present visit to Geneva he described in writing to me from the Hôtel de l'Ecu on 20 October. "You never would suppose from the look of this town that there had been anything revolutionary going on. Over the window of my old bedroom there is a great hole made by a cannon-ball in the house-front; and two of the bridges are under repair. But these are small tokens which anything else might have brought about as well. The people are all at work. The little streets are rife with every sight and sound of industry; the place is as quiet by ten o'clock as Lincoln's Inn Fields; and the only outward and visible sign of public interest in political events is a little group at every street corner, reading a public announcement from the new Government of the forthcoming election of state-officers, in which the people are reminded of their importance as a republican institution, and desired to bear in mind their dignity in all their proceedings. Nothing very violent or bad could go on with a community so well educated as this. It is the best antidote to American experiences, conceivable. As to the nonsense 'the gentlemanly interest' talk about, their opposition to property and so forth, there never was such mortal absurdity. One of the principal leaders in the late movement has a stock of watches and jewellery here of immense value—and had, during the disturbance—perfectly unprotected. James Fazy

has a rich house and a valuable collection of pictures; and, I
will be bound to say, twice as much to lose as half the conservative declaimers put together. This house, the liberal one,
is one of the most richly furnished and luxurious hotels on
the Continent. And if I were a Swiss with a hundred thousand
pounds, I would be as steady against the Catholic cantons and
the propagation of Jesuitism as any radical among 'em: believing the dissemination of Catholicity to be the most horrible
means of political and social degradation left in the world.
Which these people, thoroughly well educated, know perfectly.
. . . The boys of Geneva were very useful in bringing materials
for the construction of the barricades on the bridges; and the
enclosed song may amuse you. They sing it to a tune that
dates from the great French revolution—a very good one."

But revolutions may be small as well as their heroes, and
while he thus was sending me his Gamin de Genève I was
sending him news of a sudden change in Whitefriars which had
quite as vivid interest for him. Not much could be told him at
first, but his curiosity instantly arose to fever pitch. "In reference
to that *Daily News* revolution," he wrote from Geneva on the
26th, "I have been walking and wandering all day through a
perfect Miss Burney's Vauxhall of conjectural dark walks.
Heaven send you enlighten me fully on Wednesday, or number
three will suffer!" Two days later he resumed, as he was beginning his journey back to Lausanne. "I am in a great state of
excitement on account of your intelligence, and desperately
anxious to know all about it. I shall be put out to an unspeakable extent if I don't find your letter awaiting me. God knows
there has been small comfort for either of us in the *D. N.*'s
nine months." There was not much to tell then, and there is
less now; but at last the discomfort was over for us both, as
I had been unable to reconcile myself to a longer continuance
of the service I had given in Whitefriars since he quitted it.
The subject may be left with the remark made upon it in his
first letter after returning to Rosemont. "I certainly am very
glad of the result of the *Daily News* business, though my gladness is dashed with melancholy to think that you should have
toiled there so long, to so little purpose. I escaped more easily.
However, it is all passed now. As to the undoubted necessity of
the course you took, I have not a grain of question in my mind.
That, being what you are, you had only one course to take and
have taken it, I no more doubt than that the Old Bailey is not
Westminster Abbey. In the utmost sum at which you value your-

self, you were bound to leave; and now you *have* left you will come to Paris, and there, and at home again, we'll have, please God, the old kind of evenings and the old life again, as it used to be before those daily nooses caught us by the legs, and sometimes tripped us up. Make a vow (as I have done) never to go down that court with the little news-shop at the corner, any more, and let us swear by Jack Straw as in the ancient times. . . . I am beginning to get over my sorrow for your nights up aloft in Whitefriars, and to feel nothing but happiness in the contemplation of your enfranchisement. God bless you!'

The time was now shortening for him at Lausanne; but before my sketches of his pleasant days there close, the little story of his Christmas book may be made complete by a few extracts from the letters that followed immediately upon the departure of the Talfourds. Without comment they will explain its closing touches, his own consciousness of the difficulties in working out the tale within limits too confined not to render its proper development imperfect, and his ready tact in dealing with objection and suggestion from without. His condition while writing it did not warrant me in pressing what I might otherwise have thought necessary: but as the little story finally left his hands, it had points not unworthy of him; and a sketch of its design will render the fragments from his letters more intelligible. I read it lately with a sense that its general tone of quiet beauty deserved well the praise which Jeffrey in those days had given it. "I like and admire the *Battle* extremely," he said in a letter on its publication, sent me by Dickens and not included in Lord Cockburn's Memoir. "It is better than any other man alive could have written, and has passages as fine as anything that ever came from the man himself. The dance of the sisters in that autumn orchard is of itself worth a dozen inferior tales, and their reunion at the close, and indeed all the serious parts, are beautiful, some traits of Clemency charming."

Yet it was probably here the fact, as with the *Chimes*, that the serious parts were too much interwoven with the tale to render the subject altogether suitable to the old mirth-bringing season; but this had also some advantages. The story is all about two sisters, the younger of whom, Marion, sacrifices her own affection to give happiness to the elder, Grace. But Grace had already made the same sacrifice for this younger sister; life's first and hardest battle had been won by her before the incidents begin; and when she is first seen, she is busying herself to bring about her sister's marriage with Alfred Heathfield, whom she has herself loved, and whom she has kept wholly unconscious, by a quiet change in her bearing to him, of what his own still disengaged heart would certainly not have rejected. Marion, however, had earlier discovered this, though it is not until her victory over herself that Alfred knows it; and meanwhile he is become her betrothed. The sisters thus shown at the opening, one believing her love undiscovered and the other bent for the sake of that love on surrendering her own, each practising concealment and both unselfishly true, form a pretty and tender picture. The second part is intended to give to Marion's flight the character of an elopement; and so to manage this as to show her all the time unchanged to the man she is pledged to, yet flying from, was the author's difficulty. One Michael Warden is the *deus ex machinâ* by whom it is solved, hardly with the usual skill; but there is much art in rendering his pretensions to the hand of Marion, whose husband he becomes after an interval of years, the means of closing against him all hope of success, in the very hour when her own act might seem to be opening it to him. During the same interval Grace, believing Marion to be gone with Warden, becomes Alfred's wife; and not until reunion after six years' absence is the truth entirely known to her. The struggle, to all of them, has been filled and chastened with sorrow; but joy revisits them at its close. Hearts are not broken by the duties laid upon them; nor is life shown to be such a perishable holiday, that amidst noble sorrow and generous self-denial it must lose its capacity for happiness. The tale thus justifies its place in the Christmas series. What Jeffrey says of Clemency, too, may suggest another word. The story would not be Dickens's if we could not discover in it the power peculiar to him of presenting the commonest objects with freshness and beauty, of detecting in the homeliest forms of life much of its rarest loveliness, and of springing easily upward from everyday realities into regions of imaginative thought. To this happiest direction of his art, Clemency and her husband render new tribute; and in her more especially, once again, we recognise one of those true souls who fill so large a space in his writings, for whom the lowest seats at life's feast are commonly kept, but whom he moves and welcomes to a more fitting place among the prized and honoured at the upper tables.

"I wonder whether you foresaw the end of the Christmas book! There are two or three places in which I can make it prettier, I think, by slight alterations. . . . I trust to Heaven you may like it. What an affecting story I could have made of it in one octavo volume. Oh to think of the printers transforming my kindly cynical old father into Doctor Taddler!" (28 October.) Here may be interposed extracts from letters of two years' later date to Sir Edward Lytton. "What you said of the *Battle of Life* gave me great pleasure. I was thoroughly wretched at having to use the idea for so short a story. I did not see its full capacity until it was too late to think of another subject; and I have always felt that I might have done a great deal with it, if I had taken it for the groundwork of a more extended book." (10 April, 1848.) "But for an insuperable aversion I have to trying back in such a case, I should certainly forge that bit of metal again, as you suggest. One of these days perhaps." . . . (4 August, 1848.)

"Do you think it worth while, in the illustrations, to throw the period back at all for the sake of anything good in the costume? The story may have happened at any time within a hundred years. Is it worth having coats and gowns of dear old Goldsmith's day? or thereabouts? I really don't know what to say. The probability is, if it has not occurred to you or to the artists, that it is hardly worth considering; but I ease myself of it by throwing it out to you. It may be already too late, or you may see reason to think it best to 'stick to the *last*' (I feel it necessary to italicise the joke), and abide by the ladies' and gentlemen's spring and winter fashions of this time. Whatever you think best, in this as in all other things, is best, I am sure. . . . I would go, in the illustrations, for 'beauty' as much as possible; and I should like each part to have a general illustration to it at the beginning, shadowing out its drift and bearing: much as Browne goes at that kind of thing on *Dombey* covers. I don't think I should fetter your discretion in the matter further. The better it is illustrated, the better I shall be pleased of course." (29 October.)

". . . I only write to say that it is of no use my writing at length until I have heard from you; and that I will wait until I shall have read your promised communication (as my father would call it) to-morrow. I have glanced over the proofs of the last part and really don't wonder that the marriage of Grace and Alfred should seem rather unsatisfactory to you: some of the most extravagant mistakes occurring in Clemency's account to Warden. Whatever is done about that must be done with the lightest hand, for the reader MUST take something for granted; but I think it next to impossible, without dreadful injury to the effect, to introduce a scene between Marion and Michael. The introduction must be in the scene between the sisters, and must be put, mainly, into the mouth of Grace. Rely upon it there is no other way, in keeping with the spirit of the tale. With this amendment, and a touch here and there in the last part (I know exactly where they will come best), I think it may be pretty and affecting, and comfortable too." ... (31 October.)

". . . I shall hope to touch upon the Christmas book as soon as I get your opinion. I wouldn't do it without. I am delighted to hear of noble old Stanny. Give my love to him, and tell him I think of turning Catholic. It strikes me (it may have struck you perhaps) that another good place for introducing a few lines of dialogue, is at the beginning of the scene between Grace and her husband, where he speaks about the messenger at the gate." (4 November.)

"Before I reply to your questions I wish to remark generally of the third part that all the passion that can be got into it, through my interpretation at all events, is there. I know that, by what it cost me; and I take it to be, as a question of art and interest, in the very nature of the story that it *should* move at a swift pace after the sisters are in each other's arms again. Anything after that would drag like lead, and must. . . . Now for your questions. I don't think any little scene with Marion and anybody can prepare the way for the last paragraph of the tale: I don't think anything but a printer's line *can* go between it and Warden's speech. A less period than ten years? Yes. I see no objection to six. I have no doubt you are right. Any word from Alfred in his misery? Impossible: you might as well try to speak to somebody in an express train. The preparation for his change is in the first part, and he kneels down beside her in that return scene. He is left alone with her, as it were, in the world. I am quite confident it is wholly impossible for me to alter that. . . . BUT (keep your eye on me) when Marion went away, she left a letter for Grace in which she charged her to encourage the love that Alfred would conceive for her, and FOREWARNED her that years would pass before they met again, etc. This coming out in the scene between the sisters, and something like it being expressed in the opening of the little scene between Grace and her husband before the messenger at the gate, will make (I hope) a prodigious difference; and I will try to put in something with Aunt Martha and the Doctor that shall carry the tale back more distinctly and unmistakably to the battle-ground. I hope to make these alterations next week, and to send the third part back to you before I leave here. If you think it can still be improved after that, say so to me in Paris and I will go at it again. I wouldn't have it limp, if it can fly. I say nothing to you of a great deal of this being already expressed in the sentiment of the beginning, because your delicate perception knows all that already. Observe for the artists. Grace will now only have *one child*—little Marion." ... (At night, on same day.) ... "You recollect that I asked you to read it all together, for I knew that I was working for that? But I have no doubt of *your* doubts, and will do what I have said. ... I had thought of marking the time in the little story, and will do so. ... Think, once more, of the period between the second and third parts. I will do the same." (7 November.)

"I hope you will think the third part (when you read it in type with these amendments) very much improved. I think it so. If there should still be anything wanting, in your opinion, pray suggest it to me in Paris. I am bent on having it right, if I can. ... If in going over the proofs you find the tendency to blank verse (I *cannot* help it, when I am very much in earnest) too strong, knock out a word's brains here and there." (13 November. Sending the proofs back.)

". . . Your Christmas book illustration-news makes me jump for joy. I will write you at length to-morrow. I should like this dedication: This Christmas Book is cordially inscribed To my English Friends in Switzerland. Just those two lines, and nothing more. When I get the proofs again I think I may manage another word or two about the battle-field, with advantage. I am glad you like the alterations. I feel that they make it complete, and that it would have been incomplete without your suggestions." (21 November. From Paris.)

I had managed, as a glad surprise for him, to enlist both Stanfield and Maclise in the illustration of the story, in addition to the distinguished artists whom the publishers had engaged for it, Leech and Richard Doyle; and among the subjects contributed by Stanfield are three morsels of English landscape which had a singular charm for Dickens at the time, and seem to me still of their kind quite faultless. I may add a curious fact, never mentioned until now. In the illustration which closes the second part of the story, where the festivities to welcome the bridegroom at the top of the page contrast with the flight of the bridegroom represented below, Leech made the mistake

of supposing that Michael Warden had taken part in the elopement, and has introduced his figure with that of Marion. We
did not discover this until too late for remedy, the publication
having then been delayed expressly for these drawings, to the
utmost limit; and it is highly characteristic of Dickens, and of
the true regard he had for this fine artist, that, knowing the
pain he must give in such circumstances by objection or complaint, he preferred to pass it silently. Nobody made remark
upon it, and there the illustration still stands; but anyone who
reads the tale carefully will at once perceive what havoc it
makes of one of the most delicate turns in it.

"When I first saw it, it was with a horror and agony not to
be expressed. Of course I need not tell *you*, my dear fellow,
Warden has no business in the elopement scene. *He* was never
there! In the first hot sweat of this surprise and novelty, I was
going to implore the printing of that sheet to be stopped, and
the figure taken out of the block. But when I thought of the
pain this might give to our kind-hearted Leech; and that what
is such a monstrous enormity to me, as never having entered
my brain, may not so present itself to others, I became more
composed; though the fact is wonderful to me. No doubt a
great number of copies will be printed by the time this reaches
you, and therefore I shall take it for granted that it stands as
it is. Leech otherwise is very good, and the illustrations altogether
are by far the best that have been done for any of the Christmas
books. You know how I build up temples in my mind that are
not made with hands (or expressed with pen and ink, I am
afraid), and how liable I am to be disappointed in these things.
But I really am *not* disappointed in this case. Quietness and
beauty are preserved throughout. Say everything to Mac and
Stanny, more than everything! It is a delight to look at these
little landscapes of the dear old boy. How gentle and elegant,
and yet how manly and vigorous, they are! I have a perfect
joy in them."

Of the few days that remained of his Lausanne life, before
he journeyed to Paris, there is not much requiring to be said.
His work had continued during the whole of the month before
departure to occupy him so entirely as to leave room for little
else, and even occasional letters to very dear friends at home
were intermitted. Here are two examples of many. "I will write
to Landor as soon as I can possibly make time, but I really
am so much at my desk perforce, and so full of work, whether
I am there or elsewhere, between the Christmas book and *Dombey*,

that it is the most difficult thing in the world for me to make up my mind to write a letter to anyone but you. I ought to have written to Macready. I wish you would tell him, with my love, how I am situated in respect of pen, ink, and paper. One of the Lausanne papers, treating of free trade, has been very copious lately in its mention of LORD GOBDEN. Fact; and I think it a good name." Then, as the inevitable time approached, he cast about him for such comfort as the coming change might bring, to set against the sorrow of it; and began to think of Paris, "in a less romantic and more homely contemplation of the picture," as not wholly undesirable. "I have no doubt that constant change, too, is indispensable to me when I am at work: and at times something more than a doubt will force itself upon me whether there is not something in a Swiss valley that disagrees with me. Certainly, whenever I live in Switzerland again, it shall be on the hill-top. Something of the *goître* and *crétin* influence seems to settle on my spirits sometimes, on the lower ground. How sorry, ah yes! how sorry I shall be to leave the little society nevertheless. We have been thoroughly good-humoured and agreeable together, and I'll always give a hurrah for the Swiss and Switzerland."   * 60

One or two English travelling by Lausanne had meanwhile greeted him as they were passing home, and a few days given him by Elliotson had been an enjoyment without a drawback. It was now the later autumn, very high winds were coursing through the valley, and his last letter but one described the change which these approaches of winter were making in the scene. "We have had some tremendous hurricanes at Lausanne. It is an extraordinary place now for wind, being peculiarly situated among mountains—between the Jura, and the Simplon, St. Gothard, St. Bernard, and Mont Blanc ranges; and at night you would swear (lying in bed) you were at sea. You cannot imagine wind blowing so, over earth. It is very fine to hear. The weather generally, however, has been excellent. There is snow on the tops of nearly all the hills, but none has fallen in the valley. On a bright day, it is quite hot between eleven and half-past two. The nights and mornings are cold. For the last two or three days, it has been thick weather; and I can see no more of Mont Blanc from where I am writing now than if I were in Devonshire Terrace, though last week it bounded all the Lausanne walks. I would give a great deal that you could take a walk with me about Lausanne on a clear cold day. It is impossible to imagine anything more noble and beautiful than the scene; and the autumn colours in the foliage are more brilliant and vivid now than any description could convey to you. I took Elliotson, when he was with us, up to a ravine I had found out in the hills eight hundred or a thousand feet deep! Its steep sides dyed bright yellow, and deep red, by the changing leaves; a sounding torrent roaring down below; the lake of Geneva lying at its foot; one enormous mass and chaos of trees at its upper end; and mountain piled on mountain in the distance, up into the sky! He really was struck silent by its majesty and splendour."

He had begun his third number of *Dombey* on 26 October, on the 4th of the following month he was half through it, on the 7th he was in "the agonies" of its last chapter, and on the 9th, one day before that proposed for its completion, all was done. This was marvellously rapid work, after what else he had undergone; but within a week, Monday the 16th being the day for departure, they were to strike their tents, and troubled and sad were the few days thus left him for preparation and farewell. He included in his leave-taking his deaf, dumb, and blind friends; and, to use his own homely phrase, was yet more terribly "down in the mouth" at taking leave of his hearing, speaking, and seeing friends. "I shall see you soon, please God, and that sets all to rights. But I don't believe there are many dots on the map of the world where we shall have left such affectionate remembrances behind us, as in Lausanne. It was quite miserable this last night, when we left them at Haldimand's."

He shall himself describe how they travelled post to Paris, occupying five days. "We got through the journey charmingly, though not quite so quickly as we hoped. The children as good as usual, and even Skittles jolly to the last. That name has long superseded Sampson Brass, by the by. I call him so, from something skittle-playing and public-housey in his countenance. We have been up at five every morning, and on the road before seven. We were three carriages: a sort of waggon, with a cabriolet attached, for the luggage; a ramshackle villainous old swing upon wheels (hired at Geneva), for the children; and for ourselves, that travelling chariot which I was so kind as to bring here for sale. It was very cold indeed crossing the Jura—nothing but fog and frost; but when we were out of Switzerland and across the French frontier, it became warmer, and continued so. We stopped at between six and seven each evening; had two rather queer inns, wild French country inns; but the rest good.

They were three hours and a half examining the luggage at the frontier custom-house—atop of a mountain, in a hard and biting frost; where Anne and Roche had sharp work I assure you, and the latter insisted on volunteering the most astonishing and unnecessary lies about my books, for the mere pleasure of deceiving the officials. When we were out of the mountain country, we came at a good pace, but were a day late in getting to our hotel here."

They were in Paris when that was written; at the Hôtel Brighton; which they had reached in the evening of Friday, 20 November.

No man enjoyed brief residence in a hotel more than Dickens, but "several tons of luggage, other tons of servants, and other tons of children" are not desirable accompaniments to this kind of life; and his first day in Paris did not close before he had offered for an "eligible mansion." That same Saturday night he took a "colossal" walk about the city, of which the brilliancy and brightness almost frightened him; and among other things that attracted his notice was "rather a good book announced in a bookseller's window as *Les Mystères de Londres par Sir Trollopp*. Do you know him?" A countryman better known had given him earlier greeting. "The first man who took hold of me in the street, immediately outside this door, was Bruffum in his check trousers, and without the proper number of buttons on his shirt, who was going away this morning, he told me, but coming back in two months, when we would go and dine—at some place known to him and fame."

Next day he took another long walk about the streets, and lost himself fifty times. This was Sunday, and he hardly knew what to say of it, as he saw it there and then. The bitter observance of that day he always sharply resisted, believing a little rational enjoyment to be not opposed to either rest or religion; but here was another matter. "The dirty churches, and the clattering carts and waggons, and the open shops (I don't think I passed fifty shut up, in all my strollings in and out), and the work-a-day dresses and drudgeries, are not comfortable. Open theatres and so forth I am well used to, of course, by this time; but so much toil and sweat on what one would like to see, apart from religious observances, a sensible holiday, is painful."

The date of his letter was 22 November, and it had three postscripts.[1] The first, "Monday afternoon," told me a

[1] It had also the mention of another floating fancy for the weekly periodical which was still and always present to his mind, and which settled down at last, as the reader knows, into *Household Words*. "As to the Review

house was taken; that, unless the agreement should break off on any unforeseen fight between Roche and the agent ("a French Mrs. Gamp"), I was to address him at No. 48, Rue de Courcelles, Faubourg St. Honoré; and that he would merely then advert to the premises as in his belief the "most ridiculous, extraordinary, unparalleled, and preposterous" in the whole world; being something between a baby-house, a "shades," a haunted castle, and a mad kind of clock. "They belong to a Marquis Castellan, and you will be ready to die of laughing when you go over them." The second P.S. declared that his lips should be sealed till I beheld for myself. "By Heaven it is not to be imagined by the mind of man!" The third P.S. closed the letter. "One room is a tent. Another room is a grove. Another room is a scene at the Victoria. The upstairs rooms are like fanlights over street-doors. The nurseries—but no, no, no, no more! . . ."

His following letter nevertheless sent more, even in the form of an additional protestation that never till I saw it should the place be described. "I will merely observe that it is fifty yards long, and eighteen feet high, and that the bedrooms are exactly like opera-boxes. It has its little courtyard and garden, and porter's house and cordon to open the door, and so forth; and is a Paris mansion in little. There is a gleam of reason in the drawing-room. Being a gentleman's house, and not one furnished to let, it has some very curious things in it; some of the oddest things you ever beheld in your life; and an infinity of easy chairs and sofas. . . . Bad weather. It is snowing hard. There is not a door or window here—but that's nothing! there's not a door or window in all Paris—that shuts; not a chink in all the billions of trillions of chinks in the city that can be stopped to keep the wind out. And the cold!—but you shall judge for yourself; and also of this preposterous dining-room. The invention, sir, of Henry Bulwer, who when he had executed it (he used to live here), got frightened at what he had done, as well he might, and went away. . . . The Brave called me aside on Saturday night, and showed me an improvement he had effected in the decorative way. 'Which,' he said, 'will very much s'prise

I strongly incline to the notion of a kind of *Spectator* (Addison's)—very cheap, and pretty frequent. We must have it thoroughly discussed. It would be a great thing to found something. If the mark between a sort of *Spectator*, and a different sort of *Athenæum*, could be well hit, my belief is that a deal might be done. But it should be something with a marked and distinctive and obvious difference, in its design, from any other existing periodical."

Mis'r Fors'er when he come.' You are to be deluded into the belief that there is a perspective of chambers twenty miles in length, opening from the drawing-room. . . ."

My visit was not yet due, however, and what occupied or interested him in the interval may first be told. He had not been two days in Paris when a letter from his father made him very anxious for the health of his eldest sister. "I was going to the play (melodrama in eight acts, five hours long), but hadn't the heart to leave home after my father's letter," he is writing on 30 November, "and sent Georgy and Kate by themselves. There seems to be no doubt whatever that Fanny is in a consumption." She had broken down in an attempt to sing at a party in Manchester; and subsequent examination by Sir Charles Bell's nephew, who was present and took much interest in her, sadly revealed the cause. "He advised that neither she nor Burnett should be told the truth, and my father has not disclosed it. In worldly circumstances they are very comfortable, and they are very much respected. They seem to be happy together, and Burnett has a great deal of teaching. You remember my fears about her when she was in London the time of Alfred's marriage, and that I said she looked to me as if she were in a decline? Kate took her to Elliotson, who said that her lungs were certainly not affected then. And she cried for joy. Don't you think it would be better for her to be brought up, if possible, to see Elliotson again? I am deeply, deeply grieved about it." This course was taken, and for a time there seemed room for hope; but the result will be seen. In the same letter I heard of poor Charles Sheridan, well known to us both, dying of the same terrible disease; and his chief, Lord Normanby, whose many acts of sympathy and kindness had inspired strong regard in Dickens, he had already found "as informal and good-natured as ever, but not so gay as usual, and having an anxious haggard way with him, as if his responsibilities were more than he had bargained for." Nor, to account for this, had Dickens far to seek, when a little leisure enabled him to see something of what was passing in Paris during that last year of Louis Philippe's reign. What first impressed him most unfavourably was a glimpse in the Champs Elysées of the King himself coming in from the country. "There were two carriages. His was surrounded by horseguards. It went at a great pace, and he sat very far back in a corner of it, I promise you. It was strange to an Englishman to see the Préfet of Police riding on horseback some hundreds of yards in advance of the cortége, turning his head incessantly from side to side, like a figure in a Dutch clock, and scrutinising everybody and everything, as if he suspected all the twigs in all the trees in the long avenue."

But these and other political indications were only, as they generally prove to be, the outward signs of maladies more deeply seated. He saw almost everywhere signs of canker eating into the heart of the people themselves. "It is a wicked and detestable place, though wonderfully attractive; and there can be no better summary of it, after all, than Hogarth's unmentionable phrase." He sent me no letter that did not contribute something of observation or character. He went at first rather frequently to the Morgue, until shocked by something so repulsive that he had not courage for a long time to go back; and on that same occasion he had noticed the keeper smoking a short pipe at his little window, "and giving a bit of fresh turf to a linnet in a cage." Of the condition generally of the streets he reported badly; the quays on the other side of the Seine were not safe after dark; and here was his own night experience of one of the best quarters of the city. "I took Georgy out, the night before last, to show her the Palais Royal lighted up; and on the Boulevard, a street as bright as the brightest part of the Strand or Regent Street, we saw a man fall upon another, close before us, and try to tear the cloak off his back. It was in a little dark corner near the Porte St. Denis, which stands out in the middle of the street. After a short struggle, the thief fled (there were thousands of people walking about), and was captured just on the other side of the road."

An incident of that kind might mean little or much: but what he proceeded to remark of the ordinary Parisian workpeople and smaller shopkeepers, had a more grave complexion; and may be thought perhaps still to yield some illustration, not without value, to the story of the quarter of a century that has passed since, and even to some of the appalling events of its latest year or two. "It is extraordinary what nonsense English people talk, write, and believe, about foreign countries. The Swiss (so much decried) will do anything for you, if you are frank and civil; they are attentive and punctual in all their dealings; and may be relied upon as steadily as the English. The Parisian workpeople and smaller shopkeepers are more like (and unlike) Americans than I could have supposed possible. To the American indifference and carelessness, they add a procrastination and want of the least heed about keeping a promise or being exact, which is certainly not surpassed in Naples. They have the American semi-sentimental independence too, and none of the American vigour or purpose. If they ever get free trade in France (as I suppose they will, one day) these parts of the population must, for years and years, be ruined. They couldn't get the means of existence, in competition with the English workmen. Their inferior manual dexterity, their lazy habits, perfect unreliability, and habitual insubordination, would ruin them in any such contest, instantly. They are fit for nothing but soldiering—and so far, I believe the successors in the policy of your friend Napoleon have reason on their side. Eh bien, mon ami, quand vous venez à Paris, nous nous mettrons à quatre épingles, et nous verrons toutes les merveilles de la cité, et vous en jugerez. God bless me, I beg your pardon! It comes so natural."

On the 30th he wrote to me that he had got his papers into order and hoped to begin that day. But the same letter told me of the unsettlement thus early of his half-formed Paris plans. Three months sooner than he designed he should be due in London for family reasons; should have to keep within the limit of four months abroad; and as his own house would not be free till July, would have to hire one from the end of March. "In these circumstances I think I shall send Charley to King's College after Christmas. I am sorry he should lose so much French, but don't you think to break another half-year's schooling would be a pity? Of my own will I would not send him to King's College at all, but to Bruce Castle instead. I suppose, however, Miss Coutts is best. We will talk over all this when I come to London." The offer to take charge of his eldest son's education had been pressed upon Dickens by this true friend, to whose delicate and noble consideration for him it would hardly become me to make other allusion here. Munificent as the kindness was, however, it was yet only the smallest part of the obligation which Dickens felt that he owed this lady; to whose generous schemes for the neglected and uncared-for classes of the population, in all which he deeply sympathised, he did the very utmost to render, through many years, unstinted service of time and labour, with sacrifices unselfish as her own. His proposed early visit to London named in this letter, was to see the rehearsal of his Christmas story, dramatised by Mr. Albert Smith for Mr. and Mrs. Keeley at the Lyceum; and my own proposed visit to Paris was to be in the middle of January. "It will then be the height of the season, and a good

time for testing the unaccountable French vanity which really
does suppose there are no fogs here, but that they are all in
London."

* 61

The opening of his next letter, which bore date 6
December, and its amusing sequel, will sufficiently speak for
themselves. "Cold intense. The water in the bedroom jugs
freezes into solid masses from top to bottom, bursts the jugs
with reports like small cannon, and rolls out on the tables
and wash-stands hard as granite. I stick to the shower-bath,
but have been most hopelessly out of sorts—writing sorts;
that's all. Couldn't begin, in the strange place; took a violent
dislike to my study, and came down into the drawing-room;
couldn't find a corner that would answer my purpose; fell into
a black contemplation of the waning month; sat six hours at
a stretch, and wrote as many lines, etc. . . . Then, you know
what arrangements are necessary with the chairs and tables;
and then what correspondence had to be cleared off; and then
how I tried to settle to my desk, and went about and about it,
and dodged at it, like a bird at a lump of sugar. In short I have
just begun; five printed pages finished, I should say; and hope
I shall be blessed with a better condition this next week, or
I shall be behindhand. I shall try to go at it—hard. I can't
do more. . . . There is rather a good man lives in this street,
and I have had a correspondence with him which is preserved
for your inspection. His name is Barthélemy. He wears a prodigious Spanish cloak, a slouched hat, an immense beard, and
long black hair. He called the other day, and left his card.
Allow me to enclose his card, which has originality and merit.

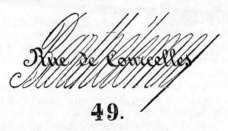

Roche said I wasn't at home. Yesterday, he wrote to me to say
that he too was a 'Littérateur'—that he had called, in compliment to my distinguished reputation—'qu'il n'avait pas été
reçu—qu'il n'était pas habitué à cette sorte de procédé—et

qu'il pria Monsieur Dickens d'oublier son nom, sa mémoire, sa carte, et sa visite, et de considérer qu'elle n'avait pas été rendu!' Of course I wrote him a very polite reply immediately, telling him good-humouredly that he was quite mistaken, and that there were always two weeks in the beginning of every month when M. Dickens ne pouvait rendre visite à personne. He wrote back to say that he was more than satisfied; that it was his case too, at the end of every month; and that when busy himself, he not only can't receive or pay visits, but—'tombe, généralement, aussi, dans des humeurs noires qui approchent de l'anthropophagie!!!' I think that's pretty well."

62 He was in London eight days, from 15 to 23 December; and among the occupations of his visit, besides launching his little story on the stage, was the settlement of form for a cheap edition of his writings, which began in the following year. It was to be printed in double columns, and issued weekly in three-halfpenny numbers; there were to be new prefaces, but no illustrations; and for each book something less than a fourth of the original price was to be charged. Its success was very good, but did not come even near to the mark of the later issues of his writings. His own feeling as to this, however, though any failure at the moment affected him on other grounds, was always that of a quiet confidence; and he had expressed this in a proposed dedication of this very edition, which for other reasons was ultimately laid aside. It will be worth preserving here. "This cheap edition of my books is dedicated to the English people, in whose approval, if the books be true in spirit, they will live, and out of whose memory, if they be false, they will very soon die."

Upon his return to Paris I had frequent report of his progress with his famous fifth number, on the completion of which I was to join him. The day at one time seemed doubtful. "It would be miserable to have to work while you were here. Still, I make such sudden starts, and am so possessed of what I am going to do, that the fear may prove to be quite groundless, and if any alteration would trouble you, let the 13th stand at all hazards." The cold he described as so intense, and the price of fuel so enormous, that though the house was not half warmed ("as you'll say, when you feel it"), it cost him very near a pound a day. Begging-letter writers had found out "Monsieur Dickens, le romancier célèbre," and waylaid him at the door and in the street as numerously as in London: their distinguishing peculiarity being that they were nearly all of them "Chevaliers de la Garde Impériale de sa Majesté Napoléon le Grand," and that their letters bore immense seals with coats of arms as large as five-shilling pieces. His friends the Watsons passed New Year's Day with him on their way to Rockingham from Lausanne, leaving that country covered with snow and the Bise blowing cruelly over it, but describing it as nothing to the cold of Paris. On the day that closed the old year he had gone into the Morgue and seen an old man with grey head lying there. "It seemed the strangest thing in the world that it should have been necessary to take any trouble to stop such a feeble, spent, exhausted morsel of life. It was just dusk when I went in; the place was empty; and he lay there, all alone, like an impersonation of the wintry eighteen hundred and forty-six. . . . I find I am getting inimitable, so I'll stop."

The time for my visit having come, I had grateful proof of the minute and thoughtful provision characteristic of him in everything. Dinner had been ordered to the second at Boulogne, a place in the *malle-poste* taken, and these and other services announced in a letter, which, by way of doing its part also in the kindly work of preparation, broke out into French. He never spoke that language very well, his accent being somehow defective; but he practised himself into writing it with remarkable ease and fluency. "I have written to the Hôtel des Bains at Boulogne to send on to Calais and take your place in the *malle-poste*. . . . Of course you know that you'll be assailed with frightful shouts all along the two lines of ropes, from all the touters in Boulogne, and of course you'll pass on like the princess who went up the mountain after the talking bird; but don't forget quietly to single out the Hôtel des Bains commissionnaire. The following circumstances will then occur. My experience is more recent than yours, and I will throw them into a dramatic form. . . . You are filtered into the little office, where there are some soldiers; and a gentleman with a black beard and a pen and ink sitting behind a counter. *Barbe Noire* (to the lord of L. I. F.). Monsieur, votre passeport. *Monsieur*. Monsieur, le voici! *Barbe Noire*. Où allez-vous, monsieur? *Monsieur*. Monsieur, je vais à Paris. *Barbe Noire*. Quand allez-vous partir, monsieur? *Monsieur*. Monsieur, je vais partir aujourd'hui. Avec la malle-poste. *Barbe Noire*. C'est bien. (To Gendarme.) Laissez sortir monsieur! *Gendarme*. Par ici, monsieur, s'il vous plaît. Le gendarme ouvre une très petite porte. Monsieur se trouve subitement entouré de tous les gamins, agents, commissionnaires, porteurs, et polissons, en général, de Boulogne, qui s'élancent sur lui, en poussant des cris épouvantables. Monsieur est, pour le moment, tout-à-fait effrayé, bouleversé. Mais monsieur reprend ses forces et dit, de haute voix: 'Le Commissionnaire de l'Hôtel des Bains!' *Un petit homme* (s'avançant rapidement, et en souriant doucement). Me voici, monsieur. Monsieur Fors Tair, n'est-ce pas? ... Alors ... Alors monsieur se promène à l'Hôtel des Bains, où monsieur trouvera qu'un petit salon particulier, en haut, est déjà préparé pour sa réception, et que son dîner est déjà commandé, grâce aux soins de brave Courier, à *midi et demi*. ... Monsieur mangera son dîner près du feu, avec beaucoup de plaisir, et il boira de vin rouge à la santé de Monsieur de Boze, et sa famille intéressante et aimable. La malle-poste arrivera au bureau de la poste aux lettres à deux heures ou peut-être un peu plus tard. Mais monsieur chargera le commissionnaire d'y l'accompagner de bonne heure, car c'est beaucoup mieux de l'attendre que de la perdre. La malle-poste arrivée, monsieur prendra sa place, aussi confortablement qu'il le pourra, et il y restera jusqu'à son arrivée au bureau de la poste aux lettres à Paris. Parceque, le convoi (*train*) n'est pas l'affaire de monsieur, qui gardera sa place dans la malle-poste, sur le chemin de fer, et après le chemin de fer, jusqu'il se trouve à la basse-cour du bureau de la poste aux lettres à Paris, où il trouvera une voiture qui a été dépêché de la Rue de Courcelles, quarante-huit. Mais monsieur aura la bonté d'observer—Si le convoi arriverait à Amiens après le départ du convoi à minuit, il faudrait y rester jusqu'à l'arrivée d'un autre convoi à trois heures moins un quart. En attendant, monsieur peut rester au buffet (*refreshment room*), où l'on peut toujours trouver un bon feu, et du café chaud, et de très bonnes choses à boire et à manger, pendant toute la nuit.—Est-ce que monsieur comprend parfaitement toutes ces règles?—Vive le Roi des Français! Roi de la nation plus grande, et la plus noble, et la plus extraordinairement merveilleuse, du monde! A bas les Anglais!

"CHARLES DICKENS,

"Français naturalisé, et Citoyen de Paris."

We passed a fortnight together, and crowded into it more than might seem possible to such a narrow space. With a dreadful insatiability we passed through every variety of sight-seeing, prisons, palaces, theatres, hospitals, the Morgue and the Lazare, as well as the Louvre, Versailles, St. Cloud, and all the spots made memorable by the first revolution. The excellent comedian Regnier, known to us through Macready and endeared by many

kindnesses, incomparable for his knowledge of the city and unwearying in friendly service, made us free of the green-room
of the Français, where, on the birthday of Molière, we saw his
Don Juan revived. At the Conservatoire we witnessed the
masterly teaching of Samson; at the Odéon saw a new play
by Ponsard, but done indifferently; at the Variétés *Gentil-
Bernard*, with four grisettes as if stepped out of a picture by
Watteau; at the Gymnase *Clarisse Harlowe*, with a death-scene
of Rose Chéri which comes back to me, through the distance
of time, as the prettiest piece of pure and gentle stage-pathos
in my memory; at the Porte St. Martin *Lucretia Borgia* by
Hugo; at the Cirque, scenes of the great revolution, and all the
battles of Napoleon; at the Comic Opera, *Gibby*; and at the
Palais Royal the usual new-year's piece, in which Alexandre
Dumas was shown in his study beside a pile of quarto volumes
five feet high, which proved to be the first tableau of the
first act of the first piece to be played on the first night of
his new theatre. That new theatre, the Historique, we also saw
verging to a very short-lived completeness; and we supped with
Dumas himself, and with Eugène Sue, and met Théophile Gautier
and Alphonse Karr. We saw Lamartine also, and had much
friendly intercourse with Scribe, and with the kind good-natured
Amédée Pichot. One day we visited in the Rue de Bac the sick
and ailing Chateaubriand, whom we thought like Basil Montagu;
found ourselves at the other extreme of opinion in the sculpture-
room of David d'Angers; and closed that day at the house of
Victor Hugo, by whom Dickens was received with infinite
courtesy and grace. The great writer then occupied in a floor a
noble corner-house in the Place Royale, the old quarter of
Ninon l'Enclos and the people of the Regency, of whom the
gorgeous tapestries, the painted ceilings, the wonderful carvings
and old golden furniture, including a canopy of state out of
some palace of the middle age, quaintly and grandly reminded
us. He was, himself, however, the best thing we saw; and I find
it difficult to associate the attitudes and aspect in which the
world has lately wondered at him, with the sober grace and
self-possessed quiet gravity of that night of twenty-five years
ago. Just then Louis Philippe had ennobled him, but the man's
nature was written noble. Rather under the middle size, of
compact close-buttoned-up figure, with ample dark hair falling
loosely over his close-shaven face, I never saw upon any features so keenly intellectual such a soft and sweet gentility, and
certainly never heard the French language spoken with the

picturesque distinctness given to it by Victor Hugo. He talked
of his childhood in Spain, and of his father having been Governor
of the Tagus in Napoleon's wars; spoke warmly of the English
people and their literature; declared his preference for melody
and simplicity over the music then fashionable at the Conservatoire; referred kindly to Ponsard, laughed at the actors
who had murdered his tragedy at the Odéon, and sympathised
with the dramatic venture of Dumas. To Dickens he addressed
very charming flattery, in the best taste; and my friend long
remembered the enjoyment of that evening.

There is little to add of our Paris holiday, if indeed too much
has not been said already. We had an adventure with a drunken
coachman, of which the sequel showed at least the vigour and
decisiveness of the police in regard to hired vehicles[1] in those
last days of the Orleans monarchy. At the Bibliothèque Royale
we were much interested by seeing, among many other priceless
treasures, Gutenberg's types, Racine's notes in his copy of
Sophocles, Rousseau's music, and Voltaire's note upon Frederick
of Prussia's letter. Nor should I omit that in what Dickens
then told me, of even his small experience of the social aspects
of Paris, there seemed but the same disease which raged afterwards through the second Empire. Not many days after I left,
all Paris was crowding to the sale of a lady of the demi-monde,
Marie Duplessis, who had led the most brilliant and abandoned
of lives, and left behind her the most exquisite furniture and

[1] Dickens's first letter after my return described it to me. "Do you
remember my writing a letter to the préfet of police about that coachman?
I heard no more about it until this very day" (12 February), "when, at
the moment of your letter arriving, Roche put his head in at the door
(I was busy writing in the Baronial drawing-room) and said, 'Here is
datter cocher!'—Sir, he had been in prison ever since! and being released
this morning, was sent by the police to pay back the franc and a half,
and to beg pardon, and to get a certificate that he had done so, or he
could not go on the stand again! Isn't this admirable? But the culminating
point of the story (it could happen with nobody but me) is that he was
DRUNK WHEN HE CAME!! Not very, but his eye was fixed, and he swayed
in his sabots, and smelt of wine, and told Roche incoherently that he
wouldn't have done it (committed the offence, that is) if the people hadn't
made him. He seemed to be troubled with a phantasmagorial belief that
all Paris had gathered around us that night in the Rue St. Honoré, and
urged him on with frantic shouts. . . . Snow, frost, and cold. . . . The
Duke of Bordeaux is very well, and dines at the Tuileries to-morrow. . . .
When I have done, I will write you a brilliant letter. . . . Loves from all,
. . . Your blue and golden bed looks desolate." The allusion to the Duc de
Bordeaux was to remind me pleasantly of a clip of his own during our
talk with Chateaubriand, when, at a loss to say something interesting to
the old royalist, he bethought him to inquire with sympathy when he
had last seen the representative of the elder branch of Bourbons, as if
he were resident in the city then and there!

the most voluptuous and sumptuous bijouterie. Dickens wished at one time to have pointed the moral of this life and death of which there was great talk in Paris while we were together. The disease of satiety, which only less often than hunger passes for a broken heart, had killed her. "What do you want?" asked the most famous of the Paris physicians, at a loss for her exact complaint. At last she answered: "To see my mother." She was sent for; and there came a simple Breton peasant-woman clad in the quaint garb of her province, who prayed by her bed until she died. Wonderful was the admiration and sympathy; and it culminated when Eugène Sue bought her prayer-book at the sale. Our last talk before I quitted Paris, after dinner at the Embassy, was of the danger underlying all this, and of the signs also visible everywhere of the Napoleon-worship which the Orleanists themselves had most favoured. Accident brought Dickens to England a fortnight later, when again we met together, at Gore House, the self-contained reticent man whose doubtful inheritance was thus rapidly preparing to fall to him.

* 63

The accident was the having underwritten his number of *Dombey* by two pages, which there was not time to supply otherwise than by coming to London to write them. This was * 64 done accordingly; but another, greater trouble followed. He had hardly returned to Paris when his eldest son, whom I had brought to England with me and placed in the house of Doctor Major, then headmaster of King's College School, was attacked by scarlet fever; and this closed prematurely Dickens's residence in Paris. But though he and his wife at once came over, and were followed after some days by the children and their aunt, the isolation of the little invalid could not so soon be broken through. His father at last saw him, nearly a month before the rest, in a lodging in Albany Street, where his grandmother, Mrs. Hogarth, had devoted herself to the charge of him; and an incident of the visit, which amused us all very much, will not unfitly introduce the subject that waits me in my next chapter.

An elderly charwoman employed about the place had shown so much sympathy in the family trouble, that Mrs. Hogarth specially told her of the approaching visit, and who it was that was coming to the sick-room. "Lawk ma'am!" she said. "Is the young gentleman upstairs the son of the man that put together *Dombey*?" Reassured upon this point, she explained her question by declaring that she never thought there was a man that *could* have put together *Dombey*. Being pressed further as to what her notion was of this mystery of a *Dombey* (for it was known she could not read), it turned out that she lodged at a snuff-shop kept by a person named Douglas, where there were several other lodgers; and that on the first Monday of every month there was a Tea, and the landlord read the month's number of *Dombey*, those only of the lodgers who subscribed to the tea partaking of that luxury, but all having the benefit of the reading; and the impression produced on the old char-woman revealed itself in the remark with which she closed her account of it. "Lawk ma'am! I thought that three or four men must have put together *Dombey*!" Dickens thought there was something of a compliment in this, and was not ungrateful.

END OF VOL. I

AUTHOR'S ADDITIONAL FOOTNOTES

* 1 (p. 4). 'I shall cut this letter short, for they are playing Masaniello in the drawing-room, and I feel much as I used to do when I was a small child a few miles off, and Somebody (who I wonder, and which way did *She* go, when she died) hummed the evening hymn to me, and I cried on the pillow —either with the remorseful consciousness of having kicked Somebody else, or because still Somebody else had hurt my feelings in the course of the day.' From Gadshill, 24th September 1857. 'Being here again, or as much here as anywhere in particular.'

* 2 (p. 6). 'The mistress of the establishment holds no place in our memory; but, rampant on one eternal door-mat, in an eternal entry long and narrow, is a puffy pug-dog, with a personal animosity towards us, who triumphs over Time. The bark of that baleful Pug, a certain radiating way he had of snapping at our undefended legs, the ghastly grinning of his moist black muzzle and white teeth, and the insolence of his crisp tail curled like a pastoral crook, all live and flourish. From an otherwise unaccountable association of him with a fiddle, we conclude that he was of French extraction, and his name Fidèle. He belonged to some female, chiefly inhabiting a back parlour, whose life appears to us to have been consumed in sniffing, and in wearing a brown beaver bonnet.' *Reprinted Pieces.*

* 3 (p. 14). The reader will forgive my quoting from a letter of the date of 22nd April 1848. 'I desire no better for my fame, when my personal dustiness shall be past the control of my love of order, than such a biographer and such a critic.' 'You know me better', he wrote, resuming the same subject on 6th July 1862, 'than any other man does, or ever will.' In an entry of my diary during the interval between these years, I find a few words that not only mark the time when I first saw in its connected shape the autobiographical fragment which will form the substance of the second chapter of this biography, but also express his own feeling respecting it when written. '20 January, 1849. The description may make none of the impression on others that the reality made on him. . . . Highly probable that it may never see the light. No wish. Left to J.F. or others.' The first number of *David Copperfield* appeared five months after this date; but though I knew, even before he adapted his fragment of autobiography to the eleventh number, that he had now abandoned the notion of completing it under his own name, the '*no wish*', or the discretion left me, was never in any way subsequently modified. What follows, from the same entry, refers to the manuscript of the fragment. 'No blotting, as when writing fiction; but straight on, as when writing ordinary letter.'

* 4 (p. 48). I take other fanciful allusions to the lady [Dora] from two of his occasional writings. The first from his visit to the city churches (written during the Dombey time, when he had to select a church for the marriage of Florence): 'Its drowsy cadence soon lulls the three old women asleep, and the unmarried tradesman sits looking out at window, and the married tradesman sits looking at his wife's bonnet, and the lovers sit looking at one another, so superlatively happy, that I mind when I, turned of eighteen, went with my Angelica to a city church on account of a shower (by this special coincidence that it was in Huggin-lane), and when I said to my Angelica, "Let the blessed event, Angelica, occur at no altar but this!"

and when my Angelica commented that it should occur at no other—which it certainly never did, for it never occurred anywhere. And O, Angelica, what has become of you, this present Sunday morning when I can't attend to the sermon; and, more difficult question than that, what has become of Me as I was when I sat by your side!' The second, from his pleasant paper on birthdays: 'I gave a party on the occasion. She was there. It is unnecessary to name Her, more particularly; She was older than I, and had pervaded every chink and crevice of my mind for three or four years. I had held volumes of Imaginary Conversations with her mother on the subject of our union, and I had written letters more in number than Horace Walpole's, to that discreet woman, soliciting her daughter's hand in marriage. I had never had the remotest intention of sending any of those letters; but to write them, and after a few days tear them up, had been a sublime occupation.'

* 5 (p. 57). To this date belongs a visit paid him at Furnival's Inn in Mr Macrone's company, by the notorious Mr N. P. Willis, who calls him 'a young paragraphist for the *Morning Chronicle*', and thus sketches his residence and himself. 'In the most crowded part of Holborn, within a door or two of the Bull-and-mouth inn, we pulled up at the entrance of a large building used for lawyers' chambers. I followed by a long flight of stairs to an upper storey, and was ushered into an uncarpeted and bleak-looking room, with a deal table, two or three chairs and a few books, a small boy and Mr Dickens, for the contents. I was only struck at first with one thing (and I made a memorandum of it that evening as the strongest instance I had seen of English obsequiousness to employers), the degree to which the poor author was overpowered with the honour of his publisher's visit! I remember saying to myself, as I sat down on a ricketty chair: "My good fellow, if you were in America with that fine face and your ready quill, you would have no need to be condescended to by a publisher." Dickens was dressed very much as he has since described Dick Swiveller, *minus* the swell look. His hair was cropped close to his head, his clothes scant, though jauntily cut, and after changing a ragged office-coat for a shabby blue, he stood by the door, collarless and buttoned up, the very personifation, I thought, of a "close sailer to the wind".' I remember, while my friend lived, our laughing heartily at this description, hardly a word of which is true; and I give it now as no unfair specimen of the kind of garbage that since his death also has been served up only too plentifully, by some of his own as well as by others of Mr Willis's countrymen.

* 6 (p. 59). 'It is with great unwillingness that I notice some intangible and incoherent assertions which have been made, professedly on behalf of Mr Seymour, to the effect that he had some share in the invention of this book, or of anything in it, not faithfully described in the foregoing paragraph. With the moderation that is due equally to my respect for the memory of a brother-artist, and to my self-respect, I confine myself to placing on record here the facts—That, Mr Seymour never originated or suggested an incident, a phrase, or a word, to be found in this book. That, Mr Seymour died when only twenty-four pages of this book were published, and when assuredly not forty-eight were written. That, I believe I never saw Mr Seymour's hand-writing in my life. That, I never saw Mr Seymour but once in my life, and that was on the night but one before his death, when he certainly offered no suggestion whatsoever. That, I saw him then in the presence of two persons, both living, perfectly acquainted with all these facts, and whose written testimony to them I possess. Lastly, that Mr Edward Chapman (the survivor of the original firm of Chapman and Hall) has set down in writing, for similar preservation, his personal knowledge of the origin and progress of this book, of the monstrosity of the baseless assertions in question, and (tested by details) even of the self-evident impossibility of there being any truth in them.'

* 7 (p. 60). Whether Mr Chapman spelt the name correctly, or has un-consciously deprived his fat beau of the letter 'r', I cannot say; but experience tells me that the latter is probable. I have been trying all my life to get my own name spelt correctly, and have only very imperfectly succeeded.

* 8 (p. 79). The allusion was to the supposed author of a paper in the *Quarterly Review* (October 1837), in the course of which there was much high praise, but where the writer said at the close: 'Indications are not wanting that the particular vein of humour which has hitherto yielded so much attractive metal, is worked out. . . . The fact is, Mr Dickens writes too often and too fast. . . . If he persists much longer in this course, it requires no gift of prophecy to foretell his fate—he has risen like a rocket, and he will come down like the stick.'

* 9 (p. 85). There is an earlier allusion I may quote, from a letter in January, for its mention of a small piece written by him at this time, but not included in his acknowledged writings. 'I am as badly off as you. I have not done the *Young Gentlemen*, nor written the preface to *Grimaldi*, nor thought of *Oliver Twist*, or even supplied a subject for the plate.' The *Young Gentlemen* was a small book which he wrote as the companion to a similar half-crown volume of *Young Ladies* (not written by him), for Messrs Chapman and Hall. He had before written for them, without his name, *Sunday under Three Heads*; and he added subsequently a volume of *Young Couples*.

* 10 (p. 87). Here is another of the same month: 'All day I have been at work on *Oliver*, and hope to finish the chapter by bed time. I wish you'd let me know what Sir Francis Burdett has been saying about him at some Birmingham meeting. B. has just sent me the *Courier* containing some reference to his speech; but the speech I haven't seen.'

* 11 (p. 93). Upon receiving this letter I gently reminded him that I had made objection at the time to the arrangement on the failure of which he empowered me to bring about the settlement it was now proposed to super-sede. I cannot give his reply, as it would be unbecoming to repeat the warmth of its expression to myself, but I preserve its first few lines to guard against any possible future misstatement. 'If you suppose that anything in my letter could by the utmost latitude of construction imply the smallest dissatisfaction on my part, for God's sake dismiss such a thought from your mind. I have never had a momentary approach to doubt or discontent where you have been mediating for me. . . . I could say more, but you would think me foolish and rhapsodical; and such feeling as I have for you is better kept within one's own breast than vented in imperfect and inexpressive words.'

* 12 (p. 99). I cannot call to mind now how I came to hear about Yorkshire schools when I was a not very robust child, sitting in bye-places near Rochester-castle, with a head full of Partridge, Strap, Tom Pipes and Sancho Panza; but I know that my first impressions of them were picked up at that time.'

* 13 (p. 101). Moore in his *Diary* (April 1837) describes Sydney [Smith] crying down Dickens at a dinner in the Row, 'and evidently without having given him a fair trial'.

* 14 (p. 103). This portrait [by Maclise] was given to Dickens by his publishers, for whom it was painted with a view to an engraving for *Nickleby*, which, however, was poorly executed, and of a size too small to do the original any kind of justice. . . . 'As a likeness', said Mr Thackeray of the work, and no higher praise could be given to it, 'it is perfectly amazing. A looking-glass could not render a better fac-simile. We have here the real identical man Dickens, the inward as well as the outward of him.'

* 15 (p. 105). We had at Twickenham a balloon club for the children, of which I appear to have been elected the president on condition of supplying all the balloons, a condition which I seem so insufficiently to have complied with as to bring down upon myself the subjoined resolution. The Snodgering Blee and Popem Jee were the little brother and sister, for whom, as for their successors, he was always inventing these surprising descriptive epithets. 'Gammon Lodge, Saturday evening, June 23rd, 1838. Sir, I am requested to inform you that at a numerous meeting of the Gammon Aeronautical Association for the Encouragement of Science and the Consumption of Spirits (of Wine)—Thomas Beard Esquire, Mrs Charles Dickens, Charles Dickens Esquire, the Snodgering Blee, Popem Jee, and other distinguished characters being present and assenting, the vote of censure of which I enclose a copy was unanimously passed upon you for gross negligence in the discharge of your duty, and most unjustifiable disregard of the best interests of the Society. I am, Sir, your most obedient Servant, Charles Dickens, Honorary Secretary. To John Forster, Esquire.'

* 16 (p. 106). I quote from a letter dated Llangollen, Friday morning, 3rd November 1838. 'I wrote to you last night, but by mistake the letter has gone on Heaven knows where in my portmanteau. I have only time to say, go straight to Liverpool by the first Birmingham train on Monday morning, and at the Adelphi hotel in that town you will find me. I trust to you to see my dear Kate, and bring the latest intelligence of her and the darlings. My best love to them.'

* 17 (p. 107). One of these disputes is referred to by Charles Knight in his autobiography; and I see in Dickens's letters the mention of another in which I seem to have been turned by his kindly counsel from some folly I was going to commit. 'I need not, I am sure, impress upon you the sincerity with which I make this representation. Our close and hearty friendship happily spares me the necessity. But I will add this—that feeling for you an attachment which no ties of blood or other relationship could ever awaken, and hoping to be to the end of my life your affectionate and chosen friend, I am convinced that I counsel you now as you would counsel me if I were in the like case; and I hope and trust that you will be led by an opinion which I am sure cannot be wrong when it is influenced by such feelings as I bear towards you, and so many warm and grateful considerations.'

* 18 (p. 109). This was the butler of Mr Gilbert Winter, one of the kind Manchester friends whose hospitality we had enjoyed with Mr Ainsworth, and whose shrewd, quaint, old-world ways come delightfully back to me as I write his once well-known and widely honoured name.

* 19 (p. 117). I have mentioned the fact in my Life of Landor; and to the passage I here add the comment made by Dickens when he read it. 'It was at a celebration of his birthday in the first of his Bath lodgings, 35 St James's square, that the fancy which took the form of little Nell in the Curiosity Shop first dawned on the genius of its creator. No character in prose fiction was a greater favourite with Landor. He thought that, upon her, Juliet might for a moment have turned her eyes from Romeo, and that Desdemona might have taken her hairbreadth escapes to heart, so interesting and pathetic did she seem to him; and when, some years later, the circumstance I have named was recalled to him, he broke into one of those whimsical bursts of comical extravagance out of which arose the fancy of Boythorn. With tremendous emphasis he confirmed the fact, and added

that he had never in his life regretted anything so much as his having failed to carry out an intention he had formed respecting it; for he meant to have purchased that house, 35 St James's-square, and then and there to have burnt it to the ground, to the end that no meaner association should ever desecrate the birthplace of Nell. Then he would pause a little, become conscious of our sense of his absurdity, and break into a thundering peal of laughter.' Dickens had himself proposed to tell this story as a contribution to my biography of our common friend, but his departure for America prevented him. 'I see', he wrote to me, as soon as the published book reached him, 'you have told, with what our friend would have called *wonderful* accuracy, the little St James's-square story, which a certain faithless wretch was to have related.'

* 20 (p. 132). By way of a novelty to help off the stock [of *Oliver*] he had suggested (17th June): 'Would it not be best to print new title-pages to the copies in sheets and publish them as a new edition, with an interesting Preface? I am talking about all this as though the treaty were concluded, but I hope and trust that in effect it is, for negotiation and delay are worse to me than drawn daggers.'

* 21 (p. 152). On this occasion, as he told me afterwards, the orchestra did a double stroke of business, much to the amazement of himself and his friends, by improvizing at his entrance 'Charley is my Darling', amid tumultuous shouts of delight.

* 22 (p. 154). Poor good Mr Fletcher had, among his other peculiarities, a habit of venting any particular emotion in a wildness of cry that went beyond even the descriptive power of his friend, who referred to it frequently in his Broadstairs letters. Here is an instance (20th September 1840): 'Mrs M. being in the next machine the other day heard him howl like a wolf (as he does) when he first touched the cold water. I am glad to have my former story in that respect confirmed. There is no sound on earth like it. In the infernal regions there may be, but elsewhere there is no compound addition of wild beasts that could produce its like for their total. The description of the wolves in *Robinson Crusoe* is the nearest thing; but it's feeble—very feeble—in comparison.' Of the generally amiable side to all his eccentricities I am tempted to give an illustration from the same letter. 'An alarming report being brought to me the other day that he was preaching, I betook myself to the spot and found he was reading Wordsworth to a family on the terrace, outside the house, in the open air and public way. The whole town were out. When he had given them a taste of Wordsworth, he sent home for Mrs Norton's book, and entertained them with selections from that. He concluded with an imitation of Mrs Hemans reading her own poetry, which he performed with a pocket-handkerchief over his head to imitate her veil—all this in public, before everybody.'

* 23 (p. 167). 'M. was quite aghast last night (9th of September) at the brilliancy of the C. & H. arrangement: which is worth noting perhaps.'

* 24 (p. 180). This word [Inimitable], applied to him by his old master, Mr Giles, was for a long time the epithet we called him by.

* 25 (p. 184). His descriptions of this school, and of the case of Laura Bridgeman, will be found in *American Notes*; and have therefore been, of course, omitted here.

* 26 (p. 196). The dinner was on 10th May, and early the following morning I had a letter about it from Mr Blanchard, containing these words: 'Washington Irving couldn't utter a word for trembling, and Moore was as little as usual. But, poor Tom Campbell, great Heavens! what a spectacle! Amid roars of laughter he began a sentence three times about something that Dugald Stewart or Lord Bacon had said, and never could get beyond those words. The Prince was capital, though deucedly frightened. He seems unaffected and amiable, as well as very clever.'

* 26A (p. 205). The ship next in rotation to the *Caledonia* from Liverpool.

* 27 (p. 218). At his second visit to America, when in Washington in February 1868, Dickens, replying to a letter in which Irving was named, thus describes the last meeting and leave-taking to which he alludes above. 'Your reference to my dear friend, Washington Irving, renews the vivid impressions reawakened in my mind at Baltimore but the other day. I saw his fine face for the last time in that city. He came there from New York to pass a day or two with me before I went westward; and they were made among the most memorable of my life by his delightful fancy and genial humour. Some unknown admirer of his books and mine sent to the hotel a most enormous mint-julep, wreathed with flowers. We sat, one on either side of it, with great solemnity (it filled a respectably-sized round table), but the solemnity was of very short duration. It was quite an enchanted julep, and carried us among innumerable people and places that we both knew. The julep held out far into the night, and my memory never saw him afterwards otherwise than as bending over it, with his straw, with an attempted air of gravity (after some anecdote involving some wonderfully droll and delicate observation of character), and then, as his eye caught mine, melting into that captivating laugh of his, which was the brightest and best I have ever heard.'

* 28 (p. 235). A young lady's account of this party, written next morning, and quoted in one of the American memoirs of Dickens, enables us to contemplate his suffering from the point of view of those who inflicted it. 'I went last evening to a party at Judge Walker's, given to the hero of the day. . . . When we reached the house Mr Dickens had left the crowded rooms, and was in the hall with his wife, about taking his departure when we entered the door. We were introduced to him in our wrapping; and in the flurry and embarrassment of the meeting, one of the party dropped a parcel, containing shoes, gloves, &c. Mr Dickens, stooping, gathered them up and restored them with a laughing remark, and we bounded upstairs to get our things off. Hastening down again, we found him with Mrs Dickens seated upon a sofa, surrounded by a group of ladies; Judge Walker having requested him to delay his departure for a few moments, for the gratification of some tardy friends who had just arrived, ourselves among the number. Declining to re-enter the rooms where he had already taken leave of the guests, he had seated himself in the hall. He is young and handsome, has a mellow, beautiful eye, fine brow and abundant hair. His mouth is large, and his smile so bright it seemed to shed light and happiness all about him. His manner is easy, negligent, but not elegant. His dress was foppish; in fact, he was overdressed, yet his garments were worn so easily they appeared to be a necessary part of him. He had a dark coat, with lighter pantaloons; a black waistcoat, embroidered with colored flowers; and about his neck, covering his white shirt-front, was a black neckcloth, also embroidered in colors, in which were placed two large diamond pins connected by a chain. A gold watch-chain, and a large red rose in his button-hole, completed his toilet. He appeared a little weary, but answered the remarks made to him— for he originated none—in an agreeable manner. Mr Beard's portrait of Fagin was so placed in the room that we could see it from where we stood surrounding him. One of the ladies asked him if it was his idea of the Jew. He replied, "Very nearly." Another, laughingly, requested that he would give her the rose he wore, as a memento. He shook his head and said: "That will not do; he could not give it to one; the others would be jealous." A half dozen then insisted on having it, whereupon he proposed to divide the leaves among them. In taking the rose from his coat, either by design or accident, the leaves loosened and fell upon the floor, and amid considerable laughter the ladies stooped and gathered them. He remained some twenty minutes, perhaps, in the hall, and then took his leave. I must confess to considerable disappointment in the personal of my idol. I felt that his throne was shaken, although it never could be destroyed.' This appalling picture supplements and very sufficiently explains the mournful passage in the text.

* 29 (p. 238). 'Runaway Negro in Jail' was the heading of the advertisement enclosed, which had a woodcut of master and slave in its corner, and announced that Wilford Garner, sheriff and jailer of Chicot County, Arkansas, requested owner to come and prove property—or—

* 30 (p. 272). Printed in the *Atlantic Monthly* shortly after his death, and since collected, by Mr James T. Fields of Boston, with several of later date addressed to himself, and much correspondence having reference to other writers, into a pleasing volume entitled *Yesterdays with Authors*.

* 31 (p. 275). In one of the letters to his American friend Mr Felton there is a glimpse of Christmas sports which had escaped my memory, and for which a corner may be found here, inasmuch as these gambols were characteristic of him at the pleasant old season, and were frequently renewed in future years. 'The best of it is' (31st December 1842) 'that Forster and I have purchased between us the entire stock-in-trade of a conjuror, the practice and display whereof is entrusted to me. . . . In those tricks which require a confederate I am assisted (by reason of his imperturbable good humour) by Stanfield, who always does his part exactly the wrong way, to the unspeakable delight of all beholders. We come out on a small scale tonight, at Forster's, where we see the old year out and the new one in.' *Atlantic Monthly*, July 1871.

* 31A (p. 281). C.D. to Professor Felton (1st September 1843). *Atlantic Monthly*, July 1871.

* 32 (p. 292). Chuffey. Sydney Smith had written to Dickens on the appearance of his fourth number (early in April): 'Chuffey is admirable. . . . I never read a finer piece of writing: it is deeply pathetic and affecting.'

* 33 (p. 299). It may interest the reader, and be something of a curiosity of literature, if I give the expenses of the first edition of 6,000, and of the 7,000 more which constituted the five following editions, with the profit of the remaining 2,000 which completed the sale of 15,000:

CHRISTMAS CAROL

1st Edition, 6,000 No.

		£	s.	d.
Dec. 1843.	Printing	74	2	9
	Paper	89	2	0
	Drawings and Engravings	49	18	0
	Two Steel Plates	1	4	0
	Printing Plates	15	17	6
	Paper for *do.*	7	12	0
	Colouring Plates	120	0	0
	Binding	180	0	0
	Incidents and Advertising	168	7	8
	Commission	99	4	6
		£805	8	5

2nd to the 7th Edition, making 7,000 Copies.

		£	s.	d.
Jan. 1844.	Printing	58	18	0
	Paper	103	19	0
	Printing Plates	17	10	0
	Paper	8	17	4
	Colouring Plates	140	0	0
	Binding	199	18	2
	Incidents and Advertising	83	5	8
	Commission	107	18	10
		£720	7	0

Two thousand more, represented by the last item in the subjoined balance, were sold before the close of the year, leaving a remainder of 70 copies.

			£	s.	d.
Dec. 1843	Balance of a/c to Mr Dickens's credit		186	16	7
Jan. to April 1844.	do.	do.	349	12	0
May to Dec. 1844.	do.	do.	189	11	5
	Amount of Profit on the Work		£726	0	0

* 34 (p. 301). A characteristic letter of this date, which will explain itself, has been kindly sent to me by the gentleman it was written to, Mr James Verry Staples, of Bristol: 'Third of April, 1844. I have been very much gratified by the receipt of your interesting letter, and I assure you that it would have given me heartfelt satisfaction to have been in your place when you read my little *Carol* to the Poor in your neighbourhood. I have great faith in the poor; to the best of my ability I always endeavour to present them in a favourable light to the rich; and I shall never cease, I hope, until I die, to advocate their being made as happy and as wise as the circumstances of their condition, in its utmost improvement, will admit of their becoming. I mention this to assure you of two things. Firstly, that I try to deserve their attention; and secondly, that any such marks of their approval and confidence as you relate to me are most acceptable to my feelings, and go at once to my heart.'

* 35 (p. 305). In a letter on the subject of copyright published by Thomas Hood after Dickens's return from America, he described what had passed between himself and one of these pirates who had issued a *Master Humphrey's Clock* edited by Bos. 'Sir,' said the man to Hood, 'if you had observed the name, it was *Bos*, not *Boz*; s, sir, not z; and, besides, it would have been no piracy, sir, even with the z, because *Master Humphrey's Clock*, you see, sir, was not published as by Boz, but by Charles Dickens!'

* 36 (p. 315). He regretted one chance missed by his eccentric friend, which he described to me just before he left Italy. 'I saw last night an old palazzo of the Doria, six miles from here, upon the sea, which De la Rue urged Fletcher to take for us, when he was bent on that detestable villa Bagnerello; which villa the Genoese have hired, time out of mind, for one fourth of what I paid, as they told him again and again before he made the agreement. This is one of the strangest old palaces in Italy, surrounded by beautiful *woods* of great trees (an immense rarity here) some miles in extent: and has upon the terrace a high tower, formerly a prison for offenders

against the family, and a defence against the pirates. The present Doria lets it as it stands for £40 English—for the year. . . . And the grounds are no expense; being proudly maintained by the Doria, who spends this rent, when he gets it, in repairing the roof and windows. It is a wonderful house; full of the most unaccountable pictures and most incredible furniture: every room in it like the most quaint and fanciful of Cattermole's pictures; and how many rooms I am afraid to say.' 2nd June 1845.

* 37 (p. 329). A characteristic message for Jerrold came in a later letter (12th May 1845): 'I wish you would suggest to Jerrold for me as a Caudle subject (if he pursue that idea), "Mr Caudle has incidentally remarked that the housemaid is good-looking".'

* 38 (p. 330). Of the dangers of the bay he had before written to me (10th August). 'A monk was drowned here on Saturday evening. He was bathing with two other monks, who bolted when he cried out that he was sinking— in consequence, I suppose, of his certainty of going to Heaven.'

* 39 (p. 350). The last two lines he has printed in *Pictures from Italy*, p. 249, 'certain of' being inserted before 'his employers'.

* 40 (p. 353). I find the evening mentioned in the diary which Mr Barham's son quotes in his Memoir. 'December 5, 1844. Dined at Forster's with Charles Dickens, Stanfield, Maclise, and Albany Fonblanque. Dickens read with remarkable effect his Christmas story, the *Chimes*, from the proofs. . . .'

* 41 (p. 357). 'A Yorkshireman, who talks Yorkshire Italian with the drollest and pleasantest effect; a jolly, hospitable excellent fellow; as odd yet kindly a mixture of shrewdness and simplicity as I have ever seen. He is the only Englishman in these parts who has been able to erect an English household out of Italian servants, but he has done it to admiration. It would be a capital country-house at home; and for staying in "first-rate". (I find myself inadvertently quoting *Tom Thumb*.) Mr Walton is a man of an extraordinarily kind heart, and has a compassionate regard for Fletcher to whom his house is open as a home, which is half affecting and half ludicrous. He paid the other day a hundred pounds for him, which he knows he will never see a penny of again.' C. D. to J. F. (25th January 1845.)

* 42 (p. 358). 'Do you think', he wrote from Ronciglione on 29th January, 'in your state room, when the fog makes your white blinds yellow, and the wind howls in the brick and mortar gulf behind that square perspective, with a middle distance of two ladder-tops and a back-ground of Drury-lane sky—when the wind howls, I say, as if its eldest brother, born in Lincoln's-inn-fields, had gone to sea and was making a fortune on the Atlantic—at such times do you ever think of houseless Dick?'

* 43 (p. 360). 'Thackeray praised the people of Italy for being kind to brutes. There is probably no country in the world where they are treated with such frightful cruelty. It is universal.' (Naples, 2nd February 1845.) Emphatic confirmation of this remark has been given by the Naples correspondent of *The Times*, writing under date of February 1872.

* 44 (p. 363). One message sent me, though all to whom it refers have now passed away, I please myself by thinking may still, where he might most have desired it, be the occasion of pleasure. '. . . Give my love to Colden, and tell him if he leaves London before I return I will ever more address him and speak of him as *Colonel* Colden. Kate sends *her* love to him also, and we both entreat him to say all the affectionate things he can spare for third parties—using so many himself—when he writes to Mrs Colden: whom you ought to know, for she, as I have often told you, is BRILLIANT. I would go

five hundred miles to see her for five minutes. I am deeply grieved by poor Felton's loss. His letter is manly, and of a most rare kind in the dignified composure and silence of his sorrow.'

* 45 (p. 372). Count d'Orsay's note about Roche, replying to Dickens's recommendation of him at his return, has touches of the pleasantry, wit and kindliness that gave such a wonderful fascination to its writer. 'Gore House, 6 July, 1845. MON CHER DICKENS, Nous sommes enchantés de votre retour. Voici, thank God, Devonshire Place ressuscité. Venez luncheoner demain à 1 heure, et amenez notre brave ami Forster. J'attends la perle fine des couriers. Vous l'immortalisez par ce certificat—la difficulté sera de trouver un maître digne de lui. J'essayerai de tout mon cœur. La Reine devroit le prendre pour aller en Saxe Gotha, car je suis convaincu qu'il est assez intelligent pour pouvoir découvrir ce Royaume. Gore House vous envoye un cargo d'amitiés des plus sincères. Donnez de ma part 100,000 kind regards à Madame Dickens. Toujours votre affectionné, Cᵉ D'ORSAY. J'ai vu le courier, c'est le tableau de l'honnêteté, et de la bonne humeur. Don't forget to be here at one tomorrow, with Forster.'

* 46 (p. 375). 'Look here! Enclosed are two packets—a large one and a small one. The small one, read first. It contains Stanny's renunciation as an actor!!! After receiving it, at dinner time today' (22nd August), 'I gave my brains a shake, and thought of George Cruikshank. After much shaking, I made up the big packet, wherein I have put the case in the artfullest manner. R-r-r-r-read it! as a certain Captain whom you know observes.' The great artist was not for that time procurable, having engagements away from London, and Mr Dudley Costello was substituted; Stanfield taking off the edge of his desertion as an actor by doing valuable work in management and scenery.

* 47 (p. 386). 'The green woods and green shades about here', he says in another letter, 'are more like Cobham in Kent, than anything we dream of at the foot of the Alpine passes.'

* 48 (p. 388). To these the heat interposed occasional difficulties. 'Setting off last night' (5th July) 'at six o'clock, in accordance with my usual custom, for a long walk, I was really quite floored when I got to the top of a long steep hill leading out of the town—the same by which we entered it. I believe the great heats, however, seldom last more than a week at a time; there are always very long twilights, and very delicious evenings; and now that there is moonlight, the nights are wonderful. The peacefulness and grandeur of the Mountains and the Lake are indescribable. There comes a rush of sweet smells with the morning air too, which is quite peculiar to the country.'

* 49 (p. 389). 'One of her [Mrs Cerjat's] brothers by the bye, now dead, had large property in Ireland—all Nenagh, and the country about; and Cerjat told me, as we were talking about one thing and another, that when he went over there for some months to arrange the widow's affairs, he procured a copy of the curse which had been read at the altar by the parish priest of Nenagh, against any of the flock who didn't subscribe to the O'Connell tribute.'

* 50 (p. 390) In a note may be preserved another passage from the same letter. 'I have been queer and had trembling legs for the last week. But it has been almost impossible to sleep at night. There is a breeze today (25th July) and I hope another storm is coming up. . . . There is a theatre here; and whenever a troop of players pass through the town, they halt for a night and act. On the day of our tremendous dinner party of eight, there was an infant phenomenon; whom I should otherwise have seen. Last night there

was a Vaudeville company; and Charley, Roche and Anne went. The Brave reports the performances to have resembled Greenwich Fair. . . . There are some Promenade Concerts in the open air in progress now; but as they are just above one part of our garden we don't go; merely sitting outside the door instead, and hearing it all where we are. . . . Mont Blanc has been very plain lately. One heap of snow. A Frenchman got to the top, the other day.'

* 51 (p. 395). This was an abstract, in plain language for the use of his children, of the narrative in the four Gospels. Allusion was made, shortly after his death, to the existence of such a manuscript, with expression of a wish that it might be published; but nothing would have shocked himself so much as any suggestion of that kind. The little piece was of a peculiarly private character, written for his children, and exclusively and strictly for their use only.

* 52 (p. 395). So he described it. 'I do not think', he adds, 'we could have fallen on better society. It is a small circle certainly, but quite large enough. The Watsons improve very much on acquaintance. Everybody is very well informed; and we are all as social and friendly as people can be, and very merry. We play whist with great dignity and gravity sometimes, interrupted only by the occasional facetiousness of the Inimitable.'

* 53 (p. 398). The close of this letter sent family remembrances in characteristic form. 'Kate, Georgy, Mamey, Katey, Charley, Walley, Chickenstalker and Sampson Brass, commend themselves unto your Honour's loving remembrance.' The last but one, who continued long to bear the name, was Frank; the last, who very soon will be found to have another, was Alfred.

* 54 (p. 402). Poor fellow! He [Roche] had latent disease of the heart, which developed itself rapidly on Dickens's return to England.

* 55 (p. 404). Out of the excitements consequent on the public festivities arose some domestic inconveniences. I will give one of them. 'Fanchette the cook, distracted by the forthcoming fête, madly refused to buy a duck yesterday as ordered by the Brave [Roche], and a battle of life ensued between those two powers. The Brave is of opinion that "datter woman have went mad". But she seems calm today; and I suppose won't poison the family. . . .'

* 56 (p. 410). Ten days before there had been a visit from Mr Ainsworth and his daughters on their way to Geneva. 'I breakfasted with him at the hotel Gibbon next morning and they dined here afterwards, and we walked about all day, talking of our old days at Kensal-lodge.' The same letter told me: 'We had a regatta at Ouchy the other day, mainly supported by the contributions of the English handfull. It concluded with a rowing-match by women, which was very funny. I wish you could have seen Roche appear on the Lake, rowing, in an immense boat, Cook, Anne, two nurses, Katey, Mamey, Walley, Chickenstalker and Baby, no boatmen or other degrading assistance; and all sorts of Swiss tubs splashing about them. . . . Senior is coming here tomorrow, I believe, with his wife; and they talk of Brunel and his wife as on their way. We dine at Haldimand's to meet Senior—which solitary and most interesting piece of intelligence is all the news I know of. . . . Take care you don't back out of your Paris engagement; but that we really do have (please God) some happy hours there. Kate, Georgy, Mamey, Katey, Charley, Walley, Chickenstalker and Baby, send loves. . . . I am all anxiety and fever to know what we start Dombey with!'

* 57 (p. 412). This was the fourth Baron Vernon, who succeeded to the title in 1829, and died seven years after the date of Dickens's description, in his seventy-fourth year.

* 58 (p. 420). Writing on Sunday he had said: 'I hope to finish the second number tomorrow, and to send it off bodily by Tuesday's post. On Wednesday I purpose, please God, beginning the *Battle of Life*. I shall peg away at that, without turning aside to *Dombey* again; and *if* I can only do it within the month!' I had to warn him, on receiving these intimations, that he was trying too much.

* 59 (p. 420). The storm of rain formerly mentioned by him had not been repeated, but the weather had become unsettled, and he thus referred to the rainfall which made that summer so disastrous in England. 'What a storm that must have been in London! I wish we could get something like it, here. . . . It is thundering while I write, but I fear it don't look black enough for a clearance. The echoes in the mountains are of such a stupendous sort, that a peal of thunder five or ten minutes long, is here the commonest of circumstances. . . .' That was early in August, and at the close of the month he wrote: 'I forgot to tell you that yesterday week, at half-past 7 in the morning, we had a smart shock of an earthquake, lasting, perhaps, a quarter of a minute. It awoke me in bed. The sensation was so curious and unlike any other, that I called out at the top of my voice I was sure it was an earthquake.'

* 60 (p. 439). 'I may tell you', he wrote to me from Paris at the end of November, 'now it is all over. I don't know whether it was the hot summer, or the anxiety of the two new books coupled with D. N. remembrances and reminders, but I was in that state in Switzerland, when my spirits sunk so, I felt myself in serious danger. Yet I had little pain in my side; excepting that time at Genoa I have hardly had any since poor Mary died, when it came on so badly; and I walked my fifteen miles a day constantly, at a great pace.'

* 61 (p. 447). Some smaller items of family news were in the same letter. 'Mamey and Katey have come out in Parisian dresses, and look very fine. They are not proud, and send their loves. Skittles is cutting teeth, and gets cross towards evening. Frankey is smaller than ever, and Walter very large. Charley is statu quo. Everything is enormously dear. Fuel, stupendously so. In airing the house, we burnt five pounds' worth of firewood in one week!! We mix it with coal now, as we used to do in Italy, and find the fires much warmer. To warm the house thoroughly, this singular habitation requires fires on the ground floor. We burn three . . .'

* 62 (p. 448). 'I shall bring the Brave, though I have no use for him. He'd die if I didn't.'

* 63 (p. 453). This was on Sunday, 21st February, when a party were assembled of whom I think the French Emperor, his cousin the Prince Napoleon, Doctor Quin, Dickens's eldest son and myself, are now the only survivors. Lady Blessington had received the day before from her brother Major Power, who held a military appointment in Hobart Town, a small oil painting of a girl's face by the murderer Wainewright (mentioned on a former page as having been seen by us together in Newgate), who was among the convicts there under sentence of transportation, and who had contrived somehow to put the expression of his own wickedness into the portrait of a nice, kind-hearted girl. Major Power knew nothing of the man's previous history at this time, and had employed him on the painting out of a sort of charity. As soon as the truth went back, Wainewright was excluded from houses open to him, and shortly after died very miserably. What Reynolds said of portrait painting, to explain its frequent want of refinement, that a man could only put into a face what he had in himself, was forcibly shown in this incident. The villain's story altogether moved

Dickens to the same interest as it had excited in another profound student of humanity (Sir Edward Lytton), and, as will be seen, he also introduced him into one of his later writings.

* 64 (p. 453). '. . . I am horrified to find that the first chapter makes *at least* two pages less than I had supposed, and I have a terrible apprehension that there will not be copy enough for the number! As it could not possibly come out short, and as there would be no greater possibility of sending to me, in this short month, to supply what may be wanted, I decide—after the first burst of nervousness is gone—*to follow this letter by Diligence tomorrow morning.* The malle poste is full for days and days. I shall hope to be with you some time on Friday.' C. D. to J. F. Paris: Wednesday, 17th February 1847.

Footnotes continued at end of Vol. II

EDITOR'S NOTES

(Quotations from Dickens's letters are, unless otherwise stated, from the three-volume edition, edited by
Walter Dexter, 1938, and are given, as are all quotations from other Dickens copyright material, by kind
permission of Mr Henry Charles Dickens, the author's
grandson.)

† 1 (p. 3). The house in which Dickens was born is now known as 393
Commercial Road, Portsmouth; it was bought by Portsmouth
Corporation in 1903 and is a Dickens Museum open to the public.
Formerly the address of the house was 387 Mile End Terrace,
Landport. The Dickens family left the house when Dickens was
nearly five months old and moved to 16 Hawke Street, Portsmouth,
where they lived from June 1812 to June 1814. The Portsmouth City
Librarian, Mr H. Sargeant, writes: 'Up to 1899 the five Mile End
Terrace numbers were duplicated in Commercial Road, but by 1901
the separate numbering had gone and Mile End Terrace was numbered in sequence. . . . No. 16 Hawke Street appeared on an Ordnance
Survey map for 1948, but had disappeared by 1951; flats have now
been erected in Hawke Street.'

† 2 (p. 47). The real life Dora of *David Copperfield* was Maria Beadnell, daughter of a bank manager in Lombard Street, whose house
Dickens visited during the four years of his fluctuating courtship of
Maria, before he became resigned to failure and gave her up—after
one last appeal for reconciliation in a letter of 13th May 1833: 'I
never have loved and I can never love any human creature breathing
but yourself. . . . Let me entreat you to consider your determination
well whatever it may be and let me implore you to communicate it to
me as early as possible.' He was seventeen when he first met her in
1829, and how infatuated with her he was may be seen from the letter
of 1855 to Forster quoted in the *Life*. That letter, as Forster says,
arose 'from the sudden reappearance of the real' Dora. Maria, now
Mrs H. L. Winter, wrote to him a letter which reached him to his
delighted surprise at Tavistock House; he replied with a long letter
(10th February 1855): '. . . Three or four and twenty years vanished
like a dream, and I opened it with the touch of my young friend
David Copperfield when he was in love. . . . You cannot remember
our old days and our old friends more tenderly than I do. I hardly
ever go into the city, but I walk up an odd little court at the back of
the Mansion House and come out by the corner of Lombard Street
. . . I forget nothing of those times . . . shall be charmed to have a
long talk with you.' But Dickens, then forty-four and at the height
of his fame, was just off to Paris; correspondence passed, talk of a
meeting alone, and eventually it seems that Mrs Dickens, at her

husband's request, called on Mrs Winter and invited her and her
husband to dinner at Tavistock House. But she was middle-aged and
talkative, and disillusionment came to Dickens; soon he avoided her
as much as was politely possible. Then he put Mrs Winter into *Little
Dorrit* as Flora Finching (as Forster indicates); he wrote to the Duke
of Devonshire, in July 1856, 'I am so glad you like Flora. It came
into my head one day that we all have had our Floras (mine is living,
and extremely fat), and that it was a half serious half ridiculous truth
which had never been told . . . some people seem to think I have done
a personal injury and that their individual Floras (God knows where
they are, or who) are all little Dorrits!'

Some of Dickens's letters to Maria, both at the time of their
youthful romance and later when she was Mrs Winter, were privately
printed in 1908 in America, as were his letters to a young bank clerk,
Henry Kolle, who was something of an intermediary for Dickens
with Maria and her parents. The *Charles Dickens and Maria Beadnell*
book prints a document which shows that Dickens and his household
wanted Mrs Winter on their side at the time of the break-up of
Dickens's marriage—a letter, dated 31st May 1858, from Georgina
Hogarth (reprinted as an appendix, vii, in *Mr and Mrs Charles
Dickens: His letters to Her*, 1935), from which these are bald extracts:
'My dearest Maria . . . Charles and his wife have agreed to live apart
in future . . . I am *perfectly convinced* that this plan will be for the
happiness of all. . . . Of course, Charles is too public a man to take
such a step as this without exciting a more than usual nine days'
wonder—and we have heard of the most wonderful rumours and
wicked slanders. . . . To a few of our *real* friends Charles wishes the
truth to be stated, and they cannot show their friendship better than
by quietly silencing with the real solemn truth any foolish or wicked
person who may repeat such lies and slanders. . . .'

† 3 (p. 66). Mary Hogarth, next younger sister of Mrs Dickens, came
to live with them at Furnival's Inn, and shortly afterwards went with
them to 48 Doughty Street when Dickens and his wife and their baby
first son moved there. Mary died suddenly, aged seventeen, seven
weeks later, in Dickens's arms, in the small second-floor room at the
back. Dickens had idolized her and the shock of her death to him was
such that not only was the appearance of *Pickwick* interrupted, but
serialization was held up of *Oliver Twist* in *Bentley's Magazine*, in
which this notice was printed: 'Since the appearance of the last
number of this work the editor has to mourn the sudden death of a
very dear young relative to whom he was most affectionately
attached, and whose society had been for a long time the chief solace
of his labours. He has been compelled to seek a short interval of rest
and quiet. The next number will be conducted by him as usual, and
the adventures of Oliver Twist will be continued.' His sorrow at her
early death always remained with him, and something of his feeling
for her is expressed in the life and death of little Nell of *The Old
Curiosity Shop*: 'Dear Mary died yesterday, when I think of this sad
story' (i. 122).

† 4 (p. 70). Forster records Dickens's relations with his publishers

rather one-sidedly; J. W. T. Ley, who is not otherwise critical of
Forster in his richly annotated edition of the *Life* (1928), writes:
'Dickens made bargains with four publishers which he afterwards
regretted, and from which he succeeded in freeing himself. In every
case we find him calling the publishers hard names because they
showed disinclination to be deprived of the just rewards of their
enterprise. In three of the four cases Forster was on his side and was
his adviser, and in his records of these disputes is invariably unjust
to the publishers.' The three cases are of course those of Macrone,
Bentley, and Chapman and Hall; the fourth case, later, was that of
Bradbury and Evans, where the dispute was grounded in Dickens's
domestic crisis of 1858 (see note † 21). His troubles in 1836-7 came
about because, in the first flush of success with *Pickwick* and his need
for ready money, he had made commitments beyond even his
capabilities of fulfilment and for fees which seemed too low as sales
mounted. Una Pope-Hennessy, in her biography, sums up the position: 'In the first place, he had sold the original series of *Sketches by
Boz* to Macrone for £150 and had just handed in another series for
which he received £150 on account. [He received for both series £400
in all.] In the second place, he had agreed to write a novel for the
same publisher; this was only partly written and overdue. In the
third place, he had contracted to supply Chapman and Hall with a
monthly sketch at £14 a number to be published under the title of
The Pickwick Papers. . . . In the fourth place, he had signed an agreement with Bentley to supply one novel for £500 and a second on the
same terms. In the fifth place, he had accepted the post of editor of
Bentley's Miscellany, which involved supplying sixteen pages of
original matter for each issue. . . .' Forster played a major part in
rearranging this programme, as he did in settling subsequent disputes
with Bentley and Chapman and Hall; he deals with these matters not
more objectively than can be expected when writing about them
many years later in the *Life*.

† 5 (p. 93). The passing of the editorship of *Bentley's Magazine* to
Ainsworth was attended by rumours critical of Forster and his part
in the Dickens-Bentley dispute. Dickens wrote to Ainsworth on 26th
March 1839 a long letter from which these sentences are extracted:
'By some means . . . the late negotiations between yourself myself
and Mr Bentley have placed a mutual friend of ours in a false
position . . . and exposed him to an accusation . . . untrue and
undeserved. . . . However painful it will be to put myself in communication once again with Mr Bentley, and openly appeal to you to
confirm what I shall tell him, I have no alternative, unless you will
frankly and openly, and for the sake of your old friend as well as my
intimate and valued one . . . avow to Mr Bentley yourself that he
(Forster) is not to blame. . . .' The version and treatment of this letter
in vol. i of the Pilgrim edition (1965) of Dickens's *Letters* may be
mentioned as an example of the excellence of that edition; apart
from providing several passages (clearly marked) not published in
the 1938 *Letters*, the editors' footnotes elucidate by quotation from
other letters, and otherwise, the background of this particular upset
in the literary and publishing world of the time.

† 6 (p. 103). Maclise's portrait of Dickens, painted for reproduction as frontispiece of *Nicholas Nickleby* (but not so used: see note * 14), is now in the National Portrait Gallery, London.

† 7 (p. 107). No. 48 Doughty Street was the home of Dickens from March 1837 to December 1839; he wrote there, as well as minor pieces, part of *Pickwick Papers* and *Oliver Twist* and *Nicholas Nickleby*. His two daughters were born there, his first son was a baby when they arrived at the house, and Mary Hogarth died there.

In 1924 the house was acquired by the Dickens Fellowship (founded by B. W. Matz in 1902) and it is now a national property held under a trust deed 'in perpetuity as a building of historic interest'. Well known as Dickens House, it has a unique assemblage (including the B. W. Matz collection) of Dickens books, manuscripts, letters, pictures, furniture and personal relics, among which is a piece from a much earlier home, the little window of the attic at 16 Bayham Street, Camden Town, where Dickens lived for some months as a child. It should be added that *The Dickensian*, established in 1905 as the magazine of the Dickens Fellowship, is published three times a year from 48 Doughty Street. (There are many branches of the Dickens Fellowship. The branch at Broadstairs is run from 'Dickens House', once the home of a lady upon whom D. based the character of Betsey Trotwood; 'Bleak House' at Broadstairs, called 'Fort House' when Dickens lived there, has Dickens rooms open to visitors during the summer.)

† 8 (p. 147). The proposed parliamentary candidature for Reading was dealt with in a pamphlet *Charles Dickens and Reading*, by E. M. Tull, and Dickens's letters in it (here quoted from the 1938 *Letters*) point to financial considerations, plus political independence, being paramount in his refusal to stand: 'My principles and inclinations would lead me to aspire to the distinction you invite me to seek. . . . But I should be bound to add—and I have no hesitation in saying it plainly—that I cannot afford the expense of a contested election . . .' (31st May 1841): and 'The sum you mention . . . is greater than I could afford for such a purpose, as the mere sitting in the House and attending to my duties, if I were a Member, would oblige me to make many pecuniary sacrifices. . . . I have very little doubt indeed that the Government would support me—perhaps to the whole extent. But I cannot satisfy myself that to enter Parliament under such circumstances would enable me to pursue that honourable independence without which I could neither preserve my own respect nor that of my constituents. . . .' (10th June 1841.)

† 9 (p. 186). Dickens's tour of the U.S.A. is recorded in much detail in W. G. Wilkins's *Charles Dickens in America*, 1911.

† 10 (p. 304). When Dickens arrived in Liverpool for the meeting of the Mechanics Institution he was met by an old friend, T. J. Thompson. An entertainment followed Dickens's speech, and Dickens as chairman found himself introducing, from the programme, 'a young lady whom I have some difficulty and tenderness in announcing—Miss Weller, who will play a fantasia on the piano'. The young lady,

Christiana Weller, made a remarkable impression on him and on his friend Thompson. On 27th February 1844 he sent her 'this bit of doggerel for your album':

> 'I put in a book, once, by hook and by crook
> The whole race (as I thought) of a "feller",
> Who happily pleas'd the town's taste, much diseas'd
> And the name of this person was Weller.
> I find to my cost that one Weller I lost,
> Cruel Destiny so to arrange it!
> I love her dear name, which has won me some fame,
> But, Great Heaven! how gladly I'd change it.'

To Thompson, Dickens wrote (28th February 1844): 'I cannot joke about Miss Weller, for she is too good. . . . Good God, what a madman I should seem, if the incredible feeling I have conceived for that girl could be made plain to anyone!' In the event Thompson became engaged to her, and after a fluctuating courtship of eighteen months they married. Mr and Mrs Thompson are only mentioned once by Forster (ii. 85), who records that Dickens's brother Frederick married Christiana's sister, Anna.

† 11 (p. 351). 'The De la Rues' (M. Émile De la Rue, Swiss banker, and his English wife, living in Genoa when Dickens and his wife were in Italy in 1844-5) get very small mention by Forster, but they have figured more prominently in later biographies. The two couples were on fairly frequent visiting terms. Mrs De la Rue suffered from attacks of frightening hallucinations, and from time to time Dickens ministered to her, apparently with some success, by mesmeric treatment. These attentions to Mrs De la Rue upset Mrs Dickens. When a little later he was contemplating taking the family to the Continent again, he wrote to Mrs De la Rue (17th April 1846): 'I need not tell *you* that *I* want to go to Genoa! But Mrs Dickens, who was never very well there, cannot be got to contemplate the Peschiere. . . . My Diary of March 19th, 1845, is lying open on my desk, and looking at it I see this entry—*Madame D. L. R. very ill in the night. Up till four.* . . . What a miserable Devil I seem to be cooped up here, bothered by printers and stock-jobbers, when there are bright Genoas (and bright patients in them). . . .' Late in 1853 Dickens was in Italy again and in the course of a long letter (5th December) to his wife referred to the De la Rues (printed in *Mr and Mrs Charles Dickens, His Letters to Her*) saying: '. . . your position beside these people is not a good one, is not an amiable one, a generous one—is not worthy of you at all . . . you have it in your power to set it right at once by writing her a note to say that you have heard from me, with interest, of her sufferings and her cheerfulness. . . .'

Among the Dickens letters in the Berg Collection in New York Public Library is one to Mr De la Rue of 23rd October 1857 (a few months before the separation of Dickens and his wife); this quotation from it is taken from Edgar Johnson's *Charles Dickens, His Tragedy and Triumph*; 'Between ourselves I don't get on better in these later times with a certain poor lady you know of, than I did in the earlier Peschiere days. Much worse! Neither do the children, elder or younger. Neither can she get on with herself, or be anything but unhappy. (She has been excruciatingly jealous of, and has obtained positive proof of my being on the most intimate terms with, at least fifteen thousand women of various conditions in life, since we left Genoa. Please to respect me for this vast experience.) What we should do, or what the girls would be, without Georgy, I cannot imagine. . . . Enough of this. We put the Skeleton away in the cupboard, and very few people, comparatively, know of its existence.'

† 12 (p. 395). The little 'Life of Christ', written by Dickens expressly for his children (also referred to in note * 51 and in vol. ii, p. 379) turned up publicly in 1934, when the manuscript and copyright were sold to the *Daily Mail* for £40,000, and a law case ensued as to distribution of the proceeds. The *Dickensian*, January 1965, notes that the manuscript has recently been anonymously presented to Philadelphia Public Library.

Notes continued at end of Vol. II